INDIA
IN THE
VICTORIAN AGE

AN ECONOMIC HISTORY
OF THE PEOPLE

BY

ROMESH DUTT, C.I.E.

LECTURER IN INDIAN HISTORY AT UNIVERSITY COLLEGE, LONDON;
LATE OFF. COMMISSIONER OF ORISSA AND MEMBER OF
THE BENGAL LEGISLATIVE COUNCIL;
AUTHOR OF "THE ECONOMIC HISTORY OF BRITISH INDIA,
1757 TO 1837," ETC.

LOW PRICE PUBLICATIONS

[A Division of D.K. Publishers Distributors (P) Ltd.]

Delhi-110052

Sales Office:
D.K. PUBLISHERS DISTRIBUTORS (P) LTD.
1, Ansari Road, Darya Ganj, New Delhi-110002
Phones: 3261465, 3278368
Fax: (011) 3264368

First Published 1904
Reproduced 1993, 1995

ISBN 81-85395-83-7

Published by: **LOW PRICE PUBLICATIONS** [A Division of D.K. Publishers Distributors (P) Ltd.] at Regd.Off.: A-6, NIMRI Community Centre, Ashok Vihar, Phase-IV, Delhi-110052.

Printed at:
Santosh Offset, Delhi-110035

PRINTED IN INDIA

PREFACE

SIX years ago, there was a celebration in London which was like a scenic representation of the Unity of the British Empire. Men from all British Colonies and Dependencies came together to take part in the Diamond Jubilee of a Great Queen's reign. Indian Princes stood by the side of loyal Canadians and hardy Australians. The demonstration called forth an outburst of enthusiasm seldom witnessed in these islands. And to thoughtful minds it recalled a long history of bold enterprises, arduous struggles, and a wise conciliation, which had cemented a world-wide Empire. Nations, living in different latitudes and under different skies, joined in a celebration worthy of the occasion.

One painful thought, however, disturbed the minds of the people. Amidst signs of progress and prosperity from all parts of the Empire, India alone presented a scene of poverty and distress. A famine, the most intense and the most widely extended yet known, desolated the country in 1897. The most populous portion of the Empire had not shared its prosperity. Increasing wealth, prospering industries, and flourishing agriculture, had not followed the flag of England in her greatest dependency.

The famine was not over till 1898. There was a pause in 1899. A fresh famine broke out in 1900 over a larger area, and continued for a longer period. The terrible calamity lasted for three years, and millions of men perished. Tens of thousands were still in relief camps when the Delhi Darbar was held in January 1903.

The economic gulf which separates India from other parts of the Empire has widened in the course of recent years. In Canada and other Colonies, the income per head of the population is £48 per year. In Great Britain it is £42. In India it is officially estimated at £2. At the last meeting of the British Association, one of the greatest of British Economists, Sir Robert Giffin, pointed out that this was "a permanent and formidable difficulty in the British Empire, to which more thought must be given by our public men, the more the idea of Imperial Unity becomes a working force." Imperial Unity cannot be built on the growing poverty and decadence of five-sixths of the population of the Empire.

For the famines, though terrible in their death-roll, are only an indication of a greater evil—the permanent poverty of the Indian population in ordinary years. The food supply of India, as a whole, has never failed. Enough food was grown in India, even in 1897 and 1900, to feed the entire population. But the people are so resourceless, so absolutely without any savings, that when crops fail within any one area, they are unable to buy food from neighbouring provinces rich in harvests. The failure of rains destroys crops in particular areas; it is the poverty of the people which brings on severe famines.

Many facts, within the experience of Indian Administrators, could be cited to illustrate this; I will content myself with one. Twenty-seven years ago, Eastern Bengal was visited by a severe calamity. A cyclone and storm-wave from the sea swept over large tracts of the country and destroyed the homes and crops of cultivators in 1876. I was sent, as a young officer, to reorganise administration and to give relief to the people in some of the tracts most severely affected. The peasantry in those parts paid light rents, and were therefore prosperous in ordinary times. With the providence and frugality which are habitual to the Indian cultivator, they had saved in previous years. In the year of distress they bought shiploads of rice out of their own savings. There was no general famine, and no large relief operations were needed. I watched with satisfaction the resourcefulness and the self-help of a prosperous peasantry. If the cultivators of India generally were as prosperous as in Eastern Bengal, famines would be rare in India, even in years of bad harvests. But rents in Western Bengal are higher, in proportion to the produce, than in Eastern Bengal; and the Land Tax in Madras, Bombay, and elsewhere is higher than in Bengal. The people are therefore less resourceful, and famines are more frequent and more fatal. The poverty of the people adds to the severity of famines.

The sources of a nation's wealth are Agriculture, Commerce and Manufactures, and sound Financial Administration. British rule has given India peace; but British Administration has not promoted or widened these sources of National Wealth in India.

Of Commerce and Manufactures I need say little in this place. I have in another work[1] traced the commercial policy of Great Britain towards India in the eighteenth and the earlier years of the nineteenth century. The policy was the same which Great Britain then pursued towards Ireland and her Colonies. Endeavours were made, which were fatally successful, to repress Indian manufactures and to extend British manufactures. The import of Indian goods to Europe was repressed by prohibitive duties; the export of British goods to India was encouraged by almost nominal duties. The production of raw material in India for British industries, and the consumption of British manufactures in India, were the twofold objects of the early commercial policy of England. The British manufacturer, in the words of the historian Horace Hayman Wilson, "employed the arm of political injustice to keep down and ultimately strangle a com-

[1] *Economic History of British India*, 1757 *to* 1837.

petitor with whom he could not have contended on equal terms."

When Queen Victoria ascended the throne in 1837, the evil had been done. But nevertheless there was no relaxation in the policy pursued before. Indian silk handkerchiefs still had a sale in Europe; and a high duty on manufactured Indian silk was maintained. Parliament inquired how cotton could be grown in India for British looms, not how Indian looms could be improved, Select Committees tried to find out how British manufactures could find a sale in India, not how Indian manufactures could be revived. Long before 1858, when the East India Company's rule ended, India had ceased to be a great manufacturing country. Agriculture had virtually become the one remaining source of the nation's subsistence.

British merchants still watched and controlled the Indian tariff after 1858. The import of British goods into India was facilitated by the reduction of import duties. The growth of looms and factories in Bombay aroused jealousy. In 1879, a year of famine, war, and deficit in India, a further sacrifice of import duties was demanded by Parliament. And in 1882 all import duties were abolished, except on salt and liquor.

But the sacrifices told on the Indian revenues. In spite of new taxes on the peasantry, and new burdens on agriculture, India could not pay her way. In 1894 the old import duties were revived with slight modifications. A 5 per cent. duty was imposed on cotton goods and yarns imported into India, and a countervailing duty of 5 per cent. was imposed on such Indian cotton fabrics as competed with the imported goods. In 1896 cotton yarns were freed from duty; but a duty of 3½ per cent. was imposed on cotton goods imported into India, and an excise duty of 3½ per cent. was imposed on all goods manufactured at Indian mills. Coarse Indian goods, which did not in any way compete with Lancashire goods, were taxed, as well as finer fabrics. The miserable clothing of the miserable Indian labourer, earning less than 2½d. a day, was taxed by a jealous Government. The infant mill industry of Bombay, instead of receiving help and encouragement, was repressed by an excise duty unknown in any other part of the civilised world. During a century and a half the commercial policy of the British rulers of India has been determined, not by the interests of Indian manufacturers, but by those of British manufacturers. The vast quantities of manufactured goods which were exported from India by the Portuguese and the Dutch, by Arab and British merchants, in the seventeenth and eighteenth centuries, have disappeared. India's exports now are mostly raw produce—largely the food of the people. Manufacturing industry as a source of national income has been narrowed.

There remains Agriculture. Cultivation has largely extended under the peace and security assured by the British Rule. But no man familiar with the inner life of the cultivators will say that the extension of cultivation has made the nation more prosperous, more resourceful, more secure against famines.

The history of the Land Revenue administration in India is of the deepest interest, because it is intimately connected with the material well-being of an agricultural nation. In the earlier years of the British Rule, the East India Company regarded India as a vast estate or plantation, and considered themselves entitled to all that the land could produce, leaving barely enough to the tillers and the landed classes to keep them alive in ordinary years. This policy proved disastrous to the revenues of the Company, and a reform became necessary. The Company then recognised the wisdom of assuring to the landed classes the future profits of agriculture. Accordingly, Lord Cornwallis permanently settled the Land Revenue in Bengal in 1793, demanding from landlords

90 per cent. of the rental, but assuring them against any increase of the demand in the future. The proportion taken by the Government was excessive beyond measure; but cultivation and rental have largely increased since 1793; and the peasantry and the landed classes have reaped the profits. The agriculturists of Bengal are more resourceful to-day, and more secure against the worst effects of famine than the agriculturists of any other Province in India.

A change then came over the policy of the East India Company. They were unwilling to extend the Permanent Settlement to other Provinces. They tried to fix a proper share of the rental as their due so that their revenue might increase with the rental. In Northern India they fixed their demand first at 83 per cent. of the rental, then at 75 per cent., then at 66 per cent. But even this was found to be impracticable, and at last, in 1855, they limited the State-demand to 50 per cent. of the rental. And this rule of limiting the Land Revenue to one-half the rental was extended to Southern India in 1864. An income-tax of 50 per cent. on the profits of cultivation is a heavier assessment than is known in any other country under a civilised Government. But it would be a gain to India if even this high limit were never exceeded.

The rule of the East India Company terminated in 1858. The first Viceroys under the Crown were animated by a sincere desire to promote agricultural prosperity, and to widen the sources of agricultural wealth in India. Statesmen like Sir Charles Wood and Sir Stafford Northcote, and rulers like Lord Canning and Lord Lawrence, laboured with this object. They desired to fix the State-demand from the soil, to make the nation prosperous, to create a strong and loyal middle class, and to connect them by their own interest with British Rule in India. If their sound policy had been adopted, one source of national wealth would have been widened. The nation would have been more resourceful and self-relying to-day; famines would have been rarer. But the endeavours to make the nation prosperous weakened after the first generation of the servants of the Crown had passed away. Increase of revenue and increase of expenditure became engrossing objects with the rise of Imperialism. The proposal of Canning and of Lawrence was dropped in 1883.

The reader will no doubt clearly grasp the two distinct principles which were held by the two different schools of administrators. One was the school of Lord Canning and Lord Lawrence, of Lord Halifax and Lord Iddesleigh, who urged a Permanent Settlement of the Land Revenue. They knew that land in India belonged to the nation and not to a landed class, that every cultivator had a hereditary right to his own holding, and that to permanently fix the Land Revenue would benefit an agricultural nation, and not a class of landlords. The other school demanded a continuous increase of the Land Revenue for the State, by means of recurring Land-Settlements, in course of which the State-demand was generally increased at the discretion of Settlement-Officers.

The Marquis of Ripon was the Viceroy of India from 1880 to 1884, and he proposed a masterly compromise between the opinions of the two schools. He maintained the right of the State to demand a continuous increase of the Land Revenue on the definite and equitable ground of increase in prices. But he assured the cultivators of India against any increase in the State-demand, unless there was an increase in prices. He assured to the State an increasing revenue with the increasing prosperity of the country as evidenced by prices. And he assured to the cultivator a permanency in the State-demand reckoned in the proportion of the field produce taken as Land Tax. Lord Ripon's scheme happily combined the rights of the State with that security to cultivators without which agriculture cannot flourish in any part of the world. But Lord Ripon left India in December 1884; and his wise settlement was negatived by the Secretary of State for India in January 1885. The compromise which had been arrived at after years of inquiry and anxious thought in India was vetoed at Whitehall; and a nation of agriculturists was once more subjected to that *uncertainty* in the State-demand which is fatal to successful agriculture.

The Half-Rental Rule still remained—in theory. But in practice it had been violated. The expenses of the Mutiny wars had vastly added to Indian liabilities, and demanded increase in taxation. Commerce could not be taxed against the wishes of British merchants and British voters; the increased taxes therefore fell on agriculture. Accordingly, from 1871, a number of new taxes were assessed on land, in addition to the Land Revenue. If the Land Revenue was 50 per cent. of the rental, the total assessment on the soil, including the new taxes, came to 56 per cent., or 58 per cent., or even 60 per cent. of the rental. And the people of India asked, what was the object of limiting the Land Revenue, if the limits were exceeded by the imposition of additional burdens on agriculture.

The late Marquis of Salisbury was Secretary of State for India in 1875. His deep insight in matters to which he devoted his attention is well known. And he condemned the weakness and the one-sidedness of the Indian Fiscal policy in a Minute recorded in 1875, which is often cited. "So far," his lordship wrote, "as it is possible to change the Indian Fiscal system, it is desirable that the cultivator should pay a smaller proportion of the whole national charge. It is not in itself a thrifty policy to draw the mass of revenue from the rural districts, where capital is scarce, sparing the towns where it is often redundant and runs to waste in luxury. The injury is exaggerated in the case of India where so much of the revenue is exported without a direct equivalent. As India must be bled, the lancet should be directed to the parts where the blood is congested, or at least sufficient, not to those which are already feeble from the want of it."

Lord Salisbury's warning has been disregarded. And while we hear so much of the prosperous budgets and surpluses since the value of the rupee was fixed at 1s. 4d., no advantage has been taken of this seeming prosperity to relieve agriculture. Not one of the special taxes on land, imposed in addition to the Land Revenue since 1871, has been repealed.

It will appear from these facts, which I have mentioned as briefly as possible, that Agriculture, as a source of the nation's income, has not been widened under British administration. Except where the Land Revenue is permanently settled, it is revised and enhanced at each new Settlement, once in thirty years or once in twenty years. It professes to take 50 per cent. of the rental or of the economic rent, but virtually takes a much larger share in Bombay and Madras. And to it are added other special taxes on land which can be enhanced indefinitely at the will of the State. The Land Assessment is thus excessive, and it is also uncertain. Place any country in the world under the operation of these rules, and agriculture will languish. The cultivators of India are frugal, industrious, and peaceful; but they are nevertheless impoverished, resourceless, always on the brink of famines and starvation. This is not a state of things which Englishmen can look upon with just pride. It is precisely the state of things which they are remedying in Ireland. It is a situation which they will not tolerate in India when they have once grasped it.

If we turn from the sources of wealth to its distribution, and to the financial arrangements of India, the same melancholy picture is presented to us. The total revenues of India during the last ten years of the Queen's reign—1891–92 to 1900–1—came to 647 millions sterling.

The annual average is thus under 65 millions, including receipts from railways, irrigation works, and all other sources. The expenditure in England during these ten years was 159 millions, giving an annual average of nearly 16 millions sterling. One-fourth, therefore, of all the revenues derived in India, is annually remitted to England as Home Charges. And if we add to this the portion of their salaries which European officers employed in India annually remit to England, the total annual drain out of the Indian Revenues to England considerably exceeds 20 millions. The richest country on earth stoops to levy this annual contribution from the poorest. Those who earn £42 per head ask for 10s. per head from a nation earning £2 per head. And this 10s. per head which the British people draw from India impoverishes Indians, and therefore impoverishes British trade with India. The contribution does not benefit British commerce and trade, while it drains the life-blood of India in a continuous, ceaseless flow.

For when taxes are raised and spent in a country, the money circulates among the people, fructifies trades, industries, and agriculture, and in one shape or another reaches the mass of the people. But when the taxes raised in a country are remitted out of it, the money is lost to the country for ever, it does not stimulate her trades or industries, or reach the people in any form. Over 20 millions sterling are annually drained from the revenues of India; and it would be a miracle if such a process, continued through long decades, did not impoverish even the richest nation upon earth.

The total Land Revenue of India was 17½ millions in 1900–1. The total of Home Charges in the same year came to 17 millions. It will be seen, therefore, that an amount equivalent to all that is raised from the soil, in all the Provinces of India, is annually remitted out of the country as Home Charges. An additional sum of several millions is sent in the form of private remittances by European officers, drawing their salaries from Indian Revenues; and this remittance increases as the employment of European officers increases in India.

The 17 millions remitted as Home Charges are spent in England (1) as interest payable on the Indian Debt; (2) as interest on railways; and (3) as Civil and Military Charges. A small portion, about a million, covers the cost of military and other stores supplied to India.

A very popular error prevails in this country that the whole Indian Debt represents British capital sunk in the development of India. It is shown in the body of this volume that this is not the genesis of the Public Debt of India. When the East India Company ceased to be rulers of India in 1858, they had piled up an Indian Debt of 70 millions. They had in the meantime drawn a tribute from India, financially an unjust tribute, exceeding 150 millions, not calculating interest. They had also charged India with the cost of Afghan wars, Chinese wars, and other wars outside India. Equitably, therefore, India owed nothing at the close of the Company's rule; her Public Debt was a myth; there was a considerable balance of over 100 millions in her favour out of the money that had been drawn from her.

Within the first eighteen years of the Administration of the Crown the Public Debt of India was doubled. It amounted to about 140 millions in 1877, when the Queen became the Empress of India. This was largely owing to the cost of the Mutiny wars, over 40 millions sterling, which was thrown on the revenues of India. And India was made to pay a large contribution to the cost of the Abyssinian War of 1867.

Between 1877 and 1900, the Public Debt rose from 139 millions to 224 millions. This was largely due to the construction of railways by Guaranteed Companies or by the State, beyond the pressing needs of India and beyond her resources. It was also largely due to the Afghan Wars of 1878 and 1897. The history of the

Indian Debt is a distressing record of financial unwisdom and injustice; and every impartial reader can reckon for himself how much of this Indian Debt is morally due from India.

The last items of the Home Charges are the Civil and Military Charges. This needs a revision. If Great Britain and India are both gainers by the building up of the British Indian Empire, it is not fair or equitable that India alone should pay all the cost of the maintenance of that superb edifice. It is not fair that all the expenses incurred in England, down to the maintenance of the India Office and the wages of the charwoman employed to clean the rooms at Whitehall, should be charged to India. Over forty years ago one of the greatest of Indian administrators suggested an equitable compromise. In a work on *Our Financial Relations with India*, published in 1859, Sir George Wingate suggested that India should pay all the expenses of Civil and Military Administration incurred in India, while Great Britain should meet the expenses incurred in England, as she did for her Colonies. Is it too late to make some such equitable adjustment to-day? India's total Civil and Military Charges, incurred in England, come to 6 millions—a sum which would be considerably reduced if it came from the British tax-payer. Is it too much to expect that Great Britain might share this burden, while India paid all the Civil and Military charges incurred in India?

These are the plain facts of the economic situation in India. Given these conditions, any fertile, industrious, peaceful country in the world would be what India is to-day. If manufactures were crippled, agriculture over-taxed, and a third of the revenue remitted out of the country, any nation on earth would suffer from permanent poverty and recurring famines. Economic laws are the same in Asia as in Europe. If India is poor to-day, it is through the operation of economic causes. If India were prosperous under these circumstances, it would be an economic miracle. Science knows no miracles. Economic laws are constant and unvarying in their operation.

The evils suggest their own remedies. The Excise tax on Indian mill industry should be withdrawn; the Indian Government should boldly help Indian industries, for the good of the Indian people, as every civilised Government on earth helps the industries of its own country. All taxes on the soil in addition to the Land Revenue should be repealed; and the Land Revenue should be moderated and regulated in its operation. The Public Debt, unjustly created in the first instance, is now an accomplished fact: but an Imperial Guarantee would reduce the rate of interest; and a Sinking Fund would gradually reduce its volume. Civil and Military Charges, incurred in England, should be borne, or at least shared, by Great Britain, as she shares them in the case of her Colonies. Civil charges in India should be reduced by a larger employment of Indians; military charges in India should be repressed with a strong hand; and India should pay for an army needed for her own requirements. All further extension of railways from State-Loans, or under guarantee of interest from the taxes, should be prohibited. Irrigation works should be extended, as far as possible, from the ordinary revenues. The annual Economic Drain from India should be steadily reduced; and in carrying out these fiscal reforms, representatives of the people of India,—of the taxpayers who are alone interested in Retrenchment in all countries,—should be called upon to take their share, and offer their assistance.

"The Government of a people by itself," wrote John Stuart Mill, "has a meaning and a reality, but such a thing as government of one people by another does not, and cannot exist. One people may keep another for its own use, a place to make money in, a human cattle farm for the profits of its own inhabitants." This statement contains a deep truth. Large masses of men are not ordinarily impelled by a consideration of other peoples' interests. The British voter is as fair-minded as the voter in any other country on earth, but he would not be a British voter, and he would not be human, if he did not ordinarily mind his own interests and secure his own profits. Parliament carries out the mandates of voters; the Indian Secretary, a Member of the British Cabinet, cannot act against the joint wishes of the Cabinet. The Members of his Council are appointed by him, and do not in any sense represent the people of India. The Viceroy of India is under the orders of the Indian Secretary of State; and the Government of India is vested in his Ordinary Council, which, in the words of Sir William Hunter, is an "oligarchy," and does not represent the people. The Members of the Governor-General's Council are generally heads of spending departments, and "the tendency is," as Sir David Barbour said before the Indian Expenditure Commission, "ordinarily for pressure to be put on the Financial Department to incur expenditure. It is practically pressure. The other Departments are always pressing to spend more money: their demands are persistent and continuous." Nowhere in the entire machinery of the Indian Government, from the top to the bottom, is there any influence which makes for Retrenchment, any force which represents the taxpayer. Fiscal reforms are impossible under this Constitution. If Retrenchment is desired, some room must be found, somewhere in the Constitution, to represent the taxpayer's interests.

The Indian Empire will be judged by History as the most superb of human institutions in modern times. But it would be a sad story for future historians to tell that the Empire gave the people of India peace but not prosperity; that the manufacturers lost their industries; that the cultivators were ground down by a heavy and variable taxation which precluded any saving; that the revenues of the country were to a large extent diverted to England; and that recurring and desolating famines swept away millions of the population. On the other hand, it would be a grateful story for Englishmen to tell that England in the twentieth century undid her past mistakes in India as in Ireland; that she lightened land taxes, revived industries, introduced representation, and ruled India for the good of her people; and that the people of India felt in their hearts that they were citizens of a great and United Empire.

ROMESH DUTT.

LONDON, *December* 1903.

CONTENTS

BOOK I

UNDER THE COMPANY. 1838-1858.

BOOK II

UNDER THE QUEEN. 1858-1876.

BOOK III

UNDER THE EMPRESS. 1877-1900.

BOOK I

UNDER THE COMPANY

1838–1858

INDIA IN THE VICTORIAN AGE

CHAPTER I

AUCKLAND AND ELLENBOROUGH

LORD WILLIAM BENTINCK left India in 1835. His seven years' rule was an era of Peace, Retrenchment, and Reform. He secured tranquillity in the East India Company's dominions, and lived at peace with the Indian Powers. He reduced the public debt, decreased the annual expenditure, and showed a surplus. He commenced that revised settlement of land revenue in Northern India which gave relief to landlords and cultivators. He admitted the educated people of India to the higher appointments in the revenue and judicial departments. He abolished the practice of Sati and suppressed the crime of Thugs. He promoted English education in India, and endeavoured to carry out the maxim that the administration of India was primarily for the interests of the people. His successor, Sir Charles Metcalfe, trained in the traditions of his school, worked in the same lines, and followed the same principles. He gave liberty to the Press of India, and earned for himself a high reputation as an able and benevolent administrator.

Henry St. George Tucker was the Chairman of the Court of Directors in August 1834, when the resignation of Lord William Bentinck was received by the Directors. Tucker had himself done distinguished service in India, and had ably managed its finances under Wellesley and

Minto. And after his retirement to England he still remained true to the interests of the people of India. He desired, when Bentinck's resignation came, to appoint a worthy successor. His choice lay between Mountstuart Elphinstone, lately returned from Bombay, and Sir Charles Metcalfe, still working in Bengal. Elphinstone, then enjoying a life of literary repose in England, declined to return to the toil and turmoil of India. And the Court of Directors, by an overwhelming majority, carried the proposal of their Chairman, that Sir Charles Metcalfe should be appointed Governor-General of India. But the ministers of the Crown demurred to the appointment. On receipt of the resolution of the Court of Directors, the Board of Control announced that the Company's nominee was ineligible to the station. It was their secret wish that the prize appointment should be given to a party man.

Great changes in administration followed thick and fast in England. The Liberal Ministry, which had declined to sanction the appointment of Sir Charles Metcalfe, went out of office towards the close of 1834. Sir Robert Peel formed a Tory Government; and the choice of that Government fell, not on Sir Charles Metcalfe, but on a Tory peer. Lord Heytesbury's appointment was made in January 1835. It was sanctioned by the Crown in February. A farewell banquet was given to him in March. Sir Robert Peel, the Duke of Wellington, and other Tory magnates attended the banquet. In April, before Lord Heytesbury had embarked for India, the Tory Government fell. The appointment of the Tory Lord was revoked by the Liberal Government which succeeded, and a Liberal lord was appointed Governor-General of India. Lord Auckland was selected to take the reins of administration from the hands of Sir Charles Metcalfe, who was acting after the departure of Lord William Bentinck. It is difficult to say if these transactions were more discreditable to the Tory party or to the

Whig party. But both parties seemed equally anxious to place party interests before the interests of Indian administration.

But the appointment of Lord Auckland as Governor-General of India had a deeper significance. It meant that the foreign policy of India must shape itself to the foreign policy of England. The Liberal party in England had come triumphantly into office in 1830, and held office—excepting a brief interruption during the winter of 1834–35—for eleven years. The strongest man in the Liberal Government during these years was the Foreign Minister, Lord Palmerston. And the strongest ambition of Lord Palmerston was to check Russia in the East. In 1838 he supported and strengthened the Turkish Government. In 1840 he made a convention with three European Powers for armed interference in support of Turkey. In 1841 he placed Egypt once more under the power of Turkey. It was easy to foresee that Lord Auckland was appointed to India to carry out this Imperial policy of England against Russia.

The East India Company has often been blamed for their wars of annexation and of conquest. But the crime of the first Afghan War cannot be laid at their door. It was undertaken without their sanction and without their approval. As early as 1835, Henry St. George Tucker, then Chairman of the Court of Directors, had induced the Board of Control to accept the principle, that England's diplomatic transactions with Persia, for the prevention of the advance of Russia, was a European question and not an Indian question. It was arranged, with that "melancholy meanness" which has so often characterised England's financial transactions with India, that India should pay £12,000 per annum for the Persian Mission, but that all power over the English envoy at Teheran and the politics of Persia should be vested in the Crown Ministers. It was not anticipated, when the Russo-Persian question was declared to be a European question, that Indian blood and Indian treasure were to be lavished on its solution.

Dr. MacNeill was appointed ambassador to the King of Persia, and placed himself in direct communication with the Foreign Minister, Lord Palmerston. In February 1837 he complained to Lord Palmerston that the agent from Kandahar had visited the Russian Minister, and had not visited the British Ambassador.[1] And in the same month he addressed another letter to Lord Palmerston, in which he justified the possible invasion of Herat by the King of Persia.

"Putting aside the claims of Persia to the sovereignty of Herat, and regarding the question as one between two independent sovereigns, I am inclined to believe that the Government of Herat will be found to have been the aggressor.

"Persia has committed no act of hostility against the Afghans, but on the death of the late Shah, the Government of Herat made predatory incursions into the Persian territories, in concert with the Turcomans and Hazarehs, and captured the subjects of Persia for the purpose of selling them as slaves.

"Under these circumstances, there cannot, I think, be a doubt that the Shah is fully justified in making war on Prince Kamran." [2]

The expected invasion of Herat by Persia took place. Dost Muhammad, the ruler of Afghanistan, gave his support to the King of Persia. He had also endeavoured to recover Peshawar from Ranjit Singh of the Punjab, and had received a Russian mission at Kabul. These were the ostensible grounds on which Lord Auckland, now Governor-General of India, declared war with Afghanistan.

The reader seeks in vain in Lord Auckland's declaration [3] any adequate cause for plunging India into a need-

[1] Letter dated Teheran, February 20, 1837.

[2] Letter dated Teheran, February 24, 1837.

[3] Declaration on the part of the Right Honourable the Governor-General of India, dated October 1, 1838.

less war. If an endeavour had been made to recover Peshawar from Ranjit Singh, the endeavour had failed, and Ranjit Singh was quite competent to defend his own. And if Dost Muhammad had supported Persia in the invasion of Herat, that invasion was "fully justified" by the conduct of the Governor of Herat, according to Dr. MacNeill's letter of 1837, quoted above. The real cause of the war was to dethrone a strong, able, and friendly ruler like Dost Muhammad, and to place on the Afghan throne a creature of the British Power. Lord Palmerston was fighting England's great rival in the East, and Lord Auckland consented to pay the cost from the taxes of India. "It was no doubt very convenient," wrote St. George Tucker, "for Her Majesty's Government to cast the burden of an enterprise, directed against Russia, on the finances of India, instead of sending the fleet into the Baltic or the Black Sea; but we are bound to resist the attempt to alienate and misapply the resources of India."[1]

The siege of Herat by Persian troops was ultimately abandoned. The ostensible reason of Lord Auckland's interference with Afghan affairs thus ceased to exist. There was yet time to abandon the contemplated Afghan War. The Duke of Wellington, who was not a peace-at-any-price man, was of opinion that the expedition should be abandoned. "I had understood," he wrote to St. George Tucker, "that the raising the siege of Herat was to be the signal for abandoning the expedition to the Indus. It will be very unfortunate if that intention should be altered. The consequence of crossing the Indus, to settle a government in Afghanistan, will be a perennial march into the country."[2]

But Lord Auckland knew better. He wrote to the Secret Committee of the Court of Directors that: "Upon receiving an authentic report that the Shah of Persia had

[1] Kaye's *Life and Correspondence of Henry St. George Tucker*, p. 511.
[2] Letter dated December 12, 1838.

relinquished the siege of Herat, I publicly announced my resolution to persevere, notwithstanding that favourable circumstance, in carrying through the course of measures which had been perfected with a view to establish the tranquillity of the western frontier of India upon a stable basis, and to raise up a permanent barrier against schemes of aggression from that quarter." The experience of sixty years enables us to judge whether the Duke of Wellington or Lord Auckland was right; and whether, by interfering in the internal affairs of Afghanistan, we "raise up a permanent barrier" against invasions, or simply demolish the existing barrier, and are led into "a perennial march into the country."

The war was carried on. The British troops marched through Sindh, because Ranjit Singh refused them permission to march through his territories in the Punjab. Kandahar was taken in April 1839; Ghazni was stormed in July; Kabul was reached in August. Dost Muhammad fled over the Oxus into Bokhara; Shah Shuja was placed on the throne. The elation in England was great; and the actors on the spot betrayed a vaingloriousness seldom manifested by British soldiers or statesmen. Sir John Keane, after capturing Ghazni, wrote to Lord Auckland: "The army under my command have succeeded in performing one of the most brilliant acts it has ever been my lot to witness during my service of 45 years in the four quarters of the globe."[1] Lord Auckland wrote to the Secret Committee of the Directors "of the flight of Sirdar Dost Muhammad Khan, and the triumphant entry of His Majesty, Shah Shuja-ul-Mulk, into Kabul, amid the congratulations of his people."[2] And His Majesty, Shah Shuja-ul-Mulk, wrote to Queen Victoria, expressing "the fullest confidence in the kind consideration of my wishes which is felt by my Royal Sister." His wishes were to found an Order of the Durani Empire,

[1] Letter dated July 24, 1839.
[2] Letter dated August 29, 1839.

and to confer the first class of the Order upon Lord Auckland, Sir John Keane, and a few others.[1]

It is not within the scope of the present work to narrate the history of the first Afghan War which is told in every school-book on Indian history, and has been fully and faithfully narrated by one of the most impartial of Anglo-Indian historians.[2] Briefly, the Afghan people resented this foreign interference in their affairs. The new Amir, Shah Shuja, smarted under the control of the British envoy. The Mullas of Kabul refused to offer up prayers for him, and declared that he was not their independent king. Sardars and chiefs of tribes became openly hostile as the stream of gold from the Indian treasury was gradually reduced. On November 2, 1841, an insurrection broke out in Kabul, and Sir Alexander Burnes was killed. On December 23 the British envoy, Macnaghten, was killed in an open meeting by Akbar Khan, son of the exiled Dost Muhammad. In January 1842 the British army of four thousand, with twelve thousand camp-followers, began their retreat from Kabul. Fighting and negotiations continued during this disastrous retreat. Akbar Khan demanded more English hostages, including the wives and children of English officers, while his troops joined the Ghilzai mountaineers in pouring a murderous fire on the retreating army. The entire force and camp-followers, sixteen thousand men, perished under the Afghan fire, or died of wounds, cold, and hunger, in the Afghan snows. One solitary survivor, Dr. Brydon, escaped.

Lord Auckland was succeeded by Lord Ellenborough as Governor-General of India in 1842. In England the Liberal Government had fallen, and a Tory Government had succeeded. The new Ministers were not responsible

[1] Papers relating to the war in Afghanistan, ordered to be printed by the House of Commons, January 21, 1840. Paper No. 24.

[2] Sir John Kaye's *History of the War in Afghanistan* would have been better known to English readers, and appeared in popular editions, if it had not been the history of a blunder and a disaster.

for this unwise and disastrous war. They could rightly throw the whole blame of it on their predecessors; and it was hoped that they would even do India the justice of relieving her of the expenses of the war. But British Ministers, Liberal or Conservative, are unwilling to face their constituencies with a demand for the cost of an unsuccessful war. The Court of Directors pressed their claims with vigour. The Court of Proprietors made a demonstration in the same direction and with equal vigour. The people of India felt the injustice of being taxed for a war beyond the frontiers of India. But all protest was vain. The cost of the first Afghan War was fifteen millions sterling, and was thrown on the revenues of India. Not a shilling was contributed by Great Britain.

In February 1842 Lord Ellenborough landed at Calcutta. Ellenborough had qualified himself for his Indian administration by his work as President of the India Board of Control. He had helped in abolishing the transit duties which had impeded the internal trade of India. And he had acted as Chairman of a Select Committee of the House of Lords, appointed to inquire into the question of Indian produce and manufactures. But Afghan affairs required his immediate attention on his arrival in India.

Ranjit Singh had died in June 1839, and there was none to oppose the march of the British army through the Punjab. General Pollock went through the Punjab and relieved Jellalabad. He defeated Akbar Khan, and in September 1842 was in possession of Kabul. The great Bazaar of Kabul, one of the finest edifices in Asia, was blown up by gunpowder; and other acts of retribution were perpetrated by the conquering army.

On October 1, 1842, exactly four years after the declaration of war by Lord Auckland, his successor issued a proclamation announcing that the victorious British army would withdraw from Afghanistan. There are some passages in this proclamation which the Duke of

Wellington might have dictated, and Lord Lawrence might have carried out, passages which are true for all time.

"To force a sovereign upon a reluctant people would be as inconsistent with the policy as it is with the purpose of the British Government, tending to place the arms and resources of the people at the disposal of the first invader, and to impose the burden of supporting a sovereign without the prospect of benefit from his alliance.

"The Governor-General will willingly recognise any Government, approved by the Afghans themselves, which shall appear desirous and capable of maintaining friendly relations with neighbouring states.

"Content with the limits Nature appears to have assigned to its Empire, the Government of India will devote all its efforts to the establishment and maintenance of general peace, to the protection of the sovereigns and chiefs, its allies, and to the prosperity and happiness of its own faithful subjects."[1]

These were wise and statesmanlike words. But Lord Ellenborough stained his administration by the policy which he adopted immediately after towards a nearer and weaker neighbour. The Amirs of Sindh had permitted the British army to pass through their country to Kabul in 1838, and from that date the Province of Sindh had acquired a value as the gateway to Western Asia. During the British occupation of Afghanistan the Amirs had rendered good service to the Indian Government; and it is lamentable to record that the conclusion of the Afghan War was immediately followed by the annexation of their country by that Government.

Major Outram had long been the British political agent in Sindh, and had dealt with the Amirs with that courtesy and kindness, joined with firmness and strength, which were a part of his character. In October 1842 the supreme power was taken from his hands and placed in those of Sir Charles Napier, a brave and distinguished

[1] Proclamation dated October 1, 1842.

soldier, but an imperious and quarrelsome man—the last man who should have been appointed to deal with Indian princes.[1] Napier was easily led to believe that some of the Amirs were guilty of disaffection to the British Government, and he declared war against them. The Amirs were defeated in the battles of Miani and Haidarabad in February and March 1843; and Lord Ellenborough, who had gone out to Asia as a peacemaker, ordered the annexation of Sindh.

No impartial historian has tried to justify this annexation of a friendly State on charges which were never proved. And it is to the credit of the Court of Directors that they passed a formal resolution, in August 1843, declaring the proceedings against the Amirs of Sindh to be unjust, impolitic, and inconsistent with the honour and interests of the Indian Government. It is more than probable that Lord Ellenborough had acted with the approval of the Tory Ministry in the matter of Sindh, as Lord Auckland had acted with the approval of the Whig Ministry in the matter of Afghanistan. The Court of Directors, however, had the right of recall, and they recalled Lord Ellenborough in 1844, after only two years' administration, against the public protests of Tory Ministers.

One more incident connected with the annexation of Sindh is interesting, rather from a literary than from an historical point of view. Sir Charles Napier, the conqueror of Sindh, had a younger brother, distinguished in letters as well as in arms. William Napier had fought under the Duke of Wellington in the Peninsular War, and his admirable history of that war is now an English classic. It is a matter of regret that the brave soldier and distinguished historian should have mixed

[1] In 1818 he had been made Governor of Cephalonia, but being of an excessively combative disposition, he became embroiled with the authorities at home. After the conquest of Sindh he became engaged in an acrimonious war of despatches with the British authorities. Later on he went out to India again, and became Commander-in-chief; but he quarrelled with Lord Dalhousie, and finally left India in 1851.

himself up with his brother's quarrels with Major Outram. The author of the "Peninsular War" published a work on the "Conquest of Sindh" in 1845; and not content with defending his brother, William Napier charged Major Outram with want of military skill, with opposition to a policy conducive to the civilisation of India, and with the advocacy of measures calculated to lead to the annihilation of a British force. The two brothers, rich in military and literary fame, sought to crush by the weight of their authority a comparatively young and obscure soldier. It is a signal instance of the justice which posterity sometimes does to true and honourable men, that James Outram survived this unworthy attack, and his fame stands higher in India to-day than that of the conqueror of Sindh. He replied to William Napier's work in his own simple style; and his book is still read by many who have forgotten William Napier's partisan work. Known early in his career as the "Bayard of India" for his high and chivalric character, Outram rose to distinction during the Indian Mutiny of 1857, and was made a baronet in the following year. And when the administration of India passed away from the East India Company to the Crown, Outram took his seat in the Council of the first Viceroy of India, Lord Canning, in 1860.

And the judgment which James Outram passed on the annexation of Sindh was the judgment of the Court of Directors, and is the verdict of impartial historians. "Solemn treaties, though forced upon them [the Amirs of Sindh] were treated as waste paper, past acts of friendship and kindness towards us in the hour of extremity were disregarded, false charges were heaped upon them, they were goaded into resistance, and the ruthless and unrelenting sword of a faithless and merciless ally completed their destruction." [1]

[1] *Conquest of Sindh*, by Lieut.-Col. Outram (London, 1846), p. 485.

CHAPTER II

HARDINGE AND DALHOUSIE

It is not the purpose of the present work to narrate the history of wars and annexations. Nor are the wars and annexations of Auckland and Dalhousie, with all the bitter controversy to which they gave rise, an attractive subject to a writer who desires to confine his story to the condition of the people. But the economic history of India is incomplete without some reference to the enormous expenditure caused by wars, or to the extension of the Empire effected by annexations. We propose therefore, in this chapter, to narrate very briefly the leading incidents of the administration of Hardinge and Dalhousie, as we have narrated the leading acts of Auckland and Ellenborough in the last chapter.

When Lord Ellenborough was recalled from India in 1844, Sir Henry Hardinge was selected to succeed him, and a better selection could not have been made. Hardinge was a brave soldier, and, like many true soldiers, was a man of peace. He had taken a distinguished part in the Peninsular War against Napoleon's forces, and had stood by Sir John Moore when he received his fatal wound in the field of Corunna. He had then taken a part in the hard-fought battle of Albuera, and had been wounded at Vittoria. He was present in the Waterloo campaign, and was in attendance on Marshal Blücher at the battle of Ligny, when his left hand was shattered by a round shot, and had to be amputated.

After the conclusion of the Napoleonic Wars, Hardinge entered Parliament, and retained his seat for over twenty years. He married the sister of Lord Castlereagh in 1821, and entered the Cabinet as Secretary at War, in succession to Lord Palmerston, in 1828. He remained a consistent Tory, and became Secretary at War once more in 1841, when Sir Robert Peel came back to power. And he held that appointment till 1844, when he was selected to succeed Lord Ellenborough in India in his sixtieth year. The appointment was no distinction for a Minister of his position and eminence; and Sir Robert Peel spoke the simple truth when he said, two years after, that in accepting the post of Governor-General of India, Sir Henry Hardinge had "made a great sacrifice from a sense of public duty."

Scarcely eighteen months had elapsed from the date of his landing at Calcutta, when he was forced into a war which was not of his seeking. Ranjit Singh, the great ruler of the Punjab, died in 1839; and the magnificent Sikh army which he had created became uncontrollable when his restraining hand was withdrawn. Like the Pretorian Guards of ancient Rome they became masters of the situation; they formed Panchyets in every regiment and obeyed no other power; and they set up and deposed men in authority. Anarchy followed with frequent revolutions; and the brother of Ranjit Singh's widow was tried and condemned by the military Panchyets, and shot by a party of soldiers. And in November 1845 the magnificent but misguided Sikh army, consisting of 60,000 soldiers, 40,000 armed followers, and 150 guns, crossed the Sutlej and invaded British India.

The commander of the Sikh army, Lal Singh, was a traitor, and probably wished the destruction of the army he led. In the first action with the British, at Moodkee, Lal Singh fled at the beginning of the battle, and so caused the defeat of his troops. The second battle, at Ferozshahar, was obstinately fought. British cannon, says an eye-witness, were dismounted, and the ammunition blown into the air; British squadrons were checked in mid career; battalion after battalion was hurled back with shattered ranks; and it was not till after sunset that portions of the Sikh position were finally carried.[1] The battle was renewed in the morning, but through the treachery or cowardice of Lal Singh his army was soon in full retreat. The third battle was won by the British at Aliwal; but the decisive contest which concluded the war was the battle of Sobreon, fought on February 10, 1846. The Sikh soldiers fought with the valour of crusaders and the determination of heroes. But Tej Singh, the Sikh commander, fled at the first assault, and is supposed to have broken the bridge over the Sutlej to prevent the escape of his army. The British victory was complete, but was dearly purchased by the loss of over two thousand troops, killed and wounded. The river, says Lord Hardinge's son, who was present at the action, was alive with a struggling mass of men. The artillery, now brought down to the water's edge, completed the slaughter. Few escaped; none surrendered. The Sikhs met their fate with that resignation which distinguished their race.[2]

The terms imposed on the conquered people proved the moderation of the conqueror. The Sikh kingdom must be dismembered so as not to be again a formidable enemy to the British Empire. But subject to this condition, Lord Hardinge (now raised to the peerage) respected the independence of the Punjab. By the treaty of March 1846 the Sikh Darbar abandoned the eastern portion of the Punjab between the Beas and the Sutlej, promised payment of a million and a half sterling or its equivalent in territory, undertook to reduce the army to twenty-five battalions of infantry and 12,000 cavalry, and surrendered all guns which had been pointed

[1] Cunningham's *History of the Sikhs*.

[2] *Viscount Hardinge*, by his son and private secretary in India, Charles, second Viscount Hardinge.

against the British army. The Sikh Darbar could not pay the stipulated sum, and a further cession of territory was therefore required. And Kashmir was thus separated from the Punjab, and made over the Golab Singh on payment of £750,000 to the British.

This treaty, concluded in March 1846, failed to safeguard the peace of the Punjab. The Sikh Darbar desired that the British troops should be maintained in Lahore to protect the Government. A second treaty of Lahore was accordingly concluded in December 1846. Ranjit Singh's widow, an able but intriguing woman, was excluded from all power, and received an annual pension of £15,000. A Council of Regency, consisting of eight Sardars, was appointed during the minority of Maharaja Dhalip Singh. A British Resident was appointed with plenary and unlimited power to control and guide the Darbar. A British garrison was maintained in the Punjab during the minority of the sovereign. And it was stipulated that the British Government should receive £220,000 a year towards the expenses of the occupation.

Five days after the conclusion of this treaty, the Governor-General wrote to the Secret Committee: "These terms give the British Resident unlimited authority in all matters of internal administration and external relations during the Maharaja's minority."[1] And in a General Proclamation which he issued on August 20, 1847, Lord Hardinge announced that he felt "the interest of a father in the education and guardianship of the young Prince."[2]

Major Henry Lawrence, an officer as brave as he was kindly and courteous, was appointed the first Resident. It is possible to conceive that if Lord Hardinge had remained in India five years longer, and

[1] Parliamentary Papers. Articles of agreement with the Lahore Darbar, 1847, p. 24.

[2] Parliamentary Papers (Punjab, 1849), p. 53.

if Henry Lawrence had remained in his post for the same period, the Punjab would have remained a strong, friendly, and enlightened Native State. But Lord Hardinge was succeeded by Lord Dalhousie within six months from the date of the General Proclamation. And Major Henry Lawrence too was compelled to leave India on account of ill-health, and was succeeded by Sir Frederick Currie.

Lord Dalhousie was a young Scotch peer, and had succeeded to the earldom in 1838. When Sir Robert Peel came to power on the fall of the Melbourne Ministry, he appointed Lord Dalhousie Vice-President of the Board of Trade in 1843, under Gladstone, who was the President. And two years after, the young earl succeeded Gladstone as President. In this capacity Lord Dalhousie had to deal with the new railways; and it is significant that he laid before the Prime Minister a scheme for treating railways as a national concern, and for bringing them completely under State control. Sir Robert Peel rightly rejected the idea of a State management of railways for England. Lord John Russell was favourably impressed with the young and industrious nobleman. And when the Liberals came to power Lord John had the magnanimity to offer to the Tory peer the post of Governor-General of India. Lord Dalhousie accepted the post, and at the early age of thirty-five succeeded the veteran Lord Hardinge in 1848.

Lord Hardinge had taken every possible precaution to secure peace and good administration in the Punjab. A British Resident had been invested with "full authority to direct and control the duties of every department." A British force had been stationed at Lahore "for the protection of the Maharaja and the preservation of the peace of the country." The British Government had power to occupy any fort or military post in the kingdom "for the security of the capital, and for maintaining the peace of the country." The Lahore State was to pay to the British Government £220,000 a year "for the maintenance of this force, and to meet the expenses incurred by the British Government." And these arrangements were to continue during the Maharaja's minority, and to "cease and terminate on His Highness attaining the full age of 16 years, or on the 4th of September of the year 1854."[1]

Maharaja Dhalip Singh was virtually the ward of the British Government; the British Government had undertaken to protect him, to control the administration of his country, and to preserve peace. And Lord Hardinge had taken adequate measures to fulfil the task imposed on the British Government. Fifty thousand men, with sixty guns, commanded the line of the Sutlej. A standing camp of nine thousand men held Lahore. Another standing camp of equal strength, with infantry, cavalry, and artillery complete, lay at Firozpur. Everything was in a state of perfect preparation to meet any contingency that might arise.

And yet no timely action was taken when trouble arose shortly after the departure of Hardinge. Dewan Mulraj's father had governed Multan for thirty years with almost independent sway. When the British Resident called for an account of his stewardship from Mulraj, he made various delays, and pretended to resign. He was taken at his word, and a successor was sent to Multan under the protection of two Englishmen, Vans Agnew and Colonel Henderson. The fort was at first surrendered, but soon after Agnew and Henderson were treacherously murdered, and Mulraj regained and kept possession of the fort. The British Resident, Sir Frederick Currie, called on the Commander-in-chief, Lord Gough, to advance with a British force from Firozpur, and to stamp out the rebellion. But Lord Gough declined, and Lord Dalhousie supported the decision of Lord Gough. The rebellion was thus allowed time to spread.

[1] Articles VI., VII., VIII., IX., and XI. of the Treaty of December 16, 1846.

One English officer did his duty promptly and well. Lieutenant Edwards was in his tent on the banks of the Indus when he heard of the murder of the English officers and of Mulraj's rebellion. He made a rush with only 400 men to Multan, but he could effect little against Mulraj's 4000 men and eight heavy guns defending the fort. All through the heat of the summer he did what it was possible for a British officer to do. He obtained levies from the State of Bhawalpur, defeated Mulraj in two battles in June and July, and drove him to the shelter of his fort. Had the higher authorities sent him aid from Lahore and Firozpur, as they were bound to do by the treaty of December 1846, the Multan rebellion would have been put down. And "had the Multan rebellion been put down," says Lieutenant Edwards himself, "the Sikh insurrection would never have grown out of it."

While no timely action was taken to put down the local rebellion, measures were adopted by the British Resident which created a general consternation among the Sikhs. Ranjit Singh's widow, the mother of Maharaja Dhalip Singh, was an intriguing woman; but she had been excluded from all share in the government, and had been removed to Sheikhpur, and had ceased to be a source of danger. According to Lieutenant Edwards, "The Rani Jhanda, who had more wit and daring than any man of her nation, was weary of scattering ambiguous voices and of writing incendiary epistles. . . . There was no longer a man found in the Punjab who would shoulder a musket at her bidding."[1] Under these circumstances the Resident's order to banish her from the Punjab to Benares was a measure of doubtful necessity, while its effect on the Sikh soldiery was instantaneous. "The reports from Raja Sher Singh's camp," wrote the Resident on May 25, "are that the Khalsa soldiery, on hearing of the removal of the Maharani, are much disturbed. They

[1] *A Year on the Punjab Frontier*, by Major Edwards, C.B.

said she was the mother of the Khasla, and that as she was gone, and the young Dhalip Singh in our hands, they had no longer any one to fight for or uphold." [1]

The postponement of the young Maharaja's marriage was another measure which created an unfavourable impression. Lieutenant Edwards saw this, and wrote to the Resident on July 28: "An opinion had gone very prevalently abroad, and been carefully disseminated by the evil-disposed, that the British meditate declaring the Punjab forfeited by the recent troubles and misconduct of the troops. . . . It would, I think, be a wise and timely measure to give such public assurance of British good faith, and intention to adhere to the Treaty, as would be involved in authoritative preparations for providing the young Maharaja with a Queen. It would, no doubt, settle men's minds greatly." [2] This wise counsel was unheeded.

Lastly, the treatment accorded to Sardar Chatra Singh, whose daughter the young Maharaja was to have married, further inflamed men's minds. Chatra Singh was the Governor of the Hazara province, inhabited by an armed Mahomedan population, warlike and difficult to control. Captain Abbot, an assistant of the Resident, was appointed to aid and advise him, but he placed himself in open opposition to the Sardar from the commencement. In August 1848 the mountaineers of Hazara, roused by Captain Abbot, closed the passes and surrounded the town where Chatra Singh was residing. The Sardar ordered the troops, stationed for the protection of the town, to encamp under the guns of the fort. Colonel Canora refused to move out of the city, and threatened to fire upon the first man that came near. Chatra Singh sent two companies of the Sikh infantry to take possession of the guns. Canora applied the match to one of the guns, missed fire, and was immediately after struck down

[1] Punjab Papers, 1849, pp. 168 and 179.

[2] *Ibid.*, p. 271.

by musket shots from the infantry. Captain Abbot called this incident the murder of Canora by the instigation of Chatra Singh. He was justly rebuked by the Resident, who wrote: "I have given you no authority to raise levies and organise paid bands of soldiers. . . . It is much, I think, to be lamented that you have kept the Nizam [Chatra Singh] at a distance from you; have resisted his offers and suggestions to be allowed himself to reside near you. . . . None of the accounts which have yet been made justify you in calling the death of Commedan Canora a murder, nor in asserting that it was premeditated by Sardar Chatra Singh."[1] Nevertheless, orders were passed in August, not to punish Captain Abbot, but to deprive Sardar Chatra Singh of the post of Governor, to resume his Jaigir, and to humiliate before the Sikh people the man whose daughter was to have been wedded to their sovereign.

All these impolitic acts roused the Sikh nation, and the rebellion of Multan began to spread. Chatra Singh's son, Sher Singh, went over to Mulraj with 5000 Sikhs, and the British force had to raise the siege of Multan. Nearly all the Sardars joined the insurrection, and the whole of the open country was in their hands.

In November 1848, seven months after the rising at Multan, Lord Gough at last moved out with his grand army. But at the first action at Ramnagar on the Chinab, he received a serious check; and the second action at Sadulapur was scarcely a victory. The third action at Chilianwala was disastrous. The British infantry proceeded to the attack when exhausted and breathless, and were compelled to make a retreat; the British cavalry, advancing without the support of guns, were similarly forced to a retreat which was soon converted into a flight; the colours of three regiments and four guns were captured by the Sikhs; and a total loss of 89 officers and 2350 men was the end of a hasty and

[1] Punjab Papers, 1849, p. 316.

ill-judged attack. Lord Dalhousie claimed this also as a victory in his public despatches, but in his private letter regretted "the lamentable succession of three unsuccessful actions" at Ramnagar, Sadulapur, and Chilianwala.

When the news of this last action was received in England, public indignation exceeded all bounds. Lord Gough was recalled, and Sir Charles Napier was appointed Commander-in-chief. Before his arrival, however, Lord Gough had retrieved his reputation by a decisive victory at Gujrat on February 20, 1849. Multan had already fallen into the hands of the British in January. The Sikh army, beaten at Gujrat, was pursued across the plains of the Punjab by Gilbert, "the best rider in India," and surrendered at Rawal Pindi on March 12. Peace was restored within one year from the date of the first trouble at Multan.

By the treaty of December 1846 the British Government had undertaken to suppress risings in the Punjab, and to protect the minor Maharaja Dhalip Singh. By a proclamation, which was issued in November 1848 with Lord Dalhousie's sanction, it was declared that the British army "entered the Lahore territories, not as an enemy of the constituted Government, but to restore order and obedience." Nevertheless, as soon as order was restored, the constituted Government was set aside. The Maharaja was dethroned and the Punjab was annexed to the British dominions. Sir Henry Lawrence, the first Resident appointed after the treaty of December 1846, protested against the annexation, and tendered his resignation. But Lord Dalhousie knew his worth as a pacificator, and induced him to withdraw his resignation. Of this great and gifted soldier we shall have more to say when we speak of the administration of the Punjab.

Another war was undertaken by Lord Dalhousie, three years after, in the eastern frontiers of the Indian

Empire. In Burma, in spite of the treaty of Yandobo, various sums of money were levied on foreign merchants, and trade with the Burmese was attended with risks and difficulties. Since 1840, therefore, the British Government had ceased to maintain an accredited agent at the Court of Ava. On September 27, 1851, British merchants at Rangoon made their complaints to the willing ears of Lord Dalhousie. The Governor-General sent a naval officer to inquire into the truth of the complaints; demanded compensation for the losses of merchants amounting to £900; and asked for the dismissal of the Burmese Governor of Rangoon. It was a repetition in Asia of the action taken by Lord Palmerston in the preceding year with reference to the losses of a Maltese Jew in Greece. Lord Dalhousie's requisitions were not complied with, and he declared war. Rangoon, Prome, and Pegu were captured, and on December 20, 1852, Lord Dalhousie closed the war by a proclamation annexing Lower Burma to the British territories.

The history of the annexation of Indian States on failure of heirs, during the administration of Lord Dalhousie, is even more singular than the history of his conquests. The ancient laws of India provided that, on the failure of natural issue, a Hindu might adopt an heir to inherit his property; and there was no distinction in the eye of the law between a natural heir and an adopted son. During the five centuries of Mahomedan rule in Northern India, Mahomedan kings and emperors had never questioned the Hindu law of adoption. On the demise of a Hindu chief, his son, natural or adopted, took out a new Sunud from the ruling emperor, and stepped into his place. On the other hand, emperors bent on conquest annexed principalities without scruple, whether the chief was living or dead, whether his son was born of his loins or adopted. Under the British rule the practice of obtaining the sanction of the Government, when a Hindu chief adopted a son, was introduced And when once this custom was recognised, the keen eye of the East India Company saw the possibility of extending their territories by refusing the sanction. Accordingly, the Court of Directors declared in 1834, that the indulgence of sanctioning the adoption of an heir should be the exception, not the rule. And the Government of India determined in 1841 "to persevere in the one clear and direct course of abandoning no just and honourable accession of territory or revenue." It was reserved for Lord Dalhousie to carry out this "just and honourable" principle into practice. With the exception of one or two very insignificant States, previously annexed under circumstances of a special nature, the policy had never been carried into practice before Dalhousie's time.

The first victim of this new policy was the House of Satara. The Rajah of Satara represented the family of the great Sivaji, the founder of the Mahratta power. The principality had been constituted by the Marquis of Hastings in 1818, when he annexed the Mahratta kingdom of the last Peshwa in the Deccan. A generation had passed since; and the last Raja of Satara had adopted a son, as he was entitled to do by the laws of his country and his race. On the death of the Raja in 1848, the Governor of Bombay, Sir George Clerk, recommended that the heir should be allowed to succeed to the State of Satara. His councillors opposed him; his successor differed from him; and Lord Dalhousie pursued the ungenerous course of annexing the State. The matter came up to the Court of Directors. The veteran Director, Henry St. George Tucker, whose name has appeared in the last chapter and will appear again in these pages, opposed the annexation. The issue, however, was never doubtful for a moment; by a large majority of votes the Court sanctioned the annexation.

The State of Karauli came up next for consideration.

The Raja of Karauli died in the same year as the Raja of Satara, and, like him, had adopted an heir before his death. Lord Dalhousie could see no difference between Satara and Karauli, and held that Karauli also had "lapsed" to the British Government. The Court of Directors, however, decided that Karauli was a "protected ally," and not a "dependent principality," and the State was therefore not to be annexed. The grounds on which the Court of Directors differed from Lord Dalhousie are set forth in their letter of January 26, 1853.

"Colonel Low gave his opinion in favour of recognising the adoption and Sir Frederick Currie supported the proposal. The Governor-General with whom Mr. Lowis expressed his concurrence, inclined rather to declaring the State a lapse to the British Government.

"The Governor-General has given a fair and impartial statement of the arguments on both sides of this important question. After having given the fullest consideration to the circumstances of the case, we have come to the decision that the succession of Bharat Pal to the Raj of Karauli, as the adopted son of Narsingh Pal, should be sanctioned.

"In coming to this conclusion we do not intend to depart from the principle laid down in our despatch of the 24th January 1849, relative to the case of Satara. . . . But it appears to us that there is a marked distinction in fact, between the cases of Satara and Karauli, which is not sufficiently adverted to in the minute of the Governor-General. The Satara State was one of recent origin, derived altogether from the creation and gift of the British Government, whilst Karauli is one of the oldest of the Rajput States, which has been under the rule of its princes from a period long anterior to the British power in India."[1]

This letter of the Directors discloses the reasons of the Company's moderation. Satara was an insignificant

[1] Karauli Blue Book, 1855, pp. 3 and 4.

Mahratta State, and its annexation involved no political risk. Karauli was a Rajput State, and its annexation might alarm the whole of Rajputana. The Indian Reform Association, led by Mr. Dickinson, a true and disinterested friend of India, drew public attention to the impolicy of annexing Karauli. A motion by Mr. Blackett was threatened in the House of Commons; and the Government of the day avoided the scandal, and bade the Governor-General hold his hand.

The large State of Sambalpur in the Central Provinces was then annexed, as the Raja had died childless without adopting an heir. But a far more important and a historic case soon came up for consideration. The Raja of Jhansi, Gangadhar Rao, died in November 1853, after adopting a son who assumed the name of Damodar Gangadhar Rao. The dying Raja announced the adoption to the two British officers stationed at Jhansi, the political agent and the commander of a contingent of troops. He delivered to them letters to the proper authorities, and commended his widow and adopted son to the British Government. Lord Dalhousie held that "the adoption was good for the conveyance of private rights, though not for the transfer of the Principality," and he annexed the State.

The State of Jhansi had rendered signal services to the British power in its earlier days. The Raja of Jhansi had saved Kalpi in 1825, and had been commended in the highest terms of praise and gratitude by Lord William Bentinck at the Darbar of 1832. He had appended to his titles the addition of *Fidwee Badshah Janujah Englistan*, "Devoted servant of the glorious King of England."

After the annexation, the widow Rani made an appeal to the British Government, alluding to the loyalty of her house; and Major Malcolm, the political agent at Jhansi, supported her statement. "The Bai does not, I believe, in the slightest degree overestimate the fidelity and loyalty all along evinced by the State of Jhansi towards our Government under circumstances of considerable temptation, before our power had arrived at that commanding position which it has since attained." And the widow herself was described by Major Malcolm as "a lady of very high character, and much respected by every one at Jhansi."[1] But Lord Dalhousie was not moved from his fixed resolve either by the past history of the State or by the position and character of its present Rani.

The annexation converted the friendly and faithful State of Jhansi into a bitter enemy; and it converted a lady of high character into a merciless and vindictive woman. For the Rani of Jhansi fomented, helped, and joined the great mutiny of 1857; she permitted at Jhansi one of the worst of the Mutiny massacres; she fought in male attire against the British troops; and she fell sword in hand, the bravest fighter of her race. The Rani of Jhansi might have lived to be an able and benevolent administrator of her little State, like so many Hindu women who have figured in modern Indian history. But a more tragic fate was reserved for her; and she is remembered as the Joan of Arc of modern Indian romance.

Smaller States were annexed one after another; but the last and greatest annexation under the Doctrine of Lapse was the kingdom of Nagpur. Raghoji Bhonsla, Raja of Nagpur, died on December 11, 1853. One of his widows adopted a young kinsman, known under the title of Appa Sahib, and the adoption was valid under the Hindu law. The Political Resident, Mr. Mansel, adhered to the standing instructions of his office; he neither forbade nor gave special encouragement to the proceeding;[2] but he recommended that the adoption should be recognised. On January 28, 1854, Lord Dalhousie recorded his minute, annexing the large and populous kingdom.

[1] Jhansi Blue Book, pp. 24 and 28.
[2] First Nagpur Blue Book, p. 56.

The extensive and valuable cotton-producing country of Berar was taken over under a different plea. The Subsidiary Force kept up at the expense of the Nizam of Hyderabad had been excessive, and £750,000 were due from him as arrears. The Governor-General intimated that he would accept Berar, as well as the rich tract between the Krishna and the Tumbhadra, in payment of the debt, and as security for future charges for contingent force. When the draft treaty was presented to the Nizam he remonstrated in vain. He asked if an alliance which had lasted for sixty years would have such an ending, and he pleaded that to take away from him a third of his dominions would be to humiliate him in the eyes of his subjects. His expostulations were in vain; he signed the treaty, and died soon after.[1]

One more act of Lord Dalhousie remains to be narrated—the annexation of the kingdom of Oudh. The misgovernment of Oudh was the reason of this annexation, and no one who reads the official literature on the subject, and weighs the evidence of unimpeachable and even sympathetic witnesses like Sleeman and Outram, will question the misrule and disorder of Oudh. Yet this misgovernment could have been remedied. General Sir William Sleeman, Resident of Lucknow from 1840 to 1854, pressed upon the Government of India his scheme for reforming the administration of Oudh, and he staked his high reputation on the success of his measure. But annexation, not reform, was Lord Dalhousie's idea; and he declared in one of his Consultative Minutes on the subject, that if the British Government undertook the responsibility, the labour, and risk of reforming a Native State, it ought to be allowed to appropriate the surplus revenue.[2] It was this rage for

[1] All subsequent proposals for the restoration of Berar to the Nizam, on payment of all debts due, proved fruitless. And quite recently Berar has been permanently leased to the Indian Government. The Nizam was soon after made a G.C.B., which the wags of Hyderabad construe in three words: *Gave Curzon Berar.*

[2] Oudh Papers (1856).

annexation which kept Lord Dalhousie from adopting prompt remedies in many cases until the evil had grown, and until he could swoop down on the offending State and include it in the Company's territory.

Lord Dalhousie placed three schemes with regard to Oudh before the Directors. He proposed that the King of Oudh should make over the province to the British Government for a limited period; or that he might be maintained in his royal state while the administration would be vested for ever in the Company; or that the State should be fully and formally annexed to the British dominions. A ruler like Bentinck would have adopted the first scheme; Lord Dalhousie himself advocated the second; the Court of Directors decided on the third. In their despatch of November 21, 1855, which has been characterised as "a specimen of the art of writing important instructions so as to avoid responsibility," the Directors issued their orders for the annexation of Oudh. And they further wished that Lord Dalhousie himself should carry out the orders before laying down his office in India. Lord Dalhousie's health had broken down after eight years' continuous work in India. He was prematurely old at forty-three, was suffering from illness, and could scarcely walk. Nevertheless, he had promised to carry out the decision of the Court of Directors, and he redeemed his promise. The province of Oudh was annexed to the British territories by Proclamation on February 13, 1856. On that last day of the same month Lord Dalhousie resigned his office as Governor-General of India. "It is well," he said to his physician, "that there are only twenty-nine days in this month; I could not have held out two days more."

We have in the preceding pages briefly narrated the history of Lord Dalhousie's conquests and annexations. During his administration of eight years he annexed eight large kingdoms or states, and the reasons assigned for these annexations were various. The Punjab was annexed because there was a rising in the country, such as the British Government itself had undertaken to quell in their treaty with the minor sovereign. Lower Burma was annexed on the complaints of British merchants trading in that country. Berar was taken over because the Nizam could not pay his debts. The kingdom of Oudh was annexed because of its misgovernment. Sambalpur was annexed because the last Raja left no heirs; and Satara, Jhansi, and Nagpur were annexed because Lord Dalhousie declined to recognise the heirs adopted by the rulers of those States.

Into the bitter controversies, of which these measures have formed the subject, it is not our purpose to enter. No impartial historian has defended Lord Dalhousie's policy and action on the ground of justice. One of the most thoughtful writers of the Victorian Age condones the crimes of Dalhousie by comparing them with the crimes of Frederick the Great of Prussia.[1] But this comparison is not altogether appropriate. Frederick's wars were against equal foes, and his crimes were almost redeemed by his high purpose to give his own country a place amongst the great nations of Europe. Dalhousie struck those who could not long resist; and he descended to an untrue interpretation of an ancient law in order to add to the already vast empire and revenues of the East India Company.

Lord Dalhousie was the last of the old Imperialist school of rulers who believed that the salvation and progress of the Indian people were possible only by the destruction of their autonomy and self-government. Brief as were his years after he retired from India, he lived to see the opinion of that school discredited, the East India Company abolished, and the Doctrine of Lapse

[1] "Lord Dalhousie, in particular, stands out in history as a ruler of the type of Frederick the Great, and did deeds which are almost as difficult to justify as the seizure of Silesia or the partition of Poland. But these acts, if crimes, are crimes of the same order as those of Frederick, crimes of ambition."—Seeley's *Expansion of England.*

disavowed by his Sovereign and Queen. A more generous confidence in the progress of the people of India by their own endeavours marked the early years of the Queen's direct rule. Within those years a Conservative Secretary of State, Sir Stafford Northcote, resolved to restore Mysore to Native rule; and another Conservative Secretary of State, Lord Salisbury, refused to annex Baroda on the ground of its misgovernment and crime. The restoration of Mysore to the old family, and the selection of a new and worthy ruler for Baroda, are amongst the wisest, as they are the most generous, political acts of British Ministers in relation to India. And no part of India is better governed to-day than these States, ruled by their own Princes.

CHAPTER III

LAND SETTLEMENTS IN NORTHERN INDIA

THE British Province of Bengal, founded by Lord Clive, was rapidly extended under the rule of Warren Hastings and the Marquis of Wellesley. Benares and some adjoining districts were annexed by Warren Hastings in 1775, on the death of the Nawab of Oudh, by a treaty concluded with his successor. Allahabad and some neighbouring districts were ceded by the Nawab of Oudh in 1801, under pressure from Lord Wellesley, and were called the *Ceded Provinces.* Delhi and Agra and the basin of the Ganges were conquered from the Mahrattas in 1803, also during the administration of Lord Wellesley, and were called the *Conquered Provinces.*

In Benares, the State-demand from the soil was permanently fixed in 1795. A pledge of a similar Permanent Settlement was given to the land-holders of the Ceded and Conquered Provinces in 1803 and 1805, but the pledge was never redeemed. For in 1808 the Special Commissioners, R. W. Cox and Henry St. George Tucker, opposed the immediate conclusion of a Permanent Settlement in these Provinces.[1] And after a long con-

[1] Henry St. George Tucker, whose name has been mentioned in the preceding chapters, was a strong advocate of a Permanent Settlement of the land revenues of India. In 1808 he had recommended a delay in the conclusion of such a settlement, not its abandonment. "I was appointed in 1807," he wrote, many years after, "to carry into execution a measure which successive administrators had considered to be essential to the prosperity of the country. Although concurring most unreservedly in the opinion that it was wise and salutary, and that it contained a vital principle which must in the end work out all the good anticipated, I ventured to counsel delay upon the ground that we were not at the moment in a state of preparation to consummate so great an undertaking; but it never occurred to my mind that the principle of the measure was to be abandoned, or that the landholders who had received from us the

troversy the Court of Directors finally declared themselves, in 1821, against the conclusion of a Permanent Settlement in Northern India. Regulation VII. of 1822 was then passed, which declared that the State was entitled to 83 per cent. of the gross rental of estates, and permitted the Settlement to be revised from time to time.

To Lord William Bentinck belongs the credit of reducing this excessive assessment, and of introducing long-term Settlements. He held a Conference at Allahabad in 1833, and the result was the passing of Regulation IX. of 1833, the basis of Land Settlements in Northern India. The State-demand was reduced to 66 per cent. of the rental, and Settlements were made for thirty years.

The great task was entrusted to Robert Merttins Bird, who performed it in the humane spirit in which Lord William Bentinck's policy was conceived. The procedure which he followed was described by himself many years after, when he was examined as a witness before a Select Committee of the House of Commons. The first process was to make a rough summary of all the land within a fiscal area. The second was to make a map including every field. The third was to make a professional survey showing the cultivated and the uncultivated land. The fourth process was to fix the Land Tax for the entire fiscal area. And the fifth and final measure was to apportion the entire amount among the villages contained within the area.

It may easily be imagined that the last two processes, the fixing of the Land Tax for a Pergana or fiscal division, and its apportionment among the villages included in the division, were watched by the agriculturists with the

most solemn pledge given in the most authentic form, were to be deprived of the promised benefit, and that in the end they were to be cast aside as an encumbrance on the earth. That pledge can never be effaced, although it remains unfulfilled."—Kaye's *Life and Correspondence of Henry St. George Tucker*, p. 222.

keenest anxiety. And indeed the weak point of the system was the assessment. For although 66 per cent. of the rental was made the rule, the rental itself was ascertained by guess-work, especially in lands held by Village Communities. "We then proceeded," said Merttins Bird, "to investigate the assessment of the Government Land Tax upon that tract, finding out, as best we could from the previous payments, and from the statements of the people themselves, from the nature of the crop and the nature of the soil, and such various means as experience furnished to us, what might be considered a fair demand for the Government to lay upon it." [1]

This method left the widest latitude to the Settlement Officer, and the greatest uncertainty in the liabilities of the agriculturist. No two Settlement Officers could form the same judgment on data which were so vague; and the assessment made at one Settlement was departed from, and generally enhanced, at the next Settlement. Agricultural prosperity was impossible when the tax on agriculture was so variable; and the accumulation of wealth, which the advocates of a Permanent Settlement had contemplated, was equally impossible, when the first signs of wealth and prosperity naturally suggested a more rigorous assessment at the succeeding Settlement.

In spite of this defect, however, the Settlement commenced in 1833 was made in a humane spirit, and gave great relief to the peasantry of Northern India, harassed by severe assessments and short settlements during the first thirty years of British rule. Merttins Bird laboured for nine years, and, on the eve of leaving India in 1842, submitted a full and exhaustive report on the results of the Settlement which was then coming to a close.

The idea of a Permanent Settlement had been abandoned. But nevertheless Bird intended and desired that the Settlement he had made should be considered permanent in the districts where most of the cultivable

[1] Fourth Report of the Select Committee, 1853, p. 30.

lands had already been brought under the plough. We glean the following facts from his lucid report.

DELHI DIVISION.

Portions of this division, irrigated by canals, were well peopled and prosperous. They had been over-assessed in some instances, but the pressure was now removed, and the Government Revenue now assessed was fair. The remaining portion which was not irrigated afforded only a precarious return to the husbandman.

"I consider, therefore, that no increase of resources can be expected from the Delhi territory on a revision of Settlement, unless Government should hereafter open a canal."

The average price of wheat was 73 lbs. for 2s.

MEERUT DIVISION.

Saharanpur District.—"This district had been partially very much over-assessed, and the measures employed for collecting the revenue had been equally harsh and illegal; some of the communities composed of the most industrious classes had been cruelly depressed. Every effort was made to effect an equalisation of the demand, and with considerable success; but a considerable inequality still remains." An increase in the Government Revenue might be made in some villages of this district after the expiry of the Settlement, but, "one-fifth of the culturable land should always be left untaxed to allow for raising artificial grasses or other fodder for cattle, and to allow for fallows and chances of dereliction." A moderate increase in the Government Revenue might be expected on the completion of the irrigation canal from Hurdwar to Allahabad.

The average price of wheat was 80 lbs. for 2s.

Muzaffarnagar District.—Some increase in the revenue might be expected at the next Settlement where low rates were now paid, but, "no Mauza [village] having brought one-half of its culturable area into the state known in the district by the term *Meesum*, and paying at the standard fixed for that rate, should be subjected to any enhanced demand."

The average price of wheat was 75 lbs. for 2s.

Bulandshahar District.—Backward, and assessment low. Increase in the Government Revenue might be expected on the completion of the irrigation canal, and also from increased cultivation and the raising of rates.

The average price of wheat was 66 lbs. for 2s.

Meerut District.—A very fine district. Increase in the Government demand might be expected at the next Settlement from increased cultivation, "but none could be looked for from enhancement of rates, except what may be obtained by the introduction of canal irrigation."

The average price of wheat was 66 lbs. for 2s.

Aligarh District.—A prosperous and well-cultivated district. Future increase of land revenue could be expected only in six Perganas named, not in others except by the introduction of canal irrigation. The Village Communities of this district had received large advances from the indigo planters, Morton and MacClintock, as well as from native bankers; and much trouble, and the sale of lands assigned for the debts, ensued.

The average price of wheat was 78 lbs. for 2s.

Agra Division.

Agra District.—Fully cultivated and assessed. "No increase of revenue can at any time be expected from this district, and the Jumma [assessment] should be declared permanent at its present amount. The only hope of any improvement in the products, or methods of cultivation, or increase of irrigation, must be founded on the agriculturists possessing an assurance that they will reap the whole return of their pains and cost."[1]

Muttra District.—Also fully cultivated. "The revenue at its present rate should be confirmed in perpetuity. There is no prospect of any further improvement unless the people be assured of reaping all the advantage of it."

Farrackabad District.—Some parts were fully cultivated, but others ought to yield an increase of revenue at the next Settlement, both from increase of cultivation and from increase of rates. The introduction of canal irrigation should also lead to an increase.

Mynpoori District.—Some parts fully cultivated and assessed, others not.

Etawa District.—Fully cultivated and assessed. "No future increase is to be expected from it, except from the introduction of canal irrigation. With this reservation the present assessment ought to be considered perpetual."

Rohilkhand Division.

Bijnaur District.—The district had been heavily assessed before, and cruelly treated by previous Revenue Officers. "Forced transfers of property to unwilling purchasers and mortgagees, forced loans extorted from recusant bankers, forced labour required for the cultivation of Mauzas [villages] which from abandonment had fallen into the management of public officers, were among the practices resorted to." These evils were now remedied, and an equitable revenue was fixed, but an equality in assessment was not yet obtained.

Muradabad District.—No information had been obtained.

[1] Paragraph 87 of Bird's Report. This was the argument used by all the advocates of a Permanent Settlement from Lord Cornwallis to Lord Wellesley, Hastings, and Minto. It is significant that after the Directors had rejected the idea of a Permanent Settlement in 1821, Robert Bird still insisted on it in 1842, in the fully cultivated districts of Northern India, as the only hope of future agricultural improvement.

Bareli District.—This district had been heavily over-assessed before, and portions of it had suffered severely from the famine of 1837. Many of the starving inhabitants had formed gangs for plunder, and many cultivators had left their homes. The assessment made at the present Settlement was moderate.

Budaon District.—The district was in a state of great distress at the time of the Settlement. The Settlement took place "when the disposition to over-assess was far from being allayed," and had therefore to be repeatedly revised. Full relief was not yet given. "No slight benefit will have been gained if Government and its servants are convinced, as I trust they now are, of the actual loss of money which is certain to follow over-assessment, and resolve to maintain those principles of moderation which have now been brought into actual practical operation for the first time."

Shajehanpur District.—The district had escaped the misery of over-assessment in past Settlements; was lightly assessed at the present Settlement, and was in a flourishing state.

Pilibeet District.—Half the district had been much over-assessed previously, but now obtained ample relief. The other half had been settled with Raja Gurnam Singh. The climate of the district was very unhealthy.

The average price of wheat was 57 lbs. for 2s.

Allahabad Division.

Cawnpur District.—Had been a good deal over-assessed before, but now obtained relief. Most parts of the district were however fully cultivated and assessed, and except by reason of canal irrigation, "the demand on Cawnpur should be considered as not liable to increase, and fixed in perpetuity."

Futtehpur District.—These remarks applied to Futtehpur District. "With exception to the increase to be gained by the introduction of canal irrigation, this district must be considered settled in perpetuity."

Allahabad District.—Had escaped the calamity of over-assessment in the past. With the exception of the increase due for canal irrigation, "this settlement should also be considered fixed in perpetuity."

The average price of wheat was 54 lbs. for 2s.

Benares Division.

Azimgarh District.—A fertile, well-irrigated, and well-cultivated district. Some portions were fully assessed and should not be considered liable to future enhancement. The remaining portions "may fairly yield an enhancement proportioned to the increase of cultivation at the close of the present term. The rates ought not to be enhanced."

The average price of wheat was 59 lbs. for 2s.

Goruckpur District.—A fertile and favourably circumstanced district and expected to yield an increase in the Government demand in the future, both from increased cultivation and from increased rate of assessment.

The average price of wheat was 62 lbs. for 2s.

The nett results of Bird's Settlement are shown in the following figures compiled from tables appended to his report. Ten rupees are taken as equivalent to a pound sterling.

Division.	District.	Total Area in Acres.	Cultivated Area in Acres.	Bird's Assessment of the Land Tax.
				£
Delhi	Delhi	364,534	174,605	36,337
	Rohtuk	844,666	474,465	62,831
	Gurgaon	1,160,437	647,353	101,424
	Hissar	1,657,975	696,147	38,020
Meerut	Saharanpur	1,018,705	606,847	100,558
	Muzaffarnagar	691,706	392,377	67,274
	Meerut	1,776,430	1,034,016	281,561
	Bulandshahar	1,025,096	592,630	95,168
	Aligarh	1,119,238	900,562	196,448
Rohilkhand	Bijnaur	1,027,533	459,409	112,237
	Muradabad	not given	not given	66,870
	Budaon	1,450,418	752,103	110,300
	Pilibeet	not given	not given	39,049
	Bareli	1,116,174	639,579	126,345
	Shajehanpur	1,309,211	651,549	102,707
Agra	Muttra	1,016,153	not given	155,728
	Agra	935,825	646,818	139,297
	Farakkabad	1,247,288	614,253	149,575
	Mynpuri	1,280,927	613,422	138,238
	Etawa	1,071,756	477,901	131,093
Allahabad	Cawnpur	1,497,795	782,276	218,154
	Futtehpur	990,584	506,905	141,893
	Allahabad	1,790,244	997,508	215,650
Benares	Goruckpur	4,560,049	1,927,234	208,354
	Azimgarh	1,652,293	773,616	151,788

When the work, thus nearly completed by Merttins Bird after nine years' labour, came before the Lieutenant-Governor of the Province, that distinguished officer wrote a thoughtful minute, dated April 15, 1842. He recognised that the Settlement had been performed with consideration and judgment, and that increase of revenues had not been the object aimed at. He approved of the introduction of four instalments in the year for the payment of revenue. And he also approved of the demarcation of boundaries and the corrections of accounts. But he doubted if the appointment of a paid watchman in every village would be welcome to villagers, and he commented in severe terms on the harsh measure which had been adopted, by over-zealous subordinate officers, to resume rent-free tenures.

"The Settlement Officer swept up without inquiring every patch of unregistered rent-free land, even those under ten Bighas [three acres] exempted by a subsequent order, which did not come out before five-sixths of the tenures had been resumed. In one district, that of Farakkabad, the obligations of a treaty and the direct orders of Government were but lightly dealt with; and in all, a total disregard was evinced for the acts even of such men as Warren Hastings and Lord Lake."[1]

Still more emphatic was the Lieutenant-Governor's condemnation of the manner in which the rights of hereditary landlords had been interfered with. The following is one of the instances cited.

"The Raja of Mynpuri, whose predecessor had received the highest acknowledgments from the British Government for his unshaken loyalty, when the district was overrun by Holkar's army in the year 1804, was, without a reference to Government, under the construction put on the right of a Talukdar, deprived entirely, he and his successors in perpetuity, of all power of interference in 116 of the 158 villages included in his Taluka, which had descended to him in regular succession before the introduction of the British rule."[2]

The Lieutenant-Governor also regarded with disfavour a constant interference in the affairs of each village. "To keep up a record of the circumstances of every field there must be a constant interference of the Executive in the affairs in every village, or, it may be said, of every villager, which would be irksome to any people, and will, I suspect, prove intolerable to the Natives of India." And generally the operations appeared to the Lieutenant-Governor to be "of a decidedly levelling character, and calculated so to flatten the whole surface of society as

[1] Paragraph 16. [2] Paragraph 18.

eventually to leave little of distinguishable eminence between the ruling power and the cultivators of the soil. It is a fearful experiment, that of trying to govern without the aid of any intermediate agency of indigenous growth; yet it is, what it appears to me, that our measures, now in progress, have a direct tendency to bring about." [1]

These remarks are of value for all time. The Settlement effected by Bird has been praised, and deservedly praised, for the great benefit it conferred on the agricultural population of Northern India. It moderated the assessment which had been excessive and oppressive during the first thirty years of British rule. And it gave the people some rest from continuous harassment by giving them a long term of settlement. At the same time it should be remembered that Bird's declared intention to make the assessment perpetual, where the lands were fully cultivated and assessed, has been disregarded by later administrators; and his desire to eventually follow the same practice in other districts, as they came more fully under cultivation, has not been fulfilled. On the contrary, the levelling character of the measures, deplored by T. C. Robertson in 1842, are more noticeable after the lapse of sixty years. The village Patwari, paid by the Government, is the master of the situation in North India to-day; and to him is entrusted the power which should legitimately belong to the representatives of the people—the Village Landlord or the Village Community. "To flatten the whole surface of society as eventually to leave little of distinguishable eminence between the ruling power and the cultivators of the soil," is not a policy of wisdom in India.

The generous and kind-hearted James Thomason succeeded Robertson as Lieutenant-Governor in Northern India in 1843, and ruled that province for ten years. Under him were trained up a number of able administrators, like John Lawrence and Robert Montgomery and

[1] Paragraphs 26, 29, 30.

William Muir, who have left their mark on the history of India, as much by their sympathy with the people as by their able administration. Thomason himself was one of the most distinguished revenue administrators of India; and while he corrected some of the evils pointed out by his predecessor, he completed the work of Merttins Bird, and closed the great Settlement in 1849. Four years later, on the very day on which an order was signed by the Queen's command to promote Thomason to the higher post of Governor of Madras, that great and good man died on September 27, 1853. Madras lost an officer whose humane policy was nowhere more needed than in that province.

Thomason's first important work, after he became Lieutenant-Governor, was his "Directions for Settlement Officers," drawn up in 1844, being the first complete Land Settlement Code compiled in India. It consisted of 195 paragraphs, and laid down the principles and procedure on which the Settlement of Northern India was conducted. A few of the provisions are quoted below.

"52. It is desirable that the Government should not demand more than two-thirds of what may be expected to be the *nett* produce to the proprietor during the period of settlement, leaving to the proprietor one-third as his profits, and to cover expenses of collection. By *nett* produce is meant the surplus which the estate may yield, after deducting the expenses of cultivation, including the profits of stock and wages of labour; and this, in an estate held entirely by cultivating proprietors, will be the profit on their *Sir* cultivation, but in an estate held by a non-cultivating proprietor, and leased out to cultivators or *Asamees* paying at a known rate, would be the gross rental"

"128. Cultivators at fixed rates have a right to hold certain fields, and cannot be ejected from them so long as they pay those rates. If they fail to pay the rent legally demandable, the proprietor must sue them summarily for the arrear, and on obtaining a decree in his favour and failing after it to collect his dues, he may apply to the Collector to eject them, and to give him possession of the land."

"129. Tenants-at-will have no right beyond the year of their cultivation."

"154. When there are many co-parceners (as in Village Communities), it is usual to select one or more from their number, and to arrange that the others should pay their revenue through them to the Government. All the co-parceners are Malguzars [revenue-payers] or Putteedars [holders of land in severalty], but the persons admitted to the engagement are the Sadar Malguzars [revenue-payers to the State direct], and are commonly called Lumber-dars."[1]

"159. It remains to point out the way in which the Record of Rights is to be formed. . . . The Record is to be permanent; it is to be, as it were, the Charter of Rights, to which all persons having an interest in the land, or seeking to acquire such interest, are to appeal. It is to be the common book of reference to all officers of Government in their transactions with the people, to the Collector, to the Magistrate, and, above all, to the Judge."

Indian administrators will recognise in these rules some of the principles which have since been embodied in the Tenancy Acts of the different Provinces of India.

The Settlement of Northern India, finally completed by 1849, at last came before the Court of Directors. And in their important Despatch, dated August 13, 1851, the Directors reviewed that great work. Merttin Bird's assessments had been revised and reduced by the exemption of many rent-free tenures, after that officer had left India; and the figures given in the Directors'

[1] From the English word *number*, these men having specific numbers in the Collector's register.

Despatch differ considerably from those quoted above from Bird's Report.

We quote the following figures from the Despatch of the Court of Directors, taking ten rupees as equivalent to a pound sterling.

District.	Total Assessment.	District.	Total Assessment.
	£		£
Saharanpur	90,443	Futtehpur	139,767
Muzaffarnagar	67,274	Allahabad	218,995
Agra	155,401	Azimgarh	135,741
Farakkabad	92,173	Juanpur	123,133
Mynpuri	138,213	Benares	81,706
Etawa	131,103	Mirzapur	67,068
Bijnaur	82,755	Delhi	35,794
Muradabad	133,463	Paniput	80,778
Pilibeet	37,589	Hissar	38,020
Bareli	100,706	Rohtuk	62,831
Shajehanpur	102,707	Gurgaon	108,848
Cawnpur	218,154		

The figures for some districts like Agra, Muradabad, Allahabad, and Gurgaon, show a very considerable increase compared to Bird's figures, possibly because the Settlement was yet incomplete when Bird submitted his Report. Other districts like Saharanpur, Farakkabad, Bijnaur, Pilibeet, Bareli, and Futtehpur show a considerable reduction.

The total land revenue demands and collections in Northern India during the last ten years of the Settlement operations are shown in the following figures:—

Year.	Demands.	Collections.
	£	£
1838–39	4,554,899	3,630,215
1839–40	4,120,668	3,565,281
1840–41	3,764,261	3,470,402
1841–42	4,161,903	3,883.357
1842–43	4,391,890	4,048,812
1843–44	4,349,415	4,110,514
1844–45	4,345,882	4,128,744
1845–46	4,301,837	4,200,341
1846–47	4,307,700	4,232,122
1847–48	4,292,166	4,248,582

The healthy results of the Settlement are seen at a glance. The period began with a large demand, and nearly a million sterling remained unrealised. The period ended with a reduced demand, and nearly the whole of it was realised.

Reviewing these facts and figures, the Directors complimented the Civil Service of India on the great task performed, and singled out Robert Merttins Bird "as being eminently entitled to our marked and special approbation."

Merttins Bird and the Civil Service deserved all the praise that was bestowed on them; but nevertheless the work was only half done. The very foundation stone of the entire structure was unstable; the fixing of the Land Tax for an entire Pergana or fiscal division was mere guess-work.

But the Land Tax was not only uncertain: it was excessive. Rule 52 of Thomason's Directions, quoted before, indicated that the Government demand might reach two-thirds of the *nett* produce. Relatively, it was a humane rule; for the British Government had demanded 83 per cent. in 1822, and 75 per cent. in 1833. But in reality it was a crushing demand which left the landlords and cultivators of Northern India resourceless. This painful truth was perceived within a few years after the Directors had complacently signed their Dispatch of 1851.

The time was approaching for commencing operations for a new Settlement. The question of the relative shares of the State and the landlords in the *nett* produce of the soil came again for anxious consideration. Experience had shown that a tax of 66 per cent., claimed by the State, was excessive and impracticable. Thomason's Rule 52 had proved oppressive, and had prevented land from becoming valuable property to its owners and tillers. It was necessary to revise Thomason's Directions, and new Rules were accordingly issued in 1855, "designed to assist the Collector in points which have been omitted from or not sufficiently detailed in the Directions to Settlement Officers, or on which different rules from those laid down in that treatise have been subsequently issued by Government." The new rules were issued in connection with the re-settlement of the Saharanpur district, and are therefore generally known as the "Saharanpur Rules."

The most important of the Saharanpur Rules is Rule XXXVI., which reduced the Land Tax from 66 per cent. to 50 per cent. of the *nett* produce or the *nett* rental of an estate. The rule is as follows.

"The assets of an estate can seldom be minutely ascertained, but more certain information as to the average nett assets can be obtained now than was formerly the case. This may lead to over-assessment, for there is little doubt that two-thirds, or 66 per cent., is a larger proportion of the *real* average assets than can ordinarily be paid by proprietors, or communities, in a long course of years. For this reason the Government had determined so far to modify the Rule laid down in paragraph 52 of the Directions to Settlement Officers as to limit the demand of the estate to 50 per cent. of the average nett assets. By this it is not meant that the Jumma [assessment] of each estate is to be fixed at one-half of the nett average assets, but that in taking these assets with other data into consideration, the Collector will bear in mind that about one-half, and not two-thirds as heretofore, of the well-ascertained nett assets should be the Government demand. The Collector should observe the cautions given in paragraph 47 to 51 of the treatise quoted, and not waste time in minute and probably fruitless attempts to ascertain exactly the average nett assets of the estates under settlement."

This rule may be said to be the basis of land assessments in India in the present day. After half a century of blunders and over-assessments, the British Government decided to limit its claims to one-half the rental or the *nett* produce of the soil; and this limit was gradually extended to all parts of India where the Land Revenue was not permanently settled. It was extended to the Central Provinces of India, and to Oudh and the Punjab, after the annexation of those provinces. And it was also formulated by the Secretary of State for India, in his despatch of 1864, for provinces like Madras and Bombay, where the revenue was generally paid by the cultivators direct, and not through intervening landlords.

CHAPTER IV

LAND SETTLEMENTS IN BOMBAY

THE British frontier in Western India rapidly advanced under the Marquis of Hastings, and the whole of the Deccan came under British rule in 1817, after the last Mahratta War. Valuable reports on the newly-acquired territories were submitted, first by Mountstuart Elphinstone in 1819, and then by Chaplin in 1821 and 1822. And these reports throw much light on the state of agriculture, and the condition of the peasantry, under the Mahratta rule.

The first and most important feature of the Mahratta Government in the Deccan, wrote Elphinstone, was the division of the country into townships or Village Communities. "These Communities contain in miniature all the materials of a State within themselves, and are almost sufficient to protect their members if all other governments are withdrawn."[1] The Patel or head of the Village Community, wrote Captain Robertson of Poona, "was, and is still, a magistrate by the will of the community as well as by the appointment of Government; he enforces the observance of what in England would be termed the bye-laws of the corporation; he formerly raised by contribution a sum of money for the expenses of the corporation as such, and for the support of his own dignity as its head; he suggested improvements for the benefit of the association, and marshalled the members to aid him in maintaining the public peace; he dispensed and still dispenses civil justice as a patriarch to those who choose to submit to his decision as referee or arbitrator; or he

[1] Elphinstone's Report, dated October 25, 1819.

presides over the proceedings of others whom either he himself or the parties might nominate as arbitrators of their disputes."[1]

The next most important feature of society under the Mahratta rule was the cultivation of the land by peasant proprietors, called Mirasdars or hereditary owners of their fields. Elphinstone tells us that "a large portion of the Ryots are the proprietors of their estates, subject to the payment of a *fixed land tax* to Government; that their property is hereditary and saleable; and they are never dispossessed while they pay their tax." "He is in no way inferior," writes Captain Robertson, "in point of tenure on its original basis, as described in the quotation, to the holder of the most undisputed freehold estate in England." The Mirasi tenure, says Chaplin, "is very general throughout the whole of that part of the conquered territory which extends from the Krishna to the range of Ghats." And Mr. Chaplin adds that "the Collector [of Poona] is very properly an advocate for preserving the rights of Mirasdars, a line of policy which he strenuously recommends in several places; but as nobody, I trust, has ever thought of invading their rights, the discussion of the question at any length would be superfluous."[2]

It is a lamentable fact that both these ancient institutions, the Village Community and the Mirasi tenure, virtually ceased to exist before the first generation of British administrators had closed their labours in the conquered territories. A fixed resolve to make direct arrangements with every separate cultivator, and to impose upon him a tax to be revised at each recurring settlement, necessarily weakened Village Communities and extinguished Mirasi rights. No impartial historian compares the Mahratta rule with its interminable wars, with the British rule which has given peace and security to the people. At the same time no impartial historian

[1] Captain Robertson's Report, dated October 10, 1821.
[2] Chaplin's Report, dated August 20, 1822.

notes without regret the decay of the old self-governing institutions, the extinction of the old tenant-rights, and the consequent increase of the burdens on the soil, which have been the results of British administration in India. It is an unwise policy to efface the indigenous self-governing institutions of any country; and the policy is specially unwise under an alien rule which can never be in touch with the people, except through the natural leaders and representatives of the people. Eighty-five years have elapsed since the British conquest of the Deccan, but the system of rural self-government, which the Village Communities represented, has never been replaced.

Land Settlements were made temporarily in different districts immediately after the conquest of the Deccan; and regular Survey Settlements were commenced by Pringle of the Bombay Civil Service in 1824-28, but ended in failure. His assessment was based on a measurement of fields and an estimate of the yield of various soils, and the Government demand was fixed at 55 per cent. of the produce. The measurement, however, was faulty; the estimates of produce were erroneous; the revenue demand was excessive; and the Settlement operations ended in oppression. "Every effort, lawful and unlawful, was made to get the utmost out of the wretched peasantry, who were subjected to torture, in some instances cruel and revolting beyond all description, if they would not or could not yield what was demanded. Numbers abandoned their homes and fled into the neighbouring Native States. Large tracts of land were thrown out of cultivation, and in some districts no more than a third of the cultivable area remained in occupation."[1]

A re-survey was commenced by Goldsmid and Lieutenant Wingate in 1835, and they founded the

[1] Bombay Administration Report of 1872-73, p. 41.

system on which land revenue administration in Bombay is based up to the present time. This date marks, therefore, the commencement of the current land system of Bombay, as 1833 marks the commencement of the current land system of Northern India. And both in Bombay and in Northern India, Settlements have been made for long periods of thirty years from these dates.

The plan adopted by Goldsmid and Wingate was very simple. They classed all soils into nine different classes according to their quality; they fixed the assessment of a district after inquiries into its circumstances and previous history; and they distributed the district demand among the villages and fields contained in the district. The owner of each field was then called upon to cultivate his holding on payment of the Land Tax fixed for his field. "The assessment was fixed by the Superintendent of Survey without any reference to the cultivator; and when those rates were introduced, the holder of each field was summoned to the Collector and informed of the rate at which his land would be assessed in future; and if he choose to retain it on those terms, he did; if he did not choose, he threw it up."[1]

It will be seen that this simple scheme entirely ignored the Village Communities of the Deccan, and extinguished the rights of Mirasi tenants to hold their hereditary lands at fixed rates. British administrators judged it wise to make a settlement directly with every individual tenant; and they imposed on each field a Land Tax according to their own judgment. The new assessment, too, was more or less guess-work, and was therefore subject to the same uncertainty which vitiated the system of Northern India. It was liable to vary as the Settlement Officer was moderate or severe. And moderation shown at one Settlement, during a time of distress, was liable to be followed by severity at

[1] Evidence of Goldfinch. Fourth Report of the Commons' Select Committee, 1853, p. 141.

the succeeding Settlement, at the first signs of prosperity. The accumulation of agricultural wealth was impossible so long as Settlement Officers retained the power of varying the Land Tax at each recurring settlement according to their own judgment. And any permanent improvement in the condition of the peasantry was impossible when the peasantry possessed no security against arbitrary enhancements of the State-demand.

The Sadar Board of Revenue and the Government of India saw this weakness in the system of the Ryotwari Settlement, which then appeared in its worst form in Madras. Ten years after the death of Sir Thomas Munro, Madras affairs were in the utmost confusion. The land assessment was raised, lowered, and raised again. The evils of uncertainty were added to the evils of over-assessment. The excessive revenue demand could not be met, and was never met. The peasantry was crushed to the ground, and there was widespread agricultural distress in the country. It was against this system that the Sadar Board of Revenue raised its voice.

A copy of the Sadar Board's letter was forwarded to Bombay. Though mainly directed against Madras, the letter was an attack on the Ryotwari System itself. And as Goldsmid and Wingate were introducing the same system in Bombay, they stood up for the system. In their able letter of October 17, 1840, they attributed the wretched state of Madras to over-taxation, and not to the Ryotwari System itself. And they contended that the Ryotwari System, properly worked, might be as beneficial to the people as the system which was introduced in Northern India by Merttins Bird. A few extracts from this remarkable letter will throw light on the land systems of Northern India, Madras, and Bombay, which were still in the process of formation at that period.

"3. In the North-Western Provinces the Land Tax is assessed upon estates generally comprising many occupancies instead of upon single fields, as here. An estate may be a single village, or occasionally only a pa: of a village; an aggregation of villages, or parts of villages; and, instead of being simply the property of one individual, is almost invariably that of many proprietors, who are jointly responsible for the payment of the Land Tax, which is assessed on the estate in the lump. In the Deccan, on the contrary, the existing divisions of land are usually fields of moderate size, capable of being conveniently cultivated by one person; these divisions have been preserved in our Settlement, and the Land Tax fixed independently upon each."

"9. . . . It appears to us that a proprietary right in land can only be destroyed by the imposition of an assessment so heavy as to absorb the whole of the rent; for as long as the assessment falls in any degree short of the rent, the portion remaining will give a value to the land, and enable its possessor to let or sell it, which, of necessity, constitutes him a proprietor. Whether or not Sir Thomas Munro disregarded the rights of the real proprietors, and recorded the land simply in the names of the actual occupants, who thus became responsible for the payment of the assessment, we do not think it necessary to inquire; but we unhesitatingly record that our Settlement recognises all existing proprietary rights, and that the proprietor has the fullest liberty to assign his land to under-tenants upon whatever terms he chooses, and which right is everywhere exercised."

"11. . . . We have adopted for the portion of the Deccan, to which our operations have as yet extended, nine classes of gradations, to one of which every peculiarity of soil has been referred; and these we have reason for believing to be sufficiently numerous."

"15. . . . The present condition of the agricultural classes, the state of the particular villages, the amount of the Government realisations, the prices of produce, and similar considerations, compared with those of preceding years,[1] affording us the chief groundwork for determining satisfactorily what abatement or addition should be made to the existing Jumma."

"39. The Board conclude their letter with a lengthened and impressive summary of the evils deemed by them inherent in the Ryotwari System, as evidenced by the wretched state of the Madras districts, which they contrast with the flourishing condition of the North-Western Provinces under the present Settlement, and thence deduce the immeasurable superiority of the village-plan of management; but, in our humble opinion, the immeasurable superiority observed in the North-Western Provinces is the result of the moderation of the Government demand; the undeniable inferiority in the Madras management arises from the error committed of imposing exorbitant and illiberal assessments."

"44. We further believe many most important elements of national prosperity to be secured by the plan of settlement now being followed in the Deccan, among which may be enumerated: a moderate and equal assessment leaving a proportion of the rent with the proprietor or holder; the settlement confirmed for thirty years; security against increase of demand, on any account whatever, during the term of the Settlement; the consequent accruement of all benefits arising from improvements to those who make them; limitation of joint responsibility to a few cases where fields are held in common, or have been subdivided by coparceners; recognition of property in the soil; perfect freedom of management with regard to rent from sub-tenants, and sale, secured to its owners; facilities for effecting sales or transfers of land afforded, by the apportionment of the assessment on fields or such limited

[1] A more effective method for preventing agricultural wealth and prosperity could not be devised than by empowering Settlement Officers to vary the assessment according to the "present condition of the agricultural classes, &c." If their condition was prosperous the assessment was enhanced; where, then, was the possibility or the motive for improvement and the accumulation of wealth?

portions of land as would, in the circumstances of the proprietors of this country, be naturally made the subject of such transfers; collection of the assessment from cultivated land only, and thus permitting the Ryot to contract and extend the sphere of his labours, according to the means at his immediate command, a privilege of immense importance in a country where the capital of the agriculturist is not only small in itself, but subject to great fluctuation from the effect of variation in the seasons."[1]

Armed with this and other Reports, John Vibart addressed the Bombay Government, defending the Bombay system against the charges of the Board of Revenue. Vibart had no difficulty in showing that in fixing the assessment, the Bombay officers proceeded on precisely the same considerations as the officers of Northern India.[2] Indeed the first impression left on the reader's mind on perusal of this correspondence is that if the assessment of Bombay was guess-work, the assessment of Northern India was guess-work also; and Northern India reproving Bombay was like Satan reproving Sin! But nevertheless there was an essential difference. In Northern India the assessment was made for an entire estate or village, and the owners of the estate or the village collectively could protest with some effect if the guess-work assessment was wrong. In Bombay, every field was separately assessed, and the humble cultivator of a field had little chance of redress if the Settlement Officer made a wrong guess.

The reader will perceive at once the great difference between a Province where old institutions like Village Communities and hereditary landlords were maintained, even in a crippled state, and a Province where they were swept away or ignored, and an absolute Government stood face to face with each individual tiller of his field.

[1] Letter of H. E. Goldsmid and G. Wingate to John Vibart, Revenue Commissioner of Poona, dated October 17, 1840.

[2] Vibart's letter to the Bombay Government, dated February 15, 1841.

It is customary with superficial writers to regard intervening landlords in India as incumbrances on the land; but thoughtful men, who have closely studied the social and economic conditions of India, have recorded a different opinion. They have recognised that, apart from the political gain of having influential bodies of men between an alien Government and an unrepresented nation of cultivators, the opinion and influence of such men, belonging to the country and to the people, leaven the administration, correct its mistakes, resist its arbitrariness, and bring it more in touch with the people. Land revenue administration in Northern India has been more successful, and land assessments have been lighter, than in Bombay and in Madras, because there were influential leaders and communities in the first-named province, who made their wishes felt, influenced the administration, and moderated taxation. The saddest mistake made in Madras and in Bombay was to ignore or to sweep away Village Communities, Polygars, Jaigirdars, and other influential bodies belonging to the people, instead of enlisting them in the cause of good administration.

"Joint responsibility for the payment of the revenue and joint village management," said Goldsmid and Wingate in their own justification, "were perhaps universal in the Deccan, but we can find no traces of joint ownership."[1] It would have been a gain to British rule, if this "joint village management," through Village Communities, which was universal in the Deccan, had been fostered and preserved. And the high admiration with which every student of history cherishes the memory of a great and good man like Sir George Wingate will not conceal from him the painful truth that, in setting aside Village Communities and making separate settlements with a hundred thousand cultivators for a hundred thousand fields in each district, Wingate made a fatal mistake. The Madras Board of Revenue

[1] Letter of October 17, 1840, paragraph 37.

protested against this mistake in Madras in 1818,—in vain. The Sadar Board of Revenue protested once more against this mistake in 1838,—in vain.

Fifteen years after this, a high administrator, a Governor of Bombay, was examined as a witness before Select Committees of the Lords and Commons. And he had the courage to state that wherever the Ryotwari System had been introduced,—sweeping aside Village Communities and intermediate landlords,—the agriculturists were a nation of paupers. Sir George Clerk's evidence is so clear and cogent, that it is necessary to quote some of his remarks.

Q. Which system of managing land is most beneficial to the people at large—by Ryots or by Zemindars?

A. They have their respective advantages, but the Ryotwari is most detrimental to the country. . . .

Q. Is not the character of the population in our dominion more generally that of the paupers?

A. Only where the Ryotwari Settlement prevails, I should say?[1]

The above evidence was given before the Lords' Committee in 1852. The same witness explained the evils of the Ryotwari System more fully before the Select Committee of the House of Commons in the following year.

Q. Will you state in a few words what the principle of the Ryotwari System is?

A. It is a very minute and detailed assessment of land under individual cultivators, in small allotments, directly by the Government, so that they are, as we found them, still paupers. There is nothing between them and the Government. . . .

Q. Your idea of the Ryotwari System is that it does not work well, either for the Government or for the natives?

[1] Report of the Select Committee of the House of Lords, 1852, p. 152.

A. Certainly not; they have no head landholders over them to acquire capital; they are of a class who never acquire capital in any country; mere cultivators....

Q. What is the system of revenue which prevails in the North-Western Provinces?

A. There has been a new Settlement carried out there of leases on long terms to Zemindars of different calibre, some holding a single village or so, and others being the many heads of a village.

Q. Was that Settlement laid down on the principle rcommended by Mr. Bird?

A. I believe so, but the principle was not new; it was much older than Mr. Bird's time; it was a very ancient mode of assessment of Land Revenue in India.

Q. Has that worked well, in your opinion?

A. I think it works remarkably well, when in forming your assessment of revenue with the heads of villages you have not infringed the rights of any Zemindar. . . .

Q. Are the Zemindars in the habit of assisting the Ryots in case of the failure of their crops?

A. Yes.

Q. In what way do they assist them?

A. They will assist them with funds, or with seed, corn, or with oxen; that is the advantage of the Village or the Zemindari Settlement.

Illustrious men like Cobden and Joseph Hume were members of the Select Committee, and it is interesting to read the witness's answers to their special questions.

Mr. Cobden: You have stated that one difficulty attending the Ryotwari System in Bombay arises from the widespread and general corruption of the native population, and that where you lose the services of Europeans, you find it impossible to obtain faithful administrators. How do you reconcile that with the statement you made in the former part of your evidence as to the general morality and truthfulness of the population of India?

A. I do not think I made use of the term wide-spread corruption of the population; I certainly meant nothing of the kind. I meant that the under-paid native agents whom you must use, in consequence of the want of funds to obtain others, are not to be trusted with the disposal of the money remitted from the revenue, or to carry out the Ryotwari System in all its minute parts.

Q. If the mass of the population be truthful and honest, where is the difficulty in finding honest agents among them?

A. You impose laborious duties upon them, and do not give them adequate salaries to maintain themselves. . . .

Mr. Hume: You have stated that the present Ryotwari System leaves the cultivators in a state of beggary, and you have expressed a doubt how far the Village System could be adopted. Is there any other step which you could recommend as a means of improving the condition of the cultivators of Bombay?

A. I do not think I expressed a doubt as to the Village System. It is the system I have always advocated and adopted.[1]

The Ryotwari Settlement went on in Bombay. The rules of the Settlement were finally gathered up in 1847 in what is known as the *Joint Report*, signed by H. E. Goldsmid, Captain Wingate, and Captain Davidson. This Joint Report of 1847 was the basis of the Bombay Settlement, as Thomason's Directions to Settlement Officers, published in 1844, was the basis of the Settlement in Northern India.

The principles of the Bombay Settlement, as explained in the Joint Report, were, *firstly*, that it was

[1] First Report of the Select Committee of the House of Commons, 1853, pp. 194–197.

based on the assessment of each field separately; *secondly*, that it granted long leases for thirty years; *thirdly*, that it abandoned the basis of produce-estimates, and substituted the basis of the value of lands for distributing the assessment.

"The cultivator's title to occupation of the fields is indestructible while he continues to discharge the assessment laid upon them, though his engagement for each be annually renewed; and by placing the assessment upon each field, instead of on his whole holding, he is enabled, when circumstances make the course desirable, to relinquish any of the former, or take up others which may be unoccupied, so as to accommodate the extent of his liabilities to his means. The fixed field assessment for the term of thirty years, introduced by our surveys, thus secures to the cultivator the full advantages of a thirty years' lease without burdening him with any condition beyond that of discharging the assessment for the single year to which his engagement extends. He has thus all the security of tenure which the longest lease could confer, without the attendant liabilities and risk which his limited capital and precarious circumstances would be quite inadequate to meet."[1]

For the purpose of estimating the value of lands, all lands were classed under nine different classes, as shown in the table on the opposite page.[2]

Fields being thus classified, it remained to determine the Government demand for a whole district, so that it might be then distributed among the fields and villages contained in the district.

"It only remains to complete the Settlement to fix the absolute amount of assessment to be levied from the whole [district].

"The determination of this point is, perhaps, the most important and difficult operation connected with the survey, and requires, beyond all others, the exercise of great

[1] Joint Report, paragraph 9. [2] *Ibid.*, paragraph 42.

Class.	Relative Value of Class in Annas or 16ths of a Rupee.	Soils of the		
		First Order.	Second Order.	Third Order.
		Of a Fine Uniform Texture, Varying in Colour from Deep Black to Dark Brown.	Of Uniform but Coarser Texture than the Preceding, and Lighter also in Colour, which is Generally Red.	Of Coarse Gravelly, or Loose Friable Texture, and Colour Varying from Light Brown to Grey.
		Depth in Cubits.	Depth in Cubits.	Depth in Cubits.
1	16	$1\frac{3}{4}$	...	...
2	14	$1\frac{1}{2}$	$1\frac{3}{4}$	...
3	12	$1\frac{1}{4}$	$1\frac{1}{2}$	...
4	10	1	$1\frac{1}{4}$	...
5	8	$\frac{3}{4}$	1	...
6	6	$\frac{1}{2}$	$\frac{3}{4}$	1
7	$4\frac{1}{2}$	$\frac{1}{4}$	$\frac{1}{2}$	$\frac{3}{4}$
8	3	...	$\frac{1}{4}$	$\frac{1}{2}$
9	2	...	...	$\frac{1}{4}$

judgment and discrimination on the part of the officer on whom it devolves. The first requisite is to obtain a clear understanding of the nature and effects of our past management of the district, which will be best arrived at by an examination and comparison of the annual revenue settlements of as many previous years as trustworthy data may be procurable for, and from local inquiries of the people during the progress of the survey. . . .

"Furthermore, to assist in tracing the causes to which the prosperity or decline of villages, or tracts containing several villages are to be attributed, independent statements of the annual revenue settlements of each village should be prepared. . . .

"And finally, with the view of affording the fullest information on this important subject, detailed figured statements should be furnished, exhibiting the source and amount of every item of revenue hitherto derived from land of every description, whether Government or alienated, comprised within the limits of the villages for which an assessment is proposed.

"The information thus collected and exhibited, with that obtained by local inquiries into the past history of the district, will generally enable us to trace the causes which have affected its past condition; and a knowledge of these, aided by a comparison of the capabilities of the district with those of others in its neighbourhood, will lead to a satisfactory conclusion regarding the amount of assessment to be imposed."[1]

It will be perceived at once from these elaborate rules how much was left to the discretion and judgment of the Settlement Officer in determining the district demand from the past history and circumstances of the district and its villages. The utmost latitude for moderation was left to a considerate officer, and of severity to an inconsiderate officer. And the fortunes of a hundred thousand tillers depended, not on fixed and customary rates, but on the different judgments of different officers. More than this, an assessment based on the past history of a district must necessarily rise after an era of prosperity; and any permanent improvement in the condition of the peasantry was impossible under a system which thus laid an increasing and deadening tax on prosperous agriculture.

This weak point in the method of assessment did not escape the Government of Bombay. The Governor of Bombay, in his Minute of November 16, 1847, remarked: "I cannot but admit that, at present, we are entirely dependent on the judgment of our Superintendents; and so we must remain until our Revenue Commissioners do something more than make their offices the channels of

1 Joint Report, paragraphs 69, 70, 74, 75, and 76.

communication between the Superintendents and ourselves." But the Revenue Commissioners themselves were powerless in the matter. The Hon. Mr. Read, Member of the Bombay Council, in his Minute of May 16, 1848, very pertinently remarked: "I concur in the Honourable the President's appreciation of what must be left to the judgment of the Superintendents of Survey. We must indeed be almost wholly dependent upon them, for I do not think that we can hope for Revenue Commissioners who can do more than exercise a very general supervision over their operations. Few Revenue Commissioners possess the knowledge, and none could devote the time necessary for a minute scrutiny into them."

It is creditable to Wingate that he exercised his irresponsible powers with moderation, tact, and humanity; that his guess-work in making assessment was performed with care and assiduity; and that his Settlement relieved the peasantry of the Deccan from that misrule and oppression from which they had suffered for twenty years. The name of Sir George Wingate is remembered in Bombay, as the name of Sir Thomas Munro in Madras, and of Robert Merttins Bird in Northern India, not because their work was free from grave faults, but because they succeeded, on the whole, in introducing some order where chaos and disorder had prevailed, and in building up systems which have lasted to our day.

The financial results of land assessments by British administrators in Bombay can be best exhibited by figures. The limits of British territory remained virtually unchanged in this province from the acquisition of the Peshwa's dominions in 1817–18, to the survey and settlement of Wingate, commenced in 1836. And yet the land revenue was increased immediately after the conquest.

In 1817–18 the Land Revenue was . .	£868,047
„ 1818–19 „ „ „ . .	1,143,041
„ 1819–20 „ „ „ . .	1,078,164
„ 1820–21 „ „ „ . .	1,818,314

In other words, the Land Revenue of the province, including the conquered dominions, was more than doubled within four years from the conquest.

Wingate's settlement, commenced in 1836, was virtually completed by 1872, and showed an increase in the Land Revenue (excluding Poona and a few other places then under a revised settlement), from £1,534,000 to £2,032,000, or an increase of 32 per cent. Figures for the different districts are given below.[1]

Districts.	Revenue Prior to Settlement.	Revenue Under the Settlement.
	£	£
Thana	166,287	211,037
Khandesh	215,946	307,869
Ratnagiri	46,440	46,572
Ahmadabad	53,752	90,474
Kaira	144,886	188,752
Surat	174,081	240,134
Broach	88,984	112,564
Panch Mahals	4,825	8,155
Karachi	19,404	31,676
Hydarabad	63,330	77,353
Shikarpur	123,931	159,263
Dharwar	113,039	156,562
Belgaum	130,744	157,026
Kishnagiri	30,555	58,283
Satara	143,656	158,543
Kanara	14,850	27,788
Total	£1,534,710	£2,032,051

[1] Compiled from Bombay Administration Report, 1872–73, pp. 49 and 50. £1 is taken as equivalent to 10 rupees.

CHAPTER V

LAND SETTLEMENTS IN MADRAS

A Ryotwari Settlement, *i.e.*, a Settlement of the land revenue with the cultivators of the soil, was made by Captain Read and Thomas Munro in the districts of Baramahal, when the East India Company first acquired those districts in 1792, and was gradually extended to other parts of the province of Madras. The first assessments were severe and oppressive. The State demanded about one-half the estimated produce of the fields, a demand which was more than the whole economic rental of the country. Thomas Munro perceived this, and in 1807 proposed to reduce the assessment to a third of the produce. The Government of Madras admitted the justice of the proposal, but could not give effect to it, for the Directors of the Company pressed for money. Orders were received from England for an additional annual remittance of a million sterling, accompanied by a threat that the Directors would take the question of reducing the establishments in their own hands in case of disobedience. The Madras peasantry, therefore, obtained no relief.

Between 1808 and 1818 the Madras Board of Revenue urged the wise plan of recognising the Village Communities of the Province. They suggested that Land Revenue Settlements should be concluded with these bodies according to the ancient custom of India. And they proved from experience that Village Settlement had succeeded wherever it was tried, and that Settlement with individual tenants had failed. But representative Village Communities had no place in the scheme of the

Company's absolute government; the Directors decided to deal with the cultivators individually, without any intermediate bodies. The ancient Village Communities of Madras declined from that date.

Sir Thomas Munro was Governor of Madras from 1820 to 1827, and within this period the Ryotwari Settlement was introduced into all parts of the Province where a Permanent Settlement of the land revenue had not already been effected with Zemindars. Munro succeeded in reducing the Government assessment to the extent he had recommended before; and his considerate measures and his untiring supervision remedied many evils.

But even the reduced demand of Sir Thomas Munro was found to be oppressive. One-third of the produce of the field represented the entire economic rent in many villages and fields. It was demanded in a fixed sum in money, irrespective of the annual yield or the prevailing prices. And it was realised, not through village elders and village corporations, but through the low-paid agents of the State, who added to the miseries of the cultivators by their cruelty and their corruption. And when Sir Thomas Munro, who had organised everything and supervised everything, was removed from the scene by the hand of death, the difficulties of the system were felt more severely than ever. For thirty years the Province of Madras became a scene of oppression and agricultural distress unparalleled even in India in that age.

The Revenue Collectors themselves witnessed the universal misery by which they were surrounded, and some extracts from their Reports[1] will illustrate the condition of the people.

Cuddapa District.—The Collector wrote to the Board of Revenue in 1828: "The Ryots are more in the hands of the merchants than perhaps you are prepared to hear.

[1] Quoted from S. S. Raghava-Iyangar's *Memorandum of the Progress of the Madras Presidency* (1893), pp. 27–32.

. . . The peasantry are too poor to more than keep up their cultivation with Takavi [Government advances], when they have met with no extraordinary losses. When they have met with such losses from the death of cattle or other cause, it is impossible to repair them without assistance from Takavi."

Bellary District.—The Collector reported in 1845: "The universal complaint and request of the Ryots is to be allowed to reduce their farms, a convincing proof that cultivation is not profitable. Ryots, formerly substantial, and capable of laying out their capital on the lands, and liquidating their Sircar [State] demand, reserving their produce until they could get a favourable price, are now sunk in debt bearing heavy interest, entirely subject to their creditors; and were it not for the aid of the Collector through his revenue subordinates, one-half, or at least one-third, of the highly assessed lands would ere this have been thrown up. Husbandry is not carried on efficiently, and consequently the land seldom returns what it ought and is capable of. The number of Patta [lease] holders has increased, but they are a poor class who seek a maintenance only in husbandry with less spirit, and by no means to be compared with the substantial farmers who have fallen into difficulties and disappeared from the rent-roll of the district. With regard to food and raiment, the majority of them are poorly clad and ill-fed, and it is impossible to arrive at any other conclusion than that poverty is the cause."

Rajamundry, afterwards called *Godavari District*, appeared, from the report of Sir Henry Montgomery in 1844, to have been on the verge of ruin. There were famines in 1830 and 1831; the seasons were unfavourable in 1835, 1836, and 1837, and calamitous in 1838, 1839, and 1840. The population, which was 695,016 in 1830, had decreased to 533,836 in 1840.

Gantur and Masalipatam.—The famine of 1833, known as the Gantur famine, was the severest on record in these parts. Captain Walter Campbell, who was an eye-witness, stated: "The description in *The Siege of Corinth* of dogs gnawing human skulls is mild as compared with the scene of horror we are daily forced to witness in our morning and evening rides. . . . It is dreadful to see what revolting food human beings may be driven to partake of. Dead dogs and horses are greedily devoured by these starving wretches; and the other day, an unfortunate donkey having strayed from the fort, they fell upon him like a pack of wolves, tore him limb from limb, and devoured him on the spot." In the Gantur portion of the Krishna district from one-third to half of the whole population perished. An epidemic broke out in the following year, and "a man in perfect health was hardly to be seen anywhere."

Nellore District.—The Ryots had become impoverished by the low prices of grain which ruled. The total cultivated area had risen from 244,319 acres in 1801 to 389,802 acres in 1850. But garden lands had ceased to be cultivated through the pressure of the assessment, owing to a fall in the prices.

North Arcot.—The Collector reported: "The Ryots are in worse condition than they were at the beginning of the century. However this may be, their present condition is indubitably bad, and must be improved. The great body of them are certainly poor; their food is deficient in quantity as well as coarse; and their clothing is scanty and poor; and their dwellings extremely mean; all this combined with gross ignorance."

South Arcot.—The Collector reported an increase in the population and in the wages of labour, and found some indications of improvement in carriages, cloths, and houses. But agriculture was in a backward condition owing to heavy and unequal assessment, and two-thirds of the cultivable lands were waste.

Tanjore District did not suffer to the same extent as other districts from agricultural depression owing to improvements in irrigation works and in communications.

Coimbatur District.—The Collector wrote in 1840, that of the ten preceding seasons nine had been bad ones, and the land revenue had fallen in consequence. The trade in coarse piece-goods exported to Bombay had improved, but trade in fine goods had been annihilated by English manufacturers. Prices of grains had increased owing to a succession of bad seasons.

Salem, Madura and Tinnevelly Districts.—The exports of cotton goods manufactured in Coimbatur, Salem, Madura, and Tinnevelly had considerably increased. The price of labour had not risen with the increase of cultivation. The Collector remarked that cheap prices had increased the consumption of luxuries.

General Condition of the Madras Ryot.—From these accounts of the condition of the different districts we turn to a description of the Madras cultivators generally, given by one of the best-known Madras officials of his day.[1] Bourdillon had served as Collector in North Arcot and elsewhere; had acquired a thorough and intimate knowledge of the people among whom he had lived; and had been chosen with Sir Arthur Cotton and other distinguished men to form the Public Works Commission which submitted their valuable report in 1852. His account of the Madras Ryot recorded in 1853 is sober and thoughtful; it exaggerated nothing; but it indicated with painful details the chronic poverty of the cultivators.

A very small proportion of the cultivators who were favourably assessed or held revenue-free lands, or possessed other exceptional advantages, were well to do, and, with an income of 30 to 40 shillings a month, were accounted to be very well off. An income of £3 to £5 a month was very rare even among these classes.

The large majority of the cultivators, however, were always in poverty and generally in debt. "A Ryot of this

[1] Description of the Madras Ryot by Mr. Bourdillon in 1853.

class of course lives from hand to mouth; he rarely sees money except that obtained from the Chetty [money-lender] to pay his kist [instalment of Government revenue]; the exchanges in the out villages are very few, and they are usually conducted by barter. His ploughing cattle are wretched animals not worth more than $3\frac{1}{2}$ to 6 rupees each [7 to 12 shillings], and those perhaps not his own, because not paid for. His rude and feeble plough costs, when new, no more than 2 or 3 shillings; and all the rest of his few agricultural implements are equally primitive and inefficient. His dwelling is a hut of mud walls and thatched roofs, far ruder, smaller, and more dilapidated than those of the better classes of Ryots above spoken of; and still more destitute, if possible, of anything that can be called furniture. His food and that of his family is partly their porridge made of the meal of grain boiled in water, and partly boiled rice with a little condiment; and generally the only vessels for cooking and eating from are of the coarsest earthenware, much inferior in grain to a good tile or brick in England, and unglazed. Brass vessels, though not wholly unknown among this class, are rare.

"The scale of the Ryots descends to those who possess a small patch of land, cultivated sometimes by the aid of borrowed cattle, but whose chief subsistence is derived from cooly-labour, either cutting firewood and carrying it for sale to a neighbouring town, or in field labour.

"The purely labouring classes are below these again, worse off, indeed, but with no very broad distinction in condition. The earnings of a man employed in agricultural labour cannot be quoted at more than 20 rupees [40 shillings] a year, including everything; and this is not paid in money but in commodities. . . .

"Taking his earnings at the highest rate, viz., 20 rupees a year, this would be equivalent in real value, using the same standard of comparison as above, to 10 pounds a year in England.[1]

[1] In other words, rupees 20 or £2 was supposed to go as far in an Indian village as £10 in England in 1840.

"The English field labourer earns on an average not less than £28 a year, including his extra gains in harvest time; and thus it appears that the real wages of a field labourer in regular employ, his command of the necessaries and conveniences of life, are in this country little more than a third of what they are in England."

We will cite the testimony of one more distinguished officer on the actual working of the Ryotwari System, under which each District Collector was entrusted with the task of realising an impossible land revenue from a hundred thousand tenants in his district! George Campbell, afterwards Sir George Campbell, Lieutenant-Governor of Bengal, and then Member of Parliament, wrote in 1852 the following account of the Madras System:—

"Only imagine one Collector dealing with 150,000 tenants, not one of whom has a lease; but each pays according as he cultivates and gets a crop, and with reference to the number of his cattle, sheep, and children; and each of whom gets a reduction if he can make out a sufficiently good case. What a cry of agricultural distress and large families there would be in England or any other country under such a system! Would any farmer ever admit that his farm had yielded anything, that his cattle had produced, or that his wife had not produced? If the Collector were one of the prophets and remained in the district to the age of Methuselah, he would not be fit for the duty; and as he is but an ordinary man and a foreigner and continually changed, it would be strange if the native subordinates could not do as they liked, and, having the power, did not abuse it. Accordingly, it is generally agreed that the abuses of the whole system, and specially that of remissions, is something frightful; chicanery and intrigue of all kinds are unbounded; while the reliance of the Madras Collector on informers by no means mends the matter."[1]

[1] *Modern India*, by George Campbell, London, 1852.

These were the early results of a policy which had ignored Village Communities, and had prescribed the collection of an impossible land revenue directly from each petty tenant. It is painful to add that the use of torture was almost universal in the Province for the prompt realisation of the assessed revenue from the miserable cultivators. Rumours of this baneful practice were heard in England; and in 1854, Mr. Blackett, M.P. for the town of Newcastle, brought on a debate upon a Motion for a Commission to inquire into the land system of Madras. He described the system as the vilest that could be devised, and asserted that the exorbitant revenue demand could only be realised by torture. The fearless John Bright took a part in the debate, and his eloquent description of the condition of the Madras cultivator, and of the treatment he received, roused indignation in the country.

The Indian Government, slow to move in the path of reform, was forced to take some action after this debate. A Commission was appointed to take evidence; and an Act was passed to enable the Commission to proceed with their task. Elliot, a judge of the Madras Small Cause Court, Norton, a Madras barrister, and Stokes, a pronounced supporter of the Ryotwari System, were appointed Commissioners. A Commission, so constituted, submitted a guarded report. They found, that the practice of torture for the realisation of the Government revenue existed in the Province; and they also found that injured parties could not obtain any redress. But they were careful not to cast any imputation on the European Officers of the Government, and they saw nothing to impress them with the belief "that the people at large entertained the idea that their maltreatment is countenanced or tolerated by the European officers of Government."[1]

The kinds of torture which were most common were:

[1] Report of the Commission, dated April 16, 1855, par. 70.

keeping a man in the sun; preventing his going to meals or other calls of nature; confinement; preventing his cattle from going to pasture; quartering a peon on him; the use of *Kittee Anundal, i.e.,* tying a man down in a bent position; squeezing the crossed fingers; pinches, slaps, blows with fist or whip, running up and down; twisting the ears, making a man sit with brickbats behind his knees; putting a low caste man on his back; striking two defaulters' heads, or tying them by the back hair; placing in the stocks; tying by the hair to a donkey's or a buffalo's tail; placing a necklace of bones or other degrading or disgusting materials round the necks; and occasionally, though rarely, more severe discipline."[1]

One thing which came out very clearly during this inquiry was that where the land was severely assessed, the cases of torture were frequent. "In Canara and Malabar," the Commission wrote, "we learn that the Land Tax is generally light, that the people are flourishing, the assessment easily and even cheerfully paid, the struggle more often being who shall be allowed than who shall be made to pay the Government dues. Land has acquired a saleable value, and allotments of waste are eagerly contended for. Who can be surprised then at hearing one and all the European dwellers in those favoured spots declare that there torture for revenue purposes is comparatively unknown?"[2]

And Bourdillon, the Collector of North Arcot, recorded his opinion that torture for the purposes of revenue "might have ceased entirely by this time, but for the exorbitant demand on the land, and some particular incidents of the revenue system in these Provinces. With a moderate assessment, land would have become a valuable property; and a man would not only have taken care not to incur the loss of it, but in case of adversity would have in itself the means of satisfying

[1] Report of the Commission, par. 61. [2] *Ibid.*, par. 58.

the Government demands upon it. Further, had the assessment been moderate, that circumstance alone would have powerfully tended to raise the character of the people; for when men begin to possess property, they also acquire self-respect and the knowledge how to make themselves respected, and will no longer submit to personal indignities."[1]

All the evils of the Ryotwari System, attended with over-assessment of the soil, as it prevailed in Madras, were known to the Indian Government. And protests were made against a system which compared so unfavourably with the system of Northern India. As stated in the last chapter, the Sadar Board of Revenue addressed a strong letter to the Governor-General of India,[2] in which they condemned the Madras System. They pointed out the fraud and oppression practised by every low-paid officer of the State, and deprecated the harassing and inquisitorial searches made into the means of every cultivator. The system, they said, was found in connection with the lowest state of pauperism and dependence. "Every man must be degraded in his own opinion and relegated to a state of perpetual pupilage. The honest manly bearing of one accustomed to rely on his own exertions, can never be his—he can never show forth the erect and dignified independence of a man indifferent to the favour or frown of his superior." But neither the censure of the Sadar Board, nor the melancholy reports continually received from District Collectors, induced the Madras Government to reform its wretched land administration. It is remarkable that while sweeping reforms were effected in other Provinces by men like Bird and Wingate, no large acts of reform, no great remedial measures, no statesmanlike policy to improve the condition of the people, emanated from the authorities of Madras. Madras has often been called the Benighted Province of India, and never was this opprobrious term

1 Report of the Commission, Appendix C. 2 Letter dated March 20, 1838.

more richly deserved than during the first half of the nineteenth century. The light that slowly dawned elsewhere in India failed to penetrate the thick gloom which hung over the Coromandel Coast; and in the vast array of official documents which have been handed down to us from those times, we seek in vain for any great ideas of reform, any sweeping measures of improvement, in Madras.

Madras officials still adhered to their system, and, indeed, extended it from time to time, as permanently settled estates were sold up for inability to pay the revenue. The eagerness with which this policy was pursued in the middle of the nineteenth century has been described by an official of the time. "Meet a Ryotwari Collector in his own house, at his hospitable board, he will admit that the sale of a great Zemindari which he had just achieved was brought about by dexterous management; that the owner had been purposely permitted to get into the meshes of the Collector's net beyond his power of extrication; that the sale could easily have been obviated, nay, perhaps was uncalled for." And instances are cited by the same writer which are painful to read in these days.[1]

Thomas Munro, the real author of the Ryotwari System, never anticipated the methods which came into operation under that system. He had said before the

[1] *Madras, its Civil Administration*, by P. B. Smollett, London, 1858. In Tinnevelly District, the proprietor of the ancient Chocumpati estate came to the Collector to arrange a settlement of the arrear due from his estate; but he was seized as a disaffected and dangerous character; was kept in confinement as a political offender without any specific charges being preferred against him; and his estate was confiscated. In Nellore District the Mahomedan Jaigirdar of Udaigiri was similarly confined for life for alleged treason without a trial; and his estate was also confiscated. In Gantur District the great Vassy-Reddy possessions, yielding a revenue of £60,000 a year, were sold for £500 for arrears which had accrued during the management of the estate by Government Officers as trustees. In Masalipatam District the Nedadavole estates, worth £3000 a year, were sold for £1200. In Vizagapatam District the ancient Zemindari of Golgonda, worth £1000 a year, was sold for £10. And as these and other estates were sold one by one, the Ryotwari System was introduced in the lands.

House of Commons in 1813: "The principle of the Ryotwari System is to fix an assessment upon the whole land of the country; the assessment is permanent; every Ryot who is also a cultivating proprietor of the land which he holds is permitted to hold that land at a fixed assessment as long as he pleases; he holds it for ever without any additional assessment."

But the assessment was fixed too high; and the consequence was that the State-demand had to be lowered, raised, and lowered again, according to the variation of the seasons, and the condition of the people. The history of the Province during thirty years was thus a history of varying assessments—new *Hukm-namas*, or orders being continuously issued, altering the assessments. Famine or distress led to a reduction; the first signs of prosperity caused a rise! Modern history scarcely furnishes a parallel to such an arrangement, under which a large, industrious, and civilised population were rendered incapable of improving their condition or acquiring agricultural wealth, by a system of assessments which was kept up to the highest paying capacity of the country from year to year.

The evils of the system were fully exposed during the Parliamentary inquiries of 1852 and 1853, preceding a fresh renewal of the East India Company's charter. Madras officials were examined in course of those inquiries, and they spoke in no uncertain voice.

Malcolm Lewen, who had served twenty-five years in India as Collector, Judge, and Member of Council, stated before the Select Committee of the House of Commons: "I think that the system of revenue has a great connection with the morality of the country; I think there are systems of revenue in Madras now which tend very greatly to sap the morality of the country as well as to impoverish it." "The Tahsildars," he added, "who go about to make inquiries, have almost entirely under their control the amount of assessment which is raised for the Government in all Ryotwari Districts. The consequence is that whenever those people go to a village, the first thing the Ryots of a village do is to endeavour to buy them over to get a low assessment."[1]

James William B. Dykes, who had been employed in revenue work in the district of Salem, stated before the House of Commons that throughout that Province the evils of the Ryotwari System were (1) irregularity in assessments which were increased if the cultivators improved their lands; (2) uncertainty of tenure, and (3) the obscurity of the revenue rules which were never made known to the ignorant cultivators.[2]

The Administration of Madras was then forced to adopt a large remedial measure in 1855, similar to that which had been adopted in Northern India in 1833, and in Bombay in 1835. An extensive Survey and Settlement were determined upon; and in their well-known order of 1855, the Madras Government anticipated the happiest results from this Settlement.

"An accurate survey and careful settlement of the land revenue will remove the evils. Each man's payment will be certain; as a general rule there will be no remissions to be intrigued for or purchased; and thus the scope for cringing and bribery on the one part, and of corruption on the other, will be very greatly diminished; and there is no doubt that, under such a system, a larger revenue may be obtained than at present, with less inconvenience to the people. Not only will the greater proportion of the payments now made to the Government Officers be saved to the Ryot, but by an equal distribution of taxation, those who now pay exorbitantly will be relieved from such extra exertion, and the burden will be laid on those who now, unfairly, evade it. Nor is this all; it is morally certain that, with a

[1] First Report of the Select Committee of the House of Commons, 1853, p. 286.
[2] Fourth Report, p. 124.

moderate and fixed assessment the occupation of land will rapidly increase. At present, cultivation is undoubtedly repressed by the heavy burdens on the land direct and indirect; but when these are lightened, not only will the properly agricultural classes extend their holdings, but numbers of the trading classes will apply their acquisitions to agriculture.

"Further, it is certain that the high assessments and the absence of accurate accounts give occasion to very extensive fraud and the concealment of cultivation. Occasionally instances of this are brought to light on a large scale, so as to prove its existence, and it is well known to all revenue officers that it exists largely, but is concealed through the purchased connivance of the subordinate officials. With reduced assessments, there would be less of this fraudulent evasion, because there would be less inducement to pay for such connivance; and with an accurate survey and clear and simple accounts such fraud would become difficult and dangerous.

"There seems no reason for doubt that, with a vast extent of unoccupied land, with a peaceful and industrious population, scantily fed and scantily employed to the extent of being led to cross the sea in search of employment, though peculiarly averse to leaving home, with roads and other means of communication being every year improved and extended; under all these circumstances it seems clear that such a reduction of assessment as would make agriculture profitable would be speedily followed by a vast extension of cultivation. To these expectations are to be added the more partial causes which will make it practicable to enforce the fair claims of the revenue on extensive tracts now evading them; and lastly it must be noticed that the measures proposed must of necessity occupy a very considerable length of time. It can hardly be expected that the survey and settlement of this extensive Presidency can be accomplished in less than 15 or 20 years, and thus only one-fifteenth or one-twentieth of the revenue will have to be dealt with in each year, and there will be full time for the restorative agencies called into existence by the new measures to come into operation. On the whole, considering the present depressed condition of the Presidency, it seems fair to anticipate with confidence, that the result of these measures, instead of a falling off, will be an accession to the revenue, while as respects the payers and the public the good will be enormous; the revenue will be derived from resources double or treble those upon which it is levied now, and will be paid with corresponding ease and absence of privation."[1]

We have made this long extract, because this document opens a new chapter in the history of Madras land administrations. The results of the Survey and Settlement, recommended in 1855, will be narrated in a subsequent chapter.

[1] Order No. 951, dated August 14, 1855.

CHAPTER VI

LAND SETTLEMENTS IN THE PUNJAB

A PORTION of the Punjab was annexed to the British dominions by Lord Hardinge in 1846, after the first Sikh War; and the remainder was taken over by Lord Dalhousie after the second Sikh War in 1849. And we have a clear and lucid account of the condition of the Province, under its former Sikh ruler sas well as under British rule, in the First Punjab Administration Report, published in 1852.

Under the great Ranjit Singh, who had consolidated the Province into a strong and powerful kingdom, men who distinguished themselves by their courage and high capacity were deputed to the remoter districts for the collection of revenue, armed with pretorian and proconsular power. Among them was General Avitable who held down Peshawar with an iron hand, as also the doughty Hari Singh who kept the fierce and turbulent mountaineers of Hazara in unwilling submission. In the districts nearer to Lahore, Kardars or agents were employed to collect the revenue; and their most important proceedings were subject to review by the Lahore Ministry.

Written law there was none; but a rude and simple justice was dealt out. "Private property in land, the relative rights of land-holders and cultivators, the corporate capacities of Village Communities, were all recognised. Under the direction of the local authorities, private arbitration was extensively resorted to. The most difficult questions of real and personal property were adjudicated by these tribunals. . . . The Maharaja constantly made tours through his dominions. He would listen to complainants during his rides, and he would become angered with any Governor in whose province complaints were numerous. At court also, he would receive individual appeals."[1]

The taxation was heavy. "But in some respects the Government gave back with one hand what it had taken with the other. The *employés* of the State were most numerous; every village sent recruits for the army who again remitted their savings to their homes. Many a highly-taxed village paid half its revenue from its military earnings; thus money circulated freely."[2]

The Land Tax under Maharaja Ranjit Singh was in theory assumed to be one-half the gross produce, but in practice "may be said to have varied from two-fifths to one-third of the gross produce. The proportion prevailed in all the provinces which the Sikhs had fully conquered, and which were fairly cultivated, and may be said to have been in force in all their Cis-Indus possessions, except the province governed by Dewan Mulraj. Beyond the Indus, owing to the distance from control, the less patient character of the population, the insecurity of property, and the scarcity of population, the revenue system pressed more lightly on the people."[3]

The Land Tax, such as it was, was raised not in money but in kind; and it was therefore proportionate to the produce of the fields in good years as well as in bad years. Under such a system cultivators were not called upon to pay a fixed and immutable sum when their harvest had failed; nor were they required in years of low prices to pay a revenue calculated on the basis of high prices.

The second treaty of 1846, concluded in December of that year, provided that a British Resident should control the civil and military affairs of the Punjab; and

[1] Punjab Administration Report, 1852, paragraph 28.
[2] *Ibid.*, paragraph 31.
[3] *Ibid.*, paragraph 233.

Henry Lawrence was appointed the first Resident. There is no brighter name in the Indian annals of this period, renowned for able administrators and brave soldiers, than Henry Lawrence the Pacificator. Born in 1806, he had seen service in the first Burmese War of 1825; he had controlled Sikh chieftains at Peshawar and helped Pollock's advance into Afghanistan in 1842; and he had taken a part in the battle of Subraon which concluded the first Sikh War in February 1846. There was no man in India who knew the Sikhs better or had more influence with them than Henry Lawrence; and there was none who felt a greater respect for their virtues, or a truer desire to maintain their position, dignity, and independence.

As Resident, Henry Lawrence was practically the ruler of the Punjab; and he secured the assent of the Council of Regency, consisting of eight Sardars, in all his measures of reform. One reform was of doubtful benefit to the people—the substitution of the British system of collecting land revenue in money for the old system of payment in kind. The State-demand was nominally reduced; but the cultivators found no relief under the summary settlements and money assessments made by British officers. In other respects, however, Lawrence was more successful and more in touch with Sikh institutions. A simple code of laws, founded on Sikh customs, was framed by fifty selected heads of villages under the supervision of Sardar Lehna Singh. Oppressive duties and Government monopolies were abolished. Able and efficient officers, selected by Henry Lawrence, carried out his ideas, and controlled the administration in different parts of the Province. And Sardars, Chiefs, land-holders, and the people generally, appreciated his administration, and accepted the rule of the great Pacificator.

Unfortunately, the two men, who had secured peace in the Punjab, left India not long after. Henry Lawrence was compelled by ill-health to leave the country at the close of 1847. And Lord Hardinge made over the reins of

Government to Lord Dalhousie early in 1848. The troubles which arose soon after, and which were allowed to grow until they culminated in the second Sikh War, have already been narrated in another chapter.

Sir Henry Lawrence, now knighted for his distinguished services, hastened back to India on hearing of these disturbances, and stood by Lord Gough in the hard-fought field of Chilianwala in January 1849. The next battle, at Gujrat, fought in February, broke the power of the Sikhs; and the question of the ultimate fate of the Punjab came up for decision. Henry Lawrence was against British annexation; his brother John Lawrence is said to have been for it.[1] On March 29, 1849, the Proclamation was issued announcing that the sovereignty of the Punjab had passed over to the Queen of England.

Sir Henry Lawrence had tendered his resignation as soon as he had heard of this decision, partly from his avowed view of the injustice of the annexation, but mainly from the belief that the arrangement that would ensue would be harsh to the conquered people. But Lord Dalhousie knew the value of the Pacificator's work, and would not let him go. He sent his Secretary to Sir Henry, desiring him to continue in his leading position in the Punjab, "if only for the special reason that it would ensure his having the best opportunity for effecting his great object—the fair and even indulgent consideration of the vanquished; the smoothing down of the inevitable pangs of subjugation to those proud and brave enemies, with whose chiefs and leaders no man was so familiar as he, or so appreciative of what was noble in their character."[2]

[1] This is the accepted belief, but John Lawrence himself denied it eighteen years after. He wrote to Sir Stafford Northcote, Secretary of State for India, as follows: "I may say, with perfect truth, that I have never been connected with any great measure of annexation, except as regards that of the Punjab; and, in that case, I was only concerned in carrying out the measure, and not in the policy of annexation itself." —Letter dated June 25, 1867. Quoted in Bosworth Smith's *Life of Lord Lawrence* (1885), vol. ii. p. 385.

[2] *Sir Henry Lawrence, the Pacificator.* By Lieutenant-General M'Leod Innes (1898), p. 113.

To this appeal, urged on such a reason, Sir Henry could not but yield. Lord Dalhousie entrusted the administration of the Punjab to a Board, consisting of Sir Henry Lawrence as President, his brother John Lawrence, and Charles Mansel who was soon succeeded by Robert Montgomery. Sir Henry conducted the political work; John Lawrence was in charge of civil and revenue administration; Mansel and his successor Montgomery superintended the administration of justice.

The Board did not work smoothly or harmoniously. Henry Lawrence, impelled by his generous instincts, strove to maintain for the fallen Sardars a high position and status in the new British Province, and to recognise in them the aristocracy of the country as they had been. John Lawrence tried to carry out the narrower view of Lord Dalhousie that the Sardars deserved little but maintenance; that none should intervene between the people and their alien rulers. Henry Lawrence endeavoured unceasingly to recognise the natural and influential leaders of the people. John Lawrence, charged with revenue administration, was anxious to have a tighter grip on the Land Tax paid by the Cultivators; and saw in the due recognition of the old Sardars an alienation of the revenues supposed to be due to the State only.

The two brothers, who had the highest personal regard for each other, became estranged in their official relations; and the work of the State suffered. "My brother and I," wrote John Lawrence to the Secretary to the Governor-General, "work together no better than we formerly did. Indeed, the estrangement between us has increased. We seldom meet, and still more seldom discuss public matters. . . . What I feel is the mischief of two men brought together, who have both strong wills and views diametrically opposed, and whose modes and habits of business do not conform."[1]

[1] Letter of December 5, 1852. *Life of Lord Lawrence*, by Bosworth Smith (1885), vol. i. p. 332.

Both brothers tendered their resignation. Lord Dalhousie had to choose between them, and he had little hesitation in choosing. He abolished the Board of Administration; made John Lawrence the Chief Commissioner of the Punjab; and transferred Sir Henry Lawrence to the less responsible and humbler post of Agent at Rajputana.

The decision of Lord Dalhousie fell as a thunderbolt on the Punjab. "Grief was depicted on every face. Old and young, rich and poor, soldiers and civilians, Englishmen and Natives, each and all felt that they were about to lose a friend. Strong men, Herbert Edwards conspicuous amongst them, might be seen weeping like children; and when the last of those moments came, and Henry Lawrence, on January 20, 1853, accompanied by his wife and sister, turned his back for ever upon Lahore and upon the Punjab, a long cavalcade of the Native Chiefs followed him, some for five, some for ten, others for twenty or twenty-five miles out of the city. They were men, too, who had nothing now to hope from him, for the sun of Sir Henry Lawrence had set, in the Punjab at least, for ever. But they were anxious to evidence, by such poor signs as they could give, their grief, their gratitude, and their admiration. It was a long, living funeral procession from Lahore nearly to Amritsar. Robert Napier, now Lord Napier of Magdala, was the last to tear himself away from one who was dearer to him than a brother. 'Kiss him,' said Henry Lawrence to his sister, as Napier turned back at last, heart-broken towards Lahore. 'Kiss him, he is my best and dearest friend.' When he reached Amritsar, at the house of Charles Saunders, the Deputy Commissioner, a new group of mourners and a fresh outburst of grief awaited him; and thence he passed on into Rajputana." [1]

We shall hear of Sir Henry Lawrence once more in this narrative. On July 22, 1857, when British rule in

[1] *Life of Lord Lawrence.* By Bosworth Smith (1885), vol. i. pp. 335–336.

India was threatened by the outbreak of a great rebellion in Northern India, when the death or resignation of Lord Canning might at any day leave India without a guiding hand, the Court of Directors thought it proper to name a Governor-General in case of a vacancy. Their choice fell on the man who had proved himself a valiant soldier in times of war, and a sympathetic administrator in times of peace. And they resolved that "Sir Henry Montgomery Lawrence, K.C.B., be appointed provisionally to succeed to the office of Governor-General of India on the death, resignation, or coming away of Viscount Canning, pending the arrival of a successor from England." But the honour of the selection came too late; Sir Henry Lawrence had fallen on July 4 at Lucknow—the most generous of British administrators then in India, after the great Englishman whom he had been selected to succeed.

Apart from the personal interest which attaches to the story of the life of Henry Lawrence, his public policy will have an abiding interest for all Indian administrators. He represented in his generation a distinct school of administrators—the school founded in the preceding generation by Elphinstone and Bentinck—the school which had almost become obsolete under the Imperialism of Auckland and Dalhousie. "This school," says General M'Leod Innes, "which gave special consideration to the feelings, traditions, and modes of thought of the Native Community, demanded a fair recognition of the claims of Native States, and urged the need for wise and generous treatment of the natural leaders of the people." [1]

Lord Dalhousie never understood, never appreciated, this school. He was an Imperialist. He held that the best administration for the people of India was the direct administration of alien rulers; that all intervening chiefs and leaders were an obstruction to good administration and a hindrance to reforms. He made the mistake, which

[1] *Sir Henry Lawrence, the Pacificator.* By Lieut.-General M'Leod Innes 1898), Introduction..

has been made again and again by British rulers in India, of ignoring old leaders and old institutions, and of trying to substitute the direct and personal rule of British officials. And in removing Sir Henry Lawrence from the Punjab, Lord Dalhousie virtually uprooted his policy swept aside the natural leaders of the people, and brought a nation of cultivators directly under the Government. The policy was neither wise in itself, nor has it conduced to good administration during the fifty years which have since elapsed.

National institutions are the results and the outer expressions of national needs. The people of India developed Village Communities, and lived under Polygars and Zemindars, Jaigirdars and Talukdars, Sardars and Panchyets, because they needed them. Their social organisation was built up according to their social requirements; they felt themselves securer and happier under their born leaders or within their Rural Communities. It is unwise for any rulers to disturb such arrangements, it is especially unwise for alien rulers to neglect the organised institutions of a people.

The want thus created has not yet been remedied. No proper self-governing institutions have yet taken the place of the old Village Communities. No natural leaders of the people adequately represent their wishes and opinions in the government of Madras, Bombay, or the Punjab. Those Governments are less influenced and less benefited by public opinion than the Government in Bengal where society was early saved from dislocation by the action of Lord Cornwallis. Assessments have been severer and harsher in Madras and Bombay in the absence of Village Communities and of intermediate chiefs. In the Punjab, where the leaders of the people were unwisely ignored half a century ago, the so-called cultivating proprietors of the soil have not prospered. And the Government is exerting at the present day to save them from a new class of leaders—speculators, shroffs, and money-lenders—the worst aristocracy that any country can have.

It is a simple truism that some sort of representation, some form of self-government, is needed to safeguard the interests and promote the welfare of all nations, in Asia as in Europe. The forms of self-government which prevailed in India were not the forms with which Englishmen were familiar; but they served their purpose. They might have been fostered, corrected, and improved; but their effacement left a blank. In critical times, the want makes itself felt; British Rule does not obtain adequate support; Imperialism itself does not find a national basis. General M'Leod Innes has pointed out in the work already cited that, in the dark days of the Indian Mutiny, Cis-Sutlej Sikhs, as well as the Mussulmans of Multan and the frontier, rendered valuable services and furnished strong contingents under the specific guidance of their chiefs. But the leaderless Sikhs of the Punjab rendered none till after the capture of Delhi. But the Indian administrator notes this want in times of peace no less than in time of war—the want of popular co-operation in influencing and popularising an alien administration.

John Lawrence carried out the policy of Lord Dalhousie. "Assess low," he wrote to Nicholson, "leaving fair and liberal margin to the occupiers of the soil, and they will increase their cultivation and put the revenue almost beyond the reach of bad seasons. Eschew middlemen. They are the curse of the country everywhere."[1]

But the assessment was not low. As in other Provinces of India, it was raised rapidly after British occupation. In 1847–48 the Land Revenue of the Punjab was £820,000. Within three years after British annexation it went up to £1,060,000. The fall in prices added to the distress of the cultivators now required to pay their revenue in money. The complaints during the year 1851 on the part of the agriculturists was loud and

[1] *Life of Lord Lawrence.* By Bosworth Smith (1885), vol. i. p. 341.

general. "There has been a very general demand among the agriculturists for a return to grain payments, to a division or appraisement of the crops every season. The Board have resisted this call, but have directed the suspension of revenue wherever it appeared desirable."[1]

The following figures for the different districts of the Punjab are compiled from the First Administration Report:—[2]

Division.	District.	Land Revenue, 1850–51.	Land Revenue, 1851–52.
		£	£
Lahore	Lahore	38,060	40,614
	Amritsar	86,872	102,473
	Dinanagar	89,927	94,041
	Wazirabad	108,338	114,018
	Shekhpura	31,916	38,322
Jhelum	Gujrat	59.382	59,859
	Jhelum	69,548	72,091
	Rawalpi ii	82,481	82,056
	Shahpur	41,231	34,381
Leia	Leia	48,444	54,357
	Khungarh	49.534	48,463
	Dera Gazikhan	45.574	47,280
	Dera Ismaelkhan	48,968	50,656
Multan	Multan	56,430	60,359
	Jhung	27,878	34,962
	Pak Pattan	25,757	38,312
	Peshawar	89.307	71,929
	Hazra	18,854	16,815
	Total	£1,018,502	£1,060.989

[1] Punjab Administration Report, 1852, paragraphs 264, 266, and 270.

[2] Paragraph 274 of the Punjab Administration Report of 1852.

This First Punjab Report, from which we have made frequent extracts in the preceding pages, was from the facile pen of Sir Richard Temple, known as the Knight of the Pen in India. John Lawrence, a solid worker and a great administrator, had not the gift of a lucid style; and he felt the want. When he first met Richard Temple in 1851 at Simla, and examined some of his settlement reports, he was mightily pleased. "Here is the very man we want as Secretary," he said to his friends. "He can understand what I say, and put it into first-rate form!" Forthwith Temple was appointed to write the Punjab Report which Henry Lawrence and John Lawrence had already partly drafted; but the new Secretary recast the whole; and the First Punjab Report stands

To "assess low" was John Lawrence's first principle in land administration: and he soon perceived that the demand of one-third the gross produce, payable in money, was oppressive to the peasantry. Within a few years the Punjab Administration corrected the mistake. The Land Tax of the Punjab was reduced to one-fourth, and then to one-sixth of the gross produce. The wisdom of this measure was proved by the extension of cultivation, the rise of revenue, and the increase of actual collections.

The figures for 1856–57 and 1857–58 show a considerable increase in revenue as compared with the figures given above, as also a very satisfactory rate of collection:—[1]

	Demand.	Collection.
1856–57 . . .	£1,485,000	£1,452,000
1857–58 . . .	£1,465,000	£1,452,000

A regular Settlement of the Land Revenue was commenced soon after the annexation of the Punjab and was approaching completion when the East India Company was abolished in 1858. One-sixth of the produce was demanded as the land revenue in the Settlements of Lahore and Amritsar districts, concluded between 1860 and 1872; while by later rules, framed under the Land Revenue Act of 1871, the Government demanded one-half the actual rents paid by ordinary tenants at will in average years.

We have now dealt successively with Northern India, Bombay, Madras, and the Punjab. For a general view of the last results of the East India Company's Land Revenue Administration in India, we cannot refer our

apart from all other Indian reports as a readable and entertaining document. In 1854, when Temple returned from England to his work, John Lawrence had become Chief Commissioner of the Punjab. "Very glad," he said to Temple, "to have got you in your proper place at last! I am glad of your opinion, and, of course, very glad of your pen; but remember, it will be *my* policy and *my* views—not yours. Your day may come; it is mine now: every dog will have its day."—Bosworth Smith's *Life of Lord Lawrence*.

[1] Punjab Administration Report for 1856–57 and 1857–58, par. 37.

readers to an abler document than to a return submitted by the India House itself in 1857.[1] It is signed by John Stuart Mill, then Examiner of India Office correspondence; and though probably it was compiled by his clerks, it bears traces of his philosophic finish and precision. Some extracts are given below.

John Stuart Mill on Indian Land Systems.

Bengal.—"In the Lower Provinces of the Bengal Presidency the land is held by Zemindars, on payment of an annual sum fixed in perpetuity, the estates being liable to be sold in default of payment under the provisions of Act I of 1845. The only land at the disposal of Government consists of estates which have been thus sold, and purchased on the public account. The rate of Land Tax cannot be given, but is believed to amount on the average to about half the rental."

Northern India.—"First. All the inhabited part of the country is divided into portions with fixed boundaries, called Mahals or estates. On each Mahal a sum is assessed for the term of twenty or thirty years, calculated so as to leave a fair surplus profit over and above the net produce of the land; and for the punctual payment of that sum, the land is held to be perpetually hypothecated to the Government.

"Secondly. It is determined who are the person or persons entitled to receive this surplus profit. The right thus determined is declared to be heritable and transferable, and the persons entitled to it are considered the proprietors of the land from whom the engagements for the annual payment of the sum assessed by the Government on the Mahal are taken.

"Thirdly. All the proprietors of a Mahal are, severally and jointly, responsible in their persons and property

[1] Return to an Order of the House of Commons dated June 9, 1857, showing under what tenures, and subject to what Land Tax, lands are held under the several Presidencies of India.

for the payment of the sum assessed by the Government on the Mahal. When there are more proprietors than one it is determined according to what rule they shall share the profits, or make good the losses on the estate. If the proprietors are numerous, engagements are only taken from a few of the body, who, on their own parts and as representatives of the rest, undertake to manage the Mahal, and to pay the sum assessed upon it.[1]

"The rate of assessment was in the first instance limited to two-thirds of the nett produce of each Mahal or estate, but on the revision which is about to take place on the expiration of the thirty years which formed the first term of settlement, it has been determined[2] to restrict the demand of the State to one-half of the average nett assets."

Madras.—"The revenue systems in force in the Madras Presidency are the Zamindari, Village joint rents, Ryotwari, and Ulangu."

"The Zamindari tenure prevails chiefly in the Northern Cercars, though there are large proprietary estates in other districts, as Madura, Nellore, North Arcot, &c."

"In the Village-renting system the villagers stand in the Zemindar's position, and jointly hold from the Government. The village is rented to the whole body, or a section of them, for a term of years, and they make their payments direct to Government, managing their affairs independently, and allotting the lands for cultivation among themselves."

"Under the Ryotwari System every registered holder of land is recognised as its proprietor, and pays direct to Government. He is at liberty to sublet his property, or to transfer it by gift, sale, or mortgage. He cannot be ejected by Government so long as he pays the fixed assessment, and has the option annually of increasing or

[1] These three Rules are taken from Thomason's *Directions for Revenue Officers*, referred to in a previous chapter.

[2] By the Saharanpur Rules of 1855.

diminishing his holding, or of entirely abandoning it. In unfavourable seasons remissions of assessment are granted for entire or partial loss of produce. The assessment is fixed in money, and does not vary from year to year, except in those cases where water is drawn from a Government source of irrigation to convert dry land into wet, or one into two-crop land, when an extra rent is paid to Government for the water so appropriated; nor is any addition made to the assessment for improvements effected at the Ryot's own expense. The Ryot under this system is virtually a Proprietor on a simple and perfect title, and has all the benefits of a perpetual lease without its responsibilities, inasmuch as he can at any time throw up his lands, but cannot be ejected so long as he pays his dues; he receives assistance in difficult seasons, and is irresponsible for the payment of his neighbours. . . . The Annual Settlements under Ryotwari are often misunderstood, and it is necessary to explain that they are rendered necessary by the right accorded to the Ryot of diminishing or extending his cultivation from year to year. Their object is to determine how much of the assessment due on his holding the Ryot shall pay, and not to reassess the land. In these cases where no change occurs in the Ryots holding a fresh Potta or lease is not issued, and such parties are in no way affected by the Annual Settlement, which they are not required to attend."

"The Ulangu-renting system prevails only in Tanjore and Tinnevelly, and is not general in either; its peculiarity consists in the Government demand being dependent on the current price of grain. On the introduction of the system, a certain grain assessment was fixed on each village, and also a standard rate, according to which the grain demand was to be commuted into money; but it was, at the same time, arranged, that if current prices in any year rose more than 10 per cent. above the standard commutation rate, or fell more than 5 per cent. below it, the Government, and not the Ryot, was to receive the profit and to bear the loss. The advantages of the system are that the Government participates with the Ryot in the benefit of high prices, while the latter is relieved from loss when the prices are much depressed; its disadvantage consists in the difficulty that is experienced in obtaining accurate and fair returns of the current prices which are taken throughout the year."

Bombay.—"Under the Bombay Presidency, the revenue management may be described in general terms as Ryotwari, implying that, as a general rule, the occupants of Government lands[1] settle for their land revenue or rent with the Government Officers direct, and not through a middleman. It should be understood, however, that throughout the Presidency, instances not unfrequently occur in which the Government revenues of entire villages are settled for by individual superior holders under various denominations, or by a copartnery of the superior holders."

"A revision of assessment is now in progress throughout the Presidency, by which the amount payable on each field is determined according to its quality, and the amount so fixed is not liable to alteration for a term of thirty years."

Punjab.—"In the Punjab, one and the same man is usually absolute proprietor and generally the sole cultivator, though he may occassionally lease out a few fields to tenants. He is saddled with no rent. He has to provide for the cost of cultivation and for the Government demand; the rest of the produce he may devote to the maintenance of his family and the accumulation of his capital. But these men, well maintaining their individuality, do yet belong to Village Communities. A village is not inhabited by a certain number of Ryots

[1] The expression "Government lands" is not a happy one. The occupants of the land in Bombay were its *proprietors*,—as clearly and unmistakably as in Madras. Government was only entitled to a Land Tax which was a portion of the nett produce of the fields.

each unconnected with the other, but by a number of persons of common descent, forming one large cousinhood, having their own head man accustomed to joint action and mutual support."

"The British Government has from the first decided on levying the Tax by money payments assessed for a number of years. The Peasant Proprietors compound with the State for a fixed period, such assessment and compounding being technically called a Settlement. But the Proprietors do not engage individually with the Government, but by villages. The brotherhood, through its headmen or representatives, undertakes to pay so much for so many years; and then, having done this, they divide the amount among themselves, assigning to each man his quota. Primarily each man cultivates and pays for himself, but ultimately he is responsible for his coparceners, and they for him, and they are bound together by a joint liability. The Punjab System, therefore, is not Ryotwari, nor Zamindari, but the *Village System.* In the hills, and occasionally elsewhere, the Zamindari System, and near Multan something approaching the Ryotwari System, may be found. But the Village System is the prevalent one, especially in the most important districts."

Summary.—The account given above may be summed up in a few words. In Bengal, land was held by landlords paying a fixed and unalterable Land Tax to the Government. In Northern India it was generally held by landlords paying a Land Tax revised at each new Settlement. In Madras and Bombay it was generally held by Peasant Proprietors who paid a Land Tax revised at each new Settlement. In the Punjab it was generally held by Peasant Proprietors living in Village Communities, each village collectively paying the Land Tax which was revised at each new Settlement.

And under these various arrangements the Land Tax gradually became a uniform rate, at least in theory In Bengal it was about one-half the rental in the middle of the nineteenth century. In Northern India it was fixed at one-half the rental by the Saharanpur Rule of 1855. In Bombay and Madras Sir Charles Wood fixed the Land Tax at about one-half the economic rent in 1864. And in the Punjab the Government demand was reduced to one-half the rents ordinarily paid by tenants at will.

This, then, is the theory of the Indian Land Tax. *Where the Land Tax is not permanently fixed, one-half of the actual or economic rent may be claimed as the Land Revenue.*

CHAPTER VII

RAW PRODUCE AND MANUFACTURES

WHEN the East India Company's Charter was renewed in 1833, it was provided that the Company should thenceforth "discontinue and abstain from all commercial business," and should stand forth only as administrators and rulers of India. The beneficial results of this provision became manifest before many years had elapsed. The Company felt a greater interest in the trades and manufacturers of India when they were no longer rival traders. And on February 11, 1840, they presented a petition to Parliament for the removal of invidious duties which discouraged and repressed Indian industries.

A Select Committee of the House of Commons was appointed to report on the petition. Lord Seymour was in the chair; and among the Members of the Committee was Mr. Gladstone, then a young man of thirty, and a stern and unbending Tory. Mr. Brocklehurst, Member for Macclesfield, then a great centre of British silk manufacture, was also on the Committee, and represented the interests of the British manufacturer. Much valuable evidence on Indian produce and manufacture was recorded, and has been published in a folio volume of over six hundred pages. It is possible, within our limits, only to refer to such portions of this evidence as are specially relevant to the present work.

J. C. MELVILL.

Military Expenditure and Home Charges.—Melvill said, the amount defrayed by the Company for the Queen's troops employed on the Indian establishment was £1,400,000, and the Company had also agreed to raise and maintain such further men as might be necessary to keep at all times an effective force of 20,000 in India. The portion of the Indian revenues spent in England was, on the average, £3,200,000 a year, and this included the dividends of shareholders, interest on debt, furlough allowances, pensions, the expenses of the Board of Control and the Court of Directors, and their establishments.

Opium.—Opium was grown in British territory, Benares, and Patna, and in the Native State of Malwa. The Benares and Patna opium was the monopoly of the Company, and the Government of Bengal got a large revenue from this monopoly, selling the opium at a profit of more than 200 per cent. Malwa opium paid a heavy transit duty of £12, 10s. the chest on passing into British territory for exportation, and the Government of Bombay derived a substantial revenue from this transit duty. The two kinds of opium met in the market of Canton for sale in China.

Salt.—The Government realised a large revenue from salt manufactured in the Company's territory, and a heavy duty on salt manufactured in Native States and coming into British territory. The Company had the monopoly in salt as in opium.

Sugar.—In 1836, Parliament passed an Act, allowing Indian sugar to be brought to England at the same duty as sugar from the West Indies, *i.e.* 24s. a cwt. The principle of the law was that the Indian sugar might come, if importation was prohibited at the place from which it came. The Governor-General had prohibited importation into Bengal; Bengal sugar therefore came to England on payment of 24s. per cwt.; and the quantity had increased from 101,000 cwt. in 1835 to 519,000 cwt. in 1839. The Governor-General had passed an Act in 1839 prohibiting importation into Madras, so that Madras also was about to enjoy the same privilege as Bengal. There was no chance of the same privilege being extended to Bombay for some time.

Rum.—There was a duty of 15s. a gallon on Indian rum imported into England, as against a duty of 9s. only on West Indian rum, although the latter was stronger.

Tobacco.—There was a duty of 3s. per pound on Indian tobacco imported into England, as against 2s. 9d. on West Indian tobacco. The difference caused much hardship; and it was believed that by equalising the duty the consumption of Indian tobacco could be greatly promoted.

Coffee.—In 1835 the duty upon Indian coffee was equalised with the West Indian duty of 6d. per pound; and the consumption of Indian coffee in England had largely increased in consequence.

Cotton, Silk, and Woollen Goods.—British cotton and silk goods, conveyed in British ships to India, paid a duty of 3½ per cent.; and British woollen goods a duty of 2 per cent. only. But Indian cotton goods, imported into England, paid a duty of 10 per cent.; Indian silk goods a duty of 20 per cent.; Indian woollen goods, a duty of 30 per cent.

As the import of cotton goods from India into England had died out, the import of raw cotton had increased. In the five years ending in 1813, the cotton-wool annually imported from India had been 9,368,000 lbs. on the average. The annual average of the five years ending in 1838 was 48,329,660 lbs.

"Native manufactures have been superseded by British?" Melvill was asked.

"Yes, in great measure," was his reply.

"Since what period?"

"I think, principally since 1814."

"The displacement of Indian manufactures by British is such that India is now dependent mainly for its supply of those articles on British manufacturers?"

"I think so."

"Has the displacement of the labour of native manufacturers at all been compensated by any increase in the produce of articles of the first necessity, raw produce?"

"The export of raw produce from India has increased since she ceased largely to export manufactures; but I am not prepared to say in what proportion."

"Have the natives of India, weavers, for instance, when thrown out of employment, the same facility in turning their attention to other matters as people in this country have, or are particular trades at all mixed up with the peculiarities of caste?"

"Particular trades are, I believe, mixed up with the peculiarities of caste. I have no doubt that great distress was the consequence in the first instance, of the interference of British manufactures with those of India."[1]

Tea.—It was known to the Court of Directors, as early as 1788, that the tea plant was a native of India; but no attempts were then made to encourage its cultivation. In 1835, Lord William Bentinck brought to the Court's notice that the tea plant was indigenous in Assam, and could be grown elsewhere in India; and the Court gave its sanction to an experimental establishment in Assam for the cultivation and manufacture of tea. Ninety-five chests of Assam tea, about 4000 lbs., had recently arrived in London, and had been pronounced good; and applications from many persons, who had formed themselves into a company, had been referred by the Court of Directors to the Indian Government. The growing of tea in Assam by private enterprise and capital thus dates from about 1840.

Andrew Sym.

This witness held grants of land from the East India Company in India, to the extent of about 60,000 English

[1] Questions 577, 578, 583, 584, and 633.

acres, and gave evidence mainly about the growing of sugar-cane and the manufacture of sugar. The cultivators grew the cane, expressed the juice, boiled it, and then sold it to the factory. There it was made into *Shukkur* by mechanical pressure, boiled into syrup, and then evaporated into sugar.

The witness had much to say about the displacement of Indian labour by the introduction of English manufactures—clothing, tools, implements, glassware, and brass articles. The people of India deprived of their occupations, turned "to agriculture chiefly."

C. E. Trevelyan.

A more important witness was Sir Charles Trevelyan who, after a distinguished service in India under Lord William Bentinck, had become Assistant Secretary to the Treasury in England.[1]

While in India, he had helped in abolishing vexatious transit duties which had impeded the internal trade. And in his evidence before the Select Committee he pleaded for the removal of those unequal and prohibitive import duties in England which kept out India's manufactures.

Population of British India.—The population of Bengal was generally calculated at 30 millions; that of Northern India under British Rule at 30 millions; that of Madras about 14 millions; and of Bombay about 3 millions. Total for British India, 77 millions. The ordinary price of labour was 2 anas, or 3d. a day. Land in Bengal was tilled by cultivators who held it under landlords. "The theory of Indian agriculture is, that as long as the Ryot, who is the occupant of the soil, con-

[1] Later on he went out to India as Governor of Madras in 1859; was recalled in 1860 for his protest against new taxes; and was Finance Minister of India in 1862 to 1865 under Lords Elgin and Lawrence. He married Macaulay's sister, and to his son we owe the *Life and Letters of Lord Macaulay*.

tinues to pay the rates of rent fixed by usage in his district, he is not liable to be ousted; but this rule is constantly broken through."[1] All restrictions against Europeans holding land in India had been removed; and it had been expected that Europeans would purchase lands and settle in India. "But that has ended in disappointment. The climate does not suit them; they do not look to ending their days there."[2]

Sugar and Rum.—The equalising of the duty on sugar was useless until the duty on rum was also equalised. "It is a mere mockery to give equality in one respect only; in order to establish equality you must equalise the duty on all the articles manufactured from the sugar-cane."[3]

The inequality in the duty on rum, besides being injurious to the manufacture of both sugar and rum, created a sore feeling, a feeling among the people of India that their interests were being sacrificed to those of more favoured countries.

> *Mr. Gladstone.*—When you speak of dissatisfaction existing among the natives, are you to be understood that you do not allude to the body of cultivators, or the population, but to that which may be fairly called the commercial class?
>
> *Mr. Trevelyan.*—I mean that those among them, particularly the commercial class, and the educated natives of Calcutta, who know something of the relations between India and the mother country, feel it as a grievance; that it goes to add to the sum of grievances which the natives feel; and that the feeling extends from the better informed class to the body of people, but without the body of the people well knowing the grounds.[4]

For the rest, the witness said that the Bengal sugar,

[1] Question 1624.
[2] Question 1513.
[3] Question 1499.
[4] Question 1789.

grown in the valley of the Ganges, had a vast home consumption. The 30 millions of Bengal, the 30 millions of British Northern India, and some 40 millions beyond, consumed the Gangetic sugar. Witness understood that the people of Central Asia too derived their supply of sugar from the valley of the Ganges, until that sugar met the beet-root sugar of Russia.[1]

Cotton Goods.—Indian cotton manufactures had been to a great extent displaced by English manufactures. "The peculiar kind of silky cotton formerly grown in Bengal, from which the fine Dacca muslins used to be made, is hardly ever seen; the population of the town of Dacca has fallen from 150,000 to 30,000 or 40,000, and the jungle and malaria are fast encroaching upon the town. The only cotton manufactures which stand their ground in India are of the very coarse kinds, and the English cotton manufactures are generally consumed by all above the very poorest throughout India. . . . Dacca, which was the Manchester of India, has fallen off from a very flourishing town to a very poor and small one; the distress there has been very great indeed."[2]

Tea.—Tea was grown in Assam, at first experimentally, by the Government, and since then by the new Assam Company. There was a dearth of local labour, and the Company engaged hill-coolies and took them from a distance to Assam to do work in the gardens. Witness believed that the contracts were for three years, but he had no precise information.

Indigo.—Hill-coolies went annually to the indigo planters of Bengal to find employment in the manufacture of indigo, "just as the Irish come over into this country to get in the harvest." The coolies did not take their families with them, and they returned home after the indigo season was over.

River Steamers.—All the steam navigation was still in the hands of the East India Company. The steamers

[1] Question 1699.

[2] Questions 1824 and 1825.

used were very small ones, and drew less than two feet water. There was a Steam Tug Company for drawing vessels up and down the Hughli River, which made a good dividend.

Roads.—Roads were seldom repaired at all, except along the main lines. But they seldom became entirely impassable for the country carts, which were stoutly made, except in the rains.

Raw produce.—Mr. Trevelyan recommended that the raw produce of India should be freed from all unequal duties in the English market. "We have swept away their manufactures; they have nothing to depend upon but the produce of their land, and I think it would be extremely unjust not to give equal privileges in the market of the mother country to that."[1]

Henry Gouger.

Henry Gouger was a merchant who had lived in India many years, and was the proprietor of works near Calcutta for the manufacture of cotton-twist, the distilling of rum, the expressing of oil from seeds, a foundry and a paper mill. His evidence therefore was of great value.

Cotton-twist.—700,000 lbs. weight of yarn was annually spun, of numbers varying from 20 to 50. The cotton used was all grown in India and selected with great care, and the machinery was worked by Indian labourers under European superintendence. There were 100 power looms, but their use was discontinued in order to employ the whole of the power steam for the manufacture of yarns which was more profitable. The lower numbers sold rather better than English yarns, the higher numbers on a par with them. But on the whole the profits of the business were not proportionate to the enormous cost. "I am inclined to think," said the witness, "there never will be another manufactory for spin-

[1] Question 1950.

ning cotton yarns, in consequence of the great expense attending the building of the present one."[1]

Coal.—Witness used coal from his own mine at Burdwan. The coal was sold at 16s. per ton in Calcutta; it was not so good as English coal, but being cheaper was generally used in the steamers in India. The cost of the Burdwan coal at Calcutta was 12s. or 13s. the ton; the price of Newcastle coal at Calcutta was 25s.

Sugar.—The juice of the cane, boiled by the growers into Goor, was brought by them and sold at the manufactory to be made into sugar. Fine Benares sugar sold at 11 or 12 rupees (24s.) for 80 lbs. weight. The price was lower before the duties were equalised. Sugar was carried to England as dead weight and the freight was £4, 10s. the ton.

Rum.—West Indian rum paid a duty of 9s. per gallon on import into England, while Indian rum paid a duty of 15s. the gallon. Rum was distilled in India both from Goor, and from molasses, the refuse of Goor. From 80 lbs. of molasses 3⅓ gallons of rum, London proof, could be obtained; a much larger quantity could be made from 80 lbs. of Goor. A gallon of rum could be supplied at Calcutta at 10 annas, *i.e.* 1s. 3d.

It might be profitable to extract sugar from Goor and then to convert the refuse, the molasses, into rum; but that was not the general practice.

Silk.—Bengal raw silk, imported into England, sold at about 16s. the pound. Corahs, or silk piece goods made in India, sold at about 16s. or 17s. the pound. The export of raw silk from India was declining. In 1828–29 it was to the value of £920,000. In 1829–30 it was £800,000. In 1830–31 it was £720,000. In 1831–32 it was only £540,000. Probably an increase had taken place in the manufacture of silk goods in India, and the export of silk goods from India had also increased.

[1] Question 1981.

G. G. de H. Larpent.

Larpent, Chairman of the East India and China Association, was then examined. The Association was formed in 1836 with the object of rendering assistance to all parties concerned in the East India and China trade. He gave his evidence at great length on the import of sugar and rum from different countries into England, and he spoke strongly on the decline of the cotton and silk manufactures of India.

Cotton goods.—Mr. Larpent supplied the Committee with the following figures relating to the import of Indian cotton goods into England, and the export of English cotton goods into India.

Cotton Piece Goods Imported into Great Britain from the East Indies.

1814	1,266,608 pieces.
1821	534,495 ,,
1828	422,504 ,,
1835	306,086 ,,

British Cotton Manufactures Exported to India.

1814	818,208 yards.
1821	19,138,726 ,,
1828	42,822,077 ,,
1835	51,777,277 ,,

In spite of this decline in the Indian manufacture, and the increase of British manufacture, British cotton goods were still imported into India on payment of an *ad valorem* duty of 3½ per cent., while Indian cotton goods imported into England were subjected to an *ad valorem* duty of 10 per cent. Quoting from Mr. Shore, witness read: "This supersession of the native for British manufactures is often quoted as a splendid instance of the triumph of British skill. It is a much stronger instance of English tyranny, and how India has been impoverished by the most vexatious system of customs and duties imposed for the avowed object of favouring the mother country." Mr. Larpent did not agree with Mr. Shore in these observations to the full extent; but they showed the feeling of a distinguished servant of the Company, a feeling which was likely to prevail among the people of India.[1]

Silk goods.—British silk goods were admitted into Calcutta on payment of a duty of 3½ per cent., Indian silk goods were subjected to an import duty of 20 per cent. in England. Corahs or Indian silk piece goods in the grey (unprinted), were imported into England mainly for being printed in England and then exported to other European countries. The following figures were given for Corahs imported into England.

	For Home Consumption.	For Re-export.
	Pieces.	Pieces.
1838 . . .	16,000	310,000
1839 . . .	38,000	352,000

Bandannas or Indian printed pocket-handkerchiefs were imported into England in considerable quantities. Mr. Larpent pleaded strongly for the equalisation of duties between Great Britain and India with regard to silk goods. Mr. Brocklehurst, one of the members of the Select Committee, represented British silk manufactures, and necessarily desired the continuance of unequal duties to the advantage of England.

Mr. Brocklehurst.—You give your opinion without reference to the effect it would have on the British produce?

Mr. Larpent.—I have no doubt there would be, to a certain extent, a rivalry in competition with the silk manufactures of this country; but I submit on principle

[1] Question 2743.

that India ought to be admitted as one of our own possessions. The argument has been used that while our manufactures are allowed to go into India at a very reduced duty, we ought to have admitted theirs on as low a duty.

Mr. Brocklehurst.—Is there any colony of this country whose manufactures are admitted on so low a scale as those of India?

Mr. Larpent.—There is no colony of this country whose manufacturers are of a magnitude calling for it. We have destroyed the manufactures of India. [And then the witness quoted the views of the Court of Directors, stated in Lord William Bentinck's minute of May 30, 1829: "The sympathy of the Court is deeply excited by the report of the Board of Trade, exhibiting the gloomy picture of the effects of a commercial revolution productive of so much present suffering to numerous classes in India, and hardly to be paralleled in the history of commerce."] [1]

But Mr. Brocklehurst was not convinced. The use of Indian silk handkerchiefs in England troubled his soul, and he returned again and again to the subject.

Mr. Brocklehurst.—Are you aware that they have already so far displaced silk handkerchiefs made in this country, that attempts are now making to introduce a spurious article from waste silk as a substitute?

Mr. Larpent.—I have heard that an article is introduced made of waste silk; and that as I stated before, the ingenuity and science of the parties who are making those goods, will probably introduce into the home market a quantity of goods at a low price, which will be in very general use.

Mr. Brocklehurst.—Driving the British manufacturer to make inferior articles to maintain his ground in competition?

[1] Questions 2750 and 2751.

Mr. Larpent.—The articles alluded to are those made here; the British manufacturers have made those inferior articles.

Mr. Brocklehurst.—It would be more desirable perhaps that India should produce the raw material, and this country show its skill in perfecting that raw material?

Mr. Larpent.—The course of things in India is decidedly leading to that; and it is in the main articles such as we have already alluded to, that we do think every assistance should be given to the agricultural produce of India; but I submit that as this is the last of the expiring manufactures of India, the only one where there is a chance of introducing the native manufactures, at least let it have a fair chance, and not be oppressed with the duty of 20 per cent., in favour of the British manufactures.[1]

MONTGOMERY MARTIN.

A still more sturdy champion for India was Montgomery Martin. He had travelled ten years in the colonies of the British Empire, mainly at his own expense; had gathered facts, figures and statistics; and had compiled the first complete History of the British Colonies in five large volumes. He had lived in India; studied Indian questions on the spot; and also edited the voluminous and valuable statistical account of Eastern India left by Dr. Francis Buchanan.

"I have examined at considerable length," he said, "and for a series of years, the trade of India. I have taken the utmost pains to arrive at correct conclusions by examining various documents which the Honourable Court of Directors of the East India House, with their

[1] Questions 2763, 2764, and 2771.

"The last of the expiring manufactures of India" has not been saved. India to-day exports annually over seventy million pounds in goods, mostly raw produce. Scarcely over a hundred thousand pounds of this is silk manufactures.

usual liberality, permitted me access to. And I have been impressed with the conviction that India has suffered most unjustly in her trade, not merely with England but with all other countries, by reason of the outcry for free trade on the part of England without permitting to India a free trade herself." And he added that, "on all articles except those where we are supplanting the native manufacturers, and consequently impoverishing the country, there is a decreasing trade."[1]

Cotton goods.—In 1815 the cotton goods exported from India were of the value of £1,300,000. In 1832 they were less than £100,000. In 1815 the cotton goods imported into India from England were of the value of £26,300. In 1832 they were upwards of £400,000. "We have during the period of a quarter of a century compelled the Indian territories to receive our manufactures; our woollens, duty free, our cottons at 2½ per cent., and other articles in proportion; while we have continued during that period to levy almost prohibitory duties, or duties varying from 10 to 20, 30, 50, 100, 500, and 1000 per cent. upon articles, the produce from our territories. Therefore, the cry that has taken place for free trade with India, has been a free trade from this country, not a free trade between India and this country. . . . The decay and destruction of Surat, of Dacca, of Murshedabad, and other places where native manufactures have been carried on, is too painful a fact to dwell upon. I do not consider that it has been in the fair course of trade; I think it has been the power of the stronger exercised over the weaker."[2]

Evidence such as this brought about a keen controversy between the witness and Mr. Brocklehurst, the representative of the British manufacturer.

Mr. Brocklehurst.—The fact being that weavers, either

[1] Question 3876.
[2] Questions 3877 and 3879.

in the one country or the other, must be sacrificed, and that sacrifice having already taken place in India, you wish to revive the population of India at the expense of this country?

Mr. Martin.—I do not wish to revive it, but I wish to prevent continued injury to India. But it does not necessarily follow that the weavers of England would be destroyed by admitting the natives of India to compete with them in this country, because the natives of India have no power looms, and no means of employing skill and capital to the extent that the manufacturers of Glasgow and Manchester have.

Mr. Brocklehurst.—The questions that have been asked refer entirely to fine fabrics which cannot be woven by power. The question is, whether we are to give up fine weaving in this country, or to retain it?

Mr. Martin.—If it is only to be retained at the expense of injustice to India, my answer is, that England ought to act with justice, no matter what the result may be. That she has no right to destroy the people of a country which she has conquered, for the benefit of herself, for the mere sake of upholding any isolated portion of the community at home.

Mr. Brocklehurst.—When the transfer of India to the Government of this country took place in 1833,[1] the destruction of weaving in India had already taken place, and therefore it is not a question of destruction, for that is past; and we have it in evidence that India is an agricultural rather than a manufacturing country, and that the parties formerly employed in manufactures are now absorbed in agriculture. Does it occur to you that there is an opening in this country, if manufacturers are displaced, for the people to turn to agriculture?

[1] The transfer of India to the Government of Great Britain did not take place in 1833. The British Government obtained control over the administration of India half a century before that date, by Pitt's India Act of 1774, and was responsible for Indian administration. In 1833 a new Act was passed renewing the Company's Charter but prohibiting their trade.

Mr. Martin.—I do not agree that India is an agricultural country; India is as much a manufacturing country as an agricultural; and he who would seek to reduce her to the position of an agricultural country seeks to lower her in the scale of civilisation. I do not suppose that India is to become the agricultural farm of England; she is a manufacturing country, her manufactures of various descriptions have existed for ages, and have never been able to be competed with by any nation wherever fair play has been given to them. I speak not now of her Dacca muslins and her Cashmere shawls, but of various articles which she has manufactured in a manner superior to any part of the world. To reduce her now to an agricultural country would be an injustice to India.[1]

Woollen Manufactures.—For twenty-five years British woollen manufactures had been admitted almost duty free in India, but the manufactures of India made of goat's wool paid a duty of 30 per cent. *ad valorem.* The result was that from 1828 to 1838 the total importation from India had not averaged more than £28,000 per annum. By stopping this trade British manufacturers were not benefited, as the shawls of England were mostly made on the continent.[2]

Shipbuilding.—There was a marked decrease in shipbuilding in India. In 1795–96 six ships were built in Calcutta, with a tonnage of 4105 tons, and five large vessels of 500 to 600 tons each were on the stocks. In 1797–98 several vessels were launched from the dockyards of Calcutta. But shipbuilding had now (1840) been entirely given up in Calcutta. A dockyard had been founded by the Parsees at Bombay, and for three generations the splendid dock establishment at Bombay had been under Parsee management. The fine vessel *Asia* was built by Naoroji Jamsetjee, and Parsee gentlemen were studying shipbuilding in the English dock-

[1] Questions 3918, 3919, and 3920. [2] Question 3957.

yards. Nevertheless, English-built ships, manned by lascars, proceeding to ports with which England had reciprocity treaties, were not treated as British ships. This was a direct impediment thrown in the way of shipbuilding in India. The Charter of the East India Company of 1833 declared that the natives of India were British subjects, and it was a hardship and injustice to them that they were not considered such in the matter of merchant ships.[1]

Home Charges.—Witness submitted a table showing the Home Charges, or the amount of Indian revenues spent in England, during twenty years, from the renewal of the Company's Charter in 1813 to the renewal of their Charter in 1833.[2] Figures showing the Home Charges for five subsequent years, 1834 to 1837, have been taken from another part of the report.[3] Figures showing the revenues of India have been taken from a Parliamentary

Year.	Home Charges.	Revenues of India.
	£	£
1814-15 . .	2,446,016	17,297,280
1815-16 . .	2,048,030	17,237,819
1816-17 . .	2,042,809	18,077,578
1817-18 . .	2,023,996	18,375,820
1818-19 . .	2,369,947	19,459,017
1819-20 . .	1,861,381	19,230,462
1820-21 . .	2,306,187	21,352,241
1821-22 . .	3,203,511	21,803,108
1822-23 . .	3,326,406	23,171,701
1823-24 . .	2,027,420	21,280,384
1824-25 . .	2,182,132	20,750,183
1825-26 . .	2,362,360	21,128,388
1826-27 . .	2,975,141	22,383,497
1827-28 . .	2,694,219	22,863,263
1828-29 . .	2,719,579	22,740,691
1829-30 . .	2,613,527	21,695,208
1830-31 . .	2,399,573	22,019,310
1831-32 . .	2,475,569	18,317,237
1832-33 . .	2,233,559	18,477,924
1833-34 . .	2,053,141	18,267,368
1834-35 . .	3,063,322	26,856,647
1835-36 . .	2,959,975	20,148,125
1836-37 . .	3,090,582	20,999,130
1837-38 . .	2,979,514	20,858,820

[1] Questions 3987 and 3992. [2] Appendix 60. [3] Appendix 1.

Return.[1] The table, which we have thus compiled, shows the proportion of the Home Charges to the total revenue of India for the twenty-four years ending in the year of the accession of Queen Victoria.

A small portion of these Home Charges, about one-fifth, was for stores supplied to India from England. The remaining sums, said Montgomery Martin, "are absolute charges upon the revenues of India, and for which no return whatever is made to India. . . . It is a curious calculation to show, that estimating the sums of money drawn from British India for the last thirty years at three millions per annum, it amounts, at 12 per cent. (the Indian rate of interest), compound interest, to £723,997,971; or, if we calculate it at two millions per annum for fifty years, the abstraction of fructifying capital from Hindustan amounts to the incredible sum of £8,400,000,000." [2]

Silk Manufactures.—The silk manufactures of India should be freed from the unequal import duty placed upon it in England, and there was the greater reason for this because they really did not compete with the silk manufactures of England or any other country.[3]

Alexander Rogers.

Flax and Hemp.—Alexander Rogers was a large proprietor of factories in India, and was introducing the culture of flax for the fibre, the natives of India having so long cultivated that plant for the seed. The first specimens of Indian flax were expected to arrive from India on June 10, 1840. "If we once succeed with flax, hemp and flax are so similar in their process of cultivation that there will be no difficulty whatever with hemp." [4]

Silk.—Witness also imported Indian silk into England extensively. The duty on British silk manufactures in India was 3½ per cent.; that on Indian silk manufactures

[1] Returns of the Gross Revenue, &c., in India since 1792, ordered by the House of Commons to be printed, June 22, 1855.

[2] Question 4137. [3] Question 4162. [4] Question 4256.

in England was 20 per cent. and upwards. This difference paralysed the Indian silk industry. Reduction of duty on Indian silks would not affect British manufactures, as the reduction of duty on French silks had not affected it. The Indian silk piece goods which would be introduced in England were of the heavier kind, the Corahs, which were very little manufactured in England. On the other hand, "the advantage to England would be that of supplying the natives with the means to purchase twice or threefold the quantity of our goods in return."[1]

Sugar.—Witness built a sugar manufactory at a cost of £2700 at Sericole, in Jessore District, near his indigo factory. He expected a profitable return, hoping for an equalisation of the duties on sugar and rum, which were produce of the same cane. His profit was 11¼ per cent., which was unsatisfactory, as money lent in India without risk would bring in 10 per cent., and at compound interest much more. If the duty on rum was equalised his profit would be more; if it was not equalised he would give up the sugar business.

J. M. Heath.

Iron.—The Association with which witness was connected began operations at Porto Novo, 120 miles south of Madras, in 1833, built blast-furnaces, put up a forge for making malleable iron, and had greatly extended their ironworks. Steel could not be made from English iron; England was entirely dependent on Sweden and Russia for every bar of iron that was to be converted into steel; India could supplement the supply, for Indian iron could be made into steel. Witness imported Indian iron in the shape of pig iron in order to be converted into bars; but the duty on the import of iron ore into England was prohibitive. "The duty upon a ton of iron

[1] Questions 4384, 4385, 4388, 4415, 4418.

ore is 5s. Now it takes about two tons of iron ore to make a ton of bar iron; a ton of bar iron pays a duty of 2s. 6d., whereas the duty upon the ore required to make a ton of bar iron is 10s. English iron going to India paid no duty at all."[1]

HORACE HAYMAN WILSON.

Books.—The distinguished Sanscrit scholar and Orientalist had been out in India for twenty-four years, and on his retirement he was made Librarian to the East India Company and Professor of Sanscrit at the University of Oxford. He stated in his evidence that books printed in India paid a duty of £2, 10s. per cwt., and pleaded for the removal of the duty.

JOSEPH TUCKER.

Silk Manufactures.—Joseph Tucker, belonging to a London firm of silk printers and dealers in silk handkerchiefs, desired to maintain the duty of 20 per cent. on Indian silk manufactures in order to protect the British industry. He said that the British people still used British manufactures only; but Frenchmen preferred the Indian article; and the export of British silk goods into France was decreasing, and that of Indian Bandannas and other silk handkerchiefs into France was increasing And he gave the following figures from a Parliamentary Return.—See table on opposite page.

The witness further explained that "When British goods first went to France, Indian goods were prohibited and consequently British goods had a preference with French buyers; hence perhaps the large quantity. As soon as the prohibition was taken off, and in fact previous to that, slightly, the trade had been affected. But im-

[1] Questions 4610 and 4676.

Exported from the United Kingdom to France.		
Year.	British Silk Goods.	Indian Bandannas and other Handkerchiefs.
	£	£
1832 . . .	50,600	29,500
1833 . . .	36,300	60,400
1834 . . .	32,700	77,700
1835 . . .	16,800	114,400
1836 . . .	15,600	107,600
1837 . . .	10,000	174,500
1838 . . .	9,400	202,200
1839 . . .	5,500	168,500

mediately the prohibition was taken off, the British trade to France was entirely annihilated."[1]

The preference given by a single European nation to a single Indian manufacture had aroused the jealousy of English dealers and manufacturers. This jealousy is manifest in the evidence of the last four witnesses, all silk manufacturers, who were examined by the Select Committee, and to whose evidence we now turn.

THOMAS COPE.

Silk Manufactures.—No witness gave his evidence in a more plain, straightforward manner than Thomas Cope, silk-weaver of Macclesfield.

Mr. Brocklehurst.—What would be the effect upon this branch of your trade if the present duty on East Indian silk goods were reduced from 20 to 3½ per cent.?

Mr. Cope.—In my opinion, it would have the effect of destroying this branch of trade; and if so, it would rob of their employment, and consequently of the means of living honestly by their labour, all those parties which I have before named, and would make them destitute and reckless, and cause them to become a burden to the

[1] Question 6379.

rest of society, whose burdens are already too heavy. It would throw out of employment a large amount of capital, and would give into the hands of foreigners that employment by which we ought to be supported.

Mr. Hogg.—You are of opinion that justice to the English operatives in silk requires that all foreign manufactured silk should be excluded from this market?

Mr. Cope.—My opinion is that in justice to the English operative there should be a duty imposed upon the importation of these goods which would put them on a level with ourselves. Now, if the Hindustanee can live at 1½d. or 2d. a day, and if an Englishman cannot live at less than 2s. a day, we think it very hard that the weaver in India should send his goods here and compete with us upon such very unfair terms.

Mr. Elliott.—Do you think that a labourer in this country, who is able to obtain better food than that, has a right to say, we will keep the labourer in the East Indies in that position in which he shall be able to get nothing for his food but rice?

Mr. Cope.—I certainly pity the East Indian labourer, but at the same time I have a greater feeling for my own family than for the East Indian labourer's family; I think it is wrong to sacrifice the comforts of my family for the sake of the East Indian labourer because his condition happens to be worse than mine; and I think it is not good legislation to take away our labour and to give it to the East Indian because his condition is worse than ours.[1]

It is needless to remark that manufacturers like Cope determined the policy of Great Britain towards India; the British Parliament and the Indian Government were merely the servants of the manufacturers and voters of Great Britain.

[1] Questions 6483, 6577, 6582.

JOHN PROUT.

Silk Manufactures.—John Prout was another silk-weaver of Macclesfield, and represented the views of British silk manufacturers.

Mr. Brocklehurst.—Do you conceive that the reduction of the duty upon East India silk manufactures and Bandannas would be an injury to your trade?

Mr. Prout.—I do conceive it to be a great injury, and it is the opinion of the trade of Macclesfield generally, because it is part of a system of policy which gives to the foreigner the home market, to the destruction of our own branch of industry.[1]

JOHN FRANCIS.

Silk Manufactures.—John Francis, a silk manufacturer of Norwich, was equally strong against Indian silks because they were competing successfully with British manufactures. And he spoke bitterly of the East India Company which had petitioned for the equalisation of duties.

Mr. Elliott.—In leaving off the silk trade in which you were formerly engaged, were you induced solely by the state of the trade, or were there any other circumstances?

Mr. Francis.—Solely from the state of the trade; I can go to the India House, when their sales of Corahs are on, and buy a piece for a less price than I can now buy a pound of silk to make it.

Mr. Irving.—How do you account for that?

Mr. Francis.—Only from the cheapness with which the Indians can send their goods here.

Mr. Brocklehurst.—Would you think the best remedy for this state of things would be to encourage India to send the raw material and let the British industry work upon it?

Mr. Francis.—To be sure.

[1] Question 6630.

And the witness added that forty years before (about 1800) the East India Company brought raw silk from India, and sold it in England to be manufactured in England. Now the Company were "indifferent to British industry," and let the silk be manufactured in India to get rid of it better.[1]

Mr. Brocklehurst even tried to get out of the witness that Indian manufacturers were comfortable, growing raw material and earning 1½d. a day.

Mr. Brocklehurst.—You do not suppose that they are uncomfortable; they live according to what they have been accustomed to all their lives?

Mr. Francis.—Certainly not.

Mr. Brocklehurst.—It may be comfort if they have no better?

Mr. Francis.—*Yes, it may be comfort to be starving, but I cannot think so.*[2]

John Poyton.

The last witness examined by the Select Committee was John Poyton, a silk weaver of Spitalfields.

Silk Manufactures.—Very few Bandannas were manufactured at Spitalfields, and India did not compete with that place at all. But, nevertheless, the witness objected to the lowering of the duty on Indian silk manufactures, because "if the duty is lowered, there will be less made in the country, and those that are now employed in making Bandannas will turn their hands to something else, and of course they will become competitors with us upon the goods that we now make."[3]

We have not been able to find out if any specific recommendations were submitted by the Select Committee of the House of Commons on the evidence re-

[1] Questions 6814, 6815, 6836, 6852, 6853, 6854.
[2] Questions 6889 and 6890. [The italics are ours.]
[3] Question 6946.

corded by them. But we have before us the Report submitted by the Select Committee of the House of Lords. For the East India Company's petition was presented to both Houses, and the Select Committee of the Lords had examined Melville and Larpent and Trevelyan, and some other witnesses whose evidence before the Commons' Committee has been referred to in this chapter. Lord Ellenborough, afterwards Governor-General of India, was the Chairman of the Lords' Committee, and his Report, professing the utmost concern for the people of India, nevertheless denied them the relief and justice which they sought. His lordship pointed out the peculiar claims of India upon the justice and the generosity of Parliament in his usual florid style.

"Possessed of a population four times greater than that of the United Kingdom, and of all the rest of the British Empire in all parts of the world, defraying from its own resources the whole charge of its civil government and of its military defence, subjected to the rule of British-born subjects in all the higher and more lucrative and honourable offices of the State, India is further required to transmit annually to this country, without any return except in the small value of military stores, a sum amounting to between two and three millions sterling."[1]

After these eloquent observations Lord Ellenborough recommended the equalising of duties on the import of West Indian and East Indian tobacco, but declined to make a similar recommendation with regard to rum. The cotton manufactures of India had already died out, and his lordship recommended that the inequality in duties between Great Britain and India should be removed. But the silk manufactures of India were still competing with those of England, and Lord Ellenborough would not recommend equalising the duties on this article—"the last of the expiring manufactures of India."

[1] Report of the Select Committee of the House of Lords, p. xviii.

CHAPTER VIII

COFFEE, SUGAR, AND COTTON

THE year 1848 was a year of political revolutions among the nations of Europe. France expelled her king and established her Second Republic. Germany showed her impatience of the despotism of petty princes by insurrectionary movements, and secured important constitutions. Italy declared a premature war against Austria, established a republic at Rome in pursuance of the ideas of Mazzini, and made her first great but unsuccessful effort to secure national independence. Austria witnessed an insurrection at Vienna, and Hungary rose under the valiant and patriotic Kossuth. In Ireland the continuous agitation for the repeal of the Union led to a rebellion. Everywhere there were indications of the passing away of the old order of things, and the rise of popular institutions and popular power.

Side by side with these political movements there was much commercial and agricultural distress in Europe. In England the contest between the landed classes who wished to keep up the price of corn, and the manufacturing and working classes who wanted cheap bread, was decided by the repeal of the corn laws in 1846. A great impetus was thus given to British manufactures; and the vague dream of a self-contained empire dawned on the minds of the people. Was it possible to make England independent of foreign nations? Was it possible to obtain her supplies from her own dependencies? Indian tea was slowly replacing China tea; was it possible for India to produce the necessary supply of coffee? Sugar plantations in the West Indies had declined after the emancipation of slaves; was it possible for India to supply sugar for the consumption of Great Britain? American cotton fed the looms of Lancashire; was it possible for India to supply that raw material to the extent required? Parliamentary inquiries were made.

SUGAR AND COFFEE COMMITTEE.

A Select Committee of the House of Commons was appointed in 1848, with Lord George Bentinck as the Chairman, to inquire into the condition and prospects of "Sugar and Coffee Planting in Her Majesty's East and West Indian Possessions and the Mauritius." The Committee examined many witnesses, and submitted their evidence with eight reports, covering over two thousand printed folio pages. Lord Palmerston was the first witness examined, but had little to say directly about the trade of India. John Bagshaw, a Member of Parliament, was examined on the same day, and dwelt at length on the many disadvantages under which India suffered in competing with other British Possessions.

"*First:* Three millions sterling and upward annually taken from the revenue of India towards the payment of the Home Charges of the East India Company, without any return whatever;

"*Second:* Fortunes accumulated in India by the Civil and Military Services, seldom if any remaining in that country annually increase the capital of Great Britain from the resources of India;

"*Third:* The well-known fact that of the revenue raised in British India, the largest portion of it is from the land, by which its produce is necessarily burdened; this amounts to nearly thirteen and a half millions sterling;

"*Fourth:* The difficulties which importers are subject

to from the way in which duties are levied at the Custom Houses of England." [1]

John Bagshaw deplored the extinction of the cotton manufactures of India within the preceding thirty years. In 1816–17 "India not only clothed the whole of that vast population, but exported £1,659,438 worth of goods." Thirty years later the whole of this export had disappeared, and India imported four millions sterling of cotton goods. "The people of India might buy British manufactures which were imported into India at a duty of 2½ per cent., but the manufacturers of India were entirely precluded from getting their goods into consumption here by the prohibitory duty which was exacted."

Sugar was not produced in England, and some healthy change in the tariffs with regard to this article had therefore been permitted. The result was marked and instantaneous. "There has been no instance of such growth," said Bagshaw, quoting from an Indian newspaper, "in any article of commerce at any preceding period. There has been no development of the resources of India to be compared with this sudden increase. Last year we [India] supplied England with one-fourth the sugar she consumed; and there can be no doubt that India would in time be able to supply the whole of the home demand." It is needless to add that this hope was never realised; and sugar manufacture declined during the last half of the nineteenth century with almost every other manufacture.

Colonel Sykes, a distinguished Director of the East India Company, had carefully studied Indian facts and figures. He spoke of the Economic Drain from India of £3,300,000 to £3,700,000 a year, and remarked truly: "It is only by the excess of exports over imports that India can bear this tribute." Henry St. John Tucker, then Chairman of the East India Company, said that this Economic Drain was an increasing quantity, "because our

[1] First Report.

Home Charge is perpetually increasing."[1] The expression of regret from the Chairman of the Company was no doubt genuine, but brought no redress. A cynic might remark that, as the flow of wealth from India to England increased in volume, England paid back the debt by copious streams of sympathy and regrets.

Nathaniel Alexander, an East Indian merchant, dwelt on the great increase in the consumption of Indian sugar in England, but spoke guardedly on its future prospects. The Indian sugar trade had been profitable before 1846, but had not been so latterly; and if that trade declined it was difficult to conceive how the country would draw its annual tribute from India. "I may say generally," said the witness, "that up to 1847 the imports [of India] were about £6,000,000, and the exports about £9,500,000. The difference is the tribute which the Company received from the country, which amounts to about £4,000,000."[2]

Both Alexander and Sir George Larpent, of whom we have spoken in the last chapter, pointed out to the Committee that, while the West Indies and the Mauritius were mainly sugar-producing countries, India was mainly a sugar-consuming country, and exported only a small portion of her annual produce of sugar. India, therefore, could never compete with other countries in exporting sugar for any length of time. "The equalisation of duties in 1836," Larpent said, "became profitable solely because the quantity from the West Indies had, during that period, greatly declined, from 200,000 tons, I think, in the year 1831, to 110,000 tons in 1840 and 1841. It

[1] First Report.

[2] *Ibid.* The truth was clearly perceived over fifty years ago that the annual Economic Drain from India for Home Charges compelled that country to export more than she could import. Trade between India and England was not natural but forced. Matters have become worse after half a century. The manufactures of India have declined; while the Home Charges have increased from three to seventeen millions sterling. India meets this terrible annual demand largely by exporting wheat and rice, the food of the people; and the result is greater poverty and more frequent famines.

was that which gave an impulse to India and a profit to India; it is nothing but the high prices of sugar here that can lead to a profitable exportation from India."[1]

More than one witness deposed that the system of assessing land, according to their estimated value, had the effect of discouraging the cultivation of valuable products like sugar. The Chairman of the East India Company, Henry St. George Tucker, said: "Sir Thomas Munro's plan was to obtain as much revenue from the country as possible; and he assessed different articles of produce according to his idea of their probable value. He raised the assessment upon articles which were expected to be very productive. Whether he succeeded or failed in that I will not undertake to say, because a reduction of the produce may have taken place from other causes; but certainly in consequence of this assessment upon sugar, I think a very great check and discouragement was given to the cultivation of the article in the Madras territory."[2]

Robert Christian, a coffee planter of Ceylon, gave an interesting account of the commencement of coffee plantation in that island.

"It was about 1837 when we first embarked; the inducements were in a great measure the falling off of the production of coffee in the West India Islands, and the large protecting duty which British plantation coffee then enjoyed; and the high prices, of course consequent upon those circumstances." Previous to this the people of Ceylon grew coffee, and exported the article without the help of European capital or agency. In 1838 Ceylon exported to England 2500 tons of coffee, grown entirely by the people of the island. Nine years later, the crop of 1847 was 12,482 tons, of which 7173 tons were grown by the Cingalese and 5309 tons by European planters.[3]

In their concluding report, the Select Committee

[1] Second Report. [2] First Report. [3] Sixth Report.

dwelt on the great distress and loss caused to sugar plantations by the emancipation of slaves, and the difficulty of obtaining free labour; and they recommended a differential duty of 10s. in favour of sugar, the produce of British possessions.

Cotton Committee.

A more important Select Committee was appointed in the same year to inquire into the growth of cotton in India. India was known from ancient times for her cotton fabrics with which she had supplied the markets of Asia and of Europe. And when England, with the help of her power looms and her protective tariffs, had suppressed that industry, the hope was still entertained that India would continue to grow the raw material required for the factories of Lancashire. Endeavours were therefore made to extend and improve the growth of cotton in India, with the idea that Great Britain would thereby have both the raw material and the manufacture in her own hands, and be thus independent of America and other foreign countries. The Select Committee, which was appointed in 1848, was therefore entrusted with a task of the very highest importance; and one of the most illustrious men of England was the chairman of the Committee. John Bright, who had already won distinction as the colleague of Cobden in the agitation which led to the repeal of the Corn Laws, was in the chair; and it was in the course of this inquiry that he obtained that intimate knowledge of Indian affairs, which marked his public utterances during the rest of his life. It may be said without exaggeration that John Bright filled the same place in the House of Commons in the middle of the nineteenth century that Edmund Burke had done in the last decades of the eighteenth. Their endeavours to render justice to a vast Eastern Dependency will live in the memory of mankind, when England's Empire shall have passed away. And their published utterances will be read as among the finest specimens of English prose, possibly when the present English language shall have ceased to be a spoken tongue.

Before the Select Committee had gone very far in recording evidence on the subject of the cultivation of cotton, the connected question of the assessment of the soil in India forced itself to their notice.

Francis William Prideaux, then Assistant-Examiner of India Correspondence, read from the petition of the Manchester Chamber of Commerce on the subject of land assessments: "Amongst the obstacles to the better cultivation of cotton, none are more obvious than the Land Tax, the tenure under which land is held, and the want of roads and the means of conveyance. Your Memorialists believe that your honourable Court is itself impressed with the conviction that the Land Tax in the present cotton-growing districts is imperfect, and has more than once begun reforms which have been abandoned almost as soon as begun; but until the injustice of levying a heavier assessment upon cotton than upon other crops be abandoned, and the tenure of land be placed upon a wise and equitable basis, all hope of so improving the quality of cotton as to procure for it prices which will stimulate further culture will be futile."[1]

The influence of British manufacturers had so far prevailed that all duties on cotton exported into England from Bengal had been abolished in 1836, those on Bombay cotton in 1838, and those on Madras cotton in 1844. But the Court of Directors declined to reduce the land assessment in order to stimulate the cultivation of cotton.

The next witness was Dr. John Forbes Royle, who had been for nine years in charge of the Botanical

[1] Select Committee's Report, p. 6.

Gardens at Saharanpur, and in 1837 had published a valuable essay on the Antiquity of Hindu Medicine, explaining the nature and extent of the chemical and surgical knowledge possessed by the ancient Hindus. He deposed that Surat cotton was 30 per cent. lower in price at Liverpool than American cotton, and that Indian cotton was generally shipped in a dirty state. American cotton grew better on the red soil, and Indian cotton on the black soil, in India. In the American States of Alabama and Louisiana, they got 400 lbs. of clean cotton per acre, while in India not more than 100 or 150 lbs. The cultivation of cotton had much increased in Northern India since the new settlement of 1833, which gave long leases to cultivators. It was desirable to introduce the saw-gin into India, but Manchester spinners would not use the Indian cotton if the American cotton was cheap. Indian cotton was used in two ways in England; it was either manufactured into cloths, or used as wadding, *i.e.* people wore coats padded with cotton in the cold weather. The importation of English cotton goods into India was increasing, and was superseding the manufactures of India more and more every year.

Thomas Bazley, President of the Manchester Chamber of Commerce, furnished a table showing the proportion of Indian cotton to American cotton imported into England—the proportion of the Indian supply to the total British import varying between 8 and 15 per cent. The figures for ten years from the date of Queen Victoria's accession are given on the next page.

The same witness deposed that while the spinner obtained from 1 lb. of Surat cotton only 12 ounces of yarn, he obtained from 1 lb. of American cotton 13½ ounces of yarn. The price of the latter was therefore between 3½d. and 6d. the lb. when Indian cotton was between 3d. and 5d.

Towards the conclusion of his evidence, Thomas

Import of Cotton Wool into England, Scotland, and Ireland.

Year.	From the United States.	From British Possessions in the East.
	lbs.	lbs.
1837 . . .	320,351,716	51,577,141
1838 . . .	431,437,888	40,229,495
1839 . . .	311,597,798	47,170,640
1840 . . .	487,856,504	77,010,917
1841 . . .	358,214,964	97,368,312
1842 . . .	405,325,600	96,555,186
1843 . . .	558,735,600	68,820,570
1844 . . .	517,218,622	88,639,608
1845 . . .	626,650,412	58,437,426
1846 . . .	382,526,000	34,270,800

Bazley explained in a few words an Englishman's idea of the trade between England and India. "In India," he said, "there is an immense extent of territory, and the population of it would consume British manufactures to a most enormous extent. The whole question with respect to our Indian trade is whether they can pay us, by the products of their soil, for what we are prepared to send out as manufactures."[1]

Robert Crawford, a merchant who had been resident in Bombay, gave figures showing the extent of cotton cultivation in some Bombay districts during twelve years, from 1834 to 1845. In Broach cotton cultivation was 3 per cent.; in Surat it was 22 per cent.; in Kandeish it was 10 per cent.; and in Sholapur it was 3 per cent. of the total cultivation on assessed lands. Asked as to the nature of land-assessment in Gujrat, witness said: "As the Government and their officers may justly claim the credit of getting all the revenue they can possibly get, it follows that the land is let at a rack-rent." And the witness, quoting from the report of Mr. Davies, collector of Broach, said: "As the present state of the market does not unfortunately give him [the cultivator]

[1] Select Committee's Report, p. 57.

that reimbursement to enable him to keep up his stock, it far less enables him to reckon upon any profits; the inference is too obvious that he mainly depends upon remissions and balances for his escape from ruin."[1]

The same witness also deposed to the evil effects of the Navigation Laws, requiring ships to be manned by English seamen. "I have known times," said the witness, "when it would very well have suited for a ship belonging to the port of Bombay manned by lascars to come to this country if she could have sailed upon the same terms as an English ship does."[2]

A more important witness was Major-General Briggs. He had entered the service of the Company in 1801, and had worked thirty-two years in India. He had served under men like Sir John Malcolm and Mountstuart Elphinstone, and had been Commissioner of Mysore and Resident of Nagpur. He had written the most valuable and exhaustive work on the Land Tax of India, and had advised Lord William Bentinck in regard to the Settlement of Northern India. And he had studied Indian history from the original sources, and produced a scholar-like translation of Ferishta's "History of India" which is still a standard work.

Major-General Briggs spoke of the enormous consumption of cotton in India, and of the capacity of that country to "produce sufficient cotton for the consumption of the whole world." And he considered that the two great obstacles which prevented a larger export of Indian cotton to England were the Land Tax, and the want of road for conveyance.[3] Questioned on the first subject, he said: "The Land Tax of India, as well as all direct taxes, have been founded upon the principle of an Income Tax; a portion of the income, whether in grain or in money, has usually been considered the right of the sovereign;" and under the Hindu rule the portion was originally fixed at a tenth of the produce.[4]

[1] Select Committee's Report, pp. 96 and 97.
[2] *Ibid.*, p, 104.
[3] *Ibid.*, p. 121.
[4] *Ibid.*, p. 123.

The Settlement of Northern India begun by Lord William Bentinck in 1833 "preserves the institutions of the people, and is most advantageous both to the Government and to the cultivator if it were made permanent." On the other hand, the land assessment in Madras was excessive, even after Sir Thomas Munro's reductions made in 1827; the Government demand was not, and could not be paid in full; it was left to the discretion of the Collector as to how much he could collect. And "when it is left to the discretion of the Collector, it is practically left to the discretion of a host of subordinate officers scattered throughout the country." The fixed assessment was never paid; remissions were annually made; the peasants were "in a very impoverished state."[1]

General Briggs strongly recommended a corn-rent, *i.e.* an assessment based on the produce of each year; and he held that the Ryotwari System might be workable under such a rule. Fifty per cent. of the produce was not more than the surplus produce or nett produce if taken in corn; "but as the tax is a money tax, it must of course very frequently represent the whole of the produce."[2]

Thomas Williamson, who had been Revenue Commissioner of Bombay, brought the strongest charge against the British system of land assessment when he said that the prosperity of the entire people depended upon the will and the inclination of one man, the Collector and Assessing Officer. "The prosperity of a whole district," he said, "mainly depended upon the personal qualifications of the officer managing it." But District Collectors were not always efficient or considerate; Gujrat had been very severely assessed till within recent years; and all land improvements had been checked. In Broach heavy arrears accumulated; remissions were made by favouritism; and corruption in various ways had its influence over the amount. The people were generally exceedingly

[1] Select Committee's Report, pp. 126 and 129. [2] *Ibid.*, p. 136.

poor and depressed; their agricultural stock had diminished; and the produce of cotton diminished. "These are the general consequences and indications of over-assessment."[1]

George Gibberne had been Collector of Gujrat, and left the country in 1826, and had revisited it in 1840 as Judicial Commissioner. He saw very little improvement in the condition of the people after the lapse of fourteen years; and altogether it appeared to him "that the wealthy inhabitants had fallen off." The assessment had been generally speaking too high: "In all the different districts that I have been in as a Collector, I think there is scarcely enough, certainly not sufficient left to enable the Ryot to lay by anything for himself, or to become a capitalist."

"Have you known any districts," witness was asked, "in which the cultivation has evidently been very much diminished in consequence of the weight of the assessment?" "I cannot say," he replied, "that I have known any; they seem stationary instead of improving; the Ryots have nothing else to do but to cultivate even if they get no profit; they must cultivate their field for food for themselves and families; they are so wedded to the country or to the village to which they belong that they would pay the rent if they could without gaining a farthing for themselves. There are no great signs of improvement."[2]

Francis Carnac Brown had been born of English parents in India, and, like his father, had considerable experience of the cotton industry in India. He produced an Indian *Charka*, or spinning wheel, before the Select Committee, and explained that there was an oppressive Moturfa Tax which was levied on every *Charka*, on every house, and upon every implement used by artisans. The tax prevented the introduction of saw-gins in India.

Francis Brown held a high opinion of the Indian system of growing cotton, and said that he would as

[1] Select Committee's Report, pp. 154 to 157. [2] *Ibid.*, pp. 200 to 203.

soon send for American planters to teach Indians in this art as he would send for Belgian farmers to teach British farmers in the art of growing wheat. He substantiated his opinion by the testimony of an American planter, Mr. Mercer, who had been sent to India to improve its cotton cultivation. In 1845–46, Mr. Mercer had represented, (to quote from the Bombay Government Circular of January 28, 1847), "That the experimental farms were only a useless expense to Government; that the American system was not adapted to India; that the natives of India were, from their knowledge of the climate and capabilities of the soil, able to cultivate better and much more economically than any European." [1]

On the question of the assessment of land, the evidence of Francis Brown was emphatic. The Madras cultivator "obtains no profit whatever beyond his food, after paying his assessment." There were millions of human beings who were cultivators in Madras, and they realised nothing beyond a mere existence or the means of existence. The pressing wants of nature, the necessity of getting food, drove them to cultivation, and wherever they planted their feet they came under the Government assessment. And the assessment was so high that it could never be realised in full. "The estimation," said the witness, "in which a native has always appeared to me to be held, is, that he is a creature born to pay to the East India Company." [2]

Charged with stating opinions so unfavourable to the Government of India, Francis Brown said: "I do not wish to detract from the credit of the East India Company—but there is the country; and I ask let it be looked at with the eyes, the understanding, and the honesty of Englishmen, and let the Government of the East India Company be judged by that examination. . . . I solemnly declare that I have seen the people of Malabar perish, and become pauperised as a country

[1] Select Committee's Report, p. 235. [2] *Ibid.*, pp. 241 to 243.

under the operation of the Government. . . . The Government of the country has generally tended to the impoverishment and abasement of the people."[1]

Contrasting the land system of America where cotton cultivation was extending, with that of India where cotton for the purpose of export was dwindling, witness said: "Land in America is put up to sale at a dollar an acre, a man purchases the fee-simple of it outright, and there is an end of all charge. But the state of things in India is diametrically opposite to this; there is no proprietary right; and consequently a man is not induced to lay out that money, or to make those exertions for his own benefit, which have been the natural stimulus applied to the production of cotton in America."[2]

It is to the credit of Francis Brown that he was one of the first to sound the note of alarm at the destruction of forests in India and consequent decrease in rainfall. It was a subject which was little understood then, and witness read the following passage from Baron Humbolt's Personal Narrative: "By felling the trees that cover the tops and the sides of mountains, men in every climate prepare at once two calamities for future generations, the want of fuel and scarcity of water."[3]

With regard to the ancient irrigation works of India, Francis Brown said: "There are throughout the whole of Southern India from Ganjam to Cape Comorin, the most extraordinary remains of tanks that it is possible to imagine." The East India Company's Government had allowed all these valuable works to go out of repair, except Tanjore, where irrigation had been attended with the most favourable results. Major Arthur Cotton had vainly pressed the importance of irrigation works on the Company's Government; and Francis Brown believed that much of India could be made by means of irrigation what the valley of the Nile had long been."[4]

[1] Select Committee's Report, pp. 262 and 263.
[2] *Ibid.*, p. 264.
[3] *Ibid.*, p. 269.
[4] *Ibid.*, p. 270.

The Directors of the East India Company, no doubt, considered Francis Brown as an enthusiast, if not a firebrand. But reading his evidence after the lapse of over half a century, it is impossible to deny that this clear-sighted Englishman, born and bred in India, perceived some of those great evils which the administrators of India could not or would not see. Nor was it likely that Indian officials should allow the evidence of such men as Francis Brown to go unchallenged. Three days after Mr. Brown's examination, Ross Mangles, who had been Revenue Secretary to the Indian Government, and was now a Member of Parliament and a Director of the East India Company, offered himself for examination. There was probably no man then in England who could have defended the Company's revenue administration more stoutly; and it is impossible to read his evidence without noting the vehemence of his conviction and the lucidity of his thought. But, nevertheless, Ross Mangles defended only the theory of the Indian Land Tax; of its abuse in practice none knew more than he.

In the Permanently Settled Province of Bengal, he said, the Government revenue paid by Zemindars was, on an average, about one-half of the rental of their estates. The Government demand in tracts not permanently settled was often 75 per cent. of the rental. In Madras the Ryot was the proprietor, and paid the land revenue direct to the Government, but the great evil of the Ryotwari System was the eternal meddling and yearly fixing of rates. "It must open the door to a vast quantity of bribery, extortion, and oppression."[1]

On the second day of his examination Ross Mangles had some discussion with John Bright, the Chairman of the Select Committee, and with George Thompson, one of the members of the Committee, which it is interesting to follow.

George Thompson.—Are you prepared to justify on

[1] Select Committee's Report, p. 276.

moral grounds the assumption on the part of the Government, whether British or any other, of a proprietary right on the soil of all India, supposing they rule over all India?

Ross Mangles.—I do not think that that is a question connected with the revenue; I never have assumed or alleged that the Government was the proprietor of the soil of India, and I do not believe that it is the proprietor of the soil in India.

George Thompson.—Is it not virtually so when it takes upon itself to demand 75 per cent. of the natural rent of the land over all the country?

Ross Mangles.—A portion of the rent from time immemorial has been the right of the State for public purposes.

John Bright.—Speaking of the mode of collecting the rent through Collectors, can you say at all, supposing the produce of a certain quantity of land to be 100, whether there be any fixed proportion which the Collector is understood to be authorised to fix as the amount of the assessment to the Government?

Ross Mangles.—I have explained to the Committee that of late years it has been found extremely dangerous to make the *produce* the basis of the settlement, and the Collectors have been enjoined on every occasion to endeavour to find what the *rent* is, and to make that the basis.

John Bright.—If the assessment was an annual assessment, as it is throughout a large portion of the Company's Government in India, would such an increase of the assessment in such a case [*i.e.* in case of improvements effected by cultivators] be calculated to improve the cultivation still further, or to discourage the cultivator from making improvements?

Ross Mangles.—The natural effect would be discouragement. I am as much opposed to annual settlements as the honourable Chairman can be.

These passages are important, as they throw light on some great principles recognised as long ago as 1848.

(1) The Government did not claim to be the proprietor of the soil; Zemindars and Ryots were recognised as proprietors.

(2) The Government claimed a portion of the economic rent as the Land Revenue.

(3) The portion was not fixed. It amounted to about 50 per cent. in permanently settled estates, and approached 75 per cent. where there was no permanent settlement.[1]

For the rest Ross Mangles held with John Stuart Mill that the Land Revenue of India, being a portion of the rent, did not enter into the cost of production of articles grown on the soil, and could not therefore have any deterrent effect on the cultivation of cotton.

John Sullivan, who had been Member of the Government of Madras, and President of the Board of Revenue, also defended the Indian Land Revenue system, but complained against the annual Economic Drain from India. "As to the complaints which the people of India have to make of the present fiscal system, I do not conceive that it is the amount altogether that they have to complain of. I think they have rather to complain of the application of that amount. Under their own dynasties, all the revenue that was collected in the country was spent in the country; but under our rule, a large proportion of the revenue is annually drained away, and without any return being made for it; this drain has been going on now for sixty or seventy years, and it is rather increasing than the reverse. . . . Our system acts very much like a sponge, drawing up all the good things from the banks of the Ganges, and squeezing them down on the banks of the Thames. . . . They [the people of

[1] This uncertainty has been subsequently removed, at least in theory. The Saharanpur Rules of 1855, and the Secretary of State's Despatch of 1864, fix 50 per cent. of the rental as the approximate Government demand in temporarily settled estates, Zemindari and Ryotwari.

India] have no voice whatever in imposing the taxes which they are called upon to pay, no voice in framing the laws which they are bound to obey, no real share in the administration of their own country; and they are denied those rights from the insolent and insulting pretext that they are wanting in mental and moral qualifications for the discharge of such duties."[1]

Some other less important witnesses are examined, but it is unnecessary to prolong this analysis. Enough has been said to indicate the nature of the evidence placed before the Select Committee; and on this evidence John Bright and his colleagues submitted their report on July 17, 1848.

They reported that for sixty years, *i.e.* since 1788, the Court of Directors had made experiments in India for extending the cultivation and export of cotton, and had introduced American gins, sent out American cotton growers, and had established experimental farms for this purpose. The Directors still believed that the obstacles which retarded cotton cultivation in India could be overcome.

The result of the experiments satisfied the Select Committee that India had the capacity to supply cotton of an improved quality to an indefinite extent, but the Committee did not expect that this effect would be achieved by the means adopted. American cotton, long-stapled, was not so well suited to the Indian manufacturer as the Indian cotton, and the fluctuating demands for exportation were not a sufficient inducement for the introduction of a variety adapted to a foreign and distant market.[2]

The miserable condition of the cultivators of India received the attention of the Select Committee. The

[1] Report of the Select Committee, p. 402.

[2] Cotton, like sugar, was grown in India mainly for consumption in India; and the people of India, very rightly, produced those articles mainly with an eye to their national requirements, rather than to the demands of Lancashire looms.

great mass of cultivators in Madras and Bombay were "almost wholly without capital, or any of those means which capital alone can furnish, by which industry may be improved and extended. They are in reality a class of cultivators in the most abject condition."

There was difference of opinion on the question as to how far this depressed condition of the cultivators was due to the Government Land Revenue demand. On the one hand the principle was urged that so long as the Government demand was limited to a part of the economic rent, no depressing result on the cultivation of soil could ensue. On the other hand, evidence had been given that districts with large populations under the control of single officers were in practice badly administered; that imprudent zeal, inefficiency, or grave errors had affected the prosperity of entire districts, and that "the whole system is depressing, if not destructive to any spirit of improvement on the part of the agricultural population."

The two principles "*of moderation in the Government demand, and certainty as to the amount and tenure*" were recommended as the basis of land settlements in India.

Lastly the Select Committee commented on the lamentable want of roads in India, and they referred to the evidence of Ross Mangles himself, a Director of the East India Company, showing how little had been done to improve internal communications. The witnesses examined had also recommended the construction of railways in India from the centres of export and import to the interior.

CHAPTER IX

TEA, SALT, AND OPIUM

JOHN BRIGHT'S report was submitted in 1848. Five years after, the East India Company's Charter came up for renewal. And, as usual, a thorough inquiry into the Company's administration was made by Select Committees of both Houses of Parliament in 1852 and 1853. We shall have to refer to this inquiry when dealing with the general administration of the Company; but some interesting facts about the production of tea, salt, and opium, elicited during this inquiry, should find a place in the present chapter.

TEA.

The most important evidence on the culture of tea was given by Dr. Royle of Saharanpur Botanical Gardens, whose evidence before the Cotton Committee has been referred to before. He had recommended the cultivation of tea to the Indian Government in 1827 and 1834; it was first undertaken by the Indian Government in 1835; and in 1842 the first tea was manufactured. At the time when the witness was examined (1853) the cultivation of the plant was going on to a considerable extent all through the North-West Himalayas, and also in Assam.

Not more than 10,000 lbs. had been grown in Kumaon in any year yet, but the cultivation was extending. The whole of the mountains from Sikkim, through Nepal and Kumaon up to the Kangra valley and even to Kashmir, was suited to the cultivation of tea. Dr. Jameson, who had been employed by the East India Company, had reported that "nowhere could the tea plant thrive with greater luxuriance than it was doing in the Kangra valley. Tea was not an article of general consumption by any part of the population of India."[1]

The Government of India had transferred all their interest in the growth of tea in Assam to a Company, and a Company was proposing to purchase from the Government the tea cultivation in Kumaon.[2]

SALT.

Among the sources of the Company's revenues in British India, their monopoly in salt and opium was not the least important. Salt was prepared in Bengal by the Company's agents, and a duty of 5s. per Maund (82 lbs.) was added to the cost of production before the article was placed in the market. A duty of 4s. per Maund was raised on salt obtained from mines in the Punjab; while salt prepared in Native States had to pay a duty of 4s. or 5s. before it passed into British territory.

Madras salt was formed by solar evaporation on the margin of the sea, and was cheaper than Bengal salt; and the Company derived a considerable revenue by selling it at 2s. the Maund. In Bombay the Government permitted manufacturers to remove the salt from the pans on payment of a duty of 1s. 6d. the Maund. Salt imported into India from England or other countries paid a duty of 5s. or 6s. the Maund, so that the importers might not under-sell the duty-paying Indian salt.[3]

The net revenue of the Company derived from salt manufacture rose from £800,000 in 1793 to nearly

[1] Commons' Fourth Report, 1853. Dr. Royle's evidence.
[2] Lords' Third Report, 1853. Edward Thornton's evidence.
[3] Commons' Fourth Report, 1853. Prideaux's evidence.

£1,300,000 in 1844. The total quantity of salt manufactured by the East India Company in these fifty-two years is estimated at a little over two hundred million Maunds; and the total revenue derived from the manufacture at sixty millions sterling.[1]

From what has been stated before, it will appear that the East India Company endeavoured to hold the balance evenly between the salt manufactured by them in India, and the salt imported from Great Britain. The House of Commons had dictated this policy by a Resolution of their Select Committee in 1836; and it was the object of the Company to comply with this Resolution. But in working out the principle the Company went too far, and gave an undue advantage to the British manufacturer. For they included the expenses of securing and protecting revenues in the "cost price," and thus added to the selling price of the Bengal salt. The British manufacturer obtained the full advantage of this blunder, and the sale of British salt went up by leaps and bounds. Two witnesses,[2] both interested in the sale of British salt in India, supplied the Select Committee with figures which are given below.

British Salt imported into Calcutta, in Maunds (82 lbs.).						
1845–46.	1846–47.	1847–48.	1848–49.	1849–50.	1850–51.	1851–52.
502,616	352,835	752,998	459,803	694,447	1,012,698	1,850,762

British Salt sent to India in Tons.				
1847.	1848.	1849.	1850.	1851.
25,754	15,507	27,640	36,341	61,711

[1] Commons' Fourth Report, 1853. Aylwin's evidence.
[2] D. C. Aylwin and W. Worthington. Commons' Fourth Report, 1853.

The great increase in the import of British salt alarmed the Bengal Board of Revenue; and they submitted an able and lengthy letter[1] pointing out the unfairness of enhancing the price of the Bengal salt by including in the "cost price" various charges which did not fall within the definition of cost.

Lord Dalhousie, then Governor-General of India, dealt with the important subject in an able Minute,[2] from which we make the following extracts:—

"The representatives of the Board of Revenue, in my humble judgment, have established that, under the existing system, no injustice is done to the importer of salt, but that great and growing injustice is inflicted on the native producer of the article."

"The direct effect of this has been to enable imported salt to compete with native manufactured salt so successfully that it is thrusting the latter out of the market, while, if the selling price of native salt were, what it would be in the hands of native traders, it might still hold its ground."

"The Government, in my opinion, should be far less ashamed of confessing that it has committed a blunder than of showing reluctance to remedy an injustice lest it should at the same time be convicted of having previously blundered."

"It may be too that the imported salt, with the many advantages which it is shown to enjoy in its import over other articles of commerce, may still drive the native salt out of the market, even at its readjusted price. If this should prove to be the case, the Government will have to consider the question under that new aspect. Its present duty is obvious."

"So great a change, however, cannot with propriety be carried into effect until a reference shall have been made to the Honourable Court of Directors. Let this be

[1] Letter No. 685, dated June 29, 1852.
[2] Minute dated September 11, 1852.

done by next mail, and as the case is urgent, an early reply should be requested."

A reference [1] was accordingly made to the Court of Directors, explaining the injustice done to the Indian salt, and demanding sanction for redress.

While the authorities in India were thus endeavouring to readjust the "cost price" of Indian salt so as to give it a fair chance of competing with imported salt, the importers of British salt were not idle. British manufacturers, professing a desire to supply the people of India with their superior article, petitioned the House of Commons for a total abolition of the duty on imported salt. And they hoped that, if that measure were adopted, the impure Indian salt would be driven out of the market, and the population of India would be consumers of British salt.

The merchants, manufacturers, tradesmen, and others of the city of Manchester held that "a constant supply of salt, of good quality and at a reasonable price, is of the utmost importance to the extensive population of India." The duty of £7 per ton imposed in India on imported salt was not less than 2000 per cent. upon the value of the article, and was "highly oppressive towards the native population of India." It was therefore prayed that British salt might be imported to India either free, or on payment of a nominal duty.

The inhabitants of Northwich, in the county of Chester, stated that 600,000 tons of salt were annually made in the salt districts of Cheshire, and gave employment to 5000 Englishmen. That if British salt could be sent to India on the same duty as other produce, a quantity for the consumption of India could be sent from Cheshire "pure in quality, certain and sufficient in supply, and low in price."

The inhabitants of the borough of Droitwich complained that the manufacture of salt by the East India

[1] Letter of the Indian Government, dated September 17, 1852.

Company in India was a "manifest violation or evasion of Act 3 & 4 William IV., cap. 85, by which the Company were required to close their commercial business"; that the duty of £7 per ton of salt imported into India limited the import to 50,000 tons per annum, while the consumption in India ought to be over 800,000 tons; and that it was the duty of the East India Company to collect their revenues in India "without excluding the British merchant from the benefit of a market to which he has natural and paramount claims to be admitted."

The mayor, alderman, and burgesses of Wych, otherwise Droitwich, in the county of Worcester, also complained that the East India Company by their enormous duty of £7 per ton "excluded British salt from the Indian market."

The Chamber of Commerce of the city of Gloucester also pointed out that the manufacture of salt by the East India Company was a "manifest violation and evasion of Act 3 & 4 William IV., c. 85," and protested against the exclusion of the British merchant "from the benefit of a market to which he has natural and paramount claims to be admitted."

The merchants, manufacturers, and tradesmen of St. Helens held that a plentiful supply of good salt at low price was "of the utmost importance to the well-being of the people of India," that Indian salt was of inferior quality and costly, and that "if the salt manufactured in England could be imported into India free of duty, or upon the same terms as other commodities at an *ad valorem* duty, and free from all excise imposts when imported, a sufficient supply to meet the wants of that country would be easily sent."

The inhabitants of Winsford, in the county of Chester, submitted a petition word for word the same as the petition from Northwich referred to above.

The Chamber of Commerce of Worcester complained that the manufacture of salt from the inexhaustible springs of Worcestershire was materially circumscribed from the ports of British India being virtually closed against British salt. "An enlightened and humane policy would provide for and encourage unfettered importation on payment of a reasonable duty for revenue only; whereas the restrictions imposed by the Indian Government are made to protect a monopoly of its own of inferior salt, carried on, as your petitioners are advised, in direct violation of Act 3 & 4 William IV., c. 85."

The Chamber of Commerce of Bristol submitted a vigorous and well-argued petition on the hardship caused by the salt tax in India. "The price to the consumer here [in England] is but about 30s. per ton instead of £21 per ton as in India; and if it were necessary to abolish the salt tax at home some years since, it appears to your petitioners that the millions of her Majesty's subjects of India have a much stronger claim for its remission in their case, wretchedly poor as they are, and essentially necessary as salt is to their daily sustenance, and to the prevention of disease in such a climate."

The merchants, shipowners, and tradesmen of Liverpool held it to be "the sacred and solemn duty of the Government to afford to the people of that country [India] the same fostering care as is and ought to be afforded to the people of this country." And they were of opinion that "the abolition of the duty on salt in British India would be not only a great boon to the people of that country, to which justice and humanity entitle them, but would also tend greatly to improve and strengthen the mercantile interests of this country generally by increasing particularly the demand for cotton and other goods of English manufacture."[1]

It is clear from the extracts given above, that the merchants and salt manufacturers of England joined an organised movement on this occasion primarily and

[1] Commons' Fourth Report, 1853, Appendix 2, and Fifth Report, 1853, Appendix 3.

mainly in their own interests. But it is nevertheless true that they honestly believed their interests in this instance to be the same as those of the tax-payers of India. It would have been a happy event for India if this prayer had been heard, and the duties imposed, both on manufactured salt and imported salt, had been withdrawn. The result would probably have been different from what the manufacturers of England expected.

The Select Committee of the House of Commons had abundant evidence before it to show how the salt tax operated in India. In a petition submitted by the Madras Native Association, and signed by T. Ramaswami and others, the petitioners described the state of things in Madras:—

"That in the year 1806 the Government established an agency for the control and management of the salt department, the first consequence of which was the doubling of the price of the article, which was then fixed at 70 rupees (£7) the garce, when the average consumption for the space of three years amounted to 31,685 garces, at the end of which time, in the year 1809, the price was again raised from 70 to 105 rupees (£10, 10s.) the garce, being three times as much as it had been prior to the Government monopoly. But as the enhanced price naturally decreased the consumption, the price, in 1820, was again fixed at 70 rupees (£7); but after a course of eight years the price was again fixed at 105 rupees (£10, 10s.), which was still further raised to 180 rupees (£18) in 1844; but in the same year it was reduced 120 rupees (£12), at which price it has ever since continued. But this being the wholesale price, it is of course sold to the retail dealer at an advance, who necessarily adds his profit, to be paid by the consumer."

"And the consequence is that either the people go without salt altogether or substitute an unwholesome article, obtained from common earth impregnated with saline particles, which they manufacture at the risk of punishment; the procurement of salt other than that of the monopoly being prohibited under the penalty of fine and corporal punishment, inflicted at the discretion of the Collector or his Tahsildar."[1]

Similarly, in a petition submitted by the British Indian Association of Calcutta, and signed by Raja Radha Kant Deb Bahadur and others, the harshness of the salt operations was fully exposed:—

"The selling price of salt is arbitrarily fixed by the Government, and is at all times so high that, though the country has abundant resources for the manufacture of the article, English merchants can afford to import it. The dearness of the article induces even those who live near the salt manufactures to use earth scraped from the salt lands; while those who reside in the interior have recourse to the alkali found in the ashes of burnt vegetables. The officers employed in the salt department are vested with judicial powers contrary to all principles of justice and policy, and necessarily employ them very irregularly and vexatiously. The subordinate officers are furnished with opportunities, on pretence of preventing smuggling, of harassing the carriers of salt and the refiners of salt-petre. Your petitioners are of opinion that, among other reforms required in this department, it is desirable that the Government, if they cannot immediately afford to forego so odious a source of revenue, should fix an unvarying rate of impost on the manufacture of salt, say 200 rupees [£20] on every 100 maunds [8200 lbs.], whereby not only the poor will be greatly benefited, but the laws will be rid of the anomaly of judicial excisemen, and the traders of the harassment caused by the subordinate officers of salt Chowkis. But as salt is the necessary of life, the duty on salt should be entirely taken off as soon as possible."[2]

Cultivators from Bombay submitted their petition to the Bombay Government against the oppressive salt

[1] Commons' First Report, 1853, Appendix 7. [2] *Ibid.*

tax on November 26, 1852; and Rustomjee Viccajee, who was examined by the Select Committee of the House of Commons in the following year, quoted from this petition. The petitioners urged that the produce of their fields supplied them with food enough for eight months in the year; that during the remaining four months they subsisted on vegetables, "which they season with chillies, and salt when the latter was free from duty; but when it was made subject to duty, they were obliged to forego even this poor comfort."[1]

The evidence, given by many distinguished and experienced officials, was not less strong than the evidence which came from the inhabitants of Bengal, Madras, and Bombay.

Robert Bird, who had served for thirty years in India as a Judicial and Revenue Officer, and was the author of the great Land Settlement of Northern India, was asked if the Salt Tax was as oppressive as it was represented to be.

"I do not know," he replied, "how oppressive it is represented to be, but that it is a very severe duty there is no doubt whatever. It is a duty of very nearly 300 per cent., or perhaps 250 per cent., upon the cost of production of the article, but it is only levied on the frontier. When Lord Auckland came up to the Western Provinces, as he was in the habit of doing, to discuss with me all the operations I was engaged in, he spoke to me about this, and said that great complaints were made about the hardships inflicted upon the people as regarded the salt duty, especially the ill-effect produced and the disrepute brought upon the Government by the palanquins of females, in which females are carried across the frontier, being searched for salt. . . . I could only say, that if they were not to be searched, we should have more Lot's wives brought into the Western Provinces than you ever saw in any country; that every woman's

[1] Commons' Fourth Report, 1853, p. 27.

palanquin would be filled with salt from top to the bottom."[1]

Frederick Halliday, who was then Secretary to the Government of India in the Home Department, and shortly after was appointed the first Lieutenant-Governor of Bengal, spoke of the corruptions and extortions inevitable in such a system as that of the Company's salt monopoly in India. He was of opinion that if that monopoly was withdrawn, and the people of India were allowed to manufacture their own salt, imported salt would have no chance in India.

"The present price of the Government manufactured salt in Bengal is very much raised to the consumer in the market by the necessary want of economy, not to say extravagances, connected with the Government system of manufacture, and by those many peculations, and extortions, and corruptions, which are inevitable in such a system, and carried on with such instruments. It has seemed almost certain under those circumstances to persons informed upon the subject, that if the Government were to withdraw, and if there were no duty imposed, and the whole were left perfectly free, the native manufacturers in Bengal would forthwith completely and entirely undersell the imported salt, and there would not be a grain of salt imported into Bengal."[2]

It is needless to add that all memorials and agitation against the Salt Tax failed. The salt revenue was not given up.

OPIUM.

The only other article in which the Company retained a monopoly was opium. And the method of raising a revenue from the article was clearly explained before the Select Committee by F. W. Prideaux, who

[1] Commons' Fourth Report, 1853. [2] *Ibid.*

was employed at the India House as Assistant-Examiner of India Correspondence.[1]

In Bengal the cultivation of poppy was altogether prohibited except for the purpose of selling the juice to the Government. Cultivators, wishing to cultivate the plant, were permitted to do so only on condition of their delivering the juice to the Government at a fixed price. The juice was then sent to the two principal factories, one at Patna and one at Benares, where it was manufactured into opium and then sent down to Calcutta. It was there sold by auction, and the Government revenue consisted in the difference between the price it had cost the Government, and the price which was realised for it from the merchants who exported it to China.

In Bombay no poppy was cultivated and no opium was manufactured; the Company's opium revenue was derived from the opium grown and manufactured in the Native State of Malwa. Merchants of that State sent the opium to the British port of Bombay for export to China; and the British Government realised a duty of £40 on each chest (123 lbs.) of opium on its passage through British territory. Previous to 1843, the Malwa opium used to pass out of India by way of Sindh; but after the British conquest of Sindh in that year, there was no exit for that opium except through British territory, and on payment of the duty on the transit which formed the opium revenue of Bombay. The conquest of Sindh had thus a pecuniary value in increasing the opium revenue of Bombay.

In Madras no opium was produced.

There has been much controversy in England as to whether the Opium Revenue can really be called a tax on the people of India, whether the wars undertaken in China for maintaining the revenue were justifiable, and whether the opium monopoly should still be retained by

[1] Commons' Fourth Report, 1853.

the Indian Government at the present time. The object of the present work is to place facts before our readers to enable them to form their own judgments, and we have no desire to enter into these controversies. No sound economist will, we think, deny that a Government monopoly, which excludes the people from a profitable industry, and stops cultivation, manufacture and trade in a paying article, is a tax on the people, in the truest sense of the word. No impartial historian has defended Lord Palmerston's wars in China in order to force the Chinese to admit Indian opium into their ports against the wishes of their Government. And no sober statesman desires to keep up the Government monopoly in this article, if it can be safely dispensed with.

At the same time, as opium is not a general article of food, the people of India do not consider the Government monopoly in the article to be nearly as hurtful to the people as the salt monopoly. There is no strong feeling in India against the first as there is against the second. Still they believe the Government would do well to abolish the monopoly as a monopoly, and derive a legitimate income by imposing heavy duties on the manufacture and sale of the article, as duties are imposed on the sale of all intoxicating drugs and liquors. The British Indian Association fairly represented the opinion of the people of India in their Petition to the House of Commons.[1]

"Justice requires that the interference of the Government with the cultivation should cease, and that revenue derived from the drug should be in the shape of fixed duties on manufacture and exportation, but principally on the latter, as is in some measure the case with regard to Malwa opium. By the adoption of this principle, the cultivators will possess that freedom of action which all men possess under Governments which are not constituted on arbitrary and despotic principles; and whatever is lost by such an arrangement will be more than

[1] Commons' First Report, 1853, Appendix 7.

made up by the saving that will ensue from the abolition of the expensive establishments which are now neccssary."

The appeal, however, was in vain. Neither the East India Company, nor the Government of the Crown which succeeded in 1858, was willing to surrender the monopoly, or exchange it for a tax on the production and exportation of opium.

CHAPTER X

TARIFFS, IMPORTS, AND EXPORTS

VARIOUS Acts were passed from time to time between 1833 and 1853 by the Indian Legislature to regulate Trade and Navigation and to fix the Tariff.[1] The duties which were levied in 1852 on some of the principal articles imported into India are shown in the following table:—

Articles.	Import Duty.
Books, British	Free.
Books, Foreign	3 per cent.
Coffee	7½ per cent.
Cotton and silk piece goods, British	5 per cent.
Cotton and silk piece goods, Foreign	10 per cent.
Cotton thread, twist, and yarn, British	3½ per cent.
Cotton thread, twist, and yarn, Foreign	7 per cent.
Horses and other animals	Free.
Marine stores, British	5 per cent.
Marine stores, Foreign	10 per cent.
Metals, British	5 per cent.
Metals, Foreign	10 per cent.
Beer, ale, and similar fermented liquors	5 per cent.
Salt	5s. per maund (82 lbs.) in Bengal. 6s. per maund in Madras
Spirits	3s. per Imperial Gallon, London proof.
Tea	10 per cent.
Wines and Liquers	2s. per Imperial Gallon.
Woollens, British	5 per cent.
Woollens, Foreign	10 per cent.
Manufactured articles	5 per cent.
Articles not named	3½ per cent.

[1] 1836 . Act, 2, 3, 14, 22, 25, 32.
1837 . Act, 5, 14, 16, 17, 32.
1838 . Act, 1, 5, 19, 29, 31.
1839 . Act, 5, 13, 15, 20.
1840 . Act, 13.
1841 . Act, 6, 10, 13, 18, 23.
1842 . Act, 3, 4, 11, 15.
1843 . Act, 14, 25.
1844 . Act, 6, 15, 16, 20, 21.
1845 . Act, 7, 9, 24, 32.
1846 . Act, 2, 9.
1848 . Act, 6, 17, 16, 23.
1849 . Act, 5, 8, 13.
1850 . Act, 5, 10, 11, 24, 27, 28.
See Commons' Report, 1852, Appendix 5.

Appendix 3 of the Commons' Report of 1852, from which the above figures are compiled, also gives us the value of the imports and exports of Bengal, Madras, and Bombay, for sixteen years from 1834–35 to 1849–50. In the following two tables we have taken a pound sterling as equivalent to 10 rupees.

IMPORTS.

Year.	Merchandise and Treasure imported into			
	Bengal.	Madras.	Bombay.	Total.
	£	£	£	£
1834–35 . .	2,645,355	656,405	2,852,369	6,154,129
1835–36 . .	2,857,530	585,088	3,485,694	6,928,312
1836–37 . .	3,395,423	672,985	3,504,747	7,573,157
1837–38 . .	3,512,788	732,466	3,427,317	7,672,572
1838–39 . .	3,851,183	778,536	3,621,876	8,251,596
1839–40 . .	4,568,378	795,714	2,412,408	7,776,501
1840–41 . .	5,509,563	837,079	3,855,551	10,202,193
1841–42 . .	5,252,527	745,887	3,631,485	9,629,900
1842–43 . .	5,563,897	660,593	4,822,403	11,046,894
1843–44 . .	6,226,848	767,504	6,618,122	13,612,475
1844–45 . .	7,515,355	1,235,455	5,755,727	14,506,537
1845–46 . .	6,223,623	1,022,211	4,337,603	11,583,438
1846–47 . .	6,649,671	1,029,003	4,157,911	11,836,586
1847–48 . .	5,418,584	1,108,817	4,043,606	10,571,008
1848–49 . .	5,770,623	1,065,271	5,713,412	12,549,307
1849–50 . .	6,498,035	1,027,441	6,171,218	13,696,696

An examination of the figures set forth herein suggests some observations. It will be perceived at once that while the imports and exports of Bengal and Bombay advanced by rapid strides, those of Madras showed a very poor increase. The imports of Bombay and of Bengal increased from two and a half millions to six millions; the imports of Madras increased from £600,000 to a million. Exports from Bombay increased from three to six and a half millions, and from Bengal from four to ten and a half millions, while exports from Madras increased only from a million to a million and a half. These striking differences were not due to any extension of territory in Bengal and Bombay; for there were few important additions to those Provinces between 1834 and 1849. The difference was mainly due to the impoverished

EXPORTS.

Year.	Merchandise and Treasure Exported from			
	Bengal.	Madras.	Bombay.	Total.
	£	£	£	£
1834-35 . .	4,158,598	992,485	3,037,077	8,188,161
1835-36 . .	5,593,896	1,152,968	4,467,740	11,214,604
1836-37 . .	6,849,527	1,351,416	5,303,173	13,504,117
1837-38 . .	6,905,809	1,072,640	3,604,986	11,583,436
1838-39 . .	6,954,381	1,111,719	4,056,573	12,122,675
1839-40 . .	7,000,943	1,355,914	2,976,411	11,333,268
1840-41 . .	8,206,771	1,133,466	4,481,832	13,822,070
1841-42 . .	8,225,539	1,423,064	4,691,689	14,340,293
1842-43 . .	7,436,369	1,327,308	5,003,942	13,767,621
1843-44 . .	10,076,904	1,230,255	6,692,393	17,999,553
1844-45 . .	10,218,740	1,706,516	5,771,796	17,697,052
1845-46 . .	10,102,755	1,476,981	6,264,965	17,844,702
1846-47 . .	9,519,797	1,584,316	4,965,192	16,069,307
1847-48 . .	8,866,928	1,491,558	4,379,947	14,738,435
1848-49 . .	9,819,742	1,946,311	6,862,190	18,628,244
1849-50 . .	10,502,244	1,345,522	6,435,776	18,283,543

condition of Madras under its wretched land system, which we have described in another chapter.

Another striking fact which we note in the above figures is the great disproportion between the imports and the exports of British India. The difference was two millions in 1834–35, and increased to over four and a half millions in 1849–50. The figures represent the trade of British India not with Great Britain only but with all countries of the world. But other countries gave a fair return for what they received; Great Britain exacted a tribute from India for which she made no commercial return. And the difference of two to four millions a year between India's imports and exports represented the annual drain of wealth from India.

In the preceding tables we have exhibited figures

showing the trade of India down to 1850. We are able to place before the reader the figures for the last eight years of the Company's rule, 1851 to 1858, from a more recent source.[1] The excess of exports continued during the first five years, but imports exceeded during the last three years, two of which were years of the Indian Mutiny.

Trade of India with all Countries.

Year.	Import of Merchandise.	Import of Treasure.	Total Imports.	Total Exports.	Excess of Exports.
	£	£	£	£	£
1851	11,558,789	3,811,809	15,370,598	18,705,439	3,334,839
1852	12,240,490	5,052,059	17,292,549	20,798,342	3,505,793
1853	10,070,863	6,831,377	16,902,240	21,519,863	4,617,623
1854	11,122,659	4,871,954	15,994,613	20,778,435	4,783,822
1855	12,742,671	2,028,256	14,770,927	20,194,255	5,423,328
					Excess of Imports.
1856	13,943,494	11,301,288	25,244,782	23,639,435	1,605,347
1857	14,194,587	14,413,697	28,608,284	26,591,877	2,016,407
1858	15,277,629	15,815,436	31,093,065	28,278,474	2,814,591

It is needless to say that the excess of imports over exports was only temporary. By 1864, as we shall see in a future chapter, India's exports once more exceeded her imports, and the difference increased to an alarming figure with the lapse of years.

Somewhat over one-half the entire trade of India was with Great Britain. Thus between 1841 and 1855, when the total imports of India ranged between ten and seventeen millions, the imports from the United Kingdom alone were between five and ten millions. And in the last three years, 1856 and 1858, when the imports rose to between twenty-five and thirty-one millions, the imports from the United Kingdom ranged between fourteen and eighteen millions. In the export trade of India the share of Great Britain was

[1] Statistical Abstract relating to British India, 1840 to 1865.

somewhat less. The total for India between 1841 and 1855 ranged between thirteen and twenty-one millions, and the exports to Great Britain were between five and eight millions; while in the three subsequent years, India's exports to the United Kingdom rose to ten millions when her total exports were between twenty-three and twenty-eight millions.

Our space forbids us from attempting to show how the import and export of all the different articles of merchandise rose or fell during these years; but a history of some of the principal articles of trade is important, as throwing some light on the industries of the people of India. Cotton twist and yarn, cotton goods, silk goods and woollen goods, machinery and metal manufactures, were among the most important imports of India; and the fluctuations in the consumption of those articles during ten years are shown in the following figures:—

Imports into India from all Countries.

Year.	Cotton Twist and Yarn.	Cotton Goods.	Silk Goods.	Woollen Goods.	Machinery.	Metal Manufactures.
	£	£	£	£	£	£
1849	909,016	2,222.089	123,505	111,815	18,064	203,997
1850	1,131,586	3,371,618	112,601	156,154	8,079	166,139
1851	1,039,329	3,642,361	111,554	218,848	20,066	245,393
1852	1,391,134	4,770,779	126,064	205,505	14,337	246,701
1853	1,130,500	3,667,433	110,546	142,027	26,457	217,187
1854	1,306,913	4,432,525	116,955	144,473	52,788	286,671
1855	1,274,098	5,403,244	197,510	171,065	126,303	312,304
1856	1,414,274	4,948,005	138,768	133,998	435,512	788,859
1857	1,191,974	4,911,353	106,333	143,797	244,433	558,329
1858	943,920	4,782,698	108,023	261,589	465,453	378,989

It will be seen from these figures that the import of cotton goods was more than doubled within six years, from 1849 to 1855; and though a further increase was arrested during the years of the Indian Mutiny, the figures went up with a bound to eight millions in 1859.

The increase in the import of machinery and metal manufactures is also remarkable.

The following figures show the fluctuations in the principal exports from India during the same ten years.

Exports from India to all Countries.

Year.	Cotton (Raw).	Cotton Goods, Twist and Yarn.	Silk (Raw).	Silk Goods.	Wool (Raw).
	£	£	£	£	£
1849	1,775,309	690,584	713,632	302,322	55,591
1850	2,201,178	742,320	666,094	441,749	48,925
1851	3,474,489	673,549	619,319	355,223	68,335
1852	3,619,989	819,049	688,640	260,225	100,612
1853	3,629,494	930,877	667,545	315,305	172,110
1854	2,802,150	769,345	640,451	326,571	205,601
1855	2,428,764	817,103	500,105	263,453	207,263
1856	3,314,951	779,647	707,706	341,035	272,942
1857	1,437,949	882,241	782,140	281,450	314,216
1858	4,301,768	809,183	766,673	158,224	387,104

Year.	Grains.	Sugar.	Opium.	Indigo.	Jute.
	£	£	£	£	£
1849	858,691	1,814,404	5,772,526	2,093,474	68,717
1850	757,917	1,925,603	5,973,395	1,838,474	88,989
1851	752,295	1,823,789	5,459,135	1,980,896	196,936
1852	869,002	1,801,660	6,515,214	2,025,313	180,976
1853	889,160	1,729,762	7,034,075	1,809,685	112,617
1854	1,413,654	948,582	6,437,098	2,067,769	214,768
1855	1,742,530	1,135,699	6,231,278	1,701,825	229,241
1856	2,896,262	1,359,104	6,200,871	2,424,332	329,076
1857	2,587,456	1,786,077	7,056,630	1,937,907	274,957
1858	3,790,374	1,175,771	9,106,635	1,734,339	303,292

The fluctuations of these articles of export are significant. The export of raw cotton rose in ten years from under two millions to over four millions. There was a continuous desire in England to extend and improve the cotton cultivation of India, so that England might rely on her own possession rather than on America for the requirements of her looms and factories. We shall see in a subsequent chapter that the Civil War in America in the early 'sixties came as a providential help to these endeavours. America sent little cotton during that war; and the export from India rose to near thirty-six millions in 1864, and to a still higher figure in the following year. But the hope vanished when peace was once more established in the United States. American cotton once more replaced Indian cotton in the British factories; and the export from India fell as suddenly as it had risen.

Throughout the century just expired, there was no thought of fostering the weaving industry in India, or of instructing the people to manufacture for themselves by means of the power loom, or of improving their old hand loom. A truly national Government, one working for the good of the nation, would have sought to preserve the old national industry of India by introducing new and improved methods; and the patient, industrious, and skilful artisans of India would undoubtedly have learnt the lesson, and preserved their old industry under new methods.

Referring once more to the table given above, we find that while the export of raw silk remained stationary and that of raw wool showed an increase, Indian silk manufactures, which had provoked so much jealousy among the silk weavers of England, showed a marked decline from 1857 and 1858 from which they never recovered afterwards. On the other hand, the export of food grains showed a steady and alarming increase, and the figure rose in ten years from less than a million to nearly four millions. It was a natural result, when handicrafts and manufactures declined, and India had to pay her annual tribute to England as well as for her imports, that she sent out a continuously increasing share of the food supply of the people. By the end of the century, the export of rice and wheat and other food grains had reached the high figure of twelve millions sterling a year.

The export of Indian sugar already began to show a decline in the last years of the Company's rule, and dwindled into a very small figure, under £170,000 sterling, by the close of the century. On the other hand the export of jute steadily increased, specially from the time of the Crimean War. The large supply of flax which England had obtained from Russia before was interrupted during the war, and Indian jute thus obtained a start which it has more than maintained since. By the end of the century the export of raw and manufactured jute from India rose almost to ten millions sterling.

The export of indigo was also large; but it is painful to state that acts of lawlessness and coercion stained the records of the industry. Such acts on the part of the European indigo planters of Bengal caused much irritation among the people, and at last brought their own remedy in most parts of Bengal. Cultivators struck; many indigo firms failed; and the manufacture of the indigo declined, as will be explained in a subsequent chapter. And the discovery of a chemical equivalent in Germany towards the close of the century gave the final death-blow to this old industry.

Mutarfa Tax.

Speaking about Indian industries it is satisfactory to note that the oppressive and harassing Mutarfa Tax on trades and professions had been abolished by 1853 all over India, except in the benighted Province of Madras. The Madras Native Association in their Petition to the House of Commons[1] described the Mutarfa as a "tax upon trades and occupations, embracing weavers, carpenters, all workers in metals, all salesmen, whether possessing shops which are also taxed separately, or vending by the road side, &c., some paying impost on their tools, others for permission to sell—extending to the

[1] Commons' First Report, 1853, Appendix 7.

most trifling articles of trade and the cheapest tools the mechanic can employ, the cost of which is frequently exceeded six times by the Mutarfa, under which the use of them is permitted." And the Association went on to state that "it falls more heavily upon the indigent than upon the wealthy, while the discretionary power under which it is collected affords a wide field for the perpetual practice of inquisitorial visits, extortion and oppression, as suits the pleasure or the cupidity of the irresponsible collectors, with whom it is no unusual thing to resort to imprisonment and fetters in order to compel their exactions." And "the whole sum raised by this impost is but little above £100,000 sterling."

There was no exaggeration in the above statement. A witness, J. W. B. Dykes, who was a magistrate and revenue officer, and had himself collected the tax in Madras, spoke in stronger terms of its oppressiveness.

Q. The tax is only levied upon those who are engaged in commercial dealings?

A. It is levied upon every one almost who does not cultivate land. . . . If an old woman takes vegetables to market, and sells them at the corner of the street, she is assessed for selling vegetables. If a man is a cloth merchant, he is assessed. But no tax is levied upon European traders. Perhaps, next door to this man who is making a few rupees a year, there is a European trader making hundreds, but he pays nothing.[1]

Such an invidious tax could not be continued in any part of India after the Parliamentary inquiries of 1853; and it was accordingly abolished. And the Income Tax, which was imposed shortly after the administration of India had been assumed by the Crown, was more just and equitable, because it was imposed on all classes of men, and because, eventually, people with poor incomes were excluded from its operation.

[1] Commons' Fourth Report, 1853.

CHAPTER XI

IRRIGATION AND RAILWAYS

GREAT irrigation canals, constructed by Mahomedan rulers in Northern India, had fallen into disrepair during the wars of the eighteenth century, and attracted the notice of the servants of the East India Company shortly after they had acquired Northern India in 1803. A Committee of Survey was appointed under Lord Minto's administration in 1810 to inquire into the state of the old canals both east and west of the Jumna; but the Chief Engineer and the Surveyor-General were divided in opinion, and "poured over the survey report such a flood of contradictory learning" that the first scheme of restoring the canals perished under its weight.[1]

Lord Hastings approached the question in a more practical manner. As a result of his tour in Upper India in 1815 he wrote hopefully of the scheme of restoring the old canal west of the Jumna:—

"I will only say that my own inspection has fully convinced me of the facility and the policy of immediately restoring this noble work. Setting aside the consideration of its certain effect, in bringing into cultivation vast tracts of country now deserted, and thereby augmenting importantly the landed revenue of the Honourable Company, the dues to be collected for the distribution of the water from it would make a most lucrative return." [2]

[1] Sir John Kaye's *Administration of the East India Company* (1853), p. 278.

[2] Minute dated September 21, 1815.

Lieutenant Blaine accordingly commenced the restoration of the *West Jumna Canal*, and saw the waters return to Delhi after a suspension of half a century, but his work did not go much farther. In 1823 Colonel John Colvin was appointed General Superintendent of Irrigation at Delhi, and the work proceeded rapidly towards completion. During the great famine of 1837 the gross value of the crops saved by the water of this canal was estimated at a million and a half sterling. The main line of the canal was 445 miles in length.[1]

The East Jumna Canal then attracted attention. That work, too, had been constructed by Mahomedan emperors, and the fame of two British engineers, Colonel Robert Smith and Colonel Baird Smith, is connected with its restoration. The first-named officer, Robert Smith, completed the work according to its original design in 1830; but much still remained to be done, and many serious defects were discovered. Captain Cautley rectified these errors; and he was succeeded by Baird Smith, whose high administrative work in another department will be referred to in a subsequent chapter. He completed the necessary improvements and additions; and the completed work, 155 miles in length, has been described with a legitimate pride by Colonel Baird Smith himself in the pages of an Indian Review:—

"Most beautiful in all parts it truly is, with its broad road, smooth as an English lawn, its double rows of trees drooping over the stream, its long graceful sweeps, its rich bordering of the most luxuriant crops, its neat station houses, and the peculiar care with which all its works are maintained. It is certainly one of the most interesting and attractive of Indian sights."

The history of the *Ganges Canal* belongs to the last years of the Company's rule. The great work was commenced by Lord Auckland, but was unfortunately sus-

[1] *Memorandum of the Improvements, &c.* Being a Return to an Order of the House of Commons, dated Febrnary 9, 1858.

pended by his successor, Lord Ellenborough. Lord Hardinge, however, recognised the merits of the magnificent scheme, and gave it his sanction and approval; and the Court of Directors, encouraged by the financial results of the East and West Jumna Canals, consented to the expenditure of over a million sterling over this great enterprise. The rule of the East India Company was swept away before the work was completed; but what was done in their time is described in their own Memorandum:—

"The total length of the Ganges Canal and its branches, when completed, will be 898½ miles, and it will furnish abundant irrigation for an area of 4½ million acres. The canal, in the words of the Lieutenant-Governor of the North-Western Provinces, 'presents a system of irrigation unequalled in vastness throughout the world; while the dimensions of the main channel, and the stupendous works of masonry which occur in its course, more particularly in the section between Roorkee and Hardwar, render the work eminently one of national distinction and honour.' The amount expended on it up to the 1st May 1856 had reached the sum of £1,560,000; and, when completed, the total cost will fall little short of two millions. The canal has but just begun to be brought into operation; but it is estimated by Colonel Baird Smith, the Director, that the annual produce of the land already watered by it is of the value of from £150,000 to £200,000; and that when the canal is in full operation, the value will ultimately reach the enormous sum of seven millions sterling. From the 30th April 1856 the canal had been carried so far that the water flowed continuously through 449½ miles of the main trunk and terminal branches."[1]

The Punjab was annexed by Lord Dalhousie in

[1] *Memorandum of the Improvements, &c.*, 1858.

1849, and was then found to contain canals of two kinds —inundation canals and permanent canals.

"The inundation canals are cuts from the rivers, which are empty during the winter, because the water is then not high enough to enter them; but as the water rises in the spring, from the melting of the snows, these channels fill, and remain full till late in autumn. The fertility of the South-Western Punjab mainly depends on these canals; and in a former age they appear to have been conducted from all the rivers; their course being traceable by the ruins, not only of villages, but of cities and public buildings, which depended for existence on their fertilising influence. Such of these canals as were found in working order at the annexation have been maintained, improved, and enlarged; and plans and estimates have been formed for the restoration of others. As yet, however, a greater part of the funds which could be spared for the purpose have been devoted to the construction and improvement of permanent canals."[1]

The only important permanent canal which the East India Company undertook in the Punjab was the *Baree Doab Canal*, about 450 miles in length. To John Lawrence and to Lord Dalhousie, India is indebted for this magnificent work. John Lawrence continuously pressed on the Indian Government the expediency of constructing roads and canals, promising that such expenditure would soon return itself tenfold in increased revenue. "If we wish to feed the thousands of human beings," wrote the Lahore Board, "whom the change of rule must necessarily throw out of employment, we cannot more readily do so than by cutting new canals, and improving the beds of the old ones."[2] "Everywhere," responded Lord Dalhousie, "I found lands of vast extent, fertile properties now lying comparatively waste, but wanting only water to convert them into plains of the richest

[1] *Memorandum of the Improvements, &c.*, 1858.

[2] Lahore Board to the Supreme Government. Letter dated November 29, 1850.

cultivation."[1] And the Court of Directors gave them "cordial assent to the undertaking"—the Baree Doab Canal—but with a caution that the work should be carried out with "due regard to economy."[2]

Baird Smith had become the most distinguished authority on irrigation in Northern India, and he took advantage of a furlough to Europe to visit Italy, and examine the great canal works of Lombardy and Piedmont. And the East India Company paid his expenses for a similar scientific visit to the United States of America. It is needless to add that the Baree Doab Canal was pushed on vigorously. By May 1856, more than 325 miles had been excavated; and the work was expected to be completed in 1859. The total cost was estimated at a million sterling, and the expected return at £120,000, or 12 per cent. on the outlay per annum.[3]

The province of Bombay does not boast of large rivers, except the Narbada and the Tapti, which water a few districts only; and there is little scope for irrigation by canals in the uplands of the Deccan. And sufficient attention was not paid by the Company's servants to irrigation by means of wells and reservoir tanks. In Sindh, cultivation was dependent on the rise of the Indus, whose waters were distributed by a network of old canals; and the Company spent £25,000 annually in keeping these canals in working order.

Madras was rich in the remains of reservoir tanks, built by old Rajas and Polygars; and Dr. Francis Buchanan had observed and described them in course of his journey from Madras to the West Coast as early as 1800.[4] A

[1] Minute dated December 6, 1850.

[2] Court of Directors to the Governor-General. Letter dated April 25, 1851.

[3] *Memorandum of the Improvements, &c.*, 1858.

[4] Every province in India has its distinct irrigation requirements. In the alluvial basins of the Ganges and the Indus the most suitable irrigation works are *canals* from these rivers; while away from the rivers, *wells* are the most suitable. In Bengal with its copious rainfall, *shallow ponds* are the most suitable works, and these were numerous in the olden times, sometimes of very large dimensions. In Madras and Southern India, where

systematic restoration and preservation of these ancient works, and the excavation of new works of the same kind where most needed, would have changed the face of the country within fifty or sixty years, and the Company might have handed over the Southern Province to the Crown with its agriculture safeguarded, and its population protected from famines. But irrigation was sadly neglected; and when, sometimes, a Collector undertook the restoration of an old reservoir, it was mainly with the purpose of adding to the heavy assessment of his district.

There are, however, a few tracts in the Province of Madras where irrigation by means of canals on a large scale is possible, and these tracts are the deltas of the great rivers—the Godavari, the Krishna, and the Kaveri. Thoughtful men perceived, early in the nineteenth century, the possibility of utilising these great rivers, and irrigating their deltas; and the name of Sir Arthur Cotton is imperishably connected with the first great canal works in the South, as those of Baird Smith and his colleagues are in the North.

Coleroon is one of the branches of the Kaveri; and the old *Coleroon Works,* constructed by the ancient Hindus, can be traced from the second century of the Christian Era. When the country came under British administration in 1801, the old works were found to be very defective; the bed of the river was rising by the deposit of silt; and the extent of irrigated land was diminishing. The success of the Jumna Canals in Northern India at last suggested the improvement of the Coleroon Works in the South; and from 1836 the work was regularly and vigorously prosecuted. The total expenditure on the Upper and Lower Coleroon anicuts

the soil is undulating, and the underlying rock retains the water, the most suitable irrigation works are reservoirs made by putting up large embankments, and thus impounding the water descending from the hill slopes. Such were most of the old reservoirs of Madras. See Voelcker's *Improvement of Indian Agriculture*, 1893.

came to upwards of £80,000; and a further sum of £100,000 was spent on subsidiary works for conveying irrigation over the district of Tanjore, and portions of Trichinopoly and South Arcot. The lands irrigated from the Coleroon and Kaveri increased from 630,000 acres to 716,000 acres; and the land revenue was increased by £44,000 per annum, giving a return of over 24 per cent. on the outlay.[1]

The East India Company took credit to themselves for the successful and profitable results of this great work, but the real credit is due to Sir Arthur Cotton, who first conceived the idea, and commenced the construction, of the Upper Coleroon Dam against much opposition. Born in 1803, he had come out to Madras in 1821; and before his final retirement from India in 1860, he had won for himself a reputation higher than that of any other engineer who has ever worked in India. "The permanent prosperity of Tanjore," wrote Baird Smith, the great irrigation man of Northern India, "is without doubt to be attributed in large measure to that first bold step taken by Colonel Cotton in the construction of the Upper Coleroon Dam, under circumstances of great difficulty, with restricted means, against much opposition, and with heavy personal responsibilities."[2]

The great reputation won by Arthur Cotton by the Coleroon Works marked him out as the fittest man to undertake the task on which his fame mainly rests, the *Godavari Works*. He selected a place a few miles below the ancient Hindu capital of Rajamundri, and he constructed his magnificent anicut in four sections, taking advantage of two islands in the river. The total estimated expenditure was £264,000; but the East India Company looked at it as a profitable speculation, and ex-

[1] *Memorandum on the Improvements, &c.*, 1858.

[2] *General Sir Arthur Cotton, his Life and Work*, by his daughter, Lady Hope (London, 1900), p. 52.

pected an increase of land revenue by £300,000, or over 100 per cent. per annum.[1]

There remained, then, the *Krishna River;* and the anicut across that river was commenced in 1853. The cost was originally estimated at £155,000; and an increase of £60,000 in the land revenue, or 39 per cent. on the outlay, was expected per annum.[2]

These were the principal irrigation works undertaken by the East India Company before 1858, when they ceased to exist. The works were constructed at a great expense; and the Company could fairly claim an adequate return on their outlay by a moderate rate on the water they supplied. It will be noticed, however, from the figures given above, that the Company went further, especially in the benighted Province of Madras; they raised the land revenue as much as it was possible to raise it, leaving the unfortunate cultivators as permanently poor as they were before. This policy would scarcely be considered wise or generous in a landlord dealing with his tenants; it was distinctly ungenerous and unwise in the Government of a great country dealing with a vast agricultural population. The growth of wealth and the accumulation of capital among a people should ever be the foremost aim of an enlightened Government.

The history of railways in India is different in its character from the history of irrigation works. Irrigation works paid, and more than paid, from the very commencement; railways did not give an adequate return on the

[1] *Memorandum on the Improvements, &c.*, 1858.

The work with its extensions cost much more in the end, and neither the East India Company, nor the Crown Administration which succeeded, was willing to find money for this beneficial and profitable *irrigation work*, while they squandered money over *railway works*. Sir Arthur Cotton spoke of it before the Select Committee of 1878 when he was examined as a witness.

"It has taken thirty-two years to obtain £700,000 for them—£20,000 a year for works which from the very first had been a most prodigious success. . . . The only dispute is whether they yield 27, 28, or 40 per cent.; and now after thirty-two years only 700,000 acres out of one million are irrigated. . . . During this time there was not the least question about £500,000 for sixty miles of railway to Nagpur, which it was acknowledged would not pay 4 per cent."—*General Sir Arthur Cotton, his Life and Work*, by Lady Hope, p. 276.

[2] *Memorandum on the Improvements, &c.*, 1858.

outlay. Irrigation works were converted into a source of revenue by the Government; railways led to a permanent loss to the Government year after year. Irrigation secured crops, increased the produce, and averted famines in years of drought; railways helped the conveyance of food to afflicted tracts in famine years, but did not add to the produce of the land.

It might naturally be expected that, under these circumstances, the Government of an agricultural country like India would be more partial to irrigation works than to railways. But Englishmen in their own country were more familiar with railroads than with canals; and they made the mistake of judging the needs of India accordingly. British manufacturers, too, thought that railways would more quickly open up the interior of India to their commodities than canals; and the administration both of the East India Company and of the Crown was subjected to a continuous Parliamentary pressure to extend and multiply railway lines in India, even at a loss to the revenues of the country. There was no counter pressure from the people of India, who had no votes and no representatives in the Executive Government; and irrigation works were thus treated with comparative neglect, while railways were multiplied beyond the urgent needs or the resources of the country.

Two private associations called the East Indian Railway Company and the Great Indian Peninsula Railway Company, were formed in 1845; but the projectors found it impossible to raise the necessary funds for their schemes without the assistance of Government. After much discussion the Directors of the East India Company consented to grant assistance in the shape of guaranteeing interest on the railway capital. The terms of the agreement were that, if the nett receipts from the railways were less than 5 per cent. on the capital expended, the Government of India would make good the difference from the revenues of India. If, on the other hand, the nett receipts from the railways were more than 5 per cent., one half of the excess would go to the railway companies, and the other to the Government of India. To take an example, if the railway traffic yielded 4 per cent. on the capital expended, the Government of India would pay 1 per cent. to make up the guaranteed rate of interest. If, on the other hand, the traffic yielded 7 per cent. on the outlay, the shareholders of the railway company would keep 6 per cent., and would pay the Government of India 1 per cent. The management remained with the railway company.[1]

It was also stipulated that the railway companies could surrender the works on giving six months' notice, and the Government would have to repay the whole amount expended by them. And the Government was empowered, after the expiration of twenty-five and fifty years respectively, to purchase the lines at the market value of the shares. Lastly, at the expiration of ninety-nine years, the land and works lapsed to the Government, who would have to purchase the engines and carriages at a valuation.[2]

East Indian Railway.—In 1854, only 37½ miles of this line were open for traffic; and in February 1855 the length opened was 121 miles, from Calcutta to Raniganj. Lord Dalhousie then drew up a scheme of a general system of trunk railways for India; and another contract was entered into, by which the same railway company agreed to extend the line to Delhi, and accepted 4½ per cent. as the guaranteed interest on their capital spent on this extension. But the Indian Mutiny occurred before any extension was opened for traffic, and the administration of the East India Company terminated after the mutiny.

Great Indian Peninsula Railway.—The line from

[1] Juland Danver's Report to the Secretary of State for India, dated March 12, 1860, paragraph 4.

[2] *Ibid.*, 1860, paragraph 4.

Bombay to Kalyan, 37 miles, was completed in 1854. In November of that year, the same railway company agreed to construct extensions at a minimum interest of 4½ per cent. on the outlay, but this rate was increased to 5 per cent. whenever shares were issued; 54 additional miles were done before the mutiny of 1857.

Madras Railway.—The first section of this line, from Madras to Arcot, 65 miles, was opened to the public in July 1856. No further extension was constructed within the period of the East India Company's administration. And no other lines except the three named above were opened for traffic before November 1858, when the Indian Empire passed under the direct administration of the Crown.

All the three lines described above were losing concerns, and the sums which the Government of India had to pay to the railway companies from year to year, to make up the guaranteed interest, are shown below.[1]

Amounts Paid by Government on Account of Guaranteed Interest.

Year.[2]	East Indian Railway.	Great Indian Peninsular Railway.	Madras Railway.
	£	£	£
1849	5,602	...	...
1850	17,471	3,063	...
1851	37,185	6,319	...
1852	45,234	16,310	...
1853	52,071	22,825	...
1854	88,884	25,002	9,703
1855	195,730	30,259	18,115
1856	297,390	60,370	42,510
1857	354,511	116,612	81,139
1858	433,968	175,289	109,267
Total . . .	£1,528,046	£456,049	£260,734

1 Juland Danvers, 1860, paragraphs 32, 48, and 60.

2 The sums paid to the East Indian Railway Company were for financial years, 1849-50, 1850-51, &c., and not for calendar years, 1849, 1850, &c., as shown above.

The loss to the people of India increased, as the railway lines were extended, from year to year. But so long as the interest was guaranteed, the railway companies made their earnings, and new companies were started to open lines in every part of India. The Sindh Railway Company, including the Punjab in their operations, the Bombay, Baroda and Central Indian Railway Company, the Eastern Bengal Railway Company, the Great South of India Railway Company, and the Calcutta and South-Eastern Railway Company, were all formed before the extinction of the East Indian Company's administration, but the lines undertaken by them were not opened.

This delay irritated British manufacturers and merchants; and in 1858 a Committee of the House of Commons was appointed " to inquire into the causes that have led to the delay." The Committee, after due inquiry, reported that the delay was owing to Government supervision of the works, to the distance of India from home, to insurrection and mutiny, and to the natural difficulties of the country. And the Committee added :—

" First, that the Government has acted wisely in committing to private enterprise the execution of these great public works ;

" Secondly, that a guaranteed interest on the requisite capital was indispensable to induce the public to invest their money in undertakings of this magnitude and novelty ;

" And thirdly, that in order to protect Indian revenue from undue expenditure, Government control over the railway operations is requisite, and even valuable to the interests of the shareholders themselves."

It is possible to conceive that if the people of India had been represented on this Committee, or even if many Indian witnesses had been examined by them, the Committee would have formed a different opinion. They might have come to the finding that, in order to protect Indian revenue from undue expenditure, railway lines on the guarantee system should not be undertaken in India except on the ground of absolute political necessity; that all other lines should be left entirely to private enterprise; and that canals were more suited to the needs of India, both as a means of cheap transit to the people and as a protection against droughts and famines.

CHAPTER XII

ADMINISTRATION

THE Company's Charter, renewed in 1834, was to expire in 1854. A fresh renewal was contemplated, and the usual inquiries into the past administration of the Company were instituted by Select Committees of both Houses of Parliament. The evidence taken by the Select Committees, and published in the shape of Blue Books, are the most valuable materials for the history of India during the early years of Queen Victoria's reign.

A Select Committee of the House of Lords sat in 1852; examined Cosmo Melvill, Sir George Clerk, John Stuart Mill, and other important witnesses; and submitted their Report in June 1852. And a Select Committee of the Lords sat again in 1852–53; and submitted three Reports in August 1853. Among the witnesses examined by this Committee were Lord Hardinge, Lord Gough, Sir Charles Napier, Sir Edward Ryan, Sir Erskine Perry, Sir Charles Trevelyan, Frederick Halliday, George Campbell, Alexander Duff, John Marshman, and Horace Hayman Wilson—names well known in India.

Similarly, a Select Committee of the House of Commons, consisting of the Chancellor of the Exchequer, Lord John Russell, Sir Charles Wood, Cobden, Gladstone, and other Members sat in 1852. They examined Lord Elphinstone, Lord Ellenborough, Lord Hardinge, Sir George Clerk, Cosmo Melvill, Henry Thoby Prinsep, and other witnesses; and submitted their Report in June 1852. And a Select Committee of the Commons, consisting of the Members named above and other Members like Macaulay, Lord Stanley, and Lord Palmerston, sat during the Session of 1852–53. They examined Sir George Clerk, Sir Edward Ryan, Sir Erskine Perry, Sir Charles Trevelyan, Frederick Halliday, Hay Cameron, Merttins Bird, Dr. Royle, John Sullivan, John Marshman, and other witnesses; and submitted six Reports between May and August 1853.

We do not propose to give within the limits of the present chapter anything like a summary of this evidence, submitted with eleven Reports, and covering four thousand folio printed pages. All that it is possible for us to do is to place before the reader the views and opinions of some of the most eminent men of the day on some of the most important questions of their time. There is a distinct advantage in reviewing the Indian administration of the early Victorian Age by help of the opinions of those who took a share in that administration. We not only clearly understand the system which was followed, but we also see how the system worked. We not only learn the rules which guided the administrators, but we also get a living picture of the administration itself, from the very men who spent twenty or thirty or forty years of their lives in carrying on the work, amidst the vast population of the Indian Empire.

Double Government.

The India Act of 1834, following Pitt's India Act of 1784, organised a double government for India. The powers of administration were left with the twenty-four Directors of the East India Company; the powers of control were placed in the hands of a Board of Control consisting of men appointed by the Crown. The Company ceased to be traders, and stood forth simply as administrators in India from 1834. And it was declared that all the powers of the Directors of the Company should be subject to the control of the Board, except in respect of the appointment of servants and officers specified in the Act. The Court of Directors originated everything; the Board of Control controlled everything. For convenience of work, the twenty-four Directors divided themselves into three Committees, viz. the Committee of Finance, the Committee of Political and Military Affairs, and the Committee of Revenue and Judicial matters.[1]

There was, however, one important subject in which the Court of Directors had no power of initiative. The Board of Control made peace or war without consulting the Directors, acting through a Secret Committee of the East India Company. "All proceedings of a great political nature, involving peace and war, may be said to be under the immediate direction of the Minister of the Crown, acting in communication with the chief authority in India through the Secret Committee of the East India Company, which so far acts entirely independently of the Directors of the East India Company."[2]

It thus happened that India was often involved in war through the action of the President of the Board of Control—a Member of the British Cabinet—without the knowledge of the Court of Directors. If the Court of Directors had any power in the matter, Lord Auckland's Afghan War, "which ended in the loss of 15,000 men, and an expenditure of many millions of money, might have been prevented." "The Court of Directors have no knowledge whatever of the origin, progress, or the present state of the war in Burma. I have twice asked for the papers, and I have been given to understand that it was not thought desirable to communicate them to the Court."[3]

It is scarcely necessary to point out that, by this unsatisfactory arrangement, Imperialist British Ministers like Lord Palmerston could, and did, involve India in

[1] Cosmo Melvill's Evidence, Commons' Report of 1852.

[2] Evidence of Col. Sykes, himself a Director of the East India Company, Commons' Report of 1852.

[3] Sir T. H. Maddock's Evidence, Commons' Report of 1852.

expeditions and wars for the Imperial interests of England; and the Court of Directors had to find money for such wars undertaken without their consent or knowledge. The Court of Directors have many sins to answer for; and they hastened their own end by the annexations of Indian States effected by an untrue interpretation of the ancient law of India. But it should be said in justice to that body that for the worst Indian wars of the early Victorian Age—the wars in Afghanistan, in Sindh, and in Burma—the Court of Directors are not answerable.

Leaving aside this undoubted defect in the constitution of the Government, the double system answered well enough in practice. It kept the Directors of the Company under a necessary control, and it avoided the evil of vesting Crown Ministers with irresponsible and despotic powers. The wisest and ablest Governor-General of the period declared that "the system of double government is much wiser than bringing the Crown more prominently forward."[1] And the most thoughtful and far-seeing English philosopher of the nineteenth century approved of the system. John Stuart Mill had been for thirty years an Assistant Examiner of Indian Correspondence, from 1823 to 1852, and he therefore spoke with authority on the system under which he had worked.

John Stuart Mill's Evidence.

"It is next to impossible to form in one country an organ of government for another which shall have a strong interest in good government; but if that cannot be done, the next best thing is, to form a body with the least possible interest in bad government; and I conceive that the present governing bodies in this country for the affairs of India have as little sinister interest of any kind as any government in the world."

[1] Lord Hardinge's Evidence, Commons' Report of 1852.

"The Court of Directors who are the initiating body, not being the body which finally decides, not being able to act but by the concurrence of a second authority, and having no means of causing their opinion to be adopted by that authority except the strength of their reasons,—there is much greater probability that a body so situated will examine and weigh carefully the grounds of all proceedings, than if the same body which had the initiative gave the final order."

To carry on the Government of India solely through a Secretary of State "would be the most complete despotism that could possibly exist in a country like this; because there would be no provision for any discussion or deliberation, except that which might take place between the Secretary of State and his subordinates in office, whose advice and opinion he would not be bound to listen to; and who, even if he were, would not be responsible for the advice or opinion that they might give."[1]

Fifty years have passed since John Stuart Mill gave this opinion, and our experience of these fifty years proves the foresight and wisdom of the great philosopher. The administration of India has certainly improved in many respects, within these fifty years, owing to larger experience; but there can be little doubt that the irresponsible government of the Secretary of State has also been attended with many hurtful results. There is no real control over the Secretary of State's action, similar to that which was exercised on the Court of Directors by the Board of Control; no periodical inquiries are made into the present administration, as inquiries were made into the Company's administration at every renewal of their Charter; and no jealous and salutary criticism, like that to which the Company was subject, restrains and corrects the action of the present Indian Government. And the results of this irrespon-

[1] John Stuart Mill's Evidence, Lords' Report of 1852.

sible administration have not been altogether happy. To confine ourselves to financial matters only, the annual revenues of India averaged thirty millions sterling in the last five years of the Company's administration; and out of this sum, only three and a half millions were remitted to England for Home Charges. By the last year of Queen Victoria's reign, 1900–1901, the revenues had been nearly doubled, amounting to fifty-five millions excluding railway and irrigation receipts, although the extent of the empire remained much the same,[1] and the wealth and income of the people had certainly not increased. And a sum exceeding seventeen millions was remitted to England as Home Charges. This enormous economic drain (increased fivefold in less than fifty years) would have been impossible under the rule of the East India Company.

Opinion of British Merchants.

British merchants and manufacturers always desired India to be well governed, but never had, or could have, that "strong interest in good government" which alone could ensure it. They naturally looked primarily at their own trade and manufacturing interests; and they believed that if the East India Company were abolished, and India were placed directly under a Crown Minister, it would be possible to secure further facilities for British trade with India, by means of pressure brought on the Crown Minister. It does not surprise us, therefore, that Manchester, Birmingham, and Liverpool differed from the opinion of Lord Hardinge and John Stuart Mill, and suggested the government of India through a Crown Minister.

The City of Manchester, in Public Meeting assembled, "believe that no security can be given for the reform of abuses in India, but by a thorough reform of its home

[1] Upper Burma and Beluchistan yield little revenue.

government; and entertain the opinion that the Court of Directors and Proprietors of the East India Stock should be entirely disconnected from the Government of India, which, for the future, should in this country consist of a Minister and a Council appointed by the Crown, and directly responsible to the Imperial Parliament."[1]

The Liverpool East India and China Association pointed out the necessity of "improved means of internal communication for produce and merchandise to and from the seaports of India"; protested against the excessive land-tax of India and against the suppression of the gold standard; asked for a better administration of justice and of the police; exclaimed against delays in the Customs department; and "would in all humility suggest the expediency of extending to India in some form the immediate authority and supervision of the Board of Control."[2]

The inhabitants of Birmingham in Public Meeting assembled were more peremptory in their demands and prayed that the Parliament would "abolish the existing system of a double government, and establish a home administration appointed by the Crown, and directly responsible to the Imperial Parliament."[3]

The administrative policy of the British Empire is determined, not by philosophers and statesmen, but by the merchants, manufacturers and the voters of Great Britain. And when the manufacturers and merchants of Great Britain desired a Crown Government for India, the introduction of that form of government was only a question of time.

[1] Commons' First Report, 1853, Appendix 7.
[2] Commons' Fourth Report, Appendix 2.
[3] *Ibid.*

Demand for Representation.

Faintly, and from far across the seas, was heard the first demand for representation from the people of India.

The Madras Native Association and the Native Inhabitants of the Presidency of Madras suggested that the Council of Madras "be composed of officials and non-officials in equal number, six or seven of each; the former to be nominated by the Government on taking their place at the Council Board in virtue of their office, the Advocate-General being one; and the latter to be selected by the Governor out of a list of eighteen or twenty-one persons chosen by the votes of the rate-payers in Madras, and of persons eligible to serve on the grand and petty juries, or in such other manner as your Honourable House may deem preferable. That as the official members, in conjunction with the casting vote of the Governor when requisite, could always carry any point of absolute importance, there could be no hindrance to the safe working of the suggested plan, while a sufficiency of information on all subjects would be afforded." [1]

The Members of the Bombay Association, and other Native Inhabitants of the Presidency of Bombay, submitted "that the time has arrived when the Natives of India are entitled to a much larger share than they have hitherto had in the administration of the affairs of their country, and that Councils of the Local Governments should, in matters of general policy and legislation, be opened, so as to admit of respectable and intelligent Natives taking a part in the discussion of matters of general interest to the country, as suggested by Lords Ellenborough, Elphinstone, and others." [2]

The Members of the British Indian Association and other Native Inhabitants of the Bengal Presidency submitted for the consideration of Parliament "the propriety

[1] Commons' First Report, Appendix 7.
[2] *Ibid.*

of constituting a Legislative Council at Calcutta, composed of seven members—three selected from among the most respectable and qualified Native Inhabitants of each Presidency to represent the Natives thereof—one member appointed by the Governor of each Presidency from among the senior Civil Officers on its establishment to represent the interests of the Government—and one member appointed by the Crown."[1]

While Indian Associations thus put forward their cautious and almost timid claims for representation, they also urged their claims for a larger share of employment in the higher offices, according to that famous clause in the Act of 1833 which was so much applauded in the House of Commons, and so consistently ignored in India. And English witnesses testified to the violation of the promise made to the Indian people. Hay Cameron, Legal Member of the Governor-General's Council from 1843 to 1848, was emphatic on this point.

Lord Monteagle.—As far as declaration goes, could there be any much stronger declaration of the general eligibility of the Natives than that which is contained in the 87th clause of the last Act?

Hay Cameron.—No, it seems to me very strong and very clear. . . .

Lord Monteagle.—Taking the clause in the larger sense in which you interpret it, have the practical results been such as to realise the expectations of the framers of the clause?

Hay Cameron.—No, quite the reverse. Not a single Native that I am aware of has been placed in any better position in consequence of that clause in the statute, than he would have been in, if no such clause had been enacted.[2]

The evidence of Sir Charles Trevelyan was still more emphatic. He referred to the Imperial nations of the past—to the Macedonians and the Romans—and showed

[1] Commons' First Report, Appendix 7. [2] Lords' Second Report, 1853.

how lasting empires had been founded by placing conquered nations "on a complete footing of equality" with the conquerors; and he gave his opinion that "the best mode of retaining our Empire over India is by employing the Natives in posts of trust and emolument; but that for that purpose they should be educated so as to qualify them better to perform those duties."[1]

The Act of 1833 was passed in the full tide of true Liberalism, only a year after the first Reform Act was passed in England. Since then, true Liberalism had ebbed, and the tide of Imperialism had swollen in England, and a regard for the people had abated in India. Francis Robinson, who had been a judge and a Member of the Board of Revenue in India, testified to this melancholy fact.

"There is a strong feeling of dislike," he said, "on the part of the ruling race in India to the people who are ruled over; the fact was known no better to any man than to the late Lord William Bentinck who first attempted to stem the current of that feeling, and to raise the Native population in the scale of society."

"Do you wish the Committee to understand," Francis Robinson was asked, "that the regard paid to the feelings of the Natives has or has not been increased greatly since particular attention was drawn to the subject by the measures of the Governor-General, Lord William Bentinck, himself?"

"I think," answered Francis Robinson, "there has been a reaction upon that point. Since the time of Lord William Bentinck there has been a reaction."[2]

Two decades had passed since the reforms of Lord William Bentinck. He had endeavoured to open out new positions of trust and responsibility to the people by the creation of such posts as those of Principal Sudder Amins, Deputy Magistrates and Deputy Collectors.

[1] Lords' Second Report, 1853.
[2] Commons' Fourth Report, 1853.

But after he had left India, little further progress was made. The number of Indians employed in Civil Administration in 1828, the year of Lord William's arrival in India, and in 1849, *i.e.* twenty-one years after, is shown in the following statement.[1]

	1828.	1849.
Principal Sudder Amins	...	64
Sudder Amins	157	81
Munsiffs	86	494
Deputy Magistrates	...	11
Deputy and Assistant Collectors	...	86
Sub-Collector's Assistants	...	27
Abkaro (Excise) Superintendents	...	15
Tahsildars	356	276
Sheristadars	367	155
Mamlatdars	9	110
Daftardars	2	19
Kamavisdars	57	...
Adalatus	...	5
Mir Munshis	...	1
Educational	14	479
Various	149	990
Total	1197	2813

Less than three thousand Indians found employment in Government services in British India in 1849. Less than a thousand of them held any posts of honour, trust, and responsibility.

Executive Administration.

The principal changes introduced by the Act of 1833, which came into operation in April 1834, provided that Bengal and Agra should be formed into separate Governments. Bengal still remained directly under the Governor-General, Lord William Bentinck; while Sir Charles Metcalfe was appointed the first Governor of Agra. A Legal Member was added to the Governor-General's Council, and Macaulay was the first Legal Member who was sent out to India. Hitherto each Province—Bengal, Madras, and Bombay—had enacted its own *Regulations;* henceforth the Governor-General,

[1] Commons' Report of 1852, Appendix 3.

with the aid of his Council, was enabled to pass *Acts* applicable to all India.

Bengal still remained without a separate Governor; the Governor-General of India was also the Governor of Bengal; and Henry Thoby Prinsep was gazetted Secretary both to the Government of India and to the Government of Bengal.[1]

Madras and Bombay were, in theory, made more directly subordinate to the Governor-General, but uufortunately there was little inclination to interfere with the virtual independence of the administration of those Provinces. "The Governor-General in Council in Calcutta very seldom interferes with the internal arrangements of the Madras and Bombay Governments; he does so in finance when an expenditure in money is required, and in Legislative Acts; but in revenue, police, and judicial matters, he seldom, if ever, interferes."[2]

When the Punjab was annexed in 1849, it was made into a fifth Province, and was placed under a Board consisting of the two Lawrences and Mansel, as has been described in a previous chapter. The Board was disestablished after three years, and John Lawrence was made chief Commissioner of the Punjab in 1852.

Each of the Provinces was divided into districts; and district officers, combining in themselves criminal, revenue, and executive duties, still conducted the administration in the primitive method organised by Warren Hastings and Lord Cornwallis in the previous century. The more important criminal cases were tried by judges, who, with their Indian subordinates, disposed of all civil cases.

JUDICIAL ADMINISTRATION.

Each Province had two superior Courts, the Sudder Court consisting of the Company's civil servants, and

[1] Prinsep's Evidence, Commons' Report of 1852.
[2] Lord Hardinge's Evidence, Commons' Report of 1852.

the Supreme Court consisting of judges appointed by the Crown. There was a concensus of opinions that the Courts should be amalgamated.

Sir Erskine Perry, who had been puisne judge, and then Chief Justice of the Supreme Court of Bombay between 1841 to 1852, thought it "extremely desirable to amalgamate them, and one of the first institutions for the improvement of India would be to let all the justice of India run in the Queen's name. . . . The system which I suggest would, to a great extent, prevent that collision of Courts which now takes place."

Sir Edward Ryan, who had been puisne judge, and then Chief Justice of the Supreme Court of Bengal between 1827 and 1842, also thought that "the amalgamation of the Supreme Court and the Sudder Court is desirable. The notion which I entertain is this, that it would be desirable to unite the Queen's Judges with the Company's Judges in one Court, and such Court should be an appellate Court for the Presidency in which it is established."

Sir Edward Gambier, who had been puisne judge, and then Chief Justice of Madras between 1836 and 1850, said: "Every suggestion which I might make would probably have reference to what I think a most desirable measure, the union of the two Courts at the Presidency, the Supreme Court and the Sudder Adalat Court."[1]

The opinion of the Bar was as emphatic as that of the Bench, and John Farley Leith, an English barrister who had taken up practice in the Privy Council in London after retiring from Calcutta, described the advantages of the proposed amalgamation very clearly. "There should be associated with the Company's Officers, who are members of the Covenanted Civil Service of India, professionally educated English judges. . . . The Covenanted Service Judges would bring into practical use all their

[1] Evidence of Sir Erskine Perry, Sir Edward Ryan, and Sir Edward Gambier, Commons' First Report, 1853.

experience and knowledge of the institutions of the country and the people, their manners and their usages, and you would then have an educated, practical lawyer to exercise his judgment on the facts and law, guided by a legal mind accustomed to accurate investigation and logical reasoning." [1]

The British Indian Association of Bengal also submitted "that the Sudder Court and the Supreme Court should be amalgamated as soon as possible." [2] In accordance with this strong and unanimous opinion the Courts were amalgamated, and converted into the High Courts of Calcutta, Madras, and Bombay, when the Company's Charter was renewed.

A Law Commission had been appointed after the passing of the Act of 1833, and Macaulay, the first Legal Member of the Governor-General's Council, was its first President. The Commission first set to work to frame a Penal Code for India. Macaulay had the Code Napoleon and other materials before him; and the Indian Penal Code was drafted and submitted in 1837. It was then submitted to legal authorities in England and in India, and the observations of the Indian Courts were reviewed in 1847 by the then remaining members of the Law Commission, Elliot and Hay Cameron. The matter then slept for some time, and the draft was subsequently so altered by Bethune, then Legal Member, that it came to be called the Bethune Code.[3] The Code, however, was not passed into law till after the abolition of the East India Company's government.

The Law Commission of 1848, then consisting of Elliot and Hay Cameron, also prepared a Criminal Procedure Code; but that too was not passed into law till after the extinction of the Company's administration. It was Lord Canning, the first Viceroy of India under the Crown,

[1] Commons' First Report, 1853. [2] *Ibid.*, Appendix 7.

[3] Sir Edward Ryan's Evidence and Sir Erskine Perry's Evidence, Lords' First Report, 1853. And Frederick Halliday's Evidence, Commons' First Report, 1853.

who passed the Penal Code and the Criminal Procedure Code of India, as well as a Code of Civil Procedure.

In the absence of codified law, the Company's judges and magistrates performed their work as best they could; and Indian officers, appointed to responsible judicial posts, displayed an ability, judgment, and capacity for judicial work, which won the admiration of the highest authorities. Sir Edward Ryan was "very much struck with their capacity and their power of administering justice"; and Sir Erskine Perry cited and supported the opinion of two leading barristers practising in India that "the judgments of the Native judges were infinitely superior to the judgments of the Company's judges who sat in appeal."[1]

Nevertheless the Indian judges were still badly paid. A European judge, said Sir Erskine before the Lords' Committee, received about £3000 a year, a Munsiff received £120. And examined by the Commons' Committee in the same year, Sir Erskine stated his opinions still more emphatically.

"I think as connected with the judicial service, in point of both intellectual and moral capacity, there is no judicial employment to which they might not attain. In the case of Zilla judges, where I was suggesting the employment of English barristers, I think it would be very advisable for the Native interests, and for the good government of India, that Natives should be associated with English judges in those posts. . . . I think the great instrument you have in your hands for securing good conduct in your Native officials is the same which you have applied to the English officials in India. By all accounts you have a very trustworthy English service throughout the country; you have obtained it by giving them very large remuneration; by applying the same principle to the Native employés you would secure exactly the same kind of service in my opinion."[2]

[1] Evidence of Sir E. Ryan and Sir E. Perry, Lords' First Report, 1853.
[2] Commons' First Report, 1853.

It is greatly to the credit of Sir Erskine Perry that, although he was merely a judicial officer in India, he could see beyond the precincts of law courts, and judge the character of the people by their ordinary transactions in their daily sphere of life. Immediately after the remarks which we have quoted above, we find Sir Erskine's views about the commercial integrity of the people of India.

"Their commercial integrity has always been very famous; it is quite remarkable what a principle of mercantile honour has prevailed among them, such as to give security to their paper from one end of India to the other; the sanctity of mercantile books was such that in the Native courts of justice, the production of the books was quite conclusive as to the veracity of any transaction in dispute."

And we are tempted here to quote the testimony of another Englishman, a contemporary of Sir Erskine Perry, who knew the people of India, not so often in law courts or in commercial offices, as in their village homes. The name of Colonel Sleeman is still remembered in India as a high and distinguished officer who travelled from province to province and from village to village to secure order, to repress crime, and to stamp out the criminals known as Thugs. "I have had before me," said Colonel Sleeman, "hundreds of cases in which a man's property, liberty, and life has depended on his telling a lie, and he has refused to tell it."[1] Few Englishmen, who have mixed with the people of India only in law courts and offices, will subscribe to this opinion; few of them who have known them in their village homes will deny it. For it is a simple truth, which every observer can verify for himself, that in their everyday life, in their family relations, as in their social and commercial transactions, the vast population of India are as simple and honest, faithful and truthful, as any nation on earth.

[1] *Rambles and Recollections of an Indian Official.*

Police Administration.

The least successful feature in British administration in India was, and is to this day, the Police. Frederick Halliday, who became soon after the first Lieutenant-Governor of Bengal, described the Police administration of India in his time at great length.

"The truth is, that the subordinate officers of the Police are generally very much underpaid, and being exposed to great temptations, are extremely corrupt. . . . Immediately under the Magistrate or Deputy Magistrate there is a Daroga or Thanadar who, till comparatively late years, was paid at the rate of 25 rupees (50s.) a month; he has large powers, and is stationed in the centre of a jurisdiction of 200 to 300 square miles. . . . Under the Daroga is an officer called the Muharrar or clerk, whose business it is to take down depositions in writing, and to keep the records belonging to the Police Station; he also undertakes precisely the same duties as the Daroga whenever the Daroga is not present, or when deputed by the Daroga to perform them; his salary is 8 rupees (16s.) a month. There is also a Jamadar, whose salary is 8 or 10 rupees (16s. or 20s.) a month, and who performs similar duties (except those of writing), subject to the directions of the Daroga; and there are some ten to twenty-five constables or Barkandazes, who receive from 4 to 5 rupees (8s. or 10s.) a month, and who, upon a pressure of business, are sometimes deputed alone to make investigations into occurrences under the orders of the Daroga. Below all these, who are paid officers of the Government, there are the watchmen of the village." Further on Halliday said: "I cannot say that crime is diminishing. It is diminishing in atrocity; for instance, Dacoities (robberies by gangs) in the Lower Provinces are as numerous as ever; in the immediate neighbourhood of Calcutta more numerous; but they are greatly diminished in cruelty and atrocity."[1]

Another witness, Robert Torrens, who had served as Magistrate, Judge, and Commissioner of Police in India, referred to the combination of the Police and Judicial duties in the same officer as a source of much evil.

Lord Harrowby.—The same man has to hunt out the crime and the criminal and to decide upon the crime afterwards?

Torrens.—He has.

Lord Harrowby.—That is objectionable, not only in theory, but found to be so in practice?

Torrens.—I think, highly so; in my experience it has been so.[2]

Village Communities.

It is somewhat remarkable that no British administrator of this period seriously endeavoured to improve the police and general administration of the country by accepting the co-operation of the people themselves and their Village Communities. India had been the earliest home of Village Communities, and for centuries and thousands of years these self-governing Communities had maintained order and peace, and settled disputes in villages, even when there was anarchy in the realm.

In Madras Province, it was reported as early as 1812, that "under this simple form of Municipal Government the inhabitants of the country have lived from time immemorial. . . . The inhabitants give themselves no trouble about the breaking up and divisions of kingdoms; while the village remains entire, they care not to what power it is transferred, or to what sovereign it devolves; its internal economy remains unchanged."[3]

[1] Lords' First Report, 1853.
[2] Lords' Third Report, 1853.
[3] Fifth Report, 1812, p. 85.

In the Province of Bombay, it was reported in 1819 that "these communities contain in miniature all the materials of a State within themselves, and are almost sufficient to protect their members if all other governments are withdrawn."[1]

And in Northern India, Sir Charles Metcalfe had stated in 1830 that "the Village Communities are little republics, having nearly everything they want within themselves. They seem to last where nothing else lasts. Dynasty after dynasty tumbles down, revolution succeeds to revolution, Hindu, Pathan, Moghal, Mahratta, Sikh, English, are masters in turn, but the Village Communities remain the same. . . . The union of the Village Communities, each one forming a separated little State in itself, has, I conceive, contributed more than any other cause to the preservation of the people of India through all revolutions and changes which they have suffered, and it is in a high degree conducive to their happiness, and to the enjoyment of a great portion of freedom and independence."[2]

It is a lamentable fact that these ancient and self-governing institutions have declined, and virtually disappeared, under the too centralised administration of British rulers. Some degree of trust in the leaders of the villages, some powers in revenue, criminal and police administration, and a careful and sympathetic supervision for the prevention of abuses, would have enabled these Communities to render good service to the present day. No system of successful self-government has been introduced after the old forms were effaced; no representatives of the village population help the administration of the present day; and an alien Government lacks that popular basis, that touch with the people, which Hindu and Mahomedan Governments wisely maintained through centuries.

[1] Elphinstone's "Report on the Territories conquered from the Peshwa," 1819.

[2] Sir Charles Metcalfe's Minute, dated November 7, 1830.

Education.

Western Education is perhaps the greatest of blessings India has gained under British Rule. It was not without much hesitation that the Directors of the East India Company consented to impart English education to the people of India. When in 1792, Wilberforce proposed to add two clauses to the Charter Act of that year for sending out schoolmasters to India, he encountered the greatest opposition in the Court of Proprietors, and the clauses were withdrawn. And the proposal gave rise to a memorable debate among the Directors.

"On that occasion, one of the Directors stated that we had just lost America from our folly in having allowed the establishment of schools and colleges, and that it would not do for us to repeat the same act of folly in regard to India; and if the Natives required anything in the way of education they must come to England for it."[1]

The only educational institutions, therefore, founded up to 1792, were a Mahomedan College founded by Warren Hastings at Calcutta in 1781, and a Sanscrit College founded by Lord Cornwallis at Benares in 1792. The objects of these institutions, however, were mainly to train law officers—Maulavis and Pandits—to help English judges in the judicial administration of the country. The disinclination to spread education among the people continued for twenty years more; and it was in 1813 that the British Parliament for the first time ordered a sum of £10,000 to be appropriated to the education of the people of India in the three Provinces. Nothing, however, was done to apply this fund for ten years more, *i.e.* till 1823.[2]

In the meantime, private enterprise had started English education in Bengal. "There were two persons who had to do with it; one was Mr. David Hare, and the

[1] J. C. Marshman's Evidence, Lords' Second Report, 1853.
[2] Sir Charles Trevelyan's Evidence, Lords Second Report, 1853.

other was a Native, Ram Mohan Roy. In the year 1815 they were in consultation one evening with a few friends, as to what should be done with a view to the elevation of the Native mind and character. Ram Mohan Roy's proposition was that they should establish an Assembly or Convocation, in which what are called the higher or purer dogmas of Vedantism or ancient Hinduism might be taught. . . . Mr. David Hare was a watchmaker in Calcutta, an ordinary illiterate man himself, but being a man of great energy and strong practical sense, he said, the plan should be to institute an English school or college for the instruction of Native youth. Accordingly he soon drew up and issued a circular on the subject, which gradually attracted the attention of the leading Europeans, and among others, of the Chief Justice, Sir Hyde East. Being led to consider the proposed measure, he entered heartily into it, and got a meeting of European gentlemen assembled in May 1816. He invited, also, some of the influential Natives to attend. Then it was unanimously agreed that they should commence an institution for the teaching of English to the children of the higher classes to be designated the Hindu College of Calcutta. A joint Committee of Europeans and Natives was appointed to carry the design into effect. In the beginning of 1817 the college, or rather school, was opened; and it was the very first English seminary in Bengal, or even in India, as far as I know.[2]

In 1832, *i.e.* ten years after the educational grant of £10,000 had been ordered by Parliament, the Bengal Government appointed a Committee of Public Instruction. The Committee established Mahomedan Colleges at Agra and Delhi with Sanscrit classes attached; and they also commenced an extensive system of printing Sanscrit and Arabic classics and translating European science into those languages. And the Committee made

1 Rev. Alexander Duff's Evidence, Lords' Second Report, 1853.

an annual grant to the Hindu College of Calcutta, which had been established six years before, and this assured its usefulness and success.[1]

Mountstuart Elphinstone was a friend of English education, and presided at a public meeting in Bombay in 1820, and a society for the promotion of education was formed. He obtained a grant of £5000 for this society for printing works and purchasing prizes, and all education in the vernacular languages was conducted during the next sixteen years through the agency of this society. An inquiry into the state of education in Bombay disclosed that in 1832 there were 1705 schools and 35,143 scholars in that province.[2]

Elphinstone's proposal to found a college at Bombay for the training of young civilians, with a department for the training of Indian officials, failed to obtain the sanction of the Directors of the East India Company. The first English school was opened in Bombay in 1828, the year after Elphinstone's departure; and the great Elphinstone Institution of Bombay was not opened till 1834.

In Madras, a few educational institutions supported by missionaries were in existence in 1828, but there were none supported by the Government. A Hindu named Pachiapa had left a large charity for religious uses; and Mr. Norton, Advocate-General of Madras, succeeded in collecting about £70,000 or £80,000 under his will. In 1839 a central educational institution was founded out of this money, and a Board of Indian Members was appointed for the management of the charity.[3] The Pachiapa College still continues to be one of the most flourishing and successful educational institutions in Madras.

An English college was established at Delhi through the exertions of Sir Charles Trevelyan.

[1] Sir Charles Trevelyan's Evidence, Lords' Second Report, 1853.
[2] J. S. Cotton's *Mounstuart Elphinstone and the Making of South Western India.*
[3] Norton's Evidence, Lords' Second Report, 1853.

The arrival of Macaulay in India gave a fresh impetus to English education. With his support and assistance Lord William Bentinck passed the famous Resolution of March 7, 1835, by which the English language was established as the language of superior education in India. The Committee of Public Instruction was enlarged; Macaulay was appointed its President; Sir Edward Ryan, Hay Cameron, and other members were added; and three distinguished Indian gentlemen of the time, Radha Kant Deb, Rosomoy Dutt, and Nawab Tahawar Jung, were also enrolled as members.[1]

The generous desire to foster English education in India was not, however, shared by all successors of Lord William Bentinck. Lord Ellenborough, who went out to India as Governor-General in 1842, was very mistrustful as to the effects of English education in India, and he attributes the same timid opinions to Dwarkanath Tagore, one of the foremost Indian publicists of the time.

"I recollect having had a visit from the late Dwarkanath Tagore, who was the most intelligent Native that ever appeared in this country, and one of the most intelligent in his own country. I had read in the newspaper that morning a speech which Dwarkanath Tagore had made on the subject of the education of the Natives of India; and when he called upon me, I said: 'I see you have been making a speech about education.' He said: 'Have they printed it?' I said: 'Yes, they print everything, but you and I know in this room we need not talk as if we were talking for publication, but we may say exactly what we think. You know that if these gentlemen who wish to educate the Natives of India were to succeed to the utmost extent of their desire, we should not remain in this country for three months.' He said: 'Not three weeks;' and perfectly true was his judgment."[2]

[1] Trevelyan's Evidence, Lords' Second Report, 1853.

[2] Lord Ellenborough's Evidence, Commons' Report of 1852.

Lord Ellenborough's successor, Lord Hardinge, was an abler administrator and a wiser statesman. He established a hundred schools in the different Districts of Bengal for imparting education in the vernacular, as a preliminary step to higher education in English. And he passed the famous Resolution for the selection of candidates for public employment from those who had been educated in the institutions established. Pandit Iswar Chandra Vidyasagar, the most distinguished educationist and literary man of his time, helped Lord Hardinge in making excellent selections.

Lastly came the famous Educational Despatch of 1854, which virtually accepted the system built up by Bentinck and Hardinge, and laid down rules for a system of education in the vernaculars of India, leading up to higher education in English. The principle is clearly enunciated in these words: "While the English language continues to be made use of, as by far the most perfect medium for the education of those persons who have acquired a sufficient knowledge of it to receive general instruction through it, the vernacular languages must be employed to the far larger class, who are ignorant of, or imperfectly acquainted with English." [1]

For the promotion of higher education in English the Despatch approved of the establishment of Universities in India. "The time has now arrived for the establishment of Universities in India, which may encourage a regular and liberal course of education by conferring academical degrees as evidences of attainment in the different branches of art and science, and by adding marks of honour for those who may desire to compete for honorary distinction. The Council of Education, in the proposal to which we have alluded, took the London University as their model; and we agree with them, that the form, government, and functions of that University, (copies of whose Charters and Regulations we enclose for

[1] Educational Despatch of July 19, 1854, paragraph 14.

your reference), are the best adapted to the wants of India, and may be followed with advantage, although some variation will be necessary in points of detail."[1]

Arrangements were made through grants in aid and in other ways, to impart education through the vernaculars to the generality of the people. And encouragement was also given to the indigenous schools for imparting elementary knowledge to the great mass of the people.[2]

The Universities of Calcutta, Madras, and Bombay were founded accordingly by Lord Canning; and the system sketched out in this famous Despatch is the system which is pursued in India to the present day. Universities have since been founded at Allahabad and Lahore; and over four million boys were attending educational institutions in British India in the last year of Queen Victoria's reign.

Elementary Education.

Most of the four million boys who attend schools in British India at the present day only receive an elementary education in reading, writing, and arithmetic; and this elementary education was not originated by British administrators, but is indigenous in India. Sir Thomas Munro and Mountstuart Elphinstone reported, after inquiries made early in the nineteenth century, that elementary education had been much more diffused in India from time immemorial than it had been in Europe; and that Indian boys, attending their indigenous schools, showed great powers of mental calculation in simple arithmetic.[3] The Brahmans and the upper classes of India considered it a part of their religious duty to give some education to their children, and the classes engaged

[1] Educational Despatch of July 19, 1854, paragraphs 24 and 25.
[2] *Ibid.*, paragraphs 41 and 46.
[3] Sir Erskine Perry's Evidence, Lords' Second Report, 1853.

in trades and commerce trained their boys in letters and in accounts, to befit them for their hereditary duties. British administration has recognised, helped, and subsidised this ancient system of elementary education; but the help given is still inadequate. One of the most pressing wants of the present day is a more liberal help to village primary schools and a wider extension of primary education to cultivating classes, so that every cultivator and labourer in India may find it possible to learn reading, writing, and arithmetic in his own village at a nominal cost. Sir Erskine Perry complained of the smallness of grant in 1853, and pointed out that with such an inadequate grant the Government could not "place schools in every village." The educational grant continues to be inadequate to the present day, and the duty to "place schools in every village" remains still unfulfilled.[1]

Female Education.

The education of girls has not kept pace with the education of boys, if it be judged by the test of attendance in schools. In a country where girls are generally married between the age of ten and fourteen, they seldom attended schools in olden times, and can do so only in very small numbers at the present time; their education must be largely carried on by a system of tuition at home. Drinkwater Bethune, Legal Member of the Governor-General's Council, made a very praiseworthy and successful endeavour to start a girls' school in Calcutta, to which he devoted £10,000 from his own personal funds;[2] and Bethune School is to this day the most successful institution for girls in India, and teaches up to the highest standard of University

[1] The total educational grant for the whole of British India with its population of 230 millions was a little over a million sterling in the last year of Queen Victoria's reign. Out of this £664,000 came from Government funds, and £484,000 from local and municipal funds.

[2] Marshman's Evidence, Commons' Sixth Report, 1853.

Examinations. The Indian Universities, following the example of the London University, bestow degrees on women, and lady graduates take their degrees in Calcutta, Madras, and Bombay. In Primary Schools little boys and girls are often taught together, and the total number of girls attending schools in the last year of Queen Victoria's reign in British India was somewhat under half a million.

As has been said before, this figure is not a correct index to the spread of female education in India. Girls and girl-wives, belonging to the upper classes, generally receive education at home. And among the lower and unlettered classes, women receive instruction in religious truths and moral duties and in their national traditions and literature, to a much larger extent than in Europe. It may be safely asserted that the mind of the unlettered Indian woman in her village home is at least as well instructed in her religion, as well informed in her national traditions and literature, as the mind of the poor European woman who knows her Bible, and reads occasional stories in penny magazines.

Public Press.

A large mass of correspondence between the Court of Directors and the Indian Government, which was published in 1858 as a Return to an Order of the House of Commons, enables us to trace the interesting history of the Public Press in India.

As early as 1791, under the administration of Lord Cornwallis, one William Duane was arrested by the Bengal Government for deportation to Europe for writing an offensive paragraph in *The Bengal Journal*. The Supreme Court held that the Government was within its rights; William Duane was warned and released; but he repeated his attack in *The World*, and was sent to Europe in 1794.

Notices were taken of other attacks in subsequent years, and in 1799 some regulations were passed by the Government of Lord Wellesley to keep the Press in order. No paper was to be published until it had been previously inspected by a Government Official. And the penalty for offending against this and other rules framed was "immediate embarkation for Europe"! The regulations were approved by the Court of Directors.

Many editors were censured for objectionable articles and paragraphs between 1801 and 1818, and many offending writers were compelled to apologise to the Government. New and milder Regulations were passed in 1818 by the Government of the Marquis of Hastings. But editors were still prohibited from publishing "animadversions" on public measures, "discussions" tending to alarm the Native population, as well as "private scandal and personal remarks" tending to excite dissension.

For a number of years after these Regulations were passed, the Government took notice of offensive writings in numerous instances; and Lieutenant-Colonel Robinson was ordered by the Commander-in-Chief to a court-martial in 1822 for writing a violent letter to the Government, in defence of what he had written in the *Calcutta Journal* under the anonymous title, "A Military Friend."

In Madras and Bombay also, notice was frequently taken of writings in the Press.

"A free Press," said the Directors in 1823, "is a fit associate and necessary appendage of a representative constitution. Wherever a Government emanates from the people, and is responsible to them, the people must necessarily have the privilege of discussing the measures of the Government; and whenever the people choose representatives to make laws affecting their persons and property, the right of animadverting on the mode in which this trust is discharged belongs, of course, to the party delegating it. But in no sense of the terms can the Government of India be called a free, a representative, or a popular Government; the people had no voice in its establishment, nor have they any control over its acts."

"The Governments in India exercise a delegated authority, derived from the Court of Directors and the Board of Control. The Government of India resides in this country [England], and is, of course, responsible to the English public, in common with the Government of England. It is in this country, therefore, and not in India, that its measures ought to be discussed."[1]

Such was the opinion held by the Directors in 1823 with regard to the Public Press of India. It must be stated, however, that what was known as the Public Press of India then, was the Press of the small European community in India. It neither represented nor defended the interests of the people; and the people of India had no Press of their own of any influence, at that time or for thirty years after. And thus it happened that, when Lord William Bentinck strove for the advancement of the people of India, and employed them in responsible offices under the Company, he was attacked by the Press of India as no Governor-General has since been attacked.

Lord William's principal adviser, Macaulay, shared a similar fate; and he refers to the Public Press of India of his time in these memorable words: "That public opinion means the opinion of five hundred persons who have no interest, feeling, or taste in common with the fifty millions among whom they live; that the love of liberty means the strong objection which the five hundred feel to every measure which can prevent them from acting as they choose towards the fifty million."[2]

[1] Letter from the Chairman and Deputy Chairman of the East India Company to the Right Hon. C. W. W. Wynn, dated January 17, 1823.

[2] Trevelyan's *Life and Letters of Lord Macaulay*. John Stuart Mill expressed a similar opinion of the English Press in India as late as 1852. In his evidence before the Lords' Committee he said: "As long as the great mass of India have very little access to the Press, it is in danger of being an organ exclusively of individual interests. The English newspaper Press in India is the organ only of the English society, and chiefly that part of it unconnected with the Government. It has little to do with the Natives and with the great interests of India."

Lord William Bentinck's successor, Sir Charles Metcalfe, signalised his short administration by giving liberty to the Press, such as it was, in 1835. This truly liberal and bold measure gave violent offence to the Directors of the East India Company. They wrote:—

"This proceeding is in opposition to all our previous orders, to the solemn decisions both of the Supreme Court at Calcutta and of His Majesty's Privy Council, delivered, in both cases, after full arguments on both sides of the question, to the recorded opinions of all preceding Governments of Bengal, Madras and Bombay."

"We are compelled to observe that this proceeding must be considered the more unjustifiable, inasmuch as it has been adopted by a Government only provisional."

"We should then be prepared at once to avail ourselves of the power entrusted to us by Act of Parliament, and disallow your new law when passed, were we not aware that the immediate repeal cf such a law, however ill-advised and uncalled for its enactment may have been, might be productive of mischievous results. We shall therefore wait for the deliberate advice of the Governor-General in Council after the arrival of Lord Auckland, your present Governor-General, before we communicate to you our final decision. But you are in possession of our sentiments, and we shall not be sorry to find, that by returning to the former system you have rendered our interference unnecessary."[1]

Fortunately, Sir Charles Metcalfe was not the man to be moved from his convictions by the "sentiments" of the Directors, and not likely to return to the former system on account of their threats. And when Lord Auckland came to India two years after, people both in England and in India had already been reconciled to the liberty of the Press, and the good work of Metcalfe was not undone.

[1] Letter dated February 1, 1836.

Twenty years after, during the troubles of the Indian Mutiny, it was considered necessary to warn one English newspaper,[1] for articles likely to inflame the minds of the people; and three Indian newspapers were prosecuted. The publishers of two of them[2] were discharged on their expressing their regret and entering into recognizances. The publisher of the third[3] was found not guilty and acquitted. Some restraints which were then placed on the Press were subsequently withdrawn.

1 *The Friend of India.* 2 *Durbeen* and the *Sultan-ul-Akhbar.*
3 *Samachar Sudha Barshan.*

CHAPTER XIII

INDIAN FINANCE. GENESIS OF THE INDIAN DEBT

THE evidence recorded by the Parliamentary Committees, from which we have made large extracts in the preceding chapter, was placed before the public in 1852 and 1853. The inquiry into the administration of Indian affairs by the East India Company was thorough and complete. There was a strong opinion, specially among the merchants and manufacturers of Great Britain, that the Crown should assume the direct administration of India. Ministers of the Crown, who had so often made war and peace in India without consulting the Directors, were nothing loth to assume direct management of Indian affairs. Nevertheless, the nation felt some hesitation in setting aside a Company which had built up the Indian Empire for them. Accordingly a compromise was effected.

The Company's Charter was once more renewed; but the Act of 1853 did not fix any definite term for the renewed Charter. It declared, simply, that the Indian territories should remain under the Company in trust for the Crown until the Parliament should otherwise direct. The number of Directors was reduced from twenty-four to eighteen, and the Crown assumed the power of appointing six out of these eighteen Directors. And the Board of Control retained its power of control.

Other changes were made by the new Charter Act. It authorised the appointment of a Governor or a Lieutenant-Governor for Bengal. That Province, which had so long been ruled by the Governor-General himself, had its first Lieutenant-Governor in 1854. The Act also authorised the formation of another Presidency or Lieutenant-Governorship. Accordingly the Punjab was placed under a Lieutenant-Governor in 1859. Among the other important changes, effected by this Act, we may mention that the Council of the Governor-General was enlarged for legislative purposes by the addition of Legislative Members. And the right of patronage to Indian appointments was taken away from the Court of Directors. It was henceforth to be exercised according to regulations framed by the Board of Control, and these regulations threw open the Civil Service of India to general competition.

With these changes, some of which curtailed the powers of the Company and added to the influence of the Crown, the Double Government which had been so strongly supported by John Stuart Mill was continued. It lasted for a few years longer, until the Indian Mutiny gave the British nation and the British Parliament a suitable occasion and an ostensible reason for setting aside the Company altogether. In closing our account of the Company's rule in India, we shall, in the present chapter, briefly review their financial administration.

The figures showing the revenues and expenditure of India, during the twenty-one years which elapsed from the accession of Queen Victoria to the abolition of the East India Company, are an interesting study, as they faithfully reflect the political history of the period. The following statement has been compiled from official records.[1] They will show the proportion of the total revenues which was derived from the Land Tax, and the proportion of the total expenditure which was incurred in England as Home Charges.

[1] The figures for the first two years have been obtained from a Return to an Order of the House of Commons, ordered to be printed June 22, 1855, and from the Commons' Committee's Report of 1852, Appendix 12. The figures for the other years have been taken from the Statistical Abstract relating to British India, 1840 to 1865, presented to both Houses of Parliament.

Year.	Land Revenue.	Gross Revenue.	Expenditure in England.	Gross Expenditure.
	£	£	£	£
1837-38 . .	11,853,975[1]	20,858,820	2,304,445	19,857,970[2]
1838-39 . .	12,303,200	21,158,099	2,615,465	21,306,232
1839-40 . .	12,273,982	20,124,038	2,578,966	22,228,011
1840-41 . .	12,313,840	20,851,073	2,625,776	22,546,430
1841-42 . .	12,154,587	21,837,823	2,834,786	23,534,446
1842-43 . .	13,322,880	22,616,487	2,458,193	23,888,526
1843-44 . .	13,228,850	23,586,573	2,944,073	24,925,371
1844-45 . .	13,224,054	23,666,246	2,485,212	24,293,647
1845-46 . .	13,386,517	24,270,608	3,044,067	25,662,738
1846-47 . .	13,995,717	26,084,681	3,066,635	26,916,188
1847-48 . .	14,437,254	24,908,302	3,016,072	26,746,474
1848-49 . .	14,274,270	25,396,386	3,012,908	26,766,848
1849-50 . .	15,248,694	27,522,344	2,750,937	26,960,988
1850-51 . .	15,382,442	27,625,360	2,717,186	27,000,624
1851-52 . .	15,391,664	27,832,237	2,506,377	27,098,462
1852-53 . .	15,365,250	28,609,109	2,697,488	27,976,735
1853-54 . .	15,838,649	28,277,530	3,262,289	30,240,435
1854-55 . .	16,419,031	29,133,050	3,011,735	30,753,456
1855-56 . .	17,109,971	30,817,528	3,264,629	31,637,530
1856-57 . .	17,722,170	31,691,015	3,529,673	31,608,875
1857-58 . .	15,317,911	31,706,776	6,162,043	41,240,571

It will be seen from these figures that in the first year of Queen Victoria's reign India showed a surplus, even after paying over two millions as Home Charges. This was due to the careful administration of Lord William Bentinck, and to the reforms and retrenchment effected by him and his successor, Sir Charles Metcalfe. But Lord Auckland arrived in India in 1838, and initiated the ambitious policy dictated by Lord Palmerston. And from that year India lost her surplus and showed a deficit, which continued under the administration of his successor, Lord Ellenborough.

The Sikh wars of the two next Governors-General, Hardinge and Dalhousie, made matters worse; and it was not until the conclusion of the last Sikh War, and

[1] Adding to this sum the revenues from Excise, Sayer, and Mutarpha, the total comes to £12,671,743, as shown in *The Economic History of British India* (1757–1837), p. 405.

[2] Deducting from this sum the expenditure incurred in England, the gross expenditure in India comes to £17,553,525, as shown in *The Economic History of British India* (1757–1837), p. 405.

the annexation of the rich province of the Punjab, that India once more showed a surplus in 1849–50. But the young Imperialist who ruled the destinies of India soon lost the surplus. Before the close of Dalhousie's administration the gross expenditure of India went up by leaps and bounds to over thirty millions in 1853–54; and in spite of Dalhousie's annexations of Nagpur and other rich states, India continued to show a deficit up to the year of his departure, 1855–56.

Lord Canning showed a surplus in the first year of his administration, owing mainly to the annexation of Oudh, which had been effected immediately before his arrival. But the surplus was changed into a heavy deficit of ten millions in 1857–58, the year of the Indian Mutiny.

Another interesting but melancholy fact which we learn from the foregoing table is the steady increase of the expenditure in England—the Home Charges. Great Britain and India were equally gainers by the establishment and maintenance of the British Empire in India, and the cost of the Empire should have been shared by the two countries. And it would have been an act of strict justice if India had been charged nine-tenths of that cost incurred in India, and England had paid the remaining one-tenth, which was then incurred in England. But the sword of the conqueror is thrown into the scale to-day as it was in the days of Brennus; and financial arrangements are never dictated by strict justice between a subject and a ruling race. To India the annual Economic Drain was a pure loss; the money flowed out of the country never to return again; it went from a poor country to fructify the trades and industries of a rich country.

"With reference to its economical effects upon the condition of India," wrote a distinguished officer whose meritorious work in India we have reviewed in Chapter V. of this book, "the tribute paid to Great Britain is by far the most objectionable feature in our existing policy. Taxes spent in the country from which they are raised are totally different in their effects from taxes raised in one country and spent in another. In the former case the taxes collected from the population at large are paid away to the portion of the population engaged in the service of Government, through whose expenditure they are again returned to the industrial classes. They occasion a different distribution, but no loss of national income."

"But the case is wholly different when the taxes are not spent in the country from which they are raised. In this case they constitute no mere transfer of a portion of the national income from one set of citizens to another, but an absolute loss and extinction of the whole amount withdrawn from the taxed country. As regards its effects on national production, the whole amount might as well be thrown into the sea as transferred to another country."

"The Indian tribute, whether weighed in the scales of justice or viewed in the light of our true interest, will be found to be at variance with humanity, with common sense, and with the received maxims of economical science. It would be true wisdom, then, to provide for the future payment of such of the Home Charges of the Indian Government, as really form the tribute, out of the Imperial Exchequer. These charges would probably be found to be the dividends on East India stock, interest on Home Debt, the salaries of officers and establishments and cost of buildings connected with the Home Department of the Indian Government, furlough and retired pay to members of the Indian Military and Civil Services when at home, charges of all descriptions paid in this country connected with British troops serving in India, and a portion of the cost of transporting British troops to and from India." [1]

In another work,[2] tracing the rise and consolidation

[1] *Our Financial Relations with India*, by Major Wingate. London, 1859.

[2] *Economic History of British India* (1757 to 1837), pp. 46, 69, 113, 291, and 408.

of the British Empire in India down to the accession of Queen Victoria, we have seen that the total revenues of India, from the commencement of the British rule down to 1837, exceeded the total expenditure incurred in India, in spite of the high pay of British officials and the wasteful expenditure of Indian wars. The figures which we have given in the present chapter show a similar excess of the income over the expenditure incurred in India during the first twenty-one years of the Queen's reign from 1837 to 1858. Therefore, if India had been relieved of Home Charges from the commencement of British rule, India would have had no Public Debt when she was transferred from the Company to the Crown in 1858, but a large balance in her favour. The whole of the Public Debt of India, built up in a century of the Company's rule, was created by debiting India with the expenses incurred in England, which in fairness and equity was not due from India. If the financial relations between India and Great Britain during the century had been referred to an impartial judicial tribunal, there can be little doubt what the verdict of that tribunal would have been. Great Britain had gained far more from India than was represented by the Home Charges; Great Britain should in equity and fairness have borne those charges; and India morally and justly had no Public Debt in 1858, but, on the contrary, could claim credit for excess payments made.

In justice, however, to the East India Company, it should be stated that the Home Charges under their administration was comparatively small, and was a little over one-tenth of the annual revenues of India. In the twenty years preceding the Mutiny the revenues rose from twenty millions to thirty-one millions, and the Home Charges rose from two and a half millions to three and a half millions. One of the saddest results of the administration of India under the Crown is that the Home Charges have been permitted to increase by leaps and bounds, not only absolutely, but relatively to the revenues, the Crown Government being irresponsible. The result justifies the opinion of John Stuart Mill, quoted in the last chapter, that the administration of India through a Secretary of State and his Council "would be the most complete despotism that could possibly exist" under British rule.

The total Indian Debt, bearing interest, was little over 7 millions in 1792, and had risen to 10 millions in 1799. Then followed Lord Wellesley's wars, and the Indian Debt rose to 21 millions in 1805, and stood at 27 millions in 1807. It remained almost stationary at this figure for many years, but had risen to 30 millions in 1829, the year after Lord William Bentinck's arrival in India. That able and careful administrator was the only Governor-General under the East India Company who made a substantial reduction in the Public Debt of India, and on the 30th April 1836 the Indian Debt was £26,947,434.[1]

The following table shows the Public Debt of India for twenty-one years, from the year of Queen Victoria's accession to the abolition of the East India Company. The figures have been compiled from official records.[2]

The increase of 2½ millions in the total Debt in 1839–40, shown in the table, was not a real one;

[1] This was the "Registered Debt." Besides this, there were Treasury Notes and Deposits, making the total "Indian Debt," £29,832,299. Add to this the "Home Bond Debt," and the total Debt of India on April 30, 1836, was £33,355,536.

[2] The Commons' Committee's Report of 1852, Appendix 2, gives figures for seventeen years, from 1833–34 to 1849–50. The Statistical Abstract gives figures for twenty-six years, 1839–40 to 1864–65. For ten years, therefore, 1839–40 to 1849–50, we have figures in both the records, but the figures do not agree. The total debt for 1839–40, for instance, according to the Commons' Report, was £32,438,078, while according to the Statistical Abstract, it was £34,484,997. Some portion of the total debt must have been left out in the table given in the Commons' Report, Appendix 2. I have taken my figures for two years only from the Commons' Report, *i.e.* for 1837–38 and 1838–39, as the Statistical Abstract gives no figures for those years. For the remaining nineteen years, 1839–40 to 1857–58, I have taken my figures from the Statistical Abstract, as being the more correct record of the total debt of India.

Year.	Indian Debt.	Debt in England.	Total.
	£	£	£
1837–38 . . .	30,249,893	3,522,825	33,772,718
1838–39 . . .	30,231,162	1,734,300	31,965,462
1839–40 . . .	32,750,697	1,734,300	34,484,997
1840–41 . . .	34,187,827	1,734,300	35,922,127
1841–42 . . .	36,670,173	1,734,300	38,404,473
1842–43 . . .	38,744,340	1,734,300	40,478,640
1843–44 . . .	40,149,151	1,734,300	41,883,451
1844–45 . . .	41,203,150	2,299,600	43,502,750
1845–46 . . .	41,592,249	2,299,600	43,891,849
1846–47 . . .	44,584,625	2,299,600	46,884,225
1847–48 . . .	45,957,613	2,799,600	48,757,213
1848–49 . . .	47,151,018	3,899,500	51,050,518
1849–50 . . .	50,035,268	3,899,500	53,934,768
1850–51 . . .	51,109,815	3,899,500	55,099,315
1851–52 . . .	51,215,193	3,899,500	55,114,693
1852–53 . . .	52,313,094	3,920,592	56,233,686
1853–54 . . .	49,762,876	3,920,592	53,683,468
1854–55 . . .	51,615,528	3,915,592	55,531,120
1855–56 . . .	53,848,922	3,915,317	57,764,239
1856–57 . . .	55,546,652	3,915,317	59,461,969
1857–58 . . .	60,704,084	8,769,400	69,473,484

the apparent rise is simply due to two different systems of keeping the accounts followed in the two records from which the figures have been taken, as has been explained in the footnote. But from 1840–41 Lord Auckland's unfortunate Afghan War began to tell on the finances of India, and the total Debt of India rose from 34½ millions to 43½ millions by 1844–45. The East India Company were not alone in protesting against the expenses of the Afghan War being thrown on the finances of India; there were many members of the House of Commons who agreed with John Bright when he said: "Last year I referred to the enormous expense of the Afghan War—about 15 millions sterling—the whole of which ought to have been thrown on the taxation of the people of England, because it was a war commanded by the English Cabinet, for objects supposed to be English."[1]

The annexation of Sindh by Lord Ellenborough, and

[1] John Bright's speech made on August 1, 1859.

the Sikh Wars of Lord Hardinge and Lord Dalhousie brought fresh liabilities, and the total Debt of India rose to 55 millions by 1850–51. There was a fluctuation after this, and endeavours were made to reduce the Debt, but it rose in the last year of Lord Dalhousie's administration to 59½ millions. The Mutiny which occurred in 1857 raised the Debt in one year by 10 millions, so that on April 30, 1858, the total Debt of India stood at 69½ millions sterling.

If ever there was a case of justifiable rebellion in the world, says an impartial historian,[1] it was the rebellion of Hindu and Mussulman soldiers in India against the abomination of cartridges greased with the fat of the cow and the pig. The blunder was made by British Administrators, but India paid the cost. Before this, the Indian Army had been employed in China and in Afghanistan; and the East India Company had received no payments for the service of Indian troops outside the frontiers of their dominions. But when British troops were sent to India to suppress the Mutiny, England exacted the cost with almost unexampled rigour.

"The entire cost of the Colonial Office, or, in other words, of the Home Government of all British colonies and dependencies except India, as well as of their military and naval expense, is defrayed from the revenues of the United Kingdom; and it seems to be a natural inference that similar charges should be borne by this country in the case of India. But what is the fact? Not a shilling from the revenues of Britain has ever been expended on the military defence of our Indian Empire."

"How strange that a nation, ordinarily liberal to extravagance in aiding colonial dependencies and foreign states with money in their time of need, should, with unwonted and incomprehensible penuriousness, refuse to help its own great Indian Empire in its extremity of financial distress."

[1] Lecky's *Map of Life*.

"The worst, however, is not yet told; for it would appear that when extra regiments are despatched to India, as happened during the late disturbances there, the pay of such troops for six months previous to sailing is charged against the Indian Revenues, and recovered as a debt due by the Government of India to the British army pay-office."

"In the crisis of the Indian Mutiny, then, and with the Indian finances reduced to an almost desperate condition, Great Britain has not only required India to pay for the whole of the extra regiments sent to that country, from the date of their leaving these shores, but has demanded back the money disbursed on account of these regiments for the last six months' service in this country previous to sailing for India."[1]

But a greater man than Sir George Wingate spoke on the subject of the Mutiny expenditure in his own frank and fearless manner. "I think," said John Bright, "that the 40 millions which the revolt will cost, is a grievous burden to place upon the people of India. It has come from the mismanagement of the Parliament and the people of England. If every man had what was just, no doubt that 40 millions would have to be paid out of the taxes levied upon the people of this country."[2]

We make these extracts and mention these facts, not to recall an almost forgotten controversy, but simply with the object of clearly explaining the genesis of the Indian Debt. The popular impression is that the Indian Debt arose out of capital spent by England for the conquest and administration of India, and for the development of her resources. The facts explained in the present chapter will show that that was not the genesis of the Indian Debt up to 1858. India had paid for her own conquest and her own administration; and what little English gold had found its way to India down to the last year of the

[1] *Our Financial Relations with India*, by Major Wingate. London, 1859.
[2] John Bright's speech on East India Loan, March 1859.

Company's rule was an insignificant portion of the tribute India had paid for a century. It is impossible to calculate even approximately what this payment amounted to. Sir George Wingate reckons it at 100 millions from the beginning of the nineteenth century down to 1858, without calculating interest. Montgomery Martin reckons it at over 700 millions during the first thirty years of the century, calculating compound interest at Indian rate of 12 per cent. And these calculations exclude the sums remitted from India in the eighteenth century.

It was this tribute, exacted as Home Charges, which was the genesis of India's debt. India paid for her own administration; paid also for the frequent wars of conquest and annexation in India. But she could not pay the full tribute demanded over and above these local expenses. Deficit occurred year after year, and thus a Debt was piled up which amounted to sixty millions when Lord Dalhousie left India. And the first year of the Mutiny expenses brought it up to seventy millions when the East India Company was abolished.

The fresh charges which were thrown on India, owing to the transfer of the Government, will be described in the next chapter. The Empire of India was purchased by the Crown from the Company, but the people of India were charged with the purchase money. The value received by the shareholders of the Company's stock was not paid by the British Crown which won an imperial property, but was added to the Indian Debt.

Would England at least guarantee this Debt thus accumulated? That would reduce the annual interest on the Debt by over a million sterling, and would so far relieve the tax-payers of India. Lord Stanley, afterwards Lord Derby, cautiously suggested it in 1859.

"I am aware the uniform policy of the Parliament and the Government of this country has been to decline all responsibility in regard to the Debt of India, which has been held to be a charge only on the Indian Exchequer. Dealing with the present state of affairs I may say at once that I am not going to recommend any change in that policy. I know well the alarm which any such proposition would create, and I know the refusal which it would inevitably receive. But this is a question which will recur again and again, and which will have to be considered in the future as well as in the present."

"I would likewise ask the House to bear in mind that if ever the time should come when the established policy in this respect should undergo a change, and when a national guarantee should be given for these liabilities, that guarantee would operate to reduce the interest paid upon the Indian Debt by no less than £750,000, or even £1,000,000, which, formed into a sinking fund, would go far to pay off the whole."[1]

Six months after it was John Bright himself who opposed the idea of giving an Imperial guarantee to the Indian Debt. And his reasons were characteristic.

"I do not oppose an Imperial guarantee because I particularly sympathise with the English tax-payers in this matter. I think the English tax-payers have generally neglected all the affairs of India, and might be left to pay for it. . . . But I object to an Imperial guarantee on this ground—if we left the Services of India, after exhausting the resources of India, to put their hands into the pockets of the English people, the people of England having no control over Indian expenditure, it is impossible to say to what lengths of unimagined extravagance they would not go; and in endeavouring to save India may we not go far towards ruining England?"[2]

Even John Bright did not see that the people of England would have very soon ceased to neglect the affairs of India, and would have obtained a real control over Indian expenditure, if some share of the liability of the Indian Debt had been thrown on them.

[1] Lord Stanley's speech on East India Loan, February 1859.
[2] John Bright's speech, August 1, 1859.

CHAPTER XIV

END OF THE COMPANY'S RULE

"My parting hope and prayer for India is, that, in all time to come, these reports from the Presidencies and Provinces under our rule may form, in each successive year, a happy record of peace, prosperity, and progress." With this pious wish Lord Dalhousie had concluded the memorable review of his eight years' administration of India before he sailed for England.

"We must not forget that in the sky of India, serene as it is, a small cloud may arise, at first no bigger than a man's hand, but which, growing bigger and bigger, may at last threaten to overwhelm us with ruin." With these almost prophetic words Lord Canning had replied to the Court of Directors at a parting banquet in London, before he sailed for India.

Lord Dalhousie's bright picture of peace, prosperity, and progress was destined to be obscured for a time; Lord Canning's fears of a dark cloud threatening to overwhelm the Empire were destined to prove a true prophecy.

The causes of the Indian Mutiny of 1857 are no longer hidden in obscurity. "As a body," wrote John Lawrence, "the native army did really believe that the universal introduction of cartridges destructive to their caste was only a matter of time . . . such truly was the origin of the Mutiny.[1] And we know now from the equally high authority of Lord Roberts[2] that the belief of the native army was not altogether unfounded, and

[1] Letter on the trial of the King of Delhi, dated April 29, 1858.
[2] *Forty-one Years in India.*

that the cartridges introduced were greased with the fat of the pig and the cow.

It is also beyond a doubt that political reasons helped a mere mutiny of soldiers to spread among large classes of the people in Northern and Central India, and converted it into a political insurrection. Lord Dalhousie's vast and rapid annexations had created an impression in India that the East India Company aimed at universal conquest; that they disregarded treaties and the laws of the country in order to compass their object. The minds of the people were unsettled; and leaders of the insurrection issued Proclamations dwelling on the bad-faith and the earth-hunger of the alien rulers. In Jhansi State, which had been annexed by Lord Dalhousie, the Dowager Rani was the life and soul of the insurrection, fought in male attire against British troops, and died on the field of battle. In Oudh, which had also been annexed by the same ruler, vast masses of the population gathered round the mutinous soldiers, and made their deposed king's cause their own.

It is not within the scope of the present work to narrate the thrilling incidents of that eventful war, which have been told by Sir John Kaye and Malleson in their great work, and have also been described in more recent and smaller works of great merit. The heroism of the small band of Englishmen who stood at Lucknow against surging masses of insurgents, and the tragic death of that truest and best of English soldiers, Henry Lawrence, "who tried to do his duty"; the unflinching courage with which a handful of warriors held their ground through weary months on the historic ridge of Delhi, until the master hand of John Lawrence denuded the Punjab to deal that memorable blow which decided the fate of the Empire; the rapid and successful march through Central India, and the prolonged and arduous operations in Rohilkhand and Oudh; all these are portions of English history and have been woven into English literature. The Poet-

Laureate of the Victorian Age has sung of Lucknow in lines which will never be forgotten; and popular writers of the present day tell the heroic story of John Nicholson and the capture of Delhi.

Still less is it within the scope of this book to dwell on the darker incidents of the Mutiny; and Englishmen as well as Indians sincerely wish that those incidents could be expunged altogether from history, at least as recorded in school books meant for boys. Wars there have been in India since the days of Clive and Wellington; but never has there been a war stained, on one side as on the other, by such wanton cruelty and crime as in 1857. The mutineers, rising as they believed in defence of their caste and religion, disgraced and blackened their cause by the inhuman, brutal, and barbarous massacre of defenceless women and children. On the other hand, British troops burnt down villages along their route of many hundreds of miles, turning the country into a "desert"; British conquerors massacred the inhabitants of Delhi after the mutineers had escaped; and British Special Commissioners executed thousands of citizens in Northern India, guiltless of the Mutiny. In the words of a living historian, "the contest seemed to lie between two savage races, capable of no thought but that, regardless of all justice or mercy, their enemies should be exterminated. Deeds of cruelty on one side and on the other were perpetrated, over which it is necessary to draw a veil."[1]

None felt the horror of these proceedings in India more than Lord Canning; none deplored them in England more than the Queen. "There is a rabid and indiscriminate vindictiveness abroad," wrote Lord Canning to the Queen, "even amongst many who ought to set a

[1] Rev. Dr. Frank Bright's *History of England*, period IV. (1893), p. 328. See also Return ordered by the House of Commons to be printed, February 4, 1858; Montgomery Martin's *History of the Mutiny of the Sepoy Troops in 1857*; Bosworth Smith's *Life of Lord Lawrence* (1885), vol. ii., chapters iv. and v.; Sir Charles Aitchison's *Lord Lawrence*, and other works dealing specially with the Mutiny transactions.

better example, which it is impossible to contemplate without a feeling of shame for one's countrymen." "Lord Canning will easily believe," replied the Queen, "how entirely the Queen shares his feelings of sorrow and indignation at the unchristian spirit shown also to a great extent here by the public towards India in general."[1]

The rule of the East India Company was doomed. The British nation had already made up their minds on the subject, and the Indian Mutiny gave them a suitable occasion. Lord Palmerston had become Prime Minister in 1855, and had concluded the Crimean War with his accustomed vigour. His Government had returned with a larger majority after the general election of 1857; and in the same year he intimated to the Chairman of the East India Company that it was the intention of the Government to propose to Parliament a Bill for placing the Government of India under the direct authority of the Crown.

Ross Mangles, then Chairman of the East India Company, and the Deputy Chairman, Sir Frederick Currie, replied on December 31, 1857. They expressed the surprise of the Court that her Majesty's Government, without imputing to the Company any blame in connection with the Mutiny, and without instituting any inquiry by Parliament, intended to propose the immediate suppression of the Company. They held that "an intermediate, non-political, and perfectly independent body," like the Company, was an indispensable necessity for good government in India. And they could not see how it was possible to form such a body if the Members of the new Government were to be nominated by the Crown.[2]

The Company also submitted a formal petition, drawn up by the clear-sighted John Stuart Mill, to the House of Commons and the House of Lords. The document, pro-

[1] *Life of the Prince Consort*, vol. iv. page 146.

[2] Return to an order of the House of Lords, ordered to be printed February 22, 1858.

ceeding from the pen of a writer so thoughtful and philosophical, interests us to the present day, and one or two passages deserve to be quoted.

Referring to the Double Government carried on by the Directors of the Company, and by a Minister of her Majesty's Government presiding over the Board of Control, John Stuart Mill urged with reason: "That, under these circumstances, if the administration had been a failure, it would, your petitioners submit, have been somewhat unreasonable to expect that a remedy would be found in annihilating the branch of the ruling authority which could not be the one principally at fault, and might be altogether blameless, in order to concentrate all powers in the branch which had necessarily the decisive share in every error, real or supposed. To believe that the administration of India would have been more free from error, had it been conducted by a Minister of the Crown without the aid of the Court of Directors, would be to believe that the Minister, with full power to govern India as he pleased, has governed ill, because he had the assistance of experienced and responsible advisers."

With reference to the proposed Council of the Secretary of State for India, he urged: "That your petitioners cannot well conceive a worse form of government for India than a Minister with a Council whom he should be at liberty to consult or not at his pleasure. . . . That any body of persons, associated with the Minister, which is not a check, will be a screen. . . . That your petitioners find it difficult to conceive that the same independence in judgment and act, which characterises the Court of Directors, will be found in any Council all of whose members are nominated by the Crown. . . . That your petitioners are equally unable to perceive how, if the controlling body is entirely nominated by the Minister, that happy independence of Parliamentary party influence, which has hitherto distinguished the administration of India and the appointment to situations of trust and importance in that country, can be expected to continue."

And lastly, against the reproach levelled against a Double Government, the petitioners urged: "It is considered an excellence, not a defect, in the constitution of Parliament, to be not merely a double but a triple Government. An executive authority, your petitioners urge, may often, with advantage, be single, because promptitude is its first requisite. But the function of passing a deliberate opinion on past measures, and laying down principles of future policy, is a business which, in the estimation of your petitioners, admits of and requires the concurrence of more judgments than one. It is no defect in such a body to be double, and no excellence to be single."

The petition was submitted in vain; Lord Palmerston introduced his Bill for the abolition of the Company's rule, and the future Government of India. It was provided in that Bill that the home administration should be conducted by a President and a Council of eight persons who were to be nominated by the Crown; that members of the Council should hold office for eight years; and that two of them should retire by rotation each year. The second reading of the Bill was carried by a large majority. But before the Bill could be passed, Lord Palmerston's Government fell over the Conspiracy Bill, intended to protect the French Emperor against the machinations of political refugees in England.

Lord Derby then formed a Conservative Government; and Benjamin Disraeli, Chancellor of the Exchequer, introduced his new India Bill, which was complicated, unworkable, and grotesque. It provided that the India Council was to consist of members partly nominated by the Crown, and partly elected by the citizens of Manchester and other places, and holders of the East India Stock. Mr. Disraeli's scheme died of ridicule. And Lord Palmerston said of the Bill, what had been said of *Don Quixote*, that whenever he saw a man laughing in the streets, he was sure that man had been discussing Mr. Disraeli's Bill! When the House of Commons met after Easter, no one could be found to support the Bill.

The two Bills were carefully examined by the Court of Directors; and they submitted to the Court of Proprietors an able Report proceeding once more from the logical and fearless pen of John Stuart Mill. One paragraph deserves to be placed before our readers.

"The means which the Bills provide for overcoming these difficulties [of the government of one nation by another] consist of the unchecked power of a Minister. There is no difference of moment in this respect between the two Bills. The Minister, it is true, is to have a Council. But the most despotic rulers have Councils. The difference between the Council of a despot, and a Council which prevents the ruler from being a despot is, that the one is dependent on him, the other independent; that the one has some power of its own, the other has not. By the first Bill [Lord Palmerston's Bill] the whole Council is nominated by the Minister; by the second [Disraeli's Bill] one-half of it is nominated by him. The functions to be entrusted to it are left, in both, with some slight exceptions, to the Minister's own discretion." [1]

The argument is unanswerable. And after the experience of half a century many thoughtful men will be inclined to hold that a strong and independent deliberative body might have tempered the action of the Crown Minister, and secured a better administration of Indian affairs. The Directors of the Company formed such a body, but they represented the interests of the Company's shareholders, not of the Indian people. That was the defect of the old system; that was the evil which required a remedy. But in the task of reorganisation which Parliament undertook in 1858, this defect was not remedied. The power of the Court of Directors was destroyed, but no

[1] Report approved by the Court of Directors on April 6, 1858. Return to an order of the House of Lords, ordered to be printed May 3, 1858.

independent deliberative body, representing the people of India and safeguarding their interests and their welfare, found place in the new scheme of administration.

Mr. Disraeli's Bill was dead; and it was necessary now to frame a new one. It was then resolved that the principles of the new scheme should be discussed in the House, and that a Bill, the joint production of both parties, should be introduced. This was done; and the new Bill became law in August 1858, and is known as an *Act for the better Government of India.*

The Act consists of 75 sections, and as it still regulates the administration of India, it is necessary to refer to the more important clauses.

The territories of the East India Company were vested in her Majesty the Queen, and the powers exercised by the East India Company and the Board of Control were vested in the Secretary of State for India. He was to have a Council of fifteen members who would hold office during good behaviour,[1] and each member was to have a salary of £1200 a year out of the revenues of India. The pay of the Secretary of State and all his establishment would similarly be charged to India.

The Secretary of State was empowered to act against the majority of the Council except in certain specified matters. And on questions of peace and war (which had hitherto been dealt with by the Board of Control through the Secret Committee of the Court of Directors), the Secretary of State was empowered to send orders to India without consulting his Council, or communicating them to the members.

The Governor-General of India and the Governors of Madras and Bombay would henceforth be appointed by her Majesty the Queen; and the appointments of Lieutenant-Governors would be made by the Governor-General subject to the approbation of her Majesty. Rules

[1] Members are now appointed for ten years, on the nomination of the Secretary of State himself, and are eligible for reappointment.

should be framed by the Secretary of State for admission into the Civil Service of India by competition.

The strangest clauses of this Act are the financial clauses. It was provided that the dividend on the capital stock of the East India Company, and all the bond, debenture, and other debt of the Company in Great Britain, and all the territorial and other debts of the Company, should be "charged and chargeable upon the revenues of India alone."[1]

By this singular clause the capital stock and the debts of the East India Company were virtually added to the Public Debt of India; and the annual tribute which India had so long paid as interest on the stock was made perpetual. The Crown took over the magnificent empire of India from the Company without paying a shilling; the people of India paid, and are still paying, the purchase money. It was an act of injustice towards a British Dependency unexampled in the history of the British Empire.[2] It was an act of injustice which pressed heavily on the people, after the expenditure of forty millions sterling for suppressing the Mutiny had been saddled on them.

One salutary financial provision was made by the Act. "Except for preventing or repelling actual invasion of her Majesty's Indian possessions, or under other sudden and urgent necessity, the revenues of India shall not, without the consent of both Houses of Parliament, be applicable to defray the expenses of any military operation carried on beyond the external frontiers of such possessions by her Majesty's forces charged upon such revenues."[3]

[1] Section 42.—*Act for the better Government of India.*

[2] Numerous instances will occur to students of English history of Great Britain incurring heavy expenditure for colonies and dependencies; in no instance was the entire cost charged to such dependencies. As late as 1900, the British Government took over Nigeria from the Royal Niger Company, paying £565,000 as purchase money; and the sum was not charged to Nigeria. More recently Great Britain has spent over two hundred millions sterling to protect or extend her South African Empire; it is doubtful if more than a fraction of it will be realised from South Africa.

[3] Section 55.—*Act for the better Government of India.*

This just and salutary principle has unfortunately been violated but too often; and the expenses of expeditions to Egypt and Abyssinia, of wars in Afghanistan and for the conquest of Burma, have been charged to India.

The Board of Control ceased to exist under the Act; and the East India Company continued to exist, only to receive out of the revenues of India the dividend on their stock.

To the mass of the people of India the provisions of this new Act were little known. But they knew of the Queen of England, and cherished her name with affection and esteem; and they hailed the news that the Indian Empire was taken under her own administration. A Proclamation, suitable to the occasion, was issued; and the Proclamation itself is dear to the people of India because the sentiments conveyed therein were the sentiments of the Queen herself.

For the first draft of the Proclamation did not please her Majesty. She asked the Prime Minister, Lord Derby, to write it: "Bearing in mind that it is a female Sovereign who speaks to more than a hundred millions of Eastern people, on assuming the direct government over them, and after a bloody war, giving them pledges which her future reign is to redeem, and explaining the principles of her government. Such a document should breathe feelings of generosity, benevolence, and religious toleration, and point out the privileges which the Indians will receive in being placed on an equality with the subjects of the British Crown, and the prosperity following in the train of civilisation."

Such were the sentiments of the Queen towards her Indian subjects; the new Proclamation was drafted according to her wishes; and it was one which was worthy of the occasion. The people of India regard this Proclamation as a Charter of their Rights, and it is necessary therefore to quote the entire document, which is not a long one.[1]

PROCLAMATION BY THE QUEEN IN COUNCIL TO THE PRINCES, CHIEFS, AND PEOPLE OF INDIA.

"Victoria, by the grace of God, of the United Kingdom of Great Britain and Ireland, and of the Colonies and Dependencies thereof in Europe, Asia, Africa, America, and Australasia, Queen, Defender of the Faith.

"Whereas for divers weighty reasons, we have resolved, by and with the advice and consent of the Lords Spiritual and Temporal and Commons in Parliament assembled, to take upon ourselves the government of the territories in India, heretofore administered in trust for us by the Honourable East India Company:

"Now, therefore, we do by these presents notify and declare that, by the advice and consent aforesaid, we have taken upon ourselves the said government; and we hereby call upon all our subjects within the said territories to be faithful, and to bear true allegiance to us, our heirs and successors, and to submit themselves to the authority of those whom we may hereafter, from time to time, see fit to appoint to administer the government of our said territories, in our name and on our behalf.

"And we, reposing especial trust and confidence in the loyalty, ability, and judgment of our right trusty and well-beloved cousin and councillor, Charles John Viscount Canning, do hereby constitute and appoint him, the said Viscount Canning, to be our first Viceroy and Governor-General in and over our said territories, and to administer

[1] It was one of the happiest days of my boyhood when I heard this Proclamation read by the highest English official in one of the district towns of Bengal on November 1, 1858, on which day it was read in all district towns in India. Hindus and Mussulmans had gathered there, and hailed the Proclamation with shouts of joy; and Brahmans held up their sacred threads and exclaimed *Maharani Dirghajibi Haun*—"May the Great Queen live long." I remember the scene as if it happened but yesterday.

the government thereof in our name, and generally to act in our name and on our behalf, subject to such orders and regulations as he shall, from time to time, receive from us through one of our Principal Secretaries of State.

"And we hereby confirm in their several offices, civil and military, all persons now employed in the service of the Honourable East India Company, subject to our future pleasure, and to such laws and regulations as may hereafter be enacted.

"We hereby announce to the Native Princes of India that all treaties and engagements made with them by or under the authority of the Honourable East India Company are by us accepted, and will be scrupulously maintained, and we look for the like observance on their part.

"We desire no extension of our present territorial possessions; and while we will permit no aggression upon our dominions or our rights to be attempted with impunity, we shall sanction no encroachment on those of others. We shall respect the rights, dignity, and honour of Native Princes as our own; and we desire that they, as well as our own subjects, should enjoy that prosperity and that social advancement which can only be secured by internal peace and good government.

"We hold ourselves bound to the Natives of our Indian territories by the same obligations of duty which bind us to all our other subjects, and those obligations, by the blessing of Almighty God, we shall faithfully and conscientiously fulfil.

"Firmly relying ourselves on the truth of Christianity, and acknowledging with gratitude the solace of religion, we disclaim alike the right and the desire to impose our convictions on any of our subjects. We declare it to be our royal will and pleasure that none be anywise favoured, none molested or disquieted, by reason of their religious faith and observances, but that all shall alike enjoy the equal and impartial protection of the law; and we do strictly charge and enjoin all those who may be in authority under us that they abstain from all interference with the religious belief or worship of any of our subjects on pain of our highest displeasure.

"And it is our further will that, so far as may be, our subjects, of whatever race or creed, be freely and impartially admitted to offices in our service, the duties of which they may be qualified, by their education, ability, and integrity, duly to discharge.

"We know, and respect, the feelings of attachment with which the Natives of India regard the land inherited by them from their ancestors, and we desire to protect them in all rights connected therewith, subject to the equitable demands of the State; and we will that generally, in framing and administering the law, due regard be paid to the ancient rights, usages, and customs of India.

"We deeply lament the evils and misery which have been brought upon India by the acts of ambitious men, who have deceived their countrymen by false reports, and led them into open rebellion. Our power has been shown by the suppression of that rebellion in the field; we desire to show our mercy by pardoning the offences of those who have been thus misled, but who desire to return to the path of duty.

"Already in one province, with a view to stop the further effusion of blood, and to hasten the pacification of our Indian dominions, our Viceroy and Governor-General has held out the expectations of pardon, on certain terms, to the great majority of those who, in the late unhappy disturbances, have been guilty of offences against our Government, and has declared the punishment which will be inflicted on those whose crimes place them beyond the reach of forgiveness. We approve and confirm the said act of our Viceroy and Governor-General, and do further announce and proclaim as follows:—

"Our clemency will be extended to all offenders, save and except those who have been, or shall be, convicted of having directly taken part in the murder of British subjects. With regard to such, the demands of justice forbid the exercise of mercy.

"To those who have willingly given asylum to murderers, knowing them to be such, or who may have acted as leaders or instigators in revolt, their lives alone can be guaranteed; but in apportioning the penalty due to such persons full consideration will be given to the circumstances under which they have been induced to throw off allegiance; and large indulgence will be shown to those whose crimes may appear to have originated in too credulous acceptance of the false reports circulated by designing men.

"To all others in arms against the Government we hereby promise unconditional pardon, amnesty, and oblivion of all offence against ourselves, our crown, and dignity, on their return to their homes and peaceful pursuits.

"It is our royal pleasure that these terms of grace and amnesty should be extended to all those who comply with these conditions before the first day of January next.

"When, by the blessing of Providence, internal tranquillity shall be restored, it is our earnest desire to stimulate the peaceful industry of India, to promote works of public utility and improvement, and to administer its government for the benefit of all our subjects resident therein. In their prosperity will be our strength; in their contentment our security; and in their gratitude our best reward. And may the God of all power grant to us, and to those in authority under us, strength to carry out these our wishes for the good of our people."

BOOK II

UNDER THE QUEEN

1858–1876

CHAPTER I

CANNING, ELGIN, AND LAWRENCE

An era of Peace, Retrenchment, and Reform succeeded the Crimean War. Lord Palmerston, the most unquiet of Foreign Ministers, was forced to be a peaceful Prime Minister when the nation wanted peace. Great events succeeded each other in the world's history. Italy won her independence in 1860. America cemented her Union in blood, shed in a great civil war. Prussia wrested provinces from Denmark, and entered on her career of aggrandisement. Russia planned her march eastward. Lord Palmerston witnessed all this, and did not move. The rise of great nations called forth his jealousy, but did not provoke his interference. He died in 1865, when there was peace in his country.

For Englishmen had entered on a period of domestic reforms. The great fiscal reforms of Mr. Gladstone, then Chancellor of the Exchequer, removed bit by bit all restraints on trade. Mr. Cobden concluded his Commercial Treaty with France in 1859. The Paper Tax was removed in 1860. Other taxes were repealed, and yet the revenues went up by leaps and bounds with the expansion of trade.

A Reform Bill was introduced after Lord Palmerston's death, but was defeated. But the nation demanded the measure; and a Reform Bill, introduced by Mr. Disraeli, was passed. Mr. Gladstone succeeded him as Prime Minister in 1868, and his first administration was marked by other reforms. The Irish Church was disestablished. The first Irish Land Act was passed. A system of National Education was organised. An Army Reform was effected.

The Ballot Act was passed. The High Court of Justice was established.

Indian history reflects this peaceful progress during the first eighteen years of the Crown Administration. Lord Canning became the first Viceroy of India. Few of those who had protested against his "clemency," and had petitioned for his recall, knew of the task he had performed, or the trial he had undergone. It often happened during the dark days of the Mutiny that the silent and indefatigable worker passed the best part of the day and all the night at his desk. One winter morning he had worked from midnight till midday, without rest and without interval for breakfast; he then fell back exhausted, the action of the brain had ceased. Nor was it Lord Canning alone who bore this burden. His wife, the faithful partaker of all his anxieties, often shared his labours. She sat up, far into the night, copying secret letters and despatches which were not allowed to pass through the ordinary official channels. They bore the burden together; and they came out triumphant.

The Mutiny was at last over. A great Darbar was held at Allahabad on November 1, 1858, and Lord Canning read the Queen's Proclamation to the assembled men. This greatest of all Indian Darbars was dignified without ostentation, impressive without vaingloriousness. At another Darbar, held at Cawnpur, the new Viceroy made a welcome announcement. The rule against adoption which had brought princely dynasties to a close, was abolished. The Government of the Queen recognised the ancient right of adoption in Indian princes. Every ruling chief in India breathed more freely when they heard this announcement. The nation received the new administration of the Crown with acclamation.

Proceeding on his journey, Lord Canning visited the great cities of Northern India and the Punjab, and reached the frontier town of Peshawar in February 1860. Retracing his steps, he paid a short visit to Simla, and returned to Calcutta in the heat of May. His health had been undermined by incessant labours; but no considerations of health kept him from his duty. Another arduous tour was undertaken in autumn; and the Viceroy held a Darbar at Jabalpur to meet Holkar and Sindia and other chiefs of Central India. It was necessary for him to be everywhere, to meet the princes and the people of India after the Mutiny. It was necessary to reassure them and to consolidate the empire in their good wishes and loyalty.

A great sorrow fell on Lord Canning in 1861. On his return from a fresh tour in Northern India he found his wife seriously ill. Lady Canning had caught the Terai fever on her journey from Darjeeling; she rapidly sank under the fatal illness, and died in November. Then the strong heart of the indefatigable worker broke. "I went into the death chamber," writes his private secretary, "the proud, reserved man could not restrain his tears, and wrung my hand with a grip that showed how great his emotion was." In March 1862 Lord Canning left India—a dying man.

In no period of modern Indian history—except under the beneficent rule of Lord William Bentinck—were so many great reforms crowded within so short a period as during the administration of Lord Canning. But the greatest of his task was to promote the agricultural wealth of India—to secure to the tillers of the land the profits of cultivation. The land question is at the root of the prosperity of all agricultural nations; and Lord Canning's generous endeavour to solve that question in the interests of the people will be narrated in a future chapter. It is enough to mention here that the Bengal Rent Act of 1859 extended to the agricultural population of the Province a protection they had never enjoyed before; and the provisions of this Act were before Mr. Gladstone when he framed his first Irish Land Act ten years after. More than this, Lord Canning sought to protect agriculture in all the Provinces of India from harassing re-settlements and increasing State-demands. If that wise measure had been adopted, India would have witnessed less of those recurring famines which are the saddest feature of Indian history during the last quarter of the nineteenth century.

High education also received the Viceroy's attention. The Universities of Calcutta, Madras, and Bombay were established in 1857 on the model of the London University. The inspiring influences of a Western Education reached a larger circle of the population. Indian society responded to this stimulus. The greatest writers of Bengal, Iswar Chandra Vidyasagar, Madha Sudan Datta, and Bankim Chandra Chatterjea, made their mark in the early 'sixties. Never, since the time of Lord William Bentinck, was so much of high aspiration and healthy ambition manifest among the people as in the early years of the Queen's Government, and under her first Viceroys.

In legislation, too, Lord Canning's administration stands apart from all subsequent times. The Indian Penal Code, which had been drafted by Macaulay and the first Law Commission in 1837, was passed in 1860. Codes of Civil and Criminal procedure were passed; and the Police was organised and regulated by a new Act.

The Governor-General's Council, as reconstituted by the Act of 1861, consisted of five Ordinary Members. Lord Canning distributed the work among the Members, and placed each of them in charge of a separate department. The Council was thus converted into a Cabinet, of which the Governor-General was the head. The Member in charge of a department dealt with all ordinary questions, and only placed serious matters before the Governor-General for his consideration. When there was a disagreement in opinion, the question was brought up for discussion before the Council. This system of administration, first introduced by Lord Canning.

obtains to the present day. Its only defect, which should have been rectified since the time of Canning, is, that there is no representation of popular opinion in the administration of the empire.

Judicial administration was reorganised. High Courts were established in Calcutta, Madras, and Bombay, in 1861, by the amalgamation of the Company's Courts and the Queen's Courts. Sir Barnes Peacock, a distinguished lawyer, sat as Chief Justice of the High Court at Calcutta. Rama Prasad Roy, son of the distinguished Raja Ram Mohan Roy, was appointed the first Indian Judge of the Calcutta High Court, but died shortly after his appointment. The most distinguished of his successors was Dwarka Nath Mitra, whose sound judgment and fearless independence commanded the respect and admiration of all.

The army was reconstructed, and India was garrisoned with 70,000 European troops and 135,000 Indian troops. This vast army has been considerably increased since, and has been made a reserve for Great Britain's Imperial requirements in Asia and in Africa.

But the most difficult problem which faced Lord Canning was finance. It had been decided by the British Government to throw the whole cost of the Mutiny Wars on the Indian finance; and the Debt of India increased by over forty millions sterling. The annual interest of this Debt was enormous, and Indian tax-payers were called upon to meet the demand. James Wilson, a sound political economist, and for some time Financial Secretary to the Treasury, was sent out as the first Financial Member of the Governor-General's Council. He created a State paper currency, and he imposed a Licence tax and an Income tax to meet the growing expenditure.

Lord Canning's work in India was done. Public opinion in England and in India had lost its bitterness. Englishmen had come to form a juster estimate of the first and greatest of Indian Viceroys. "In that land of the West," said a parting address given to Lord Canning, "if justice and humanity be ever honoured, you cannot but hold a distinguished place." But Lord Canning was not destined for higher honours. He died in June 1862, in the fiftieth year of his age. His body was buried in Westminster Abbey, close to the remains of his illustrious father. England's long roll of bright names has not many that are brighter than George Canning the Prime Minister, and Charles Canning the first Viceroy of India.

Lord Elgin arrived in India in March 1862, and proved himself a worthy successor to Lord Canning. He pursued the same policy of peace, and he felt the same sympathy with the people of India. His father is better known to Englishmen for those priceless sculptures he brought from Athens, known as the "Elgin Marbles." The son was of about the same age as Lord Canning, and had been his fellow-student at Oxford; and he had distinguished himself as Governor-General of Canada from 1847 to 1854. While on his way to China with British troops in 1857, he had heard of the Indian Mutiny; and had promptly diverted the Chinese expedition to the aid of India. Five years after, he came to India as Viceroy and Governor-General. Much was expected from a ruler who knew his work, and who sympathised with the people. But he died in the year after his arrival, and therefore left no mark on Indian administration.

The question then arose, who was to succeed Lord Elgin? Dalhousie and Canning had sacrificed themselves to the toil of Indian administration, and had returned to their country only to die. Elgin had fallen before he was two years in India. The idea suggested itself that a constitution, seasoned by long residence in India, was best suited for Indian work. And the claims of Sir John Lawrence were paramount. True, he was not a peer. True, that no Indian civilian except Sir John Shore had ever been confirmed as Governor-General before. But exceptional circumstances compelled a departure from the usual rule.

The Act for the Better Government of India had been passed by Lord Derby's Government in 1858; and his son, Lord Stanley, was the first Secretary of State for India. The Conservative Government fell in 1859, and Sir Charles Wood became Secretary of State for India under the Liberal Government which succeeded. He had been President of the Board of Control when India was ruled by the East India Company; he had reorganised education in India by his famous Despatch of 1854; and he brought to his new office an intimate knowledge of Indian affairs, combined with a sound judgment and a determined wish to do justice to the people. His Under-Secretary, Lord de Grey, afterwards became Marquis of Ripon and Viceroy of India.

Sir John Lawrence had been appointed a Member of the India Council in 1859, and had worked under Lord Stanley and Sir Charles Wood for four years, when the death of Lord Elgin created a vacancy in India. Public opinion in England pointed to the veteran of the Punjab as the most worthy successor; and Sir Charles Wood had seen enough of him to come to the same opinion. On the morning of November 30, 1863, Sir Charles looked into the room of Sir John Lawrence at the India Office and said: "You are to go to India as Governor-General. Wait here till I return from Windsor with the Queen's approval." The same evening Sir Charles returned with the royal approval.

Sir John Lawrence arrived at Calcutta in January 1864. He knew the people of India as few Englishmen ever knew them; and he was fortunate in his Councillors. Henry Sumner Maine, perhaps the greatest English jurist of the time, was his Legal Member. The veteran Sir Charles Trevelyan, who had been the colleague of Bentinck and Macaulay thirty years before, was his Finance Minister. And Robert Napier, afterwards Lord Napier of Magdala, was his Military Adviser.

One restless subordinate gave him some trouble. Sir Bartle Frere, then Governor of Bombay, was an Imperialist. He had drawn up a paper attacking Sir John Lawrence's frontier policy. The paper was meant for Lord Elgin or his yet unknown successor. It fell into the hands of Sir John Lawrence when he succeeded Elgin. Lawrence defended himself in his own manly style. And when the papers went up to the Secretary of State, Sir Charles Wood justly remarked: "Nothing could be more precipitate and rash than Frere's tirade against the Punjab policy."[1] In lavish expenditure, and in vast schemes of improvement also, Sir Bartle Frere was as rash as Lawrence was cautious and economical. And the new Viceroy had much to do to restrain his precipitate subordinate.

A great Darbar was held in Lahore in October 1864. Lawrence spoke to the assemblage of six hundred Princes and Chiefs of India in their spoken tongue—a feat which no other Governor-General before or after him could have performed. A short war with Bhutan ended in the British annexation of the Doars, on condition of payment of half the revenue to the Bhutan State. A severe famine visited Orissa in 1866; the relief operations were inadequate; and the loss of life was severe. The land question was eternally before the Government. Lord Canning had conferred security of tenure to the cultivators of Bengal; Lawrence pursued the same useful policy in Oudh and in the Punjab. And agreeing with Lord Canning, Sir John Lawrence recommended a Permanent Settlement of the State-demand from the soil in all Provinces of India. His aim was to form a strong middle class, and to promote the agricultural wealth of the people. For those were days when the welfare of the people was the *first* consideration with the rulers.

The expenditure on the Army was reduced by Sir John Lawrence from £13,182,000 at the commencement of his administration to £12,990,000 at its close. Nevertheless

[1] Bosworth Smith's *Life of Lord Lawrence* (1885), vol. ii. p. 300.

there was a recurring deficit; and the total deficit during his five years' rule came to nearly 3¾ millions sterling. Taxes imposed on the people had reached their limit. Taxes imposed on commerce evoked an opposition from British merchants which the Government could not face. "If the Licence Tax is vetoed," wrote Sir John Lawrence to the Secretary of State in 1867, "I cannot conceal from myself the conviction that all taxation which can affect, in any material degree, the non-official European community, will be impracticable. So far as their voices go, they will approve of no tax of the kind. They desire that all taxation should fall on the natives."[1]

And, writing privately to Sir Erskine Perry, then a Member of the Indian Council, Sir John Lawrence said: "The difficulty in the way of the Government of India acting fairly in these matters is immense. If anything is done, or attempted to be done, to help the natives, a general howl is raised, which reverberates in England, and finds sympathy and support there. I feel quite bewildered sometimes what to do. Every one is, in the abstract, for justice, moderation, and such like excellent qualities; but when one comes to apply such principles so as to affect anybody's interests, then a change comes over them."[2]

One unjust addition to the Indian Debt was strongly but unsuccessfully opposed by Lawrence. Great Britain had a little war of her own with King Theodore of Abyssinia in 1867. Robert Napier, then Commander-in-Chief of the Bombay army, was sent to the expedition; and the banner of St. George, in the florid language of Mr. Disraeli, was planted on the mountains of Rasselas. But the cost was enormous, and a large portion of it was meanly and unjustly thrown on India, with its disorganised finances and its annual deficits. "I believe I am right," wrote Sir John Lawrence, "that all the expenses of the British troops employed in the Mutiny who came from England, were

[1] Bosworth Smith's *Life of Lord Lawrence*.
[2] *Ibid.*, vol. ii. pp. 411, 412.

paid out of the revenues of India. I recollect very well that, in 1859 and 1860, India was even charged for the cost of unreasonably large numbers of men who were accumulated in the depôts in England, nominally for the Indian service. . . . In the present case, India has no interest whatever in the Abyssinian expedition, and it appears therefore to me that she should pay none of its cost."[1] Lawrence asked for simple justice, but he asked in vain.

It remains only to say a few words about that frontier policy with which the name of Lawrence is so intimately connected. Sir Charles Wood had ceased to be Secretary of State for India in 1866. He had retired in ill-health from the India Office, and was called to the Upper House with the title of Lord Halifax. Lord de Grey—afterwards Marquis of Ripon—succeeded him in February 1866. But the Liberal Government fell shortly after; and Lord Cranborne—afterwards Marquis of Salisbury—became Secretary of State for India in July 1866. He, too, held that office only for a short time, and was succeeded in March 1867 by Sir Stafford Northcote. And Northcote was succeeded by the Duke of Argyll in 1868, when the Liberals again came into power.

It was in keeping with the spirit of the times that all the Secretaries of State under whom Sir John Lawrence worked—Sir Charles Wood, Lord de Grey, Lord Cranborne, Sir Stafford Northcote, and the Duke of Argyll—agreed with him in his frontier policy. All of them approved of his unalterable resolution to hold to the strong natural frontiers of India, and not to seek a new frontier in the limitless mountains of Afghanistan.

For Lawrence maintained that to extend the western limits of India was to go half-way to meet the dangers we professed to fear; that it was to leave our natural frontier of an unpassable river and mountain walls for a frontier which was everywhere and nowhere; that it would compel us to fight the enemy away from our base with a hostile

[1] Bosworth Smith's *Life of Lord Lawrence*, vol. ii. p. 390.

population around us; that it was to make enemy of the Afghans who wanted only to be left alone to be our friends; and that it would be wasting millions of the Indian money, sorely needed by a population crying aloud to be saved from the tax-gatherer on the one hand, and from actual starvation on the other. Accordingly, when there was a scramble for the Afghan throne after the death of Dost Muhammad in 1863, Lawrence held firmly to his policy—a policy of Masterly Inactivity, as it has been described—until the Afghans had settled their quarrels. And in 1868, when Shere Ali, one of the sons of Dost Muhammad, had succeeded in winning his father's throne, Sir John Lawrence, with the full approval of the Government in England, recognised him as the *de facto* ruler of Afghanistan.

But this policy of Sir John Lawrence, wise, consistent, and successful, was not to pass unquestioned. Sir Bartle Frere, who had attacked his Punjab frontier policy in 1863, was now a Member of the India Council. He was a disciple of the "forward school," and he found a strong colleague in Sir Henry Rawlinson, another Member of the India Council. And Rawlinson raised the question once again in his famous Memorandum, proposing measures "to counteract the advance of Russia in Central Asia, and to strengthen the influence and power of England in Afghanistan and Persia." It is remarkable that no disciple of the forward school ever proposed that England should pay for strengthening her influence and power in Afghanistan and Persia. If such a proposal had been made, British tax-payers would have known how to deal with it. Every proposal of the forward school was based on the assumption that the people of India should pay the cost.

Sir Henry Rawlinson's Memorandum was forwarded to Sir John Lawrence. Lawrence replied to Rawlinson, as he had replied to Bartle Frere five years before. And the covering Despatch to the several Minutes, recorded on this occasion, clearly formulates the *Lawrence policy* for all time to come.

"We object to any active interference in the affairs of Afghanistan by the deputation of a high British officer with or without a contingent, or by the forcible or amicable occupation of any post or tract in that country beyond our own frontier, inasmuch as we think that such a measure would, under present circumstances, engender irritation, defiance, and hatred in the minds of the Afghans, without, in the least, strengthening our power either for attack or defence. We think it impolitic and unwise to decrease any of the difficulties which would be entailed on Russia, if that Power seriously thought of invading India, as we should certainly decrease them if we left our own frontier and met her half-way in a difficult country, and, possibly, in the midst of a hostile or exasperated population. We foresee no limits to the expenditure which such a move might require, and we protest against the necessity of having to impose additional taxation on the people of India, who are unwilling, as it is, to bear such pressure for measures which they can both understand and appreciate. And we think that the objects which we have at heart, in common with all interested in India, may be attained by an attitude of readiness and firmness on our frontier, and by giving all our care and expending all our resources for the attainment of practical and sound ends over which we can exercise an effective and immediate control.

"Should a foreign Power, such as Russia, ever seriously think of invading India from without, or, what is more probable, of stirring up the elements of disaffection or anarchy within it, our true policy, our strongest security, would then, we conceive, be found to lie in previous abstinence from entanglements at either Kabul, Kandahar, or any similar outpost; in full reliance on a compact, highly equipped, and disciplined army within our own territories or on our own border; in the contentment, if not in the attachment of the masses; in the sense of security of title and possession, with which our whole policy is gradually imbuing the minds of the principal chiefs and native aristocracy; in the construction of material works within British India, which enhance the comfort of the people while they add to our political and military strength; in husbanding our finances and consolidating and multiplying our resources; in quiet preparation for all contingencies which no Indian statesman should disregard; and in a trust in the rectitude and honesty of our intentions, coupled with the avoidance of all sources of complaint which either invite foreign aggression or stir up restless spirits to domestic revolt."

CHAPTER II

MAYO AND NORTHBROOK

LAWRENCE was made a peer on his retirement, and he had a worthy successor in India. Lord Mayo was an Irish nobleman of ancient descent, and possessed all the kindly sympathies and generous impulses of his countrymen. His genial and affable disposition disarmed opposition; his strong capacity for work secured efficient administration; and his faithful adherence to the interests of peace enabled him to continue the policy of his predecessor. His dignified demeanour impressed all, and he moved among the princes and chiefs of India, a king among men.[1]

Born in Dublin in 1822, Lord Mayo had entered Parliament in 1847, and had served as Chief Secretary for Ireland on three occasions before he went out to India. He was Mr. Disraeli's selection, and as the Conservative Government fell towards the close of 1868, people expressed a doubt if the succeeding Liberal Ministry would uphold the choice. It is needless to say that Mr. Gladstone declined to listen to party clamour, or to rescind the appointment. And during the three years of Lord Mayo's Viceroyalty in India, he had the hearty support of the Liberal Ministry.

Lord Mayo took charge of the Indian Administration at Calcutta on January 12, 1869. And we can form some idea of his Viceregal work in India if we pause awhile to take note of his "Cabinet," and his seven departments. Lord Mayo himself held the "portfolio" of the Foreign

[1] As a junior officer, I attended Lord Mayo's reception of the King of Siam at the Government House in Calcutta in the winter of 1871-72. The Viceroy's princely presence and dignified courtesy no doubt impressed his royal guest, as it struck every one present on the occasion.

and the Public Works departments. The able jurist, Fitz James Stephen, was the Legal Member of his Council, and presided over the Legislative department. Sir Richard Temple, with his varied Indian experience, was his Finance Member. Barrow Ellis was the Home Member, and Sir John Strachey the Revenue Member. Each Member dealt with the current duties of his department, and only brought important matters to the notice of the Governor-General. Once a week he held his Council, consisting of all the Members, and "in this oligarchy all matters of Imperial policy are debated with closed doors."[1]

In this brief but pithy sentence we detect all the strength and all the weakness of Indian administration. The "oligarchy" comprised the ablest British officials in India, but has never, within a half century of the Crown administration, admitted an Indian within its body. Neither the revenue, nor the finance department, nor any other department, has ever been entrusted to an Indian. The people of India have no place within the Cabinet; no consultative body of representatives has been organised to advise the Cabinet; no constitutional method has been devised to bring the Cabinet in touch with the people. The best of Governments, composed of the ablest of administrators, must fail of success when the people are so rigidly excluded from the administration of their own concerns.

Only two months after his arrival in India, Lord Mayo received the new Amir of Afghanistan in the famous Umbala Darbar. Sher Ali, who had now secured his position as the ruler of Kabul, came in the hope of obtaining a fixed subsidy from the Government of India. Lord Mayo presented him with the sum of £100,000 which had been already promised, gave him hopes of help and support when desirable, but rightly declined a fixed subsidy. "We have distinctly intimated to the Amir," wrote Lord Mayo, "that under no circumstances shall a British soldier

[1] Sir William Hunter's *Earl of Mayo* (Oxford, 1891), p. 86.

cross his frontier to assist him in coercing his rebellious subjects. That no fixed subsidy or money allowance will be given for any named period. That no promise of assistance in other ways will be made. That no treaty will be entered into obliging us under every circumstance to recognise him and his descendants as rulers of Afghanistan. Yet that, by the most open and absolute present recognition, and by every public evidence of friendly disposition of respect for his character, and interest in his fortunes, we are prepared to give him all the moral support in our power; and that in addition, we are willing to assist him with money, arms, ammunition, native artificers, and in other ways, whenever we deem it desirable so to do."[1]

This was strict adherence to the "Masterly Inactivity" of Lord Lawrence; and Lord Mayo acknowledged this in a letter to Lord Lawrence, written immediately after the Umbala Darbar. "I adhered rigidly to the line laid down—*i.e.* no treaty engagements which may, hereafter, embarrass us, but cordial countenance and some additional support as it may seem advisable. I believe that when you sent Sher Ali the money and arms, last December, you laid the foundation of a policy which will be of the greatest use to us hereafter. I wish to continue it."[2]

But Lord Mayo did something more than merely continuing the policy of his predecessor. He developed it in order to secure peace in the Indian frontiers on a firm foundation. His distinctive foreign policy was to establish a ring of friendly and independent kingdoms on the frontiers of India, without interfering with their internal administrations, and without seeking to bring them under British domination. "I have frequently laid down," wrote Lord Mayo, "what I believe to be the cardinal points of our frontier policy. They may be summed up in a few words. We should establish with our frontier States of

[1] Sir William Hunter's *Life of the Earl of Mayo* (1876), vol. i. pp. 259 and 260.

[2] Bosworth Smith's *Life of Lord Lawrence* (1885), vol. ii. p. 478.

Khelat, Afghanistan, Yarkand, Nepal, and Burma, intimate relations of friendship. We should make them feel, that although we are all powerful, we desire to support their nationality. That when necessity arises, we might assist them with money and arms, and perhaps even in certain eventualities with men. We should thus create in them outworks of our Empire, and by assuring them that the days of annexation are passed, make them know that they have everything to gain and nothing to lose by endeavouring to deserve our favour and support."[1]

In pursuance of this clear, sound, and sensible policy, Lord Mayo sent Douglas Forsyth to discuss and settle matters with Russian Ministers at St. Petersburg in October 1869, and the Oxus was fixed as the northern boundary of the Amir's dominions. Lord Mayo also succeeded in inducing the Shah of Persia to demarcate the boundary between his kingdom and Beluchistan. And he authorised a British officer to settle the internal dissensions in Beluchistan. Towards Nepal he maintained a firm and friendly attitude; and in Upper Burma he restrained the warlike propensities of the king, and established closer commercial relations. Happy it were for India if the firm and friendly attitude towards surrounding countries had been always maintained by Lord Mayo's successors.

In the internal administration of India, and especially in financial matters, Lord Mayo's success was less pronounced. Sir John Lawrence, a stern economist, had failed to secure a surplus; and Lord Mayo succeeded only by adding to the taxes. The fault lay not with them, but with British Ministers, who had thrown burdens on the Indian revenues which Great Britain ought to have shared. The Public Debt of India in 1870 was 102 millions sterling, and the interest on this heavy debt had to be paid. Lord Mayo increased the Income Tax from 1 to 2½ per cent. and then to 3⅛ per cent.; and he enhanced the duty on salt in Madras and in Bombay to secure a surplus.

[1] Sir William Hunter's *Life of the Earl of Mayo* (1876), vol. i. pp. 283 and 284.

But more permanent alterations were effected under the administration of Lord Mayo in the Indian financial system. In the first place, the principle was clearly recognised and carried into practice, that Reproductive Works should be undertaken by loans, so that the annual revenue might be devoted entirely to current expenditure. This policy led to large and unjustifiable expenditure on railways, as we shall see in a subsequent chapter; and no adequate sinking fund was provided to reduce the increasing Debt.

The second change was what is known as Lord Mayo's Decentralisation Scheme. Previous to his time, there were no fixed allotments for the different Provinces of India, and Provincial Governors sought to obtain as much as they could for their own Provinces. He who clamoured most, got most; and Sir John Lawrence had found the utmost difficulty in restraining Sir Bartle Frere from undertaking vast and expensive works for Bombay. By the Constitution of December 14, 1870, Lord Mayo made fixed grants to Provincial Governments for the period of five years, and Provincial Governors administered their own Provinces, as best they could, within the allotments made. There was still a scramble for larger grants once in five years when the allotments are made, but a scramble once in five years was better than a yearly competition among the Governors.[1]

[1] The grants at first fixed in 1870 by Lord Mayo for the different Provinces were these—

	£
Bengal	1,168,592
North-West Provinces	640,792
Punjab	516,221
Madras	739,488
Bombay	880,075
Oudh	206,948
Central Provinces	261,263
Burma	275,332
Total	£4,688,711

But in a few years it was found necessary to modify this scheme, and to give each Province a *fixed share* in the Land Revenue and other sources of revenue, instead of a *fixed grant*.

The third and the most unfortunate financial change introduced under Lord Mayo's administration was a large increase in Provincial taxes, as distinguished from Imperial revenues. As far back as 1861 the Finance Minister of Lord Canning had referred to the necessity of relieving the Imperial revenues of India by empowering each Province to levy Local Rates within its limits. In 1865 the Finance Minister of Sir John Lawrence had pointed out in his Budget Speech, that the actual proceeds from Local Rates in the year 1864-65 was 2½ millions sterling. Lord Mayo's Decentralisation Scheme led to large additions to these Local Rates.

When allotments were made for the different Provinces under the Decentralisation Scheme, each Province was allowed less than its requirements, with the express desire that the deficit should be made good by increased Local taxation. The Imperial Exchequer was relieved by multiplying the centres of taxation, as well as by adding to the volume of the taxes. The old sources of the revenues continued; while each Province now imposed new cesses, mostly on land, to add to its own Provincial revenues. This scheme, which will be more fully explained in a subsequent chapter, had been considered and rejected by Lord Lawrence. Its unfortunate adoption by Lord Mayo largely added to the State-demand from the soil, and thus unsettled the rule, which had been adopted in 1855 and 1864, of limiting assessment to one-half the rental.

In the midst of these manifold labours the life of the indefatigable worker was cut short by the knife of an assassin. Lord Mayo went on a visit to the Andaman Islands, a penal settlement; and on February 8, 1872, he was stabbed to death by a convict, in the prime of his life, and in the fulness of his vigour and manhood.

Happily, he was succeeded by another statesman equally eminent, and equally true to the policy of peace. Lord Northbrook was born in 1826, in a family distinguished in Europe for careful and successful commercial transactions. He had acquired a knowledge of India as Under Secretary of State for that dependency. He had adopted the sound views of Lawrence and Mayo on the Indian frontier question. And in his financial administration he had the help and advice of his cousin, Sir Evelyn Baring, who, as Lord Cromer, has since earned a reputation second to none in the British Empire.

Lord Northbrook's administration, like those of his two predecessors, was a reign of peace. But the administration of a country like India is never unattended with difficulties; and in the second year of his rule Lord Northbrook had to announce to the Secretary of State his serious apprehensions of an impending famine in Bengal.[1]

The terrible mortality caused by the Orissa famine of 1866, and by the famine of Northern India in 1869, was still fresh in the minds of the people; and Lord Northbrook was determined to prevent a repetition of such fatal results in 1874. Ample and timely measures of relief were undertaken; and for once in the history of India, the measures adopted were completely successful. Bengal, with its Permanent Settlement and low rental, was more resourceful than any other Province in India; the people were able to help themselves to a greater extent than elsewhere; and the measures of relief were, therefore, more efficacious in preventing deaths. The inquiries, made after the famine, showed that no mortality whatever was due to the famine.

The misrule of the Gaekwar of Baroda was another source of trouble. He was charged also with having instigated an attempt to poison the British Resident. Lord Northbrook gave him a fair trial. Three Englishmen and three Indian Princes formed the tribunal, and Sergeant Ballantyne went out from England to defend the Gaekwar. The tribunal was not unanimous in its verdict, and Sergeant Ballantyne believed to the end of his life

[1] Letter of the Viceroy in Council, dated October 30, 1873.

that the Gaekwar was guiltless of the alleged attempt. But he had proved himself unfit to rule, and Lord Northbrook, faithful to the Queen's Proclamation against further annexations, placed a young boy of the ruling house on the throne of Baroda. The experience of a generation has vindicated the wisdom of the measure. Baroda, under its own Government, is one of the best administered States of India. The young prince has lived to prove himself one of the most enlightened rulers in the country.

The Prince of Wales, now his Majesty Edward VII., visited India in the winter of 1875–76, as his brother, the Duke of Edinburgh, had done five years before. And the people of India showed their affection to the royal house by demonstrations of loyalty as sincere as they were universal.

But the fair sky of India was slowly darkened by a little cloud which had arisen in the West. The arduous endeavours of Canning and Lawrence, Mayo and Northbrook, to maintain the peace of India among strong and friendly powers, and to adjust the finances of a poor and resourceless country, were little appreciated in England. Once again the idea rose in the minds of British Imperialists that Russia must be checked in the East. Once again the thought came to them that India should be made to pay for this Imperial game.

Sir Bartle Frere, as Governor of Bombay, had vainly urged a Forward Policy in 1864; his attack on Lawrence's frontier policy had fallen into Lawrence's hands, and had been effectively answered. Sir Henry Rawlinson had once again raised the question in 1868, Lord Lawrence had once again replied. But now, when an Imperial reaction had set in in England, Sir Bartle Frere saw his chance; and his famous memorandum of 1874 revived the question. This third endeavour succeeded, because the times were propitious.

Sir Bartle Frere urged in June 1874 that British agents

should be placed at Herat, Kandahar, and Kabul; and that instead of maintaining a strong and friendly Afghanistan, a preponderating British influence should be established in that country. The veteran Lord Lawrence replied in November 1874 that the policy advocated by Sir Bartle Frere would be likely to facilitate rather than stop the advance of Russia; that it would turn the Afghan races against the British; that British officers stationed in Afghanistan would be assassinated; that the assassination would be followed by fresh wars. With almost prophetic vision the old seer sketched out in 1874 the very events which actually happened five years after. But his warnings were disregarded; and his unequalled experience and knowledge of the Afghans and the Punjab frontier were ignored. Sir Bartle Frere replied to Lord Lawrence in January 1875; and Lord Salisbury, who had once scoffed the alarms of the forward school with the keenest sarcasm, now accepted the views of Sir Bartle Frere. Lord Salisbury had succeeded the Duke of Argyll as Secretary of State for India when the Conservatives came into power in 1874. And he wrote to Lord Northbrook, suggesting the establishment of a British Agency at Herat, then at Kandahar, and eventually at Kabul.[1]

Lord Northbrook was faithful to Lord Lawrence's views. He had read Lord Lawrence's reply to Sir Bartle Frere. And he had written to Lord Lawrence to express his complete agreement.[2]

When, therefore, Lord Northbrook received Lord Salisbury's Secret Despatch in February 1875, he replied by telegraph that the time and circumstances were unsuitable for taking the steps proposed. And in June 1875 he sent a formal reply to Lord Salisbury's despatch showing that the policy which had been pursued since the days of Lord Canning, and pursued successfully, was to create a strong

[1] Despatch dated January 22, 1875.

[2] Letter dated December 18, 1874, quoted in Bosworth Smith's *Life of Lord Lawrence* (1885), vol. ii. p. 479.

Afghanistan, over whose ruler British influence was powerful enough to keep him from foreign aggression. The letter[1] was signed by Lord Northbrook and the Members of his Council—Lord Napier of Magdala, Sir Henry Norman, Sir Arthur Hobhouse, Sir William Muir, and Ashley Eden.

Lord Salisbury's rejoinder, dated November 1875, is one of the least creditable documents which have ever been penned by a British Minister.

"The first step, therefore, in establishing our relations with the Amir upon a more satisfactory footing, will be to induce him to receive a temporary Embassy in his capital. It need not be publicly connected with the establishment of a permanent Mission within his dominions. There would be many advantages in ostensibly directing it to some object of smaller political interest, which it will not be difficult for your Excellency to find, or, if need be, to create."[2]

Lord Northbrook's reply to this strange despatch was strong as it was dignified. He urged that if a permanent Mission was to be sent to Afghanistan, it was better to candidly inform the Amir of its true nature and object. But the step was not necessary.

"We are convinced that a patient adherence to the policy adopted towards Afghanistan by Lord Canning, Lord Lawrence, and Lord Mayo, which it has been our earnest endeavour to maintain, presents the greatest promise of the eventual establishment of our relations with the Amir on a satisfactory footing; and we deprecate, as involving serious danger to the peace of Afghanistan, and to the interests of the British Empire in India, the execution, under present circumstances, of the instructions conveyed in your Lordship's despatch."[3]

The same mail which brought this earnest and

[1] Dated June 7, 1875.
[2] Secret Despatch, dated November 19, 1875.
[3] Letter dated January 28, 1876.

dignified remonstrance to England, conveyed also Lord Northbrook's resignation of his high office.

With Lord Northbrook's administration ended the period of peace and reforms which had commenced in 1858. With Lord Lytton's administration began an era of restless Imperialism

CHAPTER III

LAND REFORMS IN NORTHERN INDIA

GREAT as were the reforms of Lord Canning in every department of Indian administration, his greatest were those which benefited the agricultural and landed classes of India. His Bengal Rent Act of 1859 not only gave an adequate protection to the cultivators of Bengal, but helped his successors to pass similar Rent Acts for other Provinces of India. A brief account of the land reforms effected in Northern India by Canning and Lawrence is given in this chapter.

BENGAL.

When the land revenue of Bengal was permanently settled by Lord Cornwallis in 1793, a provision was made in the Act empowering the Government to take action for the adequate protection of the cultivators. Inquiries were made from time to time into the condition of the cultivators, but for a period of over sixty years the cultivators of Bengal did not obtain the promised protection. This was not owing to the negligence of the Company's servants who administered Bengal; it was owing rather to the extreme difficulty of finding a proper basis of legislation between the classes and the masses.

The difficulty was at last overcome by Lord Canning. His Bengal Rent Act (Act x. of 1859) is considered the Charter of the Bengal Cultivators. It divided the settled cultivators of Bengal into three classes. For those who had held lands at the same rents since 1793, the law declared that the rental should remain unaltered for all the time to come. For those who had held lands at the same rents for twenty years, the law presumed that they had paid the same rents since 1793 until the contrary was proved. And, lastly, to those cultivators who had held lands for twelve years, *the right of occupancy* was conceded; and their rents could not be raised in future except on specific and reasonable grounds laid down in the law.[1]

This law created a revolution in Bengal. And the population of Bengal are at the present time more resourceful and prosperous than elsewhere in India, *firstly*, owing to the limitation placed on the State-demand from landlords in 1793, and, *secondly*, owing to the limitation placed on the landlord's demand from tenants.

Oudh.

The Province of Oudh has a history of its own. When the Province was annexed by Lord Dalhousie in 1856, the landlords or Talukdars were found to be the virtual proprietors of their estates, and Village Communities were less developed than in other parts of Northern India.

The British Government overlooked this difference. Settlement Officers tried to set aside Talukdars in many cases, and to make settlements with village proprietors. This, however, could not be effected in the majority of cases; and out of the 23,543 villages of Oudh, 13,640 were settled with Talukdars in 1856, and 9903 were settled with village proprietors.[2] This disregard of the old leaders of the people in a newly annexed Province was neither a just nor a wise act. The Oudh Talukdars felt that their rights had been confiscated; and when the Indian Mutiny broke out in the following year, they joined the Mutiny.

The war ended, all lands were confiscated by Lord Canning by his Proclamation of March 1858, which has

[1] The Right of Occupancy has been extended to other cultivators, and the rights of tenants-at-will assured, by subsequent legislation.

[2] Baden-Powell's *Land Systems of British India* (1892), vol. ii. p. 201.

become historic. The Governor-General singled out six loyal landlords whose rights were to be respected; and he held out a promise of "reward and honour" to others who might establish their claims.

"The Governor-General further proclaims to the people of Oudh that, with the above-named exceptions, the proprietary right in the soil of the Province is confiscated to the British Government, which will dispose of that right in such manner as it may deem fitting.

"To those Talukdars, Chiefs, and Landholders, with their followers, who shall make immediate submission to the Chief Commissioner of Oudh, surrendering their arms and obeying his orders, the Right Honourable the Governor-General promises that their lives and honour shall be safe, provided that their hands are not stained with English blood murderously shed. But as regards any further indulgence which may be extended to them, and the condition in which they may hereafter be placed, they must throw themselves upon the justice and mercy of the British Government."[1]

The greatest admirers of Lord Canning will admit that this Proclamation was a mistake. Wholesale confiscation was probably never his object; and a Proclamation ordering a wholesale confiscation was uncalled for and impolitic. The Proclamation created an impression that the British Government would set aside the Talukdars of Oudh in their future land settlements, to a greater extent than had been done in 1856. And it justified the fears that the new rulers would sweep away the old land system of the country, in order to have a clean slate on which they would record their yet unknown land policy.

Lord Ellenborough, who had become President of the Board of Control on the return of the Conservatives to power in 1858, saw the mistake. Another man in his place would have secretly pointed out the mistake of the

[1] Oudh Papers, ordered by the House of Commons to be printed, May 7, 1858.

Governor-General, and directed its modification in a future Proclamation. But to indulge in eloquent platitudes was one of Lord Ellenborough's weaknesses; and this was an opportunity which his lordship was not likely to miss. In April 1858 he indicted his celebrated letter to Lord Canning.

"Suddenly, the people [of Oudh] saw their King taken from amongst them, and our administration substituted for his, which, however bad, was at least native; and this sudden change of government was immediately followed by a summary settlement of the revenue, which, in a very considerable portion of the Province, deprived the most influential landholders of what they deemed to be their property, of what certainly have long given wealth, and distinction, and power to their families.

"We must admit that, under the circumstances, the hostilities which have been carried on in Oudh have rather the character of legitimate war than that of rebellion, and that the people of Oudh should rather be regarded with indulgent consideration than made the objects of a penalty exceeding in extent and in severity almost any which has been recorded in history as inflicted upon a subdued nation.

"Other conquerors, when they have succeeded in overcoming resistance, have excepted a few persons as still deserving of punishment, but have, with a generous policy, extended their clemency to the great body of the people.

"You have acted upon a different principle; you have reserved a few as deserving of special favour, and you have struck, with what they will feel as the severest of punishment, the mass of the inhabitants of the country.

"Government cannot long be maintained by any force in a country where the whole population is rendered hostile by a sense of wrong; and if it were possible so to maintain it, it would not be a consummation to be desired." [1]

Every sentence in this rebuke is just. But it was hard

[1] Letter of the Secret Committee of the Court of Directors to the Governor-General of India, dated April 19, 1858, paragraphs 13, 14, 15, 16, and 20.

on Lord Canning, who had borne the continued strain of the most serious disaster that has ever befallen British rule in India, who had struggled manfully against it and had triumphed over it, and who had restrained the fierce passions of his own countrymen and extended clemency to his opponents—it was hard on him to be censured for one serious mistake, more in the wording than in the object of his Oudh Proclamation.

The censure of Lord Ellenborough was a serious matter. He was a member of the British Cabinet; and his disapproval, publicly endorsed by the British Ministry and telegraphed to India, weakened the authority of Lord Canning when he required support and encouragement. Englishmen felt this. They did not desire it to appear that the saviour of the Indian Empire had received a censure from the British Cabinet. The difficulty of the situation was removed when Lord Ellenborough resigned his seat in the Cabinet.

In India, thoughtful and responsible men had perceived Lord Canning's mistake. Sir James Outram, then Chief Commissioner of Oudh, had induced Lord Canning to add a clause that the Government would view liberally the claims of those Oudh landlords who would promptly return to obedience. Sir John Lawrence, then Chief Commissioner of the Punjab, declared that "to tell men that all their lands and property were confiscated, to allow them no *locus penitentie*, was to drive them to despair."[1] Lord Ellenborough's censure certainly had the effect of completely rectifying the mistake. The right of property in Oudh was recognised. The Talukdars, returning to obedience, were restored to their lands. The mistake which had been made in the Punjab in 1849, and in Oudh in 1856, of levelling down the leaders of the people, was not repeated. The first regular Settlement of lands was commenced in 1860, and completed in 1878. The Settlement was for thirty years.

[1] Bosworth Smith's *Life of Lord Lawrence* (1885), vol. ii. p. 179.

It was reserved for Sir John Lawrence to extend to the cultivators of Oudh something of the same protection which Lord Canning had extended to the cultivators of Bengal. The first Oudh Rent Act (Act xix. of 1868) was passed when the first Settlement was still in progress. Without creating new rights, or recognising occupancy tenants, it gave fixity of tenure to ex-proprietary tenants; and it prohibited the enhancement of rents in respect of their holdings except by order of a court of law and equity.[1]

North-West Provinces.

The Land Settlement of the country known as the North-Western Provinces under the able direction of Robert Merttins Bird, the Directions for Revenue Officers issued by Thomason, and the final decision of Lord Dalhousie in 1855 to reduce the State-demand to one-half the rental, have been narrated in a preceding chapter. The only important change made during the subsequent period, which is the subject of the present chapter, was the passing of the Land Revenue Act (Act xix. of 1873) under the administration of Lord Northbrook. It simplified the law by repealing or modifying over fifty preceding Regulations and Acts; and the revised Settlement was concluded under the provisions of this new Act. The older methods of survey were replaced by a cadastral survey; the rental of each estate was revised and corrected by Settlement Officers after local inquiry; and between 45 and 55 per cent. of the rental thus fixed was demanded as the Government Land Revenue.

The reader will notice the importance of the changes thus introduced. The earlier method of assessment, followed by Bird and Thomason, was to proceed *from aggregate to detail;* the revenue of a fiscal circle was fixed at

[1] Later legislation has extended tenant rights in Oudh.

first, and was then distributed to the villages situated within the circle. The later method, introduced by rules framed under Act xix. of 1873, was to proceed *from detail to aggregate;* the rental of each estate was corrected and fixed by inquiry; and the Government Revenue, assessed on the revised rentals of estates within a fiscal circle, was the revenue of that circle. In other words, the revenue demand in a fiscal circle was fixed by guess-work under the old system; it was fixed on the basis of the revised rentals under the new system.

Nevertheless, the method, under which the actual rentals were fixed, was wrong in principle, and oppressive in practice. If a landlord was supposed to be lenient, the Settlement Officer might, by revising the rental of £1000, bring it up to £1200, and fix the Government Revenue at £600. Such a proceeding taught the landlord to be severe where he was inclined to be lenient; and it inspired him with a motive to screw up his rents which it is the first object of British Administration to prevent.

Another violation of the Half-Rental Rule was introduced when Local Cesses were multiplied under Lord Mayo's Decentralisation Scheme of 1870. The Half-Rental Rule was laid down by Lord Dalhousie's Government with the clear and unmistakable object of leaving to the landed classes one-half of the income from their estates, and the Land Revenue was limited to the other half. But when, in 1871, Local Cesses of 10 per cent. of the Land Revenue were imposed on estates in addition to the Land Revenue, the object of the Half-Rental Rule was defeated. The new scheme virtually added to the tax on land; it removed the clear limit which Lord Dalhousie had fixed; and it gave to Provincial Governments indefinite powers to add to the State-demand from the soil. All provinces of India suffered alike from the multiplication of Local Cesses on the land in 1871.

PUNJAB.

Sir John Lawrence made a valiant and successful endeavour to secure the Punjab cultivators in their tenant-rights. When the time came for a revised Settlement, many landlords, who had failed to register themselves as such at the Settlement of 1853, put forward their claims. To recognise them as landlords would be to degrade those who held under them to the position of tenants-at-will. And it was estimated that in Amritsar District, out of 60,000 heads of families, no less than 46,000 would be so degraded by a recognition of the claims of the landlords. A Tenant Bill was accordingly introduced to protect the cultivators; and on October 18, 1868, a great debate took place at Simla on this Bill. Sir Henry Maine gave it his hearty support in a memorable speech; and Sir John Lawrence desired it to become law. The opposition collapsed; and the Tenant Act (Act xxvii. of 1868) saved the cultivators of the Punjab, while recognising the claims of the landlords.

"The Act regulated and defined the position of tenants with rights of occupancy; it protected them against enhancement except under peculiar conditions; it recognised their power to alienate tenures; it limited the privilege of the pre-emption and gave the option to the landlord; and, with almost prophetic apprehension of the points at issue in Ireland, it defined the improvements which might be made by the tenant, and specified the compensation which he might look to receive."[1]

It is only necessary to add that three years after the Tenant Act was enacted, the Punjab Land Revenue Act (Act xxxiii. of 1871) was passed during the rule of Lord Mayo; and Settlements in the Punjab were made according to rules framed under this Act.

[1] W. S. Seton Karr, quoted in Bosworth Smith's *Life of Lord Lawrence* (1885), vol. ii. p. 423.

We have in the present chapter very briefly reviewed the legislation which was undertaken by Lord Canning and his successors to secure tenant-rights to the cultivators of Northern India. No more useful or beneficial legislation was ever undertaken by the British Government in India. The wise administrators of the day did not desire to set aside the landed classes. On the contrary, they respected their rights while they also extended protection to those who actually tilled the soil under them. Nor did Canning and Lawrence introduce new ideas and new rights for the Indian tenants. On the contrary, they only defined, improved, and *codified* those rights which Indian cultivators had always enjoyed *by custom* for centuries and thousands of years. The historian of the Indian people dwells with pleasure on the legislation of these years—legislation which respected the great and protected the weak, and which was based on the unwritten customs and the ancient rights of India. The credit of this wise and beneficent legislation was principally due to Lord Canning who first gave the protection of law to Bengal cultivators, and to John Lawrence who extended the same protection to the cultivators in Oudh and the Punjab. History recognises the heroic services of these two men in saving the British Empire in India in the dark days of 1857; but history scarcely condescends to note the services which they rendered to the voiceless tillers of Northern India by their strong determination to save their interests and secure their welfare. It is the special privilege of the chronicler of the economic condition of the people to recognise, fully and emphatically, this almost unnoticed work of the two greatest of Indian administrators.

And while those eminent rulers limited the demands of the landed classes from the cultivators of the soil in Northern India, they exerted with equal courage to limit the demands of the Government itself on the landed classes. For they held, and rightly held, that there could be no permanent prosperity, no accumulation of wealth, and no adequate motive for improvement in an agricultural country, if the Government of the country demanded a continuous increase of the Land Revenue at each recurring Settlement. Canning and Lawrence desired to limit the increasing demand in order that the people might be prosperous, and the revenue of the State might increase with the general prosperity of the people. Canning and Lawrence failed because narrower views prevailed with the succeeding generation of statesmen,—with men who were less in touch with the people and thought less of the people when the empire was safe. The story of this controversy has a melancholy interest, and will be narrated in the following chapter.

CHAPTER IV

PROPOSED PERMANENT SETTLEMENT FOR INDIA

THE famine of 1860 was the severest calamity that had visited the people of Northern India since the famine of 1837. It affected an area of 25,000 square miles, and a population of 13 millions. Delhi, Agra, Allahabad, and other towns suffered severely. The Government opened relief works for the able-bodied men and women who could work. Gratuitous relief was provided at the expense of the charitable public for those who could not work. The mortality was less than in 1837.

When the great calamity was at last over, Lord Canning appointed Colonel Baird Smith to inquire into its causes and its extent. No better man could have been selected. Baird Smith had distinguished himself as the Chief Engineer at the recapture of Delhi in 1857. But his fame rested chiefly on those great irrigation works in Northern India by which he had extended the limits of cultivation and added to the food of the people. He entered upon his new task with all his wonted energy and zeal. After an exhaustive inquiry into the condition of the famine-stricken tracts, he submitted three reports in May and August 1861. And he may be said to have discovered some facts which are true of all Indian famines.

In the first place, he clearly showed that the famine was due, not to want of food in the country, but to the difficulty of the starving people in obtaining the food. And in the second place, he also pointed out that the staying power of the people depended greatly on the land system under which they lived.

"No misapprehension can be greater than to suppose

that the settlement of the public demand on the land is only lightly, or, as some say, not at all connected with the occurrence of famines. It lies, in reality, far nearer to the root of the matter, because of its intimate and vital relation to the every-day life of the people and to their growth towards prosperity or towards degradation, than any such accessories as canals, or roads, or the like, important though these unquestionably are. It is no doubt quite true that not the best settlement, which mortal intellect could devise, would cover the skies with clouds, or moisten the earth with rain, when the course of nature had established a drought. But given the drought and its consequences, the capacity of the people to resist their destructive influence is in direct proportion—I would almost say geometrical proportion—to the perfection of the settlement system under which they are living and growing."[1]

A careful and exhaustive comparison of the famines of 1837 and 1860 confirmed Colonel Baird Smith in this belief. The areas affected by the two famines were about the same; the population affected by the later famine was larger; and the other conditions were worse in 1860. Nevertheless, the sufferings and deaths in 1860 were far less than in 1837, because the land system introduced in Northern India, since 1833, was infinitely better than the previous system.

"Foremost, then, among the means whereby society in Northern India has been so strengthened as thus to resist, with far less suffering, far heavier pressure, from drought and famine in 1860–61 than in 1837–38, I place the creation, as it may almost literally be called, of a vast mass of readily convertible and easily transferable agricultural property, as the direct result of the limitation for long terms of the Government demand on the land, and the careful record of individual rights accompanying it

[1] Report of August 14, 1891, paragraph 36.

which have been in full and active operation since the existing settlements were made."[1]

Relying on the facts and figures he had collected, and on his careful inquiries into the state of Northern India as it was then and as it had been before, Colonel Baird Smith recommended a Permanent Settlement of the Land Revenue as a protection against the worst effects of future famines, and as a means of increasing the general revenue of the country with the general prosperity of the people.

"The good which has been done by partial action on sound principles is both a justification and an encouragement to further advances; and entertaining the most earnest conviction that State interests and popular interests will be alike strengthened in an increasing ratio by the step, the first, and, I believe, the most important remedial measure I have respectfully to submit for consideration, is the expediency of fixing for ever the public demand on the land."

"It may be supposed that a great sacrifice of public revenue is involved in the concession of a perpetually fixed demand on the part of Government. It is to be observed, however, that, with a single exception to be noticed separately, the recent tendency of the measures of Government has shown a different conviction, and indicated a belief that its interests are best secured, not by general enhancement, but by general lightening of its demand on the land. . . . The land would enjoy the benefit of such accumulations, and as a necessary consequence of the increased prosperity of that class which must always be the very core of Native society, and with the strength of the weakness of which the social fabric generally must always have the acutest sympathy, trade and commerce and general wealth would not only increase, but as years passed on the community must grow stronger and stronger, and the risk of its collapsing under any such calamities as that we are now considering would gradually become

[1] Report of August 14, 1861, paragraph 60.

less and less. Assuming, then, that the results of the measure would, in some degree at any rate, realise these anticipations, it seems unreasonable to suppose that an intelligent and powerful Government could fail to participate in them. Its intelligence would direct it to the least offensive and most effective means of sharing in the general prosperity; and its power would insure the fair trial and ultimate success of those means. There would be no real sacrifice, therefore, I believe, but, on the contrary, a marked increase of the public resources, from the creation of the increased private property to which, it is conceived, that a Perpetual Settlement of the public demand must lead."[1]

Such was the first remedial measure suggested by Colonel Baird Smith, and he also urged the extension and completion of irrigation works and of roads and communications. Lord Canning sent Colonel Baird Smith's Report to all the Provincial Governments for their careful consideration.

Punjab Report.

The Government of the Punjab was the only Government in Northern India which demurred to the immediate introduction of a Permanent Settlement, because the Province had been brought under British rule only twelve years before, and cultivation was still backward in many of the districts. The new Lieutenant-Governor said:—

"The Punjab is not half cultivated; there are immense waste tracts almost unpopulated; the communications are incomplete; and the resources generally but partially developed. Hence, even admitting that it were wise to abandon the prospective right of Government to a share of the increased rent in a Province which had attained to an average degree of agricultural advancement, it might still be prudent to maintain it in one which remained in a backward state."

[1] Report of August 14, 1861, paragraphs 62 and 64.

"On a view of the whole subject, as it affects the Punjab, the Lieutenant-Governor considers that, if it be prudent in a country like the Punjab, which is still in a backward state of cultivation, which cannot be said to pay its entire military expenses, and the civil institutions of which are not adapted to the most advanced state of society, to declare the Land Tax liable to no future increase, still the existing and prospective inequalities of distribution are so many and great as to render its perpetuation very inadvisable." [1]

Report from the North-West Provinces.

Northern India has been under British rule for sixty years; and the opinion in favour of introducing a Permanent Settlement in the well-cultivated districts was strong and unanimous.

William Muir, then Senior Member of the Board of Revenue, and afterwards Lieutenant-Governor of the Province and Finance Minister of India, summed up the benefits of a Permanent Settlement under six heads.

(1) Saving of the expenditure of periodical settlements.

(2) Deliverance of the people from the vexations of resettlements.

(3) Freedom from depreciation of estates at the close of each temporary settlement.

(4) Prosperity arising from increased incentive to improvement and expenditure of capital.

(5) Greatly increased value of landed property.

(6) Content and satisfaction among the people.[2]

And the junior Member of the Board of Revenue, R. Money, foresaw no financial loss to the Government from this measure.

"I am of opinion that no amount of direct land

[1] Letter from the Punjab Government to the Government of India, dated April 25, 1862, paragraphs 6 and 16.

[2] Minute dated December 5, 1861, paragraph 30.

revenue which might possibly be hereafter assessed in excess of the demand which will be fixed at the approaching settlement, could bear any proportion to the increased sources of revenue which will, directly or indirectly, be gradually developed when the utmost possible simplification of the tenure of land shall have been affected and its stability assured."[1]

Agreeing in these opinions, the Lieutenant-Governor of the North-Western Provinces recommended the conclusion of a Permanent Settlement in a long and carefully considered Minute.

"I do not in the least doubt that the gradual and cautious concessions of a guarantee of permanency to the settlement of the land revenue in the North-Western Provinces, generally, will be productive of all the advantages which Colonel Baird Smith and Mr. Muir, in even greater detail, have depicted. Judging by the effect of settlements for long periods, it may be safely anticipated that the limitation of the Government demand in perpetuity will, in much larger degree, lead to the investment of capital in the land. The wealth of the agricultural classes will be increased. The prosperity of the country and the strength of the community will be augmented. Land will command a much higher price. The prospective loss which the Government will incur by relinquishing its share of the profits, arising from extended cultivation and improved productiveness, will be partly, if not wholly, compensated by the indirect returns which would be derived from the increased wealth and prosperity of the country at large.

"Nor should the minor advantages of freeing the people from the vexation and exaction which are inseparable from a periodical settlement of the Land Revenue, of saving the large expenditure which each revision of settlement entails upon the Government, and of removing the temptation which the approach of each revision holds out

[1] Minute dated December 21, 1861, paragraph 11.

to land proprietors of temporarily deteriorating their property, be disregarded. These are all burthens which bear, with more or less severity, on the Government and on the people, and if they can be got rid of without lasting detriment to the revenues of the state, few will be found to offer any opposition.

"It must also be admitted, I think, that the settlement of the Government demand in perpetuity will be politically wise. It is true that in Behar, and also in some of the districts of the Benares province, notably Ghazipur, which are permanently settled, the rebellion of 1857–58 was not less general or less determined than in other parts of these provinces which are under temporary settlement. But these manifestations of feeling must be regarded as having been the result of exciting causes, having but a transient influence, and can hardly detract from the force of the conviction that the absolute limitation of demand upon their land will be received by an agricultural people with the highest satisfaction, and will produce, if anything can, feelings of attachment to the Government, and of confidence in its desire to promote the best interests of the country.

"But it certainly appears to me that the introduction of a Permanent Settlement must be subject to certain conditions, exceptions, and reservations, and that some years must pass away before the measure can be consummated. Precipitancy in a matter of this vast importance is to be deprecated as pregnant with injury both to the Government and the people."[1]

The "conditions, exceptions, and reservations" which the Lieutenant-Governor, G. F. Edmonstone, laid down, were, that a revision of the existing settlement should be made before it was declared permanent; that some wild or backward districts should be excepted for many years to come from this measure; and that "the rates of water rent should be raised in order to make some compensation

[1] Minute dated May 27, 1862, paragraphs 7 to 10.

to the Government for relinquishing prospective accessions to its land revenue on the recurrence of periodical settlements."[1]

BENGAL REPORT.

The Lieutenant-Governor of Bengal, Cecil Beadon, had already expressed his opinion, as a Member of the Governor-General's Council, in support of the proposed measure. As Lieutenant-Governor of Bengal he confirmed this opinion in a separate communication.

"Although, strictly speaking, the Board are right in saying that a settlement of the Land Revenue, as between the Government and the person admitted to settlement, is a mere matter of contract, and that legislation is not necessary to give validity to a permanent any more than to a transitory one, yet the Lieutenant-Governor has no doubt that the enunciation of a lasting principle, in reference to the settlement of the Land Revenue in several large divisions of the Lower Provinces of Bengal, to say nothing of the rest of India, would most fitly be confirmed as in 1793, by legislative enactment."[2]

FINANCE MINISTER'S OPINION.

Sir Bartle Frere, then a Member of the Governor-General's Council, supported the proposal. But the most significant support which Lord Canning received was from the Finance Member of his Council, Samuel Lang. With the extreme caution, natural and commendable in a financier, he declined to accept the assurance that the prospective loss in land revenue caused by a Permanent Settlement would be made good by increased revenues

[1] Minute dated May 27, 1862, paragraph 37.

[2] Letter from the Government of Bengal to the Government of India, dated June 25, 1862. It should be explained that large portions of Bengal, like Orissa and Chota Nagpur, not being under British rule in 1793, had not been included in the Permanent Settlement of Lord Cornwallis. Cecil Beadon's recommendation, quoted above, was to extend the Permanent Settlement to these "large divisions."

from other sources. But he gave his support to the proposed measure on higher considerations which cannot be better stated than in his own emphatic words.

"We do not exist as a Government merely to get the largest revenue we can out of the country, or even to keep the mass of the people in a state of uniform dead level, though it should be a tolerably happy and contented one, as a peasant tenantry under a paternal Government.

"If we give a Permanent Settlement, as Mr. Beadon proposes, we lay the foundation for a state of society, not perhaps so easily managed, but far more varied and richer in elements of civilisation and progress. We shall have gradations of society, from the Native noblemen of large territorial possessions down, through the country gentleman of landed estate, to the independent yeoman, the small peasant proprietor, the large tenant with skill and capital on a long lease, the small tenant on a lease, the tenant-at-will, and the day labourer.[1]

"In some districts one class will preponderate, in others a different one, and, on the whole, I do not doubt that, although there may be more hardships, inequalities, and collisions, there will be more life, activity, and progress, than there ever will be where the Government was all in all.

"If the Crown in England had kept the fee-simple of all lands forfeited by successive civil wars or seized from the Church, there might have been a revenue which would have gone far to carry on the Government without taxes, but would England ever have been the country it is?

"If we have any business at all in the East, it is to try and found something better than the old approved patterns

[1] The two kinds of society here depicted are precisely those which exist at the present day in the Ryotwari tracts of Bombay and Madras, and in the permanently settled districts of Bengal. In the former we find a dead level of peasant proprietors under the Government, but *not* tolerably happy or contented. In Bengal we find gradations of society, the nobleman of territorial possessions, the country gentleman of landed estate, the occupancy cultivator with his rights secured, the tenant-at-will, the day-labourer.

of Oriental despotisms,[1] and to give India the chance at least, of becoming a great independent and intelligent community.

"Nor do I see any reason to fear the effect on revenue.

"It may be true that we shall not get so much revenue as if we had kept the increase of rent in our own hands, at any rate for the next twenty or thirty years, while it is almost certain to be rapidly increasing.

"But I have no fear of our being able to get revenue enough provided certain conditions are observed in regard to our land settlement; and I am by no means sure that it is desirable that a Government should appropriate a larger share of the income of a country, or get money more easily, than is really essential to meet the proper objects of a Government."[2]

MINUTE OF SIR JOHN LAWRENCE.

These reports and others from the Central Provinces, Madras, and Bombay,[3] came up before the Secretary of State for India. Sir Charles Wood gave a careful consideration to the question, as well as the cognate question of Redemption of the Land Tax which had also been occupying the attention of the Government for some years past. The question of Redemption fell through; but the question of a Permanent Settlement was calmly and ably discussed.

Sir John Lawrence, who was then a Member of the Secretary of State's Council, was opposed to the policy of

[1] Oriental despotism in India, whatever its faults, permitted gradations in society, and fostered Village Communities, Zemindars, Polygars, Jaigirdars, Mirasdars, Sardars, and Talukdars.

[2] Minute dated April 7, 1862. "It is sometimes said, half in jest, half in earnest"—Baird Smith had written—"that the sure effect of a full Indian exchequer is a war." It would be more correct to say that a sure effect of surpluses, secured by overtaxation, has been additional military expenditure, unjust burdens thrown on India, and larger Economic Drain from India.

[3] The opinions of the Governments of the Central Provinces, Madras, and Bombay, will be quoted in the three succeeding chapters.

Redemption, but strongly supported the policy of a Permanent Settlement.

"I recommend a Permanent Settlement because I am persuaded that, however much the country has of late years improved, its resources will be still more rapidly developed by the limitation of the Government demand. Such a measure will still further encourage the investment of money in the land, and will give still greater security to the land revenue itself, which, in years of great calamity, occurring every now and then, has suffered largely, though the loss has been more or less of a temporary character. It is also very desirable that facilities should exist for the growth of the middle class in India connected with the land, without dispossessing the present yoeman and peasant proprietors. There are many men of much intelligence, spirit, and social influence among those classes, who are yet so poor that they find it difficult to maintain a decent appearance. It is no remedy for this state of things to confer great and exclusive benefits on a few individuals, especially when the very benefits are conferred at the expense of the rest of the community. What is really wanted is to give the intelligent, the thrifty, and the enterprising among them, the opportunity of improving their condition, by the exercise of such qualities; and this can best be done by limiting the public demand on the land. When such men acquire property, and are in a thriving state, they are almost certain to be well-affected to the Government, and will use their influence, which will generally be considerable, in its favour. Feelings of race and religion have great influence on the people of India, but love for their lands has still greater. Thousands, probably millions, of the people of Northern India, the most warlike of all its races, are descended from ancestors who gave up their religion to preserve their land. It is on the contentment of the agriculturists, who form the real physical power in the country, that the security of British rule, to a large extent, depends. If they are prosperous, the military force may be small, but not otherwise."[1]

Despatch of Sir Charles Wood.

These sentiments and reasons were cordially endorsed by the Secretary of State for India in his memorable despatch of July 9, 1862, from which we make the following extracts:—

"Her Majesty's Government entertain no doubt of the political advantages which would attend a Permanent Settlement. The security, and it may almost be said, the absolute creation of property in the soil, which will flow from limitation in perpetuity of the demands of the State on the owners of land, cannot fail to stimulate or confirm their sentiments of attachment and loyalty to the Government by whom so great a boon has been conceded, and on whose existence its permanency will depend."

"It is also most desirable that facilities should be given for the gradual growth of a middle class connected with the land, without dispossessing the peasant proprietors and occupiers. It is believed that among the latter may be found many men of great intelligence, public spirit, and social influence, although individually in comparative poverty. To give to the intelligent, the thrifty, and the enterprising, the means of improving their condition, by opening to them the opportunity of exercising these qualities, can be best accomplished by limiting the public demands on their lands. When such men acquire property, and find themselves in a thriving condition, they are certain to be well affected towards the Government under which they live. It is on the contentment of the agricultural classes, who form the great bulk of the population, that the security of Government mainly depends. If they are prosperous, any casual outbreak on the part of other classes or bodies of men is not likely to become an

[1] Minute dated July 5, 1862, paragraph 15.

element of danger, and the military force and its consequent expense may be regulated accordingly."

"That this general improvement will be accelerated by a Permanent Settlement, her Majesty's Government cannot entertain any doubt. A ready and popular mode of investment for the increasing wealth of the country will be provided by the creation of property in land, and all classes will benefit by the measure. On the agricultural population, the effect will be, as pointed out by Colonel Baird Smith in the able paper already referred to, the elevation of the social condition of the people, and their consequent ability, not only to meet successfully the pressure occasioned by seasons of distress, but in ordinary times to bear increased taxation in other forms without difficulty; the feeling of ownership, or in other words, the absolute certainty of the full enjoyment of the reward for all the labour and capital which they may invest in the land, will be sure to call out all their energies for its improvement. Her Majesty's Government confidently expect that a people in a state of contentment and progressive improvement will be able without difficulty to contribute to the revenue in other ways to such an extent as more than to compensate for the disadvantage of foregoing some prospective increase of that from land."

"After the most careful review of all these considerations, her Majesty's Government are of opinion that the advantages which may reasonably be expected to accrue, not only to those immediately connected with the land, but to the community generally, are sufficiently great to justify them in incurring the risk of some prospective loss of land revenue in order to attain them, and that a settlement in perpetuity in all districts in which the conditions absolutely required as preliminary to such a measure are, or may hereafter be, fulfilled, is a measure dictated by sound policy, and calculated to accelerate the development of the resources of India, and to ensure, in the highest degree, the welfare and contentment of all classes of her Majesty's subjects in that country."

"They consider that the direct mode of making a Permanent Settlement is preferable to the indirect one of obtaining a similar result by conceding to the landholders the right to redeem their assessment. They do not believe that the power to redeem the land revenue is necessary to induce the landholders to incur expenditure in the improvement of their property. What is really required, in order to call into effective action their enterprise and capital, is not an exemption from all payments to the Government on account of their estates, but the fixing of those payments in perpetuity, at a moderate and certain amount. In Bengal, where a Permanent Settlement was made with the Zemindars seventy years ago, the general progress of the country in wealth and prosperity, notwithstanding the depressed condition of the peasantry caused by errors and omissions in the mode of making the settlement, has been most remarkable. Such errors in the existing state of our knowledge, regarding the rights and interests of the subordinate occupants of the soil, would not be permitted to recur."

"Her Majesty's Government have, therefore, determined to limit the power of redeeming the Land Revenue to such cases as are referred to above in paragraph 26, but they have resolved to sanction a Permanent Settlement of the Land Revenue throughout India. It will, however, still remain to be determined how far any particular district is in a condition to warrant the particular application of the measure at the present time."[1]

Sir Charles Wood and Earl de Grey.

When Sir John Lawrence went out to India as Viceroy, he took up the great land question with his accustomed promptness. And in March 1864, he recorded a Minute,

[1] Despatch dated July 9, 1862, paragraphs 47, 48, 53, 58, 59, and 63.

stating in general terms the manner in which he proposed to introduce a Permanent Settlement in Northern India, Oudh, and the Punjab.

On March 24, 1865, the Secretary of State for India, Sir Charles Wood, wrote his reply. He divided Indian districts into three classes, viz.:—

(1) Districts where agriculture was backward;

(2) Districts fairly cultivated and fully developed; and

(3) Districts with estates fairly cultivated, and also estates imperfectly developed.

He decided that a Permanent Settlement should be introduced at once into the second class of districts, and refused in the first class districts. In regard to the third class of districts he stated that her Majesty's Government "are prepared to authorise an immediate settlement on perpetuity, after revision, for all estates in which the actual cultivation amounts to 80 per cent. of the cultivable or Malgoozaree area." Estates not so fully cultivated "should be treated in the ordinary manner, and settled for a term not exceeding thirty years."

On August 3, 1865, the Viceroy in Council forwarded copy of correspondence with the Government of the North-West Provinces on the question of Permanent Settlement in relation to canal irrigation.

On March 17, 1866, the Secretary of State for India, Earl de Grey and Ripon, recorded his reply, approving of the instructions given by the Indian Government to the Lieutenant-Governor for the Permanent Settlement of the North-West Provinces, and suggesting the following rule with regard to canal irrigation:—

"A rule might be laid down that no Permanent Settlement should be concluded for any estate, the assets of which would, when canal irrigation shall have been carried to the full extent at present contemplated, exceed, in the opinion of the officers of the Settlement and Irrigation Departments, the existing assets in a proportion exceeding 20 per cent."

Sir Stafford Northcote.

On March 23, 1867, the Secretary of State for India, Sir Stafford Northcote, reaffirmed the decision of her Majesty's Government to introduce a Permanent Settlement. Her Majesty's Government, he wrote, were prepared to sacrifice the prospect of an increase in land revenue "in consideration of the great importance of connecting the interests of the proprietors of the land with the stability of the British Government." And he laid down two rules to restrict Permanent Settlement in undeveloped tracts and estates:—

"First.—No estate shall be permanently settled in which the actual cultivation amounts to less than 80 per cent. of the cultivable or Malgoozaree area; and

"Second.—No Permanent Settlement shall be concluded for any estate to which canal irrigation is, in the opinion of the Governor-General in Council, likely to be extended within the next twenty years, and the existing assets of which would thereby be increased in the proportion of 20 per cent."

Final Rejection of the Proposal.

Inquiries went on with a view to ascertain what districts or parts of districts in Northern India could be permanently settled under the conditions laid down by Sir Stafford Northcote. In 1869 some cases were reported in which it was shown that a Permanent Settlement, even under the conditions laid down, would cause prospective loss to Government. This was not a new argument; for Sir Stafford Northcote had foreseen such loss, and had declared it to be the final and deliberate decision of her Majesty's Government that "this sacrifice they were prepared to make in consideration of the great importance of connecting the interests of the proprietors of the land with the stability of the British Government." But every passing year of peace weakened the desire to make the sacrifice; and the objection which had been foreseen and disregarded in 1867 seemed to have a greater weight in 1869. A third condition was accordingly recommended in addition to the two laid down in 1867; and this third condition practically amounted to this, that the Permanent Settlement should be deferred as long as the land continued to improve in value.

A difficulty was then presented by the depreciation of the rupee. This, too, had been foreseen by Sir Charles Wood; but the difficulty appeared more formidable to the authorities in the 'seventies than it had appeared in the 'sixties. And, for a time, the idea of a Permanent Settlement was dropped.

At last came the final decision. The Secretary of State for India in his despatch No. 24, dated March 28, 1883, gave the *coup de grâce* to the recommendation made by Lord Canning twenty-one years before. The despatch said, "I concur with your Excellency's Government that the policy laid down in 1862 should now be formally abandoned."

It will appear from the preceding narrative that the final rejection of the proposal of a Permanent Settlement of the land revenue of India was due, not to any new difficulties discovered in course of the inquiries made, but to a change in the spirit of the Government policy. The proposal was first dictated by a desire to improve the material condition of the people; "to encourage," in the words of Lord Lawrence, "the investment of money in the land;" to promote "the gradual growth of a middle class in India;" to foster the accumulation of capital and of resources which would help the people in years of difficulties, droughts, and distress. These benevolent objects were lost sight of by a new generation of administrators. In the years succeeding the Sikh wars and the wars of the Indian Mutiny, her Majesty's Government had desired to sacrifice a prospective rise in the land revenue "in consideration," as Sir Stafford Northcote put it, "of the great importance of connecting the interests of the proprietors of the land with the stability of the British Government." The years of peace which followed, and the loyal devotion of the people of India to her Majesty's Government, weakened, instead of strengthening, this desire; and in 1883, after an uninterrupted peace in India of a quarter of a century, it was no longer considered necessary to make the sacrifice. Never has the loyalty of a nation been worse rewarded; never has the peacefulness of a people led more clearly to the withdrawal of a boon proposed in years of trouble and anxiety. It is a bad lesson for a Government to teach and for a people to learn.

CHAPTER V

LAND SETTLEMENTS IN THE CENTRAL PROVINCES

The large tract of country known as the Central Provinces of India has an area of nearly ninety thousand square miles, and a population of over nine millions.[1] It came under British Rule at different dates. In the last Mahratta war, which took place in 1817, the troops of the Raja of Nagpur attacked the British force at Sitabaldi, but were repulsed with loss. The Raja disclaimed any connection with his rebellious troops, and cemented his friendship with the British by the cession of the Sagor and Narbada Territories, which thus came under British Rule in 1818. Subsequently, Lord Dalhousie annexed the State of Sambalpur on the death of the Raja in 1849 without an heir; and in 1853 he annexed the State of Nagpur, on the demise of its ruler, the claims of the adopted heir being set aside. All these scattered territories, with the exception of Sambalpur, were united under one Administration by Lord Canning in November 1861, and were henceforth called the Central Provinces of India. And Sambalpur was added in 1862. It is necessary to say a few words here on the early administration of these separate tracts, previous to their union in 1861 and 1862.

Sagor and Narbada Territories.

When the Territories of Sagor and Narbada came under British Rule in 1818, they were first placed directly under the rule of the Indian Government, and were subsequently placed under the Lieutenant-Governor of the

[1] According to the Census of 1901. Berar has since been added to the Central Provinces.

North-West Provinces. In 1842 they were under an Agent directly under the Government of India, and on a later date they were once more transferred to the Lieutenant-Governor of the North-West Provinces. And this state of things continued till the Union of 1861.

The early administration of the Sagor and Narbada Territories was not successful. British administrators made the mistake which they had made in Madras and elsewhere. They assessed the lands too high, demanded an impossible revenue, impoverished the people, and retarded the progress of the country. The mistake was found out at a later date, and was condemned in the strongest terms.

Hoshangabad and Seonee Districts.—The first five-year settlement of Seonee and Hoshangabad, made in 1821, "probably was the worst settlement ever made. Major Macpherson had to deal with a depopulated country and an impoverished and dispirited people. . . . Major Macpherson expected an amount of improvement in five years which has not taken place in forty-five. . . . It was soon found that this assessment was extravagantly high, and could not be paid. . . . Major Macpherson, however, had chastised Hoshangabad with whips, and Seonee he scourged with scorpions."[1]

The assessment fixed by Major Macpherson in 1821 was £10,359 for an area which had been assessed by the Mahratta Government at £2277 only. In 1825 another five-year settlement was made, and the assessment was still further increased to £13,877, which was seven times what the Mahrattas had demanded. The enormous demand could never be realised, and remissions had to be allowed. "But the remissions were not sufficient, and very strenuous efforts were made to collect the revenue by any means, so that to this day a most lively recollection of the tortures and cruelties then suffered lives in the minds of the Zemindars."[2]

[1] *Settlement Report of Hoshangabad*, 1855, by Charles Elliott, paragraphs 46, 47, 48, and 49.
[2] *Ibid.*, paragraph 50.

A third five-year settlement brought little redress. At last, in 1836, a twenty-year settlement was made at a reduced assessment of £6192, which was still nearly three times the old Mahratta demand.

Narsinghpur District.—The operations of the first fifteen years were as bad at Narsinghpur as at Seonee and Hoshangabad. "It is no exaggeration to say that the first fifteen years of our administration were engrossed in one continuous struggle to keep together and support the agricultural community under an almost unbearable pressure of land revenue demand. Our first settlements were founded on the later Mahratta assessments, which, as has already been stated, had been most unduly strained to meet an extraordinary crisis. . . . When our officers attempted a rigid system of collection on so unsound a basis, and the temporary prop afforded by the consumption of the Narbada field force was withdrawn, the whole unsubstantial fabric broke down, and the impolicy of the assessment was shown by the entire desertion of numerous villages." [1]

The first assessment was £66,769. The results were disastrous, and the Malguzars or revenue-payers were ruined. Heavy remissions had to be allowed, and considerable reductions were made at the triennial settlements of 1830 and 1833. The twenty-year settlement of 1836 was made at a reduction of £5313.

Damoh District.—In this district, unfortunately, the twenty-year settlement, made in 1835, increased, instead of reducing, the previous assessment made in short term settlements. The assessment fixed in 1835 was £30,514. "Several of the Malguzars at this settlement threw up their leases, and it was only by the adoption of very determined measures that the difficulty was got over. . . . Landed property quite lost its value. Scores of villages remained under *khas* management year after year." [2]

[1] *Settlement Report of Narsinghpur*, 1866, by Charles Grant, paragraph 55.

[2] *Settlement Report of Damoh*, 1866, by A. Russell, paragraph 60.

Sagor District.—In this district also, the long term settlement which followed the short settlements, did not bring any relief. "The Government demands press so heavily upon the people that all enterprise has been crushed, and there is not the slightest attempt at improvement. I have personally satisfied myself that in many instances the Government demand exceeds the gross rental assets of some villages.

"The people have lost heart to that extent that in some instances the rightful owners of hereditary descent refused on any terms to accept the proprietary rights of villages.

"The widespread misery and distress throughout this division of the district must be seen to be appreciated, especially at Dhamonee and the part of Benaika Patna.

"The impression conveyed to me on inspecting these tracts was, that the Paganahs were dead, so vast was the desolation, and so scarce the signs of life or of human beings."[1]

"The Government of India strongly condemned this state of things at Sagor, after half a century of British administration. "In 1834," they wrote, "the twenty years settlement was still not sufficiently moderate; and the same benefits did not accrue from this long settlement as in other districts of these Territories. Heavy reductions were granted, and the assessment was thus further reduced. It is to be remarked that although the Government of the day pressed the necessity of reduction, its orders were carried out by the local anthorities with a niggardly hand, and concessions made in driblets. Had the reductions been granted promptly, the district, it is probable, would have been recovered."[2]

And the Secretary of State for India wrote from London: "Even in a stronger degree than former reports

[1] *Settlement Report of Sagor*, by Col. Maclean, 1867, paragraphs 93 and 94.

[2] Letter No. 353, dated November 30, 1867, from the Government of India (Foreign Department) to the Chief Commissioner of the Central Provinces.

from the same quarter of India, this report gives evidence of the evils committed by over-assessment since the district came under British Government."[1]

These extracts will sufficiently indicate the state of the Sagor and Narbada Territories during the early decades of the British Rule. Short settlements and heavy assessments were the rule at first; and it was Robert Merttins Bird, known as the Father of Land-Settlements in Northern India, who pressed for the introduction of a long settlement in 1834. He submitted a vigorous report on the unhappy state of these Territories, brought about by persistent attempts "to prop up by temporary expedients a revenue confessedly excessive."

Robert M. Bird's general report.—"An excessive system of fraud and speculation," he went on to say, "is said to have been introduced, and the cultivators rarely receive the benefit of that which is foregone by the Government, but have been forced to pay all that could be collected from them. On the other hand, a system of interference has been introduced, which, by destroying all confidence, has driven away capital from the land. The stores of the merchant have been opened, and grain forcibly taken away to be given out to the cultivators for seed, without any payment being made to the merchant, or any assistance afforded him for the subsequent recovery of the property of which he has been thus despoiled.

"This spoliation is stated to have occurred in favour of cultivators to whom the bankers have refused to make advances from past experience of their fraud and unfaithfulness. Capitalists, having obtained decrees against agriculturists, were not permitted to sell their cattle or imprison their persons, because, it was supposed, either of these measures would leave the land uncultivated. There is little use in following out the narrative of this system throughout all its ramifications of detail. It is sufficient to say, that an ample collection of facts, openly stated

[1] Despatch No. 33, dated April 30, 1868.

by the Natives, and which could not be denied by the European officers, afforded abundant proof that, in the vain hope of propping up an exorbitant assessment, and under the mistaken notion of practical skill in the management of details, a system of mischievous interference in the private arrangements and concerns of individuals had almost universally prevailed." [1]

It was after the submission of this report, and under the orders of the Indian Government, that a long settlement for twenty years was concluded in these Territories. We have seen before that this long settlement brought relief to some districts where the assessment was reduced while in other districts it brought none, because the local officers were still wedded to the principle of exacting the highest possible revenue from the land. The long settlement was allowed to last until the new administration of the Central Provinces was formed in 1861.

Nagpur State.

This State was under the Mahratta rulers of the Bhonsla family for over a hundred years, from 1743 to 1853. But within this period it had come under the management of British officers during twelve years, from 1818 to 1830, during the minority of the ruling prince. British administrators mistook the enhancement of the Land Revenue as a sign of efficient administration. Within these twelve years the Land Revenue of the State was very considerably enhanced; and in one district, Chanda, it was doubled. When the State was restored to the Raja on his attaining his majority, the Land Revenue had risen to £253,000. [2] The Raja's ad-

[1] Bird's report on the Sagor and the Narbada territories, dated October 31, 1834.

[2]

	£
Districts Nagpur and Warda	166,400
,, Chanda	48,500
,, Bhandara	38,100
Total	£253,000

"The fiscal result of twelve years of British management was satis-

ministration was not so rigorous as that of the British; and to us it is satisfactory to note, that the Land Revenue fell to £224,170 by the time of his death in 1853. The State was then annexed by Lord Dalhousie.

The administration of the newly annexed State during the first eight years, from 1853 to 1861, was not successful. Short term settlements did not add to the prosperity of the people, nor did they add to the revenues of the State. In 1861 the annexed State was united with contiguous districts and formed into the Central Provinces.

SAMBALPUR STATE.

This State was ruled for centuries by a dynasty of the Chohan Rajputs, who had established their power in many parts of India before its conquest by the Mahomedans. After a brief interruption, a descendant of the Chohan dynasty was restored to the throne in 1817 by British influence, and the State was placed under the political control of the Bengal Government. The Land Revenue of the State was about £10,000 sterling.

On the death of the last Raja without an heir, Lord Dalhousie annexed the State in 1849, and it was administered by the Government of Bengal until 1862. It thus happened that, when the administration of the Central Provinces was formed in 1861, Sambalpur District did not form a part of it, but still belonged to Bengal. And after its transfer to the Central Provinces in 1862, it was for some years the scene of disturbances created by a pretender. The district of Sambalpur was thus excluded from the great Settlement of the Central Provinces which was concluded between 1863 and 1867; and the land system of Sambalpur is to this day different from that of the other parts of the Central Provinces.

factory, and the revenue handed back to the Raja was considerably higher than that taken over from him."—J. B. Fuller's *Note on the Central Provinces Settlement*.

Formation of the Central Provinces.

On November 2, 1861, Lord Canning recorded the Resolution creating the Central Provinces Administration. One or two extracts from this Resolution are given below.

"The Governor-General in Council, having had under consideration the administrative arrangements of the Province of Nagpur and those of the Sagor and Narbada Territories, resolves that the time has now arrived for consolidating these several districts under one central jurisdiction."

"Therefore the Governor-General in Council,—holding, firstly, that it is desirable that the Sagor and Narbada Territories should cease to be administered as an adjunct of the North-Western Provinces, and that they should possess an Administration sufficient in itself and permanent in its nature; and, secondly, that these Territories may be joined with the Province of Nagpur under one Local Government, with the greatest advantage to the management of the resources, and to the development of the capabilities of the whole area,—has resolved to constitute a separate Chief Commissionership for the Nagpur Province and the Sagor and Narbada Territories, to be designated the Chief Commissionership of the Central Provinces." [1]

Sambalpur District was added to the Central Provinces in April 1862; Nimar District in May 1864; and Bijragogarh in May 1865.

Colonel Elliot, an old and worn-out officer, was appointed the first Chief Commissioner; but upon his absence, in the first instance on furlough, and subsequently on his removal, Sir Richard Temple (then Mr. Temple) was placed in charge, and ruled the Province until 1866. He had served his apprenticeship under Thomason the great revenue administrator and ruler of Northern India; he

[1] Resolution of November 2, 1861, Foreign Department, paragraphs 1 and 5.

had worked under the Board of Administration and under Lawrence in the Punjab; and he now had the opportunity of establishing his reputation as an able and sympathetic ruler by his administration of a newly created Province. The times were in his favour; there was a desire to deal with India considerately, and even generously, during the first decade of the Queen's direct administration; and the influences of Canning and Lawrence, of Sir Charles Wood and Sir Stafford Northcote, were all for improving the material condition of the people, and attaching them to British Rule.

Proposed Permanent Settlement.

While Mr. Temple was still officiating in his new post, the proposal of Colonel Baird Smith, referred to in the last chapter, for a Permanent Settlement of the land revenue, came before him for his consideration. It is needless to state that the proposal received Richard Temple's hearty support, and his reply to the Indian Government,[1] which is not a very lengthy one, is given below in full.

"Your No. 2038 of the 7th October 1861, and subsequent letter, No. 1474 of the 20th March 1862, requiring the opinion of the Officiating Chief Commissioner on the question of a Permanent Settlement of the land revenue, discussed in paragraphs 62 to 82 of Colonel Baird Smith's Famine Report, and as to the value of a legislative sanction for settlement for terms of years where existing settlements are not of a character to be made permanent, have, up to the present time, remained unanswered. The subject was very important, and the changes in the administration of these provinces rendered it impossible to accord that attention to it which it merited. The Officiating Chief Commissioner having, however, now fully considered it, in reference to its bearing on the peculiar condition of the districts comprised in the Central Provinces, is pre-

[1] Letter No. 532, dated July 22, 1862.

pared to submit his opinion, and has accordingly desired me to report as follows:—

"2. In the first place it may, the Officiating Chief Commissioner remarks, be superfluous to state that here, as elsewhere, a Permanent Settlement would effect only the land tax itself. It would fix the assessment for ever, and it should be more accurately termed the permanent and perpetual limitation of the direct State-demand on the land. It would in no wise effect the fundamental right and property of the people in the land. That right and property will be fixed absolutely and immutably, whether the land tax be limited to a certain sum for ever, or not. The value and interest of such right and property will indeed be greater or less, according as the State-demand is fixed for a short or long term, or for ever. But under any circumstances, the nature and essence of the right and property itself will remain the same.

"3. Here, then, as elsewhere, in the above sense, the principle of a Permanent Settlement is applicable. It would have an effect altogether beyond immediate calculation, in stimulating the industry, enterprise, and self-reliance of the agriculturists, the application of capital, the accumulation of wealth. Where the assessments were fair, it would be accepted as a great boon by the people. On the other hand, the State, no doubt, will subject itself to prospective loss by surrendering all future right to increase its land revenue. But on the other hand, such loss would be more than compensated by the gradual, if not rapid, increase of all the other branches of the revenue. These branches entirely depend on the growth of wealth in the mass of the people. A Permanent Settlement will contribute more than any measure that could be devised to augment that wealth. It follows that a Permanent Settlement will cause all other heads of revenue, except land tax, to increase. Now, in these provinces more than one-third of the total income is derived from taxes other than the land tax; the other taxes are increasing, the land tax alone remains stationary. In a fiscal point of view, then, there can be no fear for the success of a measure which would, while restricting the land tax, cause all other taxes to rise. Again, it is quite true that the value of the money will continue falling, and that prices of produce will rise more and more throughout these provinces. Thus the agriculturists will, in a short time, receive much more for their produce than they ever did before. On the other hand, the price of labour will rise, and that will greatly enhance the State expenditure. All the salaries and the establishments of the lower grades, at least, will be gradually raised, and the cost of the public works will be greatly enhanced. There might appear to be some risk then, if Government, while anticipating increased expenditure, were to limit the land tax, the main source of revenue. But it will, in reality, be quite safe to trust to increase of other taxes. It was declared, quite irrespectively of the Permanent Settlement, in the Joint Report of Colonel Elliot and Mr. Temple, that "*it is rather from the miscellaneous taxes than from the land tax that increase of resources is to be expected.*"

"4. A Permanent Settlement, then, so far as it can be introduced, will be, firstly, good for the people, and secondly, good equally for the State. The questions remaining are—To what extent could it be applied? And *When could it be introduced?* Now, it is to be ever remembered that in these provinces the railways, the roads, and the navigation will certainly work great changes, while similar results are not here to be expected from irrigation. But this prospect exists here, in common with the rest of India, neither more or less. If, then, the prospect of material improvement does not bar the concession of a Permanent Settlement elsewhere, neither should it have that effect here. So far, then, as railways, roads, and navigation are concerned, the Central Provinces seem as much entitled to the advantage of a Permanent Settlement as other provinces of India. But further, it is to be borne in mind that the amount of culturable waste in these provinces is enormous, and though this condition may exist more or less everywhere, it is peculiarly prevalent here. Not only are vast tracts of culturable waste vaguely claimed by parties with doubtful title, but within the legitimate boundaries of many, even perhaps the majority of estates and villages throughout these provinces, there is a large proportion of culturable waste. Now, although the inducement held out by a Permanent Settlement to reclaim the waste is one of the cardinal benefits of that measure, still it is but fair to the State that this privilege should be kept within *moderate* bounds. It would be right to allow every estate permanently settled a just margin of waste as a field for extending cultivation. But it would not be right to allow a Permanent Settlement to an estate which might include a large or indefinite area of waste, at present quite beyond the means of the owner to reclaim, but capable in the future of being rendered valuable by a variety of contingencies.

"5. Thus in these provinces there are many estates and villages, many entire tracts, and some entire districts, where a Permanent Settlement could not at present be properly introduced. Such districts are Raepore, Belaspore, Sumbulpore, Sironcha, Bhundara, Mundla, Seonee, Chindwara, Baitool. All these districts are in a transition state; and influence will, it is hoped, sooner or later, be brought to bear, which shall change the entire face of them.

"6. On the other hand, there are some districts in each of which a Permanent Settlement might be introduced into *parts*, but not the *whole*, with as much benefit and as much reason as into the other parts of India. And into these the introduction of the measure has been recommended. These districts are Nagpore, Chandah, Natchengaon (Kowta), Jubbulpore, Saugor, Dumoh, Nursingpore, Hoshungabad. All these districts (excepting Saugor and Dumoh) have large portions of their area continuously and highly cultivated and subject to the same kind of development as the rest of India. The Saugor and Dumoh districts are more rugged, and do not possess long strips of cultivation like those just named; but in other respects their position is the same. As regards past assessments, some have been too high and others too low, but this circumstance is not peculiar to these districts, and is but too common everywhere. On the other hand, for the Jubbulpore, Saugor, Dumoh, Nursingpore, and Hoshungabad districts, there are the fiscal data year by year during thirty-five years of British rule. For the Nagpore, Natchengaon, and Chandah, besides the British assessment, there are the data of the assessments made during the Regency exercised by Sir R. Jenkins and his officers.

"7. Such being Mr. Temple's views on this question, I am further to state that he sees no reason why they should not be applied in the course of the settlement now in progress. The state and circumstances of the operations connected with that settlement were reported at some length in my No. 11[1] of 30th ultimo; it is, therefore, unnecessary to enter into great detail on this point. The Officiating Chief Commissioner would merely submit that, should his Excellency the Viceroy in Council be pleased to approve, *firstly*, the general principles of the question as above laid down; and *secondly*, the application of them at once to such of the districts in the Central Provinces as are advanced enough to receive them, then he would solicit that sanction be accorded to the following specific measures:—

"8. (i.) That, when in the course of the present settlement it shall appear to the authorities engaged in making the settlement that an estate is, in the sense explained above, fitted for a Permanent Settlement, in such estate the assessment be made in perpetuity.

"9. (ii.) That one of the chief conditions of fitness for

[1] To Government Foreign Department.

this boon be that at least three-fourths of the culturable area is under cultivation.

"10. (iii.) That it be competent for Settlement Officers to hold out a promise, in certain cases, that on estates attaining that advanced state in which three-fourths of the land is under cultivation a revised assessment be made and declared permanent.

"11. Thus, if a permanent assessment be really desired by the people, then this system would induce every landholder to increase his cultivation so as to secure the boon, and thus the greatest possible stimulus might be imparted to agricultural industry."

Settlement of 1863–67.

While the question of a Permanent Settlement continued the subject of debate for many years, a new Settlement of the Central Provinces was commenced in earnest. The principles of this Settlement had been laid down, as long ago as 1854, by a Proclamation issued by the Government of the North-Western Provinces, for the Sagor and Narbada Territories which were then under that Government. No action had been then taken. It was after the formation of the Central Provinces in 1861 that the old Proclamation of 1854 was taken as the basis for a Settlement of the Land Revenue throughout those Provinces.

The main principle laid down by this Proclamation, and afterwards accepted for the Central Provinces generally, was the recognition of proprietary rights in the Malguzars or revenue-payers. This has often been described as the conferring of a new gift; but it was a new gift only in so far as it admitted, in theory, a right which was enjoyed by the Malguzars in practice. "I do not know," said Mr. Chisholm, one of the ablest Settlement Officers of the time, "any rights appertaining to landed property which the Malguzar individually, or he and his sharers jointly, did not exercise, except the power of sale and mortgage. He could not transfer his village, merely because the Native Government, from a short-sighted policy, declined to recognise any absolute right in land; but while he remained in possession, he was absolute as regards all the internal arrangements of the village—settling cultivators, dispossessing them, increasing rent, planting groves, constructing tanks—in fact wielding all the authority in the management of the village which appertains to holders elsewhere under the most indisputable titles."

Nevertheless it was a great gain when this right, which had been exercised in practice, was expressly admitted; and when power was also given to the Malguzars to sell or mortgage their property. "It is now the intention of Government," said the Proclamation of 1854, "to make another twenty years' settlement, and to confer the Zemindari right on such persons as may appear to have the best right to such a gift." And it was added in the same Proclamation: "Every proprietor shall enjoy the free right of transfer or division." It was the pleasant duty of Richard Temple to carry this principle into operation in the Settlement which he carried through.

The proprietary rights of Malguzars having been recognised, the next question was: What portion of their rental should be claimed as Government revenue? The Saharanpur rules had laid down that, in Northern India, the land revenue should be limited to one-half of the rental; and this rule had been extended to the Sagor and Narbada Territories.[1] But what was the rule for Nagpur which now formed the larger portion of the Central Provinces?

For Nagpur, the Government of India had sent directions [2] to leave the Malguzars from 35 to 55 per cent. of the gross rental. And it was added that "the Governor-

[1] By N.W.P. Government Order, No. 74, dated February 16, 1855.
[2] By Letter No. 2279, dated June 28, 1860.

General in Council would be disposed to leave the Malguzars in all cases 40 per cent. for expenses of management and proprietary rights, and to extend the limit in special cases to 50 per cent." These instructions were liberally interpreted by Richard Temple; and in the Settlement Code which he issued, with the sanction of the Governor-General, for application throughout the Central Provinces without any reservation,[1] the only principle of assessment he laid down was the half-rental principle of the Saharanpur rules.

These, then, were the two main principles of the Settlement of the Central Provinces:—

(1) The recognition of proprietary rights in Malguzars and tenant's rights in cultivators;

(2) The limitation of the land revenue to one-half of the rental of estates.[2]

It is painful to record that the second principle was not adhered to in the assessments made. The exact method by which the rental value of each estate was ascertained has been described by two subsequent Chief Commissioners of these Provinces.[3]

In so far as these two accounts can be reconciled, it is clear that Settlement Officers did not accept the actual rental of estates. They estimated what the rental should be from their own calculations; they based the land revenue demand on these estimated rentals; and they communicated the demand to the landlords who were left to raise their rents to the estimated rentals. A more reprehensible system of encouraging landlords to screw up their rents from helpless and ignorant cultivators can scarcely be conceived. In Bengal, in Oudh, and in the Punjab, Lord Canning and Sir John Lawrence had striven

[1] *Vide* paragraph 135 of his Administration Report for 1862–63.

[2] Sambalpur, still in a state of disorder, did not receive the benefit of this Settlement, and a Ryotwari Settlement was subsequently made in that district.

[3] Letter No. 501 S, dated May 18, 1887, and Letter No. 1862, dated April 11, 1901.

to restrict the enhancement of rents by private landlords by special legislation. But Settlement Officers in the Central Provinces and elsewhere adopted a method which encouraged landlords to screw up their rents.

The actual proportion of the rental, so calculated, which was demanded as land revenue, was also higher than 50 per cent. in most districts, as the following list will show.[1]

Percentage of Rental taken as Land Revenue.

District	Per cent.	District	Per cent.
Seonee	under 50	Warda	79
Hoshangabad	under 50	Chindwara	66
Narsinghpur	under 50	Betul	64
Jabalpur	50	Bhandara	60
Sagor	51	Chanda	60
Damoh	54	Bilaspur	57
Mandla	56	Raipur	53
Nimar	64	Sambalpur (Ryotwari Settlement)	
Nagpur	78		

It will thus be seen that the principles laid down for the assessment of the land revenue were violated in a two-fold manner. In the first place, the rental accepted as the basis of assessment was higher than the actual rents received by the landlords; and in the second place, the proportion demanded as revenue exceeded 50 per cent. of this rental in most districts, and was fixed at 78 per cent. in Nagpur itself. Once again the orders of the Government "were carried out by the local authorities with a niggardly hand," and the people had no redress against the violation of rules by the very officers for whom the rules had been framed.

One benefit, however, the people obtained from this Settlement. The Settlement lasted for thirty years, and the cultivators and landlords enjoyed some rest after the harassment of previous operations.

[1] Letter of the Chief Commissioner of the Central Provinces to the Governor of India, No. 1862, dated April 11, 1901.

CHAPTER VI

LAND SETTLEMENTS IN MADRAS

In a previous chapter we have described the Land Revenue administration of Madras during the last twenty years of the East India Company's Rule. In 1855 the Government of Madras resolved on a survey and settlement of the Province. It was proposed to reduce the Land Tax so as to promote the extension of cultivation. And it was hoped that the Government Revenue would increase with the increase of cultivation.

Views of the Directors.

The Directors of the East India Company, who had noted the happy results of the new settlements in Northern India and in Bombay, welcomed this proposal. And in 1856 they gave their formal sanction in a letter,[1] from which we make the following extracts :—

"With your letter, dated the 11th October (No. 44) 1855, you have submitted to us a Minute of Consultation, dated the 14th August 1855, showing the final result of the consideration which has been given, during the last ten years, to the question of a general survey and revision of assessments in the districts subordinate to your Presidency."

"The urgent necessity of a survey, with a view to the reassessment of the Land Revenue in the greater portion of the districts under your Presidency is, we consider, established beyond the possibility of doubt."

"The officers engaged in the duty of fixing the assess-

[1] Letter to the Governor of Fort St. George, dated December 17, 1856.

ment should always bear in mind that as you have expressed it—'the right of the Government is not a rent which consists of all the surplus produce after paying the costs of cultivation and the profits of the agricultural stocks, but a land revenue only, which ought, if possible, to be so lightly assessed as to have a surplus or rent to the occupier, whether he, in fact, let the land to others or retain it in his own hands.'"

"We are therefore of opinion that the assessment should be proportioned to the *nett*, and not to the *gross* produce."[1]

"The grain assessment having been determined, and converted into money at a fair and moderate rate, we should prefer that the assessment so fixed should be declared unalterable for a term of thirty years (as in Bombay and the North-West Provinces), at the expiration of which period both the amount of the grain assessment, and the rate of its conversion into money, would be subject to readjustment according to existing circumstances."

"You are of opinion that they (the proposed measures) will be followed generally, but surely, by a great extension of cultivation, and you anticipate with confidence the result, 'instead of a falling off, will be an accession to the revenue.'"

"We are disposed to concur in these expectations, and the probability of their realisation is borne out by the actual results of the revisions of assessment under the Presidency of Bombay, as well as by the effects of the introduction of reduced rates into the district of South Arcot."

Views of Sir Charles Wood.

The words which we have put in italics are important. They show that the East India Company did not claim the entire *nett* produce or rent of the soil, but only a portion of it as Land Revenue. They desired to have two-thirds of

[1] The *nett* produce is what is left to the cultivator after deducting the costs of cultivation and the profits of the agricultural stocks.

the *nett* produce as Land Revenue in Ryotwari tracts, as two-thirds of the rental had been claimed as Land Revenue in Northern India before 1855. In that year Lord Dalhousie's Government reduced the Land Revenue to one-half the rental in Northern India. And nine years after, when the administration of India had passed from the Company to the Crown, Sir Charles Wood, Secretary of State for India, similarly fixed one-half the *nett* produce as the limit of Land Revenue in Southern India. We quote two passages from the important Despatch of 1864, which lays down this rule, and which has never been published.

"I am accordingly prepared to give my full support to the proposition of Sir William Denison, that the *nett*, and not the *gross* produce, should be adopted as the unit of which the Government is to take a fraction."

"I have to communicate to your Excellency in Council my deliberate opinion that *the share of the nett produce, which may be fairly taken as the due of Government, should be assumed at one-half*, and not one-third, as proposed in Sir William Denison's Minute." [1]

From 1864, therefore, *i.e.* from the commencement of the Settlement which had been sanctioned in 1856, but which did not begin till several years after, the clear rule of assessment for the Madras Government was to fix the Government demand so as to leave one-half the *nett* produce of fields to the cultivators, and to claim the other half as Land Revenue.

Principle of Permanency.

One other remark is suggested by the Directors' letter of 1856. It entirely ignored the principle of permanency which underlay the Ryotwari System. Sir Thomas Munro, the real author of that system, had declared emphatically

[1] Revenue Despatch to Madras, No. 7, dated February 24, 1864, paragraphs 11 and 15. The italics are our own.

before the House of Commons that the principle of the Ryotwari System, as of the Zemindari System of Bengal, was the permanency of the State-demand. "With respect of permanency there is no difference between the two systems; but the Ryotwari leaves the Government an increasing revenue arising from the waste in proportion to its cultivation."[1] And, for more than forty years after Munro's examination, the Madras Government, while claiming an impossible Land Revenue and varying the actual collection from year to year, had never questioned that a fixed and permanent demand was the principle of the Madras System. The Court of Directors, without referring in any part of their letter to this principle, simply ignored it by prescribing a revision of the assessment after every thirty years.

The principle, however, could not be thus tacitly ignored. After receipt of the Directors' letter, the Madras Board of Revenue declared that the principle of a permanent assessment was still the principle of the Ryotwari System. "A general opinion prevails in England," they wrote in 1857, "that the Bombay Settlement for thirty years secures a far greater permanency of tenure to the landholder than the present Ryotwari tenure of Madras. This is altogether an error, for a Madras Ryot is able to retain his land, *perpetually without any increase of assessment*, as long as he continues to fulfil his engagements."

When, therefore, in 1861, the Madras Government was asked by Lord Canning to report on Colonel Baird Smith's recommendation of a Permanent Settlement of the land revenues, the Madras Government naturally replied that the Madras system *was* a Permanent Settlement. The difference in opinion between the Governor and the Members of his Council was, whether the Land Tax would be a *permanent grain rent*, or a *permanent money*

[1] Evidence given in 1813 before a select Committee of the House of Commons.

rent. The letter[1] is so remarkable that it is necessary to give it in full.

PROPOSED PERMANENT SETTLEMENT.

"I am directed by the Honourable the Governor in Council to acknowledge receipt of your letter No. 2035, dated 7th October 1861, requesting his opinion 'upon the advantages of a Permanent Settlement as applicable to the various districts of the Madras Presidency,' and 'as to the value of a legislative sanction for terms of years in districts in which his Excellency in Council may not consider the existing settlements of a character to be made permanent.'

"2. I am to premise that by a 'Permanent Settlement' this Government understand the Governor-General in Council to intend no more than fixing the Land Tax in perpetuity, in other words to bar the Government in all time to come from increasing the assessment on all land brought under the settlement.

"3. The words 'Permanent Settlement' are, however, very generally applied to Zemindari settlements under Regulation XXV. of 1802 of the Madras, and Regulation I. of 1793, of the Bengal Code. To any extension of this mode of tenure in this Presidency the Government are wholly opposed, for, among other reasons, the weighty objection, that it alienates from the State all waste land. It is to this source that this Government look for a gradual increase in its land revenue, and it is essential that this source of future revenue should not be lost to the State.

"4. This being understood, I am to explain briefly the present state of the land tenure in this Presidency under the prevailing Ryotwari system, to which alone the proposals contained in your letter are applicable.

"5. This mode of administration was introduced in 1792 by Colonel Read; and was subsequently worked out

[1] Letter from the Madras Government to the Indian Government No. 241, dated February 8, 1862.

by Sir Thomas Munro. In 1812, the Home Government ordered it to be generally introduced, and it has since formed the prevalent tenure of this Presidency, the revenue derived from Zemindaries being in round numbers half a million sterling, while that drawn from Ryotwari estates is three and a half millions.

"6. There can be no question that one fundamental principle of the Ryotwari system is that the Government demand on the land is fixed for ever.

"7. When first settling the Salem district in 1796, Colonel Read issued a Proclamation to the Ryots, in which the following rule appears: 'The Putkut Nellum (or holding) being measured and valued, the assessment of every individual field in it, when at full rate, is fixed for ever, that is to say, the Government is never to require more or receive less, nor you to pay less or more than the present rate, unless when those fields actually "dry" shall hereafter be converted into wet at the expense of Government, when the rates will be proportionately raised, according to the consequent increase of the produce, and in like manner fixed for ever. But if you carry on such works at your own expense, plant topes, &c., you may depend on receiving the advantages accruing from these and from every other improvement of your lands while you continue to pay the established rates, those constituting, except in the case above mentioned, the annual demand upon them on the part of the Sircar for ever. Upon these principles you may rent out lands, which you may raise in value by tillage and manure, at rates greatly exceeding the Sircar rates, if there be a demand for them, while you will continue to pay the fixed rates to the Sircar for ever.'

"8. Similarly, in 1802, Sir Thomas Munro, when issuing instructions to the Collectors of the Ceded Districts, expressed himself as follows: 'When a country has been surveyed, the individual (Ryotwari) supersedes both the village and district settlement. The rent of every field being fixed, each cultivator takes or rejects what he pleases, and the rents of all the fields occupied in the course of the year in any one village form what is called the settlement of that village.' Again, in 1806, when explaining the manner in which a Ryotwari settlement was conducted, he says: 'When a district has been surveyed, and the rent of every field permanently fixed, the Kulwar (individual) settlement becomes extremely simple; for all that is required is to ascertain what fields are occupied by each Ryot, and to enter them, in his Potta: their aggregate constitutes his rent for the year. He cannot be called upon for more: but he may obtain an abatement in case of poverty or extraordinary losses. He has the advantage of knowing in the beginning of the season, when he ploughs his land, the exact amount of what he is to pay; he knows the fixed rents of the different fields which he cultivates, and that the demand upon him cannot exceed their total amount; he knows the utmost limit of his rent, not only for the present, but for every succeeding year; for it cannot be raised unless he takes additional land; and he is thereby the better enabled to provide for the regular discharge of his Kists, and against the losses of bad by the profits of good seasons.' In 1818 the Board of Revenue issued detailed instructions for the general introduction of Ryotwar as ordered by the Home Government. One of the distinguishing characteristics of the system, they said, was, 'that the assessment was a permanent maximum rent fixed on each field.'

"9. At a later period the permanency of the Ryotwari settlement has, on several occasions, been acknowledged in unmistakable terms.

"10. In the Madras Administration Report of 1855–56, Ryotwari is thus explained: 'Under the Ryotwari system every registered holder of land is recognised as its proprietor, and pays direct to Government. He is at liberty to sub-let his property or to transfer it by gift, sale, or mortgage. He cannot be ejected by Government so long as he pays the *fixed* assessment and has the option annually of increasing or diminishing his holding, or of entirely abandoning it. In unfavourable seasons remissions of assessment are granted for entire or partial loss of produce. The assessment is fixed in money, and does not vary from year to year, except in cases where water is drawn from a Government source of irrigation to convert dry land into wet, or one into two crop land, where an extra rent is paid to Government for the water so appropriated; nor is any addition made to the assessment for improvements effected at a Ryot's own expense. The Ryot, under this system, is virtually a proprietor on a simple and perfect title, and has all the benefits of a perpetual lease without its responsibilities, inasmuch as he can at any time throw up his lands, but cannot be ejected so long as he pays his dues: he receives assistance in difficult seasons, and is not responsible for the payment of his neighbours.' A similar description of Ryotwari was given to the House of Commons by the Home Government in 1857.[1]

"11. The Revenue Board in 1857, in a report to Government on the new survey and settlement, wrote as follows: 'It may not here be out of place to notice that a general opinion prevails in England that the Bombay Settlement for thirty years secures a far greater permanency of tenure to the landholder than the present Ryotwari tenure of Madras. This is altogether an error, for a Madras Ryot is able to retain his land in *perpetuity, without any increase of assessment*, as long as he continues to fulfil his engagements.'

"12. In the same year, the Government, in a review of the Hon. Mr. Rickett's report, expressed themselves thus strongly: 'The proprietary right of a Ryot is perfect, and as long as he pays the *fixed assessment on his land* he can be ousted by no one; there is no principle of Ryotwari

[1] Return showing under what tenures, and subject to what land-tax, lands are held under the several presidencies of India (Mr. William Ewart); ordered, by the House of Commons, to be printed, 22nd June 1857.

management more fixed or better known than this, and the Government deny that any right can be more strong.'

"13. It is thus abundantly clear that the distinguished feature of Ryotwari is the limitation in perpetuity of the demand of the State from the land. The Ryots have thus all the advantages of the Zemindari tenure, while the State has a valuable reserve of waste land, whence, as cultivation extends, its resources will be augmented so as to meet the increasing demands on its finances which the progress of the country will entail; and in practice this leading principle of Ryotwari has never been infringed. The assessments have, as in South Arcot, Bellary, Cuddapah, &c., been reduced, but in no instance have they ever been raised; nor in the recent pressure for money has so obvious a source as increasing the land-tax been ever suggested as being open to the Government.

"14. Had matters been left in this position, the Government would now have had merely to report that the Ryotwari proprietors of this Presidency already possessed the advantages which the Governor-General in Council appears willing to concede, although these were not secured to them under legislative sanction.

"15. But in 1855, when the survey and settlement now in progress were introduced, an important modification was made in the tenure of the land.

"16. The object of this operation was to revise the assessments, which were generally too high. In order to give the Ryot in all cases a valuable proprietary interest in the soil, and to induce extended cultivation, 30 per cent. of the gross produce, carefully computed in the manner prescribed, was to be 'taken as *the maximum of the Government demand*,' and it was thought that 25 per cent. would be the average. The Government were of opinion that the assessment should be fixed in grain for a term of fifty years, and that the commuted value of the latter should be periodically adjusted every seven or ten years, according to its average money value in those periods. The Home Government objected to this arrangement, and gave the preference to an assessment in money, unalterable for thirty years. The subject was further discussed by the Government, who ultimately decided that the assessment should be revised after fifty years, if then deemed expedient. This decision, however, has not as yet been authoritatively intimated to the people.

"17. It will thus be seen that, while the leading characteristic of Ryotwari tenure is the permanency of the assessment, the revised assessments now being introduced are subject to revision after fifty years.

"18. The alternatives proposed in your letter under reply have received the careful consideration of Government, and I am to state briefly the conclusions at which they have arrived.

"19. His Excellency the Governor is favourable to the imposition of a permanent grain rent, but would reserve to Government the power of periodically determining the money value of that rent, if at any future time a material alteration in the value of money should render such a measure expedient.

"20. The Honourable Members of Council, on the other hand, support the old Ryotwari principle of a permanent money assessment, that is to say, an assessment based on a certain portion of the crop, and converted into a money payment at a fair commutation rate fixed once and for ever.

"21. I am to request attention to the minutes which accompany this letter, and contain the views of the President and Members of the Council.

"22. The Government are not in favour of settlements under legislative sanction for terms of years. Such settlements would hamper the Government without materially improving the position of the Ryot; and it would be better, both for the State and the people, either that the settlements should be in perpetuity, or that the Government should have the power at any time of acting as the exigencies of the State may require. The Government would not alter the assessment except under the pressure of necessity, and that necessity might occur in the course of the series of years fixed by law for the unalterable duration of the Settlement."

The New Settlement.

While the principle of permanency in the Government demand was admitted in this letter, it was abandoned in practice. Settlements were made for thirty years, and at the expiry of the term the Land Revenue payable by each cultivator was liable to enhancement. And no specific and definite grounds for the enhancement of the State-demand were laid down, corresponding to the grounds laid down by law in 1859 and 1868, for the enhancement of rents by private landlords in Bengal.

The fiscal results of the new operations during fifteen years, from 1861 to 1875, are shown in the table on the opposite page.[1]

It will appear from these figures that the area under cultivation, as well as the Gross State-demand on the land, increased about 20 per cent. in fifteen years. But these figures do not indicate correctly the pressure of the Land Tax. In the first place, the new lands brought under cultivation were poorer in fertility and produce than the lands which were already under the plough in 1860, and the increase in production therefore was not 20 per cent., and scarcely came to half of that. In the second place, the price of the produce was lower at the end of the fifteen years than at its commencement, and what the cultivators actually got by the sale of their produce was therefore less for each garce[2] than it was before. No wonder, therefore, that remissions had to be made from the

[1] The figures are taken from the Madras Board of Revenue's resolution, No. 542, dated December 6, 1900, Appendix 1. Ten rupees are taken as equivalent to a pound sterling.

[2] Prevailing price 1861 to 1865, rupees 194 per garce.
Prevailing price 1871 to 1875, rupees 155 per garce.

Land Revenue in Madras, Excluding Malabar and South Canara.

Year.	Occupied Area in Acres.	Assessment Thereon.	Total Ryotwari Demand.	Cesses, &c.	Gross Demand.
		£	£	£	£
1861	15,800,000	3,200,000	3,220,000	70,000	3,290,000
1862	16,400,000	3,230,000	3,380,000	70,000	3,450,000
1863	17,000,000	3,210,000	3,430,000	70,000	3,500,000
1864	17,300,000	3,180,000	3,360,000	50,000	3,410,000
1865	17,500,000	3,190,000	3,410,000	80,000[1]	3,490,000
1866	17,800,000	3,180,000	3,520,000	150,000	3,670,000
1867	18,200,000	3,230,000	3,300,000	180,000	3,480,000
1868	18,400,000	3,240,000	3,400,000	220,000	3,620,000
1869	18,800,000	3,270,000	3,600,000	260,000	3,860,000
1870	19,200,000	3,300,000	3,710,000	290,000	4,000,000
1871	18,900,000	3,220,000	3,560,000	400,000[2]	3,960,000
1872	19,000,000	3,220,000	3,670,000	420,000	4,090,000
1873	18,800,000	3,190,000	3,540,000	420,000	3,960,000
1874	19,200,000	3,230,000	3,760,000	420,000	4,180,000
1875	19,200,000	3,250,000	3,530,000	410,000	3,940,000

Government demand at the end of the period to the same extent as at the beginning. The Survey and Settlement of Madras, therefore, from which so much benefit had been expected, scarcely gave the relief that was needed. Some good was no doubt done. In the first place, the Land Tax was in a great measure equalised. In the second place, settlements for thirty years gave the cultivators relief from annual inquiries, harassment, and trouble. But judging the State-demand in relation to the total produce of the Province, and to the prices of that produce, it was undoubtedly a heavier taxation on the people in 1875 than it was in 1860. And the terrible Madras famine of 1877 proved fatally how little the new Settlement had added to the security and the staying power of the cultivators.

Better results might have been secured if the rule of 1864 of limiting the State-demand to one-half the nett produce of fields had been scrupulously adhered to. But in making settlements over large districts with 150,000

[1] Land cess first appears.
[2] Village service cess first included.

holdings, summary and expeditious methods were necessarily adopted. Individual cultivators were never allowed a chance of proving what total produce they obtained from their fields, what the expenses of their cultivation were, and what nett income remained to them. It was often assumed, in a general way, that one-third of the total produce should cover the cost of cultivation. It was assumed that 28s. covered the cost of cultivating an acre of good land, and 12s. was all that was allowed for cultivating an acre of ordinary arenaceous sandy soil. Every cultivator in Madras knew, and Englishmen with any experience of the Province knew, that this was inadequate."[1]

It was on such inaccurate calculations, made collectively for vast areas of the country, that the Government assessment was based. It was then proclaimed to the puzzled cultivator, who often found that the assessment really swept away the greater portion of the nett income from his field. But he had no right of appeal to any independent tribunal; he must either pay the assessed tax or quit his ancestral field.

But it was not the Madras cultivator alone who was puzzled. The successors of Sir Charles Wood, who had laid down the clear rule of 1864, were no less puzzled by the method in which it was ignored in practice. Lord Hobart, Governor of Madras, proposed in 1874 to close the settlement operations altogether, and to revert to a simpler method. And Sir Louis Mallet, Under Secretary of State for India, recorded two long and suggestive minutes exposing the absolute want of any guiding prin-

[1] Mr. Bowden, a landlord of considerable experience, wrote on December 5, 1895, to the Collector of his District: "The idea that the cost of cultivating an acre of poor land is less than the cost of cultivating a better class of land, is purely mythical." Mr. Master wrote in his report on the Western Delta, paragraph 79: "I cannot ascertain that the outlay on the poorer soil is much smaller than the richer." Mr. Meyer wrote: "The tendency to make the cultivation expenses roughly proportionate to the value of the land is one of the weak points of the Settlement Department." And the Madras Board of Revenue, in their Resolution of December 6, 1900, paragraph 36, wrote: "Nor does it assert that the gradation of expenses in proportion to produce is absolutely accurate in all its details."

ciple in the Madras operations. We will quote one significant passage from the first of these minutes.[1]

SIR LOUIS MALLET'S MINUTE.

"In a return to the House of Commons in 1857 on Indian Land Tenures, signed by Mr. John S. Mill, I find the following general statement: 'Land throughout India is generally *private property* subject to the payment of revenue, the mode and system of assessment differing materially in various parts.'

"On the occasion to which I have already referred, viz., the correspondence with Madras in 1856, the Court of Directors emphatically repudiated the doctrine of State proprietorship, and affirmed the principle that the assessment was revenue and not rent; the revenue being levied upon rent, as the most convenient and customary way of raising the necessary taxation, which in a self-contained country, possessed of vast undeveloped agricultural resources, is perhaps the soundest, simplest, and justest of all fiscal systems.

"Sir C. Wood, in 1864, reaffirmed this principle, but went beyond the Court by fixing the rate of assessment at 50 per cent. of the nett produce, fully recognising, however, that this was merely a general rule, and that in practice the greatest possible latitude must be given.

"The principle thus established appears to rest, then, upon a solid, scientific ground; but launched, as it necessarily was, in language and under circumstances which really almost reduced it to an abstract proposition, (for the application of the principle was entirely left to the judgment of the Settlement Officers, and the tasks given them altogether beyond the power of any human beings to discharge, except in the roughest manner), one cannot wonder that the whole administration has drifted into the chaos in which these papers show it now to be.

[1] Dated February 3, 1875. The italics are our own.

"One is tempted to ask if rent—economic rent, pure and simple—is alone to be taxed; why, instead of the costly, cumbrous, capricious, and when all is said, most ineffectual settlement system, we cannot leave the assessments to take care of themselves, and take whatever percentage on the rental of the land we want, wherever we find it. I can only suppose that the answer would be, that in truth the 50 per cent. of the nett produce has been a mere paper instruction, a fiction which has had very little to do with the actual facts of the administration, and that *in practice the rates levied have often absorbed the whole rental, and not infrequently, I suspect, encroached on profits also.*"

CHAPTER VII

LAND SETTLEMENTS IN BOMBAY

THE first general Land Settlement of Bombay, commenced in 1836, has been described in an early chapter of this work. It was conducted with considerate judgment by Sir George Wingate; and as it was concluded for thirty years, it gave the cultivators much relief after the frequent and severe assessments of preceding years. But its essential defect was that the assessment was left entirely at the discretion of the Survey Officer; and cultivators were not protected against undue enhancements at future revisions.

Before the expiry of the first thirty years' settlement, the question of a Permanent Settlement came up for the consideration of the Bombay Government. Colonel Baird Smith's proposal of 1861 was forwarded by Lord Canning to the Governor of Bombay. The Governor, while rejecting the proposal, accepted the principle of basing the assessment on "a just and moderate proportion of the gross produce." [1]

PROPOSED PERMANENT SETTLEMENT.

"It is a maxim of the Natives of this country that the perfection of financial administration may be measured by the extent to which an equitable land tax is made to contribute to the support of the State, and that the excellency of a Government may be estimated by the absence of direct and indirect taxation.

"2. I have never doubted the truth of this opinion, seeing that the Native feels that, in return for the payment

[1] Minute dated March 3, 1862.

which he makes to the State, he acquires the right to occupy or possess his land, and that in that right he receives an equivalent which to his mind deprives his payment of the essential characteristics of a tax.

"3. This financial system is one of the most ancient institutions of this country, and is founded on the right of the State to a share in the produce of the land; a right which is proved not only by the universality of the practice, but by the fact that exemption from the obligation to pay is regarded as a much cherished privilege, which has either been forcibly acquired in olden times, or has been directly conferred by the State upon the possessor as a reward.

"4. It is frequently the case that the title of the holders or occupants of the land to enjoy the usufruct of the soil has become more or less complete, and their rights of occupancy more or less permanent, according to usage and a variety of circumstances. But exemption from payment of a share of the produce is nowhere the rule, but the exception; and I consider it would be generally impolitic, by fixing permanently at their present money value the demand of the State on the land, to transgress a principle of finance so sound and correct as the one I have adverted to, because it is the tendency of prices and wages to increase, consequently the expenses of administration must increase. If, therefore, the income of Government from the land be stationary, or nearly so, which, by fixing the assessment permanently, must be the case, recourse must be had to increased taxation, both direct and indirect.

"5. It will be perceived that in these observations I advert only to the fixity of settlement in respect to the money demand, and I desire it to be understood that I do not advocate any variation in the just and moderate proportion of the gross produce on which the present assessments are based. But, as the prices of produce are yearly increasing, I see no infringement of the original conditions of the settlement, nor will it be so felt by the ryot, if, on the expiration of this experimental settlement, the Government Land Tax should be readjusted according to those increased prices and to other circumstances, provided that no revision is made within such long period of time, or otherwise than on considerations of the most sound character, and upon well-established facts.

"6. This a thirty years' settlement, such as has been introduced into a considerable portion of this Presidency, and is in progress throughout the rest of it, fulfils. The moderation with which the assessment has been fixed, has given the right of occupancy a high marketable value; and, under the settlement in some districts, the prosperity of the people has increased in a marked degree. But I do not concur with the late Colonel Baird Smith, that to intensify these results, which are similar to those described by him as having taken place under the settlement of the North-West Provinces, we should here have recourse to a Permanent Settlement of the Land Tax; and it appears to me that more is due to those other elements of our settlements which he enumerates, viz., 'security of titles, moderation of assessment,' and, above all, 'the recognition and careful record of rights,' than to the mere 'protracted fixity of the public demand.'

"7. For in this Presidency it had long been sought to perfect a Ryotwari system by acknowledging no others than the Government and the poor peasant, and imposing on the latter all the burdens that he could stagger under in support of the former. That system naturally proved detrimental to the lands and all their inhabitants, excepting here and there the usurer. The result was that which must infallibly ensue under any Government which itself lives from hand to mouth, keeps no surplus money for advances, and maintains no stores for use, when in hard times seed corn is needed. Constant remissions, and still further decline of villages, became the ordinary characteristics of provinces which had already undergone the harassing and depopulating effects of more than two centuries of wars and plunder. The authorities at length resolved on retrieving a position for agriculture. It would have been better, in my opinion, to have recognised some dormant tenures, and to have resuscitated others. But habit and the example set by predecessors, whose wars, recklessness, and oppressions had, generally speaking, exterminated the more respectable classes of landholders, served to keep out of view this best element of the success which depends on the possession of capital or of good credit. So they did the next best thing with a people who are not generally Mahomedan spendthrifts, but industrious Hindus. After a survey, they imposed a very moderate assessment. This is now in operation, and is to endure for a period of thirty years. It is obvious that this being the first attempt on this side of India, within the limits of British dominions, to apply to cultivation a method of extending and improving it, and to population an encouragement to immigrate and increase, it would be an utter disregard of the rights of the Government in Land Tax if the present settlement were to be viewed as the limit of our demand. All that is here wanted, short of the reconstruction of such classes as Zemindars and Meerasdars, with their worth and influence, is to allow such a duration of settlement (and thirty years is not amiss for the purpose) as will combine the objects of increasing at future periods the moderate and just demands of the Government, while reconciling the Ryot, for his own sake, to devote his industry and the utmost of his small means to the improvement of his long holding.

"8. It is, in my opinion, another good reason for not settling our Land Tax permanently, that there can be no doubt in any unprejudiced mind that the lands are not yet held, generally speaking, as they might without difficulty be declared to be held, on a title still more highly esteemed and cherished. However well satisfied the Ryot may be with the security of his right of his occupancy under the Revenue Survey Settlement, the term Meeras conveys to his mind a sense of ownership, which no assurance, that so long as he pays the Government revenue he will not be disturbed in the possession of his fields, can give him. This was recently illustrated to me in a forcible manner by an intelligent Patell, who, in answer to a question put to him, with a view of eliciting the estimation in which he relatively held his 'Meeras' and 'Ghatkoolee land,' replied: 'The Meeras is mine; the Ghatkoolee is yours.' And, again, as was emphatically said in my hearing, on another occasion, by a Native District Deputy Collector, and at the same time by an experienced Mamlutdar, 'they hold affectionately to meeras'—(*meeras ko bohut dil lugta*).

"9. With reference also to the possibility of having hereafter permanently to impose new taxes, I object to the proposal for abandoning the right of Government to the improved value which increased prices should give to the right of the State to a share of the produce of the fertile soil worked at small cost in money and labour—a right which has been reserved to it from ancient times, and which has, until recently, enabled it practically to exempt the people of this country from the burdens of taxation which press so heavily on the communities of Europe.

"10. I shall lament to see a departure from this wise system, nor do I see the necessity of the proposed measure, for the agricultural classes are, on all hands, admitted to be improving, and to be becoming gradually possessed of some capital; and those works of irrigation, which must mainly be the mainstay to protect them in seasons of drought, can only be undertaken on an organised system, which no present Permanent Settlement would ensure being ever executed, but which it is the duty of the Government to undertake whenever it has available resources.

"11. No legislative enactments have been found necessary in this Presidency to give effect to the thirty years' settlement now in operation, and none appears to be necessary."

The Revised Settlement.

It will be seen from paragraph 5 of this Minute that the Government of Bombay was opposed to "the fixity of settlement in respect to the money demand," but did not advocate "any variation in the just and moderate proportion of the gross produce on which the present assessments are based." In principle, therefore, the Bombay Government was opposed to a Permanent Settlement of the land revenue reckoned in money, but was inclined in favour of a Permanent Settlement of the revenue reckoned in produce. As the prices of produce were then increasing, the Government looked forward to a proportionate increase in the land revenue at the next settlement.

It would have been a gain to the cultivators of Bombay if this principle, of an increase in the land revenue in proportion to the increase of prices, had been acted upon, when the time for the next settlement arrived four years later. But in vast operations, carried on by single officers, such principles are apt to be forgotten unless they are laid down by legislation and guarded by independent tribunals. The idea spreads among the under-paid and uneducated subordinates that the Government desires as high a revenue as can be screwed out of the cultivators; a temporary season of prosperity induces the superior officers to demand a large increase in revenue; and an undue enhancement is inevitable when the new rates are fixed without consulting the cultivators, and without appeals to Land Courts.

And this is what happened in course of the Revision Settlement commenced in 1866. The Civil War in America had interfered with the import of American cotton into Lancashire, and had largely stimulated cotton cultivation in Bombay. There was a sign of temporary prosperity which officials mistook as permanent. And the officers employed in survey and settlement effected a high and unreasonable increase in the Land Revenue demand.

The distinguished Indian patriot, Mr. Dadabhai Naoroji, gave timely warning in his evidence before a Committee of the House of Commons in 1873. He said that the signs of prosperity were hollow and ephemeral, and that the enormous increase in the land revenue was oppressive and unjustifiable. Complaints against the new assessment were also universal in the Deccan; but the warning was unheeded.

Agrarian Disturbance.

The Nemesis came at last. After the conclusion of the Civil War, America once more began to export her cotton to England; cotton cultivation declined in India; prices and wages fell. Cultivators in the Deccan were unable to pay the new and enhanced revenue demanded; money-lenders refused to lend when the credit of cultivators was low, and the law in favour of creditors was restricted. Agrarian disturbances, such as have seldom been known under the British Rule, followed in 1875. Rioting was committed; shops and houses were burnt down; stocks were destroyed. A Commission was then appointed to inquire into the matter, and a civilian of Northern India sat with two civilians of Bombay to inquire into the causes of the disturbance. It is no discredit to the Bombay civilians to state that the ablest and the most independent report submitted was the Memorandum compiled by the Northern civilian, Auckland Colvin, afterwards Sir Auckland Colvin, Lieutenant-Governor of Northern India, and Finance Minister of India.

Auckland Colvin's Views.

Auckland Colvin pointed out in his Memorandum[1] the extent to which the revenue had been enhanced in the settlements recently concluded.

"The result would seem to be that, in the villages of the above five Talukas, of which the printed reports are before me, the increase in thirty years was as follows:—

Taluka.	Collections of First Period of Initial Settlement.	Revised Assessment at Expiry of Thirty Years.	Percentage of Increase in the Thirtieth Year over the Collections of the First Period.
	Rupees.	Rupees.	
Indapur . . .	65,220	124,506	90
Haveli	64,452	134,189	108
Pabal	66,508	152,228	85
Supa	48,856	81,943	68
Bhimthari . .	43,407	129,842	199

"The real increase is considerably greater, because the collections of the *first decade* were considerably in excess of the collections of the *first year* of the old survey. Finally a statement furnished by Colonel Francis shows the percentage of increase between the assessment in the *last* year of the old Settlement and the *first* year of the new—a single year—to be as follows:—

Taluka.	Percentage.
Indapur	56
Pabal	48
Haveli	66
Bhimthari	63
Supa	32

"The highest percentage of increase in any district in the North-West Provinces between the first year of the

[1] *Memorandum*, dated November 8, 1875.

old and the new Settlement (a period of thirty years) has hitherto been thirty-six; and this is in the exceptional, because recently reclaimed districts of Gorakhpur and Basti; the average for the Province is 16 per cent."

"I think the above considerations justify me in placing the *excessive enhancement of the revised settlements* as third among the special causes which have combined to disturb the relations of debtor and creditor in the Poona district."

The vast difference between the enhancements made in Northern India and those made in Bombay, as pointed out by Auckland Colvin, tells its own tale. But Colvin also described in some detail the defects of the Bombay system, and the inadequate checks imposed by the rules.

"Finally, as bearing on the relation of the enhanced assessments to the economic condition of the people, I venture to think that the Bombay administrative procedure, if I understand it rightly, is apt to press hardly on the Ryot. I should not have felt justified in advancing this opinion if I did not find myself supported by a recent expression of opinion by His Excellency the Governor in Council, which I will presently quote. The assessment seems to me to be based too purely on arithmetical data, and to be applied with too little regard to the conditions of the agricultural body who are expected to pay it. Now that the tenures have been defined and recorded, the Survey Department naturally looks to enhanced revenues as its *raison d'être*."

"The officers again to whom the assessment is confided have nothing, and never at any time can have anything, to do with the administration of the Collectorates; the officers to whom the charge of Collectorates is confided have not, and never have had anything to do with survey or assessment. Hence we find the spectacle of Collectors, and Revenue Commissioners contending against the rates imposed by the Survey Department."

"The Bombay Government, by laying down a maxim of

enhancement, has recently tried to meet this anomaly, but has cut rather than solved the difficulty. So large an increase as 100 per cent. on an individual holding, or of 66 per cent. on a village, is still allowed without special sanction of Government."

Views of the People.

It is necessary to make one more extract from a remarkably able document drawn up by the Poona Sarvajanaika Sabha,—one of the best informed and most important Political Associations in India. The Poona Riots Commission quotes from Chapter 3 of the report of the Sabha, and the following passage shows how the Bombay assessments violated the very principles of land assessment laid down by the Court of Directors in 1856, and by the Secretary of State for India in 1864.

"The assessment should consist of a portion of the *nett* profits of land, after deducting the expenses of cultivation, including the wages of the cultivator and his family, and the charges for the purchase and renewal of agricultural stock. It has been shown before that the present assessment of the Government, and the charge of the Khote profits in Konkan Districts absorb from one-half to one-third of the gross produce, which by all accounts means that the Government assessment is a rack-rent in the worst sense of the term. In the Desh districts also it has been shown that the Ryot is enabled to continue the cultivation of land from year to year, not because he receives any fraction of the proprietor's rent, or true farmer's profits, but chiefly, if not solely, because he earns the wages of himself and family in its cultivation. *In fact there is no surplus produce left,* after paying the cost of cultivation (including his wages and the charge for the renewal of agricultural stock) and the assessment of Government."

Action of the Government.

These clear and convincing facts and arguments were urged in vain. They led to no substantial change in the method and procedure of settlements. They led to no remedial measures affording security to cultivators against undue enhancements. They led to no rules for the strict enforcement of the principles of the Land Tax laid down by the Court of Directors and the Secretary of State. The Government declined to frame such rules for its own servants as had been framed to restrict the powers of private landlords in Bengal. The Government sought to relieve the cultivators of the Deccan only by restraining money-lenders. That was the object of the Deccan Agriculturist's Relief Act of 1879.

The Act enabled Courts to go behind the letter of the bond in the case of small debtors, to lay down what amount they should pay, and to grant them a discharge for the balance. To debtors owing larger sums it gave the full protection of an Insolvency Act. The Act further provided that agriculturists should not be arrested or imprisoned in execution of a decree for money; that their immovable property should not be attached or sold in execution of a decree unless it had been specifically mortgaged; and that even in such cases the Court might direct the lands to be cultivated by the debtor for a number of years on behalf of the creditor, after which the debt was discharged.

So far as the Survey and Settlement Officers were concerned, their powers were made even more absolute than before. In 1873 an appeal in an assessment suit was preferred in the High Court of Bombay, and the High Court decided the suit against the Settlement Officer. Immediately after, a bill was introduced in the Bombay Council to exclude the jurisdiction of the High Court and of all Civil Courts in matters relating to land assessments. The member in charge of the bill did not disguise its object, but explained it in these memorable words: "It is not expedient that the general policy of Government in relation to the Land Revenue should be questioned, or that the details of revenue assessments should be questioned, by Civil Courts." The Bombay revenue Jurisdiction Act was accordingly passed in 1876, excluding the jurisdiction of Civil Courts in matters of assessment. The private citizen in India is permitted by the British Government, and by British Laws, to seek redress against the Government itself in impartial Courts of Justice. But the millions of the peasant proprietors of Bombay and of Madras, subject to an enhancement of the State-demand at each Revision Settlement, are debarred from seeking justice in Courts, or before any independent tribunal, against the blunders or the undue severity of the assessing officer.

Three years after the passing of this Act, the Bombay Land Revenue system was comprehensively treated and legalised in the Revenue Code of 1879. It was an excellent Code, and it clearly affirmed the cultivator's rights of inheritance and transfer in respect of their holdings. But the Code gave no protection against undue enhancements, and no security against excessive assessments in violation of the principles laid down in 1856 and 1864.

Summary of Land Reforms in India.

We have in these five chapters briefly described the land administration of the different provinces of India during the first eighteen years of the Crown Administration. A great many real reforms were effected. Protection was given to the cultivators of Bengal, Oudh, and the Punjab, against unjust enhancement of rent by private landlords. The system of settlements in Northern India was improved, and assessments were made on the tangible basis of the rental of villages. Relief was given to Madras cultivators by the introduction of the thirty years' settlement rule. Help was given to Bombay cultivators by the Agricultural Relief Act and by the Revenue Code, both passed in 1879. And in the Central Provinces, the recognition of proprietary rights in Malguzars, and the long term settlement begun in 1863, were a boon to the harassed population.

The cardinal defects from which agriculture still suffered may be summed up in a few words.

(1) Enhancements were not limited by definite and specific rules at Revision Settlements.

(2) Assessments were not made according to the Half Rental Rule, but often absorbed the whole rental in Madras and Bombay.

(3) No independent tribunals watched the enforcement of rules.

(4) Special cesses on land, in addition to the Land Revenue, violated the Half Rental Rule.

CHAPTER VIII

TRADE AND MANUFACTURE

LORD CANNING undertook a great reform in the Indian Tariff. In February 1857, a year after his arrival in India, he addressed the Court of Directors on the subject. He proposed to equalise the duties on British and foreign merchandise, on raw and manufactured articles. He desired to exempt from duty a large number of articles which produced little revenue. He wished to abolish export duties, and to augment import duties. The proposals remained in abeyance during the Mutiny of 1857; and, in 1858, the East India Company ceased to rule.

Lord Stanley, the first Secretary of State for India under the Crown, replied to Lord Canning in April 1859. The liabilities of India had vastly increased in consequence of the Mutiny, and the financial difficulties were greater Lord Stanley, therefore, modified Lord Canning's proposals, so as to secure a larger revenue. British and foreign manufactures should be treated equally by raising the duties on British goods to the foreign rates. Duties on petty articles should *not* be abolished. Export duties should *not* be abandoned. Import duties should be increased.

Before receipt of this despatch, the Indian Government had already passed Act vii. of 1859, raising the duties on British goods to foreign rates, and taking power to levy the increased duties even on current contracts. And on receipt of the Secretary of State's despatch, Lord Canning replied that the Act recently passed was virtually in accordance with the instructions contained in the despatch.

But the Act gave great dissatisfaction to British merchants in India; and when James Wilson, the first Indian Finance Minister, went out to India, he had instructions to try and allay the irritation which had been caused.[1] Accordingly, in 1860, he abolished the export duties on Indian raw products, and considerably reduced import duties on manufactures. British merchants were conciliated; and India suffered a loss of revenue at the time of her sorest need.

In the same year, a committee was appointed to inquire into the subject of Indian tariffs generally. Two British merchants of Calcutta and Bombay formed the committee, and Ashley Eden, afterwards Lieutenant-Governor of Bengal, presided. The committee submitted their report in 1860, and suggested a uniform tariff and important customs reforms. A second committee was appointed in 1867, and submitted a revised tariff. A third tariff was prepared in 1869, and in the following year Lord Mayo's Government passed Act xvii. of 1870. The Act fixed the import duties generally at 7½ per cent. on manufactured goods and raw material, at 3½ per cent. on twist and 5 per cent. on piece goods, at 1 per cent. on iron and 10 per cent. on tobacco. The principal export duties were 6s. on a Maund (82 lbs.) of indigo, 3d. on a Maund of grain, 4 per cent. on lac, and 3 per cent. on oils, seeds, cotton goods, hides, and spirits.

Further changes were made in the following year by Act xiii. of 1871. The principal import and export duties, fixed by the Act, are given on p. 338.

Valuable evidence on the operation of these duties on trade was given before the Select Committees of the House of Commons which sat in 1871, 1872, 1873, and 1874. It is necessary therefore to refer to some portions of this voluminous evidence.

John Nutt Bullen, a prominent Calcutta merchant who had sat on Ashley Eden's Tariff Committee of 1860,

[1] See Sir Bartle Frere's evidence before the Select Committee of the House of Commons, 1871.

Import Duties.

Apparel, arms, cabinet-ware, candles, carriages, clocks, cotton, &c.	7½ per cent.
Cotton twist	3½ ,,
Piece goods	5 ,,
Medicines	7½ ,,
Colouring materials	7½ ,,
Fruits, glass, skins, jewellery, ivory, and leather	7½ ,,
Beer	1½d. per gallon
Spirits	6s. ,,
Wines	3s. ,,
Iron	1 per cent.
Other metals	7½ ,,
Naval stores, oils, paints, perfumery, porcelain, provisions, and oilman's stores	7½ ,,
Silk	7½ ,,
Sugar	7½ ,,
Tobacco	10 ,,
Woollen piece goods	5 ,,

Export Duties.

Cotton goods	3 per cent.
Grain of all sorts	4½d. per maund.
Hides	3 per cent.
Indigo	6s. per maund.
Shell lac, lac dye	4 per cent.
Oils	3 ,,
Seeds and spices	3 ,,

complained of the export duty of 4½d. per maund (82 lbs.) of grain, and said it fell on the grower of rice, and was, to that extent, an addition to the Land Tax. The import duty of 5 per cent. on cotton piece goods was, he considered, moderate and unobjectionable.[1] There were only two or three cotton spinning and weaving mills in Calcutta.

Sir Bartle Frere spoke guardedly on the effect of keeping down the import duty on cotton piece goods in order to foster the sale of British goods. "There is this difficulty," he said "that the interests of India and of England on that point seem rather at variance. No doubt some considerable increase of revenue might be realised by increasing the import duties, say, upon piece goods and yarns, but the direct result of that would be to

[1] Select Committee's Report, 1871; Question, 6014.

diminish consumption and to stimulate production on the spot."[1]

On the other hand, Walter Cassels, who had been a Bombay merchant and a member of the Bombay Legislation Council, argued that even the small import duty of 5 per cent. on cotton piece goods operated as a protective duty. And he looked with a jealous eye on the growth of the cotton spinning and weaving industry in Bombay. "I say they are protective duties. I do not advocate their abolition solely for that reason. I do not know whether you are aware that, for instance, in the Bombay Presidency there are 12 cotton mills, employing (a very small amount, of course, for Manchester) 319,394 spindles, 4199 looms, and 8170 hands, consuming, I think, 62,000 bales of cotton of 400 lbs. each annually."[2]

British administrators in India marked with satisfaction, rather than with jealousy, the growth of the infant cotton industry of Bombay; but in matters of Indian administration they were the servants of the British merchant and the British voter. The veteran Sir Charles Trevelyan, who had served India with credit and distinction under a former generation of rulers, and who had, at a later period of his life, been Governor of Madras and Finance Minister of India, spoke with some warmth against the sacrifice of legitimate Indian revenues under the mandate of British manufacturers. "Although the trade of India," he said, "increased in these ten years from £60,000,000 to £106,000,000, the Customs yielded £1,013,500 less. If Customs Duties are a legitimate source of revenue, so small an amount as £2,400,000 for the whole of India is simply ridiculous."[3]

Lord Lawrence, too, felt deeply on this point. As Viceroy of India he had tried to raise the export duties on jute and other Indian products in 1865, to get a little

[1] Select Committee's Report, 1871; Question 5608.
[2] *Ibid.;* Question 7962.
[3] *Ibid.;* 1873; Question 923.

additional revenue and save the country from a deficit. But British interests had been too strong for him, and the Secretary of State for India had disallowed his proposals. Eight years after, when he was questioned as a witness by Mr. Fawcett, he guardedly expressed his painful impressions of the influence of British trade over the financial policy of India.

Henry Fawcett.—With reference to export duties; if an attempt was made to increase the export duties, to put an export duty, for instance, upon cotton or upon jute, it would, *pro tanto,* place the trade of India in a, comparatively speaking, unfavourable position, and would bring to bear against the Government of India the very powerful pressure of the commercial classes in England, would it not?

Lord Lawrence.—That is quite true.

Henry Fawcett.—Do you think, considering that India is scarcely represented at all in this House, that it is only indirectly represented in the House, and that the commercial classes of England are powerfully represented in it, that any Government would, for one moment, be likely to resist an opposition, brought to bear upon them from people who have votes, against putting on such an export duty?

Lord Lawrence.—I think not.

Henry Fawcett.—Therefore, considering how India is governed, that India is governed by the House of Commons, and that India is governed by the Secretary of State, who, after all, is a Member of the Cabinet whose existence depends upon the votes of the House of Commons, you cannot rely upon the imposition of an export duty as giving you an increase of revenue in India, can you?

Lord Lawrence.—I am afraid not.[1]

It is necessary to make one more extract here from Mr. Fawcett's examination of Lord Lawrence to indicate the extent to which the Secretary of State and his Council

[1] Select Committee's Report, 1873; Questions 5580 to 5582.

did, and could, safeguard Indian interests against British commercial interests. The passage in question illustrates a painful truth which is as relevant to-day as it was thirty years ago.

Fawcett.—With regard to the relations between the Secretary of State and his Council, I understood in your previous examination that you said, speaking, for instance, as a typical case in reference to the Indo-European Telegraph, that when it was proposed to throw the whole expense of that telegraph on India, instead of making England bear a part of it, there would be no use in the Council of the Secretary of State objecting, because they had no political influence, and they were unable to resist the pressure which was brought to bear upon the Secretary of State from outside?

Lord Lawrence.—I said that was the practical result; I think the Council did act in many cases as a very considerable buffer between the people pressing on expenditure in India and the Secretary of State, and in many ways helped the Secretary of State to resist that pressure; but when it came to be a very important matter, in which the interests and the feelings of merchants in England were enlisted, then, I think, the Council could not resist it with any effect.

Fawcett.—But were they not appointed, and was not this great charge thrown upon the revenues of India, with no other object than that they should resist? That was the chief object with which they were appointed, was it not? If not, the duties which they performed might be performed, as they are in other Government Departments, by the permanent officials, the Under-Secretaries. Why, therefore, should they not, if they thought that this expenditure was wrong, say: "We are receiving a salary from the revenues of India; we care nothing about the political pressure that may be brought to bear upon the Secretary of State; no power on earth shall induce us to sanction an expenditure of money which we think is wrong, so far as the interests of India are concerned"?

Lord Lawrence.—"I think if you had no Council that practically there would be a great difficulty in that way. The Council may not be a perfect machinery, or a perfect buffer between those who want unduly to put expenditure on India and the Secretary of State, still they do a great deal in that way. I am sure from my experience of the five years that I was in Council, that had there not been a Council, a very great deal would have been put on India, which was not put on it, in consequence of the remonstrances of the Council.

Fawcett.—But still, without now discussing whether the Council do any good whatever, or whether it would not be desirable completely to abolish them, I want to know why was it not their first duty to the interests of India to resist—and how can it be said that they were not disregarding an important trust if they did not resist—this political pressure that you refer to, and did not say that no power on earth should induce them to sanction an expenditure which they thought wrong towards the people of India? For what other purpose did they receive their salaries except to do that?

Lord Lawrence.—That seems theoretically a very simple way of acting; but I think in practice it is extremely difficult; and I think, moreover, that if the Council had acted in that kind of way, they would not have succeeded. Some movement would have been made in Parliament, or elsewhere, whereby they would have been perhaps done away with, or their powers would have been so shackled that, in point of fact, they would have been less able to work than they hitherto did work.[1]

The total imports and exports of India during the last years of the Company's administration have been given in a preceding chapter. We exhibit below the figures for the first nineteen years of the Queen's administration, from

[1] Select Committee's Report, 1873; Questions 5597 to 5599.

1859 to 1877. These figures are taken from the "Statistical Abstracts relating to British India" annually published and presented to Parliament.

Trade of India with all Countries.

Year ending in	Import of Merchandise.	Import of Treasure.	Total Imports.	Total Exports.
	£	£	£	£
1859	21,728,579	12,817,071	34,545,650	30,532,298
1860	24,265,140	16,356,963	40,622,103	28,889,210
1861	23,493,716	10,677,077	34,170,793	34,090,154
1862	22,320,432	12,951,985	37,272,417	37,000,397
1863	22,632,384	20,508,967	43,141,351	48,970,785
1864	27,145,590	22,962,581	50,108,171	66,895,884
1865	28,150,923	21,363,352	49,514,275	69,471,791
1866 [1]	29,599,228	26,557,301	56,156,529	67,656,475
1867	29,038,715	13,236,904	42,275,619	44,291,497
1868	35,705,783	11,775,374	47,481,157	52,446,002
1869	35,990,142	15,155,954	51,146,096	54,457,745
1870	32,927,520	13,954,807	46,882,327	53,513,729
1871	34,469,119	5,444,823	39,913,942	57,556,951
1872	32,091,850	11,573,813	43,665,663	64,685,376
1873	31,874,625	4,556,585	36,431,210	56,548,842
1874	33,819,828	5,792,534	39,612,362	56,910,081
1875	36,222,113	8,141,047	44,363,160	57,984,549
1876	38,891,656	5,300,722	44,192,378	60,291,731
1877	37,440,631	11,436,120	48,876,751	65,043,789

It will appear from these figures that, during the first two years after the Mutiny, India received much more than she sent out, and that during the two succeeding years her imports were about equal to her exports. This equilibrium did not last long; in the year ending in April 1863 India exported nearly six millions more than her imports, and this difference went up to over sixteen millions in 1864, and to twenty millions in 1865. The difference decreased then for five years; but after 1870 it settled down to a figure generally between fifteen and twenty millions sterling a year. This heavy and impover-

[1] The official year terminated on April 30 up to 1866. From 1867 the official year terminated on March 31. Therefore the figures for the year ending in 1867 are for eleven months only, from May 1, 1866, to March 31, 1867.

ishing Economic Drain from India, which followed so soon after the commencement of the Crown administration, presented a melancholy contrast to the comparatively light tribute which India had paid under the Company's administration. For the difference between the imports and the exports of India during the last years of the Company's administration was something between three and four millions a year, as we have seen in a previous chapter.

Within twelve years after the change in administration, the Economic Drain from India had increased fourfold. India suffered this steady and increasing drain, and prepared herself for those frequent and widespread famines which marked the last quarter of the nineteenth century. They were the natural economic results of a continuous drain such as no country on earth could bear.

And while India suffered, the British nation, as a nation, did not gain. The manufacturers and operatives of Great Britain, who formed the nation, would have obtained larger profits from an increasing trade with India if the country had grown in wealth and prosperity. But a poor people are poor consumers of foreign articles. The total merchandise imported into India from all countries of the world showed a slight increase from 36 millions in 1868 to 37½ millions in 1877. Over one-half of this was British produce, and the consumption of British produce therefore scarcely increased a million in ten years.

The true character of the trade with India will appear more clearly if we pass in review the principal articles of import and export. The principal imports are exhibited in the table on the opposite page.

The import of cotton goods into India, which was arrested during the Mutiny years at a figure under five millions sterling, went up by a bound to eight millions in 1859, and rose to double that figure in ten years. The people of India did not use much more cotton clothing in 1869 than they did in 1859; and the increase of imports indicated a corresponding decrease in Indian manufacture.

Imports into India from all Countries.

Year.	Cotton Twist and Yarn.	Cotton Goods.	Silk Goods.	Woollen Goods.	Machinery.	Metal Manufactures.
	£	£	£	£	£	£
1859	1,714,216	8,088,927	147,740	294,258	587,566	447,011
1860	2,047,115	9,651,813	224,116	358,557	871,531	454,457
1861	1,748,183	9,309,935	259,596	222,813	870,251	386,748
1862	1,472,484	8,772,916	198,442	245,650	553,883	383,694
1863	1,270,301	8,360,229	342,111	296,221	506,518	424,188
1864	1,529,001	10,416,662	456,781	611,570	585,516	418,673
1865	2,191,440	11,035,885	443,949	867,831	554,156	608,104
1866	1,961,144	11,849,214	357,380	583,132	586,182	647,205
1867	2,572,700	12,524,106	415,070	576,481	601,740	359,422
1868	2,698,350	14,999,917	423,598	601,957	1,057,861	Not separately given
1869	2,779,934	16,072,551	486,518	764,173	793,183	
1870	2,715,370	13,555,846	466,593	596,713	555,742	
1871	3,357,393	15,687,476	425,527	583,220	447,543	
1872	2,424,522	15,058,811	480,948	514,194	405,835	
1873	2,628,296	14,605,953	560,646	719,530	517,316	
1874	2,628,959	15,155,666	608,374	668,911	1,002,347	
1875	3,157,780	16,203,560	710,478	557,585	1,185,943	
1876	2,794,769	16,450,212	708,866	869,760	1,391,667	475,338[1]
1877	2,733,514	15,991,719	584,789	811,652	882,373	440,190

From an economic point of view, the people had gained by obtaining cheaper clothing, while they had lost to a much larger extent by the loss of their weaving industry. For the loss was not replaced by any new industry; and millions of weavers sank to the level of agricultural labourers, and increased the pressure on the soil.

The same remark applies to the consumption of silk and woollen goods. The imports of the former increased from two to six hundred thousand pounds, and of the latter from three to eight hundred thousand pounds—displacing to that extent the weaving industries of India.

The fall in the imports of the last year, *i.e.* of the year ending March 31, 1877, was owing to a widespread distress in Southern India, which deepened into the terrible famine of 1877. Twenty years of peace had brought no prosperity to India; and the year chosen by Lord Lytton for his Delhi

[1] Described from 1876 as "Hardware, cutlery, and plated ware."

Durbar festivities was unhappily a year of the worst famine that India had yet known within the century.

The table on p. 347 shows the principal exports from India to all countries of the world between 1859 and 1877. We have selected only those articles the export of which exceeded two millions sterling in 1877.

The first article of export in the table is raw cotton, and the extraordinary variation in the quantities exported is both striking and instructive. Great Britain, desirous of creating a self-contained empire, had long endeavoured to obtain from the tablelands of Berar and Bombay the cotton required by the looms of Lancashire. A Parliamentary Committee had been appointed, as our readers will remember, in 1848, and John Bright, Chairman of the Committee, had held out no hopes of India largely adding to her supply to the cotton mills of England. The idea of a self-contained empire had proved a dream; England had to obtain her raw material from the country which grew it cheapest and best; and America produced the best cotton for the Lancashire looms. When the British nation were settling down to this sane economic conclusion, the Civil War of America suddenly disturbed and restricted the supply of cotton from that country. India then came to the rescue; and she supplied what America failed to supply. The export of cotton from India rose from ten to eighteen millions sterling in 1862–1863; to thirty five millions in the next year; and to thirty-seven millions in the year following. There were people who hoped at the time that Great Britain might dispense with American cotton in the future, and that her Indian Empire would henceforth supply the requirements of the Lancashire operatives. But the hope was soon dispelled. Peace returned to America; and trade returned to its natural channel. The export of Indian cotton fell as suddenly as it had risen; and by 1866–67 it had fallen no less than twelve millions. It was unfortunate for Bombay that the revision of her land-settlements began in the very

Exports from India to all Countries.

Year.	Raw Cotton.	Indigo.	Rice, Wheat, and other Grains.	Hides and Skins.	Jute.[1]	Opium.	Seeds.	Tea.
	£	£	£	£	£	£	£	£
1859	4,094,100	2,118,016	2,801,871	544,680	917,523	10,827,642	2,059,445	60,533
1860	5,637,624	2,021,288	3,588,562	444,537	623,995	9,054,394	1,548,721	127,771
1861	7,342,168	1,886,525	3,350,877	661,725	768,715	10,184,713	1,785,526	151,981
1862	10,203,470	1,647,503	4,039,938	794,137	724,455	10,553,912	1,206,331	192,442
1863	18,779,040	2,126,870	3,727,910	904,289	882,084	12,494,128	1,833,851	223,763
1864	35,864,795	1,756,158	4,325,377	897,575	1,618,244	10,756,093	2,032,832	271,229
1865	37,573,637	1,860,141	5,956,408	725,236	1,410,702	9,911,804	1,912,433	301,022
1866	35,587,389	1,861,501	5,247,918	609,803	1,083,522	11,122,746	1,750,197	309,899
1867	16,458,277	1,798,599	3,651,832	659,342	1,040,876	10,431,703	1,787,996	378,126
1868	20,092,570	1,823,226	3,961,225	988,282	1,309,537	12,330,799	2,160,572	729,714
1869	20,149,825	2,893,823	4,574,708	1,252,898	1,891,899	10,695,654	1,994,888	983,757
1870	19,079,138	3,178,045	3,221,454	1,691,330	1,984,495	11,693,330	2,308,942	1,080,515
1871	19,460,899	3,192,503	4,468,958	2,020,819	2,577,553	10,783,863	3,522,305	1,139,703
1872	21,272,430	3,705,475	4,865,748	2,525,925	4,117,308	13,365,228	2,728,788	1,482,186
1873	14,022,858	3,426,824	6,073,635	2,921,910	4,142,548	11,426,280	1,508,339	1,590,926
1874	13,212,241	3,555,300	6,548,346	2,618,358	3,436,015	11,341,857	2,361,451	1,754,618
1875	15,257,342	2,576,302	5,488,169	2,677,767	3,246,882	11,956,972	3,235,950	1,963,550
1876	13,280,959	2,875,065	6,421,137	2,944,933	2,805,340	11,148,426	5,462,388	2,183,881
1877	11,746,184	2,962,786	7,988,189	3,000,552	2,636,647	12,404,748	5,319,447	2,620,140

[1] The figures for the years 1859 to 1867 show both raw and manufactured jute,—as they have not been given separately in the *Statistical Abstract*. Roughly, three-fourths or more were exported raw, and one-fourth or less was manufactured. The figures for the subsequent years, 1868 to 1877, represent only the value of the raw jute exported.

years when accidental causes had brought about a temporary prosperity. Settlement Officers were induced to make those enormous enhancements in the Land Tax which have been described in another chapter, and which led to hardship and misery, and to rioting and disturbance, in 1875. The incident illustrates forcibly the evils of a varying Land Revenue demand in a country which is mainly agricultural. A nation of cultivators can never permanently improve their own condition if the State is ever ready to screw up its demands with the first signs of prosperity.

While the export of raw cotton underwent these variations, the export of Indian cotton goods, including twist and yarn, slowly improved. In 1858–59 the value of the export was £813,604; in 1863–64 it had risen to £1,167,577; in 1869–70 it was £1,298,757; and in 1876–1877 it had risen to £1,935,198, or nearly two millions. This aroused the jealousy of Manchester, and led to fiscal legislation which will be described in a future chapter.

The export of rice, wheat, and other food grains rose from under three millions to nearly eight millions in the nineteen years under review. Such a rise, in a country maintaining its commercial independence, is an indication of prosperity; but the commerce of India was forced and artificial. India had to meet a heavy drain which flowed annually into Great Britain without a direct commercial equivalent; she was unable to meet this demand by manufactured articles; and she met it therefore with the food supply of the people to a larger extent than she would have otherwise exported.

It is instructive, if somewhat painful, to watch how this process works. The annual Economic Drain to Great Britain is met directly from the revenues of India. A great part of the revenues of India is derived from the soil in the shape of the Land Revenue. The Land Revenue is realised, generally, from cultivators in Southern India, and from landlords in Northern India who in their turn exact rents from their tenants. Cultivators pay their revenue or their rents by selling a large portion of the produce of their fields, keeping an insufficient stock for their own consumption. Exporting merchants have their agents all over the country to buy what the cultivators are compelled to sell; and railways rapidly transport these purchases to seaports whence they are exported to Europe. India presents a busy scene to the winter globe-trotter when these transactions take place in every large town and market; but under the cheering appearance of a brisk grain trade lies concealed the fact that the homes and villages of a cultivating nation are denuded of their food to a fatal extent, in order to meet that annual tribute which England demands from India.

It thus happens that, even on the eve of great famines, the export of food goes on as briskly as ever, because the grain has to be sold to meet a rigid Land Revenue demand. In 1876–77, when India was on the brink of one of the severest famines of the century, she exported a larger quantity of food grains, as will appear from the foregoing table, than she had ever done in any preceding year. And even a province, actually suffering from famine, will continue to export food to an extent which bears some proportion to the amount of the Land Revenue realised from the province during the famine.

There are other far-reaching results of the demand of Indian rice and wheat in Europe which it is interesting to watch. The demand has had some effect in extending cultivation; and where the Land Revenue is permanently settled, this means a substantial increase to the wealth of the people. There can be little doubt that the people of Bengal are more resourceful in the present day than they were a century ago, owing to the large increase of cultivation in Bengal. The same remark can scarcely be made in respect of Madras and Bombay, where extension in cultivation leads to increase in the Land Revenue, sometimes out of proportion to the benefits obtained. It is sometimes forgotten that the lands last taken up are inferior in productive powers; and increase in the Land Revenue in proportion to the cultivated area is an increase out of proportion to the produce. When such blunders are committed, the extension of cultivation makes the people poorer, not richer.

Again, the demand of Indian produce in Europe affects the prices of the food grains. As the population of India is mainly a grain-producing nation, the rise in the price of food grains is an economic gain to the nation. But in this case also, a reservation has to be made. The signs of agricultural prosperity often induces Settlement Officers to screw up the Land Revenue, and the cultivators are left poorer when the prices fall again. All these considerations show the effects of a varying Land Revenue on the welfare of an agricultural nation.

The export of hides and skins went up from half a million sterling to three millions. This was an economic gain to the people in one way, but involved a loss in another direction; for the export of so much of skins indicated the decline of the leather industry in India. The export of jute also went up from a million to three or four millions in the early 'seventies. Most of the jute was grown in a few districts in Bengal; and while this new article of export added to the resource of cultivators, it restricted the area of land under rice cultivation.[1]

The export of opium was steady, and even showed an increase during the period under review; and as the Government had the monopoly of that article, the profits from the export was a gain to the revenues of India.

The export of seeds increased from two to five millions during the nineteen years, and this was a loss of manure to India. The refuse of oil seeds, after the oil is expressed,

[1] Mymensingh is one of the great jute-producing districts in Bengal, and nearly a third of the rice lands was under jute in the years 1887 to 1890 when I was in charge of that district.

is one of the best manures that can be used; and if the seeds had been used in India and the oils exported, an ample supply of manure would have been available for the purposes of cultivation. To export the entire seed is, in the words of Dr. Voelcker, "to export the soil's fertility."[1]

The indigo and tea exported were mainly grown and prepared by British capital and by Indian labour. The profits of the capital went to the shareholders in England; the wages of labour remained with the people of India. The many acts of coercion and oppression, by which an unwilling peasantry was forced to grow indigo by planters in Bengal, led at last to a serious disturbance and rioting in 1860. Dina Bandhu Mitra, an Indian writer, exposed the oppression in a drama of remarkable power; and the Rev. James Long translated it into English, for which public-spirited act he was fined and imprisoned by the High Court of Calcutta. The Hon. Ashley Eden, afterwards Lieutenant-Governor of Bengal, supported the cause of the oppressed cultivators; and an inquiry made by a Commission disclosed the many evils of the system. The question came up through Lord Canning to Sir Charles Wood, then Secretary of State for India, and that strong and upright administrator exerted himself to remove the evils which had stained the history of this industry. Large classes of the Bengal cultivators freed themselves, and refused to grow indigo under compulsion. The figures given in the table above will show that the export of indigo steadily went down between 1859 and 1862, and that it was not till 1869 that it showed indications again of a steady rise. A different cause—the invention of artificial indigo—finally ruined this industry in India at the close of the century.

On the other hand the export of tea showed no fluctuations, but a steady and rapid rise—the export increased fortyfold in nineteen years, from £60,000 in 1858–59, to over 2½ millions in 1876–77. The rise was continuous

[1] Dr. Voelcker's Report on Indian Agriculture.

and uninterrupted—every year within this period ended in a larger export than the preceding year. Many wild wastes in hills and valleys have been thus converted into gardens, and hundreds of thousands of poor people have found employment in these gardens. But a dark stain is cast on this industry by what is known as the "slave-law" of India. Ignorant men and women, once induced to sign a contract, are forced to work in the gardens of Assam during the term indicated in the contract. They are arrested, punished, and restored to their masters if they attempt to run away; and they are tied to their work under penal laws such as govern no other form of labour in India. Hateful cases of fraud, coercion, and kidnapping, for securing these labourers, have been revealed in the criminal courts of Bengal, and occasional acts of outrage on the men and women thus recruited have stained the history of tea-gardens in Assam. Responsible and high administrators have desired a repeal of the penal laws, and have recommended that the tea-gardens should obtain workers from the teeming labour markets of India under the ordinary laws of demand and supply. But the influence of capitalists is strong; and no Indian Secretary of State or Indian Viceroy has yet ventured to repeal these penal laws, and to abolish the system of semi-slavery which still exists in India.

CHAPTER IX

RAILWAYS AND IRRIGATION

RAILWAY operations were commenced in India under an arrangement, calculated to lead to extravagance, and not calculated to secure the comfort of passengers. Private companies working under a State guarantee of profits at 5 per cent. or 4½ per cent. on the outlay, were not likely to observe economy in the outlay, or to seek the convenience of travellers. If there was extravagance and waste in construction, the shareholders nevertheless got their guaranteed profit on all the money that was spent, wisely or unwisely. If traffic decreased and the earnings fell short of the guaranteed rate, the difference was made good from the revenues of India, *i.e.* from taxes paid by the people.

The experience of twenty years showed that these apprehensions were not unfounded. There was an extravagance in the construction of lines, and a disregard for the comfort of travellers, perhaps unexampled in the history of railway enterprise in any other country. And these facts were proved by witnesses of the highest rank and position, examined by the Parliamentary Committees of 1871, 1872, 1873, and 1874, of which we have spoken in the last chapter.

Juland Danvers and William Thornton, who were examined together in March 1872, were, from their position, the most important witnesses on the subject of Indian railways. Danvers was the Government Director of Indian Railways; and, while he admitted the extravagance and waste which had proceeded from the guarantee system, he nevertheless denied that "any other system would have enabled the Government at the time to have constructed the system of railways that has been carried out in India." Thornton was precisely of the contrary opinion, and held that "the guarantee system has not served any purpose whatsoever which might not have been better served without it."[1]

Speaking at a subsequent examination, Thornton said: "I do believe that unguaranteed capital would have gone into India for the construction of railways, had it not been for the guarantee. Considering how this country is always growing in wealth, and what an immense amount of capital is seeking investment which it cannot find in England, and goes to South America and other countries abroad, I cannot conceive that it would persistently have neglected India. I conceive that, as a result of the capital going to India and not being guaranteed—and it being known that if the investors made great mistakes, they would have to take the consequence of those mistakes—very much greater care and very much greater economy would have been adopted in the construction of the railways." "But," said Thornton, "when once Companies had been guaranteed, then there was no chance of unguaranteed Companies coming forward."[2]

It is difficult to believe, but nevertheless it is true, that the contracts were so hastily and carelessly drawn up, that they afforded no protection to the Government or to the Indian revenues on important points. "I think," said Thornton, "that the contracts are a perfect disgrace to whoever drew them up, for they contradict themselves two or three times in the course of their several clauses, and they are seldom appealed to for the protection of Government interests without turning out to be practically worthless for that purpose." "This is the necessary result of the way in which they are drawn up that, a railway having been commenced on the understanding that a certain guarantee would be given by the Government whatever

[1] Report of 1872; Questions 1863 and 1864.
[2] *Ibid.*; Questions 3030 and 3031.

the railway might cost, the Government is practically bound to continue the guarantee of interest upon the expenditure. Therefore, of course, the undertakers of the railway, the Company, are deprived of one of the great inducements to economy; they know that whatever blunders they make, those blunders will not prevent their getting full current interest on their expenditure."[1]

Lieutenant-Colonel Chesney, who had been auditor of railway accounts for six years, and was afterwards President of the newly established Cooper's Hill Engineering College, testified to the costliness and the carelessness of the work done under the guarantee system. "Railways," he said, "began in India in the year 1848, when the first staff of engineers were sent out; and I need hardly say that in those days engineers in England were not accustomed to make economy their first consideration. These gentlemen were sent out to make the railways, and there was a kind of understanding that they were not to be controlled very closely. . . . Then, too, the system of audit was extremely imperfect; it was what is called technically a post audit—nothing was known of the money expended till the accounts were rendered. The result of the system was that on one railway, the East India Railway, four millions sterling out of twenty millions had been disallowed from the capital account. The only thing to be done, however, under those circumstances, was to allow it, and bring it all into the capital account again, because, under the contract as it was worded, it was quite impossible to disallow it finally, and it was quite understood that whatever was spent must be eventually passed."[2]

Higher officials than Colonel Chesney spoke of the extravagance of the railway operations in India under the guarantee system. The Right Hon. William N. Massey, who had been Finance Minister of India under Lawrence and Mayo, said: "The East India Company cost far more,

[1] Report of 1872; Questions 1856 and 1857.
[2] *Ibid.*; Question 2623.

if not twice as much, as it ought to have cost; enormous sums were lavished, and the contractors had no motive whatever for economy. All the money came from the English capitalist, and so long as he was guaranteed 5 per cent. on the revenues of India, it was immaterial to him whether the funds that he lent were thrown into the Hooghly or converted into brick and mortar. The result was these large sums were expended, and that the East India Railway cost, I think (I speak without book), about £30,000 a mile. . . . It seems to me that they are the most extravagant works that were ever undertaken."[1]

Sir John Lawrence, as Viceroy of India, had condemned the extravagance of the Indian railways in the strongest terms, and had recorded that "the history of the actual operations of Railway Companies in India gives illustrations of management as bad and extravagant as anything that the strongest opponent of Government agency could suggest as likely to result from that system."[2] As a witness before the Parliamentary Committee of 1873, Lord Lawrence repeated his condemnation of railway extravagance in India, and also of the ill-treatment of passengers.

"I think it is notorious in India among almost every class that ever heard talk on the subject, that the railways have been extravagantly made; that they have cost a great deal more than they are worth, or ought to have cost."

"With a guarantee of 5 per cent., capitalists will agree to anything; they do not care really very much whether it succeeds or fails; 5 per cent. is such a good rate of interest that they are content to get that, and not really look after what is done. Hence one of the reasons why the cost of the railways has been more than it ought to have been."

"The Natives in my time, (and I see little difference to

[1] Report of 1872; Question 8867.

[2] Quoted in Lord Mayo's Despatch, dated March 11, 1869.

this day in spite of all the attempts of the Directors of the Companies to improve the system), greatly complained of their treatment on the railways; and I myself believe that though it is difficult to prevent abuse of power under such circumstances, yet the Government could be more effective in that respect than the Companies. . . . The Natives complained very much in this respect; and on inquiry that I used to make in India, both official and private, I was confirmed in the view that these statements of the Natives were to a considerable extent true." [1]

Our extracts have been long. But it is necessary to quote one more passage to show that even when the Indian Government declined to incur fresh railway liabilities, the Secretary of State for India had the power, no doubt under pressure from British traders, to sanction new schemes against the wishes of Indian authorities. This is revealed by the evidence of General Richard Strachey, who spoke with an experience of many years in the Public Works Department of India.

Fawcett.—But your evidence with regard to these bad bargains that have been made with various Companies tends to show this, that the people of India may be taxed in so many different ways. They may be taxed locally by local authorities; they may be taxed by the Governor-General; and the Secretary of State may carry out a scheme even against the wishes of all the authorities of India, and although he may know nothing whatever about India, and may never have spent an hour in it, which may entail heavy financial burdens on the people of that country?

General Strachey.—"There is no doubt that that is the unfortunate result of having a Despotic Government, managed in the sort of way that the Government of India is; and, for myself, I do not exactly see that there is any remedy for it.[2]

[1] Report of 1873; Questions 4589, 4777, 4781.
[2] Report of 1872; Question 6774.

It did not strike General Strachey in 1872, and it has not struck British administrators during the thirty years which have since elapsed, that the people of India, whose money was thus squandered, might have been consulted to some extent, even by a Despotic Government. If this had been done even in 1872, when the Parliamentary inquiry was made, the vast amount of capital which has been spent within the last thirty years on State Railways and Guaranteed Railways, greatly in excess of the available resources of the country, might have been reduced. But one of the gravest defects of the Indian administration is its rigid exclusiveness; there is no room in the entire machinery of the Indian Government for any effective control by the people of their own concerns.[1]

In a Minute, dated August 16, 1867, Lord Lawrence had calculated the total loss which the people of India had suffered from the construction of railways. "It is estimated," he wrote, "that while the Companies will have to supply 81 millions for the railways now under construc-

[1] Five years ago (in 1898) I had the privilege of being examined as a witness by the Indian Currency Committee, of which the Right Hon. Sir Henry Fowler was the Chairman; and I may be pardoned if I quote some portion of my own evidence to elucidate the remarks which I have made above.

"An endeavour ought to have been made during those years of peace (1878 to 1898) to bring down our Public Debt, so that we might borrow again when it was necessary to do so. And I further say that the people of India—say one financial representative from each of the five great Provinces—ought to be consulted by the Government; they should form a Committee; and some place should be found for them in the Viceroy's Executive Council, in order to advise the Viceroy and the Finance Minister in preparing every year's budget. A systematic endeavour should be made to reduce the Public Debt in every year of peace."

"I remember the condition of India twenty years ago. At that time all the main lines had been opened. The new lines which have been opened since have not added much to the development of trade; they have been constructed rather with regard to local interests."

"But all this is adding to our indebtedness, and it is a losing concern —according to your own showing—according to the last report published for the year 1897-98. We have lost 57 Crores of Rupees (thirty-eight millions sterling), and of that 28½ Crores (nineteen millions sterling) have been lost within the last twenty years. We should not abandon the railway system altogether, but we should be cautious, and I think the representatives of the people should be consulted before any new lines are sanctioned."

Questions 10,727, 10,728, and 10.742.

tion, the Government contribution will be $7\frac{1}{2}$ millions for land, loss by exchange, and supervision; $14\frac{1}{2}$ millions for interest paid in excess of nett revenues; and $4\frac{1}{2}$ millions in interest paid on those payments of guaranteed interest."

The Guarantee System was eventually abandoned. "The main system of Indian railways is nearly completed," said the official chronicler of Indian progress,[1] "and the State Railways, which are now under construction or proposed, will, for the most part, supplement the existing trunk lines. There are now open in India 5872 miles of railway which have cost about £97,000,000, giving an average expenditure of £16,536 per mile. . . . As no more lines will be entrusted to Companies, all railway construction will eventually be in the hands of the Government. Lines are now open from Calcutta to Multan and Bombay, and from Bombay to Madras. The completion of the latter line was effected on the 1st of May 1871, on which day the Great Indian Peninsula [railway] joined that from Madras."

"The whole amount of guaranteed capital which has been raised to the 31st March last was £94,725,000, of which £92,417,000 had been expended. The sum expended direct by the Government amounted to £5,398,000, making a total expenditure of upwards of a hundred million pounds sterling."

"But the railways are now almost completed, so that, with the cessation of heavy outlay on construction, the financial position may be expected to improve."

The writer of the above report anticipated a cessation of heavy outlay on construction in the future. It were well for India if his anticipation had been realised. It were well for the overtaxed population if, after the main lines had been completed, and a hundred millions had been spent on railways, the minor lines were left to private enterprise from 1874. The country could afford to wait,

[1] *Moral and Material Progress and Condition of India*, 1872-73. Ordered by the House of Commons to be printed, June 2, 1874, page 75.

and the country should have waited, in view of its resources and its liabilities. But this was not to be. The fatal facility with which the Indian Government could borrow in the English market made the construction of railways more rapid from 1874 than in the preceding years. And before the close of the century the mileage of railways in India had gone up from less than six thousand to over twenty thousand.

Railways helped the distribution of food supply in times of famine, but did not add to that supply. It was irrigation works which added to production and secured crops in years of drought. Hindu and Mahomedan rulers had therefore paid the greatest attention to irrigation works. And the remains of such works in every part of India, canals in Northern India, extensive tanks in Bengal, and large reservoirs in Southern India, still attest to the foresight and prudence of the ancient rulers. British administrators took up the work after some hesitation; and the excellent results achieved before the close of the Company's rule have already been described in another chapter. But the British nation, more familiar with railways than with canals in their own country, did not adequately realise the supreme importance of irrigation works in India; and did not extend them with the eagerness with which railway lines were multiplied.

Sir Arthur Cotton, the architect of the magnificent Kaveri and Godavari works, was one of the few men of his time who saw the great need of canals in India, both for irrigation and for transit. And he stated his convictions before the Parliamentary Committee with the pardonable exaggeration of an enthusiast. "On every important line of country in India," he said, "you can carry a canal, that is to say, on every line where there is great population." And he elucidated his remarks in the following words:—

"My great point is this, that what India wants is

water carriage; that the railways have completely failed; they cannot carry at the price required; they cannot carry the quantities; and they cost the country three millions a year, and increasing, to support them. That steamboat canals would not have cost more than one-eighth that of the railways; would carry any quantities at nominal prices and at any speed; would require no support from the Treasury; and would be combined with irrigation."[1]

It is due to two other eminent administrators, Sir Charles Trevelyan and Lord Lawrence, to state that they also recognised the importance of irrigation works for India. "Irrigation is everything in India," said Sir Charles Trevelyan; "water is more valuable than land, because when water is applied to land it increases its productiveness at least sixfold, and generally a great deal more, and it renders great extents of land productive which otherwise would produce nothing, or next to nothing."[2]

For twenty years and more, Lord Lawrence had been an advocate of irrigation works in India. He believed irrigation to be infinitely more important for the wants of the country than railways; but he could not make head against the general and deadening indifference on the subject. Railways, therefore, had proceeded faster, even under his administration, than irrigation works.

On one point, however, he was particularly strong; he would not impose a compulsory water-rate; he would make it optional with the cultivators to take water if they liked, and pay for it. "I would almost rather not make a canal at all, however much I desired to do so, rather than make it obligatory on them [the people] to take water."[3]

As the construction of railways by private companies under the Guarantee System was slowly abandoned, the

[1] Report of 1872; Questions 8429 and 8560.
[2] Report of 1873; Question 813.
[3] *Ibid.*; Question 4458. The spirit of Lord Lawrence's administration has passed away, and a compulsory water-rate has been imposed in Madras and elsewhere.

expenditure by the State increased from year to year. Irrigation works had, on the other hand, been generally undertaken by the State from the commencement, and the State expenditure therefore virtually represents all that was spent on irrigation. We extract the following figures from the *Statistical Abstract*, showing the expenditure on railways and on irrigation from Imperial Funds, not charged to revenue accounts.

	State Railways.	Irrigation Works.
	£	£
Spent up to March 1870 . . .	743,862	2,695,465
" " 1871 . . .	449,372	718,438
" " 1872 . . .	644,620	983,854
" " 1873 . . .	1,413,649	770,920
" " 1874 . . .	2,354,625	1,198,682
" " 1875 . . .	3,014,180	1,235,391
" " 1876 . . .	3,165,184	1,105,445
" " 1877 . . .	2,865,861	943,423
" " 1878 . . .	3,984,968	806,084
" " 1879 . . .	3,327,888	794,654
" " 1880 . . .	2,680,493	598,837
Total	£24,644,702	£11,851,193

It will be observed that while the total expenditure on railways by Guaranteed Companies and by the State came to 125 millions sterling down to March 1880, the total expenditure on irrigation works was only twelve millions sterling. It was this disproportion between the two classes of public works which irritated and grieved Sir Arthur Cotton; and after the terrible Madras famine of 1877, he found an opportunity to rouse the attention of the British public to the unwisdom of their policy in India.

Indian economic questions, not directly touching the interests of British traders and manufactures, seldom receive public attention in England. Sir Arthur Cotton had done all that man could do to rouse public attention to the importance of irrigation in India. And in spite of the practical proof he had given by his Kaveri and Godavari works, he might have gone to his grave unheard by the British public, if he had not enlisted the sympathy and co-operation of one of the foremost Englishmen of the day. John Bright came to his rescue.

At a great meeting at Manchester, held in January 1878, Mr. Bright supported the scheme of Sir Arthur Cotton to construct a number of navigable canals all over India at a cost of thirty millions sterling. This troubled the souls of officials. John Bright could not be ignored. The bold scheme for which he had stood sponsor could not be disregarded. Over a hundred millions had been spent on railways which Englishmen understood. But irrigation they did not understand; and to spend thirty millions on irrigation appeared to them waste of money. To take up the question of irrigation all over India seemed to the average Englishman something like taking a leap in the dark.

Lord George Hamilton, then a young man of thirty-two, and Under Secretary of State for India, expressed these apprehensions in his speech. "Seeing that, except in the delta, these irrigation works had all failed, he thought it was wrong for any one to support a gigantic agitation to force the Government into incurring an enormous expenditure, and yet keep back these notorious facts. Specially was he sorry to find that Sir Arthur Cotton had received countenance from such a high quarter as the right hon. gentleman, the member for Birmingham. His eloquence was so great that it seldom failed to influence the public mind."[1]

[1] Lord George Hamilton's speech, January 22, 1878. Lord George, in the course of this speech, spoke of Sir Arthur Cotton in terms which the latter resented. In a reply which he sent to the Secretary of State, Sir Arthur wrote: "Whether it is quite becoming, or for the furtherance of the public service, for a young man who had never been in India, had never seen a tank, an irrigated area, or a mile of steamboat canal, or spoken to a Ryot in the irrigated districts, and was consequently, of necessity, very ignorant of the whole subject, to speak before the House and the world in such contemptuous terms of an officer old enough to be his grandfather . . . is a point which I beg respectfully to offer for the consideration of the Right Hon. the Secretary of State and his Council." Lady Hope's *Life of Sir Arthur Cotton*, London, 1900.

Henry Fawcett "strongly deprecated any partisan feeling in discussing the question whether railways or works of irrigation were the better calculated to yield a profitable return, and to prevent the recurrence of famine."

John Bright then rose and asked, with all the weight of his high authority: "Why should not this Committee be appointed for the express purpose of ascertaining from such evidence as we can get in England, and if necessary, such as we can get from India, how it is that after so many years of possession—one hundred years of possession of this very part of the country—still we have got no further than this, that there is a drought, and then a famine? . . . We hear that there has been nine millions or sixteen millions sterling spent on such works [irrigation]. What is that in India? The town of Manchester alone, with a population of half a million, has spent two million pounds already, and is coming to Parliament now to be allowed to spend $3\frac{1}{2}$ millions more: that will be $5\frac{1}{2}$ millions to supply the population of that town and its immediate surroundings with pure water and a sufficient quantity of it. But in India we have two hundred millions of population subject to the English Government, and with a vast supply of rainfall, and great rivers running through it, with the means—as I believe there are the means—of abundant irrigation."

Sir George Campbell, who had entered Parliament after retiring from his high office in Bengal, sneered at Sir Arthur Cotton, and "thought there was some truth in the saying regarding him, that he had water on his brain!" But General Sir George Balfour spoke of the great and single-hearted irrigationist with esteem and admiration. Standing up before the House he would say that he did not believe that a single work that Sir Arthur Cotton had executed had ever been a failure. "Sir Arthur Cotton was a man of mighty genius; he was a man who had done much for the people; he had been a great benefactor to India; and his name would go down to posterity as one who had done great things for that country."

The inquiry asked for could not be refused. And on January 22, 1878, a select committee was appointed. Lord George Hamilton was the chairman. Twelve witnesses were examined, including Lord Northbrook, Lord Napier, and Sir William Muir; but it is needless to say that Sir Arthur Cotton was the most important witness. It was his scheme which was on its trial.

Sir Arthur put the whole case before the Committee in a few words at the commencement of his evidence.

"The Railway account now stands thus:—

Cost of works . . .	£112,000,000
Cost of land . . .	8,000,000
Debt now	50,000,000
Total . .	£170,000,000

for which we have about 7500 miles, or at the rate of £23,000 per mile. At the present cost to the Treasury in interest on share capital $4\frac{1}{2}$ millions, and on land and debt at 4 per cent., 3 millions; total, $7\frac{1}{2}$ millions. From which, deducting nett receipts, $4\frac{1}{2}$ millions, leaves *three millions a year as the loss on the money sunk.*"

"The capital spent on the water-works, including the Toombhadra, is £16,000,000. The accumulation of interest against the Bari Doab, the Ganges, and other canals, are much more than balanced by those to credit on the Kaveri, Krishna, and Godavari works, which have at least 10 millions to their credit, leaving a balance in their favour of 5 millions. So that the money sunk may be taken at £11,000,000, the interest of which at 4 per cent. is half a million, against which we have a nett profit over working expenses of about a million, leaving *a nett gain to the Treasury of half a million a year on irrigation works.*"[1]

[1] Question 2205.

But the great point which Sir Arthur Cotton made was that railways were no protection against famines. "I am afraid we must reckon that out of the 40 millions affected by the famine in Madras, Mysore, Hyderabad, and Bombay, 4 or 5 millions have perished, after spending 120 millions on railways besides incurring a debt of 50 millions sterling."[1] And he pointed out forcibly that railways did *not* provide food for man and beast; did *not* carry the whole traffic of the country; did *not* carry it cheaply enough; did *not* pay interest on cost and debt; did *not* drain the country, and did *not* provide drinking water for the people. All this was and could be done by irrigation works.

Why then were irrigation and navigable canals neglected? If these canals provided cheaper means of transit, why did the Indian Government not construct them?

"I want to know what is in your mind," asked Sampson Lloyd, a banker of Birmingham and a member of the Committee, "why any man should dread cheap transit?"

"Because," answered Sir Arthur Cotton, "it would stultify the railways, that is the sole point. Only think of a canal by the side of the Eastern Bengal Railway which carries some 200,000 tons, and a canal by the side of it carrying 2,000,000 tons, and swarming with passengers and goods. What a terrible affront to the railway that must be."[2]

The reply is a good illustration of the vehemence of Sir Arthur's convictions; but there was truth in what he urged. Englishmen had not appreciated the peculiar needs of India for cheaper transit as well as for irrigation. They had not realised that securing crops in years of drought was of far more greater importance in India than means of quick transit. Having already constructed a vast system of railways along the main lines of communication, they hesitated to venture on navigable canals

[1] Question 2204. [2] Question 2269.

which would compete with railways as a means of transit, and would deduct from the profits which the Government had guaranteed to Companies, or were deriving on their State lines. Nature had provided India with great navigable rivers which had been the high roads of trade from ancient times. And a system of canals, fed by these rivers, would have suited the requirements of the people for cheaper if slower transit, and would at the same time have increased production, ensured harvests, and averted famines. But Englishmen made a geographical mistake. They needed few canals in their own country, and they therefore neglected canals in India.

The principal lines of navigation which Sir Arthur Cotton recommended were (1) from Calcutta to Karachi, up the Ganges and down the Indus; (2) from Coconada to Surat, up the Godávari and down the Tapti; (3) a line up the Tumbhadra to Karwar on the Arabian Sea, and (4) a line up the Ponang, by Palaghat and Coimbatore.

Other witnesses were almost as eloquent as Sir Arthur Cotton himself on the benefits of canals for the purpose of navigation; and they also showed that, what Lord George Hamilton had called "failures," were not failures. Sir William Muir, who had been Lieutenant-Governor of Northern India, and then Finance Minister of India, said:

"I do not think I have expressed with sufficient emphasis the great value which I attach to the advantages derivable from the large canals such as the Ganges Canal and the Jumna Canals. The extent of prosperity which has been conferred upon the districts through which they pass is very great in a general point of view; and the degree in which the people are preserved from the distress and privations of famine is beyond all calculation a benefit to the country. The advantage also which I spoke of before in saving land revenues, which would otherwise be in arrear and lost, is also great. And further, there is an advantage in the country being protected and being preserved from deterioration, which is incidental to land which is affected by famine, that is to say, being protected from the secondary effects of famine which are liable to continue for considerable periods after the famine itself has passed away. Altogether the general improvement and advancement of the Doab, which is due specially to these canals, is a matter which, apart from their immediate financial returns, cannot be overlooked, and must be borne in mind in determining the general advantages derivable from canal irrigation."[1]

But Lord George Hamilton's Committee failed to grasp the importance of irrigation works from this broad and statesmanlike point of view. And they returned again and again to the narrower view, based on the immediate financial return of works constructed. A few paragraphs from the Select Committee's Report are quoted below.

"Sir Arthur Cotton proposes the summary and indefinite suspension of nearly all railway schemes and works. He would, however, devote ten millions annually for the next ten or twenty years to irrigation works, mainly canals (Question 2722), the main canals to be of such dimensions as to permit navigation. By such an expenditure he estimates that ten thousand miles of main line navigation would be constructed at a cost of thirty million sterling, dealing with the most populous districts, whilst the remainder of this vast sum was to be spent on feeders or subsidiary works.

"Sir Arthur Cotton estimates that such an expenditure would give a large return to Government (Question 2751), though your Committee were unable to ascertain the data of this conclusion, especially as he does not deem it to be within his province to consider how, or at what rate of interest, the money expended would be raised. Neither has he in any way attempted to estimate or make provision for the immediate rise in the cost of material

[1] Question 2885.

and labour which so sudden and simultaneous an expenditure throughout India must inevitably produce.

"The figures already embodied in this report show how few of the most carefully examined irrigation schemes have proved remunerative, and these returns are more than confirmed by Sir Arthur Cotton himself, who, in reply to a question asking him to indicate what works constructed by the Government of India during the last twenty years, other than those in the Madras Delta, had proved remunerative, replied, 'None of the great works pay yet' (Question 2214).

"It is evident to your Committee that this scheme, though of gigantic dimensions, is of too shadowy and speculative a character to justify their noticing it, except for the purpose of emphatically rejecting it."

It will appear from these extracts that the Select Committee singled out the Madras Deltas as the only remunerative works; and that, from their narrow point of view, even the Ganges and Jumna works, which had increased the prosperity of the people, prevented famines, and saved the land revenues from loss in years of drought, were not remunerative.

It is worthy of note that shortly after Lord George Hamilton's Committee had come to this decision, the Madras Famine Commission commenced its inquiries in a more thorough and systematic manner in India and in England. And the Famine Commission came to a conclusion diametrically opposite to that of Lord George Hamilton, both as regards the immediate returns, and the broad results of irrigation works. "The result has been," so the Famine Commission wrote in respect of irrigation works, "a great advantage to the State, regarded merely from the direct financial return on the money invested; and apart from their value in increasing the wealth of the country in ordinary years, and in preventing or mitigating famine in years of drought."[1]

[1] Famine Commissions Report, 1880.

And the people of India—those who paid the cost of railways and irrigation works alike—would undoubtedly have given their support, if they had been consulted, *firstly*, to Sir Arthur Cotton's proposal to stop the further extension of State Railways and Guaranteed Railways, after the main lines had been completed, and *secondly*, to the construction of carefully considered irrigation works for the benefit of cultivation and the prevention of famines. Sir Arthur Cotton's plans undoubtedly were "shadowy and speculative"; for schemes drawn up in London, even by a man of his genius and Indian experience, must be only tentative in their nature. But a close and careful examination would have shown us how far these schemes were practicable, and were likely to be beneficial. And the construction of such useful works, twenty-five years ago, would have averted the worst effects of the famines of the last years of the century. But Lord George Hamilton's Committee had given their verdict; and the occasion created by Sir Arthur Cotton's foresight and John Bright's large-hearted sympathy passed away, not to return again within the century.

CHAPTER X

FINANCE AND THE INDIAN DEBT

THE system of presenting the annual accounts underwent alterations from time to time, between 1858 when the Queen took over the direct administration of India, and 1877 when she assumed the title of Empress of India.

In the accounts presented to Parliament for 1859–60, the interest on guaranteed railway capital was for the first time shown as a charge on the revenues of the year.

In 1867–68, the policy of constructing large "Productive Works" with borrowed money, and of excluding the capital so borrowed from the ordinary revenue and expenditure accounts, was sanctioned. It was by such exclusion that a surplus was shown in the accounts under Lord Mayo's administration. The capital borrowed was shown under the heading of Debt for Productive Public Works; and the interest on the debt was shown in the ordinary revenue and expenditure accounts.

In 1870–71 the system of allotting to the different Provincial Governments certain grants of money, with the responsibility of meeting therefrom certain charges, was inaugurated under Lord Mayo's decentralisation scheme. In that year the only financial effect was an advance of £200,000 to provide those Governments with a working balance. But from 1871–72 to 1875–76 certain receipts, estimated at about £650,000, were deducted from the expenditure, and both sides of the account were reduced to that extent; while expenditure to the amount of £500,000 was shown in a lump sum as Allotments for Provincial Services.

From 1871–72 the statement of Nett Income was

abandoned; revenues were shown in the gross, and expenses of collection were included in the expenditure.

From 1876–77 the system of showing the Allotments to Provincial Governments was altered. Instead of one sum being shown as Allotments to Provincial Services, the receipts and expenditure were exhibited in detail under the proper headings. From the same year also, the annual revenue from Productive Public Works, and the annual charge for interest and working expenses in connection with them, were shown.

From 1877–78 a new heading of Provincial Rates was introduced, under which were entered the receipts from the special taxation imposed upon land in 1877. A further change was made in the following year by bringing into the general revenue account all the Local Funds previously accounted for separately, a corresponding charge being entered under various headings on the other side.[1]

The figures on the next page, showing the revenues and expenditure of India during the nineteen years which elapsed from 1858–59 to 1876–77, are taken from the *Statistical Abstracts* for India annually presented to both Houses of Parliament. Under the head of revenue we show the Land Revenue separately; and under the head of expenditure, we exhibit separately the portion of it incurred in England.

It will appear from these figures that the gross revenues of India increased from 36 millions to 51 millions in eighteen years, *i.e.* by the end of 1875–76; and the portion of it spent in England, *i.e.* the Home Charges, increased within the same period from 7½ millions to 10 millions.

Then followed the eventful year, 1876–77, when there was a decrease of Land Revenue on account of

[1] Henry Waterfield's *Memorandum* on Changes made in the form of the Accounts, dated April 20, 1880. The official year ended on the 30th April up to 1866. It ended on the 31st March from 1867. Therefore the figures for 1866–67 in the table on the following page are for eleven months only, 1st May 1866 to 31st March 1867.

Year.	Land Revenue.	Gross Revenue.	Expenditure in England.	Gross Expenditure.
	£	£	£	£
1858–59	18,123,658	36,060,788	7,466,136	51,056,930
1859–60	18,757,400	39,705,822	7,239,451	51,861,720
1860–61	18,508,991	42,903,234	7,745,848	48,154,087
1861–62	19,684,668	43,829,472	7,624,476	44,870,232
1862–63	19,570,147	45,143,752	7,252,317	44,053,122
1863–64	20,303,423	44,613,032	6,894,234	44,982,006
1864–65	20,095,061	45,652,897	6,998,770	46,450,990
1865–66	20,473,897	48,935,220	6,211,178	47,332,102
1866–67 (11 months)	19,136,449	42,122,433	7,545,518	44,639,924
1867–68	19,986,640	48,534,412	8,497,622	50,144,569
1868–69	19,926,171	49,262,691	10,181,747	53,407,334
1869–70	21,088,019	50,901,081	10,591,013	53,382,026
1870–71	20,622,823	51,413,686	10,083,004	51,098,506
1871–72	20,520,337	50,110,215	9,850,912	48,614,512
1872–73	21,348,669	50,219,489	10,547,908	50,638,386
1873–74	21,037,912	49,598,253	10,265,557	54,959,228
1874–75	21,296,793	50,570,171	10,604,994	54,500,545
1875–76	21,503,742	51,310,063	9,898,683	53,911,747
1876–77	19,857,152	55,995,785	13,467,763	58,178,563

the Madras famine. The somewhat sudden increase in the figures, representing the gross revenue and the gross expenditure of that year, is due to the inclusion in the accounts of the receipts and charges for interest in connection with Productive Works, as has been already explained. The whole of the nett railway receipts is shown on the revenue side from that year; and the whole of the Guaranteed Interest and Profits paid to Companies is shown on the expenditure side.

The total Debt of India just before the Mutiny in 1856–57 was 59½ millions, and in the following year it rose to 69½ millions sterling. As the whole charge of the Mutiny wars was thrown on India, the Public Debt rose in 1860 to over a hundred millions. And as the construction of railways was undertaken by the State after the Guarantee System was abandoned, and railway lines were recklessly extended with borrowed capital, the Public Debt rose rapidly from 1870.

It is necessary to explain that the figures for

Year.	Indian Debt and Obligations.	Debt in England.	Total.
	£	£	£
1858–59	66,082,031	15,089,277	81,171,308
1859–60	71,969,460	26,138,000	98,107,460
1860–61	71,901,081	29,976,000	101,877,081
1861–62	72,418,859	35,095,300	107,514,159
1862–63	72,656,135	31,839,100	104,495,235
1863–64	72,207,645	26,310,500	98,518,145
1864–65	72,352,455	26,125,100	98,477,555
1865–66	71,437,251	26,946,400	98,383,651
1866–67	72,526,815	29,538,000	102,064,815
1867–68	71,289,111	30,697,000	101,986,111
1868–69	71,168,289	31,697,900	102,866,189
1869–70	72,989,638	35,196,700	108,186,338
1870–71	81,372,859	37,627,617	119,000,476
1871–72	82,754,841	39,012,617	121,767,458
1872–73	82,484,476	39,012,617	121,497,093
1873–74	81,837,043	41,117,617	122,954,660
1874–75	81,738,564	48,597,033	130,335,597
1875–76	84,759,776	49,797,033	134,556,809
1876–77	83,537,992	55,397,033	138,935,025

1870–71 were revised at the instance of the Select Committee on Indian Finance so as to include some obligations not previously exhibited, and this plan was followed in subsequent years. The total Debt of 139 millions at the close of 1876–77 includes the money borrowed and spent by the Government on State Railways and Irrigation Works, but does not include the money spent by private companies under guarantee of interest from the Indian revenues. Down to 1876–77 the Government had spent about 24 millions on State Railways and Irrigation Works; that is to say, £14,651,353 on State Railways, and £9,651,618 on Irrigation Works.

It is also necessary to explain that the figures given above do not include the East India Stock of twelve millions sterling, forming the capital of the East India Company on which India still paid interest.

We have seen in a previous chapter that the East India Company had piled up a Public Debt of 69½ millions during the century of their rule in India. It is painful to observe that the Administration of the Crown *doubled this Debt in nineteen years,* bringing it up to 139 millions—not including the East India Stock.

Let us suppose once again that an independent and impartial tribunal—an International Arbitration Court not composed purely of British or of Indian judges—had to deal with this Indian Debt of 139 millions in the memorable year 1877, when the Queen assumed the title of Empress of India.

There can be little doubt what the verdict of the Court would have been. The arbitrators would have made a clean sweep of the Company's Debt of 69½ millions, as made up of a part of the unjust demand of an annual tribute which India should not have paid.[1] They would probably have given an award to Great Britain for the Mutiny Debt of 40 millions—the cost of British troops employed in India—after deducting from it the cost of Indian troops employed in Imperial wars in Afghanistan, China, Persia, and Abyssinia; and the balance against India, if any, would have been small. And lastly, the arbitrators would have allowed the Public Works Debt of 24 millions to stand—with perhaps an injunction against the borrowing of more capital for such works—as minor railway lines could wait until taken up by private enterprise, and irrigation works could be annually extended from the ordinary revenues of the empire. A hundred millions of the so-called Public Debt of India would thus have been struck off as not justly due from India. And the balance[2] would soon have been extinguished from the revenues of India, once freed from the payment of interest of this enormous and unjust liability. There would have been no National Debt; for there need be no National Debt in India.

[1] See *Economic History of British India, 1757 to 1837*, chapter xxiii.

[2] We assume there would be balance against India, not reckoning the whole of the tribute paid by India during the century of the Company's rule, and not reckoning interest. If this was reckoned, the balance would be largely against Great Britain.

The institution of a National Debt was unknown in India under her old rulers. Hindu and Mahomedan kings sometimes borrowed money from bankers on their own credit, as English kings in the olden days borrowed money by pledging their Crown jewels, or assigning specific revenues for the discharge of the debt. So late as 1688, the year of the English Revolution, England had scarcely any National Debt—the amount was less than a million.[1] And it would have been better if British rulers of India had followed the Indian precedent, or the old English precedent of the seventeenth century, instead of importing into India the more recent European institution of a National Debt.

Modern European nations create National Debts mainly to extend their conquests and colonies, and to maintain their position among rival nations. India seeks no conquests; she has no rivals in Asia; her position under a strong and good government is invulnerable. The cost of the British conquest of the country had been defrayed from her annual revenues; the cost of useful public works could be met from those revenues. There was no need for creating a permanent National Debt in such a country; and there was no need for continuously increasing it when peace had followed the Mutiny wars, and the administration had been assumed by the Crown. Lord Lawrence endeavoured to meet all expenditure from the annual income. Lord Mayo's plan of constructing Public Works with borrowed capital was a mistake. When money is easily borrowed it is easily spent, and the Debt accumulates.

The alarming growth of Debt and expenditure in India attracted the attention of Mr. Gladstone, the greatest British financier of the nineteenth century. He wished to arrest it, and he moved for a Select Committee on Indian Finance in 1871. It would have been well for India if Mr. Gladstone himself could have sat on that Com-

[1] £664,263.

mittee; but as Prime Minister of Great Britain he could not do so. He did what was possible when he appointed Mr. Henry Fawcett as one of the members. Select Committees sat for four years, from 1871 to 1874, and unfortunately discontinued their inquiries soon after the Liberal Government was upset in 1874. No final recommendations and no great remedial measures therefore ensued. But the evidence recorded during the four years is valuable, and has been referred to in preceding chapters. And it is interesting to turn again and again to this evidence, given by men who conducted the administration and directed the finances of India a generation ago.

One of the most important witnesses examined was the Right Honourable W. N. Massey, who had been Finance Minister of India from 1865 to 1868. And he impressed on the Committee, in the strongest words he could use, the necessity of limiting the expenditure in India to the annual income.

"The principle of English Finance is,—adjust your income to your expenditure. In my opinion the contrary principle should be adopted in Indian finance. The truth is that your resources are so limited, that if you should outrun the constable a little, you are at once landed in a deficit. You cannot expand any of your taxation; you cannot create new taxation with the exception of the Income Tax. I wish to say that in round terms, for there is no new source of taxation, as far as I am aware, that it is possible for you to invent. Therefore it is that I would most earnestly impress upon all Indian financiers the expediency of accommodating their expenditure to their income." And referring to the Duke of Wellington's reply to the Court of Directors in 1834, *to make the expenditure keep within the income*, the witness said, "I wish the spirit of the Duke of Wellington's reply was made applicable to the present administration throughout the whole of India." [1]

[1] Report of 1872; Questions 8583 and 8612.

Still more emphatic was the evidence of another Finance Minister of India, Sir Charles Trevelyan. He had been the colleague of Lord William Bentinck and Macaulay in Indian administration forty years before; he had been Governor of Madras and had been recalled from that post for protesting against increase of taxation; and he had then been Finance Minister of India from 1863 to 1865. A venerable man of sixty-six years, he still spoke with the fire of youth; and a veteran administrator of India both under the Company and under the Crown, he protested against the increased expenditure of the Crown Government.

"Do you think," he was asked, "that, since the direct administration of affairs by the Secretary of State for India in Council, there has been a greater disposition to give way to demands for expenditure of Indian finances?"

"Yes, no doubt," he replied. "The Queen's Government has shown itself profuse and squeezable. . . . I refer to the great point which was made in the transfer of the Government, of building up the personal independence of the Members of the Indian Council by a life tenure of office, and the arrangement that was made to continue in the Council the exclusive control over payments out of the revenue which had attached to the East India Company. But as regards expenditure, it has all gone for nothing. . . . The influences which press upon the Government outside, through the Press and through their influential supporters, have altogether been too strong, and every safeguard has been overborne."[1]

"Stout resistances," said Sir Charles on a subsequent day, "which the East India Company opposed to the demands of the Queen's Government in former days, show that a substantial barrier did exist; and I can answer for those resistances having been, to a great

[1] Report of 1873; Questions 415 and 416.

extent, effectual. . . . The most striking comparison is that between the administration of Public Works under the Queen and their administration under the Company." [1]

Four times had Sir Charles Trevelyan, as Governor of Madras, protested against the increase of expenditure and taxation. In 1859, he had protested against a tax on tobacco; and "from that time," he said in his evidence, "two conflicting policies prevailed in India; one the policy advocated by me of *reduction of expenditure;* the other, which was the favourite of Calcutta and in England, *increase of taxation.*" His second and third protests were also submitted in the same year; but it was his fourth protest, dated March 20, 1860, which cost him his high post. "Taxes," he wrote, "are a portion of the property of the community taken by the Government to defray necessary public expenditure. The Government therefore has no right to demand additional taxes unless it can be shown that the object cannot be secured by a reduction of unnecessary expenditure. In other words the reduction of expenditure is the primary mode for making good deficiency. . . . If we use the strength which our present advantages give to force obnoxious taxes upon the people, we shall place ourselves in a position towards them which will be totally incompatible with a simultaneous reduction of the native army. We cannot afford to have a discontented people and a discontented army upon our hands at the same time." [2] It was the publication of this Minute, urging obvious but unpalatable truths, which led to Sir Charles Trevelyan's recall. But a man like him could not be spared by the Indian administration; and three years after his recall, he was sent back to India as Finance Minister.

In urging reduction, Sir Charles did not fail to see the difficulties in its way. Practically all Great Britain

[1] Report of 1873; Question 965.
[2] *Ibid.;* Questions 1281 and 1282.

as well as official India was interested in increased expenditure; the people of India who were interested in reduction had no voice and no hand in the administration of their own concerns. Trevelyan boldly faced this difficulty, and the most valuable portion of his evidence is that in which he recommended that the people should be consulted before new taxes were imposed.

"I am of opinion," he said, "that as in other countries where the same principle has been carried out, Representation must be commensurate with Taxation. I think there ought to be, first, Provincial Councils, *i.e.* eight quasi-representative Councils, (I do not say that they should be appointed by popular election at first), at the chief seats of the eight Local Administrations; then there should be Zilla or County Councils, each district being represented by its notables and confidential men. And lastly there should be Town and Village Municipalities, and the principle of direct election should be introduced within such limits as may be safe and expedient."

"The Natives are by no means deficient in public spirited liberality; the country is covered with ancient works, tanks, caravansaries, and works of various kinds, which have been constructed by individual munificence; and the extraordinary liberality of Parsees and others, who have acquired fortunes during the late time of mercantile activity, is well known. If the Councils were merely consultative, the members would never become emancipated from the control of the European official Presidents. The Natives should not always be made to go in leading strings. It is the old story of not allowing a boy to go into the water till he can swim; he never will learn to swim unless he goes into the water and incurs a little risk and paddles about. At first, no doubt, they will be timid and frugal; but a little done willingly is better than a great deal done under compulsion, or done for them. Give them the raising and spending of their own money, and the motive will be supplied, and life and reality will be imparted into the whole system. All would act under a real personal responsibility under the eye of those who would be familiar with all the details, and would have the strongest possible interest in maintaining a vigilant control over them. And it would be a school of Self-Government for the whole of India —the longest step yet taken towards teaching its 200,000,000 of people to govern themselves, which is the end and object of our connection with that country."[1]

Thirty years have passed since the above evidence was recorded, but even Consultative Provincial Councils have not been created yet to give the people of India some voice in the administration of their finances. Expenditure has not been reduced; taxes have not been lightened; and there is more widespread poverty, with more frequent and severer famines to-day, than thirty years ago.

With regard to the capacity of the people of India, Sir Charles Trevelyan, with his more than forty years' knowledge of India, had no misgivings.

"The Natives," he said, "have all the qualities to make them good revenue officers. From Todar Mall, Akbar's Minister, who made the first revenue survey of India, and Purnea, who made Mysore so flourishing . . . down to Madhava Rao, and a very remarkable man, although less known to fame, Ramia Ayangar, the Natives are specially qualified for revenue functions. The whole of the appointments to the Customs might be filled by Natives."

"Then there is the great judicial department; it stands *a fortiori*, that if they are fit to be Judges of the High Court, they are fit for the subordinate appointments."

"They have shown practical talent [in engineering]; and on the main point of all, that of irrigation, nothing can be better than the ancient irrigation works of

[1] Report of 1873; Questions 863 and 866.

Southern India; in fact, they have been a model to ourselves. Sir Arthur Cotton is merely an imitator, on a grand scale and with considerable personal genius, of the ancient Native Indian engineers." [1]

Other great administrators, distinguished by their work in various provinces in India, also felt the necessity of consulting the people in some way or other in the matter of assessments and taxation.

"There seems to me a great necessity," said Sir Bartle Frere, who had been Governor of Bombay, "for having some means of ascertaining directly from the cultivators their views regarding assessments, which used to be ascertained by general communication with them, and for which there has been every year less and less facility, as our officers become more completely occupied and less able to put themselves in intimate communication with the taxpayers. I think that it would be very desirable that, before every revision of assessment after the expiration of the thirty years' leases, there should be some means of directly ascertaining what the cultivator and the cultivating class have to say upon the subject." [2]

"In India," said Sir Robert Montgomery of Punjab fame, "we set aside the people altogether; we devise and say that such a thing is a good thing to be done, and we carry it out without asking them very much about it." "I think if each local Governor had a Consultative Native body, which he would select from year to year or from time to time, and before which he would put certain points or questions, whether on taxation or on law, which might affect their welfare generally, he would get a most excellent opinion from them; and with that opinion, and the opinions of the officers of the Local Government, he would be able to arrive at the right decision." [3]

[1] Report of 1873; Questions 851 and 1547.
[2] Report of 1871; Question 454.
[3] *Ibid.*; Questions 1774 and 1831.

Robert Elliot, who spoke with an intimate knowledge of the people of Madras and Mysore, regretted that there was no channel of communication between the Government and the people, and suggested the formation of Councils of the People. "I would first of all accustom the people to the idea that the Government had something to communicate to them, and they to the Government, and you might develop that system gradually towards Representative Institutions."[1]

"If there were a Local Council of the composition that you describe," Sir Charles Trevelyan was asked, "such taxes as were passed by the Bombay Legislature, viz., a tax on the non-agricultural rural population, or such a tax as the one on feasts or on marriages, would not be passed by any freely chosen representative body?"

"They certainly would not have been passed," replied Sir Charles Trevelyan; "and that is a striking example of calling the Natives to our Councils."

"And very possibly, if the Government should recommend them an unobjectionable tax in itself, they may say, 'We will not burden the people of this Province; this sum of money must be provided for by a reduction of expenditure in some other item;' you would not interfere with their decision in the matter?"

"No."

"You would give them independence, subject to veto on any measure they may pass?"

"Yes; it would be their own affair?"[2]

A paper was handed in by Mr. Gay to the Finance Committee[3] comparing the taxation of 1856–57, the year before the Mutiny, and 1870–71, the twelfth year of the Crown Administration. The limits of the empire had not been extended within this period; the resources of the people and their industries and manufactures had not

[1] Report of 1872; Question 3454.
[2] Report of 1873; Questions 1444 to 1446.
[3] Report of 1872, page 518.

increased; the taxable wealth of the country and the material condition of the people had not improved; and yet there was increase in taxation, specially in salt and in assessed taxes, which is startling. We note some of the items below:—

Heads of Revenue.	1856-57.	1870-71.
	£	£
Land Revenue	20,046,748	24,170,151
Assessed Taxes	108,833	2,072,025
Customs	1,191,985	2,610,789
Salt	3,610,223	6,106,280
Opium	4,988,434	8,045,459
Other Heads of Revenue	1,974,687	6,371,521
Total	£31,920,910	£49,376,225

Twelve years of Crown Government had increased the taxation by more than 50 per cent. "During the last twelve years," wrote the Bombay Association in their petition to the House of Commons, dated March 29, 1871, "the salt tax has been raised 100 per cent. in Madras, 81 per cent. in Bombay, and 50 per cent. in other parts of India; the duty on sugar has been enhanced 100 per cent.; the Abkari or excise on spirits 100 per cent.; the stamp has been repeatedly revised and enhanced, and is now so complicated, vexatious, and excessive, as frequently to lead to a denial of justice; customs duties have been increased several times; heavy court fees and a succession tax of 2 per cent. have been recently imposed; a local land cess of 6¼ per cent., village service cess at the same high rate, rural town cess, taxes on trades and callings, house-tax, tolls; and a considerable variety of municipal and local rates and taxes, amounting in the aggregate to an extremely large and oppressive sum, have been levied in different parts of the country. It is now proposed to impose fresh Local Taxes to supply the deficiency caused by the conduct of the Government of India in curtailing the grant of several Provincial

Services. Your Petitioners submit that over-taxation has, for many years of British Rule, been the bane of India; and that strenuous endeavours have not been made by the authorities to reduce the public expenditure, which has been increased from year to year, until the augmentation now amounts to the vast sum of 19 millions over and above the expenditure of 1856–57."[1]

And Mr. Dadabhai Naoroji, the patriotic Indian representative who appeared as a witness before the Finance Committee, placed before the Committee with equal force and cogency the fact of the extreme poverty of the people of India, their decadence in wealth and resources under British Rule, and the heavy and growing taxation of the country.

"I may put this great financial fact before the Committee," he said. "The United Kingdom out of its resources (I use Lord Mayo's word) obtains 70 millions, from which about 27 millions being deducted for interest on Public Debt, there remains about 43 millions for the ordinary wants of the Government. This amount is about 5½ per cent. of the income of the country of 800 millions. The British [Indian] Government out of its resources obtains 50 millions, from which about 8 millions being deducted for interest on Public Debt, Railways, &c., there remain 42 millions for its ordinary wants; this makes 14 per cent. of the income of the country of 300 millions. So that the Indian Government is two and a half times more expensive than the Government of the United Kingdom."[2]

It is painful to note that these protests from the people of India led to no reduction in expenditure and in taxation. On the contrary, Lord Mayo's Decentralisation Scheme, which will be specially referred to in the succeeding chapter, led to the imposition of various new taxes by the Provincial Governments. And every proposal made by Sir Charles Trevelyan and other able

[1] Report of 1871, page 512.

[2] Report of 1873; Question 6727

administrators, to allow the people some voice in limiting taxation and reducing expenditure, was disregarded.

For the cry from England was for fresh lines of railways and fresh expenditure in India; and official India was bent on increased expenditure, rather than reduction. And as if the requirements of India were not more than enough for the resources of that country, other burdens like the cost of the Chinese War and of the Abyssinian War, the cost of telegraph lines and military charges properly payable from English estimates, were again and again thrown on India.[1]

For there was no body of men in the Constitution of the Indian Government who could effectually resist such unfairness, in the manner in which the Directors of the East India Company had endeavoured to resist it before 1858. The Secretary of State was a Member of the British Cabinet, and could not resist the joint wishes of the Cabinet; the Members of his Council, not representing the people of India, failed to resist British influences and British demands; and the Viceroy of India and his Council, unsupported by Indian representatives, had to carry out the mandates which came from England. How entirely the interests of India were sacrificed, whenever there was sufficient pressure put on the India Council, will appear from the statements of Lord Salisbury himself, who was once more Secretary of State for India in 1874, when he gave his evidence before the Finance Committee.

Henry Fawcett.—Then it comes to this simply—without saying whether any one is justified or not in doing it—that throughout the existence of an administration, the Secretary of State for India is aware that India is being unjustly charged; that he protests and protests, again and again; that the thing goes on, and apparently no remedy can be obtained for India unless the Secretary of State is prepared to take up this line

[1] See the evidence of Samuel Laing, formerly Finance Minister of India, Report of 1872; Questions 7518, 7519, 7676, 7677, &c.

and say—"I will not submit to it any longer; I will resign"?

Lord Salisbury.—It is hardly so strong as that, because the Secretary of State, if his Council goes with him, can always pass a resolution that such and such a payment is not to be made; but, of course, *any Minister shrinks from such a course, because it stops the machine.*

Henry Fawcett.—You have these alternatives; you must either stop the machine, or you must resign, or you must go on tacitly submitting to what you consider to be an injustice?

Lord Salisbury.—Well, I should accept that statement barring the word "tacitly." I should go on submitting with loud remonstrances.[1]

These extracts disclose the real weakness in the machinery of the Indian Government. There is no effective resistance to financial injustice towards India; no possible opposition to increasing taxation and expenditure. The system of taxation without any form of representation has failed in India as in every other civilised country. And future statesmen will be forced, before long, to introduce some form of representation in the financial administration of India, to save the country from calamities which no longer threaten, but have actually overtaken the Indian Empire.

[1] Report of 1874; Questions 2234 and 2235.

CHAPTER XI

LOCAL CESSES ON LAND

We have in the last chapter dwelt upon the general increase of Public Debt and Taxation in India during the first nineteen years of the Queen's Administration. It is necessary, however, to make a special reference to the Local Taxes which were multiplied in every Province of India within this period. The objects of these Local Taxes were twofold. Ostensibly they were imposed for the greater development and improvement of the country by the construction of roads and the extension of education. But an equally important object was to relieve the Imperial Revenues of those charges, and throw them more and more on the new Local Taxes. The objections to this scheme were also twofold. In the first place, they greatly added to the burdens on an overtaxed population. And secondly, as the new cesses were imposed on the soil, they violated the limits which the East India Company and Sir Charles Wood had fixed for the Land Revenue, both in permanently settled tracts, and in provinces where settlements were made for thirty years on the principle of demanding half the rental.

The Local Rates which were imposed by the Company's Government on the soil were small and insignificant, and were generally based on ancient village customs. But within six months after the empire had passed to the Crown, the eyes of administrators were turned to this source of revenue. Lord Stanley, the first Secretary of State for India, called special attention to the expediency of imposing a special rate to repay the expense of schools for the rural population.[1] His successor, Sir Charles Wood, admitted the objections to the imposition of local cesses on land; but he thought that the obligations to keep up roads was a liability which everywhere attached to the proprietors of land; and in respect of education, he considered a special enactment necessary.[2] Local Rates on land, over and above the Land Revenue, were levied in the Punjab, Northern India, and the Central Provinces; and a special enactment, imposing such rates, was passed for Bombay.

Lord Lawrence, who was Viceroy of India from January 1864 to January 1869, was unwilling to empower Local Governments to impose fresh cesses on the people, and was generally against the principle of the Decentralisation Scheme which was adopted by his successor. Questioned by the Finance Committee on this subject after his retirement from India, he said: "The system which was subsequently introduced was put before me, and I carefully considered it, and I did not think it advisable to introduce it. I thought that what was wanted really in India was to keep the Local Governments in order; to make them be careful in preparing estimates and not in exceeding their estimates; in fact that what was wanted was a restriction over them in matters of large works."[3] Nevertheless, Lord Lawrence's Government had in 1867 and 1868 recommended[4] that a cess, voluntary or otherwise, should be imposed on land in Bengal for roads and rural education.

It was under Lord Mayo's Government that the question came up for final consideration. The Bengal Government made a strong protest[5] against the imposition of the proposed cess on the Zemindars with whom

[1] Despatch dated April 7, 1859.
[2] Despatch dated May 25, 1861.
[3] Finance Committee's Report of 1873; Question 4525.
[4] Letters to Bengal Government, dated October 28, 1867, and April 25 and 27, 1868.
[5] Letter to the India Government, dated April 30, 1869.

a Permanent Settlement had been made in 1793. The Government pointed out that the increased profits from extended cultivation did not benefit the Zemindars, but benefited a large class of sub-tenants and the cultivators themselves; that estates had changed hands, and new purchasers had paid their present values; that James Wilson, the Finance Minister, and Sir Barnes Peacock, Chief Justice of Bengal, had considered special cesses on the soil in Bengal to be a violation of the Permanent Settlement; that Bengal paid a higher proportion of her revenues to the Imperial Exchequer than any other province; that a special educational cess was therefore neither feasible nor proper; but that with regard to a cess for roads, "the Lieutenant-Governor hopes that a cess for this purpose would be far less unpopular than one for education."

Neither Lord Mayo's Government, nor the Duke of Argyll, who had succeeded Sir Stafford Northcote as Secretary of State for India, agreed with the Bengal Government's views.[1] The Duke of Argyll held that it was open to the Government to impose both a road cess and an education cess in Bengal, but recommended that "until the system, machinery, and incidence of local rating in Bengal has been satisfactorily established, so much only should, in the first instance, be raised as is required for roads." And speaking generally of India, the Duke of Argyll betrayed his ignorance of its agricultural conditions and its land revenue history, when he denied that "in the Land Revenue raised from the agricultural classes, the Government of India took so much from the resources of the people as to leave them unable to bear any additional burdens."

It is strange also to note that the author of the *Reign of Law* disregarded in this matter the opinions

[1] See Letter from the Governor-General in Council, dated December 31, 1869, and the Secretary of State's Reply to the Governor-General in Council, dated May 12, 1870.

of his soundest advisers who tried to explain the law to him. In his Council, the Secretary of State had men like Sir Erskine Perry, who had been Chief Justice of Bombay; Henry Thoby Prinsep and Ross Mangles, who had unrivalled experience of Indian administration; Sir Henry Montgomery and Sir Frederick Halliday, who had ruled Provinces in India. And these men spoke in no uncertain voice. Sir Erskine Perry wrote:—

"I have come reluctantly to the conclusion, after many struggles and attempts to draw fine distinctions in support of a different view, that the language and acts of Lord Cornwallis, and of the members of Government of his day, were so distinct, solemn, and unambiguous, that it should be a direct violation of British faith to impose special taxes in the manner proposed."

"In 1854, Lord Dalhousie, a man of no weak will, was most desirous to impose a local tax in Bengal for the maintenance of an improved police; but after reading Sir Barnes Peacock's masterly exposition of the pledges which Government had entered into in 1791–93, the great pro-consul was compelled to accede to the soundness of the Chief Justice's argument, and most reluctantly abandoned his projects."

"Here, then, we have the plain language of Government, the *contemporanea exposita* of its framers, the unanimous conviction of the people, and the declared acquiescence of the State in the justice of the popular interpretation during a period of eighty years. What is the answer attempted to this state of facts?"

"The Government of India allege that the language of the Permanent Settlement itself, in section vii. of Lord Cornwallis's Proclamation, is large enough to enable them to impose the taxes in question; but this argument, on close examination, proves so utterly unsound that the Secretary of State abandons it."

"Two other arguments are brought forward; *first*, that the imposition of the income-tax proves that taxes, additional to what Zemindars pay as land assessment, may be imposed on them; *second*, that educational cesses have been imposed over most parts of India in addition to the land assessment."

"As to the income-tax, it cannot be considered sound logic, when the meaning of particular pledges is in question, to argue that because a Despotic Government has on one occasion, without consulting the people, construed these pledges in its own sense, that act of the Government is a fair proof that their construction is right and just. But argument on this head may be withheld; because I understand that both the Bengal Government and the Zemindars acquiesce in the proposition that in any great emergency they are justly subject to all general taxation which is imposed on the rest of the community."

"With respect to cesses additional to Land Revenue having been imposed in other parts of India, I am compelled to observe that, in my opinion, the Secretary of State has not interpreted the facts correctly, and that the exposition of the Lieutenant-Governor of Bengal is the true one."

"I will content myself with saying that I believe the true explanation of Local Cesses for education [in the other Provinces of India] to be this: whenever they have been levied, they have been so either when settlements for terms of years were under discussion, and when the 'higgling of the market' between the Revenue Officer and the Landowner was going on, or if the settlement was already made, the cess was imposed with the acquiescence of the Landholder."[1]

And Sir Erskine Perry paid a fine compliment to the Zemindars of Bengal who had protested against the proposed Education Cess in a public meeting held in Calcutta. The speeches, he said, "though delivered in a foreign language, would have done credit, both for

[1] Sir Erskine Perry's Dissent, dated May 14, 1870.

good sense and good feeling, to any meeting of country gentlemen in England."

Other dissents were not less emphatic. Mr. Macnaughten considered that "the tax, if levied at all, ought to be general in its application, and, irrespective of the amount of Land Revenue under the Permanent Settlement, should be imposed upon the holders of all property, real and personal, of whatever description."[1]

Sir Frederic Currie admitted the unsatisfactory state of the Indian Finance; it was a cogent reason, he said, for retrenchment and economy; "but it cannot justify our laying a special tax exclusively on the Zemindars of Bengal, to do which, Sir Erskine Perry's paper shows conclusively, would be a breach of faith and the violation of the positive statutory engagement made with these Zemindars at the Permanent Settlement."[2]

Sir Henry Montgomery said: "A government should not, in my opinion, voluntarily place itself in a position laying it open to be charged with a breach of faith."[3]

Henry Thoby Prinsep, with his vast knowledge and experience of Indian administration, wrote: "I have never felt so deeply grieved and disappointed at a decision given in opposition to my expressed opinions as when it was determined, by a casting vote, to approve and forward the Despatch referred to at the head of this paper, for I regard the principles laid down in that Despatch to be erroneous, and the avowal of them to be unwise; while the policy inaugurated and the measures sanctioned will, if attempted to be carried out, alienate the entire population of India from the Government, and shake the confidence hitherto felt universally in its honesty and good faith."

"The Court of Directors, the Imperial Government, and Parliament, were all parties to the resolution to fix

[1] Mr. Macnaughten's Dissent, dated May 14, 1870.
[2] Sir Frederic Currie's Dissent, dated May 14, 1870.
[3] Sir H. Montgomery's Dissent, dated May 18, 1870.

the Government demand upon the land of the Provinces then held by the East India Company in Bengal, in perpetuity."

"The traditions of this period are now forgotten, and new ideas are about to be introduced into the financial administration of India, which, I should be sorry to think, are likely to be attributed to the change of Government which took place twelve years ago. The right of unlimited and uncontrolled taxation is always a dangerous one to assert, and who could have expected that this policy should be advocated, and such arbitrary powers claimed, by a Queen's Government?"[1]

Ross Mangles, who had been one of the strongest Directors of the East India Company, and was now one of the strongest members of the India Council, equally shrank from an act which looked like a breach of faith and a violation of truth.

"It appears to me to be very doubtful," he wrote, "as to what length the Government of India may feel themselves justified in going, under the sanction of the Despatch just sent. They may, I fear, be encouraged to take steps which may lay them justly open to charges of a breach of solemn promises. Unguarded action may destroy in a moment the credit which the British Government has won by its honourable persistence, for a period little short of a century, in the unbroken observance of its pledges; such a price would be too dear to pay for even an object so laudable as the education of the masses. We have no standing ground in India, except brute force, if we ever forfeit our character for truth."[2]

But the most authoritative Dissent on the proposed taxation in Bengal came from Sir Frederic Halliday, who had been Lieutenant-Governor of Bengal during and after the Mutiny, and knew that province better than

[1] H. T. Prinsep's Dissent, dated May 19, 1870.
[2] Ross Mangles' Dissent, dated May 25, 1870.

any other Member of the India Council. He rightly insisted that education was spreading in Bengal through the voluntary exertions of her educated men, and it would be an unwise policy to stop this natural and gratifying result of the policy of Lord William Bentinck.

"Every educated man," he wrote, "has proved a missionary of education in his neighbourhood and among his dependants; and every considerable landholder vies with his neighbour in establishing and fostering village schools; until, in 1869, one-half of the whole State expenditure for vernacular education was met by private subscriptions and contributions from a people who, only a few years back, could by no means have been made to comprehend the value of education to themselves, still less the obligation of extending it to others. Assuredly the fruits of the great measure of 1835 are already amply visible; the wisdom and foresight of its authors are strikingly vindicated; and the condition of national education in Bengal, though far indeed from perfection, is yet abundantly gratifying in the present, and full of safe and happy augury for the future."

"Things being in this position, the Government of India suddenly declared that they were entirely dissatisfied with the system . . . they could no longer wait for the end, but must have education suddenly thrust upon the masses. . . . And since the expense of this scheme must be enormous, and the public exchequer could give no kind of aid, they directed that the whole charge, amounting certainly to many millions sterling, should be thrown upon the Zemindars of Bengal by a rate of not less than 2 per cent. upon their gross rentals."

"The Zemindars remonstrated strongly . . . they pleaded the distinct and solemn promises of the Permanent Settlement of 1792, when Lord Cornwallis had exhausted the resources of language to assure them that the rate then assessed on their lands was 'irrevocably fixed for ever,' and that they should in all future time be free from 'any further demand for rent, tribute, or any arbitrary exaction whatever.' These great national pledges, they urged, had been scrupulously adhered to in many financial difficulties, and under all changes of Government, from Cornwallis to Canning, and could not now be broken without a deliberate abandonment of plighted national faith."

"All the official persons of the Province who were consulted supported these remonstrances; and the Lieutenant-Governor of Bengal transmitted them to the Government of India, and enforced them with a powerful and, as I think, unanswerable argument. But the Government of India was unmoved, and declared in reply, that it was resolved to persevere in its determination."

"When the Income Tax was first imposed in 1860, the Zemindars of Bengal were disposed, not without plausible reasons, to object to it as an infringement; but they soon gave up the point, and accepted the advice and example of the greatest of their body. The Raja of Burdwan, in a remarkable letter to the Legislative Council, announced that he would set an example to his fellows of submission to the Income Tax, because it was levied after the great Mutiny of 1857 . . . and because *it was levied equally on all classes.* That this well-timed and patriotic declaration should not be turned against its author and his brother Zemindars as a reason for setting aside the plain terms of the Permanent Settlement, and imposing upon them *a special tax, of which other classes not connected with the land are to bear no share,* cannot prove otherwise than severely and undeservedly grating and painful to their feelings."[1]

The remonstrance of the Zemindars and the Government of Bengal, and the strong dissents of some of the ablest Members of the India Council, were not uttered together in vain. An Education Cess was not imposed

[1] Sir F. Halliday's Dissent, dated May 25, 1870. The italics are our own.

on land in Bengal. But a Road Cess of $3\frac{1}{8}$ per cent. on the rental was imposed in 1871, and the new Lieutenant-Governor of Bengal, George Campbell, was principally instrumental in imposing it according to the views of the Duke of Argyll. It was said in Bengal, that a Campbell was required to carry into execution the arbitrary policy laid down by a Campbell.

Such Local Cesses had already been imposed in other parts of India where the Land Revenue had not been permanently settled. In Bombay, Sir Bartle Frere informed the Finance Committee, the cess of $6\frac{1}{4}$ per cent. on the Land Revenue, theoretically equal to $3\frac{1}{8}$ per cent. on the nett rental, had been imposed for roads and schools.

It "was deferred in some parts from an idea that it would be considered by the people as a breach of the covenant with them during the thirty years' settlement; and where nothing was said about it at the time of the introduction of these settlements, its introduction was postponed. But in all new settlements it is made a part of the original settlement, and has the same force as the Government assessment."[1]

In the Punjab, as Sir Robert Montgomery deposed before the Finance Committee, the land settlements were made on the principle that one-half of the nett profits from cultivation belonged to the proprietors, and the other half was payable to the Government as Land Revenue. An education cess of 1 per cent. and a road cess of 1 per cent. had been added to the liabilities of the landed cesses. "If more than that were taken, I think they would consider it a grievance.[2]

In the Central Provinces the addition of cesses for roads and for education to the land assessment was justified by Mr. Morris, "provided there was some direct and immediate benefit to the people."[3]

[1] Finance Committee's Report of 1871; Question 68.
[2] Report of 1871; Question 755.
[3] *Ibid.*; Question 1368.

In Oudh, the Act of 1871, increasing the previous rate of 1¼ per cent. to 2½ per cent. from the landlords, over and above the land assessments, was passed with the "consent" of the landlords. But as Sir Charles Wingfield explained before the Finance Committee, "such consent is never voluntarily given. It is obtained through administrative influence, and it is given because they feel themselves helpless, and from fear of provoking worse measures by resisting a request put to them in that way by the Chief Commissioner. And I also think that it is not a dignified thing for one party to a contract, and that the stronger party, to ask the other and weaker party to agree to a modification of the terms of the contract to his disadvantage. . . . People who were fugitives during the Mutiny, like myself, often heard many things which in other times would not have reached their ears; and I did know that the practice which had grown up in the Upper Provinces after the settlement, of getting the people by what was called their voluntary consent to pay an Education Cess or some cess of that kind, which was not in their settlement engagements, was excessively unpopular, and was regarded as a breach of the contract entered into."

Henry Fawcett.—The thirty years' settlement, in fact, becomes a meaningless farce, if after you have made a thirty years' settlement you can impose new cesses on the land simply at the free will of the Government?

Sir Charles Wingfield.—So it has always appeared to me.

Henry Fawcett.—And according to this action which the Government has taken, the proprietors in Oudh have no security whatever that if the exigencies of the Government increase, they may not find cess after cess to any amount imposed?

Sir Charles Wingfield.—Certainly none.

Henry Fawcett.—As I understand you, if it had not

been for this Decentralisation Scheme, which naturally deprives the Local Government of £350,000, which before they had been accustomed to receive, a great part of the necessity of imposing this new cess in Oudh would not have existed, would it?

Sir Charles Wingfield.—No, I understand that the Decentralisation Scheme is made the plea; and it has reduced the grant on Oudh by £15,000. And in the Decentralisation Order you will find it is particularly mentioned that the deficit must be made good by Local Governments; and they refer to the Local Taxation that either has been or is now being introduced; and Oudh is mentioned as one of the Provinces in which it is being introduced to supply the deficit.

And Sir Charles Wingfield laid his finger on the real weakness of the Decentralisation Scheme when he said: "I disapprove of the Decentralisation Scheme because it puts the Local Governments more under a direct motive to screw as much as they can out of the people; and I know by experience what crotchets and fancies Local Governors have."[1]

There could not be a stronger confirmation of the worst fears of Mr. Henry Fawcett and Sir Charles Wingfield than the action which was taken in the North-Western Provinces of India at the very time when the Finance Committee was making their inquiries in London. By the arrangements made under the Decentralisation Scheme, a deficit of £48,030 was left to be made up by Local Taxation in the North-Western Provinces. The Lieutenant-Governor was not satisfied with making up this deficit, but exercised the powers conferred upon him to gradually obtain an increase of £102,000 by Local Taxation. And he did this by imposing a cess of 10 per cent. on the Land Revenue at the revision of the settle-

[1] Finance Committee's Report of 1873; Questions 2050, 2089, 2090, 2098, and 2073.

ments, in lieu of the old cesses which came to 5 per cent. only.[1]

The same thing happened in Madras. The deficit which was left to be made up by Local Taxation by the Decentralisation Order of 1870 was £55,428. The Madras Government passed an Act in the same year by which they imposed a cess of 6¼ per cent. on the rental, estimated to bring them £342,800, instead of £197,106 produced by the old cesses. Thus, while the Imperial Government left them to make up a deficit of £55,000, they exercised their powers to obtain an increase of £145,000 sterling.[2]

These new cesses on land, with the power to add to them indefinitely, destroyed that definitiveness in land assessments which had been secured by Lord Dalhousie in Northern India in 1855 and by Sir Charles Wood in Southern India in 1864. Generations of statesmen had grappled with the difficult Land Revenue problem in India, and, after many blunders, had limited the land assessment to one-half the actual rental or one-half the economic rent. The few local cesses which were imposed on land in addition to this Land Revenue were so insignificant up to 1864, and so often based on old local customs, that they did not count; and the people of India did not consider them a violation of the Half-Rental principle. It is painful to record that the limits fixed for the Land Revenue after more than half a century of administrative experience were now lightly swept aside; and powers were given to Local Governments to add indefinitely to the cesses on land. The new policy virtually took away with one hand the priceless security which had been given by the other. The State-demand had been limited to 50 per cent. of the nett profits from agriculture; other State-demands under other names were now added to it.

[1] Report of 1873; Questions 1964 and 1965.
[2] *Ibid.*, pages 160 to 188.

CHAPTER XII

HISTORY OF TARIFFS

WHILE Indian administrators thus strove to maintain an equilibrium in the Indian finances by new taxes on agriculture, a mandate came from England in 1874 that an old and legitimate revenue, derived from a moderate import duty, should be sacrificed to meet the wishes of the manufacturers of Lancashire. We have, in preceding chapters, given some account of Indian tariffs down to 1871; but a brief connected history of Indian tariffs will help a clearer comprehension of the controversy which arose three years later.

When the Empire of India came under the direct administration of the Queen in 1858, the import duties consisted of 3½ per cent. *ad valorem* upon cotton twist and yarns, and 5 per cent. on other articles of British produce and manufacture, including cotton piece goods. The duties were double on foreign articles.

In 1859, on account of the heavy financial pressure after the Mutiny, all differential tariffs were abolished; duties on all articles of luxury were raised to 20 per cent. *ad valorem;* duties on other articles, including cotton piece goods, were raised to 10 per cent.; and those on cotton twist and yarn to 5 per cent.

In 1860, Mr. James Wilson, the first Finance Minister of India, reduced the 20 per cent. duty on luxuries to 10 per cent., and raised the 5 per cent. duty on cotton twist and yarn to 10 per cent.; so that the import tariff consisted of a uniform rate of 10 per cent. *ad valorem*, with special rates upon beer, wine, spirit, and tobacco.

In 1861, the duty on cotton twist and yarn was reduced to 5 per cent.

In 1862, the duty on cotton twist and yarn was further reduced to 3½ per cent., and the duty on cotton and other manufactures was reduced to 5 per cent.

In 1863, the duty on imported iron was reduced to 1 per cent.

In 1864, the general rate of import duties was reduced from 10 to 7½ per cent.

In 1867, a great number of articles were added to the free list, export duties were abolished from time to time, the only increase being that the duty on grain was raised in 1867.

In 1871, a new Tariff Act was passed which we have referred to in chapter viii. of this Book. The valuations were revised. The import duty on cotton twist and yarn remained 3½ per cent., and that on cotton goods 5 per cent. They were maintained, like other import duties, merely as a source of revenue, and did not operate as a protection to the infant cotton industry of India.

But Lancashire manufacturers were jealous of the new cotton mills of Bombay; and in 1874 they made an attack on the moderate import duties on cotton twist and piece goods, representing them as protective duties. The time was well chosen. The first administration of Mr. Gladstone, which had carried out great reforms in Ireland and had established a system of national education in England, had in its last stages become unpopular in the country. The position of the Ministers became so unbearable that they dissolved Parliament in 1874. A general election therefore was at hand, and the Lancashire vote counts for much at an election. The time was opportune, and on January 31, 1874, the Manchester Chamber of Commerce addressed a memorial to the Secretary of State for India.

The Memorialists urged that the duties of 3½ per cent. on yarns and 5 per cent. on British cotton manufactures imported into India were assessed on tariff rates fixed many years ago, when values ruled much higher than at present; so that the duties thus levied actually amounted to 4 per cent. on the actual price of yarn in India, and nearly 6 per cent. on cloth.

That the tax was found to be absolutely prohibitory to the trade in yarn and cloth of the coarse and low-priced sorts.

That the Chamber were informed that it was proposed to import Egyptian and American raw cotton into India (no duty being charged thereon) to manufacture the finer yarns and cloth, and would thus compete with goods received from England on which duty was levied.

That a protected trade in cotton manufacture was thus springing up in British India to the disadvantage both of India and Great Britain.

That the duties increased the cost to the Native population, or at least to the poorest of the people, of their articles of clothing, and thereby interfered with their health, comfort, and general well-being.

And the Memorialists therefore prayed that early consideration might be given to the subject of the duties levied on yarn and cotton piece goods on import into India, with a view to their abolition.

On receipt of a copy of this memorial the Government of India pointed out that the tariff had been carefully revised at the beginning of 1869, when the tariff valuations of cotton yarns and cloths were largely reduced. The Government, however, held out a promise that a committee of revision would again be convened in the following cold season.

This did not satisfy the Manchester Chamber. They reminded the Secretary of State that in their memorial they had only incidentally referred to valuations, and that their main object and prayer was the total and immediate repeal of the duties themselves. And they added:—

"The statements as to the baneful operation of these duties on commerce, and on the best interests of her Majesty's subjects, both in India and in England, are abundantly confirmed by the latest advices from Bombay, which show that, under the protection extended by the levying of duties on imports, to the spinning and weaving of cotton yarns and goods in India, *a large number of new mills are now being projected.*" [1]

According to their promise the Government of India formed a Committee in November 1874 with a view to the revision of tariff valuations. Mr. Alonzo Money, C.B., was appointed president, and all the members were English merchants or officials.

The Committee differed in their opinions on some points, but were unanimous in rejecting the Manchester demand for the repeal of import duties on cotton yarn and goods.

Lord Northbrook was then the Viceroy of India, and was a free-trader to the backbone. But he was a strong and just ruler; and would not sacrifice a source of revenue which did not operate as protection. After mature consideration of the Committee's Report, the Viceroy in Council passed a new Tariff Act in 1875.

The new Act abolished all export duties except on indigo, rice, and lac.

Retained the import duties on cotton twist and goods, being of opinion "that a duty of 5 per cent. *ad valorem* upon cotton goods cannot practically operate as a protection to native manufacture." [2]

Largely reduced valuations.

Imposed a 5 per cent. duty on the import of long staple cotton to prevent Indian mills competing at an advantage in the production of the finer goods.

[1] Quoted in India Government Resolution No. 2636, dated August 12, 1875, forming an enclosure to Despatch No. 15 of 1875. The italics are our own.

[2] *Ibid.*, paragraph 34.

Reduced the general rate of import duties to 5 per cent.

And raised the duties on spirits and wines.

The loss to the Indian revenues by the reduction of valuations in respect of cotton goods was £88,000; while the total loss to the Indian revenues effected by the new Tariff Act of 1875 was £308,000, taking 10 rupees as equivalent to a pound sterling. But, by retaining the import duties on cotton yarns and goods, Lord Northbrook saved the Indian revenues from a further loss of £800,000. Meanwhile, the General Election in Great Britain had returned a majority of Conservatives, and the Liberal Government had resigned in 1874.

Mr. Disraeli had formed a Conservative Government; and Lord Salisbury had succeeded the Duke of Argyll as Secretary of State for India. Lord Salisbury was never a vehement free-trader, but he was vehement in his desire to conciliate Lancashire. In July 1875 he wrote to the Viceroy:—

"If it were true that this duty is the means of excluding English competition, and thereby raising the price of a necessary of life to the vast mass of Indian consumers, it is unnecessary for me to remark that it would be open to economical objections of the gravest kind. I do not attribute to it any such effect; but I cannot be insensible to the political evils which arise from the prevalent belief upon the matter.

"These considerations will, I doubt not, commend to your Excellency's mind the policy of removing, at as early a period as the state of your finances permits, this subject of dangerous contention."[1]

On August 5, 1875, Lord Northbrook wired to Lord Salisbury that the new Tariff Act had been passed that day. We quote the first portion of the telegram, detailing the changes which we have already mentioned before.

[1] Despatch to the Governor-General in Council, dated July 15, 1875; paragraphs 5 and 8.

"Act for revision of customs duties passed this day.

"Export duties abolished, except those on indigo paddy, rice, and lac, which are unchanged.

"General rate of import duty reduced from $7\frac{1}{2}$ to 5 per cent. Valuations revised.

"No alteration considered necessary in import duty on cotton goods, but their valuation reduced, which diminishes duty by £88,000.

"Five per cent. import duty imposed on long staple raw cotton.

"Duty on spirits raised from 3 to 4 rupees a gallon, London proof.

"Duty on sparkling wines raised from $1\frac{1}{2}$ to $2\frac{1}{2}$ rupees, and on other wines, except claret and Burgundy, from 1 to $1\frac{1}{2}$ rupees a gallon."

And it was pointed out towards the end of the telegram that the net loss to the Indian revenues by this Act was £308,000.

Lord Salisbury was not yet satisfied. He wired back: "Provisions of Act very important. Some objectionable." And he desired to know why the Act was passed without a previous reference to the Secretary of State, according to Legislative Despatch No. 9 of 1874.

An unpleasant correspondence then ensued. Lord Northbrook and his Council explained in August 1875 that the matter was urgent and could not be delayed; and that a reference to the Secretary of State would have had the effect of disclosing the intentions of the Indian Government, and caused inconvenience to trade.

Lord Salisbury was still dissatisfied. He proposed, in November 1875, to send his Under Secretary, Sir Louis Mallet, to India, to confer with the Indian Government in regard to fiscal legislation; and he urged the gradual but complete removal of the import duty on cotton goods.

Lord Northbrook and his Council replied in February 1876 that it was undesirable to sacrifice a duty "which brings in a revenue of more than £800,000;" and that there was "no precedent of a measure so seriously affecting the future of Indian finance as the prospective removal of a tax which brings in a revenue of £800,000 per annum, having been directed by the Home Government." "It is our duty," concluded Lord Northbrook and his Council, "to consider the subject with regard to the interests of India; we do not consider that the removal of the import duties upon cotton manufactures is consistent with those interests; and we hope that the statement contained in this despatch of the whole circumstances of the case, and of the condition of the Indian finances, will show that the real effect of the duty is not what is supposed, and that it cannot be removed without danger to the Indian finances, and that the imposition of new taxes in its stead would create serious discontent."

And in a further letter, dated March 1876, Lord Northbrook protested against the restrictions imposed by the Secretary of State on the action of the Viceroy of India. "It is our duty to represent to her Majesty's Government that the withdrawal from the Governor-General in Council of the power of prompt action on the most important occasions that can arise, will, in our opinion, seriously weaken the authority and hamper the action of the executive Government of India."

Lord Northbrook, one of the soundest and wisest of Indian Viceroys, differed largely from the new policy of the British Cabinet. He could not carry out the unwise frontier policy urged by the Conservative Government; and he could not accept the fiscal policy dictated by Lancashire. He resigned his high office, and left India early in 1876.

It would interest our readers to know how far Lord Salisbury had the support of his Council in pressing for the remission of Indian import duties, and proposing to send his Under Secretary to India to carry out this scheme. This proposal had been made by wire on September 30, 1875.

Sir Erskine Perry, one of the strongest Members of the India Council, objected to this telegram. "The Government of India," he recorded, "is necessarily despotic, and the useful function of the Home Government is, by careful revision of all measures originated there, to prevent the usual concomitants of despotism, such as caprice, hastiness, injustice, from springing up. If the telegraphic wire is to convey peremptory orders during the concoction of measures in India, it will greatly enhance the difficulties of government in that country, and will increase the repugnance of statesmen of mark to accept the office of Governor-General."

Sir Henry Montgomery, who had been a Member of the Council for seventeen years, knew of no previous instance of sending the Under Secretary to confer with the Indian Government on their fiscal policy. It is startling also to learn that he, as a Member of Council, had been allowed no opportunity to see the official correspondence on the contemplated change in the fiscal policy of India. "I had no opportunity," he wrote, "of seeing any of the official or other documents, nor was I aware of the objections which the Secretary of State entertained regarding the financial policy of the Viceroy. . . . Not having seen the official proceedings of the Government of India, not being aware of the objections of the Secretary of State, and not having had an opportunity of conferring with my colleagues, I feel myself still constrained to refuse being a party to a measure which, as far as I understand it, is more likely to provoke than prevent a crisis which would deprive India at this moment of the abilities and experience of Lord Northbrook."

Even General Richard Strachey, who agreed with Lord Salisbury in the principle of abolishing the import duty on cotton goods, wrote: "My reason for objecting to the draft of the telegram first proposed to the Council was that it virtually committed the Council to opinions on subjects, the papers relating to which had not been brought before them."

Sir Robert Montgomery, Vice-President of the Council, explained that the Council did not desire to express any disapprobation of Lord Northbrook's tariff. And Lord Salisbury, who had been in such haste to conciliate Lancashire that he had forgotten to consult his own Council, recorded the very characteristic explanation: "I was at a distance from London when the above telegram was sent to the Council." "I was not aware that they had not had the opportunity of reading the papers."

When Lord Lytton succeeded Lord Northbrook as Viceroy, the path of Lord Salisbury became smoother. On May 31, 1876, he sent two letters to India. In one of them he insisted on the repeal of the import duty on cotton goods; and in the other he explained the relations of the Indian Government with the Secretary of State. Lord Salisbury had the majority of his Council with respect to both these letters, but Sir Frederick Halliday, Sir Barrow Ellis, and Sir Erskine Perry dissented on the question of the fiscal policy; and Sir Erskine Perry and Sir Robert Montgomery dissented on the letter defining the relations of the Indian Government with the Secretary of State.

It is unnecessary to go into these dissents fully. Sir Frederick Halliday wrote: "The duties should be withdrawn only as far as they are actually protective; and hereafter to such extent, and to such extent only, as they may become protective. I do not see why a valuable and very needful revenue, to which avowedly there is no objection not derived from its protectiveness, should be given up so far and so long as it is shown not to be protective."

And Sir Erskine Perry contended that the initiative

in Indian administration should be left with the Government of India, the revision with the Secretary of State. "If the initiative is to be exercised by the Secretary of State, no careful deliberation can be ensured, for no revision is possible."

But the dissenting Members were in the minority; Lord Salisbury had the majority of the Council with him in demanding the repeal of the import duties on cotton goods; and Lord Lytton was nothing loth to comply. But a new difficulty had arisen in India. The terrible famine of Madras—the severest and most fatal which had yet occurred within the century—made the Indian authorities pause. The new Finance Minister, Sir John Strachey, spoke on March 15, 1877:—

"Financial embarrassments arising from the depreciation of silver prevented any practical steps being taken last year in this direction. It was thought unwise to give up any revenue at such a time, and the Secretary of State concurred in this decision. It is with great regret that I have to announce that, for reasons similar to those which prevailed a year ago, it has been decided that nothing can be done at the present moment towards the abolition of these duties; the financial difficulties caused by the famine are so serious that we cannot sacrifice any source of income."[1]

But Lancashire was getting impatient. No political party in Great Britain could afford to neglect the Lancashire vote; and Mr. Disraeli's Government did not wish to do so. On July 11, 1877, while accounts of the terrible Madras famine were already appearing in British papers, the British House of Commons thought it fit to pass a Resolution calculated to hasten and expedite the repeal of the cotton import duty. The Resolution ran thus:—

"That, in the opinion of this House, the duties now levied upon cotton manufactures imported into India

[1] Sir John Strachey's financial statement of March 15, 1877.

being protective in their nature, are contrary to sound commercial policy, and ought to be repealed without delay, so soon as the financial condition of India will permit."

The last clause of the Resolution has no meaning. The financial condition of India, since the Mutiny, had never permitted the repeal of any source of revenue. Local cesses had been imposed on land, severe and cruel in their operation, to secure a surplus; and these should have been repealed before the finances of India repealed any other source of revenue. But this was not how the Resolution was understood, or was meant to be understood.

Lord Salisbury forwarded the Resolution of the House of Commons to the Indian Government, and referred with something like alarm to the fact "that five more mills were about to begin work; and that it was estimated that by the end of March 1877 there would be 1,231,284 spindles employed in India."[1]

Accordingly, in the following year, the Government of India made a further sacrifice of revenue by exempting from duty some imports with which Indian manufactures were supposed to compete. "These are unbleached T-cloths under 18 reed, jeans, domestics, sheetings, and drills. . . . The Government of India has determined to commence by exempting these descriptions, with the further condition that the goods so exempted shall not contain finer yarn than what is known as 30 s., that is, yarn of which 30 hanks of 840 yards each weigh 1 lb. The loss of duty, calculated on the figures of 1876-77, cannot exceed £22,227 sterling."[2]

Even this, however, did not give satisfaction to the Manchester Chamber of Commerce. They pointed out that the list of free goods required to be materially added

[1] Letter to the Governor-General in Council, dated Aug. 30, 1877.

[2] Government of India, Financial Statement, dated March 18, 1878; paragraphs 57 and 58.

to; that shirtings and longcloths made from 30 s. and coarse yarns still remained subject to impost; that in the case of yarns the objection to the fixed limits of the free list was even stronger; and that therefore "it is resolved to urge upon her Majesty's chief Secretary of State for India the desirableness of simplifying those provisions of the new Indian Budget that affect manufactured cotton, by exempting from duty all goods made from yarns not finer than 30 s., and all yarns up to 26 s. water and 42 s. mule.[1]

Lord Lytton, the new Viceroy of India, was prepared to submit to all demands unconditionally. But be it said to the honour of the Indian Civil Service that a majority of the members of his Council protested strongly against being thus bullied into submission, and compelled to sacrifice Indian revenues in a year of famine, war, and increasing taxation. And some of the minutes recorded by the dissenting members are among the finest passages in Indian official literature.

Mr. Whitby Stokes objected to the remission, *firstly*, because the financial condition of India was deplorably bad. "We have spent our Famine Insurance Fund, or what was intended to be such. We are carrying on a costly war with Afghanistan. We may any day have to begin one with the King of Burma. We have now to borrow five crores (five millions sterling) in India, and we are begging for two millions sterling from England."

Secondly, because the proposed surrender would eventually lead to the surrender of the import duty on all cotton goods. "The powerful Lancashire manufacturers will be encouraged by their second victory to new attacks on our revenue. . . . If ever we have any true surplus, we should, in my opinion, lessen some of our direct taxes rather than abolish any of our moderate import duties."

Thirdly, because the proposed repeal would be a

[1] Resolution passed at a meeting of the Board of Directors, March 27, 1878.

relinquishment of the contribution which Native States made towards the revenues of British India.

Fourthly, because no one complained against the duties except the manufacturers of Manchester. The people of India did not ask for their repeal.

Fifthly, because, by the proposed repeal, "the Manchester manufacturers would practically compel the people of India to buy cotton cloths adulterated, if possible, more shamefully than such goods are at present. The cost of the clothing of the people would thus be increased rather than lessened."

Sixthly, because Indian newspapers will proclaim in every bazaar that the repeal was made "solely in the interest of Manchester, and for the benefit of the Conservative party, who are, it is alleged, anxious to obtain the Lancashire vote at the coming elections. Of course the people of India will be wrong; they always must be wrong when they impute selfish motives to the ruling race." [1]

Mr. Rivers Thomson, afterwards Lieutenant-Governor of Bengal, dwelt on the financial difficulties of India. The estimated Budget for 1879–80 showed a deficit of £1,395,000. The proceeds of the special tax imposed twelve months before to create a Famine Insurance Fund had been misapplied to other purposes. Fresh taxation to meet future famines would excite "the very injurious suspicion that the Government has been wanting in good faith." "It is not at such a time that in my judgment any portion of the cotton duties should be repealed; and I deprecate the procedure all the more because in impending circumstances at home, the measure has all the appearance of the subordination of the reasonable claims of the Indian administration to the necessities of English politics." [2]

[1] Minute dated March 13, 1879. The keen satire of the last sentence quoted is not excelled by anything I have ever read in Indian official literature.

[2] Minute dated March 15, 1879.

Sir Alexander Arbuthnot also dwelt on the financial condition of India; and he stoutly maintained that the resolution of the House of Commons did not set the Indian Government free from the responsibility of maintaining the solvency of India. "The people of India attribute the action which has been taken by her Majesty's Government in this matter to the influences which have been brought to bear upon it by persons interested in the English cotton trade; in other words, by the manufacturers of Lancashire. It is notorious that this impression has prevailed throughout India from the time, just four years ago, when the Marquis of Salisbury informed a large body of Manchester manufacturers that the Government of India would be instructed to provide for the gradual abolition of the import duties on cotton goods.

"Nor is this feeling limited to the Native community. From communications which have been received from the Chambers of Commerce at Madras and Calcutta, it is evident that the feeling is shared by the leading representatives of the European mercantile community in those cities.

"It is equally shared by the great body of the official hierarchy throughout India. I am convinced I do not overstate the case when I affirm my belief that there are not at the present time a dozen officials in India who do not regard the policy which has been adopted in this matter as a policy which has been adopted, not in the interests of India, not even in the interests of England, but in the interests or the supposed interests of a political party, the leaders of which deem it necessary at any cost to retain the political support of the cotton manufacturers of Lancashire.

"During the rule of the East India Company, the Court of Directors furnished what often proved an effective barrier between the interests of the people of India and the pressure of powerful classes in England.

In this respect the Council of India, as the Council of the Secretary of State is called, has in no way taken the place of the Court of Directors. . . . The Council of the Governor-General, on the other hand, has large power and heavy responsibilities imposed upon it by law. . . . It will be an evil day for India when the Members of this Council fail to discharge the duty thus appertaining to them."[1]

Sir Andrew Clarke was also unable to recognise any justification for a departure from the policy on which the Tariff Act of 1875 was based.[2]

But all these strong protests were made in vain. The Governor-General of India has the power to act against the opinion of the majority of his Councillors in certain cases; and Lord Lytton somewhat strained this power to exempt from import duty "all imported cotton goods containing no yarn finer than 30 s." The only Members of his Council who supported him in this undignified surrender were Sir John Strachey and Sir Edwin Johnson.[3]

It is needless to add that the Secretary of State approved of the action of Lord Lytton.[4] General Richard Strachey supported the Secretary of State, as his brother, Sir John Strachey, had supported the Viceroy. Five other members also approved of the action taken. On the other hand, seven members, including Sir Frederic Halliday, Sir Robert Montgomery, Sir William Muir, and Sir Erskine Perry, dissented from the Secretary of State. The import duty on coarse cotton goods had been surrendered by Lord Lytton against the opinion of the majority of his Councillors. The surrender was approved by Lord Salisbury against the opinion of the majority of the members of his Council.

We have passed beyond the limits of this Book in

[1] Minute, dated March 15, 1879. [2] Minute of same date.
[3] Letter to the Secretary of State, dated March 13, 1879.
[4] Despatch, dated July 7, 1879.

referring to the events of 1879, which properly falls within the limits of the succeeding Book. We have done so in order to give the reader a connected account of the fiscal controversy which went on from 1874 to 1879. The circumstances under which the import duty was surrendered are a curious comment on the last clause of the Resolution of the House of Commons. That clause desired the repeal of the duty "so soon as the financial condition of India will permit." The duty was actually repealed when Southern India had not yet recovered from the Madras famine of 1877; when Northern India was still suffering from the famine of 1878; when new cesses on land had recently been added to the Land Revenue; when the Famine Insurance Fund created by special taxes had disappeared; when the estimated budget showed a deficit; and when troubles and a vast expenditure in Afghanistan, brought about in quest of a scientific frontier, were impending.

If the House of Commons exerted an undue pressure on India by passing its Resolution in 1877, the Indian Government was guilty of a weak betrayal of trust in carrying out that Resolution in 1879. It may be safely asserted that no Viceroy who has ever ruled India would have sacrificed the revenues of India at such a moment except Lord Lytton; and no financier who has ever held the post of Finance Minister in India would have advised and supported such a sacrifice except Sir John Strachey.

This mean sacrifice to party politics did not even secure a party triumph. The Conservatives were defeated at the general election of 1880.

BOOK III

UNDER THE EMPRESS

1877–1900

CHAPTER I

LYTTON AND RIPON

WE now enter upon the last period of the Victorian Age. The close of Mr. Gladstone's first administration in 1874 is the date, if any single date can be given, for that gradual change in men's sentiments, opinions, and aspirations, which has been called a Conservative Reaction in Great Britain. The rapid advance of the Great Powers of the world aroused new jealousies and awakened new ambitions. A great Western Republic, united once more after a Civil War, was supreme in one half of the world, and claimed an increasing share in the politics and commerce of the other half. A united Germany had arisen with the strength of a giant from the fields of Sadowa and Sedan, and dominated over the counsels of Europe. France too was rising after her defeat, and was seeking compensation in Asia and in Africa. And Russia had torn up the Black Sea Treaty, and continued her unresisted march eastwards. A feeling of unrest filled the minds of Englishmen. Domestic reforms no longer called forth the same enthusiasm as a desire for expansion. The advance of Russia towards India must be checked. England's supremacy in Asia must be maintained. The Continent of Africa was still open, and unexplored regions awaited the British conqueror. A closer union with the Colonies would restore British influence, and would enable England to present a united front to the world. All over the globe there was need for a vigorous foreign policy—a policy of expansion and of conquest—to maintain England's position among rising nations. So Englishmen felt, vaguely, but strongly and as is often the case, the first blind enterprises were neither wise nor successful.

The sound frontier policy of Lord Lawrence no longer found favour. The creed of Sir Bartle Frere found acceptance in the present state of the national mind. Lord Northbrook had rejected that creed, but Lord Northbrook had resigned. A new Viceroy, willing to carry out the new policy, was selected. The first letter of the British Prime Minister, Mr. Disraeli, to Lord Lytton, indicated to him the task he was expected to perform.

"MY DEAR LYTTON,—Lord Northbrook has resigned the Viceroyalty of India, for purely domestic reasons, and will return to England in the spring.

"If you be willing, I will submit your name to the Queen as his successor. The critical state of affairs in Central Asia demands a statesman, and I believe if you will accept this high post you will have an opportunity, not only of serving your country, but of obtaining an enduring fame."[1]

Lord Lytton was then forty-four years of age, and was Minister of Legation at Lisbon; and this was the first intimation he received of his proposed appointment to India. The letter discloses the one object of the appointment. Lord Lytton was chosen to give effect to a policy in relation to Afghanistan which Lord Northbrook had declined to carry out. The recent famines in India and the economic condition of the people find no mention in the Prime Minister's letter. These matters did not interest the British Cabinet very much.

The new Viceroy lost no time. On April 12, 1876, he took charge of his office from Lord Northbrook. On April 24 he was at Umballa, and gave the Commissioner of Peshawar the draft of a letter to be sent to the Amir

[1] Letter from Benjamin Disraeli to Lord Lytton, dated Nov. 23, 1875.

of Afghanistan. A pretext was found for sending a British Envoy to Kabul. The Amir was informed: "Sir Lewis Pelly will be accompanied by Dr. Bellew and Major St. John, for the purpose of delivering to your Highness in person at Khureeta a letter informing your Highness of his Excellency's accession to office, and formally announcing to your Highness the addition which her Majesty the Queen has been pleased to make to her sovereign titles in respect to her Empire in India."[1]

The Amir of Afghanistan was a shrewd man, and perceived the real object of the mission. He replied accordingly: "Please God the Most High, the friendship and the union of the God-given State of Afghanistan in relation to the State of Lofty Authority,—the Majestic Government of England,—will remain strong and firm as usual. At this time, if there be any new parleys for the purpose of freshening and benefiting the God-given State of Afghanistan entertained in the thoughts, then let it be hinted, so that a confidential agent of this friend, arriving in that place, and being presented with the things concealed in the generous heart of the English Government, should reveal it to the suppliant at the Divine Throne."[2] In other words, Sher Ali demurred to the proposal of a British Envoy being sent to Kabul, and desired to send an Agent to know the thoughts concealed "in the generous heart of the English Government."

Lord Lytton was irritated by this first check. He warned the Amir, through the Peshawar Commissioner, that he was rendering nugatory the friendly intentions of the Viceroy, and was voluntarily isolating Afghanistans from the alliance and support of the British Government.[3]

[1] Letter of the Commissioner of Peshawar to the Amir of Kabul, dated May 6, 1876.

[2] The Amir's Letter, dated May 22, 1876.

[3] Peshawar Commissioner's letter, dated July 8, 1876

Lord Lytton's wisest Councillors disapproved of the attitude he had assumed. Sir William Muir, Sir Henry Norman, and Sir Arthur Hobhouse, all maintained, that Sher Ali was within his right in refusing to receive an English Mission; that the reasons assigned by him were substantial; and that the reply of the British Government was almost equivalent to a threat of war. And they added that the Amir knew the real object of the Mission; and it was not dealing with him fairly if the aim of keeping a permanent Mission at Kabul was concealed from him.

The Amir replied to the Peshawar Commissioner's letter.[1] He suggested that the British Agent at Kabul, Atta Muhammad, should come to India, explain the state of affairs at Kabul, and know the wishes of the British Government. Lord Lytton accepted this suggestion.

Atta Muhammad arrived at Simla on October 6, 1876. He explained to Sir Lewis Pelly the views of the Amir at length; and he expressed the Amir's fears that the *temporary* British Mission would merge into a *permanent* one. This was exactly what Lord Salisbury and Lord Lytton had intended. Lord Lytton was annoyed at this fresh check. In his interview with the Agent he could scarcely refrain from threats. "The British Government," he said, "could only assist those who valued its assistance." "If the Amir did not desire to come to a speedy understanding with us, Russia did, and she desired it at his expense." "The British Government was able to pour an overwhelming force into Afghanistan." "If the Amir remained our friend, this military power could be spread around him as a ring of iron; if he became our enemy, it could break him as a reed." The Amir pretended "to hold the balance between England and Russia." But the Amir was only an "earthen pipkin between two iron pots."

[1] The Amir's reply, received on Sept. 3, 1876.

Atta Muhammad was dismissed with a letter for the Amir, an *aide-memoire* for his own guidance, a watch and chain, and a present of £1000. No results followed, for Sher Ali was wide awake.

More tangible results were secured in Beluchistan. Lord Northbrook had sent Major Sandeman to settle the disputes between the Khan of Khelat and his Chiefs, and to open the trade route of the Bolan Pass which had been practically closed owing to these disputes. Major Sandeman, known and honoured all along the frontier, settled the disputes and opened the trade route. His terms of agreement were accepted by the Khan of Khelat and his Chiefs, and were ratified on oath in open Darbar. Had Lord Northbrook been still in office, Major Sandeman would have retired from Beluchistan after achieving these results; but it was Lord Lytton's policy that the British force should stay. He sent his favourite military adviser, Colonel Colley, with a secret treaty; and the sixth article of the treaty provided for the permanent occupation of the Khan's territory by a British military force. The Khan of Khelat signed the treaty, and Quetta was permanently occupied by British troops. "The Khan of Khelat," wrote Lord Lytton to the Queen, "has agreed to sign with me a treaty, the terms of which will make us virtually masters of Khelat."[1] The treaty was executed at Jacobabad on December 8, 1876.

Having thus secured a foothold in the south of Afghanistan, Lord Lytton made his preparations on the eastern side of that kingdom. Colonel Lumsden had advocated the British occupation of the Kurm and Khost valleys; but Lord Lawrence had rejected the proposal. Lumsden's scheme, however, had attractions for Lord Lytton. The road from Rawal Pindi to Kohat was repaired; Cavagnari was sent to the Kurm River with orders to select a site for a military camp; and the Commander-in-chief was directed to be in readiness to

[1] Lord Lytton's letter to the Queen, dated November 15, 1876.

move to Kohat three batteries of artillery, two companies of sappers and miners, a regiment of British and two regiments of native cavalry, and two regiments of British and four regiments of native infantry.[1]

In the north of Afghanistan, too, Lord Lytton was equally active. He supplied the Maharaja of Kashmir with arms of precision; and he encouraged him to push forward troops into passes leading to Chitral. Kashmir was almost an insolvent State. British India was groaning under over-taxation, and was on the brink of the most terrible famine which had yet occurred within the century. But no considerations of economy, and no humane desire to lighten the taxation, restrained the Viceroy from these vast and expensive preparations against a danger which did not exist, and which his own action helped to create. He did what he had threatened to do; he formed a ring of iron on the south, east and north of the Amir's dominions.

On January 1, 1877, a Darbar was held at Delhi, and Lord Lytton proclaimed to the Princes and the people of India that the Queen had assumed the title of *Empress of India.* Mr. Disraeli had feebly imitated the policy of Bismarck; and the sovereign of British India assumed the august title which the sovereign of Prussia had assumed six years before. Thoughtful men in England inquired if this title added in any way to the real power of the Queen, or took away anything from the treaty rights of Indian princes.

Mr. Lowe inquired in the House of Commons if it was prudent to make a marked distinction between England and India, by giving to the Sovereign of England a title which implied obedience to law, and to the Sovereign of India a title which implied the supremacy of force. And Mr. Gladstone led the Opposition at the second reading of the Bill, and made a speech reflecting the best traditions and principles of British policy.

[1] Papers presented to the House of Lords on February 28, 1881

"If it be true, and it is true, that we govern India without the restraints of law except such law as we make ourselves; if it be true, and it is true, that we have not been able to give India the benefits and blessings of free institutions, I leave it to the Right Hon. Gentleman [the Prime Minister, Mr. Disraeli] to boast that he is about to place the fact solemnly on record by the assumption of the title of Empress. I, for one, will not attempt to turn into glory that which, so far as it is true, I feel to be our weakness and our calamity."

"I am under the belief that to this moment there are Princes and States in India over which we have never assumed dominion, whatever may have been our superiority in strength. We are now going by Act of Parliament to assume that dominion, the possible consequences of which no man can foresee."

"I ask whether the supremacy over certain important Native States in India was ever vested in the Company, or whether it was not. We are bound to ask the Right Hon. Gentleman whether their supremacy was so vested or not, and whether he can assure us upon his responsibility that no political change in the condition of the Native Princes of India will be effected by this Bill."

This was going to the root of the question. The new title, if it meant anything, meant that the Sovereign of India was about to assume powers over Indian Princes and States not secured by the treaties. The Sovereign of Prussia had assumed some powers over the States of Germany, openly and explicitly, when he had assumed the title of Emperor of Germany. The Bill before the Parliament made no specific mention of such powers. Did the new title imply such powers, or did it not?

We owe it to the categorical questions of Mr. Gladstone, and of Sir W. Harcourt, that the Prime Minister declared emphatically that no new powers over the Indian Princes and States were assumed. "The change of title," said Mr. Disraeli in answer to Sir W. Harcourt, "does not in the least affect the right and dignity or honour of Native Princes in India." The reply is important for all time to come.

It is, however, explained by the daughter and biographer of Lord Lytton that: "Treaties, made perhaps a hundred years before, and still in force, might be quoted to show that the Native Princes, although not so strong, were equal in dignity and rightful position to the Viceroy. The Nizam, the Gaekwar, and the Viceroy, had all the same salutes, than which, to native imaginations, there could be nothing more significant. The twenty-one guns ceased, after the Delhi Assembly, to be a sign of equality with the representative of the Sovereign."[1]

The fair chronicler of her father's Indian administration here confuses two things which are distinct. The Nizam and the Gaekwar never believed that they were the equals of the Viceroy in power. The assumption of a new title was not needed to convince even "native imaginations" that the Viceroy represented the greatest power in Asia. But the Nizam and the Gaekwar relied on the rights secured to them by treaties, as a poor citizen of a State may rely on his rights secured by law. And we have the Prime Minister's word for it that the assumption of the new title does not in the least affect those rights. Any interference with the autonomy of Native States, secured by treaties, is a violation of good faith to-day, as it was before the assumption of the new title.

While the Darbar of Lord Lytton was held at Delhi, amidst pomp and festivities and needless ostentation, the shadow of a great famine was already darkening over the land. If anything could have recalled the ruler of India in 1877 from a foolish and wasteful frontier policy to retrenchment and a reduction of the burdens on the

[1] *Lord Lytton's Indian Administration*, by Lady Betty Balfour, London, 1899, p. 133.

people, the terrible famine of that year should have produced that effect. It was a calamity unprecedented in its intensity within the memory of living men. Since the Queen's accession, India had suffered from great famines in 1837 and 1860, in 1866, 1869, and 1874, but no calamity so widespread and so fatal had been known in India within the century. The peasantry of Madras, with their wretched land-system, were not as resourceful as the peasantry of Bengal. Relief operations were not organised as wisely as in the Bengal famine of 1874. Large villages were depopulated. Vast tracts of country were left uncultivated. And five millions of people—the population of a fair-sized country—perished in this Madras famine in one single year.

But neither the Delhi Darbar, nor the distress in the land, diverted the Viceroy from the object he had placed before himself. There was a Conference at Peshawar between the Amir's Envoy, Nur Muhammad, and Sir Lewis Pelly, in February 1877. Sir Lewis Pelly insisted, as a preliminary condition, that British officers should reside on the frontier of Afghanistan. And he gave hopes that the British Government might then enter into an offensive and defensive alliance, recognise the Amir's heir, and support the Amir against disturbances in his dominions. But the aged Nur Muhammad declared the Amir's conviction, that to allow British officers to reside in his country would be to relinquish his own authority. The Conference came to nothing, for there was no basis of negotiation left.

Lord Lytton lost all patience. He wrote to Sir Lewis Pelly: "The British Government does not press its alliance and protection upon those who neither seek nor appreciate them. This being the case, it only remains for the Viceroy to withdraw, at once, the offers made to the Amir in the month of October last."[1] Three weeks after the receipt of this letter, the aged Nur Muhammad died.

[1] Letter to Sir Lewis Pelly, dated March 3, 1877.

His surviving colleague had no authority to continue the negotiations. Atta Muhammad, the British Agent at Kabul, was recalled. A war seemed inevitable.

Great events had in the meantime followed each other in rapid succession in Europe. The Russians had vanquished the Turks in a great war, and were near the gates of Constantinople. Mr. Disraeli had ordered the Mediterranean fleet to the Dardanelles, landed Indian troops at Malta, called out the Reserves, and occupied Cyprus with the consent of Turkey. And Russia had replied by mobilising an army in Turkestan, and despatching a Mission to Kabul.

Lord Lytton took note of these events, and acted accordingly. He arranged with the Maharaja of Kashmir for the establishment of a British Agency at Gilgit, upon the slopes of the Hindu Kush; and the insolvent State of Kashmir was made to pay for a telegraph line from this new station to the British territory. And Lord Lytton congratulated himself on his cleverness. "We shall have secured a vicarious but virtual control over the Chiefdoms of Kafristan, which will cost us nothing, by their absorption under the suzerainty of Kashmir, our vassal." [1]

The kingdom of Kabul was indeed an earthen pipkin between two iron pots. The Russian Mission was forcing itself into Kabul. The Amir, in dire alarm, wrote to General Kaufmann, declining to receive the Russian Mission. But the Russians would not turn back, and General Stoletoff reached Kabul on July 22, 1878. The Amir had to receive the Mission; and the draft of a treaty was drawn up.

In the meantime, peace had been secured in Europe by the Congress of Berlin. General Stoletoff was recalled by the Russian Government, and left Kabul on August 24, 1878. The plea for interference with Afghanistan existed no longer. But Lord Lytton had determined on sending a British Mission, since a Russian Mission had

[1] Lord Lytton to the Secretary of State. Letter dated April 9, 1878.

been received. "Neither the withdrawal of the Russian Mission, nor any assurances on the part of Russia," he wrote, "will cancel the fact that a Russian Mission has been well received at Kabul; and that Russian officers have had full opportunities of instilling into the minds of the Amir and his Councillors distrust and dislike towards England, belief in Russia's power and destiny, and hopes of assistance against us from that country."[1]

Sir Neville Chamberlain was placed in charge of the British Mission. It left Peshawar on September 12, and reached Jumrud on September 21. Its further progress was stopped by the Afghan commander, Faiz Mahammad. A conference between him and Cavagnari came to nothing, and the Mission returned to Peshawar. Upon this, Lord Lytton proposed to issue a manifesto defining the causes of offence; to expel the Amir's troops from the Khaibar Pass; to occupy the Kurm Valley; and to advance from Quetta to Kandahar. At the instance of the Home Government, however, an ultimatum was sent on October 2. As no reply was received by November 20, the date fixed, military operations were commenced on the following day.

The narration of the incidents which led up to the Afghan War of 1878 has occupied a longer space than we wished to devote to that subject. But the narration was necessary. The war upset the long-established policy of Canning and Lawrence, Mayo and Northbrook. It disturbed the peace on the north-west frontier of India, which had been maintained for nearly forty years. It was undertaken after peace had been concluded with Russia, and the alarm of a Russian invasion had ceased. And it brought about a financial disaster on India, still suffering from the effects of the Madras famine of 1877 and the northern famine of 1878. The veteran Lord Lawrence raised his voice against the war in time—before the ultimatum was sent. And some passages

[1] Minute, dated September 4, 1878.

from the letter which the aged statesman wrote to the *Times* on September 27 deserve to be quoted.

"We ought not, indeed, to be surprised that the Amir has acted as he has done. From the time of the Treaty of 1857, the late Amir Dost Muhammad Khan refused to allow us to have a Mission at Kabul, or even to send one there as a temporary arrangement, solemnly assuring us that such a step would lead to mischief, and not to peaceful relations with the Afghans. We accepted his excuses. In 1869 the present Amir affirmed the same policy."

"What are we to gain by going to war with the Amir? Can we dethrone him without turning the mass of his countrymen against us? Can we follow the policy of 1838–39 without, in all probability, incurring similar results? If we succeed in driving Sher Ali out of Kabul, whom can we put in his place? And how are we to insure the maintenance of our own creature on the throne, except by occupying the country? And when is such an occupation to terminate?"

"Such are the political and military considerations which lead me to raise my voice against the present policy towards Amir Sher Ali. Are not moral considerations also very strong against such war? Have not the Afghans a right to resist our forcing a Mission on them, bearing in mind to what such Missions often lead, and what Burnes's Mission in 1836 did actually bring upon them?"

The warning was given in vain. The hero of the Indian Mutiny, who had been hailed in England twenty years before as the saviour of the Indian Empire, was now treated with scorn. Abuse and contumely were showered upon him by platform orators, by anonymous correspondents, and by sapient writers in the ministerial press. The spirit of the age had changed. Counsels of peace were ridiculed. New Imperialism demanded a war.

On November 9, before the time given by the ultimatum had yet expired, Lord Beaconsfield disclosed the real cause which led England to this war. It was not undertaken, he said in a speech at the Mansion House, to punish the Amir for his reception of the Russian Mission, or his refusal to receive an English Mission, but for a rectification of boundary and for securing a scientific frontier. Sir Bartle Frere, then High Commissioner of South Africa, must have gloried at this triumph of the policy he had advocated for fifteen years. And he had good cause to regret that policy before the war was over.

It is not within the scope of the present work to narrate in detail the incidents of the war. British troops advanced by three routes—the Khaibar Pass, the Kurm Valley, and the Bolan Pass. Sher Ali fled to Turkestan and died. His son, Yakub Khan, signed the treaty of Gundamak on May 26, 1879, assigning the districts of Pishin, Sibi, and Kurm to the British Government. "The third article," wrote Lord Lytton, "establishes our exclusive influence throughout Afghanistan, and our paramount control over the Amir's external relations."[1] This was what Sher Ali had foreseen, and had fought against. "We have secured a scientific and adequate frontier," wrote Lord Beaconsfield to the Viceroy. "It will always be a source of real satisfaction to me that I had the opportunity of placing you on the throne of the Great Moghal."[2]

The congratulations were somewhat premature. Sir Louis Cavagnari and the British Embassy entered Kabul on July 24, 1879. The Afghans were sullen and angry. The new Amir was unpopular and was suspected of treachery. On September 2 Cavagnari sent his last telegram, which contained the words, "All well." On September 3 this gallant officer and his escort were massacred. Yakub Khan abdicated, and was deported to India. A fresh war became necessary.

[1] Despatch dated July 7, 1879.
[2] Lord Beaconsfield's letter to the Viceroy, dated August 14, 1879.

Mr. Lepel Griffin was sent to Kabul in March 1880 to undertake the diplomatic and military superintendence of affairs, in communication with the military commander, Sir Frederick Roberts. "I see no reason," wrote Lord Lytton to him, "why you should not, as soon as you reach Kabul, set about the preparation of a way for us out of that rat-trap."[1] "The sole object," he wrote to the Secretary of State, "of all the military operations I have sanctioned for this spring is to facilitate the early evacuation of the country."[2] Such were the results of the new policy, described by the very man who had adopted it.

In April 1880 the Conservative Government fell. And Lord Lytton, who had no policy of his own except the policy which had been dictated by the Conservative Ministry, resigned simultaneously with the Government. He had acted against the advice of his wisest predecessor, Lord Lawrence, and his wisest finance minister, Sir William Muir.[3] He had achieved no results, and had involved India in a loss of over twenty millions sterling. That money would have sufficed for all the more important irrigation works which Sir Arthur Cotton had recommended to the Select Committee of the House of Commons in the very year in which the Afghan War had begun. It would have saved millions of cultivators in India from distress and famine for all time.

A Liberal Government was formed by Mr. Gladstone

[1] Lord Lytton's letter to Lepel Griffin, dated February 16, 1880.

[2] Letter of February 18, 1880.

[3] It has been stated before that Sir William Muir, along with Sir Arthur Hobhouse and Sir Henry Norman, dissented from the letter written to the Amir in July 1876. In October 1876, just before leaving India, Sir William Muir wrote a second note, repeating and enforcing the opinions contained in the first, and asking that both these notes might be treated as Official Minutes. This was not done. Lord Cranbrook refused to present the notes to Parliament with other papers referring to Afghan affairs; and Sir William Muir was compelled to publish them to establish his freedom from complicity in Lord Lytton's Afghan policy. Muir's successor, Sir John Strachey, was at one time an earnest supporter of Lawrence and Mayo; but he readily became a convert to Lord Lytton's new policy.—See Colonel Hanna's *Second Afghan War*, vol. i. p. 172.

in 1880, after the fall of the Tory party. Nothing brings out in a clearer light his great influence and power than his success in stemming the tide of Imperialism for a time, and his forcing a short Liberal reaction. Never, even in his younger days, had the veteran statesman distinguished himself more by his burning eloquence and his righteous zeal, than when he denounced the "Bulgarian atrocities," and fought his Midlothian Campaign. The nation responded to the call; they returned the Liberals to power. And the second administration of Mr. Gladstone was signalised by a new Irish Land Act and a new Reform Act, and by the Liberal measures introduced by the Marquis of Ripon in India.

The Marquis of Hartington succeeded Lord Cranbrook as Secretary of State for India, and Lord Ripon took charge of his office from Lord Lytton on June 8, 1880. The Afghan War was soon brought to a close. A British brigade was defeated by the Afghans at Maiwand, near Kandahar, on July 27; but Sir Frederick Roberts marched from Kabul to Kandahar and totally routed the Afghan army on September 1. Abdur Rahman was recognised as the new Amir; and the British army retired from Kabul and Kandahar.

India enjoyed peace once more, and the budget once more showed a surplus. Mr. Fawcett and Mr. Gladstone had, in opposition, denounced the policy of charging the Indian finance with the whole cost of the Afghan War; and the Liberal Government now voted a sum of five millions from the Imperial exchequer as a contribution to that war. It was a small proportion of the total cost of the war; but it is the only instance on record of a practical recognition of the principle that the cost of expeditions beyond the frontier of India, inspired by a jealousy of Russia, should not be borne by India alone. Another sane measure was adopted by the Liberal Government. The weak Government of Lord Lytton had passed an Act to muzzle the Vernacular Press of India. Whenever the

Government of India is betrayed into blunders, there is a tendency to stifle the voice of criticism. Lord Ripon, with the approval of the Home Government, repealed this Vernacular Press Act.

It was also the pleasing duty of the Marquis of Ripon to hand over the State of Mysore once more to its Indian ruler in 1881, after the State had been under British administration for half a century. The high credit of this just and generous act does not belong to Lord Ripon, or to the Liberal Government of the time, but to the Conservative Government of 1867, and to Sir Stafford Northcote, then Secretary of State for India.

Mysore had been conquered from Tipu Sultan in 1799. And after the British Government and their ally the Nizam had carved out large slices of the conquered territory for themselves, the remainder had been made over to the old Hindu royal family by the Marquis of Wellesley. The gallant and sympathetic Sir John Malcolm was the first British Resident; and after his departure in 1804, the Indian Minister, Purnea, managed the State with an ability and success which won the admiration of the Duke of Wellington.

But the officials of Madras continued to cast longing eyes on this State, and the belief was general among the people of the State that their opposition to their Raja would be viewed with complacency by the East India Company's Government.[1] There was an insurrection in Mysore, and the management of the State was temporarily assumed by the Company's Government in 1832. Lord William Bentinck was influenced by exaggerated reports against the Raja in taking this action, and he afterwards felt that he had been misled. For after his return to England he repeatedly declared that the supersession of the Raja of Mysore was the only incident in his Indian administration which he looked back upon with sorrow.[2]

[1] See Report of the Special Committee on the Mysore Insurrection, dated December 12, 1833; paragraph 199.

[2] See Major Evans Bell's *Mysore Reversion* (1865), p. 20.

The Raja repeatedly asked for restoration; and Lord Hardinge, after a careful examination of the question, expressed a doubt if British occupation could continue after British pecuniary claims were satisfied.[1] The Court of Directors replied that the real hindrance to restoration was the hazard which would be incurred to the good government of the State.[2]

Lord Dalhousie, who succeeded Lord Hardinge, was of a different disposition. He recorded a Minute stating that the deposed Raja was sixty-two years of age, and had no son; and he trusted that, on his death, "the territory of Mysore, which will then have lapsed to the British Government, will be resumed, and that the good work which has been so well begun will be completed."[3]

Fortunately the doctrine of lapse, and the spirit which inspired that doctrine, disappeared when the Queen assumed the direct government of India in 1858. Lord Canning acknowledged the fidelity and the attachment of the old Raja, and his endeavours to preserve peace in Mysore during the Indian Mutiny; and promised to convey his wishes to the Secretary of State.[4] The question was ripe for decision in 1867 when Sir Stafford Northcote was Secretary of State; and the Conservative Government decided "to maintain the family of the Maharaja of Mysore on the throne of that province in the person of His Highness's adopted son."[5]

Eight years after, a Conservative Government was again in power, and Lord Salisbury was Secretary of State for India. And he made some remarks on the education of the heir to the Mysore throne, as proposed by Colonel Malleson, which deserves to be on record.

"Literary proficiency is not in this instance the

[1] Despatch dated August 6, 1846. [2] Despatch dated July 14, 1847.
[3] Minute dated January 16, 1856. [4] Letter dated June 28, 1860.
[5] Despatch of the Secretary of State to the Indian Government, dated April 16, 1867.

principal object to be attained. At an age when the education of other men is not complete, His Highness will be invested with powers upon the due exercise of which the happiness of large numbers will depend, and will be charged with duties which will leave to him little leisure for the pursuits of a student's life. It is of great importance that he should be well instructed in the knowledge which will help him to success in his high vocation. The principles of the government which will be administered by his authority and in his name, the special dangers and errors to which it is exposed, the blessings which if rightly directed it may confer, the warnings or the encouragement furnished by the history of other princes of his own race, are matters to which his mind should be specially turned during the remaining years of his minority."[1]

When the Liberal Party came into power in 1880, the time had arrived to restore the State. British management had reorganised the administration of Mysore, but had not been financially successful. The famine of 1877 was as severe in Mysore as in Madras; and, as in British India, a vast debt had been accumulated.

The revenues of the State were burdened with a debt of £800,000 to the Government of India, in addition to liabilities incurred for the construction of the Bangalore-Mysore Railway. And it was therefore decided that in restoring the State to the Raja, the old annual subsidy of £245,000 should be continued for five years, and the proposal to increase it to £350,000 should be kept in abeyance.[2]

The Instrument of Transfer contains twenty-four

[1] Despatch to the Governor-General in Council, dated June 17, 1875. If the education of minor rulers and chiefs had always been shaped on these principles, and if they had always been kept in touch with their own people and with the administration of their own States, they would not have turned out failures so often.

[2] Despatch from Lord Hartington, Secretary of State for India, to the Governor-General in Council, dated August 12, 1880.

clauses; and the transfer, which took place on March 25, 1881, was notified by a Proclamation to the chiefs and the people of Mysore.

In British India, the measures adopted for the further protection of cultivators were among the most beneficent acts of Lord Ripon. The Bengal Rental Acts of 1859 and 1868 required to be strengthened, and the prolonged deliberations on this subject ended in a Bill which, with some modifications, was passed by Lord Ripon's successor in 1885. For the Ryotwari tracts in Madras and Bombay, Lord Ripon proposed the judicious rule that the State-demand in settled districts should not be enhanced except on the ground of an increase in prices. These land reforms will be fully narrated in a subsequent chapter.

A small amendment which Lord Ripon proposed to the criminal law of India, by giving Indian magistrates jurisdiction to try European offenders, evoked a violent opposition. And the proposal was ultimately carried in a modified form, with a provision permitting European offenders to claim a jury. But the measure for which Lord Ripon's administration is best known is his introduction of Local Self-Government in districts and in municipal towns. In a resolution of the Financial Department,[1] the Governor-General formulated the principle in the following words: "The Provincial Governments, while being now largely endowed from Imperial sources, may well in their turn hand over to Local Self-Government considerable revenues at present kept in their own hands."

Letters were accordingly addressed to the Provincial Governments indicating branches of expenditure which appeared most suited for local control. Provincial Governments accepted the new principle, and offered their suggestions; and the Governor-General in Council then dealt with the question in greater detail. A few

[1] Resolution dated September 30, 1881.

extracts from this subsequent resolution[1] will elucidate the objects of the new scheme.

"It is not primarily with a view to improvement in administration that this measure is put forward and supported. It is chiefly desirable as an instrument of political and popular education. His Excellency in Council has himself no doubt that, in the course of time, as local knowledge and local interest are brought to bear more freely upon local administration, improved efficiency will, in fact, follow."

"There is reason to fear that previous attempts at Local Self-Government have been too often over-ridden and practically crushed by direct, though well-meant, official interference. In the few cases where real responsibility has been thrown upon local bodies, and real power entrusted to them, the results have been very gratifying."

"The Governor-General in Council desires that the smallest administrative unit—the Sub-division, the Taluka, or the Tahsil—shall ordinarily form the maximum area to be placed under a Local Board."

"The Municipal Committees will, of course, remain the Local Boards for areas included within town limits."

"The Local Boards, both urban and rural, must everywhere have a large preponderance of non-official members."

"Members of Boards should be chosen by election whenever it may, in the opinion of the Local Governments, be practical to adopt that system of choice."

"The Government should revise and check the acts of the Local bodies, but not dictate them."

"It does not appear necessary for the exercise of these powers that the chief Executive Officers of towns, Sub-divisions, or Districts, should be chairmen or even members of the Local Boards. There is, indeed, much reason to believe that it would be more convenient that

[1] Resolution dated May 18, 1882.

they should supervise and control the acts of those bodies without taking actual part in their proceedings."

"The Governor-General in Council therefore would wish to see non-official persons acting, whenever practicable, as Chairmen of the Local Boards."

These extracts sufficiently indicate the scope and object of Lord Ripon's scheme, and after a great deal of official correspondence and discussion the scheme resulted in the creation or development of three classes of Boards.

(1) Counties are called Districts in India, and District Boards were formed answering to County Councils in England. The majority of the members were elected by the people; some were nominated and appointed by the Government; and the Executive Government Officer of the District was appointed the Chairman. Roads, education, hospitals, and some ferries, were made over to these District Boards.

(2) Local Boards were formed in Sub-divisions of Districts, and were placed under the orders of the District Boards. Most of the members of Local Boards were chosen by election: some were nominated and appointed by the Government.

(3) In Municipal towns the majority of the members were chosen by election; and in advanced places the members were allowed to choose their own non-official Chairman.

A humble beginning was thus made in extending the elective system, and in giving the people of India some share in the administration of local affairs. Nothing makes British Rule in India more popular and more secure, nothing draws the people closer to an alien administration, than making them partakers in the duties and responsibilities of that administration. It was by this policy that Munro and Elphinstone and Bentinck had succeeded in consolidating the Indian Empire in the early years of the century; and it was this policy which made the administration of Lord Ripon so popular.

India in our generation has not witnessed such manifestations of loyalty and gratitude as the Marquis of Ripon evoked from the people before he left the country. Those who witnessed them have seen nothing like them in India or in any other part of the world. "His journey from Simla to Bombay was a triumphal march such as India has never witnessed—a long procession in which seventy millions of people sang hosanna to their friend." [1]

A sympathetic and wise administration, recognising the political advancement of the people, and gradually extending the forms of Self-Government and of Representation, strengthens British Rule in India, and makes the people themselves proud of the Empire. An autocratic and distrustful administration, repressing the legitimate ambitions of the people, and excluding them from the management of their own concerns, weakens the Empire, and creates a natural and universal discontent, which spreads and deepens into political danger.

[1] *Europe and Asia*, by Meredith Townsend.

CHAPTER II

DUFFERIN AND LANSDOWNE

THE success of the great Liberal leader in stemming the Conservative Reaction, which had begun in 1874, was only temporary. No statesman can battle against his times. Never had Mr. Gladstone a more arduous and difficult duty before him than during the four years of his second administration. He had an ingrained and unalterable hatred of aggression; but the nation was bent on expansion. In Afghanistan, he had the strength to withdraw from a mischievous and wasteful expedition. In Egypt, he was forced to take action against Arabi Pasha; he halted and hesitated after the victory of Tel-el-Kebir; he was compelled in the end to occupy the country. In South Africa, Mr. Gladstone had the courage to restore independence to the Transvaal Republic; and his countrymen considered this act as a shameful humiliation. In the Soudan, he had not the decision either to withdraw at once, or to advance at once; and the fall of Khartoum and of General Gordon was condemned by his countrymen a crime.

It was plain, Mr. Gladstone was not the man for the hour. He had been a Peace-Minister all his life; he would not now turn an Imperialist. He had befriended small nations all over the world; he would not annex small States now. His soul was bent on domestic and popular reforms; the nation wanted a leader who would extend the limits of the Empire. His high character, his strong personality, and his unrivalled powers, still inspired respect and admiration; but his influence declined because the nation was bent on a different policy. When, therefore, he had carried the Third Reform Act in December 1884, his work was done. The Liberal Ministry resigned in June 1885. Twice after, Mr. Gladstone became Prime Minister with the help of the Irish vote; but he was never as popular in England after 1885 as the "People's William" had been before 1874. He was not the man that England wanted for her new foreign policy.

Lord Beaconsfield had died in 1881, and Lord Salisbury had become the Conservative Leader. When, therefore, the Conservatives came into power in 1885, Lord Salisbury became Prime Minister. And he remained in that high post until 1902, except during the brief periods when the Liberals were in power—from February to July 1886, and from 1892 to 1895. Lord Salisbury was not an Imperialist himself. He desired peace, and strove for peace. But he had the capacity to yield, and to drift with the tide, when he could not oppose it. He had ridiculed a forward policy in India, and had then yielded in 1875. He prevented a war with Russia by the limitation of the Indian frontier in 1885. He avoided a war with the United States by the Venezuela arbitration in 1895. He avoided unpleasantness with Germany by the delimitation of African possessions. And he settled amicably, and with signal success, the claims of Great Britain and France, both in Fashoda and on the Niger. All these high services will be remembered to the credit of a Prime Minister who always strove for peace. But he yielded, when he could strive no longer, in the closing years of the century.

In India, the first result of this growing demand for expansion was the conquest of Upper Burma. Lord Dufferin had succeeded Lord Ripon as Viceroy of India. He was an able and accomplished statesman, possessing great tact and varied experience. He had been Under-Secretary for India from 1864 to 1866, when Lord Lawrence was Viceroy of India. His brilliant administration of Canada from 1872 to 1878 marked him out as an able administrator. He was then ambassador at St. Petersburg and at Constantinople; and he had some share in abolishing the Dual Control and establishing British administration in Egypt. In December 1884 he succeeded Lord Ripon in India, at the mature age of fifty-eight.

Complaints had been made against the King of Burma from time to time. The British Mission had been withdrawn from Ava in 1879. But the British Cabinet had advised the Indian Government to be "slow to precipitate a crisis." Negotiations for a new treaty, which took place at Simla in 1882, came to nothing. The demarcation of the Manipur frontier by Colonel Johnstone did not receive the assent of Burma. British merchants at Rangoon held a public meeting in October 1884, and urged the annexation of Upper Burma. The sins of the King were, as usual, exaggerated to inflame the public mind. Handbills were distributed describing King Thibaw as a drunkard. The Rangoon Chamber of Commerce addressed a circular letter to various Chambers of Commerce in Great Britain, desiring them to bring pressure to bear on the British Cabinet. It was suggested that British Burma should be cut adrift from India, and formed into a Crown Colony.

In the meantime King Thibaw was endeavouring to strengthen his position by negotiations with the Powers of Europe. The Court of Ava despatched a Mission to Europe in 1883; and by April 1885 it had concluded commercial treaties with France, Germany, and Italy. The French Envoy, M. Haas, who reached Mandalay in May 1885, exerted to establish a dominating French influence in Burma. Arrangements were made for the establishment of a French bank and the construction of a French railway. Lord Salisbury took note of these negotiations. He spoke to M. Waddington, the French Ambassador in London, and brought the facts to the notice of M.

Freycinet. The French Government disclaimed all knowledge of M. Haas's doings, and M. Haas was recalled. The danger was passed.

Advantage was then taken of a petty quarrel to annex the kingdom. A British Company had for years past worked the Ningyan teak forests in the kingdom of Burma. The High Court of Ava delivered judgment against the Company for having defrauded the King of revenue amounting to £73,000. The Company remonstrated, and Lord Dufferin insisted on a further inquiry. The King of Ava questioned the right of the Indian Government to raise the subject. Lord Dufferin replied by an ultimatum, demanding that King Thibaw should receive a permanent British Resident; suspend proceedings against the Company till the arrival of the Resident; regulate his external relations according to the advice of the Indian Government; and grant facilities for the development of British trade with China through Bhamo. The Burmese Government declined to discuss the Company's case with the British Government; said that a British Agent would be permitted to come and go as in former times; asserted that the friendly relations of Burma with France, Italy, and other Powers would be maintained; and declared that British commerce with China would be assisted in conformity with the customs of the country.

Lord Dufferin considered himself justified in declaring war on receipt of this reply. A great Power does not need stronger reasons for crushing a small Power. Hostilities were commenced in November 1885; there was virtually no opposition. King Thibaw was deported to Ratnagiri on the Bombay coast; his kingdom was annexed on January 1, 1886. The annexation was virtually the conquest of a new country by Great Britain; but the cost of the conquest, and of proceedings taken for years after to break down the armed resistance, was charged to the revenues of India. A railway has since been constructed from Mandalay towards China at the cost of the Indian tax-payer. But the hope of a brisk Chinese trade, which was so strong a reason of the annexation, has proved a myth.

Beyond the Western frontiers of India, the Russian attack on the Afghans at Penjdeh threatened for a time to disturb the peace between Great Britain and Russia. But the danger was averted; and a Boundary Commission, appointed in concert with Russia, delimited the Afghan frontier on the Oxus and towards Central Asia.

There was an increasing demand on the part of the people of India for representation, and for a larger share in the administration of their own concerns. The Indian National Congress was founded, and its first meeting was held at Bombay, in December 1885. And year after year, at Christmas time, it has given expression to the views and aspirations of the most moderate and the best educated men of India. Mr. W. C. Bonnerjee, a leading citizen of Calcutta, Mr. P. Mehta, a leading citizen of Bombay, and other eminent Indian leaders, cordially helped by Mr. A. O. Hume, ensured its success by their strength, their moderation, and their patriotic endeavours. There was at first some uneasiness among officials at this new movement; but the sober sense and the calm persistence of Indian leaders have removed all anxiety, and have made the Congress a representative institution of the educated people of India.

Lord Dufferin himself was not opposed to progress. He appreciated the Indian National Congress at its first formation; but ultimately he was misled as to its object and scope. He appointed a Public Service Commission with the object of opening some of the higher branches of the administration to the people of India; but some of the best recommendations of the Commission remained a dead letter. And he is believed to have recommended a system of election for the appointment of some members to the Legislative Councils of India, a recommendation which ultimately led to the India Councils Act, passed by Parliament in 1892. On the other hand, the army and military expenditure of India were vastly increased under his administration; and there was a mischievous and wasteful activity once more beyond the North-West frontier of India.

Lord Lansdowne succeeded Lord Dufferin in 1888. He, too, had been Governor-General of Canada, and therefore went out to India with considerable experience as an administrator. But he was wanting in the tact and discretion and the quiet strength of Lord Dufferin. A silly Imperialism predominated in his Council, and wasteful expenditure beyond the Indian frontiers proceeded at a more rapid pace. A distinguished administrator, who was himself behind the scenes during these years, says that while Lord Lansdowne's urbanity and high distinction conciliated and impressed all with whom he was brought into personal contact, yet, as time passed, it became evident that his thoughts were more occupied with affairs beyond the North-West frontier of India than with the interests of good government within its limits. The influence exercised over the Viceroy by his chief military and political advisers became more and more matters of universal comment. Under their influence, and probably with the approval of the British Cabinet, Lord Lansdowne renewed in substance Lord Lytton's policy, and the wars which have drained India of money and men since 1896, were due to the course of action adopted by Lord Lansdowne in the years preceding. There never was a time since 1838, when Simla was more actively the centre of ambitions, and of designs beyond the Indus. "The most favoured type of Indian official was no longer the Provincial Governor or the sagacious Resident, but that Warden of the Marches of Beluchistan, Sir Robert Sandeman, whose unique aim was to extend the zone of British influence beyond the frontier, and whose method was to participate in tribal dissensions, and to benefit by them. 'Sandemania,' which had proved so contagious, then first became epidemic in high quarters."[1]

In pursuance of this restless and ambitious policy, Lord Lansdowne took some action in regard to the State of Kashmir which created alarm in India, and brought on a discussion in the House of Commons. The post of Gilgit is over a hundred miles to the north of Kashmir; and it was Lord Lytton's policy, as we have seen before, to have a hold over this distant place through the Kashmir State. Lord Lansdowne improved on this policy; for a time he set aside the ruler of Kashmir; and he virtually controlled the affairs of that State through the British Resident.

A Resident had been first appointed in Kashmir by Lord Dufferin in 1885, on the accession of the new ruler, Maharaja Pratap Singh. Mr. Plowden became Resident in the following year, and began to assume an authority over affairs which alarmed even the Foreign Office of India. "I do not agree with Mr. Plowden," wrote the Foreign Secretary to Lord Dufferin. "He is too much inclined to set Kashmir aside in all ways." "If we annex Gilgit, or put an end to the suzerainty of Kashmir over the petty principality of the neighbourhood, and above all if we put British troops into Kashmir just now, we shall run a risk of turning the Darbar against us, and thereby increase the difficulty of the position." "If we have a quiet and judicious officer at Gilgit, who will get the Kashmir force into thorough order and abstain from unnecessary exercise of his influence, we shall, I hope, in a short time, have the whole thing in our hands without hurting any one's feelings."[2] Lord Dufferin was a cautious statesman. Plowden was transferred from Kashmir in 1888. And in the same year Lord Dufferin himself left India.

[1] Sir Auckland Colvin.

[2] Letter dated May 1888. Quoted in Mr. William Digby's *Condemned Unheard* (London, 1890).

His successor, Lord Lansdowne, acted with less tact and wisdom. Early in 1889, the new Viceroy of India deprived the ruler of Kashmir of all powers, and placed the administration in the hands of a Council to act under the advice of the British Resident. The reasons which led to this measure, as stated by Lord Lansdowne himself,[1] were these:—

(1) Unfavourable reports about the administration.
(2) Disorder in the finances.
(3) Neglect to carry out reforms.
(4) Treasonable letters alleged to have been written by the Maharaja.
(5) Offer of the Maharaja to abdicate.

The first three charges were of a general nature, and had no special application to the short time that Pratap Singh had been on the throne. His State was annually visited by hundreds of Englishmen, and they spoke of no oppression and no misery among the people. There was worse distress in the British Provinces of Madras and Orissa, in the very year when the letter was written.

The fourth charge was never proved and never relied on. Lord Lansdowne himself wrote to the Secretary of State: "We are not disposed to attach any excessive importance to these letters." And the Under-Secretary for India said in the House of Commons in April 1889: "The Government of India attach very little importance to the intercepted letters." The letters were never proved, and were probably forged by the Maharaja's enemies.

The fifth charge was based on a letter, written by the Maharaja to his brother under some pressure, and was not an abdication.

The action of Lord Lansdowne was therefore unaccountable. There was an alarm in India, and the impression gained ground that the Viceroy desired to virtually annex Kashmir in pursuance of his Gilgit policy. Mr.

[1] Letter to the Maharaja, dated June 28, 1889. Quoted in Mr. William Digby's *Condemned Unheard* (London, 1890).

Bradlaugh, M.P., who at the time took a keen interest in Indian affairs, gave expression to this alarm. He moved adjournment of the House on July 3, 1890, and brought on a debate on the subject. The motion for adjournment was lost, but the debate stayed the hands of the Indian Government. Maharaja Pratap Singh has since been restored to power, and has ruled Kashmir in peace. No charge of misgovernment or of treason has been brought against him.

Great events had in the meantime followed in rapid succession in England. Mr. Gladstone had endeavoured to pass his Irish Home Rule Bill in his third administration, February to July 1886, and had failed. Ninety-three Liberals had receded from Mr. Gladstone, and had joined the Conservatives in support of the Union with Ireland. In the general election which followed, the Conservatives and Liberal Unionists formed the majority, and Lord Salisbury became Prime Minister for the second time.

The Unionist Government lasted for six years, from 1886 to 1892. But Mr. Gladstone, now over eighty years of age, was still determined to carry through his Irish Home Rule scheme, and vehemently attacked the Government. A general election took place in 1892. The Home Rule was the leading question, and the contest was stubborn. Mr. Gladstone triumphed, and became Prime Minister for the fourth time, with a majority of forty on his side. Lord Kimberley, who had been his Secretary of State for India in 1886, was again appointed to the post, succeeding Lord Cross the Conservative Indian Secretary. But in 1894 Lord Kimberley became Foreign Secretary, and was succeeded by Mr. Fowler, now Sir Henry Fowler, in the India Office.

Great hopes were entertained in India from the return of the Liberal Government, and from Mr Fowler's accession to the India Office. His undoubted abilities and his clear grasp of facts would surely enable him to comprehend Indian questions in their true light.

Mr. Fowler had been a staunch supporter of Irish Home Rule, and would support and extend Self-Government in India. He had been President of the Local Government Board, and would make the District Boards of India real centres of popular administration. He was a man of the people, and would sympathise with the just ambitions of the people of India. These hopes were widely entertained in India, but they were doomed to disappointment. Under the influence of the times, and under the Imperialist administration of Mr. Gladstone's successor, Lord Rosebery, Mr. Fowler fast drifted into Imperialism. His administration proved more autocratic than that of his titled predecessors. He adopted with vehemence the official idea of an absolute Government in India uninfluenced by popular opinion. He resented, on occasions, with equal vehemence, the just demands and aspirations of the people. He passed no large remedial measures, made no popular concessions. He was a joy to the ruling classes; he disappointed the people of India.

Mr. Fowler continued large extensions of Indian railways on borrowed capital, beyond the resources and the immediate needs of the country. He sanctioned the mischievous activity and the wasteful expenditure of the Indian Government beyond the frontiers of India. A mission was sent to the Amir of Kabul. A delimitation of the frontier was effected. Chitral, Swat, and Wazaristan were included within the British sphere of influence. Seeds were sown for the frontier war which broke out three years after.

Mr. Gladstone's Home Rule Bill had been passed by the House of Commons in 1893, but had been rejected by the House of Lords. Early in 1894 the aged Minister had retired from Parliament; and in 1898 he passed away, mourned by the entire nation. His greatest political opponents, those who had bitterly resented his foreign policy and his Home Rule scheme, joined with his most ardent followers in doing honour to the memory of a MAN who was God-fearing, great, and good. His deep earnestness, his unrivalled powers, his high personal character, and his lifelong services to his country, had created an impression on the popular mind. Above all, it was the combination of his greatness with private Christian virtues that struck the imagination of a nation. "A great example," said his political opponent, Lord Salisbury, "to which history hardly furnishes a parallel, of a great Christian Man." They laid his remains in Westminster Abbey, where sleep England's greatest and best.

CHAPTER III

ELGIN AND CURZON

WHEN Mr. Gladstone finally retired from public life, early in 1894, the last restraint on the growing feeling for war was withdrawn. The Liberal Government continued under Lord Rosebery for a year, and fell in June 1895. Intelligent observers, who could read the signs of the times, felt that some great war, somewhere in the world, was inevitable. The air was thick with unquiet rumours. Places of amusement and public gatherings rang with the voice of defiance. The public press breathed of the expansion of the Empire. Trade looked forward to future possibilities from conquests. Workmen re-echoed the cry, and were led to hope for more profitable employment. Lord Salisbury, now Prime Minister for the third time, raised his warning voice more than once, and then allowed matters to drift. A foreigner, judging from the events of 1815, 1855, and 1895, would have said: the British nation were, on the whole, a peaceful nation, but required a little blood-letting once in forty years to make them appreciate peace.

Wars followed almost immediately. Sir Herbert Kitchener, now Lord Kitchener, conquered Dongola and moved up the Nile in 1896. In September 1896 he shattered the army of the Khalifa at Omdurman. The fall of Gordon was avenged. British supremacy was established on the sands of the Soudan. France withdrew from Fashoda.

The power of China had been broken by Japan in 1894 and 1895. European Powers crowded in to secure "spheres of influence" in that decrepit empire. Russia obtained Port Arthur and became dominant in Manchuria. Germany acquired ports and territories. England took Wei-Hai-Wei. Then followed the Boxer rising, and the war of the allied Powers in China. And European armies disgraced themselves by barbarities against an unresisting and unoffending population.

But the culminating event of these dark and unquiet times was the war in South Africa. Dr. Jameson led an expedition against the Transvaal, and was crushed in 1896. The Boers armed themselves against further attacks. The British became impatient of the pretensions of the "Nebulous Republics." A war followed, which lasted two years, which cost Great Britain over 20,000 men, and over two hundred millions of money. And amidst the horrors of the war, Queen Victoria passed away in January 1901, lamenting the disasters which closed her long and prosperous reign.

India did not escape the influences of these unquiet times. Lord George Hamilton was Secretary of State for India from 1895 to 1903. He had been Under Secretary for India from 1874 to 1878. He had been a member of an Indian Finance Committee in 1874, and had presided at the Irrigation Committee of 1878. He was familiar with Indian problems, and approached them with some knowledge of details. But he lacked the firm grasp and the abilities of his predecessor; and he had as little sympathy with the people of India and their just aspirations. During a period of unexampled calamities, of war and pestilence and repeated famines, the Secretary of State stood by without a plan of radical improvement, without a scheme of permanent utility. No large remedial measures were introduced to improve the wretched condition of a suffering nation. No action was taken to lighten the load of taxation. No adequate steps were adopted to foster indigenous trades, industries, and manufactures. No needed security of tenure and of moderate assessments was bestowed on the cultivators of the soil. On the contrary, the darkest days of distress witnessed the adoption of the worst repressive and coercive measures. The liberty of the press was restricted. Representative institutions were repressed. The admission of educated Indians into the higher services in their own country was steadily narrowed for the benefit of English boys seeking a career in the East. Never, within the preceding thirty-seven years of the government of India under the Crown, had the country suffered from greater calamities; and never had the administration been more barren of sympathetic and remedial measures, more fruitful of coercive and repressive measures.

Lord Elgin had succeeded Lord Lansdowne in 1893. His father's name was still remembered and respected in India; and the new Viceroy came, therefore, with traditions of peace and goodwill towards the Indian people. But his hand was not strong enough to restrain the influences which surrounded him. One of the most peaceful of men, he drifted into a needless and profitless war across the western frontier.

Chitral is situated among the mountains of Kafristan, a hundred miles to the north of the frontier British district of Peshawar. A British resident with a small body of troops, sent there for temporary purposes, was besieged in 1894, and relieved in 1895. The Liberal Government of Lord Rosebery had decided to withdraw from this distant, useless, and isolated post, after the triumph of the British arms. But the Conservative Government, which succeeded in 1895, decided to retain it. This decision, combined with the active operations which had gone on since Lord Lansdowne's administration, irritated and alarmed the frontier tribes. There was a general rising among the Afridi and other races; and a frontier war followed.

British troops behaved with their accustomed bravery. Highlanders and Goorkhas distinguished themselves by the capture of Dargai in October 1897. The Sikhs covered themselves with glory in desperate encounters. Forts and villages were taken; the country was desolated; and then the British troops withdrew from the wild country. There was a strong outburst of feeling in England against this useless and wasteful war, but India obtained no help from the British Exchequer.

In the meantime the people of India were passing through an unexampled calamity. A famine, wider in its area than any previous famine known in history, desolated Northern India and Bengal, the Central Provinces, Madras, and Bombay. Relief operations on a vast scale were undertaken, and were attended with varied success in the different provinces. In Bengal the people are resourceful, and could help themselves to some extent, and there was no increase in the death-rate owing to the famine. In Bombay and Madras the death-rate showed a very considerable increase. In the Central Provinces it was doubled. The total loss of life through the effects of the famine, within this one year, could be estimated by the million.

Another dread calamity visited the unhappy country in the same year. A severe bubonic plague desolated the fairest towns of Western India. The measures adopted for its prevention were harsh and obnoxious to the people without being efficacious. The military were called in to help the civil authorities to enforce these measures. There was a cry of alarm among the people, but they appealed to the Government of Bombay in vain. The operations had a tragic end. Two English officers were assassinated in the streets of Poona. Riots occurred in the streets of Bombay. The disturbance was quelled with loss of life. The murderer was arrested, tried, and executed.

But the Government had been struck with panic. Rigorous prosecutions against the press were commenced, and sentences of savage severity were passed in some cases. Two men of influence and distinction were arrested and kept in confinement without a trial. And laws were passed to restrict the liberty of the press. Magistrates were empowered to bind down editors of newspapers for good behaviour, and to send them to prison in default of security, without trial for any specific offence. Englishmen who had passed half their lifetime in India felt that the Government was acting under a needless panic, and that signs of suspicion and distrust would not strengthen the Empire. Among the people of India, the terrible year 1897–98 left other bitter memories than those of famine, war, and pestilence.

When, therefore, it was announced, towards the close of 1898, that the Hon. George Curzon was to succeed Lord Elgin as Viceroy of India, the intelligence was received by the people of India with a feeling of relief and joy. And Lord Curzon was received in India with an enthusiasm which was as sincere as it was universal. For the people felt that they were at last under the rule of a strong and able ruler, who would see things with his own eyes, and act according to his own judgment.

Lord Curzon had many of the qualifications of a good ruler. He had energy, industry, and intelligence of a high order, and had already made his mark in public life in England. Born in 1859, he had worked as Under Secretary of State for India in 1891–92, and as Under Secretary for Foreign Affairs from 1895 to 1898. He had travelled extensively in Asia, and had written on Central Asia, Persia, and the Far East. He had the gift of eloquence and an elegant style; he appreciated public praise; and he was responsive to public criticism. More than this, he had a real appreciation of oriental life; he felt an admiration for oriental art and literature which befitted him to be the ruler of a great oriental nation.

Richly endowed with all these gifts, Lord Curzon nevertheless lacked some of the qualifications of a successful administrator. A staunch and ardent Imperialist, he neither appreciated self-government nor believed in popular co-operation. Brilliant, young, and ambitious, he evinced a high regard for British power and prestige, British interests and trade in the East; but he did not evince the same anxiety for the material improvement and the political advancement of the great eastern nation whose destinies were placed in his hands. An autocratic rule was his ideal.

The time for a final judgment on Lord Curzon's Indian administration has not yet arrived. But the story of Indian administration during the Victorian Age would be incomplete without some mention of the early years of Lord Curzon's rule. And one records with pain that the first acts of Lord Curzon produced disappointment and disillusionment among the people. As far back as 1876, the Government of Bengal had introduced something like Self-Government within the Municipality of Calcutta. Fifty Municipal Commissioners were elected by the ratepayers of the town, and twenty-five were appointed by the Government. This scheme had ensured State control, while it recognised popular representation. The Municipal Commissioners had, amidst many blunders, done excellent work for the town. They had improved its drainage and water supply. They had cleansed unsanitary spots, and had made the town the resort for health-seekers from the malarial districts of Bengal. They had laid out spacious streets and improved its appearance. They had saved it from any serious attack of the plague which had raged in many other towns in India. And in the words of Sir Antony Macdonnell, who, as Lieutenant-Governor of Bengal, had seen the work of the Municipal Commissioners, they had "displayed a care and attention to their duties which is very meritorious, and has in some cases risen to devotion."

But work by popular bodies was not the ideal of the closing years of the century. It was desired to restrict the powers of the elected Commissioners. Sir

Alexander Mackenzie, Lieutenant-Governor of Bengal, introduced a Bill calculated to have this effect. The people of Calcutta protested. Lord Curzon intervened and made the Bill worse. He reduced the number of elected members to twenty-five, making it equal to the number of the nominated members. The latter, with the official Chairman, obtained the controlling power. Real popular Government was at an end. The most distinguished citizens of Calcutta, who had given years of their life to municipal work, retired from the scene. The administration of Calcutta has deteriorated since this retrogade measure was passed. And Municipal Self-Government in other parts of India has also been weakened.

Self-Government in districts and villages has not improved. Representative institutions in India, started under Lord Ripon's administration between 1880 to 1884, have found little encouragement since. The educated classes, who looked forward to a larger share in the administration of their country under British Rule, have been disappointed. The great mass of the agricultural population of India have fared no better. Tenant-right has not been strengthened. State-demands and State-enhancements have not been limited by definite rules. The power of alienating holdings has been restricted in the Punjab and Bombay. The water-rate has been made compulsory in Madras. These changes will be fully described in subsequent chapters.

A severe famine once more overtook India in 1900, and lasted for four years. Vast relief operations were once more undertaken. They were successful in the Central Provinces, but were badly managed in Bombay. And when the Famine Commission published its report, it was found that the rigorous collection of the Land Tax was largely accountable for the permanent indebtedness of the agricultural classes.

The currency of India was settled. The rupee was

raised to 1s. 4d., and then fixed at that value. And as taxes in India are collected in rupees, the process meant an increase of taxation all round. Budgets henceforth showed a surplus. The cultivators of India had the first claim of relief from that surplus. The cesses on land, which had been imposed in addition to the land revenue since 1871, required to be withdrawn. There has been no such repeal; the cultivators have obtained no relief.

There are two main principles by which the people of India judge the administration of their rulers. They demand, and rightly demand, a wider Representation and a larger share in the administration of their own concerns. And they ask, and rightly ask, for Retrenchment and a reduction in the burdens on the people. Recent administration has failed in both these principles. It has restricted Self-Government; and it has increased public expenditure and added to the taxation on the people.

The year 1903 began with a Proclamation of the coronation of King Edward VII., made at the Delhi Darbar with unseasonable ostentation and expense, at a time when India was in the fourth year of a continuous famine. The year ended with Darbars in Persia, and an expedition to Tibet. Is it possible that the cost of these last acts, undertaken to extend British power in Asia, shall be charged to the revenues of India?

CHAPTER IV

LAND ADMINISTRATION IN NORTHERN INDIA

THE principles of Land Assessment in Bengal, Northern India, and the Punjab, had been settled under the administration of the East India Company. And measures had been adopted in the early years of the Crown Government to settle the relations between landlords and tenants, and to extend protection to the cultivators of the soil. The history of the last quarter of a century is therefore a history of smaller measures, and of the further development and extension of principles already laid down.

BENGAL.

In Bengal the Rent Act of 1859 had given security of rent and tenure to the tillers of the soil. But the cultivators of the Western districts (Behar) had not derived the same benefit from the measure as their more quick-witted brethren of the Eastern districts. The experience of twenty years suggested the necessity of a further measure, to protect them from the unjust demands of their landlords. Lord Ripon's Government undertook this useful task; and the burden of the work fell on Antony Macdonnell, who was then Revenue Secretary of Bengal.

It is needless to narrate the long discussions which were held before the proposed measure took shape. The Government gave a full and even respectful hearing to the objections of landlords. Committees were held in districts and divisions to consider and revise the proposed remedies. The draft of the Bill was modified and recast from time to time. And it was ultimately passed by Lord Dufferin, after Lord Ripon's departure from India. The Tenancy Act, as passed in 1885, gave the needed protection to cultivators without infringing in any way on the just rights of landlords. The two main objects of the new law were to extend the *right of occupancy* to settled cultivators, and to extend adequate protection to *non-occupancy cultivators.*

The beneficial results of the Permanent Settlement of 1793, which limited the State-demand from landlords, and the Rent Acts of 1859 and 1885, which limited the landlord's demand from tenants, are obvious in every part of Bengal at the present day. There is an educated and influential class of landlords, who have identified themselves with the British Rule, and have always given loyal help in the cause of good administration. There is a strong and intelligent middle class, holding tenures of various degrees under the landlords, and forming the strongest element in a progressive society. And there is a resourceful peasantry, able to defend their rights, and able also to resist the first effects of a drought and a failure of crops. The rents are light; the cultivators are not under the thraldom of money-lenders; and British administrators can view with a just pride a province where their moderation has insured agricultural prosperity to a nation.

The following figures, which we quote from a recent official document, represent the proportion of rent to the produce of the soil in fourteen districts, representative of the different parts of Bengal.[1]

It will be seen that in no district is the rental as high as one-fifth of the produce. As the Bengal Government remarks: "The figures in this table indicate with sufficient clearness that rents in Bengal amount, on the average, to little more than 11 per cent. of the gross produce of

[1] Letter of the Bengal Government to the India Government, dated June 24, 1901.

District.	Proportion of Rent to the Average Produce.
24 Perganas	10 per cent.
Nadiya	7 "
Midnapur	8 "
Hughli	14 "
Birbhum	15 "
Backerganj	9 "
Noakhali	9 "
Tipera	9 "
Rajshahi	13 "
Gaya	14 "
Balasor	11 "
Muzaffarnagar	16 "
Cuttack	14 "

the land." This pleasing assurance of the Bengal Government contrasts painfully with the disclosure made by the Famine Commission of 1900, that the Land Revenue levied by the State in Gujrat is 20 per cent. of the produce. The Land Revenue ought to be half the rental under the rule of 1864, and not double the rental. The State ought to be more considerate than private landlords, not more exacting and harsh.

Northern India.

A healthy change was introduced in the method of assessing the Land Revenue. The basis of assessment, as has been explained in a previous chapter, was formerly an *estimated rental*—an approximate guess of what the lands were likely to yield. A more sensible rule was subsequently adopted of taking the *actual rental* as the basis. This was made quite clear by the rules issued by the Revenue Board in 1887, from which we make the following extracts:—

"The assessment of the revenue in each village is to be based, as far as possible, on the actual rentals recorded in village rent rolls, corrected where necessary."

"The Settlement Officer is not at liberty to add to these rent rolls any estimate on account of a prospective rise in rents or prospective increase in cultivation."

It is, therefore, clearly the object of the Government, at the present time, to limit the Land Revenue in Northern India to one-half of the *actual rental* which landlords obtain from their tenants. It is a matter for regret that this clear rule has not been adhered to, even in Settlements which have been completed after 1890.

A distinguished and public-spirited landlord of Northern India, the Hon. Nihal Chand, Rai Bahadur, Member of the Legislative Council of the Province, has done public service in bringing this fact to notice in his *Notes on the Land Revenue Policy*, published in 1903. And it is necessary to cite some facts from this publication, if only to point out the reforms which are still needed in the actual operation of the rules.

Basis of Assessment.—The actual rental of estates is the basis of assessing the Land Revenue. But the Revenue Board issued a circular, so recently as 1901, directing that where the rents are inadequate, the Settlement Officer should reject the recorded rental, and base his assessment on an estimated rental.[1] The effect of such a rule is obvious. Where the landlords are disposed to be lenient to cultivators, the rule is a reminder to them to screw up their rents. In Bengal, where the Land Revenue is permanently settled, and the State is not interested in raising rents, every Legislative Act, passed within the last half-century, has had the object of securing a moderate rental, and the leniency of the landlord is encouraged by the administration. In Northern India, on the other hand, where the State bases its Land Revenue on the rental, the leniency of the landlord is chastised, and he is called upon either to screw up his rents or to pay more than one-half of what he receives.

[1] Rule quoted in the Hon. Nihal Chand's *Notes*, p. 11.

Several instances are cited in the *Notes* to illustrate how such cases are dealt with. In the Muzaffarpur District, the actual cash rental was increased by £307[1] in the settlement of 1892. In the District of Saharanpur it was increased by £5644. In the District of Mirut it was increased by £11,906. And in the District of Badaun it was increased by £2714. Landlords and cultivators in Northern India can fairly ask that this practice should now be abandoned, when Lord Curzon has himself declared the actual rental to be the basis of the Land Revenue assessment.

Non-occupancy Lands.—A considerable portion of the estate of a landlord in Northern India is sometimes cultivated otherwise than by Occupancy Ryots. A portion is tilled by the landlord's own labourers. A portion is let to cultivators on grain rent. And a portion is let without rent to sweepers and barbers, potters and blacksmiths—men required to live in villages and carry on their hereditary professions. None of these lands escape the Settlement Officer's attention. And as there is no cash rental to form a basis, the assessment is based on an assumed rental, which is often unduly severe. In the District of Muzaffarnagar the landlords' own holdings should have been assessed at £16,565, according to the rates at which occupancy lands were assessed; but a higher rate was imposed, and the assessment was fixed at £23,970. A case is cited in which the Settlement Officer assumed 8s. per acre to be the proper rental for the purposes of his assessment; but when the landlord asked for a decree against his tenant at this high rate, his prayer was refused, and decree was given only for 6s. 6d. per acre. In other words, the Settlement Officer decreed rents at one rate, and assumed rents at a higher rate for the purpose of assessing the Land Revenue. To such unfairness and inconsistencies are Revenue Officers betrayed when there are no independent

[1] £1 is taken as equivalent to 15 rupees, its present value.

Land Courts to control their action, and to decide questions arising between the State and the people.

With regard to small bits of land held by village tenants rent free, surely a little imagination and some consideration for the customs of the people should induce Settlement Officers to altogether exempt them from assessment. The village blacksmith and the village potter have served the Indian village community from times immemorial; and as their incomes from their trade are scanty, they have been allowed to hold little bits of land without rent. The barber and the sweeper get even less from their trade; and they would leave their village probably if not attached to it by their small acreage of cultivation. It is an excellent old institution, by which villagers have grouped themselves into self-contained communities from olden times. Petty services are secured to villagers by gifts of lands, and landlords ask for no rents from such service lands. The loss to the State by exempting such miserable bits of land would be almost inappreciable;[1] while the Government would be saved from the appearance of a "melancholy meanness." Rigid rules have strangled many good old institutions in India—let the old, old village barber and village potter be spared.

Improvements.—It has been emphatically and repeatedly laid down by the Government that cultivators and landlords shall not be taxed for their own improvements. And Lord Curzon has recently repeated the assurance that the State has similarly surrendered its right to all share in improvements in which the capacity of the soil plays a part with the industry or outlay of the cultivator.[2] This is an equitable and an excellent maxim, but it is not fully carried out in practice. Settlement Officers do not always earmark the portion of the increase

[1] To take the instance of one District, Muzaffarnagar, the total lands assessed in 1892 were 701,431 acres, of which only 5669 acres were held rent free, and supported more than 5669 poor professional families.

[2] Resolution dated January 16, 1902.

in produce or rental which is due to improvements, and do not exempt it from assessment. The experience in every province in India—in Bombay and Madras as well as in Northern India—is, that this equitable rule is violated.

The Settlement Officer of Muzaffarnagar District records the following remarks: "It is impossible to allow for the addition made to the assets of an estate by irrigation from these wells. . . . It is hopeless to expect the smaller landlords to establish their claims in the way laid down; and even the larger landlords cannot do so. When they apply for compensation, and are told that *they must show that increased rents are being paid owing to the improvement*, they answer that the Settlement Officers have better information on the subject than themselves. The value of improvements cannot be judged by the increase in rent, because the circumstances affecting rents are various, and are uncertain in their operation; and conversely an increase of rents is not a necessary sign of an improvement."[1]

The italics are our own. A Settlement is made once in thirty years. Within that time a landlord, or his deceased father, may have dug thirty wells within his estate, made a few roads, cleared some jungle, probably reclaimed a marsh. Within the same period the Government has probably constructed a railway line close to the estate, and has opened a new canal-distributary through the estate, by reason of which some wells have fallen into disuse. Within the same time, also, the rupee has fallen in value, risen, and fallen again; and the prices of crops have oscillated inversely to the oscillations of the rupee. All these facts have had their effect on the rental, and have made it what it is at the time of a new Settlement. How can the landlord prove how much of the increase in the rental within the thirty years is due to the improvements made by him or his father, apart from the

[1] Muzaffarnagar Settlement Report, dated September 22, 1892; paragraph 158.

other causes? He cannot; and the State virtually sweeps away nearly all the profits of the improvements made by the landlord and the cultivator. At the settlement of Muzaffarnagar made in 1892, the State obtained an increase of over £20,000 in the Government Revenue, and the Settlement Officer made only an insignificant allowance of £1074 for improvements. No stronger reasons exist for the establishment of independent Land Courts than to assure to the cultivators and landlords the fruits of their improvements. A system of periodical re-settlements, which enables the State to derive profits from improvements made by private owners, is the surest bar to all improvements.

Secrecy of Settlement Proceedings.—Thomas Merttins Bird described in some detail, before a Select Committee of the House of Commons, the method he pursued in the great Settlement which he effected in Northern India between 1833 and 1842. It was his policy to meet villagers, to consult them, to carry on discussions with them from day to day, and virtually to obtain their assent to the assessment he made. There are men still living[1] who followed this excellent system in Madras, when the Survey and Settlement of that Province was first made after 1861. *Mais nous avons changé tout cela.* Settlement proceedings are now carried on in Northern India as if they were a State secret. The people, whose fates are determined by these proceedings, are jealously excluded from any knowledge of the proceedings. They are not consulted, they are not permitted to adduce facts, they are not allowed to know what is going on. The rents are compiled and corrected by the Settlement Officer, the Land Revenue is assessed by the Settlement Officer, the Report is drafted and submitted by the Settlement Officer—in the dark—without consultation

[1] I may mention one honoured name—that of Mr. R. K. Puckle, C.S.I., now living in retirement in London. His fame as a popular and sympathetic administrator is still fresh and green in the province in which he worked.

with the people. The Report goes to the Commissioner for his sanction, and the people wait in ignorance and silent expectation. The Commissioner sends it up to the Revenue Board, and the people are still waiting in ignorance. When the Board have approved and sanctioned the new assessment, then the Settlement Officer first discloses to bewildered landlords the new assessments on their estates which they shall have henceforth to pay.

We will suppose the landlord objects to the new assessment. To whom does he carry his objection? To the Commissioner and to the Revenue Board who have already sanctioned the Settlement. The assessment is as much their work as it is the work of the Settlement Officer; and it is obviously unfair that appeals against the assessment should be heard by them. They could hardly make large alterations in the Settlement which they have already considered, examined, and approved, without stultifying themselves.

Why should not such objections be heard by independent tribunals—Judges experienced in Land Revenue work? The answer given by the Government of the North-Western Provinces is, that to appoint such independent tribunals or Land Courts "might possibly touch the financial solvency of the Government."[1] The reason, though advanced by so high an authority as Sir Antony Macdonnell, appears to us incomprehensible. It can scarcely be that Revenue Officers strain the rules unfairly in order to secure financial solvency. And it is as difficult to imagine that British Judges of high position and repute will strain the rules in an opposite direction to bring on financial insolvency. And yet it is necessary to make one of these suppositions to justify the present practice of permitting assessing officers to hear appeals against their own work. The people of India seek for justice; and the financial solvency, as well as the prestige of the British Government, is

[1] Letter to the Government of India, dated December 22, 1900.

strengthened, not weakened, by a just administration. The people demand that the assessment of estates should be made in consultation with the assessees from the commencement; and that objections against the assessment should be heard by tribunals other than those who have made it.

Local Cesses.—We have already in a preceding chapter referred to the imposition of special cesses on land, in addition to the Land Revenue, which virtually nullifies the Half-Rental rule. Ten per cent. on the Land Revenue is charged for roads and schools in Northern India; 2 per cent. for the famine insurance fund; and 4 per cent. more for Patwaris or village officials. This makes a total of 16 per cent. on the Land Revenue, or about 8 per cent. on the rental; and this is in addition to the customary allowances to village watchmen and headmen which the people of India have paid from olden times.

The system followed down to 1872 was to assign a portion of the Land Revenue itself for these local purposes. Sir William Muir, the able and sympathetic ruler of this province, explained this principle clearly and forcibly. "The correct principle, as it appears to the Lieutenant-Governor, is that which is followed in these provinces, viz. to assign a fixed portion of the Land Revenue for local objects. This is now done always at the time of Settlement by setting apart one-eleventh of the entire demand, or one-tenth of the Imperial Land Revenue, for purposes of revenue, police, district roads, district *dak* [postal service], village education, and sanitation,—duties the discharge of which is to a large extent obligatory on Government as a superior landlord of the country."[1]

But this practice was abolished in 1872 by a distinct order. "The system of taking engagements from the proprietors to the payment of the local cesses as a part of the Land Revenue be abandoned."[2] The effect of this change in rule is manifest. So long as the local

[1] Smith's *Manual*, page 203.
[2] Revenue Board's Circular, dated July 13, 1872.

rates on land were considered a "part of the Land Revenue" they could rightly be included in the Government demand of Half-Rental. But by the rule of 1872, the Government virtually imposed the rates in addition to Government demand of half the rental. And the rates, too, have been increased from 10 to 16 per cent. of the Government demand. Large surpluses have now been secured by fixing the rupee at 1s. 4d., and the people can fairly demand that the Half-Rental rule should be honestly adhered to. The total assessment on the soil should not exceed half the actual rental.

Legislation.—A Rent Act for the North-West Provinces, now called the Province of Agra, was passed in 1873, and was amended and consolidated in 1881, under the administration of Lord Ripon. And a Rent Act was passed for the Province of Oudh in 1876. After the close of the century these Acts, both for Agra and Oudh, have been consolidated by Sir Antony Macdonnell by a comprehensive Act. His main object in passing this new Rent Act for Northern India in 1901 was the same that guided him in drafting the Rent Act for Bengal in 1885. They were *firstly* to strengthen the occupancy tenants, and *secondly*, to protect the tenants-at-will from arbitrary enhancement and ejection. To Sir Antony Macdonnell, in our generation, belongs the high credit of completing that beneficial work in Northern India, which was begun by Canning and Lawrence, to extend adequate protection to the cultivators of the soil.

PUNJAB.

The Punjab, on the other hand, has undergone changes of a questionable character. The healthy rule of settlements for thirty years, which gave cultivators and landlords peace and security for a generation after a revision, has been rescinded; and in 1895 the term of settlements was unwisely reduced to twenty years. And lastly, a law of doubtful utility was passed in 1901 to restrict the right of transfer.

In an early chapter of this work we showed that the Sardars and leaders of the people were treated with scant justice in the Punjab after its annexation in 1849. Since then, the province has been a land of small proprietors, often tilling their own land, and sometimes having tenants under them. Lord Lawrence passed an Act in 1868 to protect these tenants; and this was followed by another Tenancy Act in 1887. But the small proprietors have not been able to hold their own. In 1891 they tilled nearly 54 per cent. of the cultivated area of the province; while in 1900 the proportion had fallen to 45 per cent. Apprehensions were entertained that the land was passing away from the fine old families of the province, as well as from the sturdy tillers who had held them before. A Descent of Jaigirs Act was passed to promote the principles of primogeniture among the old families. And a Land Alienation Act was passed to save the old tribes from a landless existence. This last Act is, as remarked before, a measure of doubtful utility; it was passed against the opinion of the Lieutenant-Governor of the Province; it has the economic effect of decreasing the marketable value of land; and it can hardly in the long run benefit the tribes for whose benefit it was passed.

"The cesses in the Punjab are restricted to 12½ per cent. of the annual value [rental] which is defined as double the Land Revenue. But in practice the Land Revenue is generally less and often much less, than 50 per cent. of the assets [rental], and the cesses do not in most districts exceed 11 per cent. of the annual value."[1] But even this is a higher percentage than is levied in Agra and Oudh; and the rule of limiting the total State-demand on the soil to one-half the rental is more needed in the Punjab than elsewhere.

[1] *Moral and Material Progress and Condition of India*, 1901-2.

CHAPTER V

LAND ADMINISTRATION IN THE CENTRAL PROVINCES

THE three clear principles which were established at the great Settlement of 1863 were:—

(1) Recognition of proprietary rights in the Malguzars of the province;

(2) Limitation of the State-demand to half the rental;

(3) Making the Settlement for a long term of thirty years.

The recognition of proprietary rights was absolute and unreserved. It was not the creation of a new right, but the recognition, by the Government, of the state of things which had existed in practice. The Malguzars were virtually landlords, exercising nearly all the powers of landlords, and the State recognised them as such in the Settlement of 1863. This will appear clear from a few extracts which we shall place before our readers.

MALGUZARI SETTLEMENT OF 1863.

As early as 1853 the Secretary to the Government of the North-Western Provinces had declared:—

"Regarding the general principles of the Settlement, I am directed to intimate that his Honour has resolved that it shall be concluded on the basis of apparent or approximate proprietary right, in so far as such right can, with any approach to certainty or confidence, be traced; and that the leading object in so doing shall be to recognise fixed rights, or claims, or interests, in whatever form they may already have grown up, and to avoid an interference with them by any speculative acts or views of the officers of Government."[1]

And this declaration was repeated in the summaries appended to the Settlement Code of 1863:—

"The recognition of positive rights of ownership has hitherto been withheld. But those rights nevertheless existed, and are now to be recognised. The leading object is to recognise fixed rights or claims and interests, in whatever form they may have already grown up.

"When recognising and declaring rights, the word 'confer' is to be employed by Settlement Officers for the sake of form and expediency, in order to bar future contest or litigation."[2]

It is a matter for regret that the principle so clearly established in the Settlement of 1863 was subsequently ignored. The sympathetic spirit of the administration of Sir Richard Temple had disappeared when Colonel Keatinge became the Chief Commissioner of the Central Provinces in 1871–72. The idea gained ground that virtually all rents paid by cultivators were due to the State; and that the Malguzar was a *parvenu* on whom the Government had "conferred" a right which could be taken away again. The Ryotwari System found favour with Colonel Keatinge; the Landlord System which had grown up in the Central Provinces, and had been recognised in 1863, was in disfavour. Accordingly a proposal was made to pull down the structure which had been built up, to bring the cultivators of the Central Provinces directly under the State, and to treat the Malguzars only as servants of the State, and remunerated by the State.

Mr. Peddar, Commissioner of the Nagpur Division, had himself a leaning towards the Ryotwari System; but he raised his voice against introducing a change in the

[1] Letter to the Revenue Board, dated November 30, 1853.

[2] Summaries appended to Circular Orders of the Settlement Code of 1863, page 35.

Central Provinces which would be a breach of faith. And some passages of his elaborate letter on the subject deserve to be quoted:—

"We think that the persons, with whom the Settlement has now been made, have an equitable right to expect that its general principles will be sanctioned. The Malguzari System has been formally adopted by the Government for the whole of this Division. The Chief Commissioner [Sir Richard Temple] himself, in open Darbar, has explained that system, and has promised its introduction. Proprietary rights have accordingly been formally conferred after inquiry into the different claims to them. And on the strength of the belief thus created, obligations have in some instances been contracted. We consider, therefore, that all that can now be done is to modify the existing system in detail."

"For the same reason we would deprecate the adoption of the system suggested in paragraph 20 of the Government of India letter. To consider the entire sum payable by the Ryots for their holdings at the time of the Settlement to be Government Revenue, and to remunerate the Mukadam by a percentage on this sum, *plus* the assessment of waste land brought into cultivation during the term of Settlement, would be to go back to the former system. And I entertain no doubt that this would be the correct course. But it would be an essential change in the principle of the present Settlement, and would be looked upon as a breach of faith by the Malguzars. Their position would be changed from that of land-owners, paying half the profits of their villages as assessment to Government, to that of hereditary servants, receiving remuneration from Government."[1]

This letter must have damped the Ryotwari ardour of Colonel Keatinge, Chief Commissioner of the Central Provinces. He forwarded it to the Government of India, approving of the modifications suggested by Mr. Peddar,

[1] Letter dated April 6, 1872; paragraphs 28 and 29.

but recommending that the main principles of the Settlement of 1863 should remain intact. The Government of India yielded, and maintained the proprietary rights of the Malguzar—but gave him the option of descending to the position of a hereditary servant.[1] The Malguzar, we need hardly add, did not avail himself of this option—the fly did not come into the parlour.

Ryotwari System of Sambalpur.

The district of Sambalpur had, on account of disturbances, failed to share in the general Settlement commenced in 1863. Here, therefore, Colonel Keatinge had a free hand. Sir Richard Temple had issued orders for a Malguzari Settlement in this district; but the orders had not yet been carried out. In 1863 Sir Richard Temple had visited Sambalpur, and proclaimed in open Darbar the principles of the contemplated Settlement; but the Darbar proclamation was not binding on his successor. Colonel Keatinge had a clean slate, and he wrote on it, *Ryotwari Settlement*. Proprietary rights were denied and withheld. The revenue-payers were to be considered lessees of their villages. They were to be remunerated by permission to hold their home-farms revenue-free. They would further be permitted to keep to themselves rents of waste lands brought under cultivation during the Settlement. And in view of Sir Richard Temple's pledge to regard them as proprietors, they were made proprietors only with regard to their Bhogra lands. The Settlement was made for twelve years only, 1876 to 1888. Sambalpur has remained a Ryotwari District ever since.

It is sad to contemplate how the fates and fortunes of hundreds and thousands, and sometimes millions of people, are often determined under a non-representative Government by the whims of one official. The Malguzari System has been decided upon for the Central Provinces

[1] Resolution of the Government of India, dated June 21, 1875.

after years of anxious deliberation. It was based on customs which had grown up in the country. It had received the approbation of the Governments of Lord Canning and Sir Richard Temple. It was calculated to promote the agricultural wealth of the people. It had already been adopted in most parts of the Central Provinces. It had been promised in open Darbar at Sambalpur. The people of the district wished for it and asked for it. One man, Colonel Keatinge, desired to set aside the promises made, and to introduce Ryotwari Settlement in Sambalpur. His recommendations were not known to the people. The sanction of the Viceroy's Council was given without consulting the people. And a Ryotwari Settlement was introduced in Sambalpur. Every unbiassed man will ask himself if this system of administration can be wise, or popular; if it can secure the welfare of a nation or strengthen British Rule in India.

The Rental.

A Tenancy Act was passed in 1883. It recognised (1) Absolute Occupancy Tenants, who had full powers of transfer, and whose rents were fixed at the Settlement for thirty years; (2) Occupancy Tenants, with powers of transfer under certain conditions, and whose rents were fixed by the Settlement Officer for ten years; (3) Ordinary Tenants, with powers of transfer subject to the landlord's consent, and whose rents were fixed for seven years. The Act had the same object as the Tenancy Acts of Bengal and Northern India, viz. the protection of the cultivators; but it bears traces of the unwillingness of the Government to recognise the full proprietary rights of the Malguzar. In Bengal and Northern India, landlords dealt with their own tenants, subject to the salutary checks imposed upon them by the law; but in the Central Provinces the Settlement Officer intervened, and settled the rents which the tenants should pay to their landlords. A healthy freedom of transactions between landlords and tenants was allowed in Bengal and Northern India; an unhealthy State interference was introduced in the Central Provinces. "We do not," says Sir Antony Macdonnell in reference to Northern India, "for the purpose of assessing the Government Revenue, make a basis of our own; we proceed on the basis of actual facts which have been brought into existence by the operation of the ordinary law of rent, and the arrangement which the landlord has made with his own tenant."[1] But in the Central Provinces there is no operation of the ordinary law of rent; the Settlement Officer intervenes and makes the arrangement between the landlord and his tenant. This mischievous interference weakens the landlord and strangles the tenant-right. The Malguzar in the Central Provinces does not feel the responsibilities and the duties of a landlord when the Government Officer settles the rental for him. And the peasantry of the Central Provinces have not the independence, or the self-reliance of the Bengal peasantry; they do not know their own rights, and cannot defend them. A grandmotherly legislation makes both the landlord and the tenant weaker in the Central Provinces; nullifies the education which property gives to every owner of the land; stifles the staying power of the people; and finds them helpless and resourceless against the first outset of scarcity or famine. Nothing is more demoralising to an agricultural population than such needless intervention of the State in the ordinary transactions of agricultural industry. The right policy is that which has succeeded so well in Bengal and in Northern India. Afford adequate and ample protection to the cultivator by law; and then treat him as a responsible man, standing on his own legs, dealing with his landlord, knowing and defending his rights.

But the settling of the rental by Government officers

[1] Evidence given before the Currency Committee, vol. i. p. 211.

created for the State itself a difficulty which it had not foreseen. In the Settlement of 1863, the actual rental of estates had been disregarded; and Settlement Officers had assessed the Land Revenue on a supposed rental which they thought the lands should bear. But when they themselves fixed the rental under the new Tenancy Act, they could hardly disregard it in the approaching Settlement of 1893. They would have to accept the rental they had fixed; and the prevailing rule compelled them to limit the Government Revenue to half that rental. The administrators were in a dilemma. They could not break through the rental they had fixed. And they could not break through the rule limiting the Government Revenue to half that rental.

Settlement of 1893.

The proposal which was made in 1887, as an escape out of this difficulty, is one of the strangest documents in Indian official literature. Mr. Mackenzie, afterwards Sir Alexander Mackenzie, was then the Chief Commissioner of the Central Provinces. He was an able Bengal civilian, had been trained in secretariat work, and under the administration of Lord Ripon had drafted those important resolutions on Local Self-Government from which we have given some extracts in a previous chapter. Among many qualifications as a ruler, he lacked sympathy with the people, a respect for their aspirations, a just regard for their rights. His policy varied with the spirit of the times; and his administration of the Central Provinces, and subsequently of Bengal, was marked by some of the most retrograde measures of the closing century. In the Central Provinces he openly admitted that the Half-Rental rule had been *evaded* in 1863 by the Settlement Officer assuming a high rental; that the rule could not be *evaded* at the next Settlement because the rental was now legally defined and fixed; and that the rule therefore must be withdrawn. A few extracts from this remarkable document are given.

"Under the method of assessment which was then followed [in 1863] it was, however, practically impossible for an Officer in any part of the province, who saw that an enhancement of revenue was justifiable and sought to secure this, to give full effect to a rule restricting the Government Revenue to a definite share of the assets, unless the term assets received a very loose and general interpretation. The assets or rental value of each Mahal [estate] was in fact determined by the comparison of a number of statistical inferences, the principal of which was that obtained by the application of soil-rates to the areas under different soils in a village, which yielded the soil-rate rental. Whether this rental corresponded in any way with the real rental of the Mahal depended on the extent to which rents rose in the proceedings taken for rent adjustment after the assessment was given out."

"The system of assessment, which is being followed in the Settlement of the Central Provinces now begun, differs essentially from that of the former Settlement. Under the Tenancy Act, the rents of all Absolute Occupancy and Occupancy Tenants must be fixed by the Settlement Officer. . . . It has, moreover, become very evident that it will further fall to the Settlement Officer to fix the rents of all Ordinary Tenants. . . . It will no longer be necessary for our Assessing Officer to assume, as the assets of an estate, a rental value which may or may not be realised at rent adjustment. The rental value which he assumes for his assessment will be given effect to by him."

"It must, moreover, be realised that the system of Settlement to which the Government has now, by law, committed itself, will render it impossible to evade the operation of the Half-Assets rule in the manner followed at the last Settlement. It will no longer be practicable to adopt for the application of the Half-Assets rule a rental value which is in excess of the actual adjusted rental, and in this way to make an assessment which, while nominally at Half-Assets, absorbs in reality a very much larger proportion of the income of the Malguzars."

"Mr. Mackenzie would ask that the Half-Assets rule may be authoritatively declared inapplicable to the Central Provinces at the present Settlement, and that the Local Administration may be left to make a reasonable and moderate Settlement all round, subject to the final orders and approval of the Governor-General in Council."[1]

The Government of Lord Dufferin was unwilling to enhance the Government Revenue wholly or principally from the Malguzar's share of the assets, and suggested that the provisions of the law should be fully utilised by enhancing the rent of tenants.

"The fixing of rent by Settlement Officers under rules to be made by the Chief Commissioner under Section 82 is really the most important part of the Settlement operations. The method by which this duty is to be performed is not discussed in your letter, but it is noted that, in the Central Provinces Proceedings for March 1887, a scheme for revising rents is discussed by Mr. Fuller and Mr. Fitzpatrick, in which suggestions are made for a method (1) of raising unduly low rents to the local level, and (2) of raising all the rents of an area to a higher level when the whole of them are unduly low."[2]

Mr. Mackenzie replied in a long communication, in which he asked for a latitude of 50 to 65 per cent. of the rental to be fixed as the Land Revenue.[3] And the Government of India finally decided by allowing the latitude to the Chief Commissioner.

"The Government of India has some hesitation in

[1] Letter to the Government of India, dated May 18, 1887, signed by Secretary J. B. Fuller, who afterwards succeeded Sir Henry Cotton as Chief Commissioner of Assam.

[2] Letter of the Government of India, dated August 24, 1887.

[3] Letter to the Government of India, dated March 16, 1888.

allowing in any case so high a percentage as 65 to be taken; and would at least prefer that this maximum be restricted to those cases in which the former percentage was not at any rate below that fraction; and that in other estates 60 per cent. be taken as the highest admissible percentage."[1]

There is scarcely anything in the entire range of Indian official literature which is more painful reading to the official, or to the public, than this correspondence. In Northern India the right of settling rents with tenants was left with the landlord; in the Central Provinces this right was deliberately assumed by the State under the Act of 1883. In Northern India legislation sought to restrain landlords from enhancing rents; in the Central Provinces the State deliberately laid down the policy of enhancing rents. In Northern India the State-demand was limited to one-half the rental fixed by landlords; in the Central Provinces this rule of half-rental was cast aside because it could no longer be *evaded*, and the State assumed the power of demanding 50 to 65 per cent. of the rental, after the State-Officers had raised that rental. A policy better calculated to repress agricultural wealth and prosperity, and to prepare the Province for starvation and famines, could hardly be compassed by the wit of man.

The final blow was dealt by Lord George Hamilton, Secretary of State for India. He decided in 1895 that the period of Settlement, too, should be reduced from thirty to twenty years. The healthy rule which gave peace and rest to the agricultural population for a generation after a Settlement, a rule still observed in Northern India, Madras, and Bombay, was set aside in the Central Provinces as in the Punjab. More frequent revision of the assessment was the unsympathetic policy of the closing years of the century.

One by one the three cardinal principles of the Settlement of 1863 were whittled away within thirty-

[1] Letter from the Government of India, dated May 31, 1888.

two years. The Proprietary Rights of Malguzars were restricted, and they were stopped from settling the rental of their estates. The Half-rental Rule was abandoned. The Thirty Years' Rule was also abandoned. All the safeguards which had been provided by the Governments of Lord Canning and Sir Richard Temple for the growth of a prosperous landed class and a prosperous peasantry were removed one by one under the Governments of Lord Dufferin and Lord Lansdowne.

The settlement that followed was in accordance with the spirit of the new rules which had been framed. In a speech which the Hon. B. K. Bose, Member for the Central Provinces, made in Lord Curzon's Council on March 28, 1900, he gave the following figures showing the percentage of increase in the rental imposed on the cultivators of the different districts in the new Settlement.

District.	Percentage of Enhancement in the Rental in various Groups within the District.
Sagor	10, 8, 9
Damoh	14, 10
Jabalpur	11, 4, 3, 9 (reduced by 5 % in one group)
Mandla	(figures not available)
Seoni	12, 8, 10
Narsinghpur	4, 6
Hoshangabad	4, 5, 9, 8
Nimar	23
Betul	14, 17, 18, 14
Chhindwara	17, 9, 12
Wordha	20, 7
Bhandara	14, 15, 13
Nagpur	13, 17, 15, 14
Balaghat	16
Raipur	12
Bilaspur	13, 7
Sambalpur	(figures not available)

It will thus be seen that the Settlement Officers, true to the instructions of Lord Dufferin's Government, raised the rental throughout the Province from 3 to 23 per cent. for the purposes of the new Settlement. This increase was in addition to the enhancements which had been made by the landlords themselves before that power was taken out of their hands. Rents were screwed up all round, so that the Land Revenue based on the rental might show an increase. If landlords themselves complained that they could not collect the high rents fixed, they complained in vain. They must pay the high Land Revenue assessed on the new rents, whether they could collect the rents or not.

It is due to one distinguished officer to make some mention of his endeavour to decrease the rigour of the assessment. Antony Macdonnell came as Chief Commissioner in the Central Provinces after Alexander Mackenzie. He refrained from fixing the Land Revenue as high as 65 per cent. of the rental in any district. The percentages generally varied between 50 and 60 per cent. But the evil had already been done. The rental had already been increased. And the Land Revenue assessed on that rental showed an enormous increase over the Land Revenue fixed in 1863. We quote the following figures from the speech of the Honourable Mr. Bose, already referred to.

District.	Percentage of Increase in the Land Revenue as compared with 1863 in various Groups within the District.
Sagor	68, 42, 53, 48
Damoh	55, 73
Jabalpur	50, 44, 62, 86, 64, 77
Mandla	61, 66
Seoni	95, 97, 55, 92, 50
Narsinghpur	57, 46
Hoshangabad	69, 87, 96
Nimar	58, 56
Betul	55, 63, 57, 37
Chhindwara	45, 55, 47, 25
Wardha	26, 28
Nagpur	20, 21, 28, 24
Bhandara	40, 38, 30, 52
Balaghat	48
Raipur	82, 98
Bilaspur	102, 105
Sambalpur	34

And local taxes on the soil, which were insignificant in 1863, had risen to 12½ per cent. on the Land Revenue in addition to that revenue.

FAMINES OF 1897 AND 1900.

No serious famine had revisited the Central Provinces under British Rule. But the impoverishment of the people paves the way for famines. A failure of crops is a serious calamity in an agricultural country under all circumstances; but the effects of a famine become ten times more fatal if the people have no resources and no savings. The famine of 1897 was the most serious and fatal ever known in the Central Provinces. Districts were devastated. Cultivated lands became jungle. Large masses of the people were swept away. Both cultivation and population decreased. A question was then asked in the House of Commons by Mr. Samuel Smith, M.P., if the operation of the New Settlement would be postponed until the famine was over. Lord George Hamilton declined to postpone the Settlement Operations.

But the hand of nature is stronger than the hand of man. A fresh famine desolated the unhappy Provinces in 1900. The new Settlement with its enhanced revenue demand became impossible. The Government was forced to suspend its operation. Abatements were made in Sagor, Damoh, Jabalpur, Seoni, Narsinghpur, Hoshangabad, and Nimar. Abatements were in progress in Betul, Wardha, Bhandara, Balaghat, and Raipur in 1902. An impossible Land Revenue had to be reduced after the Province had been devastated by two famines.

The people of the Province demand, not merely temporary abatements, but permanent reforms. No new measures are required; it is only necessary to go back to the principles of 1863. All departures from those principles have proved disastrous; they have weakened the landed classes and impoverished the peasantry. Settlements should be made for thirty years, as they are made in Northern India, Bombay, and Madras. The Land Revenue should be limited to one-half the actual rental, as it is limited in the Provinces of Agra, Oudh, and the Punjab. Additional cesses imposed on the soil since 1871 should be abolished. The cultivators should have the same rights in their holdings and the same protection against enhancements as are assured to cultivators in Bengal and Northern India under Tenancy Acts. And strengthened by such protection, they should be left to settle their rents with their landlords without the intervention of Settlement Officers. The intervention of the State in settling the rent of each field has, in effect, added to the rental, and impoverished the population.

Rigid Rules and their Operation.

No task, more unsuitable for the State, can well be imagined than to intervene and settle the rent which each tiller should pay to his landlord, and no task has been worse performed. The rules for fixing the rent are so complicated that they are neither properly understood nor properly worked.[1] Poorly instructed and poorly paid Patels

[1] The complexity of the rules may be imagined from the following extracts from the *Introduction to the Central Provinces Settlement Code* issued in 1891:—

"The first step in working this system is to ascertain the various classes of land. . . . The next step is to determine the relative value of each class expressed in the number of soil units per acre. . . . A scale of factors having been framed showing the number of soil units of each land class compared with other classes, the number of soil units in each holding or village is calculated by multiplying the area of each soil class by the factor of the class. Thus, for instance, if 150 acres of land fall into three soil-classes, the factors for which are 32 for A, 16 for B, and 4 for C, the areas being respectively 50, 75, and 25 acres, the number of soil units will be—

$$\begin{array}{ll} A & 50 \times 32 = 1600 \\ B & 75 \times 16 = 1200 \\ C & 25 \times 4 = 100 \\ \hline & 2900 \end{array}$$

"If the existing rental payment was 275 rupees, its incidence per soil unit would be $\frac{275}{2900} = 1.5$ anna."

"Coming now to the second class of arguments used in rent enhance-

and Patwaris, getting three shillings to six shillings a week are expected to work according to these impossible inductive and deductive rules! As a matter of fact, they vaguely imagine that the Government wants an increase in rental, and they secure one. Two or three Assistant Settlement Officers in a District cannot efficiently check the work of Patels and Patwaris over thousands of square miles. The fixing of the rent is therefore often a poor guess work, and the mistakes are against the cultivator. And the cultivator has no independent Land Court to appeal to against the finding of the official paid three to six shillings a week.

The mistakes which are most frequently made in fixing and enhancing rents are known universally in the Central Provinces. In the first place the classification of lands is often wrong, and Patels have a habit of placing on a higher class lands which really fall under a lower class. In the second place, the crop experiments, by which the productiveness of the different classes of soil is judged, are often misleading; no adequate allowance is made for dryage and loss in harvesting. In the third place, much cultivable land is left uncultivated owing to the want of seed grain, want of bullocks, or the general poverty of the cultivator. All such land is, however, included by Government Officers in fixing the rental; and the landlord has to realise rents for lands which tenants cannot cultivate, or to pay revenue for lands for

ment, those obtained deductively from considerations based on the rise in prices, let it be supposed that prices would justify an enhancement of 33 per cent. on rents paid at a former settlement, whereas a comparison of the rental paid then and now, effected by contrasting the rate per acre in cultivation at both periods, shows that rents, considered in the aggregate, have risen by 10 per cent. only, a further enhancement of 23 on the original rental, or of 20 per cent. on the rental as it stands, is justified. The soil-unit system offers a means of distributing this enhancement equitably."

"In the hands of inductive reasoning, the system is then an instrument for arriving at the amount of an enhancement; it serves also as a means for fairly distributing an enhancement arrived at by deductive reasoning, as it reduces every Ryot's holding to, so to speak, a common denominator."

which he gets no rent.[1] In the fourth place, it is proved in the case of minor's estates, which the State administers for those minors, that State Officers are themselves unable to realise the rents they have fixed by something like 10 per cent. Private landlords necessarily bear a heavier loss. Fifthly, the instalments of the Government demand are not judiciously fixed. A large instalment is demanded in February in order to complete the collection within the financial year. Landlords press their tenants for rent in January in order to pay the revenue in February. The crops are not yet harvested in January, and the tenants have to mortgage standing crops, much under their fair value, to money-lenders in order to pay rents. Sixthly and lastly, while the law of Bengal empowers the Government to sell an estate in default of payment of revenue, the law of the Central Provinces empowers revenue officers to arrest a landlord and send him to prison for default. Such severity, unknown in the revenue laws of Bengal, is a stain on the administration of the Central Provinces.

Tenancy Act of 1898 and Needed Reforms.

A consolidating and amending Rent Act, passed in 1898, has not improved the position of the tenant. It provides that the rent of ordinary tenants shall be fixed by Settlement Officers for seven years. And provisions have been made restricting the alienation of home-farm lands by landlords, and the transfer of their right by occupancy and ordinary tenants. Such restrictions are unknown to Bengal laws, and they have the economic effect of lessening the marketable value of properties. It is not by such measures that the Central Provinces

[1] In the inquiries which I personally made in the Central Provinces in March 1903, I was informed in one District that nearly a fourth of the assessed land was left uncultivated that year. Rents could not be realised for most of these lands, but the revenue had to be paid.

can regain their prosperity after the recent calamities. It is by more liberal measures, and by going back to the healthy principles of 1863, that the agricultural population of the Province can become strong, resourceful, self-reliant, and prosperous.

CHAPTER VI

LAND ADMINISTRATION IN BOMBAY AND MADRAS

THE Land Systems of Bombay and Madras, like those of Northern India, were built up under the administration of the East India Company. The first Settlement for thirty years in Bombay was commenced by Wingate in 1836; and a Settlement of thirty years for Madras was ordered by the Court of Directors in 1855. And after the administration had passed to the Crown, it was laid down by Sir Charles Wood in 1864, that the demand of the State from the soil should be limited, as in Northern India, to one-half the nett produce or economic rent. The action which was taken in the two Provinces, down to the time of Lord Lytton's administration, to carry out these principles, has been narrated in a previous chapter. We shall now briefly continue the story to the end of the century.

BOMBAY.

The mistakes which were made in Bombay at the revision of the Settlement commenced in 1866 were among the reasons which led to the Poona Riot of 1875. Auckland Colvin, one of the Members of the Commission appointed to inquire into the causes of the disturbance, pointed out the sudden and enormous enhancements made in the Land Revenue demand. This evil was not removed. The Bombay Government did not place clear and definite limits on its own claims upon the soil. The rule of Sir Charles Wood to limit the demand to one-half the rental was virtually ignored in Settlement Operations.

The Revenue Jurisdiction Act of 1876 took away the jurisdiction of Courts of Justice in matters of assessment, and made the Settlement Officers absolute. The Agricultural Relief Acts of 1879 sought to protect cultivators from their creditors, but gave no hint of limiting the Land Revenue. The Land Revenue Act of 1879 contained no adequate provisions to limit the State-demand. And yet it was this protection which Bombay cultivators needed more urgently than any other. As Sir William Hunter said, openly and strongly from his place in the Governor-General's Council in 1879: "The fundamental difficulty of bringing relief to the Deccan Peasantry is that the Government Assessment does not leave enough food to the cultivator to support himself and his family throughout the year."

The only rule which limited the discretion of the Settlement Officer was that he should not enhance the revenue of a Taluka or group of villages by more than 33 per cent., or that of a single village by more than 66 per cent., or that of an individual holding by more than 100 per cent. Such a rule was calculated to do more harm than good.

The Revision Settlement, commenced in 1866, went on slowly, and by 1899 (the year preceding the Bombay famine), only half the villages of the Province had been revised. Out of 27,781 villages in the Province, only 13,369½ had been resettled. And the figures[1] showing the old demand, and the revised demand, indicate the enormous increase which had been secured.

The figures on the opposite page call for one or two remarks. The headings of columns 3 and 4 will show that this increase of 30 per cent. was not the result of the slow extension in cultivation during thirty years; it was obtained in the year of the revision. As Auckland Colvin

[1] Bombay Administration Report for 1898–99; Appendix II. £1 is taken as equivalent to 10 rupees. Fractions of £1 are taken as £1, or omitted.

District.	Number of Villages resettled.	Revenue realised in the Year before Revision.	Revenue demand in consequence of the Revision.	Percentage of Increase.
		£	£	
Ahmedabad . . .	444	87,310	109,294	25.2
Kaira	525	131,678	151,843	15.3
Surat	201	55,278	61,066	10.5
Panch Mahals . . .	222	11,043	11,193	1.3
Thana	824	59,772	84,13	41.1
Khandesh	2272	264,475	345,573	30.6
Nasik	959	67,768	93,194	37.5
Ahmednagar . . .	1017½	98,157	124,509	26.9
Poona	1035	96,503	127,335	32.0
Sholapur	672	83,478	112,976	35.3
Satara	962	122,264	159,267	30.3
Kolaba	1059	73,656	100,148	35.9
Belgaum	892	83,749	109,847	31.1
Dharwar	1290	129,868	187,253	44.2
Bijapar	995	81,631	109,043	33.6
Total . . .	13,369½	1,446,600	1,886,854	30.4

had pointed out in 1876, a slow increase in the Land Revenue is obtained in Bombay during the term of a Settlement; and then a sudden and additional increase is obained at the Revision Settlement. It need hardly be repeated that this sudden increase in the Land Revenue is made without consulting the cultivator. Sir Bartle Frere had expressed a desire, in his evidence before the Select Committee of 1872, that the cultivators of Bombay should be consulted, and should have their say, when a new Settlement was proposed. As a fact, however, the cultivators are not consulted; they know the revised State-demand for the first time when it is announced to them.

A system of calculating and determining the revised demand, without consulting those on whom it is imposed, is convenient for expeditious work, but is not just to the Peasant Proprietors. They have not the right or the opportunity of restraining the demand within one-half the nett produce of their fields. They cannot limit the enhancement to a rate proportionate to the rise in prices or the increase in cultivation. They have no chance of proving how far the increased demand trenches on improvements made by themselves. And they are not permitted to appeal against the new assessment to an independent tribunal, after the assessment has been proclaimed to them. The result is what might be expected. The Hon. Gokuldas Parekh, a Member of the Legislative Council of Bombay, has shown from the official figures, exhibiting the results of crop experiments made by Government Officials, that among the large class of cultivators in Gujrat, who own holdings of five acres and less and are unable to grow rich rice, the value of their out-turn is not sufficient even in ordinary years to enable them to meet the Government demand, the cost of tillage, and the maintenance expense of their families and cattle. And he also proves that, "Even a large proportion of the cultivators, holding up to ten acres, are unable to get out-turns sufficient for the payment of the cost of cultivation and their maintenance."[1]

But a higher authority than the Hon. Gokuldas furnishes us with figures for Gujrat which are painful to contemplate. The Famine Commission of 1900, of which Sir Antony Macdonnell was the President, has found that the Government Revenue in Gujrat represents one-fifth of the gross produce of the soil. This is nearly double that which private landlords in Bengal obtain as rent from their tenants ; and this virtually sweeps away the whole of the Economic Rent of Gujrat, instead of limiting the Government demand to one-half the rental as is laid down by the rule of 1864.[2]

[1] *Land Problems in India:* published by Natesan & Co. of Madras, page 147.

[2] I visited Gujrat in March 1903, and made inquiries in some villages in the districts of Kaira, Ahmedabad, Surat, and Broach. The condition of the Peasant Proprietors was wretched beyond description, and the worst of them lived in single rooms with all their family, and with hardly any articles of furniture. The cattle they used was often hired; and any property they had was often mortgaged. Calculating the Land Revenue demand in proportion to the produce, in presence of villagers and of village officials, I found that the demand often came to 30 or 40

The famine of Bombay, like the famine in the Central Provinces, brought the redress which cultivators might have expected from a just and considerable land administration. The enhancements made in the Settlement commenced in 1866 could not be maintained. Half the Province might be sold up, but the Revenue-demand could not be realised. In 1902 and 1903, therefore, the Bombay Government was engaged in lowering assessments in Gujrat. No specific rules governing the reductions have been published. The people are ignorant what limits regulate the Government-demand beyond the varying discretion of the different officials. The people are ignorant to what limits that demand will rise again in some future year, or at the next settlement. The alternate raising and lowering of the State-demand, according to signs of distress or of prosperity, is a see-saw policy which is fatal to agricultural prosperity. A general feeling exists in the country that the Government desires to take as much as it can, leaving the population permanently poor and indebted. A sullen despair prevails among the peasantry which may lead to political danger in the future.

per cent. of what the cultivators actually reaped in average years. I also visited some villages in Satara and Poona in the Deccan, where the Government demand was somewhat less. Among the cultivators whom I examined was a retired soldier who had been to Malta in 1878, and who had now settled down as a cultivator. The Land Revenue in these villages came to 20 or 30 per cent. of what the cultivators actually reaped in average years. When Government Officers declare that the Land Revenue is 20 per cent. in Gujrat and under 10 per cent. in the Deccan, they base their calculations on what the fields *can* yield, and what they *do* yield. This mistake would be impossible if the revenue were paid in kind according to the old custom of India. If the harvest was good, the Government share would be high; if the harvest was poor, the Government demand would be less. The State would benefit by the prosperity of the people, and would suffer with their poverty; and there would be a correspondence between the condition of the peasantry and the Land Revenue collection. But as the British Government has decided to demand its revenue in money, it is of the greatest importance to see that this money demand is based on a correct and careful calculation of what the cultivators do actually obtain from their fields in average years. 10 per cent. of that *actual yield* would probably represent half-rental; 30 or 40 per cent. represents more than the entire Economic Rent, and trenches on the cost of cultivation and wages of labour.

A large remedial measure is needed. The measure which would have suggested itself in the age of Canning and Lawrence would have been to enlarge and define the tenant-right, to limit enhancements to specific and definite grounds, and to provide Land Courts to assure the peasantry in half the nett produce of their fields. But the measure which suggested itself in 1901 is in keeping with those adopted in the Central Provinces and in the Punjab. A Bill was introduced to empower the Government to take away the right of transfer attached to the soil, in case of default in the payment of the Revenue. The right of transfer was inherent in Mirasi holdings since the Mahratta times. It gave a marketable value to the holdings, and increased the resources of the Peasant Proprietors. It was recognised by the British Government from the commencement of British Rule in the Deccan. It was expressly confirmed by the Land Revenue Act of 1879, which provided that, even when a holding was sold for default, the right of transfer inherent in the holding would vest in the purchaser. The Bombay Peasant Proprietors had exercised this right during eighty years of British Rule. They had enjoyed a legal sanction to the right for over twenty years. The Government now sought the power to take away this right in cases of default. The Bill did not mention any backward tracts, or backward hill tribes, to which its operation would be limited. It sought to empower the Government with respect to the entire Province, and to all Peasant Proprietors.

Never did the people of Bombay protest more emphatically against any Government measure than against this Act of Confiscation as they regarded it. All parts of Bombay shared in the protest. The mass of Peasant Proprietors felt that it was a blow struck at their recognised rights. The elected members of the Bombay Legislative Council argued against the measure forcibly, loyally, emphatically. They left the

Council Hall in a body when their protest was disregarded. The Bill was passed into law. The Bombay Land Revenue Act of 1879 was amended so as to empower the Government to resettle fields without the right of transfer when they were sold for default.

Measures like this do not add to the strength and the staying power of a nation of cultivators. They do not add to the value of their property or improve their economic condition. The Peasant Proprietors of Bombay still look forward to more liberal measures, assuring them in their rights, limiting the State-demand to half the nett produce, and limiting enhancements to specific, definite, and equitable grounds.

MADRAS.

It has been stated in a preceding chapter that a regular Survey Settlement was commenced in Madras in 1861. The Settlement was made for thirty years; and as District after District was taken up, the work continued for a long number of years. In fact, Settlement Work is thus going on continually in Madras as in Bombay; for before the last District or Taluka has been settled or revised, the time has come for a fresh revision of the first tract settled thirty years ago. This arrangment is convenient to Settlement Officers; and the people do not object to it so long as a place, settled once, is left in peace for thirty years. What they do ask for is that enhancements, made in Revised Settlements, should be made on specific and definite grounds; and that the new demand should be limited to one-half the nett produce of their fields. The results of Settlements, down to 1875, were exhibited in figures in a preceding chapter. Similar figures for the subsequent eighteen years, down to 1898, are given below from an official report:—[1]

[1] Resolution of the Madras Board of Revenue, No. 542, dated December 6, 1900, Appendix I. £1 is taken as equivalent to 10 rupees. Malabar and South Canara are omitted.

Land Revenue in Madras, excluding Malabar and South Canara.

Year.	Occupied Area in Acres.	Assessment thereon.	Total Ryotwari Demand.	Cesses, &c.	Gross Demand.
		£	£	£	£
1876	19,200,000	3,240,000	2,770,000	380,000	3,150,000
1877	19,200,000	3,250,000	3,590,000	400,000	3,990,000
1878	19,100,000	3,260,000	3,720,000	410,000	4,130,000
1879	18,400,000	3,200,000	3,660,000	410,000	4,070,000
1880	18,100,000	3,180,000	3,640,000	410,000	4,050,000
1881	18,000,000	3,170,000	3,570,000	410,000	3,980,000
1882	18,300,000	3,210,000	3,630,000	440,000	4,070,000
1883	18,500,000	3,230,000	3,740,000	450,000	4,190,000
1884	18,700,000	3,240,000	3,500,000	460,000	3,960,000
1885	19,100,000	3,270,000	3,760,000	450,000	4,210,000
1886	19,500,000	3,310,000	3,860,000	460,000	4,320,000
1887	19,700,000	3,550,000 [1]	3,900,000	590,000	4,490,000
1888	19,800,000	3,570,000	3,920,000	570,000	4,490,000
1889	20,100,000	3,610,000	3,960,000	650,000	4,610,000
1890	20,200,000	3,630,000	3,900,000	640,000	4,540,000
1891	20,200,000	3,650,000	3,680,000	660,000	4,340,000
1892	20,700,000	3,710,000	4,030,000	680,000	4,710,000
1893	21,000,000	3,880,000	4,390,000	380,000 [2]	4,770,000
1894	21,300,000	3,950,000	4,520,000	570,000 [3]	5,090,000
1895	21,500,000	3,930,000	4,680,000	590,000	5,270,000
1896	21,500,000	4,000,000	4,400,000	560,000	4,960,000
1897	21,600,000	4,030,000	4,740,000	540,000	5,280,000
1898	21,600,000	4,050,000	4,850,000	550,000	5,400,000

It will appear from these figures that a million of acres went out of cultivation after the famine year of 1877; and the loss continued for no less than seven years. It was not till 1885 that the cultivated area again came up to the figure for 1877.

But the most striking fact revealed by the foregoing table is increase in the gross demand within the eighteen years. The area under cultivation went up from 19 millions to 21½ million acres, or less than 14 per cent.; but the gross demand increased from £3,150,000 to £5,400,000, or over 70 per cent. Or if we take the increase in the assessment on the occupied area, the

[1] Irrigation charges in Godavari and Krishna transferred to land assessments.

[2] Village service was suspended for the year.

[3] £100,000 transferred to Land Revenue "Miscellaneous."

increase is from £3,240,000 to £4,050,000, or nearly 25 per cent. This large and disproportionate increase is mainly due to the irrigation of some of the Ryotwari land; and the Irrigation Cess has been consolidated with the Land Revenue, so that the cultivator cannot tell how much is demanded for the land and how much for the water supplied.

The question whether the water-rate should be a compulsory rate on all lands within reach of canals, or whether it should be an optional rate payable by those cultivators who choose to use the water, has been under consideration for many years. Lord Lawrence had declared before the House of Commons Committee in 1873: "I would almost rather not make a canal at all, however much I desired to do so, rather than make it obligatory on them [the cultivators] to take water."[1] And the Duke of Argyll, as Secretary of State for India, had strongly and emphatically maintained this view three years before, *i.e.* in 1870. His reasons against levying a compulsory water-rate on cultivators were recorded clearly in his letter to Lord Mayo,[2] from which we make the following extracts:—

"The object of the provision in question is to enable Government to secure itself against pecuniary loss in the event of a canal proving a financial failure. Such failure might ensue from three causes. A canal might not be able to supply for irrigational purposes the expected quantity of water, or, the expected quantity being available, cultivators might decline to avail themselves to the expected extent, or excessive costliness of construction might, in order to render a canal remunerative, necessitate the imposition of higher rates than cultivators could afford or would voluntarily pay. In the first case, under the proposed enactment, the loss consequent on Government having engaged in an unsuccessful speculation, would fall, not upon itself, but upon

[1] Report of 1873; question 4458. [2] Letter dated January 11, 1870.

the cultivators, whom it had disappointed. In the second cultivators would be forced to pay for water for which they had no use, or, at any rate, were not disposed to use, possibly, no doubt, from imperfect appreciation of the value of irrigation, but quite possibly also from a perfectly intelligible desire to have part of their land under dry crops, instead of all under wet. With regard to the third, none can require less than your Government to be reminded how prone to become excessive guaranteed expenditure always is; and under the provisions of the Bill all expenditure on Government canals would be guaranteed."

"To force irrigation on the people would be not unlikely to make that unpopular which could otherwise scarcely fail to be regarded as a blessing, and which, as all experience shows, Indian agriculturists, if left to themselves, are sure duly to appreciate, sooner or later, and seldom later than the first season of drought that occurs after irrigation has been placed within their reach."[1]

In Bengal, accordingly, the irrigation rate is optional to this day; and cultivators use it largely and pay for it cheerfully. But the Government in Madras has always been less liberal, and more autocratic than in Bengal; partly because it is less under the control of the Governor-General in Council, and partly also because there is less of influential and educated public opinion in the Ryotwari tracts, to leaven the administration and bring it in touch with the wishes of the people. Accordingly, the

[1] What was foreseen in the last sentence was precisely what happened in Orissa in 1896, when I was acting as Commissioner of that Division. The cultivators had neglected to take the canal water until the drought of 1896 came. Thousands of applications then poured in for the use of the canal water at the rates which had been fixed by the engineers. And cultivators bound themselves for five or six years to use the water and pay for it. Ignorant the Indian cultivators are, but nowhere in the world are the tillers more keenly alive to their own interests and their own profits than in India. The Ryots have come to consider canal water as a blessing, and are paying the water-rate voluntarily and cheerfully, where it is not unwisely forced on them as a compulsory tax.

scheme which was rejected by the Duke of Argyll in 1870, and which was condemned by Lord Lawrence in 1873, was passed into law in Madras in 1900. Instead of leaving the cultivators the option of using and paying for canal water, a law was passed making the irrigation rate compulsory on all lands supposed to be benefited by canals, even by percolation! And no option was left to cultivators to appeal to Courts of Law to show that their lands were *not* benefited.

The Water Tax is consolidated with the Land Tax. The cultivator does not know what portion of the assessment is for his holding and what portion is for the water which is supposed to benefit him. But he does know that the total assessment is so excessive as not to leave him one-half the nett produce of his holding. In many places, the assessment leaves him nothing beyond the wages of his labour and the cost of cultivation.[1] Irrigation protects him from famine; but it has not enabled him to save, or to improve his condition.

It also appears from the table given above that the cesses went up with a bound in 1887, when the irrigation charges were transferred to Land Assessments. So long as the water-rate was separate from the land-rate, cesses could be charged on the land-rate only. When irrigation charges were consolidated with land assessments, the cesses went up in one year from £460,000 to £590,000. Is it possible in Madras to separate the land-rate from the water-rate, so as to impose the cesses on the former and not on the latter?

But the greatest complaint of Madras cultivators is about the uncertainty of the assessments. In 1882, as

[1] I visited some villages in the irrigated Deltas of the Godavari and Krishna in January 1903. The crops were assured against the effects of drought; but the lands were highly assessed, and the cultivators were poor and generally in debt. Their holdings had a very poor market value, because they brought little to the peasants after paying the consolidated tax. I had the advantage of discussing the matter with a high official in Godavari District. He could not understand why lands so rich sold at such a miserable price. The reason was that the rich lands left little to the tillers after payment of Government dues.

we shall see in the succeeding chapter, the Marquis of Ripon, then Viceroy of India, sought to remove this uncertainty. He laid down the rule that in districts which had been surveyed and settled, there should be no enhancement of the Land Revenue except on the clear ground of an increase in prices. The Madras Government accepted this rule. The principle was explained in Government publications. The Madras Revenue Settlement Manual, compiled in 1887, laid down:—

"That the grain values, thus determined, should be declared unalterable."

"That the Ryots' payments should vary with the rateable money value of the standard crop, fixed every thirty years."

"The revised settlements are to be permanent as regards grain values; but to be reconsidered as regards commutation rates after thirty years."[1]

The Madrás Agricultural Committee reported in 1889: "A revaluation of soils at each recurring revision would, it is said, and we think rightly said, be fatal to improvement. We believe that the present opinion of the Government is opposed to such a revaluation, and is inclined to make the settlements permanent, so far as the grain values of soils are concerned."[2]

The Government of Madras remarked on the above report: "Nor has the Government any intention of revising the classification of soils. This principle has been repeatedly laid down, and is very clearly stated in the Settlement Manual."[3]

These assurances were as clear and emphatic as words could make them. "People had actually invested money in land," writes the Hon. Vencataratnam, member of the Madras Legislative Council, "relying on these

[1] Chapter II., sections 5 and 6; and Chapter III., section 8.
[2] Paragraph 31.
[3] Government Order, dated July 4, 1889; paragraph 20.

declarations. But when the time came for giving effect to them, the Government coolly cast them to the winds, and sought to obtain increases not warranted by a rise in prices. In the Revision Settlements of the Trichinopoly, Godavari, and Krishna Districts, the soils in the Deltaic tracts have been reclassified, and the Ryots' improvements deliberately taxed in such reclassification. The actual work of classification is practically done by a low paid agency. In the case of individual holdings, the enhancements went up to 200 or 300 per cent., and even more."[1]

As in Bombay, so in Madras, this uncertainty in the assessment militates against all improvements, and is a bar to all agricultural prosperity. What is wanted in Madras, as in Bombay, is some effective provision to limit the Land Tax to one-half the nett produce in every village and every field, and to limit enhancements of the tax to specific and definite grounds like increase in prices, or in cultivation.

The trend of land legislation in the Central Provinces and the Punjab, in Bombay and in Madras, has in recent years been sadly different from that of the earlier decades. In the early years of the Crown administration, and under the rule of Canning and of Lawrence, the one object which animated the Government was to assure the position of the cultivator, to make his tenant-right valuable, to inspire him with a feeling of self-reliance and strength, and to make him a substantial if not a prosperous member of the community in which he lived. The Bengal Rent Act of Lord Canning, the Oudh and Punjab Rent Acts of Lord Lawrence, the Settlement of the Central Provinces made in 1863, all had this one common object: to make agriculture prosperous, and to identify the interests of the Government with the interests of the landed and cultivating classes.

But recent land administration seems to aim at a

[1] *Land Problems in India*, Natesan & Co., Madras ; pages 103 and 104.

different object, to secure for the State a firmer grip on the produce of the soil, to whittle away both landlord right and tenant right, and to make an agricultural nation more dependent on the unfettered will of the Executive Officer.

The power of the Revenue Officer and the Settlement Officer has been made more absolute by legislation. The period of Settlements has been cut down from thirty years to twenty years in the Punjab and the Central Provinces. Cultivators in the same Provinces have been restrained from alienating their own holdings. The Government has taken the power of withdrawing the right of transfer in Bombay. The Government settles rents between landlords and tenants in the Central Provinces. The rule of limiting the State-demand to half the nett rent is, in practice, disregarded in Bombay and in Madras. The rule of limiting State enhancements to the specific and definite ground of a rise in prices has been withdrawn. And a compulsory water-rate, which was condemned by Argyll and Lawrence, has been imposed in Madras, and is consolidated with the land assessment.

CHAPTER VII

LAND RESOLUTIONS OF RIPON AND CURZON

THE uncertainty of Land Assessments, and the harassment caused by the revaluation of lands in Settlement Operations, were evils which successive Viceroys endeavoured and desired to remedy. Lord Mayo was of opinion that, when the quality of the soil and the quantity of the produce were once ascertained, there should be no further alterations in assessment except on the ground of fluctuations in prices. Lord Northbrook was also in favour of a self-regulating system of assessments, and was not in favour of repeating valuations at each fresh Settlement. The question was finally taken up by Lord Ripon. In his despatch of October 17, 1882, he desired to eliminate from future settlements the elements of uncertainty and inquisitorial inquiry. His object was to give the agriculturist an assurance of permanence and security, whilst not depriving the State of the power of enhancement of the revenue on "defined conditions." The reader will perceive that this was a compromise between the two opposite principles which had been held for twenty years by Indian administrators.

Men like Canning and Lawrence had held that the Land Revenue should be fixed for ever, leaving to the people of the country all future increase in the profits of agriculture. Other administrators had held that the State should claim an indefinite increase of revenue from the increasing profits from agriculture. Lord Ripon's masterly scheme met the views of both schools. He left the door open for a continuous increase of the Land Revenue with the increase of prices. At the same time, he offered to the cultivators what was virtually a Permanent Settlement of the Land Revenue as represented in produce.

To Settlement Officers Lord Ripon virtually said: You shall have a legitimate increase in the Land Revenue if there is an increase in the prices of crops. To the cultivators he said: You are secure henceforth from all uncertainty and all harassing inquiries; the Land Tax you pay shall not be an enhanced share of your produce.

Lord Ripon addressed the Governments of Madras and Bombay, offering this scheme for their acceptance. The Government of Madras accepted the proposal that in districts where the Land Revenue had been adequately assessed, *i.e.* in districts which had been duly surveyed and settled, the element of price alone would be considered in future settlements. The Government of Bombay demurred to the proposal.

After a considerable correspondence, the matter came up before the Secretary of State for India for final decision in 1885. He had disapproved of the scheme of a Permanent Settlement of the Land Revenue for India only two years before. It was hoped that the acceptance of Lord Ripon's scheme would at least give some security to the people against arbitrary and uncertain enhancements of the Land Revenue. It was hoped that after the bitter experience of a quarter of a century, the Crown Administration would at last give the harassed cultivators of India some pledge, some intelligible rule, to determine demands of the State. It was believed that the difficult problem would accept its final solution in the masterly compromise that Lord Ripon had made.

The action of the Secretary of State for India destroyed all these hopes. He looked to the interests of the Indian Land Revenue, not to the welfare of the Indian cultivators. He would frame no definite rule; he would give no pledge. "Some of the principal administrative difficulties which now exist in India," he recorded in reply to Sir Alfred Lyall, "arise in a measure from such pledges having been given on former occasions." He did not perceive that the greatest of all "administrative difficulties" in India was the wretched poverty of the cultivators; and that no progress, no improvement, no accumulation of agricultural wealth was possible without some definite rule or pledge given to the people.

Accepting the principle that it was desirable to simplify procedure and avoid unnecessary harassment to the people, the Secretary of State laid down the following rules:—

(1) The idea of a Permanent Settlement is abandoned.

(2) The State shall claim its share in the unearned increment of the value of land.

(3) Rise in prices is one of the indications and measures of this increment.

(4) Revision Settlements should be made less arbitrary, uncertain, and troublesome to the people in the future.

(5) Modifications should be made in the assessment rules, and enhancement of revenue should be made mainly on increase in the value of land.[1]

These elaborate instructions, excellent in their way, fixed no definite or intelligible rule by which the cultivators of India could measure their liabilities, or Settlement Officers could limit their enhancements. Settlements therefore went on as before; enhancements of the Land Revenue were made on grounds which the cultivators did not understand and could not contest. And how little the new rules of 1885 added to the prosperity and the

[1] Despatch dated January 8, 1885, referred to in Madras Revenue Board's Resolution, dated December 6, 1900. The original papers connected with Lord Ripon's proposals of 1882, and the Secretary of State's decision of 1885, have never been published. They contain a mass of valuable proposals, including those of Sir Alfred Lyall, regarding the Land Question in India, and their publication in the shape of a Blue Book is urgently needed as a help to reforms in Land Administration in India.

staying power of the cultivators was proved by the famines of 1897 and 1900.

Then the question was once more taken up by some men who had passed the best part of their lives in the task of Indian administration. They had retired from the Indian Service, but still felt a strong desire to help and befriend, as far as they could, their Indian fellow-subjects. They met in consultation in London, when India was still suffering from the famine of 1900, and they submitted a Memorial to the Secretary of State for India offering five suggestions to make the existing rules of land administration definite and clear, and more helpful to the Indian agriculturists.[1]

The five suggestions made in the Memorial are given below:—

Thirty Years' Rule.—"That no revision of the Land Tax of any Province, or part thereof, should be made within thirty years of the expiration of any former revision."

Half-Rental Rule.—"Where the Land Revenue is paid by landlords, the principle adopted in the Saharanpur Rule of 1855, whereby the Revenue demand is limited to one-half of the actual rent or assets of such landlords, should be universally applied."

Half-Produce Rule.—"Where the Land Revenue is paid directly by the cultivators, as in most parts of Madras and Bombay, the Government demand should be limited to 50 per cent. of the value of the nett produce, after a liberal deduction for cultivation expenses has been made, and should not ordinarily exceed one-fifth of the

1 The Memorial was dated December 20, 1900. The signatories to the Memorial were: The Right Hon. Sir Richard Garth, late Chief-Justice of Bengal; Sir John Jardine, late Judge of the High Court of Bombay; Sir William Wedderburn, late Chief Secretary of Bombay; Mr. R. K. Puckle, C.S.I., late Director of Revenue Settlement in Madras; Mr. J. H. Garstin, C.S.I., late Member of the Madras Council; Mr. J. B. Pennington, late Collector of Tanjore in Madras; Mr. H. J. Reynolds, late Revenue Secretary of Bengal; M. C. J. O'Donnell, late Commissioner in Bengal; Mr. A. Rogers, late Member of Council in Bombay; Mr. J. P. Goodridge, late Settlement Officer of the Central Provinces, and the present writer.

gross produce even in those parts of the country where, in theory, one-half of the nett is assumed to approximate to one-third of the gross produce."

Enhancement Rule.—"That when revision is made in any of those parts of India where the Land Revenue is paid by the cultivators direct to the Government, there should be no increase in the assessment except in cases where the land has increased in value, (1) in consequence of improvements in irrigation works carried out at the expense of the Government, or (2) on account of a rise in the value of produce based on the average prices of the thirty years next preceding such revision."

Local Cess Rule.—"Lastly we recommend that a limit be fixed in each province beyond which it may not be permissible to surcharge the land tax with local cesses. We are of opinion that the Bengal rate of 6¼ per cent. is a fair one, and that in no case should the rate exceed 10 per cent."

Our readers who have followed the story of Indian Land Administration in the preceding chapters will perceive at a glance that the memorialists suggested no new rules and no foreign principles. They accepted the different land systems which had grown up in the different provinces of India. They accepted the principles which had been laid down by preceding administrators. They suggested rules which were in keeping with the principles generally recognised in India. They asked for no large measures, like the extension of the Permanent Settlement, as had been done by Canning and Lawrence. And they did not demand the abolition of the local cesses imposed on land, as has been done in the present work. They desired only to limit such cesses, though the limits which they recommended have been somewhat vaguely worded in their last rule. What was meant by the rule is that when the cesses are assessed in *Rents* as in Bengal, they should not exceed 6¼ per cent. of the rental; and when they are imposed on the *Land Revenue* as in other

Provinces, they should not exceed 10 per cent. of that revenue.

The memorial was forwarded by the Indian Secretary of State to the Government of India, and the Land Question thus again came up for discussion. Lord Curzon approached the subject with a true appreciation of its national importance, and gave it his own personal consideration. It was unfortunate, however, that he did not institute any open inquiry, and he did not ask for the views and opinions of the people or of popular associations. In a matter so vitally touching the welfare of an agricultural nation, some expression of the popular opinion might have assisted the Viceroy in viewing the question from both sides; some deliberation among men familiar with land tenures in the different Provinces might have cleared many misapprehensions. Lord Curzon simply asked for the opinions of the local governments, and the local governments naturally defended the systems which they themselves worked. Their defence was summarised in a Government Resolution,[1] which was published as a final reply to the memorial.

The memorialists had not urged an extension of the Permanent Settlement. Many of them did not consider such extension desirable; and they had asked for reforms in which they all agreed, and which involved no change in the existing system. Nevertheless Lord Curzon thought it desirable to travel out of the proposals which the memorialists had made, and to condemn the proposal of a Permanent Settlement which the memorialists had not made.

"At an earlier period," says the Resolution, "the school of thought that is represented by the present critics of the Government of India, advocated the extension of the Permanent Settlement throughout India." "They [the Government of India] cannot conscientiously

[1] Resolution of the Governor-General in Council, dated January 16, 1902.

endorse the proposition that in the interests of the cultivator that system of agrarian tenure should be held up as a public model which is not supported by the experience of any civilised country."[1]

"The school of thought" referred to represents the views of such men as Lord Cornwallis and Sir Thomas Munro, Lord Wellesley and Lord Hastings, Lord Canning and Lord Lawrence, Lord Halifax and Lord Iddesleigh; and the fame of these eminent administrators, who have built up the Indian Empire by their sympathetic regard for the people no less than by their vigour and wisdom, will survive the sneers of modern Imperialism. And when Lord Curzon adds that a Permanent Settlement of the Land Revenue "is not supported by the experience of any civilised country," he forgets the history of his own country where the great Pitt made the Land Tax perpetual and redeemable in 1798, five years after Cornwallis had fixed the Land Revenue in Bengal.

But the Permanent Settlement of Bengal has a stronger justification than the Perpetual Settlement of England. In England the Settlement benefits the landed classes only, for they are the sole proprietors; in Bengal it benefits the nation—the cultivators more than the landed classes—for the cultivators are primarily the owners of the soil. In England the Settlement is an invidious limit to a tax on one out of many sources of the nation's income; in Bengal it is a protection to agriculture, which is virtually the only source of national income. In England it has had the effect of making the rich richer, and the poor poorer; in Bengal it has had the effect of helping the poor—the millions of cultivators—more than the rich. In England it has added to the wealth of a limited class; in Bengal it has made the nation more prosperous, and less liable to the effects of those famines which have cost millions of lives in other Provinces of India.

[1] Resolution, paragraphs 5 and 6.

But, as stated before, the question of extending the Permanent Settlement was never raised in the Memorial, and it is necessary to confine ourselves in the present chapter to Lord Curzon's decision on the five suggestions which were made in the Memorial. We shall take them in the order in which they have been already quoted.

Thirty Years' Rule.—Settlements are made for thirty years in Northern India, Madras, and Bombay; but the period of Settlements has been cut down to twenty years in the Punjab and the Central Provinces, as we have seen in previous chapters. The memorialists urged that the liberal and considerate rule of Settlements for thirty years should be maintained in all Provinces. Lord Curzon justifies the present difference in practice, but leaves us in hope that it will disappear in time. He says:—

"The reasons for this differentiation are familiar and obvious. Where the land is fully cultivated, rents fair, and agricultural production not liable to violent oscillations, it is sufficient if the demands of Government are readjusted once in thirty years, *i.e.* once in the lifetime of each generation. Where the opposite conditions prevail, where there are much waste land, low rents, and a fluctuating cultivation; or again where there is a rapid development of resources, owing to the construction of roads, railways, or canals, to an increase of population or to a rise in prices, the postponement of re-settlement for so long a period is both injurious to the people, who are unequal to the strain of a sharp enhancement, and unjust to the general tax-payer who is temporarily deprived of the additional revenue to which he has a legitimate claim. Whether these considerations, justifying a shorter term of settlement than thirty years, apply with sufficient force to the Punjab and the Central Provinces at the present time, and if they do apply at the present time, whether the force of their application will diminish with the passage of time, are weighty questions to which careful attention will be given by the Government of India upon a suitable occasion."[1]

The reasons alleged for the differentiation are historically wrong. The Central Provinces were less advanced in cultivation, had lower rents, and were more in need of development by railways and roads in 1863–67, when a settlement for thirty years was made, than in 1895, when a settlement for twenty years was made. Northern India and Bombay were less developed and less advanced in cultivation in 1833 and 1837, when they were settled for thirty years, than the Punjab is at the present time. The idea in those days was to permit the people to obtain the benefits of long settlements; to let them enjoy the fruits of all progress during the generation of a lifetime; and to inspire them with a motive for making improvements by leaving them alone for thirty years. A narrower desire to demand more frequent enhancements dictated the policy of 1895; and the policy stands condemned by its result. The people of the Punjab and the Central Provinces desire to see an early fulfilment of the hope held out in the last sentence of the above extract, a return to the more generous policy of Lord William Bentinck, Lord Canning, and Lord Lawrence.

Half-Rental Rule.—The declaration of the Government on this rule is contained in the following extract:—

"While the standard of 50 per cent. has nowhere been laid down as a fixed and immutable prescription, there has been, and there is, a growing tendency through temporarily settled Zemindari Districts to approximate to it, and in special circumstances a very much lower share is taken. It does not appear to the Government of India to be necessary to issue fresh regulations upon a matter in which their general policy is so clear, and where, save in exceptional cases to be justified by local conditions, uniformity of practice is now so common."[2]

[1] Resolution, paragraph 18. [2] Resolution, paragraph 13.

The Saharanpur Rule of 1855, and Sir Charles Wood's despatch of 1864 laid down 50 per cent. of the rental or the economic rent as the limit of the Land Revenue assessments, and these limits *were* exceeded in the Central Provinces and elsewhere, as we have seen in preceding chapters. The above extract is probably meant as an assurance that there is a growing tendency now to return to these limits. The people of India hope that the Half-rental Rule will not again be set aside in any Province, in any future settlements.

Half-Produce Rule.—The Government resolution has misstated the object of the memorialists in respect of this rule. The memorialists suggested a double limit: (1) that the Land Revenue should not exceed half the nett produce; (2) that it should not exceed one-fifth the gross produce in certain parts of India where it does exceed that proportion. The Government resolution replies:—

"The gross produce standard recommended by the memorialists would, if systematically applied, lead to an increase of assessments all round."[1]

The memorialists laid down no such standard for systematic application. They only laid down a *maximum limit.* The Gujrat, what is generally taken as half the nett produce, is in many villages and fields far in excess of one-fifth the gross produce. In Madras it was assumed that one-third of the gross produce would be half the nett produce, and one-third of the gross produce was therefore sometimes demanded as Land Revenue.[2] It is to correct such misleading calculations,

[1] Resolution, paragraph 17.

[2] In the Standing Information for the Madras Presidency, published in 1879, there is a rule fixing the maximum limit of the Land Revenue at *one-third the gross produce* where the soil has not been improved by the Government irrigation works. This being pointed out, the Madras Government explained in their Resolution dated March 13, 1901, that the rule was inserted through an error, and "this error appears to have been due to the misapprehension of the compiler." It is curious that this error was never corrected for over twenty years, till the memorial was submitted. And it is certain that assessments of the Land Revenue were often made at one-third the gross produce.

and to prevent over-assessment, that the memorialists, while accepting the Half-nett Produce Rule, proposed an additional limit that the Half-nett Produce should in no case exceed one-fifth the gross produce. And many over-assessed fields and villages in Bombay and in Madras would have obtained relief if the Government had accepted this second limit in addition to the Half-nett Produce Rule prescribed in 1864.

Enhancement Rule.—The object of the memorialists was the same that Lord Ripon had in view, viz. to specify and define the grounds on which the State was entitled to enhance its Land Revenue demand. They accepted Lord Ripon's rule of increase in prices as a ground of enhancement; and they added to it the improvement made by Government irrigation works as another reasonable ground of enhancement. The memorialists desired that every peasant proprietor in India should know and feel that the State did not enhance the Land Revenue except on specific and equitable grounds; and should have the same security that is now offered to the tenants of private landlords in Bengal. The Government of Lord Curzon has declined to grant him this security on the following grounds:—

"To deny the right of the State to a share in any increase of values except those which could be inferred from the general table of price statistics—in itself a most fallacious and partial test—would be to surrender to a number of individuals an increment which they had not themselves earned, but which had resulted partly from the outlay of Government money on great public works, such as canals and railways, partly from the general enhancement of values produced by expanding resources and a higher standard of civilisation."[1]

The whole of this argument is a misstatement of the point at issue. The memorialists asked for no surrender of the just rights of the State. They expressly reserved

[1] Resolution, paragraph 22.

to the State the right of enhancing the Land Revenue on the very grounds mentioned in the Government Resolution. If canals increased the produce, the State was entitled to an increase of revenue. If railways raised the prices, the State could raise its demand. If "expanding resources" and "a higher standard of civilisation" caused a general enhancement of values, the State could enhance the Land Assessment accordingly. But if none of these grounds existed, the State should not arbitrarily increase its demand at each recurring Settlement. This was the argument of the memorialists. The argument has not been met or answered.

To the cultivator of India, all the benefit he derives from "expanding resources" and "a higher standard of civilisation" is represented by the increase of produce or the increase of prices. If canals have increased his produce, if railways and roads have increased prices—he is justly liable to an increase in the State-demand. If there has been no increase in produce or in prices, if his economic condition remains precisely the same as before, why should the Settlement Officer add to his burdens because his richer neighbour can travel by rail, or his money-lender has a civil court nearer at hand? To enhance the Land Tax when the land does not produce more, and the produce does not fetch higher prices, is to tax the cultivator for a benefit he has not derived, and to make him poorer with advancing civilisation.

Local Cesses Rule.—From what has been stated in the preceding chapters, the reader will perceive that special taxes imposed on land, in addition to the Land Tax, are harsh and unfair, and violate the Half-Rental Rule and the Half-Produce Rule, laid down in 1855 and 1864. The memorialists, however, did not suggest their withdrawal, but that they should be placed within fixed limits. The proposed limits were 6¼ per cent. on the Rental or 10 per cent. on the Land Revenue. The present rates in

Northern India, in the Punjab,[1] in the Central Provinces, and elsewhere, greatly exceed these limits. The people of India have some hopes of relief from the following remarks recorded in the Government Resolution:—

"There are grounds for suspecting that the distribution is often unfair, and that the landlords shift on to the tenants that share of the burden which is imposed by the law upon themselves. In the present backward condition of so many of the people, it is not possible effectively to redress this injustice. And the question presents itself, whether it is not better, as opportunities occur, to mitigate imposts which are made to press upon the cultivating classes more severely than the law intended. The Government of India would be glad to see their way to offer such relief."[2]

Two years have nearly expired since this was recorded. Two budgets with large surpluses were framed in March 1901 and March 1902; but not one of the special cesses on land, imposed since the Decentralisation Scheme of 1871, has yet been withdrawn.

It is a lamentable truth that the peasant proprietors of Madras and Bombay, paying the Land Tax direct to the State, have, at the present day, less security than the tenants of private landlords in Bengal. The Bengal tenant pays 11 per cent. of his produce to his landlord; the Gujrat Ryot pays 20 per cent. to the State. The Bengal tenant knows the specific grounds on which his landlord can claim enhancement; the Madras and Bombay Ryot does not know the grounds on which the State will claim enhancement at the next Settlement. The Bengal tenant reckons beforehand the limits of his landlord's claims; the Bombay and Madras Ryot cannot guess what

[1] The Local Cesses on Land in the Punjab, according to Lord Curzon's Resolution, "are equivalent to 5.2 per cent. on the Rental Value." But, according to a more recent Blue Book, "the cesses in the Punjab are restricted to 12½ per cent. of the annual value." *Moral and Material Progress and Condition of India*, 1901–2.

[2] Resolution; paragraph 25.

the Settlement Officer's claims will be. The Bengal tenant can appeal to Courts against excessive demands; the Bombay and Madras Ryot can appeal to no Land Courts and no independent tribunal against unduly severe assessments. Certainty and definiteness in the rental make the Bengal tenant value his tenant-right, and enable him to free himself from the thraldom of the money-lender; uncertainty and indefiniteness in the State demand make the Madras and Bombay Ryot till his land without hope, without heart, without motive to save, and year by year he is sinking deeper in indebtedness. The Marquis of Ripon proposed to bestow on the peasant proprietor something of the security which the Bengal tenant enjoys, but the proposal was negatived by the Secretary of State in 1885. Friends of the voiceless cultivators of India again appealed for such security in the closing days of the century; the appeal was rejected by Lord Curzon in January 1902.

CHAPTER VIII

TRADE AND MANUFACTURE

All the old industries, for which India had been noted from ancient times, had declined under the jealous commercial policy of the East India Company; and when Queen Victoria ascended the throne in 1837 agriculture was left the only national industry of the people. Little was done to foster new industries after the Crown assumed the administration of India in 1858; and the last decades of the century still found the Indian manufacturer and artisan in a state of poverty and decline. A few experiments were made from time to time, but not on an adequate scale, and not in a manner commensurate with the vast interests at stake.

Cotton.—Spinning and weaving were the national industries of India down to the commencement of the nineteenth century. The spinning-wheel and the hand-loom were universally in use; and it is scarcely an exaggeration to state that nearly half the adult female population of India eked out the incomes of their husbands and their fathers by the profits of their own labour. It was an industry peculiarly suited to Indian village life. There were no great mills and factories; but each woman brought her cotton from the village market, and sold her yarn to the village weaver, who supplied merchants and traders with cloth. Vast quantities of piece goods, thus manufactured, were exported by the Arabs, the Dutch, and the Portuguese; and European nations competed with each other for this lucrative trade with India. But when the East India Company acquired territories in India, they reversed this policy. Not content with the carrying trade between India and Europe, British manufacturers sought to repress Indian industries in order to give an impetus to British manufactures. Their great idea was to reduce India to a country of raw-produce, and to make her subservient to the manufacturing industries of Great Britain. How this policy was pursued, and how it ultimately succeeded, has been narrated in another work.[1]

Later on, when power-looms had entirely supplanted hand-looms in Europe, Indian capitalists began to start cotton mills in their own country. This, again, aroused the jealousy of Lancashire manufacturers; and the fiscal policy pursued by the Indian Government in 1874 to 1879 has been told in a previous chapter. And the sad story will be continued to the close of the century in the succeeding chapter.

But hand-looms still survive in India to some extent, in spite of power-looms. The reasons are not far to seek. India is pre-eminently a country of small industries and small cultivation. Land in England belongs to great landlords; the agriculturists are mere farmers and labourers. But land in India belongs primarily to small cultivators who have their hereditary rights in their holdings; the landlord, where he exists, cannot eject them so long as they pay their rents. In the same manner, the various industries of the country were carried on by humble artisans in their own villages and huts; the idea of large factories, owned by capitalists and worked by paid operatives, was foreign to the Indian mind. And despite the great results which are achieved by capital, it is nevertheless true that the individual man is at his best,—in dignity and intelligence, in foresight and independence,—when he works in his own fields or at his own loom, rather than when he is a paid labourer under a big landlord or a wage-earner in a huge factory. And every true Indian hopes that

[1] *Economic History of British India*, 1757 *to* 1837.

the small cultivation of India will not be replaced by landlordism, and that something of the home industries will survive the assaults of capitalism.

Endeavours have been made to help the handloom weavers who still carry on their hereditary profession. Their methods are susceptible of improvement, and their output could be largely increased by the use of improved looms. Experiments are being made in different places, and specially in Madras. It is too early yet to say what the result will be; but it is confidently believed that, with necessary improvements, hand-looms will be found to answer, at least for certain descriptions of goods. Such a result would help millions of poor weavers, Hindu and Mahomedan, who have sunk to the lowest depths of poverty, and are the earliest victims of famines. And a civilised Government has no more sacred duty than to help these submerged classes, and revive one of the most ancient industries of India.

Silk.—Silk manufactures have declined from the days of the East India Company, and their export is insignificant. *Tussur* silk is grown in most parts of India, and quantities of fabrics are produced both for home use and for export. In Assam, silk still continues to be the national dress of women, and the industry is entirely a home one, each family weaving *Sarees* for its own use. Finer silks, produced by the mulberry-feeding worms, are obtained in Bengal districts, and some improvement has been effected by the adoption of scientific methods of testing the "seed" and rearing the worms. In the Punjab, however, the endeavour to reintroduce the cultivation of silkworms has ended in failure. In Kashmir, the industry is indigenous, and the State is endeavouring to develop it by the importation of sound "seed" from Europe. "The silk-weavers of India possess the very highest skill in their craft, and it is probable that under competent and energetic direction, with the assistance of capital, the industry could be revived and extended."[1]

Wool.—The manufacture of coarse blankets, used by the poor, is carried on in many parts of India. The Shawl industry of Kashmir is practically extinct, so far as elaborate and artistic products are concerned; and such shawls are produced in only very small quantities, generally to order. The Punjab is still, however, the seat of a considerable woollen manufacture, and specially of woollen carpets. And the carpet industry of Madras is also important.

Woollen mills, conducted mainly by European capital and under European management, nearly doubled their production within the last decade of the century; and there were 594 looms and 22,986 spindles in 1901. The output of the mills is chiefly used for the army and the police.

Jute.—Bengal has virtually a monopoly of the cultivation of jute, the average yield of the crop being about twenty million cwt. One half of this produce is exported to Europe, while the other half is used either for the making of home-spun cloths or bags, or in the jute mills. There were 35 mills, 8218 looms, and 171,148 spindles in 1901, and the number of looms and spindles nearly doubled in the succeeding year.

Hands Employed.—But altogether mill industry in India is still in its infant stage, and the number of people who find employment in these industries is insignificant. In the year 1901 the cotton mills of India employed 173,708 hands; the jute mills employed 64,700 hands; and apart from indigenous home industries there was no other manufacturing industry which employed as many as 20,000 hands.

In the preparation of agricultural staples for the market, indigo factories employed 173,000 workers; jute presses, 20,000; cotton ginning, cleaning, and pressing

[1] *Moral and Material Progress and Condition of India*, 1901–2, p. 227.

mills about 52,000; timber mills, 8000; coffee works, 5000; and oil mills, 4000.

Iron and brass foundries employed 18,000 persons; tile factories, 10,000; printing presses, 13,000; lac factories, 5000; silk filatures and silk mills, 14,000; and paper mills about 5000. The numbers employed in woollen mills increased only 16 per cent. in the ten years ending in 1901.

Paper.—There were nine mills in 1901, and the amount of paper produced was 47 million pounds. The Government of India obtains from these mills most of its foolscap, blotting-paper, and note-paper, but imports about £15,000 worth of paper from Europe.

Brass and Copper.—The household vessels of the Hindus are generally made of brass, though Mahomedans often use copper. The brass industry is about the only indigenous industry which is still safe from foreign competition, though large quantities of enamelled iron ware, imported from Europe, are coming into use in Hindu households. It is satisfactory to learn from an official historian of Indian industries that "the continuance of the internal demand for brass and copper ware is assured; and the skill of the artificers is so great that, with proper direction and energetic development, a large expansion of exports to Europe is possible."[1]

Wood Carving.—Apart from the work of the carpenter who exists in every Indian village and town, there is a large trade with Europe in small articles as toys, boxes, and the like, carved with artistic skill. Inlaying is also a notable art in India.

Tea.—The area under tea, of which nine-tenths lies in Assam and Northern Bengal, expanded 45 per cent. within the ten years ending in 1901. There was indeed over-production, and it has latterly become necessary to restrict the area under cultivation, and to reduce the quantity of leaf taken from the plant. The total yield

[1] *Moral and Material Progress and Condition of India*, 1901–2, p. 227.

of the crop in 1900 was over 197½ million lbs., while that in 1901 was 191¼ million lbs. The export by sea from British India in the year 1901–2 is shown in the following figures :—

Country to which Tea is Exported.	Quantity in million lbs.
United Kingdom . . .	159
Australia	8½
Persia	2½
Asiatic Turkey	2½
Russia	1½
China	1½
United States.	1
Canada	1
Other countries	2
Total	179½ million lbs.

It will thus be seen that the world, outside the British Empire, does not favour Indian tea.

The "slave law" of India, by which labourers, imported to Assam, are bound by penal clauses to serve out their term of contract, continues to mark the tea industry of that Province with an indelible stain. Much oppression and many acts of cruelty are reported from time to time; but the Government of India does not care to brave the wrath of capitalists by withdrawing these penal clauses, and leaving the labour market free as in other industries. The condition of the labourers in the gardens is often wretched; and an endeavour made by Sir Henry Cotton, late Chief Commissioner of Assam, to raise the wages by one rupee a month, evoked the opposition of tea-planters, and did not receive adequate support from Lord Curzon. A compromise was effected; the proposed increase was reduced to half a rupee; and it was to come into operation after two years. The planters, on the other hand, suggested the imposition of a cess on the exported tea, the proceeds of which were to be used to promote the sale. The Government of India descended from its dignity by accepting this proposal, and thus constituting itself agents of tea-planters for the sale of tea.

The number of persons employed in tea industry in 1901 was 606,835 permanently, and 90,946 temporarily.

Indigo.—The competition of artificial indigo threatens this industry with extinction. This will necessarily be an economic loss to India; but there has been so much of oppression and coercion by indigo planters in connection with the growth and production of indigo, that the people of India view its extinction with perfect indifference, and even with satisfaction. The value of the indigo exported in 1895–6 was £3,569,700; in 1891–2 it fell to £1,234,800.

The number of indigo factories in 1901 was given as 898, besides some 3000 vats in Madras. The number of persons employed was given as 173,000, but this is not a complete record.

Sugar.—The large imports of bounty-fed beet sugar from Germany and Austria induced the Indian Government to impose a countervailing duty in 1899,—mainly in the interests of cane sugar from Mauritius and other British possessions. This checked the bounty-fed sugar for a time, but only for a time, as the following figures will show:—

Imports.	1897–98.	1898–99.	1899–1900.	1900–1.	1901–2.
Beet sugar from Germany and Austria	2,206,064	1,526,291	872,515	1,792,590	2,936,196
Cane sugar from Mauritius, &c. .	2,029,330	2,238,619	2,063,477	3,049,046	2,491,907

It will appear from these figures that in the last year, 1901–2, imported beet sugar once more exceeded the cane sugar from Mauritius and other places. This was owing to developments in the Continental sugar-trade, and the rise of the "cartel" system. It was decided, therefore, to enact a further law to countervail the "cartel" bounty. Its effects have still to be seen.

Opium and Salt.—The Government continued to retain its monopoly over these articles. The revenue derived from opium declined within the last ten years of the century, while the salt revenue showed rather an increase.

Nett Revenue in Rupees.[1]		
Year.	Opium.	Salt.
1890–1	56,983,850	80,943,550
1891–2	61,505,670	81,771,480
1892–3	63,906,840	81,973,970
1893–4	47,509,640	87,544,710
1894–5	57,076,520	81,673,340
1895–6	50,549,810	83,408,010
1896–7	39,225,460	78,983,530
1897–8	27,906,550	81,204,780
1898–9	33,520,400	86,341,690
1899–1900	40,122,420	82,780,605

It has been stated in a previous chapter that the salt revenue is derived firstly from a duty imposed on the manufacture of salt in British India, and secondly, from a duty imposed on salt imported from Europe or from the Native States of India. The task of levying a duty on salt imported by sea was easy enough. But in order to realise the duty on salt imported from the Native States, it was necessary to maintain an Inland Customs Line. In 1870 this Indian Customs Line extended itself across the whole of British India, from a point in the north-west of the Punjab to the northern frontiers of Madras. It was a huge material barrier, 2500 miles long, consisting of thorny trees and bushes, stone walls

[1] The nett revenues are found by deducting all expenditure connected with the revenues from the gross revenues. Fifteen rupees may be roughly taken as £1.

and ditches; and it was guarded by an army of 12,000 officers.

The first steps towards abolishing this system were taken by the Government of Lord Mayo. Mr. A. O. Hume negotiated an amicable arrangement with the Native States of Jaipur and Jodhpur, under which the sole right of manufacturing salt at the Sambar Salt Lake was made over to the Indian Government. The Government of Lord Northbrook then entered into an arrangement with Jodhpur, by which all important salt sources of that State were transferred to British management. The Government of Lord Lytton took further measures to abolish the Inland Customs Line, firstly, by making the duties approximately equal in the different parts of India, and secondly, by agreements with Native States in Rajputana and Central India, under which the British Government obtained leases and control of all the important sources of salt manufacture. The work was finally completed by the Government of Lord Ripon, which equalised the salt duty throughout India at the reduced rate of 2 rupees the maund, *i.e.* 2s. 8d. on 82 lbs. Unfortunately the salt duty was again raised to 2½ rupees the maund in 1888, and it remained at that high figure for fifteen years. In March 1903 it was reduced once more to 2 rupees.

Coal.—Coal is found over a very extensive area in India, and mines are worked in different parts of the country, mostly with European capital. The rapid increase in the industry, and in the annual output in recent years, is shown by the figures on the next page.

"These figures," writes the official chronicler whom we have quoted before, "look very small if compared with the 219 millions of tons produced in the United Kingdom in 1901; but the amount is sufficient to meet the present Indian demand for coal."[1] The Indian railways use Indian coal almost exclusively; and less than 1 per

[1] *Moral and Material Progress, &c.*, 1901-2, p. 235.

Province.	Output in Tons.	
	1892.	1901.
Bengal	1,920,050	5,703,876
Assam	164,050	253,162
Burma	3,670	12,466
Rajputana	nil	12,094
Central India	88,623	164,415
Punjab	66,352	67,730
Beluchistan	13,284	22,772
Central Provinces	132,005	191,516
Nizam's Territory	149,601	421,218
Madras	61	nil.
Total	2,537,696	6,849,249

cent. of the coal they used in 1902 was drawn from abroad. Iron and steel industries are largely helped by the Indian coal, and mills all over the country depend upon it. Coal is also largely used in towns as fuel for domestic purposes. The coal mines and quarries under the Mines Act, *i.e.* those which are not less than 20 feet in depth, gave employment to 85,361 persons in 1901.

Gold.—The production of gold in India is practically confined to Mysore, which produced 529,782 ounces in 1901; and this represents 99 per cent. of the Indian yield for the year. The labour employed amounts to 21,000 hands. A very small amount of gold is obtained by sand-washing in Northern India and Burma. The Wynaad fields of Madras have proved a failure; and the amount produced in the Nizam's territory is small.

Iron.—The principal sources of ironstone are the Salem ores in Madras, the Chanda ores in the Central Provinces, and the Barakar ores in Bengal. Inquiries made by private and public agency have established both the quantity and quality of the Salem ore; but no large industry has yet commenced. The Barakar Works were started in 1865. After the failure of two companies, the Government ran the business at a loss, and then handed it over to the present company. Things are looking up;

the production of pig iron has increased, and a steel plant has been set up. Negotiations are in progress for the development of the Chanda ore. The production of iron in India was 63,000 tons in 1901, of which 57,000 were produced in Bengal.

Petroleum.—Burma supplies 98 per cent. of the mineral oil produced in India, and the remainder is almost all obtained from Assam. The total production was only 5000 gallons in 1892, while in 1901 it had risen to 633,000 gallons. There is, however, a large demand for foreign oil in India; and the Russian product has displaced the dearer American product in the Indian market. Ninety-nine millions of gallons, valued at 2½ millions sterling, were imported in 1901–2, showing that the Burma produce does not supply even a hundredth part of the total Indian demand.

Rubies.—The far-famed ruby mines of Burma have as yet yielded little profit. In 1901 the Ruby Mines Company produced gems, rubies, sapphires, and spinels of the total value of £104,500. Jade to the value of £29,000 was exported in 1901–2.

Manganese, Mica, and Tin.—Manganese to the value of £100,000 and mica to the value of £70,000 were exported in 1901–2. Tin is found in Tavoy and Mergui in Lower Burma, and also in the Shan States in Upper Burma.

A vast deal of attention is naturally directed to the mill industries of India, to tea, indigo, and coffee, and to mining industries, as European capital is largely employed in India in these forms. From the figures given above, it will, however, be seen that the number of labourers employed in these industries bears no appreciable proportion to the population of India. The problem of improving their condition finds no solution in the encouragement given to British companies in India, or in a system of emigration. Where is the country on earth which could receive, in the next ten years or twenty years, even a tenth of the Indian population of three hundred millions? The real solution of the Indian economic problem lies in relieving agriculture from excessive and uncertain taxation; in fostering those indigenous industries in which millions of Indian artisans find employment in their villages; and in helping those nascent manufactures which the people are starting with their own capital in towns. The people of India welcome the employment of British capital for the development of the mineral resources and the new industries of India. But British statesmen view things through a false perspective when the interests of British capitalists in India loom larger in their eyes than the interests of agriculture, and of those humbler industries on which the Indian nation, as a nation, depends for its existence.

We now turn to the subject of India's external trade; and the following table, compiled from *statistical Abstracts relating to British India*, shows the total imports and exports of India during the last twenty-four years of the century.

The difference between the total imports and the total exports is the distressing anomaly of the Indian commerce. The difference mounted up to about thirty millions of tens of Rupees, equivalent to twenty millions sterling, between 1891–2 and 1896–7. It represents the annual Economic Drain from India, the amount she paid from her food supply and for which she received no commercial equivalent. Famines during the closing years of the century, and the price which England paid for using the Indian army in South Africa, reduced this Economic Drain to some extent; but even during the last four years of the century the average annual Economic Drain from India was about twenty million tens of Rupees, equivalent to thirteen millions sterling.

Trade of India with all Countries in Tens of Rupees.[1]

Year ending in	Import of Merchandise.	Import of Treasure.	Total Imports.	Total Exports.
	Tens of Rupees.	Tens of Rupees.	Tens of Rupees.	Tens of Rupees.
1878	41,464,185	17,355,459	58,819,644	67,433,324
1879	37,800,594	7,056,749	44,857,343	64,919,741
1880	41,166,003	11,655,395	52,821,398	69,247,511
1881	53,116,770	8,988,214	62,104,984	76,021,043
1882	49,113,374	11,322,781	60,436,155	83,068,198
1883	52,095,711	13,453,157	65,548,868	84,527,182
1884	55,279,348	12,877,963	68,157,311	89,186,397
1885	55,703,072	13,888,197	69,591,269	85,225,922
1886	55,655,909	15,477,801	71,133,710	84,989,502
1887	61,777,351	11,053,319	72,830,670	90,190,633
1888	65,004,612	13,825,856	78,830,468	92,148,279
1889	69,440,467	13,844,960	83,285,427	98,833,879
1890	69,197,489	17,459,501	86,656,990	105,366,720
1891	71,975,370	21,934,486	93,909,856	102,350,526
1892	69,432,383	14,722,662	84,155,045	111,460,278
1893	66,265,277	17,009,810	83,275,087	113,554,399
1894	77,021,432	18,461,256	95,482,688	110,603,561
1895	73,528,993	9,581,207	83,110,200	117,139,850
1896	72,936,753	13,367,986	86,304,739	118,594,549
1897	76,117,373	13,084,563	89,201,936	118,921,592
1898	73,647,035	20,530,617	94,177,652	104,781,428
1899	72,101,528	17,895,613	89,997,141	120,211,146
1900	75,304,480	20,973,686	96,278,166	117,039,710
1901	80,894,589	24,576,762	105,471,352	121,945,960

The character of India's trade with the world will appear more clearly by an examination of her principal imports and exports. The table on the next page shows the principal imports.

In examining this table it is necessary to remember the varying value of ten rupees between 1885 and 1897. Ten rupees represented about sixteen shillings before 1885, and it only represented less than twelve shillings in 1895 and 1896. The large increase in the import of cotton manufactures between 1885 and 1897, as shown in tens of rupees, does not therefore represent a proportionate

[1] Ten rupees represented about 16 shillings between 1878 and 1885,
" " about 14 shillings between 1885 and 1890,
" " about 12 shillings between 1890 and 1897,
" " and $13\frac{1}{3}$ shillings since 1898.

Imports into India from all Countries, in Tens of Rupees.

Year ending in	Cotton Twist and Yarn.	Cotton Manufactures.	Hardware, Cutlery, and Plated Ware.	Machinery and Millwork.	Refined Sugar.	Silk Manufactures.	Wool Manufactures.
	Tens of Rupees.	Tens of Rupees.	Tens of Rupees.	Tens of Rupees.	Tens of Rupees.	Tens of Rupees.	Tens of Rupees.
1878	2,850,403	17,322,313	448,228	850,997	798,036	804,883	782,781
1879	2,779,772	14,126,784	425,453	863,455	1,480,881	924,044	878,042
1880	2,745,306	16,915,511	431,928	616,833	1,068,788	837,890	927,876
1881	3,699,177	22,910,717	552,556	769,844	1,611,157	1,397,197	1,299,130
1882	3,222,065	20,772,099	626,613	1,221,045	1,243,756	1,267,620	1,121,232
1883	3,378,190	21,431,872	791,791	1,342,398	1,086,961	1,038,180	984,873
1884	3,465,943	21,642,388	813,887	1,788,868	1,148,370	1,263,894	1,217,053
1885	3,360,420	21,197,414	844,552	1,484,124	2,140,838	1,273,354	1,234,340
1886	3,172,083	21,110,545	776,542	991,553	1,458,097	1,109,043	1,391,861
1887	3,318,377	25,846,508	865,397	1,371,459	2,080,540	1,383,735	1,528,865
1888	3,581,906	23,924,467	1,093,939	1,800,218	2,113,617	1,743,818	1,715,755
1889	3,746,797	27,764,508	1,102,205	2,316,871	1,790,939	1,682,166	1,561,950
1890	3,482,529	26,391,399	1,096,191	2,435,385	2,200,049	1,778,114	1,455,235
1891	3,768,362	27,241,987	1,197,614	2,063,863	3,399,886	1,386,362	1,818,213
1892	3,514,620	25,174,852	1,238,994	2,111,597	2,561,996	1,750,695	1,762,031
1893	2,683,850	22,942,015	1,217,754	2,359,103	2,625,683	1,801,571	1,523,243
1894	3,108,941	29,268,528	1,380,473	2,518,038	2,824,190	1,827,874	1,892,042
1895	2,851,254	29,822,374	1,332,556	2,442,433	2,875,297	1,277,420	1,541,639
1896	2,971,090	22,784,782	1,483,475	3,237,401	3,106,813	1,704,320	1,445,517
1897	3,325,871	26,424,304	1,557,742	3,510,190	3,151,829	1,366,669	1,692,535
1898	3,493,038	22,901,970	1,477,811	2,861,108	4,784,479	1,149,260	1,148,427
1899	2,551,634	24,678,086	1,430,123	3,055,931	4,016,999	1,361,794	1,523,731
1900	2,450,011	27,002,113	1,590,292	2,541,903	3,376,629	1,129,831	1,758,001
1901	2,489,215	27,346.128	1,841,473	2,257,558	5,655,211	1,665,810	2,112,576

real increase. On the other hand the value of ten rupees has been fixed at 13s. 4d. since 1898; and the increase in cotton imports, and the decrease in machinery and mill works, since that year, are real. They show the baneful effects of the excise imposed on the mill manufactures of India, which will be fully described in the next chapter.

When every civilised Government on earth is endeavouring to help home manufactures, the Indian Government has cruelly repressed the infant mill industry of India under the mandate of Lancashire, even in respect of coarse cotton fabrics with which Lancashire does not compete. The results broadly stated are—a decline in cotton manufactures, a decrease in the demand for machinery and mill-work, and an increase in the import of cotton manufactures from 23 millions to over 27 millions of tens of rupees within three years.

Silk manufacture continues to decline in India in spite of the experiments which have been referred to before; and the import of manufactured silk increased from a million to 1½ million tens of rupees between 1898 and 1901. The import of woollen manufactures nearly doubled within that period.

Reference has been made to the legislation undertaken to repress the import of bounty-fed sugar into India. Its success is seen in the decline of sugar imports in 1898–99 and 1899–1900. But it has failed in the long run, and the import of 1900–1901 exceeded the import of any previous year in the history of India.

The import of hardware, cutlery, and plated-ware shows a steady increase. But India imports raw metals in larger quantities. In 1900–1901 she imported iron and steel to the value of over three millions sterling, and brass to the value of over six hundred thousands sterling.[1] The only other large item of import, exceeding two millions sterling in value in 1900–1901 is mineral oil,

[1] Iron and steel, £3,048,421; brass, £611,422.

mostly from Russia. The import of liquors exceeds a million.[1]

We now turn to India's exports, and the following table shows the principal articles.

In examining the figures of this table it is necessary to bear in mind once more the varying value of the rupee. The apparent increase in the export of cotton and cotton goods, in grains, seeds, and other articles in the early 'nineties, is largely owing to the fall in the value of the rupee. We are on more safe ground from 1898 when the value of 10 rupees was raised to 13s. 4d. and ultimately fixed at that sum; and the increase in exports shown in the last four years of the table is real.

Cotton manufactures show only a slight increase. The unjust excise tax imposed on the rising mill industry of India retarded the natural progress of the cotton manufactures. Raw jute shows a steady increase from seven to nearly eleven millions of tens of rupees during the last three years of the century. The export of jute manufactures also increased from 5¾ millions to 7½ millions of tens of rupees.

The export of indigo has steadily decreased owing to the invention of artificial indigo in Europe; while the export of tea has steadily increased to nearly 10 million tens of rupees, or 6½ millions sterling.

Silk and wool are minor items, and have not been shown in the following table. The export of raw silk was only £354,102, and of manufactured silk only £119,203, in the year ending with March 1901. Raw wool to the value of £819,748, and wool manufactures to the value of £227,681, were exported in 1900–1901.

The export of rice, wheat, and other grains showed the most remarkable variations during the last four years of the century. The export was 14 million tens of rupees, or 10 millions sterling, in 1897–98, and it went up to 27 million tens of rupees, or 18 millions sterling,

[1] Mineral oils, £2,305,235; liquors, £1,077,939.

Exports from India to all Countries in Tens of Rupees.

Year ending in	Raw Cotton.	Cotton Twist and Yarn.	Cotton Manufactures.	Rice, Wheat, and other Grains.	Hides and Skins.	Raw Jute.	Opium.	Seeds.	Indigo.	Tea.
	Tens of Rupees.	Tens of Rupees.	Tens of Rupees.	Tens of Rupees.	Tens of Rupees.	Tens of Rupees.	Tens of Rupees.	Tens of Rupees.	Tens of Rupees.	Tens of Rupees.
1878	9,387,354	744,791	1,550,228	10,152,923	3,757,480	3,518,114	12,374,505	7,360,683	3,494,334	3,061,867
1879	7,914,091	937,698	1,644,125	9,802,363	3,097,561	3,800,426	12,993,985	4,682,512	2,960,463	3,170,118
1880	11,145,453	1,163,946	1,573,970	9,866,906	3,738,455	4,370,032	14,323,314	4,781,465	2,947,434	3,072,244
1881	13,241,744	1,330,051	1,777,975	12,711,640	3,735,646	3,934,030	13,600,148	6,392,185	3,571,581	3,099,887
1882	14,941,423	1,420,737	1,914,549	17,510,685	3,950,052	5,030,302	12,432,142	6,064,732	4,509,080	3,662,859
1883	16,055,758	1,874,464	2,093,146	14,884,812	4,444,946	5,846,926	11,481,379	7,205,924	3,912,997	3,738,842
1884	14,401,902	1,983,019	2,326,018	17,623,582	4,666,788	4,592,635	11,294,460	10,086,088	4,640,991	4,134,221
1885	13,295,124	2,506,617	2,080,017	13,895,442	4,936,510	4,661,368	10,882,606	10,752,854	4,068,900	4,137,351
1886	10,782,021	2,841,555	2,248,973	17,612,364	5,336,229	4,355,362	10,735,518	9,975,129	3,783,160	4,397,177
1887	13,475,962	3,418,008	2,436,344	18,027,614	5,149,357	4,869,815	11,077,669	9,222,870	3,691,677	4,883,143
1888	14,413,544	4,146,731	2,798,854	15,738,038	4,860,380	6,040,379	10,067,764	9,399,190	3,890,649	5,302,446
1889	15,045,679	5,318,614	2,872,631	16,152,771	4,746,007	7,897,154	10,508,082	9,564,217	3,948,595	5,473,137
1890	18,671,329	5,840,114	2,733,369	16,816,596	4,524,360	8,639,861	10,115,936	10,631,247	3,863,084	5,445,487
1891	16,533,943	6,627,165	2,869,768	19,812,212	4,698,771	7,602,010	9,261,814	9,345,990	3,073,125	5,504,293
1892	10,763,559	5,884,698	3,081,168	29,059,325	5,186,738	6,848,493	9,562,261	12,210,542	3,214,086	6,283,870
1893	12,743,883	6,864,304	3,060,054	20,007,373	5,591,991	7,944,223	9,255,014	11,633,374	4,141,179	6,620,499
1894	13,310,769	5,054,099	2,914,356	16,732,563	5,801,752	8,524,130	8,019,428	16,761,734	4,182,128	6,928,993
1895	8,708,233	5,783,626	3,599,834	17,432,503	6,560,259	10,575,977	9,064,665	14,206,042	4,745,915	7,988,599
1896	14,090,866	6,801,553	3,418,688	18,714,836	7,640,863	9,992,861	8,459,336	9,721,660	5,354,511	8,025,974
1897	12,971,960	7,262,255	2,700,924	13,848,018	7,001,730	10,550,577	8,022,923	8,014,875	4,370,757	8,495,781
1898	8,872,457	7,070,179	2,497,419	14,111,549	8,318,180	10,129,192	6,097,563	8,600,816	3,057,402	8,274,117
1899	11,190,128	6,685,396	2,462,869	27,201,260	7,450,633	6,941,245	7,126,009	11,852,012	2,970,478	8,191,115
1900	9,925,080	7,007,844	2,610,798	18,103,075	10,463,385	8,071,647	8,203,714	10,109,689	2,692,510	9,176,979
1901	10,129,647	4,243,444	2,706,330	14,069,509	11,483,583	10,867,756	9,456,436	9,018,361	2,135,980	9,682,222

in 1898–99. Our readers, who have perused the previous chapters on trades and manufacture in the present work, will not be at a loss for an explanation. The trade of India is not natural but forced; the export of food grains is made under compulsion to meet an excessive Land Revenue demand. The year 1897–98 was a year of widespread famine in India, and millions of people died of starvation. Nevertheless, the Land Revenue was collected to the amount of 17 millions sterling; and cultivators paid it largely by selling their food grains, which were exported to the amount of 10 millions sterling in that calamitous year. In the following year the crops were good. The agriculturists sold large quantities of their produce to replace their plough cattle, and to repair the losses of the previous famine year. Unfortunately, too, the Government realised the arrears of the Land Revenue with a vigour as inconsiderate as it was unwise; and vast quantities of the new produce had to be sold to meet this pressing Land Revenue demand. Both these causes operated to increase the export of food grains to a figure which it never reached before. Those who judged the prosperity of India by its revenue collection were jubilant. A Land Revenue collection of over 18 millions sterling gave them the evidence they relied upon. The usual misleading statements were made in India, and in the House of Commons, about the recuperative power of India. Few cared to inquire if the enormous exports and the enormous Land Revenue collection had left any stores of food among the people.

The Nemesis followed soon. The following years were years of scanty harvests. Bombay and the Central Provinces had been denuded of their food resources. And those Provinces suffered from a three years' continuous famine, which is unparalleled in the history of modern times.

Nature set a limit which the cultivators had not obtained from the moderation of their rulers. Population decreased in Bombay, and still more in the Central Provinces. Miles of cultivated land became waste. Jungle grew on homesteads, wheat lands, and rice lands. The Land Revenue demand of the Government could no longer be collected. Then, with a reluctant confession of blunder,[1] the demand was revised. Both in Bombay and in the Central Provinces the demand was reduced in District after District. The Land Revenue in the years immediately succeeding did not reach 18 millions sterling. The export of the food grains has never reached 18 millions sterling since.

But the relief is only temporary. There is nothing to restrain Settlement Officers from screwing up the Land Revenue demand again on the first signs of prosperity. There is nothing to give an assurance to the people as to the limits of the State demand from the produce of their fields. A system which is virtually one of adjusting the demand to the utmost paying capacity of an agricultural population demoralises the nation, and makes any permanent improvement in their condition impossible. The people ask for some rule limiting Land Revenue enhancements to definite and specific grounds. The Marquis of Ripon granted them such a rule, but it was withdrawn the month after his departure from India. Lord Curzon has declined to grant them such a rule, as we have seen in the last chapter.

The facts stated above also show the unwisdom of judging the condition of the people of India by the volume of India's foreign trade. Englishmen find this a fairly correct test in their own country, and make the natural mistake of applying it to India. Englishmen live to a large extent on their commerce and manu-

[1] "Mr. Dutt seemed to think that, in the Central Provinces, the Government of India were exacting an exorbitantly high Land Revenue. He [Lord George Hamilton] was very reluctant to dogmatise as to what was, and what was not, a reasonable Land Revenue; and he should be very sorry to say that in the past they might not, here and there, have placed the Land Assessment too high."—Report of Lord George Hamilton's speech in the House of Commons, the *Times*, April 4, 1900.

facture. The sale of their manufactures enables them to buy food from foreign markets. The profits of commerce and of the carrying trade add to their wealth. The volume of trade is a fairly correct index of their national income.

But the circumstances are different in India. The external trade is carried on by foreign merchants with foreign capital. The profits of the trade come to Europe and do not remain in India. The earnings of the foreign trade are not the earnings of the people. The volume of the foreign trade is not an index to their national income. In the year 1881–82, under Lord Ripon's reign of peace and comparative prosperity, the total imports and exports of India were 83 millions sterling. In 1900–1901, a year of famines and distress, the total imports and exports were 122 millions. Who that knows India, or has heard anything of India, will say that India earned more, or was better fed, and was more prosperous, in 1900–1901 than in 1881–82?

Commerce, even when carried on by foreign capital and foreign merchants, is beneficial to a country. It brings in articles cheaper than the country can produce. And it also brings a higher price for the home-produce than can be obtained at home. In both these ways commerce is beneficial, even though the profits of trade go to other lands. But in India, even this benefit is restricted because her foreign trade is forced, not natural. The excise imposed on cotton manufactures *restricts* the production of articles which the country could produce. And the Land Revenue system of India, as well as the Home Charges, *forces* the export of food grains, much of which the country needs for its own population. Thus large imports of cotton goods into India are secured by restrictions on the Indian industry. And large exports of food are compelled by a heavy Land Tax and a heavy Tribute.

CHAPTER IX

HISTORY OF TARIFFS

In a previous chapter we have narrated the history of Indian Tariffs down to 1879, when Lord Lytton sacrificed an important source of Indian revenue in a year of war, famine, and deficit. His successor, the Marquis of Ripon, concluded the Afghan War, established peace, and secured a surplus. And his Finance Minister, Sir Evelyn Baring, now Lord Cromer, abolished the remaining Import Duties in March 1882,—excepting those on salt and liquors.

There was some justification for the abolition of import duties in a year of peace and prosperity. Nevertheless, Lord Ripon and his Finance Minister would have acted more in the interests of the people of India, if they had, in the first instance, withdrawn the Cesses which had been imposed on land, since 1871, in addition to the Land Revenue. While agriculture, the main industry of the people, remained overtaxed, it was not fair to surrender a legitimate revenue derived from customs, which did not operate as a protection.

No fresh import duties were levied for twelve years, between 1882 and 1894, except a small duty on petroleum imposed in 1888. But the steady increase in Military Expenditure which was made after Lord Ripon's departure from India, the large addition in the army sanctioned by Lord Dufferin, and the mischievous activity of Lord Lansdowne's Government beyond the frontiers, disturbed the financial equilibrium of India. And the fall of the rupee created difficulties in remitting to England the increasing Home Charges which were paid in pounds sterling. It is remarkable how little of the increase in Indian expenditure, between 1884 and 1894, was due to improved domestic administration, and how much of it was due to extravagant military charges and impoverishing Home Charges. In 1894 the Indian Government found itself face to face with a deficit of over two million sterling.

Lord Herschell's Committee was appointed to inquire into the possibility of further taxation in India. The Committee came to the conclusion that, "Of all the suggested methods of adding to the revenue, the re-imposition of Import Duties would, according to the evidence before us, excite the least opposition, indeed it is said that it would be popular." But the Committee took care to add that any attempt to re-impose duties on cotton goods would meet with great opposition.

Accordingly, in March 1894—twelve years after the abolition of Import Duties by Sir Evelyn Baring—they were re-imposed on articles imported into India, other than cotton. A duty of 5 per cent. *ad valorem* was imposed generally on all articles with a few exceptions. Iron and steel paid 1 per cent.; petroleum, which paid 1d. per gallon; and railway materials, industrial and agricultural machinery, coal, raw materials, grains, books, and miscellaneous articles were duty free. The Bill was vigorously opposed in the Legislative Council, specially on the ground of the omission of cotton from the schedules; and Lord Elgin, in passing the Tariff Act in March 1894, hinted that it was not a final measure.

It was indeed a very temporary measure. For in December 1894 a fresh Tariff Act was passed, including cotton fabrics and yarns, on which a duty of 5 per cent. *ad valorem* was levied. But the Indian Government thought it wise to propitiate Manchester by imposing a countervailing Excise Duty of 5 per cent. upon yarns produced in Indian mills, which could compete with Lancashire yarns. As a rule, Lancashire manufactures, imported into India, are of the finer classes; and goods, produced at Indian mills, are of the coarser kinds. But in some of the medium yarns, the two supplies—Lancashire and Indian—might overlap; and a 5 per cent. Excise Duty was imposed for these "counts" in which there was an element of competition. The Indian yarns "above twenties,"—*i.e.* those of which more than 20 bundles of a specific length went to 1 lb.—were excised.

But British manufacturers were not satisfied. A debate took place in the House of Commons on January 21, 1895, and Sir Henry Fowler, Secretary of State for India, made a significant statement: "Her Majesty's Government would, in concert with the Government of India, consider the matter with a view to carry out loyally the declared intention to avoid protective injustice."

Six days after he received a deputation from Scotch manufacturers and exporters of dyed cotton goods to India, which specially brought forward two points :—

(1) That they sent cotton yarns of low counts to Burma which had to pay a duty of 5 per cent., while yarns of Number 20 and under from Calcutta and Bombay paid no duty on entering Burma.

(2) That Indian goods paid 5 per cent. excise duty only on the grey yarns from which they were made, while bleached, dyed, woven, and printed British goods paid a 5 per cent. custom duty. Thus bleached, dyed, woven, and printed Indian goods enjoyed a fiscal advantage.

On May 27, 1895, Sir Henry Fowler received another deputation of Lancashire manufacturers and exporters of cotton goods. The deputation was invited to send a statement of facts and arguments. This was duly submitted. But the Liberal Government fell in June 1895, and Lord George Hamilton became Secretary of State for India with the return of the Conservatives to power.

The Conservative party were bound by many pledges and semi-pledges to the Lancashire voters. And they went further in making concessions to the Lancashire demand than the Liberals had done. In September

1895 Lord George Hamilton addressed a letter to the Indian Government, from which we make the following extracts:—

"The Lancashire deputation lay stress on the statement that it is impossible to work fairly, to both the Indian and British manufacturer, an artificial dividing line at 20 s., or at any other count."

"It would be best for India, as well as for the United Kingdom, that the Indian ports should be free from custom duties, as they practically were from 1882 to 1894. But if the condition of the Indian finances compels the Government to retain the import duties, then it is necessary that the duties should be placed on such a footing as will not infringe pledges that have been given, or afford ground for continued complaint and attack."[1]

Slowly but surely the authorities adopted the fatal policy of putting an excise duty on all Indian woven goods. The line drawn at 20 s. count was to be removed; yarns were to be freed; and all woven goods, including the coarsest Indian manufactures with which Lancashire did not compete, were to be excised.

On January 16, 1896, Lord Elgin wired to the Secretary of State, asking his approval to a new measure imposing a 3½ per cent. duty on all woven goods, and exempting all yarns. Lord George Hamilton wired his approval on the next day; and an Indian Tariff Amendment Bill and a Cotton Duties Bill were introduced in the Governor-General's Council.

It can be easily imagined that this determination to revise the Tariff Act passed only a year before, and to subject to an iniquitous excise tax the coarse cotton goods of India, which did not compete with any European goods, raised angry protests from members of the Governor-General's Council—official and non-official, Indian and European. The debate took place on Feb-

[1] Despatch, dated September 5, 1895.

ruary 3, and covers thirty-six folio pages.[1] We only make room for a few brief extracts.

Mr. Playfair, representing the European mercantile community of Calcutta, said :—

"Nothing has been produced, therefore, to contradict the views held by honourable members, that competition on the part of Lancashire mills with the production of the coarser fabrics spun and woven in Indian mills does not exist. On the other hand, further examination in India proves that in reality no competition exists in goods made from yarns below 20 s."

"And after all, what is this Indian trade over which so much contention has unfortunately arisen? An examination of statistics shows that the powerloom spindles in India amount to $\frac{1}{25}$th, and the powerlooms in India to $\frac{1}{60}$th of the world's supply. In relation to Great Britain's equipment, which represents one-half in spindles and one-third in looms of the world's supply, India possesses $\frac{1}{12}$th part of Great Britain's spindles and $\frac{1}{19}$th part of her looms. May India not have this little ewe lamb? My lord, I have every sympathy with the depressed condition of Lancashire trade, and for the welfare of England as well as India, everything that can legitimately be done to afford relief should be granted. But, because Lancashire masters may be alarmed and discontented on account of the state of their affairs, I see no reason why they should unjustly attack a separate industry in India. The proposals under these Bills mean a remission of taxation of 51½ lakhs (or 37 per cent.) on Manchester goods, and an increase of 11 lakhs (or 300 per cent.) of taxation on Indian-made goods."

Rao Sahib Balwant Rao spoke on behalf of the Indian manufacturer :—

"No less an authority than Mr. Mill advocates a temporary protection to infant and promising industries.

[1] Papers relating to the Indian Tariff Act, 1896, and the Cotton Duties Act, 1896, presented to Parliament.

. . . But taking our stand on Free Trade alone, it cannot be made out that in the duties, as they have hitherto been levied, there can be any protection afforded to India. Properly speaking it is only 30 s. and 40 s. of the Indian goods that can enter into direct competition with Manchester."

"If the articles manufactured in India out of the yarns of 20 s. and lower were excised, no advantage is gained by any foreign dealer. . . . But at the same time millions will have to buy their coarse cloth at an unnecessarily higher price, which is sure to tell heavily on their impoverishment. Those who are best able to pay a tax, and that too in proportion to their higher comfort, will have their tax reduced, and the deficit will be filled up by the poorest."

Mr. Anand Charlu, representing Madras, also pointed out that there was no competition in the coarser goods, and to excise the coarser goods in India would be going beyond the pledges given to Lancashire. He added:—

"I beseech the responsible Ministers who have the power, if they possess the will, to see that our interests are not ruthlessly jeopardised. To them I shall say, also, that they are drifting—let me say unwittingly—beyond even the pledges given by the Secretary of State for India; for that officer has promised relief only against injustice and only against protection."

Mr. Stevens, afterwards Sir Charles Steevens, representing Bengal, said:—

"I fear it must be owned that the measure has not received the support of the public as a whole. For this there are two main reasons. *First*, the suspicion existing in some quarters that it has been called for by the exigencies of party politics in England rather than by the wants of India; *secondly*, that the trade will be disturbed to the disadvantage of important industries and of poor consumers in this country."

All these protests were in vain. Indian Legislative

Councils have no independence. Sir James Westland, the Finance Minister of Lord Elgin, was in charge of the Bills, and had little difficulty in having them passed.

Section 6 of the Cotton Duties Act of 1896 runs thus:—

"There shall be levied and collected at every mill in British India, upon all cotton goods produced in such mill, a duty at the rate of 3½ per centum on the value of such goods."

The reader will observe that this legislation altogether stands apart from any previous fiscal legislation which had ever taken place in India. In 1879 cotton duties were surrendered. In 1882 all import duties except on salt and liquors were repealed. In 1894 import duties were re-imposed, and an excise duty was imposed on such Indian goods as competed with Lancashire goods. But the surrender of 1896 went farther and deeper. It imposed an excise duty on all cotton goods produced in India. It taxed the coarse Indian fabrics with which Manchester had never competed and never could compete. It threw a burden on Indian mills which competed with no mills in Europe. It raised the price of the poor man's clothing in India without the pretext of relieving the poor man of Lancashire.

As an instance of fiscal injustice, the Indian Act of 1896 is unexampled in any civilised country in modern times. Most civilised Governments protect their home industries by prohibitive duties on foreign goods. The most thorough of Free Trade Governments do not excise home manufactures when imposing a moderate customs duty on imported goods for the purposes of revenue. In India, where an infant industry required protection, even according to the maxims of John Stuart Mill, no protection has ever been given. Moderate customs levied for the purposes of revenue only, were sacrificed in 1879 and 1882. Home-manufactured cotton goods, which were supposed to compete with imported goods, were excised in 1894. And home goods, which did not compete with foreign goods, were excised in 1896. Such is the manner in which the interests of an unrepresented nation are sacrificed.

The result of this iniquitous legislation, combined with the recent famines and currency legislation, has been disastrous. The following figures will show how the industry has been checked in the closing years of the century.

Year.	Number of Mills.	Looms.	Spindles.	Yarns, million lbs.	Piece Goods, million yds.
1898-99	175	37,288	4,455,038	512	101
1899-1900	186	38,520	4,729,570	513	98
1900-1901	190	40,542	4,932,602	353	98

New mills are struggling into existence in spite of every check, but the output in yarns and piece goods shows a lamentable decline.

In the fiscal controversy which is going on in England at the present time (1903), Protectionists, Retaliationists, and Free Traders, all appeal the good of the people of Great Britain as the final test. Protectionists urge that Protection secures the interests of the people. Retaliationists argue that it is necessary to point the revolver at the foreigner to secure justice to the people. Free Traders insist that absolute Free Trade is the only possible policy to save the overgrown population of Great Britain from dear-loaf, penury, and starvation. All parties agree in regarding the good of the people as the final aim and end of fiscal legislation; they only differ as to the method by which it can be best secured. Will Englishmen honestly apply this test to India? Will they dare to be just to the Indian manufacturer, and legislate in the interests of the Indian industries and the Indian nation?

CHAPTER X

RAILWAYS AND IRRIGATION

"RAILWAYS are now almost completed," wrote an official chronicler in 1873, "so that with the cessation of heavy outlay on construction, the financial position may be expected to improve." [1]

"Sir Arthur Cotton proposes the summary and indefinite suspension of nearly all railway schemes and works," wrote the Select Committee headed by Lord George Hamilton in 1878. "He would, however, devote ten millions annually for the next ten or twenty years to irrigation works." [2]

"Among the means," wrote the Famine Commission of 1880, "that may be adopted for giving India direct protection from famine arising from drought, the first place must unquestionably be assigned to works of irrigation." [3]

These anticipations and recommendations have been disregarded. There was no "cessation of heavy outlay" on the construction of railways. There was no "suspension" of new railway schemes and works. "The first place" among famine-prevention works was not assigned to irrigation.

The reasons are, that the Indian administration is very considerably influenced by the trend of public opinion in England, and not by the opinion of the people of India. Englishmen understand railways, and do not understand the importance of irrigation for India.

[1] *Moral and Material Progress and Condition of India*, 1872–73.
[2] Select Committee's Report.
[3] Famine Commission's Report, 1880, Part II., p. 150.

2 M

English manufacturers look to the opening of distant markets in India by means of railway extension. English merchants demand fresh facilities for trade with India by new lines of communication. British houses of trade influence Indian administration, both through Parliament and by direct correspondence with the India Office. Members of Parliament urge the construction of new railway lines by frequent questions in the House of Commons. None cares for irrigation because none in England understands its supreme importance for India. The pious intention recorded in the official report of 1873, to discontinue heavy outlays on new railway lines, was soon forgotten. Sir Arthur Cotton was ridiculed as an enthusiast and a visionary. The Famine Commission's Report slept in official archives. New railway lines were pushed on vigorously beyond the urgent needs of India, and certainly beyond her resources.

But there was a difficulty in constructing new lines in a country where the people were poor and railways did not pay. The policy of guaranteeing profits to private companies, from the revenues of India, had led to extravagance and to a disregard for the comfort of the passengers which were fully exposed before the Finance Committees of 1871, 1872, 1873, and 1874. It was then resolved that the State should itself undertake future constructions with borrowed capital. This policy was followed for a few years; but the famine of 1877 and the Afghan War of 1878 upset Indian finance, and stopped the further construction of State railways.

Endeavours were then made to induce private companies to undertake fresh lines. The endeavours failed; and the Indian Government again fell back to the vicious guarantee system. Again that policy was abandoned, and State railways were commenced; but the fall of the rupee made it necessary for the Government to curtail their gold liabilities, and State railways were discontinued.

Once more the Government appealed to private companies, and a Resolution was passed in 1893 specifying the conditions on which the Government would grant concessions to such companies. The Resolution failed to attract investors. New terms were set forth in 1896. A few lines were constructed on these new terms, and then they failed to work. Capitalists would not invest without a clear guarantee of profits from the revenues of India. "And at the present time the Government find it most difficult to take up railway schemes without a guarantee in some form or other, and are, speaking generally, *obliged to give a guarantee*, or *to find capital themselves*, for all new lines of railway."[1]

Is there not a third alternative? Now that all the main lines are completed, may not the future extension of Indian railways be left entirely to private enterprise without a guarantee? The people of India do not ask for the construction of more railways from taxes paid by them. The Famine Commission of 1897 do not think more railways are needed for famine-protection purposes, and declare that "greater protection will be afforded by the extension of irrigation works."[2] The Famine Commission of 1900 recommend an increase in the rolling stock, but do not urge the further extension of railway lines.[3] And the Special Commissioner recently sent out to India to inquire into Indian railways, admits that "so far, therefore, as railways per square mile of territory are concerned, India is rather better served than most countries outside Europe," better served than Trans-Caspian Russia or Siberia, than Egypt or Natal, than Transvaal or Orange River Colony, than New Zealand or Victoria, than New South Wales or Queensland, than Venezuela, Brazil, or the Argentine Republic. Japan alone has more railways compared to her area, because her area is

[1] Robertson's Report on the administration and working of Indian railways, 1903, p. 30.

[2] Famine Commission's Report, 1898, p. 330.

[3] *Ibid.*, 1901, p. 79.

small; but in respect of population, India has a mile of railway for every 12,231 people against a mile for 12,713 people in Japan.[1] Surely these are facts which should make us pause. We cannot enjoy the luxury of European travelling when the annual earning per head of population in India is £2, and that in England is £42. We are content to be among the foremost nations out of Europe, so far as the facilities of travelling are concerned. We can wait till private companies find it remunerative to undertake new lines, without asking for a guarantee from our taxes. We object to the revenues of India being assigned for new lines, or for guarantees on new lines. The further extension of State railways or of guaranteed railways would be a betrayal of the interests of the people of India under pressure from other quarters.

The rapid advance in railway construction in recent years will appear from the following table showing the mileage of Indian railways since the beginning of railway construction in India.

Railways in India.

Year.	Mileage.	Year.	Mileage.	Year.	Mileage.	Year.	Mileage.
1853	20	1871	5,077	1885–86	12,375	1893	18,510
1856	273	1873	5,694	1886–87	13,387	1894	18,906
1857	288	1875	6,518	1887–88	14,376	1895	19,555
1861	1588	1877	7,322	1888–89	15,241	1896	20,262
1862	2336	1881	9,891	1889–90	16,096	1897	21,133
1863	2550	1882	10,144	1890–91	16,977	1898	22,048
1865	3373	1883–84	10,828	1891–92	17,564	1899	23,528
1867	3936	1884–85	12,000	1892	17,894	1900	24,760

And the mileage for 1901 was 25,373. It will be seen that, within twenty-eight years since the official historian wrote that "railways are now almost completed," the mileage of railways has increased from five thousand to twenty-five thousand.

[1] Robertson's Report (1903), p. 35.

The total outlay on the construction of these lines is shown in the following tables which have been compiled from decennial Reports on the Moral and Material Progress and Condition of India.

Expenditure up to December 1891.	
	Tens of Rupees
State railways made by the State . . .	133,546,074
State railways made by Companies . .	28,113,763
Guaranteed Companies	49,205,868
Assisted Companies	5,607,036
Native States Railways	8,600,251
Portuguese and French Lines	1,689,068
Railway surveys, collieries, &c.	907,705
Total	227,669,765

Capital Outlay Year by Year up to December 1901.			
Year.	£	Year.	£
1892	3,240,000	1897	7,307,000
1893	3,666,000	1898	6,993,000
1894	3,526,000	1899	8,926,000
1895	4,373,000	1900	7,106,000
1896	5,213,000	1901	6,773,000

The total capital outlay down to the end of the year 1901 is given as 340,159,800 tens of rupees, equivalent to £226,773,200 sterling.[1]

It only remains to add that the Government reserved the right to purchase lines from guaranteed companies, and this right has been freely, and we think rightly, exercised within the last twenty years. The East India Railway was acquired in 1880, the Eastern Bengal Railway in 1884, the Sindh, Punjab, and Delhi Company's lines in 1885–86, the Oudh and Rohilkhand Railway in 1888, the South Indian Railway in 1890, and the Great Indian Peninsular Railway in 1900. But while the old guaranteed lines were thus purchased by the

[1] *Statistical Abstract relating to British India*, 1891–92 *to* 1900–01.

Government, other guarantees nave again been given in recent years for new lines. The Assam Bengal Railway, formed in 1892, obtained a guarantee of 3 per cent. to connect Assam with the port of Chittagong, obviously in the interests of the Assam tea gardens. The Burma Railways Company, formed in 1897, obtained a guarantee of 2½ per cent. to take over the State-railway system in Burma, and to extend the line from Mandalay towards China. The line has been carried as far as Lathio, and has brought no traffic; and the Indian money has been wasted on a scheme from which Indian tax-payers have nothing to gain.

When we turn from railways to the subject of irrigation works we turn from unwise extravagance to equally unwise niggardliness. The great schemes suggested by Sir Arthur Cotton were never seriously considered. And the total outlay on irrigation works in India, down to March 1902, scarcely amounted to 24 millions sterling against 226 millions sterling spent on railways.

The area of land irrigated from Government canals in the different provinces of India in the year 1901–1902, excluding the Sindh canals, is shown in the table on the next page.

It has been stated before that the water rate has been consolidated with the land rate in Madras, and cultivators in the Ryotwari tracts are required to pay a fixed consolidated tax year after year.

In some provinces a year of heavy rainfall means a larger distribution of canal water, while in Sindh a good rainfall means a fall in the irrigated area, because the people are not in want of irrigation water. In Orissa, where there is generally a good rainfall, the cultivators refrained, to a large extent, from using the canal water, until the drought of 1896. Then there was a rush of applications, and agriculturists entered into agreements to use and pay for the canal water for years to come.

Province.	Canals.	Acres irrigated.
Bengal	Orissa Canals	201,498
	Midnapur Canal	82,134
	Sone Canal	557,494
Agra and Oudh	East Jumna and two Ganges Canals and other Works	2,741,400
Punjab	West Jumna Canal	589,955
	Bari Doab Canal	856,041
	Sirhind British Canal	728,908
	Sirhind Native State Canal	341,553
	Chinab Canal	1,748,129
	Jhelum Canal	65,367
	Sohag, Para and Sidhnai Canals	161,885
Bombay	Nira, Mutha, and other Canals	139,040
Madras	Kaveri, Krishna, and Godavari Canal systems, about	2,500,000
	Periyar system	154,000
	Rushikulya system	84,3000
	Pennar and other Canals	not given

For all these reasons, the area irrigated in India varies from year to year.

But there are large tracts of country where no canals or other irrigation works have yet been constructed; and the famines of 1897 and 1900 once more directed the attention of the Government to a duty yet unfulfilled. At last, in 1901, measures were adopted which should have been taken twenty years before; and a Commission was appointed to inquire into the extent to which irrigation works could be extended in India. Sir Colin Scott-Moncrieff, who had served in the irrigation department in India, and had distinguished himself by his great and successful irrigation works in Egypt, was elected the head of the Commission; and the result of his labours has recently appeared in four Blue Books of very respectable size.

The second volume contains a summary of the irrigation works done in India, and the suggestions of the

Commission for future works. In the Punjab, the Commission recommend the postponement of the Lower Bari-Doab scheme, and suggest the bolder scheme of a canal from the Chinab to be carried across the valley of the Ravi.

In Sindh, the further development of the existing inundation canals is proposed. In Gujrat, the Commission make a valuable proposal to find suitable sites for storage works on the Sabarmati, Mahi, and Narbada rivers, and for the construction of canals from these reservoirs for the irrigation of Ahmadabad and Kaira. And for the Deccan they make a similar but bolder proposal that the catchment areas of all the rivers which derive their supplies from the unfailing rainfall of the Western Ghats should be examined with a view to the construction of storage works, and to the excavation of canals from these works to parts of the country urgently in need of protection.

In Madras, the extension of the Kurnool-Cuddapa canal and a complete investigation of the Tumbhadra project are recommended; and large storage works for the Kaveri and the Krishna are also proposed.

In Bengal, storage works and canals for the irrigation of Shahabad and Muzaffarpur Districts are proposed. And in Agra and Oudh, the Commission strongly recommend the construction of the Ken canal for the protection of Banda and Bandelkhand, and also a diversion of the Sarda water into the Ganges, utilising a portion of it for the irrigation of Bijnor and Budaon.

Besides these and other large works, there is a wide field for the construction of works of a humbler class, the majority of which will not cost more than £60,000, while some may cost even less than £6000. "There is a great deal to be said in favour of such works. They afford protection to many tracts which cannot be brought within the scope of larger and more ambitious schemes; they involve much less financial risk; and on most of them work can be started for the purpose of employing relief labour with some assurance that the works are likely to be completed."

Both in regard to the smaller works and the major works, the Commission strongly recommend their construction for the protection of agriculture even when they are not likely to be directly remunerative. "There are other small works which are never likely to be directly remunerative, but which we have no hesitation in recommending, as we have recommended many major works, on the ground that they afford the only means of providing protection against drought to tracts that are greatly in want of it. Foremost among these we would place the works which we have proposed in the rice-growing districts of the Central Provinces. But we hope that many works of the same kind may be possible in other tracts such as are to be found in Gujrat, Berar, Chota Nagpur, and Bandelkhand." The Government of India and the Provincial Governments, which have so often been compelled to remit portions of the Land Revenue after the devastations caused by recent famines, will no doubt feel that, even from a purely financial point of view, it is a sound and wise policy to undertake these large and small irrigation works, even when they are not likely to be "directly remunerative."

A wise suggestion is made by the Commission for the appointment of a Central Board invested with the responsibility of regularly watching and reporting progress in irrigation works in the future. The recommendation might be somewhat widened; a Central Board for all public works, including railways, might be formed; and some Indian Members, qualified by their administrative experience and their knowledge of the needs of their countrymen, should be appointed to the Board. The Public Works of India are represented by one member of the Viceroy's Council, generally an engineer. He looks at questions from an engineer's point of view, and does not know the requirements of agriculture. He is amenable to pressure for railway extensions, but is not cognisant of the desires and the needs of the people of India.

During half a century, numerous works have been constructed which the country did not urgently need, and many works have been neglected which were vital to the protection of agriculture. Gathering wisdom from past experience, the Government may now think it expedient and necessary to admit some popular element in a Board of Public Works. It would be the duty of the Board to supervise the construction of all the public works in the future; to represent the needs and requirements of railway passengers on State and Guaranteed lines alike; to adjust the water rate imposed on cultivators so as to safeguard the revenue without being unjust to the people; and generally to help the Government of India in a branch of administration which is in special need of the co-operation and help of the people.

CHAPTER XI

ROYAL COMMISSION ON EXPENDITURE

THERE was a growing feeling of uneasiness at the continuous increase of the Indian Debt and the Indian expenditure. There was a complaint that the apportionment of charge between Great Britain and India was neither just nor expedient.

Able and cautious financiers had reduced the Public Debt of Great Britain by over a hundred and fifty millions after the Crimean War, but there was no decrease in the Indian Debt. On the contrary, the cost of the Abyssinian and other wars had been unjustly charged to India, and a needless Afghan war had swelled the Indian Debt. Mr. Gladstone had marked the growing evil with pain and solicitude; he had appointed a Select Committee on Indian Finance to remedy it; but the Finance Committee discontinued its work after 1874 and achieved no results. Mr. Gladstone had also relieved the Indian Exchequer of five millions sterling, which was paid out of the Imperial Exchequer as a portion of the cost of the Afghan War of 1878. But the balance, about eighteen millions sterling, fell on India. During the long administration of Lord Salisbury, from 1886 to 1892, Indian finance went from bad to worse; Indian expenditure increased under the rule of Lords Dufferin and Lansdowne. When Mr. Gladstone formed his fourth and last administration in 1892, the people of India looked for some redress.

For the first time in the history of the British Parliament, an Indian was elected as a Member. Born in 1825, Mr. Dadabhai Naoroji had from his early youth devoted himself to social and political reforms in his own country. In 1854 he was Professor of Mathematics and Natural Philosophy at Elphinstone College, Bombay; in 1855 he visited England, and was appointed Professor of the Gujrati language at University College, London. He gave his evidence before the Finance Committee of 1873, as we have stated before. In the following year he was appointed Prime Minister of Baroda State, when Lord Northbrook seated a young prince on the throne of the deposed Gaekwar. Returning to England after a few years, he once more devoted himself to an untiring advocacy of the cause of his country. And in 1892, at the ripe age of 66, he was elected Member for Central Finsbury, and entered the House of Commons.

With a zeal and capacity for work undimmed by age, with a sincerity of patriotism which called forth the admiration even of his opponents who disagreed with his opinions and resented his vehemence, Mr. Naoroji continued his labours in the House of Commons for three years. If anything could add to the fame and influence of such a patriot, it was the absolute sincerity of his convictions, the unsullied purity of his motives, the childlike simplicity of his character, the beauty and charm of his private life. Like the great Gladstone, Mr. Dadabhai Naoroji riveted his hold on the hearts of his countrymen as much by his life-long political work as by his high and spotless private character. And men of all classes and persuasions in India were as proud of their Grand Old Man.

For three years Mr. Naoroji pressed for financial justice to India in the House of Commons, and his endeavours bore fruit. A Royal Commission was appointed in May 1895, "to inquire into the administration and management of the Military and Civil Expenditure incurred under the authority of the Secretary of State for India in Council, or of the Governor of India, and the apportionment of charge between the Governments of the

United Kingdom and of India for purposes in which both are interested." Lord Welby was the President of the Commission, and Leonard Courtney, George Nathaniel Curzon, Sir William Wedderburn, Sir Donald Stewart, Thomas R. Buchanan, William S. Caine and Dadabhai Naoroji, were among the Commissioners. Mr. Curzon resigned his seat on the Commission in the following year on being appointed Under Secretary of State for Foreign Affairs.

The Commission began their work well, and recorded a mass of valuable evidence given by such witnesses as Sir Charles Bernard, Sir David Barbour, Sir Auckland Colvin, Lord Cromer, Lord Wolseley, Lord Northbrook, Lord Roberts, Lord Lansdowne, Lord Ripon, and a number of other distinguished witnesses. All this evidence was recorded within two years, from November 1895 to July 1897. And the Commission then went to sleep for three years!

When the final report was at last submitted in 1900, there was a feeling of disappointment in England and in India. Sir Henry Fowler himself gave expression to this sense of disappointment in the House of Commons. The Commission had elicited much valuable evidence; but the majority of them hesitated to come to the obvious conclusion. They would not radically disturb the existing financial relations between Great Britain and India. They would not withdraw from the Indian tax-payer charges for which India alone was not justly liable. In the closing year of the century, a year in which India was suffering from the severest famine known in the history of modern times, her starving population failed to obtain that financial justice which they had expected from the British Parliament and from a British Royal Commission.

The majority of the Commissioners submitted a Report which, with reservations, covers 150 folio printed pages. A few of the recommendations made on the apportionment of charge deserve mention.

Civil Charges.—The majority of the Commissioners recommended that the United Kingdom should contribute £50,000 towards the expenses of the India Office, and should pay half the charges incurred at Aden and in Persia.

Employment of Indian Troops out of India.—They held that India had a direct and substantial interest in keeping open the Suez Canal, in questions affecting Siam, Persia, and the Arabian coast, and in questions affecting Afghanistan and Central Asia. That India had sole interest in punitive expeditions on her borders. That India might have a modified interest in questions affecting the East Coast of Africa as far as Zanzibar. That subject to these principles questions of apportionment of charge between India and Great Britain might be referred to a tribunal for mediation.

Naval Charges.—They found that India maintained a local marine, was responsible for the defence of her coasts, and contributed £100,000 for general naval defence undertaken by the Admiralty. They held that the contribution was not excessive.

Army Charges.—They held that the Capitation Charge of £7, 10s. on every British soldier sent out to India should be continued. But they recommended that half the cost of the transport of troops to and from India should be paid by Great Britain. On the point urged that the Indian Army was maintained largely for the Imperial purposes of Great Britain, they stated: "When the time for revising the present arrangement arrives, the exceptional position of India as to military charges should be borne in mind. If, on the one hand, she imposes a certain strain on the Imperial resources in the supply of services which she properly pays, on the other she renders services to the Imperial Government which should not be disregarded."

The only relief to India, therefore, which the Commission recommended out of the Imperial Exchequer was:—

	£
In aid of the charge for the India Office	50,000
Half the military charges for Aden	108,000
Increased contribution to the charge of the Persian Mission	5,000
Half the cost of the transport of troops to and from India .	130,000
Total	293,000

A minority of the Commissioners consisting of Sir William Wedderburn, Mr. Caine, and Mr. Naoroji submitted a separate report, covering forty printed pages, and pointing out more thoroughly the financial injustice done to India, and the redress which was needed.

The Government of Lord Salisbury acted on the report of the majority with some modifications. To contribute £50,000 from the Imperial Exchequer towards the cost of the India Office would be to enable Members of Parliament to bring on a debate on India by moving a reduction of this supply. The India Office does not appreciate such debates on Indian administration, and the proposed contribution was not made on account of the India Office.

On the other hand, the really larger questions of reduction of the Indian Debt, reduction of the Home Charges and of taxation, and reduction of the military expenditure remained untouched. The duty of relieving the Indian tax-payer of the burden of a heavy and excessive taxation remained unfulfilled. The problem of bringing to the lives of the two hundred millions of British subjects in India something of that comfort and prosperity, which are the heritage of British subjects elsewhere in the world, remained unsolved.

We conclude this chapter with a few extracts from the very valuable evidence recorded by the Commission. The evidence with appendices fills nearly 1500 folio pages, in double columns and small print. Our extracts, therefore, do not pretend to be a summary of this enormous quantity of evidence, but will only convey to readers the opinions of some notable witnesses on some important points of administration.

LORD CROMER ON A COURT OF ARBITRATION.

13,642. That is what we should like to hear?

My view of the question of the Home Charges is this: I believe there is a very general wish in this country, in Parliament, and amongst Ministers of whatsoever party, to deal not only justly, but even generously, with India; but I think it would be an extremely good thing if you could arrange in some way a Court of Arbitration to deal with these matters. It is not only that the Settlement should be just, it is of the highest importance that everybody in India should think it is just, not only Natives, but the European public, who have also to be considered, and the Government of India themselves. Under the present system, although I am not alluding to any special point, or saying that the distribution has been unjust, there is no means of making the people in India think it is just. It is supposed to be arranged between the various departments and the India Office, and the general impression, rightly or wrongly, is that the English view is advocated with greater strength, and more successfully, than the Indian view. Whether that be right or wrong, the mere fact that such an opinion exists is an evil, and therefore I should be very glad if something could be done to have some Court of Arbitration to settle these matters. That is all the more desirable, because a great many of these matters must be rather the subject of equitable compromise than anything else. Take the case of Aden, to which somebody alluded in the course of these discussions; it is perfectly impossible for anybody to make any precise calculation as to what contribution India should pay for Aden. India is very much interested in Aden, and so are Ceylon, Hong Kong, and the Straits Settlements, and English commerce generally. It is a matter of judgment how much India should pay; and it would satisfy Indian opinion, and do a great deal of good in that way, if there were some Court of Arbitration instituted to settle these matters.

13,650. Would you give power to either party to refer any question on which there was an apportionment of charge to the Board of Arbitration?

I think I should. I should make them the Court of Appeal; in fact I almost think they ought to be constituted by Act of Parliament with the necessary powers laid down specifically.

13,651. Something like the Judicial Committee of the Privy Council?

Very much of that nature, yes.

13,652. And when a question arose between Home Departments and the Indian Government as to the apportionment of any charge, would you give the power to either party to refer it to the Board of Arbitration, or would it necessarily go there?

No; I think I would give either of them the power of referring; of course, restricting myself to financial questions—nothing else but pure finance.

13,653. And in regard to these charges which have permanently to be apportioned between England and India, the military charges, and the capitation grant, would you say that they, at intervals of five or ten years, should be referred to this Board of Arbitration?

I think so. My inclination certainly would be to give the utmost possible guarantee to the Indian taxpayers and Indian public that all these questions are decided by some body of men who are quite independent, and who are not in any way biassed against them.

LORD NORTHBROOK ON WARS OUTSIDE INDIA.

14,108. Have you paid any attention to the arrangements made for the payment of troops lent by India for service out of that country?

Yes, I have had occasion to give considerable attention to this matter.

14,109. Do you think that fair treatment has been given to India in the apportionment of those charges?

I think that India has been hardly treated.

14,110. Could you go through the various cases and give us your reasons?

The cases will be found in Sir Henry Waterfield's Memorandum in the appendix, page 364. I think I might take them in the order in which he gives them there.

14,111–2. I suppose you are going to take them from paragraph 16, are you?

Paragraph 19.

14,113–4. Quite so, I see 19?

Well, I will not go back to anything before the Abyssinian Expedition. I think that in the case of the Abyssinian War it was not right to charge India with the ordinary expenditure of the expedition.

14,119. Do you remember the ground upon which the Government decided at the time that India had an interest in Abyssinia?

No, I should like to see that. I never heard of it. I believe a protest was made at the time.

14,120. I am speaking from memory now. Was it not put forward that the Government of India was concerned in this question, because Abyssinia, being within the purview of India, you may say the prestige of the English name must not be endangered by allowing any English official subjects to be taken prisoners?

The idea may have been put forward. I do not think any impartial person would have paid the slightest attention to it.

14,121. I think I remember a French critic arguing at the time that the war was for the purpose of discovering a sanatorium for English troops?

That would be a better reason than the reason

adduced as regards prestige, in my opinion. Then I come to the next case, the Perak Expedition. It was a very small one, but in this Perak case I cannot conceive any one doubting that India has been hardly treated. Here was an expedition beyond the frontier of India, and for which, in order that any portion of the Indian revenue should be applied, it is by statute necessary that there should be an address to the Crown from both Houses of Parliament. I happened to be Governor-General at the time, and I protested against this charge being put upon India. Not only was no notice taken of the protest made by the Government of India, but not even were the statutory addresses from both Houses moved so that the law was broken, and the charge so made upon India was never repaid. It has remained charged upon India from that time to this, contrary to the law, and contrary to the protest of the Government of India. That is the case of Perak; that is the second one I have got to deal with, and I think this case is perfectly clear. I do not think that any answer can be given to it. In regard to the expedition sent to Malta, the whole of the expenses, both ordinary and extraordinary, were very properly paid by the Government of England.

14,124. Have you mentioned the Egyptian operation of 1882?

I am coming to that now, that is the next case, the Egyptian Campaign of 1882. This was a case with which I individually had a good deal to do. Therefore I should not like to give any very strong opinion against the arrangement that was made. There was no doubt that, as regards keeping the Suez Canal open, India had a substantial interest. It had an interest. The question was what interest, how much the interest was. In the first instance it was intended that India should pay the whole cost of the expedition that was sent. That was when it was supposed that some very small force would have been sufficient. That was the reason why the

Government at that time thought India should pay the whole. The English Government were put to very considerable cost, and we thought that India would be put to a small cost, and we thought she might very fairly pay the small cost of the troops sent to Suez. However, the operations became very extended, and it ended in the expedition from India becoming a large expedition. The whole cost was, I think, £1,700,000, and the ultimate arrangement made between the two Governments, the Government of India and the Government of England, was that India paid £1,200,000, and England paid £500,000. That was the arrangement that was made, and it was accepted by the Government of India, but it certainly was accepted unwillingly. The Government of India thought it had been very hardly treated in the matter, and I think that, looking at it now, I must say that it would have been perhaps better if we had charged India half, that India should have paid £850,000 and England should have paid £850,000. I do not want to press that, because I myself was in the Government at the time, therefore I cannot say that I considered it at the time to be an unfair arrangement.

14,127. [Soudan War.] Would you consider that if the original plan had been carried out, India was sufficiently interested in the expedition to justify her being called upon to contribute?

If you ask me my opinion, I should say, "No, certainly not." I do not think there was a substantial interest of India in any expedition to the Soudan, but my argument rests upon this, that when by a statute the revenues of the Government of India are not to be used excepting after addresses from both Houses of Parliament, it is essential that the terms of that statute should be strictly adhered to, and, in my opinion, the continued employment of the Indian troops at Suakim as a garrison was not covered by the address. It alone could authorise the expenditure of the money, that is my point. As regards the force sent to Suakim last year, I say that certainly India should not have been charged.

14,165. Now you have gone through and brought before us the ground for the differences of opinion between the two Governments?

I should like to be allowed to sum it up before you go to the next question.

14,166. Yes, if you please.

To sum up what I have put before the Commission with respect to these cases of troops lent by India, I think certainly that, if the ordinary charges of that Abyssinian War were £600,000, that is a sum of money which India has a fair and equitable ground to claim. The whole of the Perak ordinary charges ought certainly, I think, to be paid. I will take the Suakim charges to be about £200,000, I do not know exactly what they were, but whatever the charges for Suakim were, I think the whole of the garrison charges at Suakim ought to be refunded to India. My opinion is that, on equitable grounds, £350,000 ought to be given to India in respect of the Egyptian Expedition of 1882, so that the charges should be divided between the two Governments, and I think that those sums ought, either directly, or in some other equitable manner, to be allowed to India now. I do not see any reason why it should be considered that because India has been inequitably treated, and in some cases, in my opinion, illegally treated, during many years, that that treatment should not be redressed by some action at the present time. That concludes all I have to say upon that matter.

Lord Lansdowne on the Indian Army.

15,996. Have you considered, Lord Lansdowne, from the point of view of India itself, whether, supposing she were isolated from the United Kingdom, it would be necessary to maintain a force such as is borrowed from the United Kingdom, and in the same degree of efficiency?

I should say certainly not. The Indian Army is organised with a view to the possibility of its employment upon operations which have nothing to do with the internal policy of the country or with the mere repression of tribal disorders upon the frontier.

15,997. Then would it be a fair suggestion that the difference in the cost of training that force so borrowed, between what would be necessary for Indian purposes and the standard which is kept up for Imperial and home purposes, should be borne by the home exchequer?

It is very difficult to express these things precisely in terms of money; but your question seems to me to point to the principle which I was endeavouring in my answers to the Chairman to enforce.

15,998. That we, for home purposes, for Imperial purposes, are keeping the army at a higher standard of efficiency than India, taken by itself, would require, and that we should make that consideration an element in arriving at the settlement of charge between the two countries?

Certainly an element.

15,999. That cannot be put into figures, but still it is an important element in the spirit in which we should approach this settlement?

That is my view.

Sir Henry Brackenbury on the Indian Army.

14,782. It is not the amount that either the War Office or anybody else is proposing to charge India?

I perfectly understand that; but, as I understand it, the basis of these charges generally is, that India should repay to England what it can be proved that England would not pay but for the military requirements of India, subject to what, I think, is called some sort of rebate.

Well, my personal opinion is, that it is altogether wrong that there should be any such theory as that at all, and if I might be allowed to give my reasons for that opinion, in the first place, I would say that the army in India is largely in excess of the requirements for the preservation of internal order in India. The strength of the army in India is calculated to allow of a powerful field army being placed on or beyond the Indian frontier, in addition to the obligatory garrisons required for keeping order in India. The necessity for maintaining in India that powerful field army, in addition to the obligatory garrisons, is caused by the approach of a great Military Power into a position which enables her to threaten directly Afghanistan, to which we are under treaty obligations, and indirectly to threaten the security of India. The foreign policy of India is directed entirely from England by her Majesty's Government, and it is part of British foreign policy generally. The object of British foreign policy generally, I believe, is to secure British rule over the British Empire. If it were desired to maintain British rule in India only for India's sake, then I think it would be fair to make India pay to the utmost farthing everything that could be shown was due to Britain's rule over India; but I cannot but feel that Britain's interest in keeping India under British rule is enormous. India affords employment to thousands of Britons; India employs millions of British capital; and Indian commerce is of immense value to Great Britain. Therefore it seems to me that India, being held by Great Britain, not only for India's sake, but also for Great Britain's sake, Great Britain should pay a share of the expenditure for this purpose; and in estimating what that share should be, I think that England should behave generously, because, in the first place, England is a rich country, and India is a poor country. It is not altogether a fair basis of comparison of their comparative richness and poorness, but it is one that is worth bringing to notice, and that is the income tax of India, as compared with the income tax of this country. In India you have an income tax of $2\frac{1}{2}$ per cent., about 6d. in the pound. I cannot lay my hand exactly on what that income tax produces, but I believe that the 6d. in the pound produces less than £1,000,000 sterling; in England every penny produces considerably over £2,000,000 sterling.

Sir Auckland Colvin on the Viceroy's Council.

3216. May I ask you one or two questions which Sir Ralph Knox wished to ask you, and which I shall be glad to put you even in an imperfect way? They referred to the Constitution of the Council of the Viceroy. Am I not right in thinking that the number of the Council, the Executive Council, I think you call it, is eight?

Not so many as that.

3217. Seven?

There are the Viceroy, the Commander-in-Chief, the Military Member, the Home Member, the Public Works Member, the Finance Member, and the Legal Member—seven. It varies; it is not necessarily the same; the Public Works Member is not always there.

3218. Out of that number we may say that all represent spending departments, except the Viceroy himself and the Financial Member?

I should not make that exception there; I should make no exception there. The Viceroy is in charge of the Foreign Department, which has a large political area beyond the Indus, which causes very considerable expenditure.

3219. Unless the Viceroy throws his weight on the side of economy, the Financial Member stands quite alone?

Yes.

Sir David Barbour on the Weakness of Financial Check.

2224. I think I am right in saying that in many respects the Financial Member stands alone as against the whole of the other Members of Council, in respect that he is the one to furnish funds, and the others want to spend funds?

That is the case, of course; that is necessarily the case. The different departments want money, and he has to keep some check upon them, if he can.

2225. So that, though he may be stronger in his department individually as against any particular department, he is not strong enough to resist the whole of the Council?

He cannot resist the majority.

2226. And the general feeling is that he has got to provide the funds for the necessary requirements of the others, so that he finds himself rather in antagonism with the general feeling of the Council?

Of course he must have continual controversies going on as regards particular items of expenditure; that is inevitable.

2227. And therefore, supposing the Viceroy is inclined to some military operation, and the Military Member of the Council is not actively opposed to the Commander-in-Chief, there would be at once a very large majority against the Financial Member?

Oh, yes, of course.

2301. And in the whole arrangement of the Budget and of expenditure the Indians themselves have no voice whatever?

Of course they have no direct and immediate voice; but there is no doubt that the Government of India does pay a certain attention to public opinion in India; every Government does.

2302. But they have no direct voice in the matter? No direct voice as far as I can see.

Mr. D. E. Wacha on the Growth of Expenditure.

17,743. Looking at the evidence you have given us on the increase of expenditure generally, may I ask you whether you have arrived at any conclusions on the strength of the facts as stated, which you would like to place before us?

From the foregoing examination of the progress of expenditure, it will be evident to the Commission—

(1) That the financial embarrassments which prevailed during the decade owe their origin principally to the enormous growth of military expenditure, which has led to the imposition of additional taxation, which now amounts, including the customs duties on cotton goods, to nearly 6 crores [four millions sterling].

(2) That the growth in civil expenditure is also very considerable. But so far as this is concerned there is not much cause of complaint save in one respect, namely, that the costly foreign agency absorbs a large portion of the revenue which could be considerably saved if there was more extensive employment of Indians in the higher grades of the administration. It may be observed that adequate civil expenditure of a productive character is much to be desired. I mean such as gives the taxpayers a fair *quid pro quo*, such as education for the masses, more efficient administration of justice, greater village and town sanitation, and all other works of public utility which contribute to the expansion of provincial resources and prosperity of the people.

(3) That the burden or exchange might have easily been borne, without resort to fresh and enhanced taxation, had the military expenditure been on the basis of 1884–5.

(4) That a similar growth, if allowed to go unchecked

in future, is liable to plunge the Government into fresh embarrassments, leading to further taxation, which is neither desirable in the interests of good and stable government, nor in the interests of the people, among whom there prevails sullen discontent, inasmuch as their capacity to bear further burdens has been greatly crippled. The Secretary of State writes imperative despatches for strict economy, and for exercising utmost care in public expenditure, for the danger of increasing the burdens of taxation has to be borne in mind. (*Vide* Despatch of 12th April 1888, vol. ii., Appendix, p. 141; Despatch of 3rd November 1892, vol. ii., Appendix, p. 154.)

These warnings seem to fall on deaf ears, and Secretaries of State do not enforce what they enjoin, and the despatches only remain pious intentions. At any rate, the Commission must have noticed how, in spite of them, expenditure has grown apace. Since 1892 taxation to the extent of about 3 crores [two millions sterling] has been added, while the military activity beyond the frontiers was even greater in consequence of the acquisition of Gilgit, which ultimately led to the occupation of Chitral at a cost of 1½ crore [one million sterling], and with a permanent annual charge of 25 lakhs [£166,000]. The State Secretary himself is a silent or originating party to this kind of expenditure, so that it may be truly observed that the despatches are practically of no effect, and that both the Secretary of State and the Government of India must be held equally responsible for that expenditure.

It is a well-known fact that India has no true surplus to speak of. It lives at the best from hand to mouth and is oftener than not in a condition of embarrassment from which it relieves itself only by windfalls or borrowing or by enhanced taxation which every time that it is imposed diminishes the capacity of the taxpayer, whose income does not exceed Rs. 27 [36s.] per annum.

From 1849–50 to 1894–5 there has been a net deficit of 37.62 million Rs. [twenty-five millions sterling]. In other words, during the forty-six years, Indian ances have exhibited an annual deficit of Rs. 800,000 [£533,000] on an average. The most essential fact seems to have been invariably lost sight of, that India is made a poor country by the "bleeding" it has been subjected to, and can, therefore, have but a poor revenue. That a system of administration, however well-meaning, which takes no cognisance of this essential fact, but goes on adopting a western system of Government, a system of alien Government in which the people have no voice, and which is besides known to be costly, must in the long run end in financial disaster, however long it may be in coming in. I go further and say it is a system unnatural and foredoomed to failure. Under the circumstances Indians cannot but view with the gravest apprehension any further increase of expenditure.

Mr. G. K. Gokhale on the Exclusion of the People of India from High Office.

18,331. I think you were going to offer some observations on the services.

Yes. In every department of Indian expenditure the question of agency is one of paramount importance. According to a Parliamentary return of May 1892, we have in India in the higher branches of the civil and military departments a total of 2388 officers drawing Rs. 10,000 a year and upwards, of whom only sixty are Natives of India, and even these, with the exception of such as are Judges, stop at a comparatively low level. And they are thus divided. (See table on next page.)

In addition to these the railway companies employ 105 officers, drawing Rs. 10,000 a year and more. They are all Europeans, and their total salaries come to 16 lakhs 28 thousand rupees. If we come down to officers drawing between Rs. 5000 and Rs. 10,000 a year we find that we have 421 Natives in the civil department

	Natives.	Eurasians.	Europeans.	In Thousands of Rupees.		
				Total Salaries of Natives.	Total Salaries of Eurasians.	Total Salaries of Europeans.
Civil department	55	10	1211	947	151	25,274
Military	1	1	854	12	11	13,268
Public works . .	3	4	239	33	45	3,415
Incorporated local funds	1	...	9	10	...	113
	60	15	2313	1002	207	42,070

as against 1207 Europeans and 96 Eurasians. In the military department there are 25 Natives, as against 1699 Europeans and 22 Eurasians. In the public works department there are 85 Natives, as against 549 Europeans and 39 Eurasians. And in the incorporated local funds there are 4 Natives, as against 22 Europeans and 3 Eurasians. The total salaries of officers of this class are thus divided:—Civil Department: Natives, Rs. 2,905,000; Eurasians, Rs. 650,000; and Europeans, Rs. 8,830,000. In the Military Departments: Natives, Rs. 164,000; Eurasians, Rs. 139,000; and Europeans, Rs. 13,698,000. In the Public Works Department: Natives, Rs. 537,000; Eurasians, Rs. 278,000; and Europeans, Rs. 3,962,000. And in the Incorporated Local Funds: Natives, Rs. 25,000; Eurasians, Rs. 17,000; and Europeans, Rs. 146,000. In addition to these there are, under the railway companies, 258 officers of this class, of whom only 2 are Natives, 8 being Eurasians, and 248 Europeans. Their salaries are thus divided: Natives, Rs. 12,000; Eurasians, Rs. 50,000; and Europeans, Rs. 17,100,000. In England £125,360 is paid as salaries by the Indian Government, and £54,522 by railway companies, all to Europeans. The financial loss entailed by this practical monopoly by Europeans of the higher branches of the services in

India is not represented by salaries only. There are besides heavy pension and furlough charges, more than three and a half millions sterling being paid to Europeans in England for the purpose in 1890. The excessive costliness of the foreign agency is not, however, its only evil. There is a moral evil which, if anything, is even greater, A kind of dwarfing or stunting of the Indian race is going on under the present system. We must live all the days of our life in an atmosphere of inferiority, and the tallest of us must bend in order that the exigencies of the existing system may be satisfied.

Mr. G. Subramania Iyer on Control over Finance.

18,767. Perhaps you would run through them, would you?

Yes. Before proceeding to express my views on the subject of the system of provincial finance, which is an important wheel in our financial machinery, I shall point out my remedies thus far.

There can be no doubt that one way of strengthening the financial position of India would be, as Sir Auckland Colvin says: "In some way, without undue interference with the authority of the Government of India, to establish a control emanating from what theoretically is at present the last Court of Appeal, Parliament. A Committee of the Members of Parliament, such as Sir William Wedderburn has suggested, to scrutinise the financial statement every year and to submit a report to the House of Commons before the financial statement is brought up for discussion, would in some measure secure this end. The Committee would of course pay due attention to the opinions of the non-official Members expressed in the Legislative Council of the Viceroy." It came out fully in the evidence before the Commission that the present system, by which disputes regarding the apportionment of certain charges between the two Governments are kept up for years and finally decided to the satisfaction of neither party, should be put an end to. It has been suggested that the principles which should be the general basis of apportionment should be laid down in a Treasury Minute, and that the application of these principles to instances where the two Governments might not agree, should be left to an arbitrator, or a body of arbitrators, chosen by both the Governments. This suggestion commended itself to the Marquis of Ripon and the Marquis of Lansdowne. It would be a better system I think to rest the power of final decision in the Judicial Committee of the Privy Council. The Privy Council is a tribunal well known in India, and would command from the people greater confidence than any arbitrators chosen from time to time. I have already pointed out the importance of the Members of the Secretary of State's Council being men in touch with the actual financial conditions of the day in India. To secure this end the present system of appointing them for ten years, and keeping them on for a further period if the Secretary of State chooses, should be abolished. Their term of office should extend only to five years like the Members of the Government of India and the Provincial Governors, and they should not be eligible for re-appointment. Among the Members of the Council there should always be several Indians possessing necessary qualifications and not necessarily official. They should be appointed on the recommendation of the elected Members of the Legislative Councils. They would take care to put before the Secretary of State the Indian view, which he has no means of knowing under the existing system. Coming to the constitution of the Government of India in India, I have already pointed out the desirability of the Governor-General being divested of control over any particular department, so that he may have more time than he has at present to attend to internal affairs of the country, which unfortunately do not receive the same attention that they used to receive in years previous to 1885. The Members of the Governor-General's Legislative Council should be empowered to vote on the Budget, although any decision adverse to the Government of India may be overruled by the President. There should be given greater scope for interpellation, and whenever any measure of legislation affecting finance is in contemplation, the views of the public bodies should be obtained beforehand as far as possible.

MR. SURENDRA NATH BANERJEA ON THE WIDER EMPLOYMENT OF INDIANS.

19,320. You are going to proceed to give us your opinion on the growth of expenditure?

Yes. The question of the wider employment of the people of India in the public service of their own country is more or less a financial problem. The expenditure has gone on increasing, especially in the military department; and the Indian public opinion regards the growth of military expenditure as utterly beyond what the country can bear, and as seriously interfering with legitimate expenditure on the most necessary domestic improvements. The people of India who are capable of forming a judgment on the subject are at one with Sir H. Brackenbury in the opinion that the cost of the portion of the Indian Army, in excess of what is necessary for maintaining the internal peace of the country, should be met from the British Exchequer, and the expenses of the salaries of the European portion of the Army ought to be fairly apportioned between England and India. Until this is done, the resources of India will not be found equal for the purposes of good and progressive government, and no improvement is possible in the condition of the masses. By the wider employment of the people of India in the public service, economy would be introduced, and an impetus imparted to the intellectual and moral elevation of the people. Ten years ago the Public Service Commission, presided over by the late Sir Charles Atchison, at that time Lieutenant-Governor of the Punjab, and consisting of some of the most distinguished officials and non-official representatives of the day, reported upon the question of public employment in India. The gist of their recommendations may be summarised as follows: That indigenous agency should be more largely employed in the public service; that the recruitment of the official staff in England should be curtailed, and advantage taken of qualified agency obtainable in India. In other words, the provincial service, recruited in India, should be the backbone of the administrative agency, subject to European supervision and control. "Considerations of policy and economy alike require," observed the Commission in their Report, "that so far as is consistent with the ends of good government, the recruitment of the official staff in England should be curtailed, and advantage taken of qualified agency obtainable in India." As a matter of fact, however, the higher appointments in almost all branches of the public service are held by Europeans, although more than ten years have elapsed since the Commission submitted their Report.

CHAPTER XII

INDIAN CURRENCY COMMITTEE

THE continuous fall in the value of silver after 1870 was a matter of concern to the Indian Government. The fall was no loss to the people of India. The prices of the produce of the country, estimated in rupees, rose as the value of the rupee fell; and the export trade of India rather benefited than suffered by the depreciation of silver. The revenues of the Government also increased automatically in rupees as the rupee fell in value. The Settlement Officer raised the Land Revenue demand when he found rice and wheat selling at a higher price, estimated in rupees; the Local Cesses, assessed on the Rental or the Land Revenue, rose with the rise of rents and the revenue; and the Income Tax Assessor increased his assessments when he estimated the incomes of traders and merchants at a larger number of rupees. Officials could demand some increase in their salaries in rupees as the rupee fell; European Officials in India did eventually obtain a compensation in an invidious and objectionable shape; Indian Officials failed to get an adequate increase to their humble salaries. So far as the financial administration and the monetary transactions of India were concerned, the fall in the value of silver, as compared with gold, created no difficulties, and caused no inconvenience.

But the Government of India had to remit large sums of money annually to England in gold for the Home Charges, and this remittance in gold meant an increasing amount in silver as the silver fell in value. This the Government of India considered an additional tax on

India. And instead of suggesting a reduction of the Home Charges, they proposed to artificially raise the value of the rupee, which meant a real and universal increase of taxation in India.

The fall of the rupee during the first eight years after 1870 came to be $3\frac{1}{2}$d., as shown in the following figures :—

Value of the Rupee.

	d.
1871–72	$23\frac{1}{8}$.
1872–73	$22\frac{3}{4}$.
1873–74	$22\frac{3}{8}$.
1874–75	$22\frac{1}{8}$.
1875–76	$21\frac{5}{8}$.
1876–77	$20\frac{1}{2}$.
1877–78	$20\frac{3}{4}$.
1878–79	$19\frac{3}{4}$.

In 1876, the Calcutta Chamber of Commerce strongly urged the Government of India to suspend the coinage of silver in order to stop the fall in the rupee; but the Government of India declared that the circumstances did not justify any action in relation to the Indian currency.[1]

In November 1878, when Lord Lytton was on the eve of a war with Afghanistan, he addressed the Secretary of State again on the subject, and proposed some steps for raising the value of the rupee by limiting its coinage.[2] He submitted a Draft Bill, and proposed that the Coinage Act should be modified.

The Despatch was forwarded by Lord Cranbrook, Secretary of State for India, to Sir Stafford Northcote, Chancellor of the Exchequer. And it was ultimately referred to a Committee consisting of Sir Louis Mallet, Mr. Stanhope, M.P., Sir Thomas Seccombe, Mr. Farrer, Mr. Welby, Mr. Griffin, and Mr. Arthur Balfour, M.P. These gentlemen reported on April 30, 1879, that, "having examined the proposals contained in the Despatch, they are unanimously of opinion that they

[1] Financial Despatch to the Secretary of State for India, dated October 13, 1876.

[2] Despatch, dated November 9, 1878.

could not recommend them for the sanction of her Majesty's Government."

Subsequently, on November 24, 1879, the Lords of the Treasury replied in detail to the proposals of Lord Lytton. Some portions of this able and exhaustive reply should be quoted:—

"It has not yet been established whether the variation in the relation between gold and silver may not have been caused by appreciation of the former metal as well as by depreciation of the latter, or by a combination of both."

"It appears to my Lords that the Government of India, in making the present proposal, lay themselves open to the same criticisms as are made upon Governments which have depreciated their currencies. In general, the object of such Governments has been to diminish the amount they have to pay their creditors. In the present case the *object of the Indian Government appears to be to increase the amount they have to receive from their taxpayers.* My Lords fail to see any real difference in the character of the two transactions."

"If, on the other hand, it is the case that the value of the rupee has fallen in India, and that it will be raised in India by the operation of the proposed plan, that plan is open to the objection that it alters every contract and every fixed payment in India."

"If the present state of exchange be due to the depreciation of silver, the Government scheme, if it succeeds, may relieve:—

"(1) The Indian Government from the inconvenience of a nominal readjustment of taxation in order to meet the loss by exchange on the home remittances;

"(2) Civil servants and other Englishmen who are serving or working in India, and who desire to remit money to England;

"(3) Englishmen who have money placed or invested in India, which they wish to remit to England."

"But this relief will be given *at the expense of the Indian taxpayer, and with the effect of increasing every debt or fixed payment in India, including debts due by Ryots to money-lenders;* while its effect will be materially qualified, so far as the Government are concerned, by the enhancement of the public obligations in India, which have been contracted on a silver basis."[1]

This letter from the Treasury, in reply to the Indian Government's proposals, settled the question for the time, and it was not raised again for six years. The fall of the rupee during these six years was very slight, and is shown in the following figures:—

Value of the Rupee.

	d.
1879–80	20.
1880–81	20.
1881–82	$19\frac{7}{8}$.
1882–83	$19\frac{1}{2}$.
1883–84	$19\frac{1}{2}$.
1884–85	$19\frac{5}{16}$.

It will thus be seen that between 1878–79 and 1884–85, covering the last two years of Lord Lytton's and the whole of Lord Ripon's administration, the rupee fell only from $19\frac{3}{4}$ to $19\frac{5}{16}$. But early in 1886 there was a fall in the price of silver; and Lord Dufferin, then Viceroy of India, sent an alarming telegram to the Secretary of State. "Our financial arrangements for meeting interest on loans for frontier railways, defences, and increased military expenditure have been based on the assumption that the rupee would not fall below eighteenpence. Recent fall in the price of silver, and the uncertainty regarding policy of United States of America, cause us grave anxiety. . . . We earnestly commend the question to the early consideration of her Majesty's Government. Experience seems incontestably

[1] The italics are our own. The "nominal readjustment of taxation" referred to in the last portion of the extracts would not have been needed, as the taxation adjusted itself automatically in reference to Land Revenue and other sources of revenue, as stated before.

to have shown that delay seriously aggravates the difficulties of settlement."[1]

This was followed by a letter,[2] in which Lord Dufferin and the members of his Council stated that the fall in the price of the rupee was due to speculation regarding the repeal or modification of the Bland Act in America; that an attempt should be made to secure a stable relation between the rupee and gold; and that "the present time would appear to be a favourable one for reopening the whole question." The Indian Government did not inquire how far the additional military expenditure referred to in their telegram, and the consequent increase in India's remittances to England, had helped to affect the exchange against India. Nor did they venture to suggest that the plainest remedy for the growing evil was a bold and determined reduction of the Home Charges, which had to be paid in gold.

Lord Randolph Churchill, then Secretary of State for India, forwarded both the telegram and the letter to the Treasury; and, once more, the Lords of the Treasury rejected the proposal of the Indian Government. They referred to the declaration recorded by Mr. Goschen, Mr. Gibbs, and Sir Thomas Seccombe, as the representatives of her Majesty's Government at the International Monetary Conference of 1878, that "the establishment of a fixed ratio between gold and silver was utterly impracticable." And they declared that the proposals of the Indian Government would be a benefit to English officers in India at the cost of the Indian taxpayer, as had been pointed out by Sir Stafford Northcote more than six years before.

"The Treasury find no reason stated in the despatch of the Government of India in the present year which induces them to dissent from the conclusions thus sent for on the authority of Sir Stafford Northcote as to the

[1] Telegram dated January 12, 1886.
[2] Dated February 6, 1886.

results of any attempt artificially to enhance the gold value of silver."

"Whilst it is admitted that some benefit might be derived by the European officers of our Government from the proposed measures, it is shown how injurious would be their effect upon the Indian taxpayer. Since that time the great stimulus which the fall in the value of silver is believed to have given to the export trade of Hindustan, *and the great addition which has accrued to the commercial wealth and the industries of the people*, reinforce the warning then given against rashly meddling with a condition of things which may well have brought to the people of India more of advantage than of loss. It is impossible to regard this question from the point of view either of the Indian exchequer or of the Anglo-Indian official without a corresponding regard to the general effect of the fall in the gold price of silver upon the trade and prosperity of the great mass of the population."[1]

No further action was taken by the Indian Government for some years after receipt of this reply from the Treasury. But the rupee rapidly fell in value, and it was never inquired how far this fall was caused by the continuous increase in the military expenditure and consequently in the annual drain from India, under the administration of Lord Lansdowne and Lord Elgin. The fall of the rupee during eight years from 1885–86 to 1893–94 is shown in the following figures:—

Value of the Rupee.

	d.
1885–86	18.2.
1886–87	17.4.
1887–88	16.8.
1888–89	16.3.
1889–90	16.5.
1890–91	18.0.
1891–92	16.7.
1892–93	14.9.
1893–94	14.5.

[1] Treasury to India Office, dated May 31, 1886. The italics are our own. The Treasury accepted the general belief that the fall of the rupee was rather to the advantage of Indian manufactures.

The continuous fall of the rupee induced the British Government to depart from the policy it had so long and so justly maintained on behalf of the Indian taxpayer and the Indian industries. The International Conference of Brussels in 1892 produced no change in the situation. It was considered likely that the United States would repeal the clauses of the Sherman Act, which provided for the annual purchase of fifty-four million ounces of silver. The question of the Indian currency was therefore referred to a Committee under the presidency of Lord Herschell, then Lord Chancellor. Lord Herschell's Committee reported in May 1893 in favour of closing the Indian mints, with a proviso that the Indian Government should undertake to issue rupees in exchange for gold at the rate of 16d. per rupee, and should receive British sovereigns in payment of Government dues.

An Act was accordingly passed in India in June 1893, and a notification was issued. A rise in the value of the rupee followed in the succeeding years, as the following figures will show:—

Value of the Rupee.

	d.
1894-95	13.1.
1895-96	13.6.
1896-97	14.4.
1897-98	15.3.
1898-99	16.0.

When the rupee had been brought up nearly to the value suggested by the Herschell Committee, the Government of India asked the Secretary of State, Lord George Hamilton, for measures to fix the rupee at that value.

Lord George Hamilton formed a Committee in 1898, and appointed Sir Henry Fowler as the Chairman. The object of the Committee was not to discuss the policy of raising the value of the rupee to 16d. That policy had already been accepted and acted upon. Sir Henry Fowler was himself the Secretary of State for India in 1894 and 1895, when the Indian mints remained closed, and the rupee began to rise. He was not likely to question that policy now. And the instructions of his Committee were not to reopen a discussion on the policy, but to report "whether the object the Government of India have in view can best be attained by the measures which they suggest."[1] Nevertheless, a great deal of evidence was recorded by Sir Henry Fowler's Committee as to the expediency, in the interests of the people of India, of fixing the rupee at the enhanced value of 16d. Reference to some portions of the evidence recorded will be made further on. Sir Henry Fowler and his Committee submitted their report in 1899. They recommended that the British sovereign should be declared a legal tender at the rate of 1s. 4d. per rupee. And they also recommended that the Indian Government, without undertaking to give gold for rupees at that rate, should make a gold reserve, to make it available for foreign remittances when a fall of exchange made such help necessary. An Act, making British sovereigns legal tender in India, was accordingly passed in 1899. There has been a flow of gold since into the Indian treasury and currency reserves. The amount of gold so held in April 1899 was two millions sterling; by March 1900 it had risen to seven millions. The effect of these measures on the revenues and taxation of India will be discussed in the next chapter.

The evidence recorded by Sir Henry Fowler's Committee in 1898 and 1899 fill nearly six hundred folio pages, double column. Anglo-Indian officials of high distinction and great administrative experience expressed their opinions clearly and emphatically; but one thing they did not do—they never suggested the possibility of reducing the Home Charges which had created all the difficulty. They accepted these charges as absolutely unavoidable; they were strongly against the open increase of taxation in India; and they therefore recommended

[1] Letter from the Secretary of State to Sir Henry Fowler, dated April 29, 1898.

that the rupee should be maintained at its enhanced value. Sir Antony Macdonnell's evidence fairly represents this opinion; and the following extract will explain his views.

Sir Antony Macdonnell's Evidence.

5778. Suppose now that the mints were reopened and the exchange value of the rupee fell to, say, 1s., would that at all affect your revenue?

Of course it would affect us in this way, that more revenue would have to be raised to meet the Home Charges.

5779. You mean by increased taxation?

Yes.

5780. Will you give us your opinion as to the economic effect of attempting to increase the taxation in India?

I suppose if the rupee fell to 1s. you would have, in order to make both ends meet, to raise ten or twelve crores of rupees or thereabouts. I say that it would be impossible to do that without producing such political discontent as would be an extreme cause of danger.

On the other hand, Sir Robert Giffin's evidence fairly represents the opinion of British economists. He condemned an artificial currency for India, and considered no currency good for any country which was not automatic. And he grappled with the difficulty of the Home Charges by boldly suggesting a reduction of those charges.

Sir Robert Giffin's Evidence.

10,082. The last point I shall mention with reference to this question of finance is that there is reason for suggesting in all the circumstances that the whole question of Indian expenditure should itself be reviewed.

The statements I have seen are confined almost exclusively to the question whether more taxes can be imposed in India or not, but in financial questions, the other side of the matter should be looked at also. It may be the case, and I fear it is the case, that the Imperial Government unfairly charges a great amount of expenditure to India which ought rather to be borne by the empire in general. The army in India is maintained not exclusively for the advantage of the Indian people, but also for the general benefit of the British Empire. It may then be possible to make the deficit in India more manageable than has been represented, and thus avert the supposed necessity of altering the money of India. That is perhaps trenching upon the domain of politics very much, and as we all know there has been a Royal Commission sitting for some time under the chairmanship of Lord Welby, dealing with the question of what ought to be charged to India, and what ought not to be charged in respect of military and other expenditure; but I should like to put very strongly the impression which I have formed that in this matter India substantially is not dealt with in a fair manner, and that something ought to be allowed for the advantage which the empire in general gets from the existence of the European army in India, which is not exclusively for the benefit of the Indian people. I should say that from three millions to four millions sterling is the idea that I have formed as to what ought to be deducted from the permanent charge upon India. This, then, is the main ground—*i.e.* the want of proof as to deficit—upon which I take the objection to the alteration of money in India; and, of course, there remain all the objections to the nature of that alteration itself.

Only two Indian witnesses were examined, *i.e.* Mr. Merwanji Rustomji, representing the Exchange Brokers' Association of Bombay, and the present writer, representing Bengal. Both these witnesses were against fixing the value of the rupee at the enhanced value of 16d. Mr. Rustomji recommended the rupee to be fixed at 14d., which had been its approximate value in 1893, before the mints were closed. And the present writer recommended that the value of the rupee should not be artificially fixed at all. Our readers will pardon our giving some extracts from the evidence of these two witnesses, representing the Indian opinion.

Mr. Merwanji Rustomji's Evidence.

9746. Why do you advocate 1s. 2d. as against the 1s. 4d. rate?

I advocate it on the principle that you are going for a gold standard, and I would impress upon you that it is advisable from many points of view. In the first place, take the mill industry, that is an important matter, and take the other trades in which India competes with China.—

9747. Your principal reason is that you think that a 1s. 2d. rate will be better for Indian trade?

I am taking the Indian mills, and trade carried on in competition with China.

9748. Do you think that the 1s. 2d. rate will materially lessen the competition with China, if China really begins to make railways, and so on?

What I say is, we shall be able to lay down our yarn cheaper than now.

9749. Permanently, or for a time only?

In comparison with the 1s. 4d. rupee, we shall lay down always cheaper.

Mr. Romesh C. Dutt's Evidence.

10,643. Did the proposals of the Government of India to arrest the fall of the rupee have the effect of raising its value?

Yes, I think it was 1s. 2d., if I remember rightly, in 1893, and it is now nearly 1s. 4d., so that within these last five years the value of the rupee has been enhanced by 2d. as compared with gold. With regard to the fall from 1871 to 1893 I may be allowed to explain that the Indian Government and Provincial Governments got a natural increase in their revenue in consequence of the fall. The Land Revenue and other revenues went up in this way. The price in rupees rose all round; the price of food grains rose; and as the Government in its recurring Settlements made that a ground of enhancement—because the Government as [superior] landlord is entitled to an increase if the price of the produce rises—there was a natural increase in Land Revenue. Then, also, with regard to the Income Tax; as the incomes, estimated in rupees, went up, the Government got an increase of the Income Tax. So that while there was a fall in the value of the rupee from 1871 to 1893, the Government was directly, and in a natural way, getting an increase in the revenues as estimated by the rupee.

10,661. Your first objection [to the artificial raising of the rupee] is that practically this means a general increase in taxation.

Yes, over and above the natural increase.

10,674. Then you say there is another and a still graver objection to the proposal. Will you explain that?

Millions of agriculturists and labourers in India are indebted to money-lenders and Mahajans; and the debt is, in many cases, reckoned in rupees and not in grain. To artificially enhance the value of the rupee, or to fix the value at the rate to which it has been already artificially raised, is to increase the indebtedness of the cultivators and labourers of India to money-lenders and Mahajans. The measure serves to add to the profits of the prosperous classes who feed on the distresses of the poor, and to add to the weight of the millstone which the poor and indebted classes carry round their necks. Throughout the bazaars and money-markets of India, the effect of raising the value of the rupee is to add to the profits of the rich money-lender, and to enhance the liabilities of the poor cultivator who has a debt.

10,692. Now, will you come to the matter of trinkets?

All that the poor people in India can possibly save in years of good harvest is saved, not in savings banks, which do not exist in India for the poor, but in silver jewellery and trinkets for their women. Practically, all the spare wealth which the cultivating and labouring classes have in India is in this form; and in years of scarcity and famine all this silver, or a great part of it, is sold in the affected districts in order to procure food grains. The proposal of the Government of India is virtually one to confiscate about a third of the poor man's savings in India. The value of the rupee being artificially raised, the silver bangle or bracelet in which the cultivator has invested all his savings, sells for less than what it costs; and thus by a stroke of the pen the Government of India reduces what is really the national wealth of the poor in India in order to meet its own liabilities on somewhat easier terms.

10,707. Then, will you tell us how you think these proposals have an effect on the manufactures of India?

On that point I should premise that my information is second hand, because I am not personally engaged in manufacture or trade. But I have consulted men engaged in trade, and they tell me that the raising of the value of the rupee artificially dislocates trade, and has injured manufacture. I have heard from merchants engaged in Bombay in the cotton industry, that the cotton industry is in a miserable state just now, specially in competition with the produce from China and Japan, and they impute that directly or indirectly to the closing of the mints.

British trade is prospering with other Asiatic countries having silver currencies; why should British traders demand, in the case of India, a fixed ratio between gold and silver, which they cannot demand from other Asiatic countries? The people of India do not ask for it; the people of India will not profit by it; the people of India are likely to lose in a variety of ways, as indicated above, by the artificial raising of the value of the rupee. And the Government of India, naturally representing the people, and standing forward as the protectors of their welfare, should reject a scheme which the people do not want, and cannot profit by.

10,710. You say: "The proposal of the Government of India is not the natural or the proper remedy for that increasing drain which is annually flowing from India to England, in the shape of pay, pensions, and allowances"?

The allowances are paid in England in gold, and instead of reducing its gold obligations, which is the natural and the proper remedy, the Government seeks to adopt the unnatural and desperate and dangerous remedy of converting all its remedies in India into gold. Let us suppose the case of an Indian landlord who gets his rents from his estate in rupees, and has to pay an agent in London in gold. What would Courts of Justice and Equity think if the landlord preferred suits to realise his Indian rents in gold, on the ground that he has to pay one London agent in gold? His prudent and proper course would be to minimise his London expense.

CHAPTER XIII

FINANCE AND THE INDIAN DEBT

"Two conflicting policies prevailed in India," said Sir Charles Trevelyan in 1873, in his evidence before the Select Committee on Indian Finance. "One, the policy advocated by me, of *reduction of expenditure*; the other, which was the favourite at Calcutta and in England, *increase of taxation*."

After the retirement of Lord Northbrook from India, and of the able and sympathetic Finance Minister, Sir William Muir, in 1876, the policy of increase of taxation prevailed unchecked. The Madras famine of 1877 did not lead Lord Lytton to a reduction of expenditure and a reduction of taxes. On the contrary, under the advice of his new Finance Minister, Sir John Strachey, he imposed new taxes to create a Famine Relief and Insurance Fund. "The simple object was, in fact, to provide so far as possible an annual surplus of one and a half crores, for famine relief in famine insurance expenditure. To the extent to which, in any year, the amount was not spent on relief, it was to be spent solely on reduction of debt, or rather upon avoidance of debt, which is the same thing."[1] And a pledge was given to the people of India that the proceeds of the taxes would not be expended for any purpose other than that for which they were imposed.

The pledge was broken soon after it was given. In the budget of 1878-79 the grant was made; but in the budget of 1879-80 it was suspended. The famine insurance taxes continued to be levied; but the grant

[1] Report of the Famine Commission of 1898, p. 324.

for famine relief and insurance disappeared. There was a strong protest from the public in India. The Finance Minister, Sir John Strachey, argued that whether the public accounts showed surplus, equilibrium, or deficit, the new taxes must prevent debts by the amount they yielded, and therefore fulfilled the conditions under which they were imposed. The public in India considered this argument a disingenuous evasion of a specific pledge. The Secretary of the State for India himself took exception to Sir John Strachey's argument. It was decided in 1881 that the full grant of 1½ crores of rupees should in future be entered in the budget under the head of Famine Relief and Insurance, with sub-heads for (1) Relief, (2) Protective Works, and (3) Reduction of Debt.

Thus "the original policy of devoting the whole of the grant, less actual cost of famine relief, to reduction or avoidance of debt had been changed by the acceptance of the view that a large part of the grant might be better applied to what are called Famine Protective, as distinct from Productive, Public Works."[1]

But even this new and modified purpose of the Famine Grant was not scrupulously adhered to. In the fifteen years ending with 1895-6, the Famine Grant of 1½ crores, or one million sterling a year, would be fifteen millions sterling. But the expenditure in Famine Relief, Protective Works, and Reduction of Debt was less than ten millions sterling, as shown in the following figures.

1881-82 to 1896-97.	
	£
Famine Relief	213,571
Protective Railways	4,367,287
Protective Irrigation Works	1,209,207
Reduction or Avoidance of Debt	3,551,533
Total	9,341,598

[1] Report of the Famine Commission of 1898, p. 325.

"Avoidance of Debt" is an ambiguous term. Nothing but positive "Reduction of Debt" should be shown under the last head. But taking the figures as they are given, the total expenditure fell short of the stipulated Famine Grant by over five and a half millions sterling. The Indian Debt should have been reduced by that amount. Instead of that the loss incurred on the Bengal Nagpur and Midland Railways, amounting to £2,389,397 in the fifteen years, was shown as expenditure from the Famine Relief and Insurance Grant.

Then followed six years of almost continuous famines, and famine relief expenditure largely increased. The total expenditure for the twenty-one years, therefore, from 1881-82 to 1901-02 exceeds the total stipulated grant by a million sterling, as shown in the following figures:—

1881-82 to 1901-92.	£
Famine Relief	11,906,358
Protective Railways	4,827,522
Protective Irrigation Works . . .	1,398,955
Reduction or Avoidance of Debt . .	4,132,996
Total	22,265,831

We have excluded the loss on the Bengal Magpur and Midland Railways, which, in these twenty-one years, amounted to £3,280,334. It should be noted that recent famine relief expenditure has increased the liabilities of India; the original purpose of the famine relief taxes, to keep down such liabilities by reducing the debt in ordinary years, has not been fulfilled.

The total revenues of India, including the Land Revenue, and the total expenditure, including the Home Charges, during twenty-five years, are shown in the following table, compiled from *Statistical Abstracts*:—

Year.	Land Revenue.	Gross Revenue and Receipts.	Expenditure in England.	Gross Expenditure charged against Revenue.
	Tens of Rupees.	Tens of Rupees.	Tens of Rupees.	Tens of Rupees.
1877–78	19,891,145	61,972,481	16,202,016	66,234,521
1878–79	22,323,868	65,194,020	16,794,424	63,059,922
1879–80	21,861,150	68,433,157	17,486,144	69,661,050
1880–81	21,112,995	74,290,112	17,340,712	77,921,506
1881–82	21,948,022	75,684,987	17,369,631	72,089,536
1882–83	21,876,047	70,278,337	17,335,995	69,603,500
1883–84	22,361,899	71,841,790	18,464,752	69,692,313
1884–85	21,832,211	70,690,681	17,527,406	71,077,127
1885–86	22,592,371	74,464,197	18,426,170	77,265,923
1886–87	23,055,724	77,337,134	19,829,035	77,158,707
1887–88	23,189,292	78,759,744	21,855,698	80,788,576
1888–89	23,016,404	81,696,678	21,954,657	81,659,660
1889–90	23,981,399	85,085,203	21,512,365	82,473,170
1890–91	24,045,209	85,741,649	20,656,019	82,053,478
1891–92	23,965,774	89,143,283	22,911,912	88,675,748
1892–93	24,905,328	90,172,438	26,161,815	91,005,850
1893–94	25,589,609	90,565,214	26,112,111	92,112,212
1894–95	25,408,272	95,187,429	28,775,648	94,494,319
1895–96	26,200,955	98,370,167	27,458,338	96,836,169
1896–97	23,974,489	94,129,741	26,234,255	95,834,763
1897–98	25,683,642	96,442,004	25,319,824	101,801,215
1898–99	27,459,313	101,426,693	24,487,765	97,465,383
1899–1900	25,807,584	102,955,746	24,589,269	98,793,811
1900–01	26,254,546	112,908,436	25,801,435	110,403,130
1901–02	27,432,027	114,516,788	26,052,983	107,091,423

We shall confine ourselves to the figures of the last five years to trace the exact results of the artificial appreciation of the rupee. The rupee had been raised to slightly over 15d. in 1897–98, and to 16d. in 1898–99, at which figure its value has been fixed. We show below the total revenues and the total expenditure of India for these five years in pounds sterling for the convenience of British readers.

	1897–98.	1898–99.	1899–1900.	1900–01.	1901–02.
	£	£	£	£	£
Total revenues.	64,257,207	67,595,815	68,637,164	75,272,291	76,344,525
Total expenditure	67,830,014	64,954,942	65,862,541	73,602,087	71,394,282

These figures disclose the startling fact that taxation in India has been increased by 12 millions sterling in five years mainly by the artificial raising of the value of the rupee. This was precisely the result which was foreseen by the Treasury in 1879, when the Lords of the Treasury condemned in explicit terms the object of the Indian Government "to increase the amount they have to receive from their taxpayers" by increasing the rupee. It was "a benefit to English officers in India at the cost of the Indian taxpayer," which the Treasury had again foreseen and condemned in 1886. It was a result which was foreseen and deprecated by several witnesses before the Currency Committee in 1899, including the present writer, when he pointed out that the artificial raising of the rupee "means a general increase in taxation." And this result was deplored by the Hon. Mr. Gokhale from his place in the Governor-General's Council in March 1902; he condemned, in an able and luminous speech, the continuous raising of the revenue when the country was suffering from prolonged famines and distress unexampled in the previous history of British India.

This policy of fixing the value of the rupee at 16d. has now been permanently accepted; it is not likely to be departed from again. But the people of India may fairly claim relief from those additional taxes which were imposed on them before the value of the rupee was raised. It is a common saying that you cannot burn the candle at both ends. And, as the Government of India have decided to add to the taxation of the country by appreciating the rupee, it is not just or equitable to maintain those added taxes which were imposed before this step was taken. The Indian Budget now shows a surplus, year after year, in spite of the extreme poverty of the people; it is possible to relieve that poverty to some extent by withdrawing those taxes which tell severely on the earnings of the nation.

Nothing presses so severely on an agricultural nation

as the numerous Cesses which have been imposed on the land, in addition to the Land Revenue, since 1871. The time and the occasion have come for their repeal. "The question presents itself," Lord Curzon himself has declared, "whether it is not better, as opportunities occur, to mitigate those imposts which are made to press upon the cultivating classes more severely than the law intended."[1] It will be a real and much-needed relief to the cultivators of India, after years of famine and suffering, if these imposts be now repealed, and the Land Tax be rigidly confined to the limits prescribed by Lord Dalhousie in 1855, and Sir Charles Wood in 1864 —*one-half the rental on the economic rent.*

The Famine Relief and Insurance taxes have also taken the form of additional imposts on the land. To keep these taxes is only to add to the poverty of the people, and the severity of the famines; to repeal them would be to give the agricultural population some relief. For the best insurance against famines is to permanently improve the condition of the cultivators, and to secure them against a multitude of imposts upon the land already severely taxed for the Land Revenue.

Lastly, the Salt Tax might be still further reduced. And the Excise imposed on the manufacture of cotton mills calls loudly for repeal. It is not a tax which the British Government in India can justly maintain on Indian manufactures, when the British Government at home are seeking by every means in their power to encourage and help home manufacture against foreign competition.

It has too often been the case in India that a handsome surplus in the budget has been succeeded by some needless and expensive war on the frontiers. It has also happened that such surplus has been swept away by larger demands from the Imperial Exchequer or the

[1] Resolution on the Land Revenue Policy of the Indian Government, dated January 16, 1902.

British manufacturer. As soon as the Indian budget showed a surplus under the new currency policy such demands were made. A sum of £786,000 has already been swept away, against the protests of Lord Curzon, for the increased cost of the recruitment of the British Army. Another demand of £400,000 was made for the maintenance of an army in South Africa, and was only given up when officials and the public, in England and in India, combined in a vehement protest. Lancashire manufacturers have once more referred to the Indian surplus, and demanded the repeal of the 3½ per cent. import duty on cotton goods. Complications on the Tibet frontier are arising which create a just alarm that the Indian surplus may end in ambitious and useless military expeditions. The Persian Gulf question also looms in the distance.

All this is perfectly intelligible under the present constitution of the Indian Government. Every great interest, every section of British subjects, can bring pressure to bear on the Indian Government—except only the people of India. The British Cabinet can press its demands through the Secretary of State for India, who is a member of that cabinet. British manufacturers can use their votes and work through their representatives in the House of Commons, to demand and obtain concessions. And military men have an influence in the Viceroy's council which never ceases to operate. By an irony of fate the only section which has no representation, no voice, no influence in the Indian administration is the people of India. And thus a surplus in the Indian budget, obtained by increase of taxation, is swept away, time after time, without giving the people any relief. The danger at the present moment (1903) is great, the large surplus will not appear much longer. The Indian nation expects and hopes that it will not disappear without giving some real, tangible, and substantial relief to the famine-stricken and unrepresented cultivators of India.

The total debt of India the last twenty-five years is shown in the two tables given below. In the first table the Indian Debt is shown in tens of rupees. In the second table it is converted into pounds sterling as shown in recent numbers of the *Statistical Abstract.*

Year.	Permanent and Unfunded Indian Debt.	Debt in England.
	Tens of Rupees.	£
1877–78	82,783,277	59,677,033
1878–79	86,877,821	59,029,117
1879–80	91,506,846	68,855,556
1880–81	95,782,357	71,429,133
1881–82	98,784,414	68,141,947
1882–83	100,651,862	68,585,694
1883–84	103,503,456	68,108,837
1884–85	104,450,406	69,271,088
1885–86	100,717,480	73,806,621
1886–87	101,442,979	84,228,177
1887–88	107,806,795	84,140,148
1888–89	111,585,949	95,033,610
1889–90	113,437,052	98,192,391

Year.	Permanent and Unfunded Indian Debt.	Debt in England.	Total.
	£	£	£
1890–91	78,416,801	104,408,208	182,825,009
1891–92	79,229,246	107,404,143	186,633,389
1892–93	80,214,413	106,683,767	186,898,180
1893–94	82,545,516	114,113,792	196,659,308
1894–95	81,836,145	116,005,826	197,841,971
1895–96	82,076,049	115,903,732	197,979,781
1896–97	85,158,840	114,883,233	200,042,073
1897–98	86,766,193	123,274,680	210,040,873
1898–99	87,828,906	124,268,605	212,097,511
1899–1900	88,023,665	124,144,401	212,168,066
1900–01	90,407,865	133,435,379	223,843,244
1901–02	91,925,015	134,307,090	226,232,105

There is need for the creation of a sinking fund to reduce this debt in years of peace. There is need for the co-operation of representative Indians in reducing debt and expenditure. There is need for introducing a popular element in the financial administration of India. The Governor-General's Council consists of able, experienced, and conscientious men, but they represent, nearly all of them, spending departments. They feel the needs of their departments, they urge additional expenditure; there is no counter-influence making for retrenchment. Retrenchment is not possible in India, or in any other country in the world, unless the taxpayers have some voice in the national expenditure.

In no department of the Indian administration are representative Indians better qualified to take a share than in the department of Revenue and Finance. They see and they feel the operation of the Land Tax and of every other tax. They live among their agricultural countrymen, know their troubles and their difficulties, and can voice their wishes and their views. They have a strong and almost a personal interest in effecting retrenchment. They have an inherited and traditional aptitude, excelled by no nation on earth, for accounts and finance. Their entire exclusion from the control of administration has not been attended with happy results. In no department has Indian administration been less successful—owing to this very exclusion of popular influence—than in revenue and finance.

A Finance and Revenue Board, including some Indian members elected by the Legislative Councils of the larger Provinces, could materially help the Finance Member and the Home Member of the Governor-General's Council in their arduous and difficult work. And the admission of some qualified Indians, appointed by the Government, to the Councils of the Secretary of State and the Governor-General would make the administration better informed and more in touch with the interests of the people. All British interests, all sections of the British community, have influence on the Indian administration. It is just, and it is expedient that the Indian people should have some voice and some share in that administration which concerns them more than any other class of people. In the absence of this popular element in the Indian administration, all the influences at work make for increased taxation and increased expenditure, and for the sacrifice of Indian revenues on objects which are not purely Indian; no influences are at work which make directly for reduction in expenditure and taxes, and for relieving the burdens of our unrepresented population. The evidence of distinguished Englishmen, given before the Expenditure Commission, and quoted in a previous chapter, proves how Indian money is often spent. The facts which we shall lay before our readers in the next chapter will show how such expenditure affects the material condition of the Indian people.

CHAPTER XIV

INDIA IN THE TWENTIETH CENTURY

WE propose in this concluding chapter to place before our readers some figures relating to India at the commencement of a new century. The figures have been compiled from the last published number of the *Statistical Abstract*, issued in the present year, 1903.

The *Area and Population* of India, according to the Census of 1901, are shown in the following tables.

British India.

Provinces.	Area in sq. miles.	Population.
1. Ajmir-Merwara	2,711	476,912
2. Andamans and Nicobars	3,188	24,649
3. Assam	56,243	6,126,343
4. Beluchistan	45,804	308,246
5. Bengal	151,185	74,744,866
6. Berar and Central Provinces	104,169	12,630,662
7. Bombay (including Aden)	123,064	18,559,561
8. Burma	236,738	10,490,624
9. Coorg	1,582	180,607
10. Madras	141,726	38,209,436
11. N.-W. Frontier Province	16,466	2,125,480
12. Punjab	97,209	20,330,339
13. Agra and Oudh	107,164	47,691,782
Total	1,087,249	231,899,507

Revenues and Expenditure.—The gross revenues of British India in 1901–2 amounted to £76,344,526. Deducting Railway and Irrigation Receipts, the nett revenues of British India were £53,580,985, or in round numbers 53½ millions sterling. The population of British

Native States in India.

States and Agencies.	Area in sq. miles.	Population.
1. Beluchistan Agency . . .	86,511	502,500
2. Baroda State	8,099	1,952,692
3. Bengal States	38,652	3,748,544
4. Bombay States	65,761	6,908,648
5. Central India Agency . .	78,772	8,628,781
6. Central Province States . .	29,435	1,996,383
7. Hyderabad State	82,698	11,141,142
8. Kashmir State	80,900	2,905,578
9. Madras States	9,969	4,188,086
10. Mysore State	29,444	5,539,399
11. Punjab States	36,532	4,424,398
12. Rajputana Agency	127,541	9,723,301
13. Agra and Oudh States . .	5,079	802,097
Total	679,393	62,461,549

India being under 232 milions, the taxation per head of population is very nearly 4s. 8d. per head.

The income of the people of India, per head, was estimated by Lord Cromer and Sir David Barbour in 1882 to be 27 rupees. Their present income is estimated by Lord Curzon at 30 rupees. Exception has been taken to both these estimates as being too high; but we shall accept them for our present calculation. 30 rupees are equivalent to 40 shillings; and the economic condition of the country can be judged from the fact that the average income of the people of all classes, including the richest, is 40 shillings a year against £42 a year in the United Kingdom. A tax of 4s. 8d. on 40 shillings is a tax of 2s. 4d. on the pound. This is a crushing burden on a nation which earns very little more than its food. In the United Kingdom, with its heavy taxation of £144,000,000 (excluding the cost of the late war), the incidence of the tax per head of a population of 42 millions is less than £3 10s. The proportion of this tax on the earnings of each individual inhabitant (£42) is only 1s. 8d. in the pound. The Indian taxpayer, who earns little more than his food, is taxed 40 per cent. more than the taxpayer of Great Britain and Ireland.

The total expenditure for 1901–2 charged against Revenue was £71,394,282. Deducting Railway and Irrigation expenses, the nett expenditure was £49,650,229. Out of this total the Civil Departments and charges, in India and in England, cost £15,286,181; and the Army services cost £15,763,931.

Home Charges.—Returning once more to the Gross Expenditure of £71,394,282, we find that, out of this total, a sum of £17,368,655 was spent in England as Home Charges—not including the pay of European officers in India, saved and remitted to England. The Home Charges may be conveniently divided into the following heads:—

	£
1. Interest on Debt and Management of Debt . . .	3,052,410
2. Cost of Mail Service, Telegraph Lines, &c., charged to India	227,288
3. Railways, State and Guaranteed (Interest and Annuities) .	6,416,373
4. Public Works (Absentee Allowances, &c.)	51,214
5. Marine Charges (including H.M. Ships in Indian Seas) .	173,502
6. Military Charges (including Pensions)	2,945,614
7. Civil Charges (including Secretary of State's Establishment, Cooper's Hill College, Pensions, &c.) . . .	2,435,370
8. Stores (including those for Defence Works) . . .	2,057,934
Total	17,368,655

The largest items are Interest on Debt, Railways, and Civil and Military Charges. How the Indian debt was first created by the East India Company by an unjust demand of Tribute, and how it was increased by charging to India the cost of the Afghan and Chinese Wars, the Mutiny Wars, and the Abyssinian and Soudan Wars, has been shown in previous chapters. To what extent this debt is justly and morally due from India, and how far it is entitled to an Imperial Guarantee which would reduce the Interest, are questions which we do not wish to discuss again in this chapter.

Of Railways, too, we have said enough in previous chapters. For half a century the Indian railways did not pay, but were nevertheless continuously extended. The working expenses, the interest on capital spent, and the profits guaranteed to private companies, exceeded the earnings by over 50 millions sterling—a clear loss to the Indian taxpayer. In recent years the lines have paid; but how long this state of things will continue we do not know. And it is an additional loss to India that the interest on capital and the annuities are withdrawn from the earnings of the lines in India, and paid in England to the extent of 6½ millions a year. The money does not flow back to India, is not spent among the people of India, and cannot in any way fructify the trades and industries of India.

Lastly, the Civil and Military charges include payments to the Imperial Exchequer, salaries of the Secretary of State's establishment, and also pensions of retired civil and military officers. The people of India can justly call upon their British fellow-subjects to bear a portion of the cost of an empire beneficial alike to England and to India. It is a mean policy to make India alone pay for a concern from which India alone is not the gainer, and a readjustment of the Civil and Military Charges, on the lines indicated by Sir George Wingate more than forty years ago, is urgently needed.

Wages and Prices.—The average monthly wages of able-bodied agricultural labourers in different parts of India during the last half of 1902 are shown below from official figures. (See table on next page.)

Leaving out exceptionally rich districts like Backergunj, Delhi, and Ahmedabad, and exceptionally poor districts like Fyzabad, the wages of the able-bodied agricultural labourer range from 4s. 8d. to 6s. 8d. a month. Except in very rich districts, therefore, the agricultural labourer does not get even 3d. a day; his average earnings scarcely come to 2½d. per day. Some deduction should be made from this, as he does not get employment all through the year; and 2d. a day therefore is

Province.	District.	Monthly Wages.
Bengal	Patna	6s. 8d. to 8s.
	Backergunj	10s. 8d.
Agra and Oudh	Cawnpur	5s. to 6s. 8d.
	Fyzabad	2s. 6d. to 5s. 4d.
Punjab	Delhi	10s. 8d.
Bombay	Ahmedabad	9s. 4d.
Madras	Bellary	6s. 4d.
	Salem	4s. 8d.
Central Provinces	Jabalpur	5s. 4d.
	Raipur	5s. 4d.

more than he hopes to get throughout the year. The appalling poverty and joylessness of his life under such conditions can not be easily pictured. His hut is seldom rethatched, and affords little shelter from cold and rain; his wife is clothed in rags; his little children go without clothing. Of furniture he has none; an old blanket is quite a luxury in the cold weather; and if his children can tend cattle, or his wife can do some work to eke out his income, he considers himself happy. It is literally a fact, and not a figure of speech, that agricultural labourers and their families in India generally suffer from insufficient food from year's end to year's end. They are brought up from childhood on less nourishment than is required even in the tropics, and grow up to be a nation weak in physique, stunted in growth, easy victims to disease, plague or famine.

Agriculturists who have lands are better off. They are better housed, better clothed, and have more sufficient food. But a severe Land Tax or rent takes away much from their earnings, and falls on the labouring classes also. For where the cultivator is lightly taxed, and has more to spare, he employs more labour, and labour is better paid. In Backergunj, where the land is lightly rented and the cultivator is prosperous, the labourer employed by him gets 10s. 8d. a month. In Salem, where the land is heavily taxed, and the cultivator is poor, the labourer he employs earns 4s. 8d. a month. It is this fact which appeals strongly to the Indian economist familiar with the circumstances of his fellow-villagers; it is this fact which is ignored by the Settlement Officer when he enhances the Land Tax. A moderate Land Tax relieves the landless village labourer as much as the cultivator; a heavy Land Tax presses ultimately on the landless labourer, deprives him of work, reduces his wages, and renders him an easy victim to the first onset of famines. We have in these pages again and again urged a limitation of the Land Tax within moderate and definite limits, because a moderate and definite Land Tax is calculated to improve the condition of the entire village population of British India—all the 200 millions who own lands and who labour on lands. And the Native States of India would soon follow the lead of the British Government in this matter, as they do in other details of administration.

The official compilation from which we have taken the above figures does not furnish us with the wages of unskilled labour in towns. Speaking from our own knowledge, we should say that in large towns like Calcutta and Bombay, an able-bodied unskilled labourer earns 4d. a day, or 10s. a month. A skilled labourer, like a common mason, carpenter, or blacksmith, earns 20s. to 30s. a month in towns.

The price of rice exported from Calcutta in January 1903 was about 4s. 8d. the maund, a maund being 82 lbs. The price of Delhi wheat of good quality was 40s. the candy. But in most Provinces of India, the labourers live on inferior food—Bajra and Jowar, and other coarse grains.

Foreign Trade.—The total imports of merchandise and treasure into India during 1901–2 (excluding Government stores and treasure) was £67,412,798; and the total exports from India during that year was £88,618,297, showing a balance against India of over 21 millions sterling. The United Kingdom sent goods to the value of 43 millions, or two-thirds of India's total imports. Austria sent 2½ millions, Germany 2 millions, Belgium 2 millions, Russia 2 millions, and Australasia 2½ millions. France imported into India goods worth over £900,000, and the United States nearly £800,000. Of India's total imports, no less than 22 millions were of cotton yarn and manufactures, largely from Lancashire. The next largest items are, sugar, nearly 4 millions; iron and steel, over 3 millions; machinery and mill work, 2 millions; and mineral oils, 2½ millions.

Of the exports from India, the United Kingdom took 23 millions, or one-fourth of India's total exports. Germany took 6¾ millions, France 6 millions, Belgium 3 millions, Austria 1½ millions, Italy 2 millions, the United States 5½ millions, Egypt 3½ millions, China 11¾ millions, the Straits Settlements 7 millions, and Japan 4½ millions. The largest exports were, rice and wheat, 11½ millions; raw cotton, 9½ millions; cotton yarn and manufactures, ; millions; hides, 5½ millions; jute and jute manufactures, 13½ millions; seeds, 11 millions; opium, 5½ millions; and tea, 5½ millions sterling.

Economic Condition of the People.—There was a pressing and influential demand in England for an inquiry into the economic condition of the people of India after the recent famines; but the Secretary of State resisted the demand and refused the inquiry. The latest inquiry of the nature was made fifteen years ago by Lord Dufferin's Government in 1888, but the results were never published, and were regarded as confidential. This concealment of facts does not appear to us to be a wise action; the alarming poverty and resourcelessness of the people of India are not a secret, and an evil is not remedied by being hidden from the eye. Large portions of the confidential reports of 1888 have, however, already been placed before the public,[1] and there can be no harm, therefore, in referring to them briefly in the present chapter.

In the *Province of Bombay* it is denied that the greater portion of the population live on insufficient food. But there are "depressed classes" all over the Province, and some of them live below the poor standard of the Indian workman's life and earnings. In the Ratnagiri District, with its miserable soil and heavy payments for land, "there was hardly a season in which this population did not endure without a murmur the hardships of a Deccan famine." Land is less fertile in the Deccan than in Gujrat, and "authorities are unanimous that many cultivators fail to get a year's supply from their land." In the Karnatic also, "the reporting authorities agree that there is a large number of cultivators who do not get a full year's supply from their lands." Even in the favoured division of Gujrat, the cultivator gets only a six or nine months' supply from his field, and most of it goes to the money-lender as soon as the harvest is reaped. And "some of the numerous deaths assigned to fever are caused by bad or insufficient clothing, food, and housing."

In the *Punjab* the condition of the agriculturists and labourers is no better. In Delhi Division "the diet is of a distinctly inferior class, even judged by the comparatively low standard of the country." In Gurgaon District the standard of living is perilously low, herbs and berries are consumed for want of better food, and short food is the cause of migration. The extra Assistant Commissioner of Ferozepur reports that men in many villages do not get food for two meals in twenty-four hours. The Assistant Commissioner of Lahore reports that a considerable number of the people are underfed. Two Mahomedan officers of Rawalpindi Division tell us a

[1] In "*Prosperous*" *British India*, by Wm. Digby, C.I.E., London, 1901.

still sadder story. One of them maintains that 10 per cent. of the Hindu and 20 per cent. of the Mahomedan population are weak and unhealthy from insufficient food; the other says that a great portion of the lower class of agriculturists belong to this category. "The people of Hill Tracts in Hazara," says Colonel Waterfield, C.S.I., "whether agricultural or grazing, may, I think, generally be called a poor, ill-grown, and underfed-looking race."

In the *Central Provinces*, we are told that, in Sagor, Damoh, Narsinghpur, Hoshangabad, Nimar, and Nagpur Districts, "three-quarters of the tenants are reported to be in debt, and from the details which are given, it is evident that the position of a large proportion of them is one of hopeless insolvency."

Province of Agra and Oudh.—The reports of this Province are more ample and more explicit.

The Collector of Etawa writes: "The landless labourer's condition must still be regarded as by no means all that could be desired. The united earnings of a man, his wife, and two children, cannot be put at more than 3 rupees (4s.) a month. When prices of food grains are low or moderate, work regular, and the health of the household good, this income will enable the family to have one fairly good meal a day, to keep a thatched roof over their heads, and to buy cheap clothing, and occasionally a thin blanket."

The Collector of Banda writes: "A very large number of the lower classes of the population clearly demonstrate by the poorness of their physique that they are habitually half-starved, or have been in early years exposed to the severities and trials of a famine. And it will be remembered that if any young creature be starved while growing, no amount of subsequent fattening will make up for the injury to growth."

The Collector of Ghazipur writes: "As a rule, a very large proportion of the agriculturists in a village are in debt."

The Commissioner of Fyzabad quotes Mr. Bennett's statement that, "It is not till he has gone into these subjects in detail that a man can fully appreciate how terribly thin the line is which divides large masses of people from absolute nakedness and starvation." And the Commissioner adds: "I believe this remark is true of every district of Oudh, the difference between them consisting in the greater or smaller extent of the always large proportion which is permanently in this depressed and dangerous condition."

The same Commissioner wrote in the *Pioneer* that, "It has been calculated that about 60 per cent. of the entire native population are sunk in such abject poverty that, unless the small earnings of child-labour are added to the small general stock by which the family is kept alive, some members of the family would starve." As regards the impression that the greater portion of the people of India suffered from a daily insufficiency of food, he writes: "The impression is perfectly true as regards a varying, but always considerable part of the year, in the greater part of India."

"Hunger," writes the Deputy Commissioner of Rai Bareili, "as already remarked, is very much a matter of habit; and people who have felt the pinch of famine—as nearly all the poorer households must have felt it—get into the way of eating less than wealthier families."

"I believe," writes the Commissioner of Allahabad, "there is very little between the poorer classes of people and semi-starvation; but what is the remedy?"

Is this word of despair the final utterance of British administration in India? There must be a remedy when the land in India is fertile, the people are peaceful, skilful, and industrious, and a civilised Government honestly desires to make them prosperous. It is the form and method of an absolute government—not in touch with the people, and not able to secure their well-being—

which is responsible for the failure of the administration in its highest wish and object.

The remedy lies in two words—Retrenchment and Representation.

Retrenchment would permit a reduction in the imposts on land. Agriculture, virtually the only national industry in India, should be relieved. The Cesses on land, in addition to the Land Tax, should be withdrawn. The Land Tax, where it is not permanently fixed, should be limited through the agency of independent tribunals to its theoretical incidence—half the rental or half the economic rent—which is high enough in all conscience. And the Land Tax should not be enhanced except on definite grounds laid down by law.

Other industries also need help. The Government of India should cease to act under mandates from Manchester. The Excise duty on Indian mill industry should be repealed. Moderate import duties, required for the purposes of revenue and not for protection, should be retained. And every possible help and instruction should be given to those humbler home-industries by which tens of millions of people still support themselves in their villages.

Above all, the national expenditure of India should be retrenched. The military expenditure should be limited to India's requirements; and India should obtain a contribution from the Imperial Exchequer for the additional charges incurred for Imperial purposes. Sir Robert Giffin considers three to four millions sterling a fair contribution. The Indian debt should be steadily reduced, and should obtain an Imperial guarantee. The higher services of India should be opened more freely to qualified Indians, and should not be kept as a preserve for English boys seeking a career in the East. And the Home Charges, the annual expenditure of 17 millons of Indian money in London, should be steadily reduced. It is this annual Economic Drain from the food supply of India which impoverishes the Indian population more than any other cause.

It is neither a just nor a true Imperial policy to charge the Indian taxpayer every shilling spent in London for Great Britain's Indian Empire. The empire benefits Great Britain as well as India, and it is a mean counting-house practice to debit India with the cost of establishments maintained in London to supervise Indian affairs. The annual remittance of 17 millions for Home Charges, added to the remittances made by European officers employed in India, represent nearly one-half of the nett revenues of India. No subject nation can prosper if nearly one half of its revenues is withdrawn from the country by the ruling power. And no ruling nation ultimately benefits by such an influx of gold, received without a direct commercial return. It is with nations as with individuals; the bread we earn by labour nourishes and invigorates; the food we consume without toil is poison to our system. It was through influx of gold, without commercial return, that luxury, degeneracy, and decline overtook ancient Rome, and a political and commercial atrophy supervened in modern Spain. Future historians will perceive more clearly than we do how the influx of Eastern gold, more than the rivalry of Western nations, enervates England's manufacturing industry, her commercial fitness, her strong fighting capacity. England as a sturdy, industrial, and commercial power declines under the insidious influence of Eastern gold, as England, as a free country, declines under the contagion of the despotic form of government she has established in the East. Financial justice to India would help British manufacture, firstly and directly by creating a vastly larger market for British goods among a prosperous Indian population, and secondly and indirectly, by arresting that influx of gold without a commercial return which enervates and corrupts her industrial capacity.

The second remedy we have proposed is Representation. We do not want a Parliament in India; but administration will not and cannot be successful until the people are admitted to some share in its control. The good work has already been commenced. *Legislative* Councils in every large Province admit some members elected by the people. The principle is capable of extension, and every district in a Province should be allowed to send its Representative. Madras and Bombay have *Executive* Councils; other Provinces in India should be provided with such Executive Councils, and Indian Members should find a place in them. The Governor-General's Executive Council consists of a number of able and experienced Englishmen, nearly all of them heads of spending departments. Some representation of the people, *i.e.* of the taxpayers, in the Council would strengthen the administration, and make it better informed and better able to promote the welfare of the people. And the Secretary of State in London would benefit by the advice and information which qualified Indians, admitted to his Council, could give him on grave matters of administration. For forty-five years Secretaries of State have ruled India without hearing the voice or the opinion of an Indian member in his Council Chamber at Whitehall. Such exclusive and distrustful administration is unpopular as it is unsuccessful.

The remedies suggested above are not innovations, they are necessary developments of the system which has grown up during nearly half a century. We do not like experiments in Government; we distrust new and ideal Constitutions. We desire to see progress in the lines which have already been laid down; we wish to bring the system of administration, already formed, more into touch with the lives and the interests of the people.

For the present constitution of the Indian Government is not in touch with the lives of the people, does not protect the interests of the people, and has not secured the material well-being of the people. The Democracy of Great Britain, reasonable and fair-minded on the whole, cannot interest itself in the details of Indian administration, and must necessarily look after its own interests. The Parliament of Great Britain cannot give adequate attention to Indian affairs. And the Secretary of State, who is a member of the British Cabinet, with the Councillors selected by himself, does not represent the people, does not know their needs, does not secure their interests. In India, the Governor-General and his Councillors, selected by himself, are under the orders of the Secretary of State, and are not in touch with the people. The entire policy of Indian administration, in all its important details, is shaped and controlled and regulated by the oligarchy at Whitehall and the oligarchy at Simla. There is no place in the administrative machinery where the views of the people are represented, where the interests of the taxpayer are protected. The wit and ingenuity of man could not devise a system of administration for a vast and civilised population, where the people are so absolutely, so completely, so rigorously excluded from all share in the control over the management of their own affairs. Is it any wonder that that administration — the oligarchy at Whitehall and the oligarchy at Simla — should, amidst surrounding Imperial influences, sometimes forget the over-taxed Indian cultivator, the unemployed Indian manufacturer, the starving Indian labourer?

Such was not the past in India. Hindu and Mahomedan rulers were always absolute kings, often despotic, but never exclusive. Their administration was crude and old-fashioned, but was based on the co-operation of the people. The Emperor ruled at Delhi; his Governors ruled provinces; Zemindars, Polygars, and Sardars virtually ruled their estates; villagers ruled their Village Communities. The entire population, from the cultivator upwards, had a share in the administration of the country. It is true that modern administration must necessarily be more centralised, more thorough in the supervision of every detail, more uniformly regulated, than the administration of the Middle Ages. If so, then this modern administration should necessarily contain within itself some popular element, and should be helped and sustained by popular bodies in divisions and districts. To make the present administration more centralised, and at the same time to exclude from it all popular element, is to preserve the despotism of the Middle Ages without the advantages of self-government which that despotism left to the people.

From whatever point we view this grave question, we arrive at the ultimate truth—a truth which Englishmen know better than any other nation on earth—that it is impossible to make Indian administration successful and the Indian people prosperous without admitting the people to a share in the control of their own affairs. "It is an inherent condition of human affairs," said John Stuart Mill, "that no intention, however sincere, of protecting the interests of others, can make it safe or salutary to tie up their own hands. By their own hands only can any positive and durable improvement of their circumstances in life be worked out." Indian hands have been tied up too long, and the result has not been happy. Let Indians to-day stand side by side with British administrators, and work conjointly to help their country and improve their wretched lives.

England herself stands to gain and not to lose by a constitutional government in India. Isolation does not strengthen the empire, it is already creating discontent among a numerous population which will necessarily be an increasing source of political danger. A popular form of government will arrest this evil and will strengthen the empire; it will enlist the people of India in the cause of the empire; it will make them proud of the empire as their own. More than this, it will arrest the evils which a despotic form of government creates—in

England as much as in India. It will arrest that insidious influence with which England's eastern despotism infects and poisons her own institutions and her own people year after year.

It is said of Louis XI., King of France, that on one occasion he had decided to hang his soothsayer, but that he changed his mind on being told that the duration of his own life depended on that of the soothsayer. It is certainly true, in a far higher sense, that England's destiny hangs on the destiny of India. A prosperous India will help England's trade, and a constitutional India will strengthen England's Empire. Impoverished India starves England's trade, and a despotic form of government in India spells England's decline.

INDEX

THE END